Frank Borzage

Frank Borzage

The Life and Films of a Hollywood Romantic

HERVÉ DUMONT

with a foreword by Martin Scorsese

TRANSLATED BY JONATHAN KAPLANSKY

McFarland & Company, Inc., Publishers
Jefferson, North Carolina, and London

The present work is a reprint of the illustrated case bound edition of Frank Borzage: The Life and Films of a Hollywood Romantic, *first published in 2006 by McFarland.*

Frontispiece: Frank Borzage on the set of *No Greater Glory* (1934).

Stills are from the collections of the Swiss Film Archive/Cinémathèque Suisse

This book was originally published in French as *Frank Borzage: Sarastro à Hollywood* by Edizioni Gabriele Mazzotta, Milan, and Cinémathèque Française, Paris, in 1993.

LIBRARY OF CONGRESS CATALOGUING-IN-PUBLICATION DATA

Dumont, Hervé.
[Frank Borzage. English]
Frank Borzage : the life and films of a Hollywood romantic / Hervé Dumont ;
with a foreword by Martin Scorsese ; translated by Jonathan Kaplansky.
p.   cm.
Filmography:
Includes bibliographical references and index.

ISBN 978-0-7864-4098-6 (softcover : 50# alkaline paper) ∞

1. Borzage, Frank.   I. Title.
PN1998.3.B68D8613   2009   791.4302'33092 — dc22   2006009599

British Library cataloguing data are available

On the cover: *foreground*—Frank Borzage on the set of *No Greater Glory* (1934); *background*—the final scene of *A Farewell to Arms* (1932)

Manufactured in the United States of America

McFarland & Company, Inc., Publishers
Box 611, Jefferson, North Carolina 28640
www.mcfarlandpub.com

To Jacqueline

Contents

Foreword by Martin Scorsese 1

Preface 3

Introduction: Keys to an Alchemy of Film 9

1. From Salt Lake City to Inceville 31
2. Debut at the Megaphone 43
3. In Search of a Style 58
4. Working for William Randolph Hearst 68
5. A New Status: Producer-Director 86
6. Fox Films Spurred On by Ambition 100
7. Fame Through Jacob's Ladder 111
8. Two Forgotten Masterpieces 134
9. Between Glory and Disgrace 155
10. Freedom at the Top 175
11. The Romance of the Deprived 197
12. The Warner Brothers Purgatory 227
13. At MGM: Stars and Real Life 250
14. The Mystical Dimension 269
15. The Mortal Storm 284
16. Wandering Downwards with Highlights 302
17. Republic Studios in Sublime Mode 323
18. In Semi-Retirement 342

Filmography 359
Notes 391
Bibliography 409
Index 415

Foreword
Martin Scorsese

The older I get, the more I realize that when it comes to film history, nothing can be assumed. You have to keep going back to square one, and you can never take *anything* for granted. You can never say to yourself that anyone who really cares about cinema will obviously know this film or that director. Because there are many reasons that people who do care — passionately — may not know a given film or filmmaker. Official film history is always refining things down to a few Oscar winners, important classics, and we all know what they are. In the world of advertising, the past stretches back about 24 hours ... if that. In many of the video stores, the "classics" are anything made before 1990, and the idea of watching a film in black and white or with subtitles or without sound is unheard of.

It still seems shocking to me that some people don't know who John Ford is, even who Fellini or Kurosawa are — they all have to be explained all over again. So where does that leave Frank Borzage?

Borzage, as it's often been said, was a romantic, and that's one strike against him — I haven't seen every one of his films but I have seen most of them, and I think I can safely say that there's not an ironic moment in any of them. And when I say that he was a romantic, I'm not talking about mood or the fact that he excelled at romances— he clearly *believed* in romance, in love as a transcendent state. You see it — you *feel* it — in film after film. And that's a big part of what makes him so unfashionable now. To put it bluntly, there's nothing hip about *Lucky Star* or *Living on Velvet* or *I've Always Loved You*, to name just some of my favorite Borzage pictures. They feel very far from modern life. Which means that *they* don't come to *you—you* have to go to *them*.

A few years ago, I looked at quite a few of Borzage's pictures all in a row — as many as I could find. And I was truly astonished. I was astonished by Borzage's artistry, by his passion, and by his extraordinary delicacy. Whenever he's filming two people falling in love, as in *Lucky Star* or *7th Heaven* or *A Farewell to Arms,* or two people already in love protecting each other from a hostile world, as in *Man's Castle* or *The Mortal Storm*, or many other variations in between, the action plays out in what I would call lovers' time — every gesture, every exchange of glances, every word spoken *counts*. Borzage was so tuned into the nuances between people that he was able to catch emotions that you just don't see in anyone else's movies. For instance, those scenes between Kay Francis and George Brent at the heart of *Living on Velvet—* she's humoring him, playing along with him, because she doesn't want to upset his fragile balance; he seems peaceful, but you can see that beneath the surface he's emotionally undone, that he could crack at any moment. Many of these scenes are played in close-up, and the intensity of the feelings between Francis and Brent is overwhelming. *Mannequin* is also very moving, for a different reason. Joan Crawford's character believes in an ideal of love, and Spencer Tracy knows that he can fulfill that ideal but waits patiently for her to figure it out: What might have been an ordinary melodrama in anyone else's hands becomes a study of two people motivated by faith, who finally come together as one. *Till We Meet Again* is another film that would have been completely ordinary in anyone else's hands. Ray Milland is an American pilot whose plane crashes in occupied France, and Barbara Britton is a young novice who helps him to escape. Borzage brings the relationship just one step short of a genuine love affair, and the fact that they can't act on their feelings — she's devoted her life to God and he's married with children — makes those feelings that much more poignant. In the end, she martyrs herself in order to save him, and it's like the grand consummation of their love affair. There's a spiritual power to these films, and to all of Borzage's best work — because for him, love is sanctified, untouched by the outside world. It passes through all barriers, and it's more powerful than any evil. You can feel the power of Stewart and Sullavan's love after they're gone, shaming the people who've betrayed them, at the end of *The Mortal Storm*. In *I've Always Loved You*, the bond between Philip Dorn and Catherine McLeod is conveyed through a series of grand camera movements linking them as they're making music together. And at the end of *China Doll*, the love between Victor Mature and Li Li Hua lives on in their grown daughter, setting foot on American soil years after they've both died.

Borzage was an artist, and a great one. And he is fully deserving of this wonderfully insightful, impeccably researched book. Hervé Dumont has done a wonderful job of piecing together the details of Borzage's life and his films. For those who already know his work, it will deepen your appreciation. For those who have yet to step into Borzage's universe, this book will serve as your guide.

Preface

"Frank Borzage was one of the greatest American directors of all time," declared Samuel Fuller.[1] This peremptory claim is not isolated. In a 1969 interview in Brussels, Josef von Sternberg — so stingy with praise for his colleagues! — admitted that of all those who worked in Hollywood, Frank Borzage (pronounced "bor-ZAY-guee") was without a doubt "the most worthy of his infinite admiration."[2] Having discovered *Humoresque* in a Moscow movie theater in 1925, Sergei M. Eisenstein unhesitatingly placed Borzage alongside Chaplin and Stroheim as one of "the three greatest filmmakers in America."[3] Within the profession, Marcel Carné declared his "exceptional predilection" for the filmmaker's work,[4] and William K. Howard deemed it was "even more important than that of Fritz Lang and Ernst Lubitsch."[5] Terence Fisher, the champion of British horror films, called Borzage, along with John Ford, his two "favorite directors"[6] and Yves Boisset lamented in 1959 that the creator of *The River* "still does not have the place he deserves among the luminaries in the history of movies."[7]

Film historians fully concur with this profusion of praise — with one jarring note, or rather a restriction. Like Alfred Hitchcock or Howard Hawks in the fifties, Borzage was for a long time the exclusive favorite of European movie buffs, particularly the French. Certainly, English-speaking critics of the time always recognized the quality of his films most acclaimed by the establishment and the public at large. After all, in 1920 Borzage had received the first artistic distinction for film ever given in the U.S., the Photoplay Gold Medal, and in 1927 won the first Oscar ever for directing (followed by a second in 1931). But the fact remains that no one had perceived the fundamental originality, the "poetic anarchism," the underlying provocation of his films. In the U.S., films as unconventional as *The River* (1928), *Lucky Star* (1929) and *Man's Castle* (1933) were simply ignored or drenched in sarcasm. Others were condemned in a few laconic sentences for very bad reasons: *A Farewell to Arms* (1932) was judged only in light of Hemingway's sentimental realism, and *Three Comrades* (1938) was evaluated in relation to F. Scott Fitzgerald's controversial contribution. The standard works of the era attest to this superficiality: Lewis Jacobs (*The Rise of the American Film. A Critical History*, 1939) only mentions his name among other directors who were "no less commercially proficient and who occasionally also produce arresting pictures," while Paul Rotha (*The Film Till Now*, 1949) reduces him to a "leader of the Sentimentalists and gauzed photography school."

In France, as of the late twenties, André Breton, the revered leader of the Surrealists, gathered around him fervent Borzagophiles, sensitive to this quasi-spiritual quest for purity, to the eroticism and spirit of freedom appearing in his films, for which there were no other examples in the Hollywood at the time. For the Surrealists, Borzage was a true revolutionary: one who transformed hearts and the entire perception of reality, instead of simply demonstrating on the barricades. In *La Revue du Cinéma*, forerunner to the *Cahiers* between

1929 and 1931, Jean-Georges Auriol became impassioned for *The River*. As in Japan, China and South America, it seems, various Parisian movie buffs began a cult to Borzage that would be continued by the tenants of the very early Cinémathèque Française, Henri Langlois and Jean Mitry (1936). The most perceptive of them, including future filmmaker Jean Charles Tacchella, suspected a profoundly cohesive work, due no doubt to an unusual personality, but of which almost no one was aware. After the war, as distribution of his films became rarer, Borzage became a kind of legend. His masterpieces were believed to have disappeared, surviving in the memories of veteran movie buffs as ghost films, haloed in mystery and perhaps overrated, kept alive by a few big guns of film history. For instance, Georges Sadoul often spoke of "a great man unrecognized, the equal of his contemporaries John Ford, Howard Hawks and King Vidor."[8] In fact, watching these mythical reels again or for the first time, in the fifties and sixties, was a hit and miss affair, compared to which Indiana Jones' explorations were leisurely strolls! Even in the *Cahiers du Cinéma*, where so much was done to promote the Hollywood greats, Borzage remained a blank page.

It took decades, if not more, for Frank Borzage — whose death in June 1962 basically went unnoticed — to be slowly rediscovered. In the U.S., Andrew Sarris had timidly saluted the "romantic" Borzage in his obituary, mentioning that his filmography probably needed to be reevaluated.[9] In 1980, Jean Mitry, by then an internationally renowned historian, declared that "a good fifteen films ensure him a place of honor among the greatest creators of which film history can be proud."[10] Finally, ten years later, Bertrand Tavernier and Jean-Pierre Coursodon accorded him "one of the top places in the seventh heaven of great filmmakers."[11]

For me, the baptism of fire came in 1966, when Henri Langlois paid a visit to the Swiss National Film Archive in Lausanne — then headed by Freddy Buache — with a copy of *7th Heaven* (1927) under his arm. The screening had an electrifying effect.... I had been warned, however. The rapturous pages by Ado Kyrou in his two famous books, *Le surréalisme au cinéma* (1952) and *Amour-érotisme & cinéma* (1966) had whetted my appetite. All of a sudden it confirmed the accuracy of the chapter Kyrou devoted to Borzage that began: "It is difficult to make those who have not seen these films understand the irresistible charm they radiate."[12] The screen revealed to me, magnified a hundredfold, the archetypes of the most Borzagian couple of the postwar period: Cyd Charisse and Robert Taylor in Nicholas Ray's *Party Girl* (1958). Now I had to discover classics such as *Little Man, What Now?* (1934), the uncensored version of *A Farewell to Arms* (1932), the virtually unknown *Liliom* of 1930, and finally the mythical *The River* (1928) of which only the most famous part remains. Like so many other movie buffs, for me this was the beginning of a long love story and I lay in wait, patiently — and passionately — for his films. There was a continent to update, mysteries to try to approach, then shed light on.

Until very recently, it was difficult to get a precise idea of his work, as between 1915 and 1960, this prolific man directed close to one hundred films. Approximately sixty of them have survived, spread all over the globe; fortunately all the essential titles are among the survivors. It wasn't until April 1971 that the Film Studies program at Harvard University organized a first Borzage retrospective, still quite limited in number (about ten films); the New York Cultural Film Center (Columbus Circle) followed timidly in August 1973; the National Film Theatre in London and the Toulouse Film Archives in May and in December 1975; French television (Patrick Brion's "Cinéma de minuit") in May 1976; the Luxembourg Film Archives in October 1984; the "Centre Action Cinéma" (Rui Nogueira) in Geneva in January 1985; and UCLA in April 1986. But these were only faltering attempts compared to the fabulous retrospective of all films then existing (64) undertaken by the

Madrid and Lisbon archives in April 1990. Then in October 1991, a tribute was held at the Filmmuseum in Amsterdam (40 films), and a year later, one at the Giornate del cinema muto in Pordenone (Italy), very appropriately entitled "Frank Borzage, Hollywood's Lucky Star." Need we emphasize that this "most ignored star among the classics" (Davide Turconi) never stopped growing over the years, and the reappearance in dribs and drabs of one missing reel or another still holds pleasant surprises? *Lucky Star* (1929), rediscovered in Amsterdam in 1990, is a source of marvel, as is *The Lady* (1924), an admirable melodrama thought definitively lost that reappeared (with a few scenes missing) in 1992 in Washington.

Despite these various events, publications devoted to the filmmaker can still be counted on the fingers of one hand. In 1973, Henri Agel and Michael Henry Wilson, pioneers in the field, came out with a first 63-page installment in the defunct collection *Anthologie du cinéma* in Paris.[13] The next year John Belton's famous essay in the series "The Hollywood Professionals" appeared (London–New York). Three film journals dedicated special issues to him: *Focus!* (Chicago) in 1973, *Bright Lights* (Ohio) in 1975 and *Positif* (Paris) in 1976. These publications analyzed films then visible — the tip of the iceberg — but none of them ventured into biographical considerations, and the legendary filmmaker remained hidden behind his work. This aspect is made abundantly clear in the first book entirely devoted to the filmmaker, published in 1981 in the U.S.: *Souls Made Great Through Love and Adversity. The Film Work of Frank Borzage* by Frederick Lamster (Scarecrow Press, Metuchen, N.J.). To tell the truth, it was the biases of Lamster's text that incited me to write and determined my own methodology; the author takes drastic measures to slot Borzage's filmography inside a preestablished interpretive framework, even if it means eradicating everything that doesn't fit into it. His text limits itself to the description of 44 films grouped arbitrarily by theme (westerns, society dramas), without seeking knowledge of the production history, nor the economic and cultural factors, nor of Frank Borzage himself, of whom Lamster seems unaware, to the point of not even mentioning the dates of his birth and death. In the framework of the American film industry of the past, dominated by the all-powerful studio system, such historical gaps fatally lead to aberrations in matters of judgement and interpretation. What comes to mind is the John Ford devotee who heaped praise on the Ford episode of the Civil War in the Cinerama epic *How the West Was Won* (1962) — while all the battle scenes had been filmed six years earlier, in August 1956 in Kentucky, by Edward Dmytryk for *Raintree County*, then blown up for Cinerama, owing to a lack of funds! When we know that Douglas Sirk worked uncredited on a pirate film with Errol Flynn (*Against All Flags*, signed by George Sherman) or that Billy Wilder completed John Huston's *The Barbarian and the Geisha*, we cannot be careful enough before pigeonholing creators blindly into "authorist" perspectives.

Writing about Hollywood while merely viewing films to brazenly develop a theory about an author-creator — as the *Cahiers du Cinéma* and their disciples used to do (*Movie*) — seems to me today more unacceptable than ever, even if this procedure in the past had the considerable merit of promoting the notion of author and the preeminence of direction over the film's subject. Although cultural products, these films were tributary of the circumstances surrounding their creation and reception. Putting them into context (which takes into account the traditional pragmatism of the film industry) is thus imperative, all the more so as many sources and contemporary documents, gathered in film archives, are finally available to researchers. Only after studying these contexts can a film analysis attempt to supply worthwhile answers. These circumstances led me to investigate the filmmaker's personal archives,[14] to systematically consult what was held in Hollywood studios and what was censored, and finally to locate the widow of Borzage, and his family and friends in California in order to gather first-hand recollections from them. What follows is the fruit of many research trips in Europe and the U.S. between 1989 and 1992. Considering the specificity of the personality and the richness of his filmography, I made a special effort to approach the material without too many preconceived ideas. Prudence was essential, as the interpretations of "Borzagophiles" all over the world diverge greatly. My convictions crystallized during my successive discoveries. May they contribute to the definitive reevaluation of one of the giants of filmdom and place his work in the perspective it deserves.

At the top of the list, I would like to thank Filmoteca Española in Madrid, without whom this work would never have seen the light of day, at least in its present form; thanks to the Borzage retrospective organized by Catherine Gautier in April 1990, I had the exceptional opportunity of viewing and studying at leisure almost all the still-existing work — a task that, otherwise, would have been Promethean, with prints coming from Los Angeles, Paris, Brussels, Moscow, Prague, London, Rochester, Oklahoma…. The hospitality of José María ("Chema") Prado, and above all the enthusiastic and incredibly efficient support of Catherine Gautier were essential to the undertaking.

Another ardent Borzage supporter, Freddy Buache, former curator of the Swiss Film Archive, opened doors for me abroad throughout all my inquiries by means of recommendations, letters and various forms of support. Dominique Païni, then head of the Cinémathèque Française, offered to publish my manuscript, together with Edizioni Gabriele Mazzotta (Milan). The glossy book — with color illustrations— appeared in March 1993, in conjunction with a second complete Frank Borzage retrospective in Paris (70 films) that made quite a stir in the media. The cycle was then partially resumed in Lausanne (34 films) and in Zurich. At the same time, The Mary Pickford Theater in Washington paid tribute, screening 17 films. Since then, silence — and it would have seemed that a serious rediscovery of Borzage was limited to the Old World were it not for the appearance in 1995 of some remarks in *A Personal Journey with Martin Scorsese Through American Movies* that finally gave some hope of a breakthrough in the U.S., the filmmaker's native land. Thank you, Michael Henry Wilson.

It took the overwhelming passion (an understatement, really!) of an ardent Canadian Borzagophile, Marcel Pereira of Toronto, to break the deadlock on the American continent. In 2000, this skilled researcher succeeded in convincing Mrs. Juanita Moss, widow of the filmmaker, to generously finance a translation of my text, and found a translator. This arduous undertaking was entrusted to Jonathan Kaplansky (Ottawa), the quality of whose work can be appreciated in the present edition. Parallel to this, the San Sebastian International Film Festival — Spain, once again!— decided to dedicate its 2001 retrospective to Borzage (42 films) and to publish at the same time a Spanish translation of my work with the support of the Filmoteca Española.

I was warmly received by all Borzage's relatives; some of the encounters were quite moving. Among them, Juanita Moss (Montecito, CA), the filmmaker's widow; Frank's two sisters, Dorothy Galla-Rini (San Marcos, CA) and Susan Williams (Escondido, CA); his nieces and nephews Madeline Matthey (Burbank, CA), William H. Borzage (Thousand Oaks, CA), and Raymond and Frank Borzage, Jr. (North Ridge, CA). Colleagues, actors and friends who were kind enough to assist include: William H. Clothier ASC (Studio City, CA), Anthony Coogan (Hollywood), Helen Hayes (Nyack, N.Y.), Rose Hobart (Woodland Hills, CA), Arthur Jacobson (Los Angeles), Joseph H. Lewis (Marina Del Rey, CA), Joseph L. Mankiewicz (Bedford, N.Y.), Catherine McLeod (Los Angeles), George J. Mitchell ASC

(La Mesa, CA), Jean Negulesco (Marbella), Luise Rainer (Vico-Morcote, Ticino, Switzerland), Gene Reynolds (Los Angeles), George Sidney (Beverly Hills), Robert Stack (Los Angeles), James Stewart (Beverly Hills), Patricia Stimmings (Camarillo, CA), Jean-Louis Trintignant (Mas de la Chapelle, France), Dorothy Wellman (Hollywood), Charles F. Wheeler ASC (Hollywood), Joe Youngerman (Beverly Hills).

I am particularly grateful to Kevin Brownlow (London) who unhesitatingly gave me access to up his incredible work files, and to filmmaker Jean Charles Tacchella (Paris), whose friendship, erudition and enthusiasm for film are priceless. I was fortunate enough to benefit from the knowledge, advice and friendly support of numerous well-known historians and collectors such as Medardo Amor (Valencia), Peter von Bagh (Helsinki), Rudy Behlmer (Studio City, CA), Joao Bénard da Costa (Lisbon), Luciano Berriatúa (Madrid), Herbert Birett (Munich), Hans-Michael Bock (Hamburg), Patrick Brion (Paris), James R. Curtis (Brea, CA), Geoffrey N. Donaldson (Rotterdam), Michel Eloy (Brussels), William K. Everson (New York), Christian Gilles (Paris), Pierre Guinle (Brussels), Fritz Güttinger (Zurich), Herbert Holba (Vienna), Jan-Christopher Horak (Rochester), John Kobal (London), Thomas Kramer (Zurich), Eric de Kuyper (Amsterdam), Ronny Loewy (Frankfurt), Louis Marcorelles (Paris), Miguel Marias (Madrid), Vittorio Martinelli (Rieti, Italy), Marco Müller (Locarno), Marcel Oms (Narbonne, France), James Robert Parish (Studio City, CA), Francisco Rialp (Barcelona), David Robinson (London), Markku Salmi (London), Zdenek Stábla (Prague), Davide Turconi (Montebello della Battaglia, Italy) and Michael Henry Wilson (Westlake Village, CA).

However, my work would have been unthinkable had I not been able to consult the following archives and the diligent people in charge there. In the U.S.: Academy of Motion Picture Arts and Sciences/Center for Motion Picture Study — The Margaret Herrick Library [A.M.P.A.S.], Beverly Hills (Kristine Krueger, Sam Gill, Sandra Archer, Alison G. Pinsler, Linda Harris Mehr, Val Almendariz); University of California, Los Angeles/Theater Arts Library & Film-TV Archive (Brigitte J. Kuyppers, Steven Ricci); University of Southern California/Doheny Library — Archives of Performing Arts, Los Angeles (Ned Comstock, Leith Adams); The American Film Institute/The Louis B. Mayer Library, Los Angeles (Misha Shutt, Alan Gevinson, Ruth Spencer) and John F. Kennedy Center for the Performing Arts, Washington (Susan E. Dalton); The Library of Congress/Motion Picture, Broadcasting and Recorded Sound Division, Washington (Paul C. Spehr); The Museum of Modern Art/Film Study Center, New York (Eileen Bowser, Charles Silver, Mary Corliss, Ron Magliozzi, Adrienne Mancia, Joe Gartenberg); The New York Public Library/Performing Arts Research Center, New York; American Society of Cinematographers [A.S.C.], Hollywood (Leonard J. South, George E. Turner); Directors Guild of America, Inc., Los Angeles (Selise E. Eiseman); 20th Century Fox Film Corp. Studios, Hollywood (Ellen Gameral); George Eastman House/Film Department, Rochester, NY. In Europe: Gabrielle Claes and Jean-Paul Dorchain at the Cinémathèque royale de Belgique, Brussels; Fred Junck and his Cinémathèque municipale de Luxembourg; The British Film Institute, London; Hoos Blotkamp and René Wolf of the Nederlands Filmmuseum, Amsterdam; the Bibliothèque de l'Arsenal, Paris (Emmanuelle Toulet); the Centre National de la Cinématographie, Paris; Svenska Filminstitutet, Stockholm (Rolf Lindfors); Det Danske Filmmuseum, Copenhagen (Karen Jones); Suomen Elokuva-Arkisto/Finnish Film Archive, Helsinki (Timo Matoniemi). Finally, a big thank you for the interest and help of the dynamic team of "Le Giornate del Cinema Muto" at Pordenone (La Cineteca del Friuli, Gemona), particularly to Lorenzo Codelli, Livio Jacob and Paolo Cherchi Usai.

The generous grants from Pro Helvetia-Fondation suisse pour la culture, Zurich (Luc

Boissonas, Hanne Zweifel-Wüthrich), and the Fédération des coopératives Migros—Service culturel, Zurich (Arina Kowner, Ursula Mürkens, Roger Perret) were a great help during my research in Los Angeles and New York.

Last but not least, I'm infinitely grateful to my friends Raymond Scholer and Gilles Recordon for tracking down the typos in my manuscript with untiring zeal, eagle eyes and marathon-like endurance. As for my wife Jacqueline, her pertinent advice and competent, sustained editorial support were key to the creation of this work. It is to her that I dedicate the pages that follow.

Hervé Dumont

N. B.: The asterisks preceding the titles of certain films indicate unrealized projects.

Introduction: Keys to an Alchemy of Film

"When a finger points to the moon, the ignoramus looks at the finger"
— *Zen proverb*

"Reason, religion and decency
Love destroyed all three!"

— *Shah Abdul Latif, 1689–1752*

Cinematographer William H. Clothier,[1] a seasoned veteran of the camera who strode through the Far West with John Ford and John Wayne, assured us several times that "Frank Borzage was just like his films." These remarks suggest that Borzage's filmography is both coherent and consistent. We can in fact state that throughout his life Borzage always made the same film over again and his work always reveals the same preoccupations. The style and subject of his films were not subordinate to the aesthetics or objectives of a particular studio: in his 48 years in the business, the director worked for all the big American film companies—Fox, Metro-Goldwyn-Mayer, Columbia, Paramount, Universal, RKO, Warner, United Artists and Republic. This coherence, both diegetic and formal, is in itself exceptional, especially in Hollywood's first five decades, and bears the stamp of a veritable auteur (not including his early attempts and some bread and butter work, inevitable in the studio system). A producer-director from 1923 on, Borzage was part of a tiny minority that maintained control of its films; this privilege allowed him to remain true to himself over the decades.

The opening remarks quoted above also imply that his films cannot be understood without an overview of the creator's personality, and vice versa. "Frank Borzage reflected the gentleness that made him a fine director of love scenes," wrote Raoul Walsh in his memoirs.[2] Borzage was "my beloved friend," added Tay Garnett[3] and "a most unique man," according to George Sidney.[4] The assistant Arthur Jacobson found "he was the kindest man in the business," and the widow of "Wild Bill" Wellman told us, laughing, "My late husband had a hell of a character and didn't get along with most people, but he just adored Frank, and that means something!"[5] He did not, it seems, have any enemies.

His European admirers, transported by the lyricism of his images, sometimes called him a "cursed creator," the term used to describe the nineteenth-century French poet Rimbaud. They saw Borzage as treated harshly by the Machiavellian studios. His subtle humanism, sensitivity, and gentle disposition certainly conflicted with the brutal pragmatism (if not savagery) of the movie-making world. He stands out against the money-grubbers, with a good deal of composure, health, and serenity that, in a neuroses-ridden universe, make him something of an alien. Marlene Dietrich said he was the only person in Hollywood "unaffected by the galloping 'jealousy' virus."[6] Easy-going, he preferred the company of simple people. His success brought him many fair-weather friends who took advantage of his excessive generosity and trusting nature (regarding his lifestyle, see the end of chapter 10). His humor was mischievous, his laughter contagious. Other people's compliments made him blush like a schoolboy, and, while energetic, muscular and self-assured, he revealed nothing of his emotional life or deep convictions. His few confidants describe him as extremely vulnerable, but ruled by pride: he never spoke of what moved him. "Borzage is a wonder," exclaimed Bob Baker. "A pinup from his matinee idol days shows a face so trusting you feel like hissing dire warnings about the ways of the world. But somehow, on the evidence of his films, he kept his benevolence and gentleness right to the end. He must have led a charmed life, unless he was the greatest con man of all time!"[7]

A con man, certainly not. But perhaps there was a kind of mystery.

"A most unique man," claimed George Sidney (picture dated 1925).

Borzage was above all a free agent, outside the Hollywood mainstream where action and realism were king. He wanted to film the indescribable, to praise the vitality of life like a naive minstrel ruled by a romantic temperament whose irrepressible gust would be captured on screen. He was supremely indifferent to passing fashions: he was only attracted to the universal and the everlasting.

From 1920 to 1940 for various reasons he had the wind in his sails, and apparently effortlessly reached the top of his profession. But when his kind of story fell from popularity, when the public's tastes changed and critics backed away, the economic recession restricted his freedom. Borzage sailed for a while against the current, then, unperturbed, abandoned films for outdoor sports. Not once did he try to solicit new audiences by caving in to the anguished pessimism or morbid obsessions of the postwar period. His stories remained as is. Paradoxically, they affected all social classes (rich and poor alike), groups of ideas, circles, from millions of movie buffs in the Western world and in the Orient, to the most fervent Surrealists.

Sublime Love

The central, unchanging theme of Borzage's filmography is love, a word we are tempted here to write with a capital "L." Love seen as both the unique object and subject of his films. "One suspects he felt romantic love more deeply than we mere mortals," remarked Dan Sallitt,[8] a tad envious, and his films seem to echo the notion of "sublime love," developed by Benjamin Péret. This Surrealist felt that "holy" feeling implies "the greatest degree of elevation, the cut off point where all sublimation converges, no matter what path it has taken, the geometric place where spirit, flesh and heart melt together in a perpetual diamond.... Sublime love appears as a feeling that fills the entire life of the subject, recognizing in the loved one the unique source of happiness. The object of love has become as essential to the heart as air to physical life."[9]

Borzage has been graced with vastly different labels: "Poet of the Couple," "Prince of Melodrama," "Filmland's Fairy Tale King"; MGM trailers introduce him as "Hollywood's No. 1 Director of Love Stories." The filmmaker seems to be fond of one of romantic poetry's central themes: love bringing souls together, giving birth to true life. Famous New York critic Andrew Sarris remarked two years after Borzage's death: "Frank Borzage was that rarity of rarities, an uncompromising romanticist."[10] For Ado Kyrou, another Surrealist, Borzage's masterpieces were "flashes of love in the muck of passing romance, the kind described in paperback novels!"[11] His most famous films, in fact, contain elements of the fairy tale. But fairy tales for adults. Interesting how from the first pictures he directed, in 1915–1916, the filmmaker addressed an adult public, capable of following the complexities, contradictions and torments affecting all human relationships. There is nothing of the "age of innocence" about him, this "childlike" label Edward Wagenknecht uses to describe the silent era (*The Movies in the Age of Innocence*, 1971). His works are not naive, but attest to an unquenchable quest for purity.

Charm and cruelty coexist in fairy tales. They have naive heroes without families, objects with an existence of their own (taxis, talismans, etc.) and above all, emotional power that touches people the world over. "His films are like dreams, full of paradisiacal sweetness and unutterable terror" (Richard Griffith),[12] a comparison mentioned again by J.-P. Coursodon: "Borzage was Hollywood's most consummate dreamer, one whose best work could strip the phrase 'the dream factory' of any pejorative connotations."[13] No doubt the filmmaker had the exceptional talent of creating real tales, extracting an age-old message from them as we have seen, which explains Claude Beylie's apparently contradictory but very apt expression: "romantic effusiveness colored by reality."[14] There is an overriding impression that the magical elements in his works are not gratuitous. Borzage knew nothing of parapsychology or other airy-fairy spiritualism (which shows how much he is at odds with today's sensibility!). His "romanticism" has links with Novalis rather than Hölderlin or Hoffmann. Borzage's "Hymns to the Night" are not escapist fantasy; they are songs of a visionary. For him, darkness is only for the blind, for night shelters the mystery of the sun. Nightmares are short-lived, as is death. What seems to be deliriousness is ecstasy, not madness. Of his "Beloved," Novalis says: "In her eyes I saw eternity. In the distance, the centuries receded like hurricanes. My arms around her neck, I cried for my new life, tears of rapture. It was the first, the only Dream, and ever since I've had eternal, unshakable confidence in Heaven and Night, and its light, the Beloved" ("Hymnen an die Nacht," 1797). Borzage's films do not contain "lost illusions," as people have written. His work contains no bitterness, only sadness: "I never liked downbeat stories when they are downbeat from the start of the picture. Never mind the tragic ending, as long as the stories have a lift."[15]

Yet his films remain unclassifiable.[16] The thirst for the absolute emanating from his stories always confused rationalist viewers, and still does. His audacious conclusions superbly defy all laws of plausibility by combining formal elegance with a rare imagination (isn't propriety the basis for what is plausible?). Masterpieces such as *7th Heaven* and *Lucky Star* confused critics (inasmuch as they went beyond the level of the plot). For instance, Jean Mitry, paralyzed with admiration, indulged in verbal acrobatics, describing "Hallucinations, full of images of the 'other,' of idealized love belonging to the realm of dreams rather than a naive spiritualism," celebrating Borzage as "the poet of the idyll projected by amorous exaltation into an imaginary world where the highest dreams come true."[17]

Others opt for a Lacanian analysis (such as Paul Willemen of the National Film Theater in London), which can only satisfy unquestioning supporters of this type of approach involving "suppressed desires" and "incest." In a well-known article, Jacques Segond attempted to apply the outline of *Cinderella* (as recorded by Perrault) to 14 Borzage films: the myth is fundamental, he explains, "inasmuch as it deals with both the division of society into classes and sexuality."[18] This theory is appealing, but has two major disadvantages. First of all, too many films of the time, American or other, were inspired from this outline for us to detect any properties specific to Borzage.

Certain equivalencies dealing with stepmothers, good fairies and carriages are laborious and Segond is rather quick to place exceptions in the category of "ironic subversions." Furthermore, it seems (at the risk of appearing reactionary) that the psychoanalytic interpretation of the fairy tale — and thus the films— severely restricts their impact. Freud and Bettelheim aren't of much help in interpreting the elegiac transports of *7th Heaven.*

The "Son of Light"

While we don't profess to explain the question definitively, the following reflections will hopefully provide keys that are more helpful in deciphering Borzage's work. It has been said that the filmmaker was a very secretive man. We know practically nothing about his private convictions; he didn't even reveal them to his wife. He did remark in 1940, though, that the spiritual dimension of his films interested him above all, and in the profession, he was regarded as a mystic (cf. chapter 14). Straight off this clue justifies critics who saw in his work a metaphysical quest, discernible throughout his entire career, from *The Forgotten Prayer* (1916) to *The Big Fisherman* (1959). In the U.S., these included John Belton, Fred Camper, and later their emulator Frederick Lamster. In 1972, Belton noted in his famous essay, "Souls Made Great by Love and Adversity": "Where Griffith concerns himself primarily, like Dickens, with the restitution of the family unit, or the creation of a new family-like unit, Borzage's interest lies chiefly in the salvation of his characters— not with external but internal order."[19] His extensive analysis, however, contains excesses of interpretation which we will discuss later. In France, Catholic historian Henri Agel often spoke of "the Borzagian cycle of transfiguration," particularly in "Cinéma et nouvelle naissance,"[20] an original work which extends the question of resurrection to classic films. But to date Michael Henry Wilson has provided the most satisfactory vision. He saw in Borzage's work a "supplication towards light." "What Borzage likes to suggest, no matter what script he is assigned," wrote Wilson in 1976 in a remarkable text, entitled "Le Fra Angelico du mélodrame,"[21] "is that his creatures hold the promise of another life. Therefore, they have no scores to settle down here." This spiritualist vision has convinced a number of exegetes, even diehard agnostics. Jacques Lourcelles clearly stated in 1992: "Chronologically, he was one of the first filmmakers to attain the universal —certainly more enthusiastically and in a less calculated way than Griffith. In his films we find a very pure emotion, imbued with timeless mysticism."[22]

Borzage's aims, however, extend beyond religion. The director was not baptized and did not belong to any church. This enigma may be somewhat clarified by what his family confided to us. Like his brother Bill, Frank joined the Freemasons and was an active participant in their working sessions, organized according to the Ancient and Approved Scottish Rite ("Free & Accepted Masons of California"). He was initiated into the three corporate grades of Apprentice, Companion and Master respectively on February 6, 1919, July 20, 1920, and September 14, 1920, at Culver City Lodge No. 467.[23] His regular attendance at the lodge finally allowed him to attain, on May 10, 1941 the penultimate degree in the hierarchy, the 32nd, carrying the impressive title of Master of the Royal Secret. Each grade was obtained following specific rites: initiation involved its teaching, oaths, symbols, passwords and special gestures. Those who attained the final three grades (White Masonry) held extremely important powers in their respective obediences and were entitled to lead works of superior Masonry. Incidentally, Borzage was also a member of the Shriners (Ancient Arabic Order of Nobles of the Mystic Shrine) at the Al Malaikah Loge, a symbolic organization more or less inspired by elements of Muslim esotericism, mostly known for its philanthropic work.[24] In Hollywood, the Freemasons never comprised a true lobbying group; affiliation was a matter of personal conviction and even Brothers as well known as D. W. Griffith, Cecil B. DeMille, William Wyler, Frank Capra, Merian C. Cooper, Jack Warner, Darryl F. Zanuck, Louis B. Mayer, Clark Gable, W. C. Fields, Douglas Fairbanks, Jr., Audie Murphy, Oliver Hardy, Tom Mix, Roy Rogers and Donald Crisp have remained close-mouthed on the subject. Their works only very rarely can be deciphered according to a strict Masonic perspective: going more deeply into the teaching is a matter of personal inclination. As Marcel Oms has suggested, Griffith's work offers a rather philosophical vision,[25] while Borzage undoubtedly emphasized the vertical, spiritual dimension.

On his deathbed, while relatives were encouraging him to convert to the Catholicism of his ancestors, Borzage retorted that Masonic initiation answered all his aspirations. Therefore we include here certain explanations outside the world of film, indispensable, however, due to general ignorance (or prejudice) regarding the "Sons of Light." For too long, the profound meaning of Masonry has been eclipsed, reduced to a merely humanistic and progressive entity, due to certain lodges that today are merely a kind of Sunday school of secularism, or even a club for networking. René Guénon[26] has shed light on the "operative" origins of Masonic obediences, closely tied to the Christian alchemists of the Middle Ages. Symbolically, Masonry goes back to the creation of the world; it adopted a calendar that began 4000 years bc and celebrated the construction of Solomon's Temple in Jerusalem as its first important work. We will not go into the history of these cathedral builders, custodians of holy architecture in the Western World, but simply note that the Ancient and Approved Scottish Rite belongs to a "regular" branch of Masonry, to which we refer exclusively. The ultimate goal of the Mason was simply the "construction of the ideal Temple," the entire ritual lending itself to a metaphysical transposition in the name of the Architect of the Universe (identified to the Word of Christ). While preaching a universal religion, Anglo-American Masonry remains firmly linked to the theist dogmas common to Judaism and Christianity; the Bible ("the Great Light") is mentioned in sermons in lodges, but the perfect tolerance required by the obediences excludes sectarianism, and thus all kinds of religious proselytizing — as in Borzage's films.

It has been said that in his films the quest for a loving union, for intoxicating sentiment takes on cosmic proportions. Progressively sublimated, love aspires to a supreme blessedness that transcends it. For Borzage's lovers, love is not an answer in itself, but a vehicle toward integral harmony, as it includes regeneration, and finally, redemption. This *unio mystica* is not only "ideal," because attraction is not only emotional, but also physical. With Borzage, redemption is achieved through embrace, whether it takes form (*Man's Castle*, *A Farewell to Arms*, *China Doll*) or is only fantasized about (*Till We Meet Again*). A subtle eroticism rises from the weaving of images. All that need be revealed is a bared ankle, a shoulder; for his lovers the idea of bodies uniting is omnipresent. Even if the censor had allowed it, to show a couple cavorting would have translated none of his feelings, proven nothing. "Sex? Certainly. Put in a good supply of it, but sex that is romantic," Borzage pointed out.[27] The essence of the union cannot be shown visually, and as David Thomson remarks, "Borzage knows that sexuality is a state of being, and his images steadily look forward to it,"[28] an impression summed up nicely by Mitry as "the delicate chastity of desire laid bare."[29]

Sarastro and Masonic Symbolism

The filmmaker prefers a story that includes the tale, love in various aspects and what may be called supra-human wisdom. In place of the Cinderella myth, the preceding explanations lead to more specific themes and images. Borzage's pivotal work, *7th Heaven* (1927) and thus all his films inspired from it (to a greater or lesser extent), from *Man's Castle* (1933) to *China Doll* (1957), contain disconcerting symbolic analogies with Mozart's *The Magic Flute*. Aside from Borzage, there were many Freemasons among the management at Fox, the company that produced *7th Heaven*: while the parallel we attempt to draw may be unexpected, even off-putting, it has some relevance. The deeply Masonic nature of Mozart's opera has often been analyzed.[30] "All the crowd needs to do is to take pleasure at seeing the spectacle," wrote Goethe, himself a Mason, "at the same time, those initiated will see its full signification." The story is about Tamino, a prince seeking his ideal love, the Princess Pamina, daughter of the Queen of the Night. Before being united in the Temple of Isis, the couple must undergo, separately, then together, a series of mysterious ordeals the high priest Sarastro imposes on them. Tamino and Pamina are in fact Man and Woman destined to form the Couple in the highest sense of the term (as declares the "moderator" Sarastro at the assembly of the temple). And what is the subject of *7th Heaven*? Chico is a Parisian sewage worker, but lives on the top (seventh) floor of a wretched building; Diane is an orphan forced into a criminal existence by her sister. The young man rescues the poor creature, reluctantly giving her shelter beneath the rooftops of the city (a place associated verbally with "paradise"). The couple discover themselves gradually, but as it blooms, their love encounters a sister's hatred, an officer's overtures, and above all, a war that separates the lovers physically. Every day at the same time — the "supreme hour," Chico and Diane commune in spirit. In the eyes of the world, Chico is dead in the trenches, but he returns to Diane blinded, yet "seeing." A supernatural light envelops the couple, who embrace in "Seventh Heaven."

In order to better understand what fundamentally connects *7th Heaven* to Mozart's magical opera, we must quickly digress into its symbolism. According to Masonic hermetic cosmogony, human existence is ruled by the alternating of the sun and the moon. In *The Magic Flute*, the high priest Sarastro (Zoroastre) represents the sun (he wears its emblem on his chest) — gold — and incarnates the principle of Good. His antagonist is the "evil" Queen of the Night, represented by the moon and its alchemical correlate, silver. The fundamental relationship between Sarastro and the Queen of the Night is not merely the confrontation of reason and instinct, as has been written, but in its highest sense symbolizes the relationship between divine Intellect and individual psyche, the latter being, by the nature of things, subject to the former. Vain, the Queen of the Night (the egotistical human soul) wants to abolish the supremacy of the Spirit (in the theological sense); the day when her own daughter delightedly participates with her beloved in his ascension, forming the perfect couple, her furor erupts, because the lovers' triumph irremediably brings forth the "obliteration of the Night."

Sarastro is the keeper of the Light, or, in theologic terms, the intermediary between God and men. As Borzage "places his characters in an eternity made quasi-mystical by their love" (J. Lourcelles), he guides his couple toward their "sacred" wedding. The union is such that "from the two beings that you are, you have become one" reveals Héphaïstos in Plato's "The Banquet," "because, after your death, there in Hades, instead of being two you will still be one, both of you sharing death." Symbolically (we use this in Guénon's sense, not Jung's), this marriage of principles between sun and moon, king and queen, is one of the themes of alchemy, because the union of former "man" and "woman" restores the paradisiacal state of the human being.[31] But these considerations

Charles Farrell and Janet Gaynor, the sublime lovers of *7th Heaven* (1927).

carry over to the Masonic secret and would take us too far off-topic.

The universe led by Sarastro and the Queen of the Night is made up of the four elements, grouped into two complementary dyads. In the "solar" dyad are Fire (Tamino) and, above him Air (Papageno); the "lunar" dyad comprises Water (Pamina), and further down, the Earth (the Moor Monostatos servant of the Night). In *7th Heaven*, Chico, for example, assumes Tamino's function and Diane, Pamina's; Papageno becomes the streetcleaner Gobin, and Monostatos, successively becomes Nana (the sadistic sister), then colonel Brissac. Papageno, impervious to the mystical designs of his companion in adventure, represents "ordinary" humanity that has no access to Light (which corresponds to Gobin's nature in the film, notably in the last sequence). Monostatos is the "false brother," the Tempter who adorns himself with traits of wisdom, but prefers sensual pleasures stripped of any authentic feeling. Chico's "diurnal" essence appears in his aspiration to the top (from sewer to street, from street to his seventh heaven), Diane's nocturnal aspect is linked to her troubled past. Tamino-Chico and Pamina-Diane first must seek each other out, then, once they've found each other, go beyond their initial fate, passing through a series of ordeals rendering them worthy of their new status. The man, an errant knight (as many of Borzage's vagabonds) does so by freeing himself from the veil of illusion emanating from the Queen of the Night. The woman does so by rejecting any memory of her nocturne origin, like

Borzage's Diane, Angela (*Street Angel*), Rosalee (*The River*), Mary (*Lucky Star*) and Trina (*Man's Castle*). In the Masonic lodge, the successive ordeals of applicants are represented by a purifying voyage through the four elements and their respective dangers. This transformation signifies the death of the former life and rebirth in a new one, a notion Masonry connects with conferring each grade, a new degree toward knowledge. While Mozart clearly represents the two last stages of the itinerary (the ordeals of Water and Fire), Borzage, of course, does not faithfully reproduce these ceremonies. He translates them into romantic situations, easily decipherable beneath the surface in his filmography. A more detailed description of these Masonic convergences can be found in the passages on *7th Heaven* (chapter 7) and *A Farewell to Arms* (chapter 10).

The Apotheosis of the Couple

Borzage's is a pneumatic art (in the Gnostic sense of the term); it illustrates a transformation and is destined to transform those sensitive to it. Like Mozart's characters, his lovers are fundamentally predestined towards a supreme union. First, they must possess two attributes (the famous "qualifications for initiation"), the first being the ability to love to the extent of forgetting oneself, if necessary, to the ultimate sacrifice. The second faculty is to establish a protective enclave ("a safety zone" says Trina in *Man's Castle*) in which the couple will be able to carry out the alchemical process. For even though they are "chosen," inwardly preserved from the degradation of the world, Borzage's protagonists are far from perfect. Life may have driven them to receiving stolen goods, stealing, prostitution. They begin by confusing thirst for independence with irresponsibility and selfishness, take their boastfulness for courage; for a long time, various traumas prevent their true union (*The River, Bad Girl*); sometimes, they only discover the nature of their respective feelings after having lived together (shocking overcautious censors). The basic situations can easily be seen as an aside made up of tender passion and passionate tenderness between the avatars of Pygmalion and Galatea. The man shows the way, indicates the direction, but at the critical moment it is the woman who develops decisive strength and courage. In Mozart's opera, Pamina guides Tamino through the challenges, and the sweethearts cannot accede to the doorway of the temple of Isis individually. This may all seem hopelessly outdated to fans of Woody Allen, Fassbinder or Almodóvar, but it nevertheless corresponds to the fundamental symbolism originating in the yin and yang complementarity. Very quickly, it appears that the lovers need one another, that they function reciprocally as enlighteners and that only a joint effort, transcending time, space, and perhaps even death, can lead to saving equanimity. To accede to this state, Borzage places obstacles in their path ("adversity"), which are not there simply accidentally, but to allow them to overcome their own weaknesses, leading to questioning that crushes the framework of their egos, erasing individual limitation. The lovers are projected into a jumble of oppositions that they must harmonize so as to become one. The filmmaker provides no formula, or critical commentary, but places us before an accomplished fact in the form of a visual apotheosis. This process is further explained by Frederic Lamster: "In most of the films the [spiritual] journey is unconscious. Yet by the final scenes, with a final recognition, the implications of the journey are made clear to the viewer and, more importantly, to the characters. The catharsis of stage and literary melodrama is kept, but it is not so much evil expunged as love recognized and immediate reality transcended."[32]

Adhering to the rules of the tale of initiation, Borzage's heroes are necessarily "luminously beautiful couples at war with an ugly world" (A. Kyrou); their physical beauty is the irradiation of the spiritual energy lying dormant within them, waiting to be awakened, for, as Plato says "True Beauty is the splendor of Reality." As opposed to Griffith's puritanical heroes, this beauty goes hand in hand with marked sensuality. These characters are social outcasts; pariahs, street performers, unproductive people who immediately capture Borzage's sympathy. They are doubly outside the norm (taking this overused term to designate a mathematical average), partly because due to their intrinsic qualities they stand apart from the surrounding hypocrisy and greed; partly because these same norms (prejudices, laws they must abide) are inherently foreign to them. They are indifferent to profit and "success." These are the Percevals of "authentic values," those of the heart. Outside social class (if not unclassifiable) also because their fundamental purity — which goes beyond moral innocence as a traditional criteria of melodrama — is stronger than the social condemnation surrounding them. (Visually, Borzage often emphasizes this aspect by sketchy or stylized sets and surroundings, so the heroes are not consumed by their squalor.)

The Church as an institution is always powerless, completely surpassed by the seraphic fervor of Borzage's heroes. They do not wait for the Church's blessing before going to bed (*A Farewell to Arms, Man's Castle, Liliom, Little Man, What Now?, Desire, History Is Made at Night*) and the couple's vows are addressed directly to heaven, with no earthly intermediary (*7th Heaven, Three Comrades, The Mortal Storm*), or they take part in a "foreign" ceremony (the Confucian wedding in *China Doll*). Unsurprisingly, for a long time the filmmaker was the black sheep of the Legion of Decency and several of his films were mutilated when initially or subsequently released (particularly *A Farewell to Arms, Man's Castle*, and *Strange Cargo*).

Melodrama and Social Reality

As the initiation process uses motifs of melodrama, it may be useful to outline Borzage's ambiguous link to this much derided genre, which he defended: "Critics don't seem to sense the idea that life is made up largely of melodrama. The most grotesque situations rise everyday in life.... Coincidence runs rife in the life of everyone. And yet when these true to life situations are transferred to the screen they are sometimes laughed down because they are 'melodrama.' If this is true then all life is a joke and while some humorists hold to this idea, I am not one of those who believe it so."[33] Popular melodrama prefers various dramatic situations, but rather than applying it conventionally to penetrate the drama, Borzage accentuates the truthfulness of these same situations. Potential clichés in his scripts are shattered by natural performances, and the skimpy or reactionary content is literally transformed visually. In fact, with Borzage the melodrama becomes a platform, a materia prima which lends itself to a range of extrapolations, from the individual to the cosmic. Centered around basic psychological conflict, the genre contains recognizable everyday characters with whom everyone can immediately identify. The director often insisted: "To me, stories that have the greatest appeal are just simple dramas of ordinary people."[34] It may seem contradictory to extol the ordinary, then transform it into the extraordinary, but aren't fairy tale heroes above all "anonymous," and doesn't the spirit shine "everywhere and in everything"? ("What am I? A man like you," Papageno replies to Tamino.) Once the couple is formed and secretly endowed with extraordinary qualities, the most baroque transports are permitted. Claude Beylie in some sense sums up Borzage's entire filmography when he writes that *A Farewell to Arms* "erupts like a thunderclap, makes 20 other more than honorable films pale in comparison, shows what a completely transcendent and spiritual melodrama should be, thanks to a fire dwelling within pure tragedy, unforgettable poetry, and a mirror of immaculate eroticism."[35] The hero of the classic melodrama is imprisoned in a dichotomy typical of American society, in which the individual is torn between acceptance by others, justification (success, obsession with superlatives and records) and paranoia. Melodrama as a genre scarcely goes beyond societal and moral considerations, even when imbued with religiousness as in Leo McCarey's films. Borzage is not a moralist, at least in the narrow, restricted sense. Diane escapes the police through lies (*7th Heaven*), Angela owes her salvation to the work of a forger (*Street Angel*), Bill manages to cheat a restaurant (*Man's Castle*), Frederic is a deserter (*A Farewell to Arms*), etc. Borzage at first seems to follow the intimate lines of Griffith, but he eschews sentimentality, never pitying innocent victims or evoking pastoral nostalgia or idyllic communities ruled by a nineteenth century code conduct. Virtue does not triumph over money and power. Murnau and King Vidor describe the efforts of their couples to resist the hustle and bustle of the city, the crowd, conventionality, and slow annihilation by the company of others: confronted and eroded by daily life, their love is fragile. Poignancy arises less from external situations than from a fragility inconceivable for the lovers of *Three Comrades* or *History Is Made at Night*. Borzage also avoids the fatalism and social determinism underlying John M. Stahl's work. The flamboyant hysteria that consumes Vincente Minnelli's characters is foreign to him. Douglas Sirk uses the melodrama to criticize the psycho-social motivations of the upper-middle class; his disillusioned protagonists vehemently respond to external forces, while Borzage's heroes exist independently of them, knowing that their truth lies beyond. It is not a reflex to escape, but the unshakeable conviction of those "simple in spirit."

The filmmaker is honest enough to not offer ready-made explanations and consolations to those downtrodden by existence. No miraculous solutions. His work contains no trace of Capra's simplistic philanthropy or of the complacent, pious optimism so adored by Hollywood. This same intellectual integrity prevents him from cultivating a systematic skepticism, depicting sordid aspects of life or an austere, masochistic code of morals. Perhaps part of the wide success of his films was due to this attitude of a "soulful aristocrat," freed from any reductive designs. Even plunged in the depths of misfortune, his characters still have an extraordinary certainty of something beyond them — whether interpreted as love or what is at its source. The viewer is intuitively carried away by Diane and Chico's radiant heartfelt "knowledge," the same way tales awaken in us a memory of a timeless truth. In an era as depressed as the thirties, this contribution was surely more helpful to people than the sugary adventures of a showgirl who marries a millionaire or people gassing themselves to death in the realistic films of the Weimar Republic.

Yet far from ignoring reality and social problems, Borzage is attuned to the sudden fluctuations of his era. The constant presence of social factors is one of the most noted aspects by a sector of critics and earned Borzage widespread praise, as far away as Communist China! As a teenager, Borzage personally experienced vagrancy, privation and hunger (chapter 1). He even stated in 1920: "I know the folk who go to my motion pictures are interested most of all in the problems, the joys and the sorrows of their own daily life and I hope to bring to the films a reflection of all this. I want to go beneath the surface of things."[36] The destitution in the slums of Paris (*7th Heaven*), Marseille (*The Lady*), Naples (*Street Angel*) and New York (*Humoresque, Mannequin*), the privations of farmers in Massachusetts (*Lucky Star*) had a dramatic impact, affecting generations of movie buffs. His sorrowful tramps, fallen women and underpaid employees profoundly influenced neo-realistic scriptwriters such as Cesare Zavattini and Japanese filmmakers such as Yasujiro Ozu and Kenji Mizoguchi. It has been written that *Man's Castle* records the Depression in the U.S.,

Little Man, What Now? unemployment, exploitation and inflation in the early years of the Weimar Republic, *Three Comrades* political chaos at the dawn of dictatorship in the same republic, *No Greater Glory* the threat of militarism, and so on. European film of the time, fascist or other, never dared address these questions so frankly. All this is true, yet insufficient, because close viewing shows that Borzage's priorities are elsewhere. In the end, he shows only limited interest in social mechanisms or class struggles and his distrust of ideologies is manifest. The frequent depiction of the middle class (*The Nth Commandment, Bad Girl, After Tomorrow*) does not so much illustrate the characteristics of a precise social milieu as it reproduces the situations experienced by the great majority.

Nazism in *The Mortal Storm* is not attacked so much on grounds of democracy and personal freedom, as for the way it separates people: this force destroys people's harmony, tears families apart, becoming a "diabolic" presence par excellence ("diabolos" meaning "that which divides"). The last reel of *Three Comrades* is not about beating up a fascist but about avenging a friend, making someone pay for breaking up the sacred unit. Pacifist convictions alone did not lead the director to film *A Farewell to Arms*; Borzage does not object to violence a priori, since the blackguards in *The River, Man's Castle* and *The Three Comrades*, for example, are killed off without scruples or hesitation. At first glance, a military maneuver may appear justified when it serves to halt the invader (the Germans at the Marne in *7th Heaven*), but war itself is inadmissible because its motives are futile (nationalism), and its sacrifices useless arising from politics indifferent to humanity, no matter what side they are on. We know that Borzage, anything but a "sissy," always refused to wear a uniform. Gratuitous killing, whether on the orders of a superior or simply villainous (he hated gangster films), repelled him. From the early twenties on, World War I played an incisive role in his filmography: none of his characters come out unscathed. If not murdered in the war, characters are mutilated: wounded or "false" deaths (*The Pride of Palomar, Children of Dust*), paralyzed in some way (*Humoresque, Lucky Star*), blinded (*Back Pay, 7th Heaven*). Heroism is only unconscious (*Lazybones*). Patriotic glory is pathetic and it is always the "little people" who pay (*No Greater Glory*). Borzage could adopt Lamartine's exclamation: "Nations, a pompous word for barbarity/ Does love stop where your footsteps stop?" ("La Marseillaise de la paix," 1841). Borzage avoids scenes of the battlefield, and it is no coincidence that the only two war sequences in his film career were directed by colleagues (John Ford for *7th Heaven*, Jean Negulesco for *A Farewell to Arms*). At the level of the individual, war is unconditionally condemned for its murderous intrusion in the emotional realm of the heroes. Like social distress or Hitlerian brutality, the roar of the cannons represents a threat to love and is thus (in the film's framework) a manifestation of man's spiritual degradation. They are the images of the "chaos" that the Masonic Light aims to "organize."

A closer look reveals that in the Hollywood of the early 1950s there were few rebels who rejected society's institutionalized values so effectively, few filmmakers so politically incorrect (both to the left and to the right) as Borzage. His most enduring films are characterized by a spirit of freedom, uniquely his own. Only Raoul Walsh, also underrated by the critical establishment, using different genres and having a very different temperament, shows a similar aversion to flag-waving, ideological manipulation, and sexual and spiritual hypocrisy. Both men, each in their own way, thumbed their noses at the holy trinity of the "Family, Country, Church," an unconfessed rampart of conquering materialism. Compared to them, colleagues such as John Ford, Howard Hawks and William A. Wellman look like old reactionaries!

Borzage, without evasion, captures the deathly dissoluteness of his era, but rather than stopping at the phenomena, he translates their essence: a world destroying dignity is but a sordid, deserted space not worth returning to, but of going beyond. One does not adapt to the darkness, even out of compassion. The conclusions of *Man's Castle*, *7th Heaven* and *The Mortal Storm* are clear on this subject; contrary to the protagonists of the classic melodrama, Borzage's heroes do not aspire to reenter into society. This voluntary isolation (some call it "poetic anarchism") never excludes generosity or warmth toward society's rejects. Paradoxically, the filmmaker portrays private drama with so much shuddering intensity that it reverberates on the whole socio-political framework providing it with unsuspected relief: the interruption of the idyll in *A Farewell to Arms* implicitly transforms the narrative into a pacifist tract, ten times more powerful than the sight of a heap of corpses, and the intimate drama played out in the hovels of *Man's Castle* functions as an indictment against savage capitalism. Jacques Lourcelles pertinently remarks that Borzage "goes from the individual to the collective and from the historical to the metaphysical, without losing contact with his public who follows each character's story as if it were both their own and that of all humanity. This polyphony is virtually unique in the history of film."[37] Nevertheless, what appears on the cosmic level to be a calamity becomes a necessity, metaphysically speaking. War, like any form of hostility, separation or constraining vicissitude, is finally an obstacle to be surmounted, an ordeal destined to strengthen the couple on their journey to the Temple of Isis. Ultimately, love and hate cannot be antithetical: the latter is only a temporary and passionate deviation of the former. Sooner or later, the result of hatred ends up submerged, transformed by love (the purifying snow in the last shot of *The Mortal Storm*), revealed as an unconscious accomplice of the Path, like the Queen of the Night at the end of "The Magic Flute." Significantly, the ins and outs of the ordeal, like the concrete ways of overcoming it, are less interesting than the attitudes experienced before and after the journey, for Borzage does not capture his characters' actions, but their reactions. He is the filmmaker of the state of grace.

The "Borzage Touch"

The press of the 1930's frequently used the term the "Borzage touch," indicating that the director possessed, like Lubitsch, Sternberg and Hitchcock, a style, tone and thematic all his own, recognizable in a thousand. People the world over admired his pictorial splendor and velvet-smooth images, succumbed to this unsurpassed degree of sobriety in the poignant, restrained emotion, naturalness in the supernatural. But we are hard-pressed to truly delineate this touch; the tenderness, magic, and incandescent poetry emanating from his masterpieces escape all definition. Once transposed to the screen, his most extraordinary scripts don't lend themselves to laughter, but rather to dreaming, eyes wide-opened. Starting from an often banal plot (a simple résumé of his films conveys no idea of their qualities), from dramatic situations also dealt with by others, how does Borzage manage to enchant us, to distress us the way he does? It must be that with him film writing is intimately linked to his way of being, and only some assessments of his working methods may bring elements of response.

Circa 1933 the filmmaker described his leanings: "Borzage admits a strong dislike for making conventional pictures. He can't direct a picture unless he feels it. As for making pictures mathematically, according to a set formula — well — he simply couldn't do it."[38] In other words, he could not become a talented jack of all trades such as Henry Hathaway or Michael Curtiz: a question of nature, not pride or ambition. To develop his creative potential, he did not need a good script, but the good script. Ill-intentioned or simply poorly informed writers attempted to illustrate the filmmaker's credo, taking a remark made to reporters in 1937: "The trouble with most directors is that they take the whole thing too seriously. Making a motion picture consists of going onto a set, training a camera on competent players, and letting them enact a good script."[39] People saw in these remarks resignation, abdication (before *Three Comrades* and *The Mortal Storm*!), whereas it was really modesty and a high degree of professionalism; Borzage never took himself for an "artist" but, like the majority of his Hollywood colleagues, for a filmmaker graced with luck, an artisan in the most noble sense of the term. The following paragraphs attempt to place this observation in proper perspective.

Borzage expressed himself quite early on about what motivated him to go into movies, particularly an interview granted to Peter Milne in 1922.[40] At age 28, after a world triumph with *Humoresque*, he immediately pointed out that without profound knowledge of the human heart, a director cannot reach the peak of his profession. Borzage observed that his first films already betray serious maturity and psychic equilibrium along with an authentic passion for people. Having started out with Thomas H. Ince and low-budget westerns, he soon went beyond simple action films. Each face hides a story, he thought, but as it is unknown, he must make use of the face itself, compensating the shaded areas by using his own imagination: "Characterization is what makes pictures attractive. Sincere, true characterization. There isn't enough of it in the average picture of today…. I believe in developing every character, no matter how small, that there is in my story if that development is to prove interesting. And by interesting I don't mean the blood-and-thunder sort of interest. A character doesn't have to have committed a murder or betrayed a friend, or to have won a battle in a war or politics to be interesting. It is the commonplace little things in that character's life that can be thrown up on the screen and made interesting, absorbing, living." In other words, strong characters make their own story.

Concerning the plot, he stated "I prefer a thin plot on my pictures. I like to use the majority of the film for characterizations, so I don't like to have to take up too long to unfold a plot. It gets the audience worried about superficialities instead of the real people. And I only like a few people in my plots so I can have time to make them live."[41] An agenda that we can confirm easily in *Lazybones*, *The River*, *Lucky Star*, *Bad Girl* and *Living on Velvet*. But the public is also invited to take part: it is up to them to "read" the thoughts on the faces, as it is wrong to do all the work for them beforehand. "I believe in letting the audience do part of the acting. Let the audience read the player's minds and experience some of the emotions of the characters on the screen. The story that is too obvious and the portrayal that is too obvious lack the artistry which conceals real art. The finished picture should bear no sign of consciousness and no sign of effort."[42] The camera work and editing are fluid, almost imperceptible. The narration is linear and flashbacks are rare; even if Providence spins its web at each image, a return backwards would smack of fatalism, running counter to freedom, let alone the liberating tendencies that guide his films. Like Cecil B. DeMille with his barber, Borzage tested all his stories out before a suitable audience, people who were not in the business and who went to few shows. He invited to his office, either family members or preferably, his employees: the cook, chauffeur, gardener, butler, even his wife's Japanese maid. A born storyteller, he described to them in detail his next film, acting out the crucial scenes, observing their reactions and scrupulously noting their comments.[43] And naturally, he collaborated very closely on all scripts, though they may have been signed by others.

Visual Style

On a strictly narrative level, Borzage always gave priority to the image, as can even be seen by the luxurious visuals in his last work, *The Big Fisherman* (1959). "An engraving, an illustration, even a drawing or photograph can replace ten thousand written words," he said in 1936. "This observation was valid in Confucius's time of and still is today. That is why, even though talkies have now become the supreme form of entertainment, I still feel an irresistible urge to direct a movie with no dialogue, with no other sound than incidental music. I arrange it so that my films have the least amount of dialogue possible. In the love scenes, it's almost always superfluous. How much more expressive is a look, a caress, a gesture!"[44] Patrick Brion mentions that the director's paradox is "having directed silent films (artistically if not technically) during the sound period."[45] Therefore the image conveys a work's inner, hidden dimension, the play of light and darkness that reveals the profound meaning of things. John Belton was the first to seriously concern himself with Borzage's visual style,[46] to mention to what extent the photography enriches the narrative. Starting with the type of studio lighting preferred by Borzage at Paramount and MGM in the thirties, he generalizes (which weakens his argument) seeing in the luminosity of his compositions a visual metaphor: "The light becomes an intangible force that cannot be dealt with physically. In a way, Borzage's visual style reflects his belief in the immateriality of objects and characters. His images have little to do with real things; rather, like Plato's ideal forms, they refer to an absolute and eternal reality that exists on a purely abstract level. In other words, Borzage's images often function as spiritual metaphors, revealing the director's concern for larger issues outside the action itself." In any case, this analysis helpfully mentions some particularly interesting procedures, specific to the "Son of Light."

Before going into more detail, we should mention that the filmmaker completely masters the mysteries of the camera. "Even though it never appears in his films, Borzage worked a great deal on the technical aspect; he designed his shots and his lighting extremely carefully, and [was] very helpful to all the technicians, preparing everything beforehand," recalled cinematographer Joseph Ruttenberg.[47] His colleague George Folsey added: "Frank Borzage is the easiest director in Hollywood to work with. With 20 years of experience in motion pictures and his knowledge of every camera angle, he always has four ways to film each scene."[48] His camera angles are not arbitrary.

Space is not simply decorative or neutral. Using a camera with a wide-angle lens and a soft focus tends inevitably to weaken the contours, emphasizing the immateriality and thus giving less importance to the physical setting itself (as Belton notes). Background lighting is amplified but the setting remains hazy, eliminates the depth of the field. The light, of unknown origin, is filtered, misty, playing on vast surfaces, creating a singular unity of tone. This general luminescence could well have a distant but visceral link to the golden backgrounds of Byzantine art, a reminder of the "Eternal Present." (Belton sees in it a representation of divine immanence.) Visually several of Borzage's films reveal a tendency to suppress the third dimension, to deny spatial reality. Orson Welles' depth of field creates a feeling of isolation or derision, Max Ophuls' baroque surveying with the camera renders distance practically tangible. But with Borzage, space is not an obstacle: his lovers communicate independently from it (*7th Heaven*) or use it to attest to their proximity, a very noticeable phenomenon, for example, in *Three Comrades* (chapter 13). From the time Murnau came to Fox in 1926–1927, Borzage's space shrank, becoming diaphanous, malleable, inhabited by a supernatural presence. The reality of the set may be doubtful (emphasizing a kind of studio artificiality, with procedures such as background projection or the stylized abstraction in *Liliom*, for example). Borzage does not create, in the same frame, tension or opposition between foreground and background, between characters and environment. A unifying sfumato neutralizes these conflicts, eliminating despair. The rare objects he emphasizes—the three-way mirror in *Little Man, What Now?*, the dress in *Man's Castle* or the icon in *Street Angel*—have ties to a reality that goes beyond what is represented, not fighting it. This negation of space is thematically linked to the preeminence of Time. Borzage's dramas depend on duration, and possibly their fundamental characteristic is this "interaction" between the ephemeral (the fragility of the moment) and the timeless. They take us through the fluctuations of a slow metamorphosis and the decisive steps of an existence, sometimes over generations. Most often, they document the permanence of Love, a trace of eternity in the temporal.

Without a doubt, Borzage's silent and sound movies are essentially metaphorical and /or symbolic. Stylistically his films are created around significant visual or acoustic references. Every shot, camera movement, and all lighting, is justified in and of itself. The metaphors don't only comment on the action, but often transcend it poetically to let destiny appear: the whistling of the trains in *Man's Castle*, the luna-park and the railway tracks in *Liliom*, the kepi in *No Greater Glory*, the shoes and the portrait of Jean Arthur in *History Is Made at Night*, the fading lightbulb in *Mannequin*, the plan of escape hidden in the Bible in *Strange Cargo*, etc. In his central works, Borzage uses a symbolism that conveys what can't be said, metaphysical in the etymological sense of the term ("beyond form"): the stairway and the gangplank in *7th Heaven*, the whirlpool in *The River*, the eye of the dome in *A Farewell to Arms*, the snow in *The Mortal Storm*. Exceptionally, a "bird's eye view" appears in a high-angle shot of the impromptu marriage in *7th Heaven* and the sacrificial deaths in *Three Comrades* and *Till We Meet Again*, in the shot of the painting that Janet Gaynor and Charles Farrell "look at" in *Street Angel*, the statue in *Green Light*, etc. The camera movements indicate a Eucharistic contact ("love at first sight" in *Living on Velvet*, the harmony of the pianists in *I've Always Loved You*), an intrinsic relationship between strangers (*Green Light*) or an unconscious feeling of social belonging (the beginning of *Little Man, What Now?*). At times Borzage borrows purely formal aspects of expressionism, but the realm of the night and darkness which afflict his heroes illustrates less their own confusion than a kind of cosmic imbalance, the outside (*Street Angel, Lucky Star, Till We Meet Again*). The sets represent specific places (Paris, Naples, New York, Bavaria or Guyana) only by arbitrary definition, since the filmmaker assembles authentic details to create an objectified abstraction or better, an imaginary landscape, a no man's land of the conflicts of the soul; there may be something that goes beyond "the most precise if not the most perfect expression of poetic realism in world cinema" (Mitry).[49] Jean-Loup Bourget best defined this relationship of forms and senses: "What in Borzage's melodrama appears to be symbolic may well be real, what appears to be real may well be symbolic."[50] We believe that this observation of inverse analogy is fundamental, both at the level of profound understanding of the work and in understanding its symbolism in general, as it must be seen in the "regular" Masonic perspective.

Borzage enjoys dressing up his opening and closing shots, because they "carry" the structure of the film with their inventiveness and their embrace of the universal. Various elements echo them throughout the framework, key sequences that the filmmaker, like a musician or an architect, carefully structures until the peak, according to precise and subtle laws of measurement. He doesn't fear borderline situations, and candidly seeks out the poignant, which he addresses with sincerity and sobriety. It would have been fascinating to ask the filmmaker about the cinematographic mechanisms of the "master of love," as

Truffaut did with the "master of suspense" (Hitchcock). Borzage often joked as a means of evading: the best time to film a love scene is at lunch, he claimed, when the actor is famished: it makes him look more passionate! Hitchcock certainly would have approved. When his humor was less facetious, Borzage compared feelings at the movies to dynamite: they give strength to a film, but can easily destroy it if the operator does not handle with extreme care. He advocates two ways to not burn one's fingers.

First, humor, a precious safeguard to counterbalance effusiveness each time things threaten to sink into sentimentality. Laughter as an outlet, as a diversion, to be doled out delicately at the risk of obliterating what preceded it. Comicalness or irony, never sarcasm, because the humor must bring characters together, render them more human, therefore more authentic. Examples include Papa Kantor's greed and massacre of English (*Humoresque*), Boule's temperamental taxi (*7th Heaven*), Allen John's disarming ingenuity (*The River*), Baa-baa's pilfering and her grime (*Lucky Star*).

Second, systematic underplaying is required: restrained acting. Emotions must be muted, suggested or translated allusively. The most overwhelming instant, the culminating point of the scene often is conveyed by an unexpected hand gesture, or a furtive exchange of looks, or a movement of the head. This type of elliptical acrobatics requires extremely tight editing. A patch of a door or another accessory modestly camouflages pain, an outside noise stifles a sob, a quick fade-out comes a few seconds before the emotional peak, just in time to let the viewer lose himself in fantasy. He and he alone must discover the feelings inherent in various aspects of the drama and lead them to their outcome: "Make the audience sentimental instead of the player. Make the audience act. Sentiment gives force to a picture, but it's dynamite. Don't point to it, see that it's there, but don't mention it, leave its discovery to the audience. The minute the players start being sorry for themselves, they're sunk. Sentiment is such a treacherous thing for the screen, it is so easy for it to change from a mood to an insufferable pall that it must not be allowed to express itself."[51] In *Lazybones*, Buck Jones is filmed from behind when Madge Bellamy leaves him. A consoling hand (his mother's) enters the field and rests on his arm. The emotional impact is increased tenfold by the length of the shot and the exclusion of the face. Earlier, ZaSu Pitts breathed her last breath, pressed up against her natural daughter (whose features also remain invisible). Helen Hayes hides her tears behind a photo of Cooper (*A Farewell to Arms*); only Margaret Sullavan's eyes emerge from the bandages enveloping her head (*The Shining Hour*). The stronger the emotion, the more Borzage's camera pulls back to a distance shot: Vera Gordon praying, tiny, at the back of the synagogue (*Humoresque*); Robert Taylor filmed from a bird's eye view when he carries his fainted beloved on the beach in *Three Comrades*. Another shot shows Christ in *The Big Fisherman* distancing himself from the camera as his message becomes increasingly important. At times the protagonists apply this technique: on the train station platform in *Three Comrades*, Margaret Sullavan asks her friends to turn their backs to her the minute she gets on the train. At times characters abruptly stop talking or their words become incomprehensible. Borzage excludes us from the secrets Spencer Tracy murmurs in Loretta Young's ear (*Man's Castle*). The lovers do not feel any need to share their happiness with us. The viewer fills in the missing pieces with delight and satisfaction." I like the audiences who see my picture to feel that they are eyesdropping, peeking in, as it were, on a scene which was enacted not particularly for their benefit, but because the inevitable forces of destiny willed it to happen."[52] Thus, feelings become reality: "I believe in playing against sentimentality. The smile behind the tear is much more effective than plain sentimentality. To me, romance and realism walk hand in hand."[53]

Work on the Set

Walking around his set, one would think that Borzage never encountered difficulty. Rare are those who saw him get angry: when aggravated, he would leave and smoke a pipe outside. He always found a moment to chat with everyone, and, it is said, treated the electrician's helper with the same respect as the head of the studio. As opposed to Preminger, he did not yell or rush anyone. Borzage dismissed choreographer Albertina Rasch from the set of *I Take This Woman* (1939) for shouting and swearing. His proverbial calm was contagious, good humor and jokes abounded. He encouraged card games and magic tricks between takes, and said he derived so much pleasure from filming that he wanted people to share his joy. Borzage avoided the megaphone; instead of yelling "Quiet on the set" just before shooting, he would ring a small electric bell. The pace of work was thus relaxed but nevertheless efficient; working overtime at night was not unknown: his films easily came in ahead of schedule. Dan Thomas recalled in 1937: "A casual visitor on one of his sets would think Borzage didn't have a worry in the world. He seems the most nonchalant director in Hollywood. That casualness often is deceiving, however. Frank told me that from the moment he walks on the set in the morning until he leaves at night, he never stops thinking about the picture. And if you study him closely, you can see that he is concentrating on the work at hand, even though he may be discussing the races with a friend. Even during the actual filming of a scene, he sometimes appears to be paying little attention to what's happening. But those who work with him know differently. Let the players make the slightest mistake and he detects it instantly."[54] Borzage recalls: "I used to knock myself out behind the camera, carrying the emotions of every character in front of it. But one day I caught the crew laughing at me. Today I am more conservative facially but I feel the emotions of every scene. At the end of the day I'm exhausted."[55] Madge Bellamy, a star in 1925–26, remembers with amusement the era when actors were given direction without fear of the microphone: "Borzage would weep as he directed. He would sob, 'You see him. He means everything to you. He may not love you any more! He is your whole life!— Doesn't he care for you now?' By this time Borzage would be in tears. 'He kisses you! Oh, what joy!' Frank would be too choked up to go on...."[56]

In the silent era, Borzage filmed difficult scenes by blocking his ears to avoid becoming distracted by the lines and to better record the harmony of the gestures. After 1930, observers remarked upon his habit of turning his back to the action and listening to the scene, which allowed him to measure the authenticity of the tone and determine the right take. The importance given to hearing, the melody of the voices and the overall sound quality respond to his method of directing, more intuitive than intellectual. In all cases, the oral had priority over the written. The ear must "speak" directly to the eyes. In order to stimulate his imagination, Borzage always agreed that people read the proposed subjects to him. Arriving on the set, he no longer consulted the script (which he knew by heart) but insisted that the script clerk read the dialogues aloud to him while he studied the set with an eye for placing the camera and the actors: "It is significant that he directs a picture without reading the script during production," noted Gary Cooper. "Whenever he has occasion to read the script, he calls upon the script clerk to read it to him aloud. I have talked to him about it, and he thinks it is just an old habit. That is what he says, and possibly believes; but I am sure that he does so primarily because reading is a mental process, and that it interferes with the free play of his imagination and emotions. If you ever visit a Borzage set, watch him when the script clerk reads to him. He gazes into the spot where the action is to take place and taps contemplatively on the floor with a stick he always car-

Frank Borzage with aviator Amelia Earhart (left) and Helen Hayes on the set of *A Farewell to Arms* (1932).

ries. He might ask to have it read for him a second or third time; and he comes out of his reverie only long enough to ask the question."[57] Filming delicate scenes was obligatorily done with a musical accompaniment, even until the late thirties. This profound affinity with music — even though the filmmaker was not a cultured music buff — appears at several levels. It occurs in the use of musical themes, at times parsimonious and studied (*Liliom*, *Secrets* (1933), *Moonrise*), and at others metaphorical ("Liebestod" in *A Farewell to*

Arms, the insistent call in *Man's Castle*); in the preeminence of music as an immaterial link and vehicle of happiness, constant in all his sound work (*Song o' My Heart*, *Three Comrades*, *His Butler's Sister*, *I've Always Loved You*, *The Day I Met Caruso*); and at the level of "narrative melody," in the mind-boggling mastery of timing (the very rhythm of sequences and movement, the length of the shots). "The first thing a director learns is tempo which establishes the pace of a scene, a sequence of an entire story," said Borzage. "Next, the development of a story sets up a kind of definitive rhythm that makes every incident fall naturally into place. With or without music, it is just as necessary to strike the right note."[58] Also noteworthy is his use of certain fade-ins that modulate the picture not dramatically but lyrically. They do not indicate the passage of time, but at a crucial moment maintain the meticulous phrase of emotions with a kind of purely melodic ellipsis. So the shot of Mrs. Nemecsek, crouched on the floor, holding her dead son to her (*No Greater Glory*) fades into that of the same mother walking toward the camera with the corpse in her arms. In *Lucky Star*, Charles Farrell relentlessly tries several times to walk with his crutches; these attempts are punctuated by a series of fade-ins.

Having prepared himself in depth the day before, Borzage gave the impression of knowing exactly what he would do and thus worked effortlessly; the actors, he professed, are at ease with someone who knows what he wants, and will more easily accept his ideas. Yet the cardinal rule of a director is flexibility. He must remain flexible while knowing where he is going, to never fixate on one sole concept because it is his alone: "A great picture and not self-glory is the vital and moving end for which a director is fighting."[59] And Jean Negulesco admits: "I took a great many lessons from [Borzage]. He impressed me through his kindness and attitude towards others. He was open to suggestions from everywhere and respected whatever people could bring."[60] Nor was the script sacrosanct. In fact, Borzage often improvised and modified entire passages in the midst of shooting (which brought down the wrath of expedient studios such as Warner Bros.). To be natural, dialogue had to be spoken rapidly, the lines must burst forth as if the speakers were trying to interrupt each other. It was thus essential for the actors to be able to say their lines easily, so Borzage asked the dialogue writers to not go too far from the set.

Borzage and His Actors

But the Borzage touch is most concretely manifested in his work with the actors themselves. We have seen that the filmmaker did not believe in giving excessive direction. He called on the intelligence of his actors and gave them a free rein, at least in appearance. The actor had to maintain his individuality, he believed, since if the role "stuck" to his personality, more accurate results would be obtained. If, however, the director interfered and tried to force his own idiosyncrasies on the actor, he would destroy the very qualities for which he selected the actor. At the same time, Borzage began, with *7th Heaven*, to call actors by the names of their characters, and asked them to do the same when they spoke together between shots, a subtle way of intensifying identification with their roles. *The Los Angeles Examiner* reported: "Frank Borzage is the idol of his actors and actresses, and they never miss a chance at a Borzage picture if they get it. The reason for this popularity lies principally in that he brings out not only the best but the most of people. He doesn't direct in the sense that most directors do. He says quietly: 'Now, how would you like to play that scene, how do you feel it?' And then with the answer: 'Well, go ahead and do it that way.' 'The way a person feels a part is the way to play it,' he has said. 'Then what you get is genuine.' 'Let's try again. I think you can do better.'"[61] If need be, he would act it out himself,

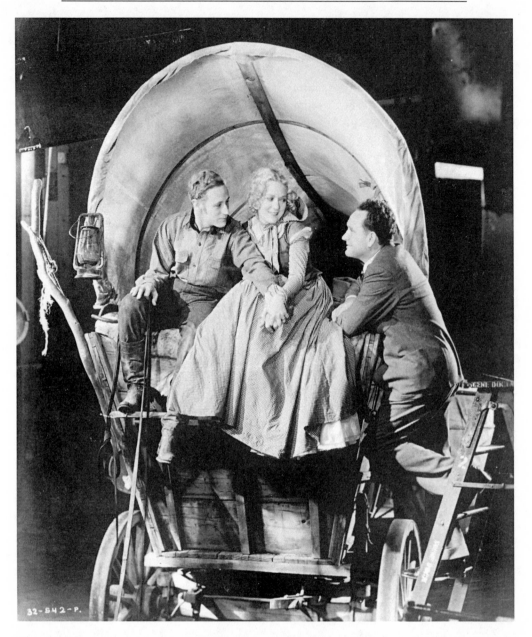

The idol of his actors: they never miss a chance at a Borzage picture if they get it. With Leslie Howard, left, and Mary Pickford, shooting *Secrets* (1933).

in a phlegmatic, neutral tone, without removing his eternal pipe from his mouth. He believed a director should only suggest and guide, not indicate. The actors were not to imitate him, but to find their own response.

On no account should the feeling risk sliding into sentimentality which arises from the artificial. Thus, throughout his career, Borzage never stopped seeking naturalness and simplicity, thinking that by following his own instincts the actor would appear true and melodrama would give way to life. To maintain invaluable spontaneity, the director rehearsed little and limited the number of takes. "I've finally learned that the first rehearsal —

always the first take — is the best. There may be a few imperfections, but the general effect is better. You get a crisp, vital quality in the acting on that first take ... the performance has spontaneity."[62] Reporting on the set of *Little Man, What Now?*, Patricia Keats provides some revealing observations: "There is never any screaming or banging or snarling on a Borzage set. Instead there is quiet calm, rather conducive to naturalness. None of that graveyard silence of a von Sternberg set nor that circus-like clanking of a DeMille set. Everyone talks naturally and no one gets unduly excited. Least of all the director himself. He kneels down by Margaret Sullavan and goes over her lines with her. He doesn't tell her how to read them, he doesn't tell her how to 'act' them. One, two, perhaps three takes is all he ever needs. This is all very bewildering to Margaret, because she feels as if she is awfully bad and that Mr. Borzage isn't even bothering with her. You see, the only other picture Margaret has made was directed by John M. Stahl who used to make as many as 58 takes of one little scene and who used to direct every word Margaret spoke and every bat of an eyelash. What a contrast in directors! No wonder Margaret, who suffers intensely from ye olde inferiority complex, was quite upset. But when Frank Borzage heard that Margaret was worrying about his lack of direction of her, he told her, 'When you cease to be natural, Margaret, I will direct you, not before.'"[63] Borzage also mentioned on several occasions how much he abhorred the term "act," as a true movie actor "lives" his role. The filmmaker maintained a privileged relationship with him, took him aside, introduced him in a low voice to his magic circle. "He was not a shouting man. Sometimes we didn't even hear what he said to the actors,"[64] complained assistant Arthur Jacobson. When an actor disagreed, he listened to him and didn't turn away before having ironed out the differences, as only a convinced actor can be convincing. A director of course had to coordinate the talents of his artists, but better to tell them what they should be feeling than what they should be doing. "When Frank Borzage directed *7th Heaven*, he talked to Janet Gaynor about each scene until his mind and hers were in tune, then he told her to go on the set and think it. The physical reaction he left to her, and she was unconscious of it," reported Welford Beaton.[65] The director explained himself in a 1934 interview: "Once they have thoroughly absorbed the mood and feeling of a scene, the rest is easy.... I love to direct. I love to get into the hearts and souls of my players and make them live the characters which they portray."[66]

Perhaps a part of the Borzage enigma resides in his noteworthy ability to bewitch, to invest his actors with ineffable gentleness, all the while seeming to leave them their freedom. Beginners are his favorite raw material, and he was a great discoverer of talent (the couples of Janet Gaynor–Charles Farrell, Sally Eilers–James Dunn, Vera Gordon, Maureen O'Sullivan, George Breakston, etc.). He had a special kind of contact with young people: his direction of children in *Humoresque* and *No Greater Glory* is astounding. Speaking of the filming of *Desire* (1936), alongside Marlene Dietrich, Gary Cooper (in the text quoted above) praised the filmmaker's genius for communicating his own mood. "Mr. Lubitsch directs with his mind. The capacity of Mr. Borzage for feeling a scene, and his ability to transmit the emotion he feels to the players, is responsible for his success in directing romantic stories, I believe. Miss Dietrich and I were called upon to enact highly emotional scenes in *Desire*. I became aware then, as never before, how his personality seems to radiate a tenderness that makes itself felt in the players and lends conviction to the scene." Asked in 1990 about her work on *A Farewell to Arms*, Helen Hayes conveyed to us her indelible impression: "Frank Borzage was so sensitive — and when we had these very intimate scenes he always kept the set closed. There was nobody around, only the people working on the set, Borzage didn't allow guests. His direction was so gentle and subtle and unobtrusive

Helen Hayes listening to Borzage's instructions, with cinematographer Charles Lang (standing, in back) and an unidentified camera man (*A Farewell to Arms*, 1932).

that I can't remember that he directed us—but of course he did! He was a very romantic man, I wouldn't say he was sentimental, but romantic, and he stirred us all into a romantic mood. That picture was a highly emotional experience for Cooper and me. I cannot tell you what he did and what he said and how he approached the actors, I just know that he lured everything from you. He was right there, inside our minds."[67] Borzage–Sarastro kept the secret of this truly alchemical operation. In his work methods, and in the content of his masterpieces, there is a dimension that goes beyond, a mystery impossible to capture, to describe, to understand. But then, isn't this mystery the essence of all art?

1

From Salt Lake City to Inceville

More than one historian has been perplexed trying to discover Frank Borzage's genealogy and nationality: sources found in film lexicons are rather scant, even contradictory. Georges Sadoul believed him to be Scandinavian,[1] Harry Carr made him out to be German[2]; still others claim his parents were Irish or even French ("Borzange").

In reality, Frank Borzage was of Italian-Austrian origin on his father's side, and Swiss on his mother's. His origins are therefore ethnically complex, with the Germanic component appearing to predominate. His father Luigi (later Louis or Lew) Borzaga was born in 1859 in Roncone, near Trente, in meridional Tyrol that at the time was part of the Austro-Hungarian Empire. (There are still German-speaking Borzaga cousins in Innsbruck). Trained as a stone mason, he occasionally left the arid valley of Adige to seek work on the northern side of the Alps, in eastern Switzerland. He met his future wife, Maria Ruegg, in Zurich, where she worked in a silk factory. Born April 23, 1860, in Ricken, she came from St. Gallenkappel (canton of Saint-Gall) and her parents, of peasant stock, had roots in several places, including the Zürcher Oberland. Her mother died giving birth to her, and Maria, an only child, was raised by her aunt. Luigi met her at a folkloric recital: the young woman was an accomplished yodeler. He spoke a Piemontesean dialect, but communicated with Maria in halting German, the rudiments of which he had learned at school; to court his beloved, however, he was faced by the xenophobic hazing of the local youths and had to fight back with his fists.

But finding work in Switzerland, as in the Tyrol, was chancy, and times were uncertain. With Europe threatened by war, in 1882 the French colonialist occupation of Tunisia resulted in the purely defensive conclusion of the Triplice between Austria, Germany and Italy. A committed Italian Nationalist, Luigi wanted at all cost to avoid being drafted by Austria. There was only one way out: from 1880 on, the demographic increase in Europe, coupled with the depression that for a decade was hitting the entire industrial world, made emigration double, and Luigi joined the ranks of the 40,000 to 60,000 people who left Italy for good every year and emigrated to the United States, his cousins Giuseppe and Max Borzaga at his side. He first worked as a coal miner in Hazelton, Pennsylvania. Resourceful and inventive, he found living conditions markedly better than in Europe and found the means to buy a house. Soon after, Luigi brought over his fiancé from Switzerland. The crossing was treacherous and the ship was stuck on a sandbank for several days. Not understanding even a trace of Italian, Maria decreed that from then on English would be their common language. After their marriage in Hazelton (June 24, 1883), the couple traveled across the country, establishing themselves temporarily in Wyoming, where Henry, their first child, was born in 1885.[3] The small family — proclaiming themselves Tyrolean —finally settled in the Mormon stronghold of Salt Lake City, on the other side of the Rockies, where they would remain until 1919. In all, Maria Borzaga brought 14 children into the world, 6 of whom died at an early age. After Henry followed Mary, and then, in 1892, Bill.[4]

Frank, the fourth of the flock, came into the world on April 23, 1894, the supposed anniversary of the birth and death of William Shakespeare! From then on, people would be tempted to place the work of the future filmmaker (born under the sign of Taurus) under the double patronage of tragedy and resurrection by love:

> I dreamt my lady came and found me dead; —
> Strange dream, that gives a dead man leave to think, —
> And breath'd such life with kisses in my lips,
> That I reviv'd, and was an emperor.
>
> (*Romeo and Juliet*, act V, sc. 1)

Verona, city of the immortal lovers, was but a stone's throw from the Borzaga's place of origin. A circumspect glance at Frank Borzage's birth chart reveals tendencies, that corroborate in quite a surprising way the major aspects of his creative activity and his private life. Principally the data reveals a personality that has an inner quest, metaphysical in nature, attracted to the symbolic, the ritual and to magic (Jupiter in conjunction with Pluto; Neptune in Gemini reasserted by the moon in Sagittarius; Mercury in Aires). His sensual, even hedonistic temperament (the sun in Taurus), conflicted with a search for subtle aesthetic models, almost deprived of material character, and this marked contradiction led to repetitive patterns which are almost obsessive. Innate romanticism, which often emerged as suffering, confusion in (emotional) sentimental life, large capacity for sympathy and altruism are the other elements that figure most prominently.[5] All his life Frank felt a particular bond with his mother, from whom he seems to have inherited kindness, sensitivity and warm simplicity, along with a secret penchant for melancholy. In the thirties, at the peak of his career, he never missed an opportunity to introduce this diminutive elderly lady whom everyone called "Curly" to the Hollywood upper crust; Maria, for so long discreet, submissive, then took great pleasure in concocting a few typically Swiss dishes such as Zurich-style "rösti" (sliced roasted potatoes) for her illustrious hosts. Above all, from his father, Frank got his tenacity, if not his stubbornness, as well as a good, communicative disposition; the father — son relationship was difficult. Above all, the son reproached his father for having saddled Maria, Frank's mother, with too many pregnancies, some of which were conceived under the influence of liquor. Nevertheless, Luigi made a brief, Hitchcock-like appearance in each of his son's films[6]; Frank's mother, his two sisters, Dolly and Sue, as well as Henry Borzage's daughter Madeline, would also very frequently work as extras, up until the forties. Official biographies erroneously give 1893 as the filmmaker's date of birth, but the birth records conserved in Salt Lake City[7] reveal the truth: to get ahead professionally, Frank, still a teenager, subtracted a year from his date of birth.

Although Catholic, the Borzagas had a good rapport with the community of the Church of Latter Day Saints. Luigi was even responsible for founding several Mormon temples. After the birth of Frank, the family moved from 907 South Washington Street to East Parley's Canyon Road, east of Salt Lake City, where the father acquired ten acres of farm land (with horses, cows, chickens and fruit-bearing trees) and built a two-story house with his own hands. Irrigating the arid earth sometimes led to friction with the Mormons; but, more positively, several Austrians and a few Northern Italians were among their neighbors. The family grew over the years: Daniel was born in 1896, Lew in 1898, Dolly in 1901 and Susan (Sue) in 1905.[8] They lived simply, seemingly self-sufficient, and although there was barely

Maria and Luigi Borzage with children in 1896 (from left: Frank, Bill, Henry and Mary).

enough money, the children wanted for nothing, although everyone had to pull their weight; every day the boys were sent to the four corners of the city to assist their father in his masonry work, while the girls were in charge of managing the vegetable garden, and the farmyard, where they raised chickens.

Evenings were a happy time: the entire family shared a passion for music. Henry, Bill, Dan and papa Luigi played the accordion spiritedly, Lew the guitar and violin, and Frank, Dolly and Sue the piano. Their repertoire consisted mainly of traditional folk tunes and of popular music; sardonic wits say that Frank left for Hollywood in order to flee from this pervasive mingling of sounds! When Bill, Dan and Lew became adults, they periodically used their instruments as a means of earning money. The "Borzage Brothers" traveled the roads of California with their accordion tunes, when they were performing on radio or working as musicians on movie studio sets. Dan, for example, was the extra and favored musician of John Ford for four decades. Ford hired him in 1924 (*The Iron Horse*) out of admiration for Frank,[9] and with the arrival of sound, most of Ford's works included a few atmospheric moments courtesy of Dan. Film buffs will remember Dan having Henry Fonda and Jane Darwell dance to the music of "Red River Valley" in *The Grapes of Wrath* (1939), and his tie-clad fiddler makes the cowboys dance in *My Darling Clementine* (1946). As for Lew, Jean Negulesco remembers[10] that Frank regularly asked his brother to play the violin before filming scenes in *A Farewell to Arms* to immerse Gary Cooper and Helen Hayes in the appropriate mood.

Despite very modest living conditions, Frank had a happy childhood. Max Falk, Hollywood correspondent from *Cinémonde* in Paris, describes these years: "In the beginning, there was a cabin. In this cabin, father Borzage, an Italian emigrant, fought against tuberculosis and poverty, while the thirteen other tenants, all Italian, played the mandolin or fife.... At the factory where Frank worked, was an old drunken carpenter. Each evening, drunk, this carpenter would recite Shakespeare, Poe, and Walt Whitman, and remembering being an itinerant actor, a traveling bard. One day, he was found dead and people realized he wasn't even wearing a shirt beneath his jacket. Seeing this man's fate pushed Frank Borzage to leave the cabin and cast himself into the wide world." Falk later claims that Borzage spent time in Italy and fought in the Italo-Turk war of 1911–12 "at the sides of Benito Mussolini and other socialist and anarchist militants" before becoming "imprisoned in Florence," then "expelled."[11] Yet the filmmaker never set foot in Italy before 1960, two years before his death! This melodramatic invention would have only been a journalistic curiosity, had various historians not copied it word for word. The fabrications concerning Borzage's beginnings appear to have increased proportionate to his fame — press agents working for the big studios were partially to blame; only with the help of the direct testimony of two of his surviving sisters, plus recourse to three rare attestations from the twenties, as well as a previously unpublished Borzage interview on tape dating from 1958,[12] were we able to reestablish the facts.

Frank's education at Ashton and at Forest Dale School was short-lived: at age twelve, he had to leave school to help his father in the building business and mix mortar along with his two elder brothers. Culture would therefore have to be acquired through experience. Like Chaplin and Capra, Borzage would develop his artistic sensitivity through direct contact with life, as opposed to through knowledge acquired in books. In the meantime, the teenager discovered a consuming passion for the stage and attended each show directed by the Canadian playwright William Mack (a.k.a. Charles W. McLaughlin, 1878–1934) that was performed locally. He made his decision: he would become an actor. The following year, with his father's intervention, Frank found work in the silver mines of Silver King, in Park City. Although everyone made fun of his ambitions, the budding wandering minstrel, stubbornly turning a deaf ear to his parents' dire predictions, saved every penny so that he could pay for an acting course as soon as possible. After about two months of working underground, opportunity knocked: Frank entered drama school in Salt Lake City. The company suggested its students set off on tour to various villages in Utah. Excited and enthusiastic, he felt he was bound for glory. "My mother wept, as all mothers do," said Borzage reminiscently in a 1958 interview (cf. note 12), "and my father was quite furious, but I went. Dad came to the train and, as I boarded it, slipped a roll of money, fifty dollars, into my hand. When you stop to consider what fifty dollars meant to him, you can

Early school days at Forest Dale School, Salt Lake City (1906).

realize his sacrifice for something he could not understand." But the feeling of euphoria was short-lived. After a 27-mile tour and a few performances in Ogden, Kaysville and Layton, the manager declared bankruptcy, having "borrowed" his latest recruit's savings. Frank returned by night, in defeat: he tiptoed back into the house and slid beneath the sheets. The next morning at dawn, pretending nothing had happened, his father knocked on the door, roused him from bed and brought him to the building site, asking no questions. Frank was the butt of gibes on all sides: the boy gritted his teeth, returned to the mine and began again to save. After all, he had been born under the sign of the bull.

The next theater company took him across Montana and he flopped in Laramie, Wyoming, but this time was unable to return home. Literally starving, he found a job in a camp for railroad men as the Chinese cook's assistant, then joined a team of unskilled road workers on the railway in the Rockies. This demanding work, carried out in both snow and rain, lasted for several months and took him as far as Oregon. He next turned up, weakened by illness and completely broke, in Denver where an old poverty-stricken black man cared for him in his cabin. Frank survived thanks to the soup kitchen, where he lingered on, helping in the kitchen and gardening in the hotel complex. He slept in public parks or in empty drainpipes. On his own, the teenager knew poverty, what it was to struggle for survival, and his experience as an itinerant laborer gradually sensitized him to the most sordid social realities, a fact later reflected in his films.

Luck finally smiled on him. Frank was 16 when he answered an ad in the paper for a well-built young man with stage experience. Gilmore Brown (1887–1960), the famous theatrical producer, future founder of the Pasadena Playhouse, was looking to add actors to his troupe. Frank arrived at the Brown Palace Hotel in Denver without an appointment. "Any wardrobe?" the producer asked him. "Well, you're looking at it!" the young man answered with a trace of insolence. With one stroke of the pen, Frank joined Gilmore Brown Stock Company of Florence, Colorado. For two seasons, he studied several Shakespearean

Theatrical breakthrough at sixteen (Borzage standing) with the Gilmore Brown Company.

plays and modern dramas in repertory; he was cast in widely divergent roles, as they were staging "Hamlet" with only five actors! In the same performance, night after night, Frank portrayed Polonius, the gravedigger, Osric, and two other roles. The public, often cowherds or shepherds, dubbed him "the crêpe hair guy" because of his curly hair that relegated him to playing tenderfoots. Brown taught him the tricks of the trade and his student, a relatively good self-learner,[13] later remembered, above all, Brown's advice about directing actors. Never shout, never rush an actor, but learn to let him feel confident, he vowed to himself for the future. In his investigation into Borzage's theatrical beginnings, Davide Turconi mentions an annotation in the *New York Daily Mirror* from August 1911 announcing the imminent departure on tour of the Gilmore Brown company with the comedy *The Tyranny of Tears* by Haddon Chambers.[14] Eight actors made up the troupe, with Borzage second to last on the list. They traveled to Aspen, Colorado (August), Hutchinson, Salina, Norton, Concordia and El Paso, Texas (October 1911–January 1912), then to Kansas and finally Phoenix, Arizona, where the company closed with Edward Rose's costume drama "The Prisoner of Zenda"; Borzage played the role of Rupert von Hentzau, and also directed the play. This particular play was Borzage's invitation to the movies. Even though the Mexican border was nearby and his old jalopy had given up on him, Frank headed west toward California; where the climate was mild and many actors were reportedly finding new jobs in factories where they made "moving pictures." His parents, impressed by his trials and tribulations, sent him a bit of money to help him reach Los Angeles.

Frank Borzage was 18 years old at the time — almost the same age as movie-making.

In the development of the American motion picture industry, 1912 was a key date, marked by the victory of independent producers over the powerful Motion Picture Patents Company (MPP), a U.S.–wide monopoly that Thomas Edison had built up in New York in 1908. The pioneer companies of Biograph, Vitagraph, Kalem, Lubin, Essanay, Pathé, Méliès and Gaumont, recognizing Edison as the lone inventor of the cinematograph, paid him royalties to produce films in America and distribute through the trust, then headed by the unscrupulous Joseph J. Kennedy, the father of the future president. Movies would be withheld from the independent producers if they did not affiliate. The parallel distribution networks decided to circumvent Edison's dictate by producing films independently — far away from onlookers, if possible. In California, for example. Besides, the sun shone permanently there and the scenery was varied. That's how Hollywood was born.

In 1912 the independent filmmakers fought back, while the Motion Picture Patents destroyed itself in legal proceedings, because its requirements and methods of intimidation (they used revolvers) did not withstand the test. For the first time, the two opposing camps cranked out an equal number of films. Three future industry giants already appeared on the horizon: William Fox, the only New York movie theater owner not to have yielded to pressure from the MPP, expanded his rental office nation-wide. Adolph Zukor started Famous Players (the future Paramount). Carl Laemmle, a German immigrant, created the basis for Universal, and various small companies gravitated toward Independent Motion Pictures. Several other companies grouped together in consortiums, as the competition looked as if it would be fierce. As of March 1912, the Mutual, presided over by Swiss magnate John R. Freuler, ensured distribution to movie houses and foreign sales of films of Freuler's American Film Mfg. Co.; Charles T. Hite's Thanhouser company, Harry E. Aitken's Reliance-Majestic Pictures, etc. In October, the New York Motion Picture Company of Adam Kessel and Charles Baumann joined the Mutual group with its subsidiary companies (Kay-Bee, Bison and Broncho).

It is difficult to date Borzage's début in motion pictures, as testimony and sources contradict each other. His first-ever appearance in film may date from November 1, 1912, when *On Secret Service* was released, a Kay-Bee two-reeler signed by Thomas H. Ince. His presence in the credits is uncertain, but historians such as Einar Lauritzen and Gunnar Lundquist mention this title (cf. filmography) and we summarize it here, with reservations. The chronology of the films lead us to presume that the teenage actor had begun to take advantage of all aspects of the situation, even with rival companies, pouncing on the smallest opportunity to scoot in front or in back of a camera. (We know practically nothing about his brief stay at Lubin Film Mfg. Co. and Rex Motion Pictures, circa 1913–14.) Whether as extra, props man, gofer, or third assistant (bringing coffee to the set), Borzage found small jobs, sometimes with Ince, sometimes with the young actor-director Wallace Reid.

Wallace Reid was on the point of becoming the idol of the American public. Having grown up in the theater, this charming, good-looking, athletic and cultured music lover, possessed all qualities necessary for success. Discovered by Vitagraph after a turbulent journey somewhat reminiscent of Borzage's, Reid shone in the Hollywood firmament from 1914–15 on (Griffith's *The Birth of a Nation*, DeMille's *Carmen* and *Joan the Woman*) before tragically succumbing to morphine, at 31 years of age. Reid is therefore responsible for Borzage's début, having developed a liking for the odd-job man in one-reel westerns — there were about forty, according to French historian Jean Mitry — filmed in Santa Barbara by American Film Mfg. Co. under Allan Dwan's supervision. His roles or his jobs were still so insignificant that no trace of them has survived. The films themselves, from 15 to 20 minutes long, were put into the can every two or three days, at maximum; the negative was then sent to Chicago for editing and titles. Borzage had no idea at the time that it was in Santa Barbara that he would first get behind a megaphone. When Reid and his mentor Dwan moved to Hollywood, moving over to Universal in 1913, Borzage followed them; he still played the cowboy in about ten Universal features signed Wallace Reid until 1914, at the sides of female stars such as Pauline Bush (Mrs. Dwan) and Dorothy Davenport (Mrs. Reid). Each morning at dawn, along with his buddies Hal Roach and Harold Lloyd, he parked himself in front of the studio gates at the corner of Sunset Boulevard and Gower Street to attract the attention of an assistant director. Harold Lloyd exhibited a range of portrait photographs, while Roach and Borzage, after finding out of what type of film was in production that morning, presented themselves, already made-up and in costume; from time to time, they got small parts, which paid between five and seven dollars. Borzage also managed to stay afloat by doing theater. The star Francis J. McDonald, whom he had seen on stage in a play entitled *The House of a Thousand Candles* by Meredith Nicholson, provided him with a steady job at Universal; Borzage would pay back the debt by offering him a part in *The Gun Woman* in 1918, and much later in *The Magnificent Doll* (1946) and *The Big Fisherman* (1959).

Although he acquired experience Universal, it was due to the influential Thomas Harper Ince (1882–1924) that Borzage got his break. "I owe him everything," he declared tersely, the day after his triumph in *Humoresque* (1920). Sadoul called Ince "one of the founders of the art of film" and claims that "for world cinema [he held] the same importance as Griffith."[15] He was the first to glorify the Wild West, a poet of space and of movement, a natural and spontaneous defender both of a genre on which he regally left his mark.

In 1911 Ince began working at Kessel & Bauman (New York Motion Picture Co.). Sent to California to film the new line of westerns, he rapidly became disgusted by the cheap junk about the Far West distributed by the Nickelodeons and persuaded his backers to a buy a huge piece of land located north of Santa Monica, a wild gorge named Santa Ynez Canyon, which had only been accessible by going along the Pacific by Malibu Beach. As Robert Florey recalls,[16] in early 1912, Ince had built, "on a promontory jutting over the ocean and the mountainous gorge, wooden barracks that could be used for offices, dormitories, refectories, dressing rooms and exteriors for westerns." Aside from the sets, which had no roofs, they built "a covered theater in which to film that had a saloon, a sheriff's office adjoining a prison, a rustic living room and two other sets." Paying them, Ince convinced the Miller Brothers of the "101 Ranch Real Wild West Show" circus to establish their winter residence in the canyon; the troupe of hardened cowboys and cowgirls, horses, stagecoaches, American buffaloes, along with several teepees — whatever was needed to portray the many adventures of the capture of the West authentically. There were even horse trainers and acrobats who could serve as stunt men. A fence was built and guards hired to distance unwanted onlookers (and gangsters hired by the competition). In this tremendous open-air studio, soon to be dubbed "Inceville," Ince filmed the defeat of the 7th Cavalry at Little Big Horn (*Custer's Last Stand*), amazing spectators and critics by the precision of the costumes and historical detail. Many of these films were not personally directed by Ince, but delegated to assistants such as Francis Ford (John's brother); the boss was content to supervise the whole operation, overseeing the initial production work and final editing. To vary his output, Ince also filmed stories set in the era of the *Mayflower* and several Civil War episodes in which Borzage did intelligent extra work (the full-length feature *The Battle of Gettysburg*, *When Lee Surrendered*, *The Pride of the South*, etc.); here he discreetly defends the cause of the Confederates, since industry from the North supported the rival magnates from the Edison trust! Another novelty was that the majority of these films released under the suggestive label of Buffalo or Broncho, then of Kay-Bee (for the initials of Kessel & Bauman) presented a two-reeler, lasting approximately a half an hour. This was a preliminary step toward the directing full-feature films—four reels or more—that were gradually being shown in movie theaters.

While he was collaborating from time to time on small Wallace Reid westerns, Borzage worked more and more often at Inceville's "western village," and once or twice at Thomas Ince Studio in Culver City (Washington Blvd), which only became operative as of January 1916. To reach Inceville, the young man and his roommate David Butler—another future filmmaker—took first the Venice–Los Angeles tram (they lived in L.A.) to the terminus, then the bus, then walked—or climbed up—the hills leading to the studio. The salary was soon raised from $12 (a novice with no personal wardrobe) to $30 a week. In 1913, Borzage's status changed. Fortified by his stage experience, one day he asked the big boss to hire him as a character actor. Mr. Ince, twelve years his senior, stared him down. "Out of the question," he answered an astounded Borzage. "I see you as a young lead. You're going to be a star!" Flattered and buoyed by such praise, Borzage did not budge. He discovered later, laughing, the reason for his sudden rise: there was an extraordinary physical resemblance between the two men. At any rate, he appeared, heading the cast, together with the seductive Rhea Mitchell in *A New England Idyll*. This Reginald Barker two-reeler, filmed in ten days, from November 2–11, 1913, marked the officially documented beginning of Borzage at Ince and may be considered his first real screen break. The following week he was filmed in *A Romance of the Sea* by Walter Edwards, a pirate romance involving the legendary Captain Blood, then in the stampedes of Scott Sidney's *Desert Gold*, in December.

The clincher follows barely one month later with the disaster movie *The Wrath of the Gods*. This time, not the Far West, but another setting particularly well-liked at the time by the public: Japanese-style exoticism, jazzed up here with a spectacular volcanic eruption illustrating the destruction of the island of Sakura which occurred January 13, 1914. They picked up on the news, since the filming of this six-reel blockbuster had already begun on the 27th of that same month; executing it was so important that Ince delegated direction to two of his pupils, Reginald Barker and Raymond B. West (for the special effects, tinted red). The film linked the recent cataclysm to the vicissitudes of a "forbidden" love between a Japanese beauty and an American castaway (Borzage). To this end, the producer secured the services of a highly rated Japanese theatrical actress, Tsuru Aoki. Her future husband, the fascinating Sessue Hayakawa (*The Bridge on the River Kwai*, 1957) played the part of the renegade's father, assassinated by islanders after having converted to Christianity. A village of Japanese fishermen settled in California provided the extras. The only white

Borzage's first breakthrough (center) on the screen in *The Wrath of the Gods* (1914), with Tsuru Aoki (left) and Sessue Hayakawa.

man in the cast, Borzage stood out —fatefully, as it were —from the rest of the group and grabbed the attention of fans. The film was astoundingly successful: in New York alone, 40,000 people converged on the Brooklyn baseball stadium, transformed into an open-air movie theater; the stadium could contain only half the spectators and riots broke out with many people wounded.

Immediately afterward Borzage and the Aoki-Hayakawa couple followed up with a series of oriental dramas traced along the lines of *Madame Butterfly*, often concluding in the form of hara-kiri: *The Geisha, A Relic of Old Japan, Nipped, A Tragedy of the Orient*. In the feature *The Typhoon*, Borzage, the young lead, portrays a Parisian playwright — along with mustache and artist's scarf — who became the rival of a Japanese ambassador (Hayakawa) in a quest for love; it all ends with the passionate murder and the guillotine for the yellow diplomat. The intrigue is of course deliciously outdated, but watching the film, we are struck by Borzage's mimicry, alternately exaggerated and finely drawn; his acting contrasting bizarrely with the theatricality of the other protagonists. This is especially noticeable when watching other of his parts in the 1910s: the actor plays his roles with so much simplicity, vulnerability and restraint that his profile seems almost displaced, unconnected to the context.

Borzage's first appearance in the cinematographic press dates from December 1914: *Photoplay Magazine* published a full page photo of him, touting him as "one of the most daring young players in filmdom," then going on to briefly describe the risks he took confronting a lion with a pitchfork in *A Romance of the Sawdust Ring*.[17] Other praised his physical prowess and painstaking struggle for realism. In the western *The Panther*, for example, filmed in Great Bear Valley west of the Sierra Nevada, he is tied to a tree and literally whipped until he bleeds by the title bandit; when director Walter Edwards yelled "cut!," the technicians gathered up the young man, lying fainted on the ground: in keeping with his role, he had not opened his mouth."[18] "His skill at carrying off all sorts of stunts helped make him greatly popular," confirmed *Picture Play*, surprised at discovering a fashionable actor dressed in evening clothes who was also an accomplished athlete.[19] Elsewhere people praised his resourcefulness. "Reel Life" tells how one day, when Borzage found himself in the middle of a forest, for the same film, he was shattered to discover he had forgotten his make-up at the hotel! Playing an unfortunate who is lost in the woods, on the brink of madness after days of, Borzage slipped away without his director's knowledge and sought out a charred stump; he made himself up so artfully with charcoal that people took him for a tubercular on the verge of death. Edwards inspected him closely in front of the camera and exclaimed, half worried, half admiringly: "Say, do you feel as bad as you look?"[20]

Athletic, six feet tall, with curly brown hair and piercingly bright blue-grey eyes, Borzage appealed to people. His roles at Ince were relatively varied, but he had such a friendly expression that he had to fight to play "bad guy" roles. He appeared as a cynical card player in *Tools of Providence* (1915) alongside the most famous cowboy of the industry, William S. Hart. When he tries to rape Hart's character's fiancé on a church bench, he is killed by a bullet that ricocheted against a bell.[21] His Brylcreemed playboy was also worthy of praise in a singularly incisive social drama for the time, *The Cup of Life* (1915), by Raymond B. West and Ince. Set in the miserable neighborhoods of the East Side, the film describes naturalistic details such as the moral and physical downfall of a woman attempting to escape her grim environment. Deserted by her rich lovers after her first wrinkles appear, she descends into filth, drugs and alcohol, while her radiant young girl's face is reflected one last time in the mirror.

Unlike his rivals, Ince did not fear tragic endings. This rather unlikely dramaturgic intransigence would not leave the young Borzage indifferent. As the months went by, Borzage observed with growing attention the entire filmmaking process. Ince had promised him to promote him to the rank of director, "when the time came." He was sensitized by the importance of natural setting in dramatizing the real (as opposed to using only sound sets). The story had to be carefully structured, but directed with enough flexibility so that the public would believe the scenes were improvised, a representation of life itself as opposed to contrived intrigues. As for the actors, their choice was dictated by the authenticity of their characteristics and not by their popularity or their professionalism. The action was linear and facts reduced to the essential. Dramatic progression was tightly edited, a matter of economics. The drama had to unfold around a few specific motives, so a great many intertitles had to be eliminated, along with any superfluous psychological developments (Ince was the first to introduce the technique of cutting in his screenplays). The story was unimportant. What mattered was to provide narration backed up by means of strong character types, judicious details and a landscape appropriate for establishing a "climate." These were the fundamental lessons Borzage learned from his years spent at the Ince school.

"Thomas Ince was less of a great discoverer of actors than David Wark Griffith," remarked the noted historian Georges Sadoul. "But he knew, nevertheless, how to recruit from American film-making some of its glories. One of his favorite actors was a still-teenage cowboy, Frank Borzage. This actor's popularity was great enough to reach Europe, but never approached, however, that of Thomas Ince's three major discoveries: Charles Ray, William S. Hart and Sessue Hayakawa."[22] According to current research, Borzage appeared as an actor in about 80 films, excluding those in which he worked as an extra with Wallace

Reid and his own directorial work; about half of these movies were filmed at Ince studios. A not inconsiderable filmography, considering his age, and one which did not end when he become his own boss. His talents as actor would still be sought out by other filmmakers up until 1917. Notable was his zesty interpretation in *A Mormon Maid*; in autumn 1916, Jesse L. Lasky productions (Paramount), then headed by Cecil B. DeMille, gave Borzage the lead in this anti–Mormon film of rarely seen virulence. Superbly photographed by Charles Rosher, energetically directed by the underrated Robert Zigler Leonard, *A Mormon Maid* shows the "Saints of the Last Days" of the 1850s as a sprawling sect under the domination of lecherous old men, more dangerous for the farmers of Utah than the American Indians. In the streets of Salt Lake City, the "Angels of Vengeance," hundreds of them armed and wearing the emblem of a giant eye on their face masks, maintain order and enforce polygamy (the iconic reference to the Ku Klux Klan is intentional). We can legitimately wonder what led Borzage, a native of Salt Lake City, to accept such work. We find in *A Mormon Maid*, strangely enough, a prototype of the situation Borzage later favored. We see in it the "innocent" couple threatened by a tyrannical collectivity (*The Mortal Storm*), flights of love through displacement (a squirrel receiving the caresses that the two partners intend for each other), and also a very marked sense of allegorical stylization that may have been influential.

FRANK BORZAGE

the juvenile lead with the Kay Bee, Broncho and Domino Companies is one of the most daring young players in filmdom. Recently he fought a battle with a lion, with no other weapon than a pitchfork in Thomas Ince's picture "A Romance of the Sawdust Ring." When it was all over, the lion subdued, the heroine rescued and the scene finished, then and then only Borzage showed the strain he had been under.

First appearance in the press (*Photoplay Magazine,* December 1914).

2

Debut at the Megaphone

In the summer of 1915, Samuel S. Hutchinson, president of American Film in Santa Barbara, offered Borzage what appeared to be a tempting contract. He suggested Borzage become the male star of a new production unit, Beauty, that specialized in sentimental comedy and vaudeville. Hutchinson claimed he was captured by the singular mix of wholesome little boy humor, energy, aplomb and tenderness the young man radiated beneath his Sunday rancher exterior. Borzage agreed because, as we have seen, he was familiar with the Santa Barbara team; perhaps he also accepted it because, very independent by nature, he sought to distance himself somewhat from Ince's studio system, where everyone was, to say the least, being constantly monitored, if not totally subjugated by the authority the crucial pioneer wielded over all his employees. He seemed to find it difficult to make it on his own, constrained by aligning himself with the pervasive style, themes and interventionist methods of the studio. Ince was actually restructuring his entire organization in order to join David Wark Griffith and Mack Sennett in the legendary Triangle Film Corporation. American Film, on the other hand, was a medium-sized company, with administrative centers in New York and Chicago. By 1912, it had moved its California studios from San Juan Capistrano to "sleepy old Santa Barbara, the town of monks and Missions and moving picture shows"—a vacation spot where it owned a complex of 12 shooting sets; there were 18 directors, between 75 and 100 actors and more than 200 technicians, carpenters and workers at the location, managed by an inexperienced studio head, P.G. Lynch, and Thomas Ricketts,[1] an artistic director overoccupied with his own projects.

The Beauty unit churned out a film a week, with three directors taking turns, each spending two weeks preparing and one shooting. But work on these insipid tracks, brief one- or two-reel playlets in which Borzage played opposite Neva Gerber (later one of the "serial" princesses) was frustrating. *Touring with Tillie*, for example, tells of the billing and cooing of two wealthy campers with a young ranch owner. The plots of *Alias James*, *Chauffeur*, *Her Adopted Father* and *Cupid Beats Fathers* (fall 1915) are hardly more encouraging, and Borzage felt he was being poorly directed by hackers. "Everything was so overdone, so unnecessary," he complained.[2] After 13 of these, no longer able to bear either the types of stories or the exaggerated mimicry in which directors forced him to indulge, the enraged actor, having just left the set after refusing to roll his eyes while looking at the camera, sought out his boss. "We'll get you another director. Who do you want?" "Well, Mr. Ince told me that some day he wanted me to direct for him and why not let me try to direct myself?" "I don't know, what kind of stories would you do?" "It doesn't make any difference." "I'll tell you," the boss said, "we have some horses here, a couple of desert horses we're just feeding, how about making some western pictures? Can you ride?" "Sure I can ride, I'm athletic, I can do practically anything I set out to do." Borzage consented on the spot, even if his experience was limited to a few outings riding the old family nag bareback in Salt Lake City. Once given the green light, he secretly sought out the Morrison brothers: Peter, Carl and Chick, authentic cowboys and rodeo champions (Chick was also one of the managers of the American Film Studio). When he explained the delicate situation, the Morrisons slapped their thighs and did their utmost to provide him with an intensive riding course that included training, using a lasso and so on. On December 18, 1915, *Motion Picture News* officially announced Frank Borzage's promotion to the rank of director, claiming it was due to "the young actor's remarkable sense of film intuition," as President Hutchinson termed it. The budding director, a mere twenty-one-year-old, would often play the lead himself, working in the Mustang production group in place of director Thomas Chatterton.

In the meantime, Borzage had already completed his first film, *The Pitch o' Chance*, released in theaters on Christmas Day 1915. The script was his own. L. Guy Wilky, who later became William C. DeMille's favorite collaborator, was assigned to the camera. Helene Rosson, youngest sister of cinematographer Harold G. Rosson and directors Arthur and Richard Rosson, as well as Jack Richardson, the oldest star of the company, played opposite him. Borzage was also responsible for the editing, which he did from the negative: there was no time to wait for a print as the laboratories were in Chicago. "I shot about five or six thousand feet on my first two-reeler and I had to get it down to length, to two thousand feet. I hadn't covered myself with close-ups or angle shots, so I had an awful hard time getting this down to two reels. Well, that really gave me a great lesson, the best lesson that ever happened to me in my life. Since then, of course, I cover myself in every way. When I make a film now, or ever since then, I protect myself from almost every angle. As a matter of fact, I edit the thing as I shoot it."[3] Miraculously, a print of *The Pitch o' Chance* has survived: it is in the Library of Congress in Washington. An exceptional document, it brings out certain paradigms in Borzage's work and therefore merits a detailed description.

The film begins with three iris ins-and-outs to rapidly introduce the characters. Rocky (Borzage), a dolt "who bets on everything, anything or nothing at all," yawns and flips a coin to find out if he wants to roll a cigarette. In the saloon, Kentuck (Richardson), the professional gambler, cigar in mouth, is concentrating on his cards. He appears cocksure, adulated and unbeaten. The blond Nan (Rosson) "who sort of belongs to Kentuck," observes her man with a sullen, resigned expression. Hair mussed, she leans forward, palm on chin, looking disenchanted. Fade to black. Rocky, fidgeting, makes a few stupid bets with a friend — does he want to take a jaunt to the city or stay on the ranch? Will the farm boy drop his bag of hay? An intertitle tells us of Kentuck's domestic arrangement: dozing on his bed he is awakened by Nan, who doggedly trails behind him to the saloon where a fourth character appears, the dancer Kate, a brunette who persists, hoping to win Kentuck's favor. The opening iris shot is from above the waist; the woman watching, detached, with a pained expression, suffering visibly despite her smile.

From then on, Borzage resists the usual black and white clichés. Nan notices her potential rival from the back of the room, gets up, momentarily giving up her place at Kentuck's side while he busily counts his money. Kate encircles him amorously, wrapping her arms around him, but he doesn't let himself become distracted. Nan returns to her place, Kate withdraws, hurt. Then Rocky makes a riotous entry into the saloon, pulling clients' hats over their eyes before going up to the bar, emitting a cry of joy and betting on a fly slowly circling before his eyes. Winning, he is drawn to the gaming table, but suddenly focuses on Nan. As she conspicuously ignores the demanding and childish Rocky, he finds a chair and starts playing poker with Kentuck: it's his lucky day! In the meantime, the two women have met up behind the players. "You're only afraid of him — while I — I love him," says Kate. Nan lowers her head, sobs: "I know it — I" and bursts into tears while Kate consoles

First steps as a director, with assistant Park Frame and cinematographer L. Guy Wilky (1916).

her affectionately. Distraught, Nan returns and sits near Kentuck; Rocky stares at her insistently. The filmmaker shoots the entire sequence around the table from the same angle: the table in gentle diagonal, the characters in medium shot, in such a way that the positioning and movement of the protagonists foreshadows what lies ahead. Kate, at the far right, determines the interaction by her ability to move. All clients in the saloon watch the action, fascinated. Rocky, as impetuous as ever, wins round after round. Worried, Nan takes the revolvers of her two opponents. Kentuck is ruined. Emotions have peaked, everyone stands up. Rocky gives his opponent one last chance: "double or nothing" for his savings—and "his" girl. Nan and Kate assess each other, each one in close profile shot. Kentuck looks as if he's going to seize his weapon, thinks, then accepts. Nan, horrified, throws herself on him and hammers away at him with her fists, while Kate takes advantage of the diversion (close-up) to extract the good cards from Kentuck's hand. She then walks around the table, going in front of the camera which visually indicating her role as "master of ceremonies," the cards hidden in her hand, while Rocky and Kentuck are busy restraining Nan. Kate, now on the extreme left, places herself once more in back of Rocky, whom she now wants to conquer. The poker game resumes, Rocky wins everything, and, with lightning speed, grabs a neighbor's revolvers and holds the enraged pack of cowboys captive. Forcefully, he orders Nan to take back the money in his hat and follow him (exit left), then leaves the establishment walking backwards from the camera.

In the next part, essentially psychological, Borzage alternates first between shots showing Kate and Kentuck alone in the saloon and the departure of Nan and Rocky. The world is collapsing for each of the protagonists. Kentuck remains grief-stricken at the bar, then sits across from Kate who observes him, sorry, worried, feeling guilty, as he downs drink after drink. Later that night, collapsed on the table, he is dead drunk; the bartender wants to throw him out the door, but Kate convinces them to let him sleep, then sits by him, caressing his face. In the meantime, Rocky accompanies Kate to her lover's cabin where she wants to pick up her personal belongings. Deeply humiliated, Nan enters the total darkness (symbolizing solitude and confusion) alone, turns on the gaslight, sits down on the bed and looks at Rocky through the window, but lowers the weapon when she sees him converse with his horse. When she returns, Rocky, still thinking about his jackpot, gaily places a hat on her head, takes her bags and helps her mount the horse (she seems unused to being treated considerately). The scene around the campfire, lit only by the intensity of the flame, is constructed symmetrically with the poker game. Rocky gets up, intending to hold Nan in his arms; she has fainted on the other side of the fire, her face buried in her hands. The couple is now no longer separated by the table, but by the emotional barrier symbolized by the fire. Man and woman are both plunged into the isolation of the black background. Embarrassed, the cowboy slowly walks around the flames and approaches her to apologize: "They call me Rocky, an' I reckon they call me right." Echoing the beginning of the bar scene, he once again draws his revolver, entrusting it to her. Then, ashamed, he disappears in the darkness to go to bed.

The next day, Rocky has prepared coffee and breakfast. Nan is seated at the edge of the frame and turns her back to him, withdrawn, disdainfully ignoring his clumsy attempts at reconciliation ("Betcha five bucks it's gonna rain; betcha ten bucks my hoss can beat your'n back to town"). At the word "town," Nan jumps up and does an about face. Rocky, saddened, makes a promise that may cost him greatly: "I'd almost quit gamblin' if I could take back that play I made last night." Nan, without a word, hands him back his revolvers. A sign of forgiveness, of trust. We see them again, headed for the city. Rocky stops his horse and reveals enough of himself to say "I reckon I've done ye enough harm, and can't do no more good. I'll be leavin' ye here — good-bye." An unexpected moment of tenderness follows: very slowly the two begin to hold hands and do not let go, even when Nan's horse turns around. Rocky (from the back) stays in the foreground, his hand still extended and open, while Nan gradually disappears at the back of the image. The filmmaker uses the depth of the frame to express their emptiness, the discovery of aloneness. As in the night scenes, the various stages of hesitation between Rocky and Nan are edited in such a way that they continually alternate with the development in the town. Borzage's mastery of this technique proves that in 1915 he had already assimilated Griffith's syntactical lessons. Indeed, the dawn light also illuminates Kentuck's clouded mind; supported by Kate, he spots the four aces spirited away during his game lying on the table; jaw clenched, he heads for the exit of the saloon. He goes home, finds the cabin empty, seizes his weapons. He explains to Kate, who joins him, distraught, but not daring to admit her failure of the day before: "I'm not thinking of her [Nan]; she went along too eagerly. I'm thinking of him, and I'm going to get him."

The last act is traditionally reserved for settling scores, but Borzage injects an original point of view. Nan arrives in the city and bumps into Kentuck at his cabin doorstep, Winchester in hand. We understand by gestures that he is telling her of his intent to kill the suspected cheater. Nan, refusing to believe her abductor is dishonest, rides hell bent for leather to warn him of the danger. Rocky wanders along the road, looking defeated. They meet again on horse (medium shot), facing one another, but Nan is now wearing her hair undone, which emphasizes the sudden blossoming of her femininity. Irritated, and having

Frank Borzage and Helen Rosson in *The Pitch o' Chance* (1915), his first directorial effort.

nothing left to lose, Rocky accepts Kentuck's challenge. Nan grabs him by the shirt, begging him not to act. Their hands brush. She gently withdraws her hand, never taking her eyes off him, then leaves, perturbed, becoming smaller once again at the center of the frame. When the action takes resumes, the film changes in tone. Brusquely, Borzage introduces a series of wide-angle shots in which the protagonists are reduced to the scale of ants, huge lyrical tableaux which he divides without transition medium-close shots. A horizontal panoramic shot toward the right follows these stampedes along a windy route which borders the side of the mountain — as if the horsemen, insignificant puppets, were only enacting a destiny beyond their control. Caught once again between gunfire, Nan warns her former lover of the arrival of Rocky. The duel is over almost immediately: landing on his feet Rocky beats his enemy who is hidden on top of a rock. But Kentuck is seriously wounded, not dead. Rocky carries him on his horses and returns to the city. Kate and her cowboys run after, bringing the wounded man to her cabin. Outside, Rocky, himself shot in the arm, refuses all help and holds out a fistful of dollars to one of the guys: "Give that to Kate. They'll need it. I can't never use that pile after the way it was played." Moving away, disgusted, he surprises Nan. She is crying, leaning against a fence. "Burning her bridges behind her," reads the intertitle. Rocky takes her hand and doesn't let go. His marriage proposal alternates with two shots showing the final hesitations of the young woman: first we see the drinking binge with the cowboys (pursuing her life as barmaid), then we see a happy family with two children. A close-up shows Nan pretending to embrace Rocky, but she is simply pressing herself against his chest, hiding her face from the camera — a technique in which, by obscuring emotion, serves to emphasize it all the more. The filmmaker will use this technique again on various occasions.

Westerns of the 1910s focused mainly on the fundamental opposition between good and evil, between living wild and living in civilization, between individual and society. In a mythical framework they develop the moral concepts of free will, choice, and so on. Of course, many introduce a love relationship between hero and heroine, but the outside action is emphasized, crucial to the couple's ultimate union. The usual western stories told at the American Film Co. are no exception.[4] However, *The Pitch o' Chance* devotes more than half its running time to simply describing their growing affection. In 22 minutes (it is his first attempt at the megaphone) Borzage reveals his skill at portraying complex emotional development that is believable. His first film depicts the humiliating drama of a woman "won at poker" as a vulgar prize, and deals with the mutual taming of the sexes and the awakening of love that is a part of mutual respect. He illustrates a form of psychological regeneration, each one acting as a catalyst in revealing the other's profound nature. The trajectory of the lovers in *7th Heaven* (1927), *Lucky Star* (1929) and *China Doll* (1957) is practically the same. Borzage automatically rejects notions of good and evil, portraying a purely moral conflict. In the beginning, Rocky is only a noisy greenhorn, a teenage case of arrested development, a shameless gambler. Kentuck is not bad; he's just a placid macho guy profoundly shaken up by his defeat; he seeks not to avenge his wounded pride, but what he wrongly perceives to be a swindle. The female characters generally support each other more than they quarrel, even though they're rivals. Their past is not lily white — we know what the codified designation of "dancer" stands for — and only love incites Kate to lend destiny a helping hand, liberating, she believes, the unhappy Nan. The above remarks show to what extent *The Pitch o' Chance* stands out from other productions of the time.

A similar diegetic universe and lyrical sensitivity is found in another American western that escaped destruction, *Nugget Jim's Pardner* (July 1916). It is also smoothly directed, although its structure is even more linear: the neophyte filmmaker develops here a humor that neutralizes any sentimentality. Hal (F. Borzage), the son of a rich East Coast businessman, lives a life of such debauchery that his father disinherits him, kicking him out. Falling over drunk, Hal hides in a cattle wagon headed for Arizona. He jumps from the train not far from Silvertown, a prospecting settlement. There, the miner Nugget Jim, a poorly shaven, potbellied grouch in his fifties (Dick La Reno), spends his days drinking, while his daughter Madge (Anna Little) has been reduced to performing in a dubious club. In vain, she begs him to give her a different life, but the father, annoyed, turns a deaf ear after pocketing her meager earnings.

Meanwhile, Hal finds the door to Old Jim's hut open, and famished, prepares himself a small feast. When Jim enters his lair, the simple opposition between the two personalities creates a comical situation which the director plays to the hilt. He shows a close-up of the miner, features frozen, teeth clenched, followed by his insolent, greedy sidekick, still busily preparing his food. Hal greets Jim distractedly, continuing to eat greedily, speeding up as he senses the threatening storm. Inside Jim is furious, but his features remain impassive, as if paralyzed by this tuxedo-clad whippersnapper's inconsiderateness and cold-bloodedness. A medium-shot frees energy too long contained: with a few punches, Jim floors the intruder. Hal wipes his chin, makes a sign of surrender and declares insolently: "Listen, Sport — how'd you like a little exercise like this *every* morning?" Jim grabs him by the throat, shakes him roughly and drags him to the edge of a stream to make him fully pay for his meal. Not in the least perturbed, Hal finishes the remainder of a sandwich before getting to work, under the prospector's orders. At sunset, Jim returns to his cabin again and sits down at the table. Hal smiles in spite of the blisters on his hands and his aching back. As if nothing had happened, he enters in turn, making himself comfortable, rolling up his sleeves, getting out the dishes, finding a chair (Jim's belongings land on the ground) and settling in unceremoniously before liberally helping himself to the food, as the dumb-founded owner watches. "You know, I like this mining business," he says, "guess I'll take you as a pardner." Fade-out.

Within a few minutes, Borzage draws the portrait of a papa's boy whose unsuspected resources and boldness elicit sympathy. Jim's reactions attest to the powerlessness of the drunken thug. We can but admire the naturalness of the actors in an era when gesticulating before the camera was the norm (even Griffith couldn't escape it, due probably to his taste for the grandiose). As the motifs of train and railway that frame the film evidently symbolize an inner journey, the dining room table is the pivot, in a way, or perhaps a battlefield, because it is there that the change of hearts occurs. After a few weeks, Hal learns coincidentally that his "partner" has a girl working in a shady dive. Surprising a tearful Madge, he knocks out the manager and takes the young woman in hand. The roles are reversed (Borzage chooses the same angles for shots used earlier): the couple enters Jim's cabin while he is eating. The drunken lout gets up threateningly, but Hal, his strength mightily increased by anger, hits him squarely and shuts him up in the next room. Madge hesitates letting her father in the door; Hal authoritatively shows him a bed, spending the night himself on the front porch. (A surprising concept: before going to bed, Hal works furiously for several minutes—the actual time of the action—to extricate the blanket placed beneath his horse's saddle). The next day, they free the father, finally sober; setting the table, the two converse and serve themselves animatedly, each attentive and good humored; the meal illustrates the new harmony. After lunch, Hal pushes Jim toward the door and forces him to prospect the stream. While the smiling young man sits down on a rock, Jim finds himself again, spade in hand, dazed, almost dreamy. During the next few weeks, the three in Nugget Jim's cabin grow more friendly, as we learn from the intertitle. The transformation is revealed in the clothing: initially the three were dressed in dark colors. Now, since returning home, Madge wears a white dress and blouse (pure once again), Hal a white striped shirt and Jim, toward the end of the film, a light shirt; what's more, he's shaved and combed his hair.

While sitting down to eat (of course), Hal discovers a missive from his elderly father: his health deteriorating, the father searched for him with the help of a detective, begging him to come home. All is forgiven... A conventional outcome that Borzage manages to go beyond by means of a beautiful farewell scene, both simple and elegant in its emotional impact. As soon as the letter arrives, the trio falls silent and communicates with their eyes; Hal drops his arms to his sides and the filmmaker groups his characters in front of the camera using cache—Madge and Hal alone, then Madge, Hal and Jim, in order to emphasize the union that occurs on two levels. Hal turns his head several times, toward one, then the other. At the station Hal, Madge and Jim look at each other successively in a long shot, hearts full of emotion. Hal climbs rapidly onto the departing train. The composition of long framing twice mixed with medium close-up shots of father and daughter is rigorously symmetrical and emphatically symbolic. Hal, from the back, is standing up on the platform of the last car of the train. The director's camera is placed in the corridor of the compartment: the hero, in the center of the image, is framed by two dark sections of the inside wall—as if under a porch looking out on luminous scenery separated only by a gallery. As the train pulls out, this fixed framing emphasizes Hal's sudden solitude—the railway track below extends across the field of vision, and the composition of the black sections evokes the disappearance of those beloved who had surrounded it in the preceding sequence. Suddenly, Hal strides across the post, jumps on the track and determinedly retraces the path; the camera remains focused on the train and he disappears from the field of vision. The End.

Nugget Jim's Pardner (1916): the final shot.

Contrary to what the title of the film might suggest, the final cliché of the gold mine as salvation is never introduced. Defying the sacrosanct filial obligation (another cliché of classic melodrama), bourgeois norms and paternal fortune, Hal returns to the two people whose lives he changed and who, in turn, have made a man out of him: the alternate title of the film is *The Caliber of Man*. His father's motive in driving him away was not only material; there was also the issue of social convenience. When stripped of everything he finds both his true spiritual dimension and true family, as on his itinerary he meets three isolated people: a wanderer, a drunkard and his bar maid. Seeing *Nugget Jim's Pardner* reminds us of Borzage's 1933 masterpiece *Man's Castle*—both films are connected by the leitmotif of the train.

But the most original rediscovery is *The Pilgrim*. Filmed in June 1916, this production uses the same actors as the preceding film but its plot is practically non-existent. The action is whittled down, with hardly any conflict and Borzage concentrates on mere characteri-zation —following a process described earlier — via gestures and looks, with the intertitles reduced to a bare minimum. Finally, Borzage provides us with an example of his concept of actor's acting. Seemingly a proponent of the Actors Studio before its time, he expresses himself mainly by his positioning, his body, his back (often turned to the camera). The tremulous sensitivity of his performance evokes Kirk Douglas or Marlon Brando forty years hence. Here *The Pilgrim* reveals a modernity that leaves the viewer stunned.

A winding road, visible inside an iris. A cowboy (F. Borzage) and his mule enter the frame and move calmly toward the camera, which remains distant, even when the individ-ual arrives in town and enters the saloon, after having doused his mount's swollen leg with water. At the bar he trades in his spurs for a bottle of rum and sits alone at a table. Wearing a beard that is a few days old, he looks savage, his lips sealed. Accompanied by a dozen noisy employees, Jim (D. La Reno) the foreman of Dudley Ranch, makes his entrance. He spots the newcomer and questions him, a monosyllabic exchange that the intertitles stress ironically: "Pilgrim?" "Yep." "Cowman?" "Yep." "Work?" "Yep." The stranger is thus hired, but refuses the offer of a welcoming drink, returning to his table and finishing his drink alone. At the end of the day, the odd fellow reaches the ranch with slow measured steps, eyeing the men's quarters disdainfully and going out to sleep next to his mule. The animal lies on the ground; the cowboy places his head on the animal's neck and affectionately slides a part of his blanket under his muzzle, as a kind of pillow. The two fall asleep, their heads touching.

A missive announces the arrival of Nita Dudley (A. Little), on the next train. This big-city woman wants to "breathe in the Far West"; the ranch is simmering with excitement, the cowboys earnestly getting dressed up, the beefy foreman combs his hair, putting on cologne and getting out his violin. But the new guy spoils the fun and holes himself up in the saloon where the hostess approaches him unsuccessfully, provoking a scuffle with Mex (J. Richardson), her jealous protector. With one violent blow, the cowboy flattens the troublemaker and prepares to leave. The Mexican takes out his knife. The saloon customers push toward the camera, shutting us out from what follows. Still impassive and not particularly appealing, the cowboy elbows his way through the crowd, plants the knife on the table, empties his glass and walks out. Mex is on the ground, immobile. The cowboy sits down on a stone in the woods and smokes, lost in thought. The incident is reported at the ranch. Curious, Nita mounts her horse to go into the city, loses her way, and falls over our cowboy who deigns, for once, to unseal his lips. "You're off the trail if you're going anywhere." She asks him to take her to the saloon. The cowboy notices, amazed, that people are crying at the Mexican's bedside and for the first time, his face registers an emotion other than irritation or indifference. Noticing him, people move away. He offers Nita a chair, settles in near his victim and spends the night tending the wound, a metaphoric process in which the wounded represents his alter ego. Nita is dozing on the chair. At dawn, he picks up the young woman who is asleep and stretches her out on a couch. She awakens in his arms, stupefied, disturbed, their intense looks erotically charged. Borzage then defines the parameters of the cowboy seated between the two people on the bed, between his past and perhaps his future.

"And the days that followed..." The couple goes for a walk; stopping at a fountain, Nina drinks from the cowboy's cupped hands. He is freshly shaved, smiling, speaking as if freed from a kind of hold. In a room at the ranch, the couple faces each other. Embarrassed in the manner of young lovebirds, they are too shy to speak and exchange long looks. From the cowboy's stammering, overflowing with tenderness, the viewer understands that he is asking for her hand in marriage. Nina leaves, then returns with her fiancé's photo. "The wedding is next month." The cowboy is literally hypnotized by the portrait (which the viewer does not see); his face distorted under his extreme suffering, his gestures become slower. He leaves. Nita catches up with him outside, a fence separating them. More intense, persistent looks; he gives her his hand. She hesitates, not sure if she should take it, finalize the farewell. An intertitle appears, a well-known four line stanza: "*The Pilgrim—* that's him walkin' / They say, with never a care. / You always see him hawkin' / 'Tween here and anywhere." The iris diaphragm of the beginning: the "eternal wanderer" slowly moves away with his mule and leaves the frame. In *The Pilgrim*, Borzage invites us to study rapports in which nonverbal communication is key. With its laconic tone and "western" decor serving only as a pretext, the action is not commented upon. The unidentified wanderer disappears as he came, taking his mystery with him. Tormented, misanthropic (for reasons which escape us), he opened himself to others for an illusory idyll. On the other hand, Borzage shows the girl, still a teenager, held captive by her contradictory flights of fancy as well as by paternal authority. Fleeting happiness, heartbreaking good-byes, secret quest. It's fascinating to watch to what point *The Pitch o' Chance, Nugget Jim's Pardner* and *The Pilgrim*, truly the beginnings of Borzage's work, already translate, although only at the experimental stage, the filmmaker's profound credo.

The film world gave early acknowledgment to the originality of Borzage's talent. In August 1916 *Photoplay Art* mentioned that "Although one of the youngest directors in the motion picture field, Frank Borzage has already won a high place for himself in the rapidly growing industry. He is a keen student of character and his productions show unusual artistic finish and individuality."[5] On a salary of $7500, he delivered no fewer than 18 films in one year, 15 of which appear to be lost today. As opposed to Ince, the director did not introduce continuity details in his scripts, but settled for a few pages of synopsis which left him entirely free to improvise according to his inspiration. The work began at 7:30 am and continued until 6:00 pm. The interior sets (saloon, hotel room, blockhouse, etc.) were erected outdoors, on raised platforms covered with only a semitransparent canvas to allow sunlight to filter in. Exteriors were filmed in the immediate vicinity of Santa Barbara, in the Coast Range mountains, in the caves of the Channel Islands, around the luxurious residences of Montecito, and occasionally, in the hills of Santa Ynez, not far from Ince Studios. Two cars were used, one for the cameras and reflectors, the other for the troupe. Besides Helene Rosson and Jack Richardson, top billing was given to Vivien Rich, a bubbly ingénue from Boston; and more often to Anna Little who was the undisputed studio star. This former equestrian, a veritable daredevil, started with Broncho Billy Anderson — the very first onscreen cowboy with Essanay — then became the most highly paid actress at Inceville. The colorful Irishman Richard "Dick" La Reno (Nugget Jim) began his film career in 1913 with DeMille's *The Squaw Man*.

The first section of Borzage's work consists mainly of half-hour-long westerns, showing the region's arid and mountainous landscapes. In these brief episodes that portray the wild west, with their condensed plots, Borzage himself plays the lead roles. The filmmaker's specific contribution is visible throughout. He introduced characterization which became increasingly important until it finally shaped the plot, had a profound intuition of the vicissitudes of the human heart and was surprisingly adept at mixing comic and tragic. He believed it was important to make the characters believable for people to be able to believe the universe in which they moved: psychological verisimilitude was always of utmost importance. A glance at the plots of other films, most of which, unfortunately, are lost, appears to confirm this impression. In *A Flickering Light* (April), Borzage expounds, for example, on a basic structure close to that of *The Pitch o' Chance*: ridiculed in the village, Jim, a drunken cowboy, marries a saloon prostitute who acts desperately grateful. During his absence, a rancher tries to take the woman by force and Jim finds them in a compromising position. Knowing and trusting his wife, however, he flattens the thug out on the carpet. Not a theatrical and predictable tragic misunderstanding, but a healthy reaction demonstrating, as always, generosity. *Jack* (May) is the name of a too-candid farm boy who believes in the promises of marriage of a flirtatious big-city woman and who builds her a house; when she drops him, he sets fire to it, barely escaping the flames. The woman, on the point of marrying a rich local squire, leaves her scandalized family at the altar and hastens to the bedside of the burned man. At times, Borzage cast himself in pathetic roles, as in *Nell Dale's Men Folks* (August), where he portrayed a mentally retarded character whom a sheriff riddles with bullets to protect his sister's escape with her outlaw lover.

But in general good humor prevailed and the filmmaker gave free rein to his vigorous, cheerful personality. *Unlucky Luke* (April) developed the theme of a gambler who wins the heart of his lady friend after losing at dice. The newspapers mention a visual ellipse that summed up the tone of the film: some onlookers, including Luke and Seth, his friend and rival, gather round a stagecoach to stare at the passengers. When the new teacher appears, the eyes of the rogues light up. They cast each other dubious looks. Luke: "I saw her first!" Without transition, the following image shows the two comrades rolling in the dust. *That Gal of Burke's* (July) is a variation on the theme of lighthearted teasing at the farm; *Matchin' Jim* (September) seduces the girls while they are playing heads or tails. Elsewhere, Borzage is capable of being more subtle: in *The Courtin' of Calliope Crew* (August), the cowboy, a braggart, accompanies a convoy of emigrants to California; when an old man dies of exhaustion, he discreetly becomes the quasi-invisible protector of his timid, puritanical daughter; even his request for marriage is by "long distance," by an intermediary letter. "The love situations are purely psychological, as the characters barely meet face to face, yet a love interest pervades the entire story, culminating in the complete surrender of [the girl]," *The Moving Picture World* characteristically remarked.[6]

Finally, *The Forgotten Prayer* (August), disconcertingly introduces religion in a passionate relationship in the middle of the desert, and bears marked similarities to one of the major themes underscoring Borzage's work, from *7th Heaven* (1927) to *Strange Cargo* (1940). Having remained alone too long in the sierra, old "Mojave" Matt realizes he has forgotten half the words to the Lord's Prayer, which he recites daily, and decides to return to civilization to freshen his memory. In an encampment slightly further on, Dan (F. Borzage) and Alice (A. Little), have been happily married for four years when Alice's former lover, Sandford, appears on the scene. When the intruder is disrespectful, Dan threatens him with his weapon and leaves him without provisions in the middle of the Mojave desert. Matt discovers him as he is dying; before he expires, Sandford whispers a bit of the next part of the prayer: "Forgive us our trespasses." Mojave Matt arrives at Dan and Alice's cabin; the two of them, embittered, are no longer on speaking terms. The old desert hermit asks Dan the rest of the biblical verse. Dan recites: "as we forgive those who trespass against us," and while Mojave Matt disappears, Dan, crying, and illuminated by the meaning of prayer, holds his wife in his arms. Borzage already transcends the underlying moralism and religiosity by showing the lovers as emotionally demonstrative; Metanoïa and embrace are intimately linked. At one point in the film, Borzage includes a shot representing the Last Supper. During the filming (April–May 1916), a budget-conscious studio executive told him there were "too many people on the set."[7] Borzage had to explain to him that since the entire American filmgoing public was not ignorant, in order to remain faithful to the New Testament, they would certainly be surprised to learn that Jesus had only invited six disciples to the last supper!

Judging by their plots, the remaining American Film productions of 1916 largely conform to the soap operas of the time. *The Silken Spider* (March) tells a dark tale of greed, heredity, and moral redemption set in high society; *The Code of Honor* (March), a spy story, focuses on the plans of a revolutionary submarine; *The Demon of Fear* (June) provides a psychological sketch on the ravages of fear and true courage. Finally, *Quicksands of Deceit* (July) is a rural melodrama in which an adopted orphan sacrifices herself for her smart half-sister. *Life's Harmony* (February), a copy of which can be found at the George Eastman House in Rochester, is reminiscent of the pastoral idylls of the Victorian era beloved to Griffith (Borzage is not in the cast). It is the drama of an old New England organist, Pringle (G. Périolat), whom the parish board summarily replaces after twenty years of loyal service. His adopted daughter Faith (V. Rich) becomes infatuated with Gordon, his young replacement. Pringle developed a special patent for the organ during his free time and now, out of work, hopes it will bring him enough money to survive. Gordon offers to submit his invention to Washington and release some capital there. But weeks go by with no news of him. A report in a newspaper denounces him as a crook. Pringle, at the end of his resources, prepares to send the inconsolable Faith back to the orphanage when Gordon appears, pockets bulging with money. A flashback explains that he was the victim of an accident who temporarily lost his memory. As for the press clipping, it was about his recently deceased brother! With its pastoral images and sometimes Rembrandt-like lighting effects, this short sentimental fable mostly sketches a portrait of an organist fallen on hard times. It touches in passing the bigotry and cowardice of certain parishioners. Qualities specific to the cinema observed in the preceding reels—a clear narrative, visual shortcuts, groupings in deep focus confirm it, but the argument leaves little room for extrapolation. It is therefore unsurprising to learn that the film was written and begun by Lorimer Johnson; Borzage only co-directed.

At the end of the year, as if in reward for his work, Borzage obtained authorization to film his first two full-length features, the five-reel westerns *Land o' Lizards* (September) and *Immediate Lee* (November). The first seems to emanate from Borzage's experience in the Santa Ynez mountains one month earlier. Returning on horse to the studio after a day of shooting exteriors, Borzage noticed that his mount had begun to limp; he examined the hoof and was amazed to discover a large gold nugget. The *Pittsburgh Reader* commented ironically, "Now Borzage is spending all the spare time his wife will allow him in the mountains looking for the spot where the horse found the gold. Here's wishing you luck, Frank!"[8]

Only fragments exist of *The Land o' Lizards*, which received special treatment ("Masterpiece De Luxe Edition") at the time of its release; it was even distributed in Europe. Some twenty minutes of the original fifty were rediscovered in Spain. The first scene of the film that was recovered tersely introduces the main character, The Stranger, played by Borzage himself. (The filmmaker seems to have a penchant for this form of archetypal anonymity, as seen in *The Pilgrim* or through the protagonists of *The Gun Woman* (1918); the anonymity of characters such as the Stranger and the Collector, would be exploited by Italy's spaghetti westerns half a century later.) A gang of outlaws led by Buck Moran is terrorizing the area of Los Huesos in Arizona. No one dares confront them. In the local saloon, one lone solitary man remains unaffected by the invasion of the pistoleros. Seated at a game of patience, Stetson on his head, cigarillo dangling from his lips, the Stranger is concentrating on his cards. His impassive expression makes him seem a difficult individual. "Perhaps he'll leave in a while, when he feels like it," an intertitle informs us. Moran and his followers, seated at the bar, observe him in the distance, almost respectful.

In the heart of the "cursed valley" where the bandits have taken hold lives an old farmer, David Moore, and his teenage son. Moore is really a gold prospector working at night, extracting the precious metal from a place known only to him. The few remaining shots suggest an emotionally strong scene: standing at his father's side, Bob removes his hat revealing a woman's head of hair; the little girl — Bobbie (Anna Little) — has lost all hope, having to hide her identity to avoid being molested by the riffraff. The father dries her tears, asking her to be patient. Borzage films this aside with tenderness into the light, by the window, carefully using a superb lighting effect followed by an iris-out. The press of the time specifically praised Anna Little's performance as a would-be boy, "one of the most appealing of her career."[9]

Ward Curtis, president of a "National Mining Company" in New York, is closely interested in Los Huesos, because his engineers suspect there are gold mines in the area. He decides to go there with his daughter Wynne, who dreams of discovering the Far West. On his arrival, the businessman searches in vain for his liaison officer. A local indicates one of three still-recent tombs at the edge of the "cursed valley." All the New Yorker has to do is discover among the residents a man courageous enough to confront the outlaws. This quest is the juiciest and most representative moment of the fragment. After the intertitle announcing the search for the "rare bird," Borzage cuts to a medium-close shot of the Stranger, perpetually seated at a table in the saloon and absorbed, reading a newspaper. The barman (off screen) gives him a box of cheap cigars. Without taking his eyes off the paper, the individual puts the cigar in his mouth; with his right hand he lights a match by rubbing it between his fingers, then pours himself a drink. Meanwhile, Curtis has unsuccessfully done the rounds of the tables. He stands in front of the stranger, who ignores him, still busy with his paper. As his cigar has gone out, he mechanically extracts a match from his pocket and lights it in his hand. But Curtis takes him by surprise, removing the butt from his lips, throwing it on the ground and saying, smiling: "You don't re-light a cigar that's gone out on its own…" Then he offers the stranger a Havana. The Stranger looks at him, enraged. Having crushed the Havana between his fingers, he removes his scarf, grabs the tie of the man addressing him and authoritatively knots the cowboy's scarf around his neck, telling him to dress appropriately for the Far West. Curtis remains stupefied, while the man across from him calls the barman, takes back the cheap cigar, lights it his own way and continues reading. "I like your way of knotting ties," the businessman tells him, visibly impressed. They sit down at the table together to talk.

The portrait of the Stranger becomes more subtle as of the following sequence, although much of the film is missing. In order to win his case, Curtis introduces his recruit to his daughter, a sophisticated city girl. The cowboy first enters Wynne's room accidentally. Scowling, his expression becomes candid and juvenile. He is gauche, vulnerable, frightened at being so close to a pretty woman, not knowing how to hold his hand out to her or what to do with his hat. Smiling rather idiotically, his gaze remains fixed on the young lady, and Curtis is satisfied to note, that his ploy has worked: the bumpkin has been seduced. Back in her room, Wynne smiles ironically. Dissolve to Bobbie Moore wearing boy's clothing, looking sad and dreamy, women's underwear in her hands. With this ellipsis, Borzage establishes a parallel between fantasy and the one true heartfelt choice. One only cares for the appearance, the other must disguise itself to hide its true nature. In Wynne's eyes, the stranger's simplicity and authenticity are ridiculous, but Bobbie sees them as positive qualities. Then, contravening the usual drama, the filmmaker gets rid of Wynne half-way through: she returns to the East Coast, weary and bored by provincial life: "The Stranger is the only picturesque thing I have seen in this land of lizards," she concludes.

The rest of the film contains major gaps. We see magnificent exteriors when the action speeds up, but basically all the intimate scenes have been cut. The gunman begins his inquiry, visits the Moores to interrogate them about the bandits. Bobbie, secretly enamored, eagerly invites him to have lunch with them. The following night, the old prospector is surprised at work and beaten to death by one of Moran's men. The hero, who camps out in the vicinity, chases the killer away, and, although hurt, manages to bring Moore's body back to the farm before collapsing. Bobbie spends the night tending to the young man. She tells the gangsters, who come looking for the stranger to finish him off, that he is now in the city. The momentary danger avoided, the wounded man rises and discovers that a woman had been watching over him. He excuses himself, confused. She explains herself.

Disfigured by an outlaw's knife: Borzage with Anna Little in *Immediate Lee* (1916).

Love at first sight. He takes the face of his loved one in his hands and gently approaches her while she waits for the embrace, as if frozen with emotion. All the Borzagian delicacy surfaces— in the lapse of a few seconds, since what follows, once again, has been destroyed!

The love-struck upholder of the law removes himself to hide in the nook of a valley. After having combed the region, a furious Moran returns to the Moore's farm. He hits Bobbie, who loses her cover. The bandits burst out laughing when they discover Bobbie's sexual identity and their chief takes this unexpected booty off on his horse. A long fight scene in the prairie follows, most of which appears to have been lost: the Stranger attracts a group of outlaws in a trap at the edge of the valley and brings several prisoners back to the city, encouraging all able-bodied men to besiege Moran's lair. In homage to Ince, Borzage photographs the massive attack in a long tilt shot, composing a lyrical dramatic panorama of surprising beauty. In his laudatory note on the film, Louis Delluc, the forerunner of international film criticism, mentions here "all sorts of juicy details like this bag of beans— in the foreground— riddled by revolvers' shots and collapsing bit by bit, like the thermometer of the battle."[10] The final images of the fragment show the Stranger breaking down a door inside the ranch where Bobbie is sequestered. The happy ending is missing, and the print's condition allows only for sketchy analysis. Even so, we can clearly note the familiar approaches and personal themes such as that of the lovers' mutual transformation: the tomboy becomes a woman (like Pauline Starke in *Until They Get Me*), the hard boiled type is transformed and opens himself to others.

Immediate Lee is the surname of the formidable pistolero, always ready to draw arms, who seduces the mistress of a cattle thief to get the crook. "The personality of Frank Borzage is strong enough to make the role of a gunman interesting whether he be hero or villain, an intense personality, quite capable of asserting itself even in minor roles. It carries the story of *Immediate Lee* by main force," lauded *Moving Picture World*.[11] *The New York Dramatic Mirror* had this to say: "There is a delectable romantic vein throughout, and an original departure from the usual plot characteristic of the Western story, making this one of the most realistic and entertaining Western pictures of the year."[12] Professionally speaking, therefore, 1916 was a happy year from all points of view. And what's more, Borzage also ended up finding, metaphorically, his gold mine — he wrote his family in Utah that he had just married "the most beautiful creature in the world," while the press announced his new "vocation"[13] to his dejected female admirers. On June 7, 1916 in Los Angeles, the filmmaker married vaudeville and movie actress Lorena B. Rogers (1901–1966). The marriage lasted 24 years, a rare feat in Hollywood, a period in which Borzage would profess veritable adoration to his soul mate. She would be his confidante, manager, often his counselor (for choosing scripts), and even sometimes his muse. Born in Chicago, of Irish origin, blond and bubbly Rena came from a well-established social milieu, much different from that of her husband. She had been educated in Dublin in a Catholic boarding school, her father was a prominent Albuquerque architect and her uncle on her mother's side, Sir Charles Cameron, was a renowned politician. Onscreen she played the ingénue in numerous burlesques of the American Vogue, playing opposite Ben Turpin.[14] Hutchinson, the president of American Film, generously gave the lovebirds a three-week honeymoon, part of which they spent with the Borzaga clan in Salt Lake City.

3

In Search of a Style

By 1917 Frank Borzage had finally become established in Hollywood; the year also marked the end of his acting career and his beginnings with the famous Triangle Film Corporation, which for three years was to play a prominent role in the evolution of the American cinema. A formidable artistic triumvirate made up of D.W. Griffith, Thomas Ince and Mack Sennett managed their own production units. Silent film stars such as Douglas Fairbanks and the Talmadge sisters made conspicuous debuts there. But the public failure of Griffith's *Intolerance* in 1916,[1] as well as a series of bad calculations and unwise investments due to the inept management of president Harry E. Aitken, put the company in the red. On the advice of Allan Dwan (who supervised production), Aitken attempted to keep the ship afloat by injecting new talent. In the summer of 1917, Ince prudently left the company for Paramount; he was preceded in his departure by Griffith and Sennett. Adversely affected by the defection of its three pillars, the Triangle attracted Frank Borzage and Jack Conway as house directors in its vast Culver City studios, located on Washington Boulevard.[2] In front of the camera Triangle managed to gather a bevy of young hopefuls, whom, it was hoped, would increase their chances of success: Gloria Swanson, William Desmond, Pauline Starke, Texas Guinan and Alma Rubens.

The circumstances surrounding Borzage's departure from American were unclear; he was replaced by Henry King, another newcomer with a promising future. In all probability, it was thanks once again to Ince that Borzage owed his introduction to Triangle. He first turns up as actor only, in the credits of one of Ince's last productions for Triangle, the sentimental farce *Wee Lady Betty*, a comedy about ghosts set in Scotland with Bessie Love, directed by Charles Miller and released in August 1917. One month later Borzage was directing his own films. After a year's experience at the megaphone, the director "was worth" $175 a week; his colleague William Beaudine, who debuted in 1916, was earning $150, Jack Conway, who had been active since 1912, $350 and Dwan, almost a veteran (he began in 1911), the impressive sum of $1000 a week. From all points of view Borzage's new position was a promotion, and the technical team of Triangle, with its immense arc light park, was far superior to the makeshift facilities in Santa Barbara. On the other hand, the director's freedom regarding choice of scripts appears to have been seriously curtailed, as Borzage had to conform to the "look" of the home studio and film a bit of everything. Evaluating this eclectic period of experimentation is difficult, since between 1917 and 1920 (with the release of *Humoresque*), it appears that only three of his fifteen films have survived. These three are again westerns imbued with Borzage's personal style.

The first, *Until They Get Me* (December 1917), is a rare gem, probably one of the most beautiful pieces of the genre to be directed in the 1910s. Flashes of raw poetry mix with haunting eroticism, and only King Vidor or Nicholas Ray were to come up with anything equivalent. In the cast were Jack Curtis, an old-timer of cowboy films,[3] the young Texan

Joe King and the ravishing sprite Pauline Starke, a sixteen-year-old fresh off the set of *Intolerance*, where she played Bathazar's favorite inside the Babylonian harem.

Borzage throws the viewer into the action without warning: "Late in the afternoon of the 7th of September 1885 in Alberta, Canada, a man in desperate need of a horse—," and the iris immediately opens on Kirby (J. Curtis), a horseman riding hell-bent for leather toward the camera. He notices a group of men sitting at the foot of two majestic oak trees of quasi-mythical dimensions, their branches covered in autumnal splendor in the underbrush: an unreal meeting place, marked by fatality. As his mount is out of breath, Kirby asks to sell him off for another. Drunk, one of the men persuades him to drink, accidentally breaks his flask of brandy, gets angry and draws his gun. Kirby is the quicker of the two, the man collapses—dead. The involuntary murderer takes aim at the others and flees in a panic after exchanging his white horse for a piebald with a tawny and white coat. These colors symbolize the hero's fundamental but tarnished innocence. Kirby finally reaches his ranch, isolated from the rest of the world ("an outpost of civilization," another metaphor evoking purity), kept by a couple of old Indians who are devoted heart and soul. The filmmaker enlightens us by reinforcing identification with Kirby through the image: when he enters right into the field (the interior of the blockhouse), he is interrupted by a subjective shot of the Indian, who appears suddenly in the half-light and blocks his way, holding a baby in his arms. The semi-darkness, the ghostlike apparition of the woman, the silence, the scene filmed in tinted orange, impalpably lets us know that he has come too late: his wife has died in labor. The camera remains fixed on the man's horrified face. By inserting a brief shot of Selwyn (J. King), a young recruit from the Royal Mounted Police galloping after him in pursuit, Borzage emphasizes all the tragic absurdity of the situation. The entire sequence reveals an extraordinary talent for striking a balance between emotions, first when Selwyn realizes his victim cannot be a cold-blooded assassin and he excuses himself, then when Kirby takes leave of his child by placing (close-up) his infant's minuscule hand in his own. Thanks to the Indians who manage to fool Selwyn, the fugitive heads for the open sea, but promises to return every year on the same date to visit his son "until they get me."

"A Ranch in Northern Montana, near the Canadian Border. The 6th of September one year later." Margy (P. Starke) enters the picture, dwarfed by a large carpet that hides her (seemingly a part of her body) as she beats the dust out of it—the caterpillar leaving its cocoon. A willful little face suddenly appears, enveloped by braids, and we learn that this little Cinderella of the Far West, outrageously exploited by the owners of the farm, is preparing to run away, just like her "sister" Diane, portraying another woman-child, in *7th Heaven*. Margy runs to saddle a horse and disguises herself as a boy, fedora pulled down over her head. But a completely gratuitous shot of her ankles, filmed from below her bed at ground level, introduces the first hint of trouble. In the meantime, Kirby, en route to his annual clandestine visit, has lost his mount. He is hurt and bleeding, with two sheriffs hot on his heels. The stocky forty-year-old hides in the barn where he seizes a saddled horse. Margy surprises him and obliges him to let her ride behind him. Kirby complies, then suddenly returns to remove her hat, exposing her long hair, now loose. His reflex remains unexplained. The man runs his hand through the little savage's luxuriant hair, a symbolic gesture foreshadowing the liberation of her femininity, and one that perhaps challenges the law. The two runaways manage to shake off the sheriffs, but when Kirby wants to get rid of the beautiful child, she clings to him provocatively, enveloping him with her arms and placing her thighs over his. Having reached the Canadian border, the couple separates. Kirby confides his secret to Margy and she, overwhelmed, presses herself tenderly against

Flashes of raw poetry mix with haunting eroticism: Pauline Starke and Jack Curtis in *Until They Get Me* (1917).

him. Kirby's blood runs over her cheek (another sexual connotation). When Selwyn and the sheriff join up with Margy once more, Kirby has managed to slip away in the bush. Margy, hypocritically pious, exchanges her overalls for a little girl's skirt, much too short for someone her age, at the request of the seductive Canadian (who remains skeptical).

Sitting astride the horse behind the virtuous police officer, she reaches the barracks of the Royal Mounted Police, hidden in the midst of vast forests (a counterpart to the "outpost of civilization," which is the fugitive's ranch). Margy is therefore designated as both an obsession and an effective link between the two opponents, each one tormented by the other. Kirby is tormented by his murder and his status as perpetual runaway, and Selwyn is tormented by his humiliating incapacity to locate him, a failure which turns to neurosis. In her "forbidden" contact with Kirby (who could be her father), Mary reveals herself to be a woman, fierce and beautiful; as she faces the young Selwyn, representing authority, she becomes a child once again.

The last third of the film, unfolding almost entirely at the outpost of the mounted police, focuses on "the warmth of Margy's presence" which illuminates life at the garrison. The girl is taken under the care of the commandant's wife. Borzage multiplies the light humorous touches in order to show the effects of the seduction: instead of doing her homework, she plays checkers with policemen thrilled to hold her hand to as they show her how to move the pawns on the checkerboard. "And after four years, Margy and the authorities at Ottawa govern the post about equally," is the ironic comment of an intertitle. She has learned to play checkers as well as how to play at being a woman. Christmas Eve marks the definitive transformation of chrysalis into butterfly: Margy appears from behind the door in a long evening gown, clinging and luminous against the dark background. Time stops. The members of the garrison remain open-mouthed, as if intimidated by her resplendent grace ("She's the Breath of Heaven"). From then on, the roles are reversed: Margy, now conscious of her erotic power, loses her innocence to some extent; she becomes a simpering young woman before Selwyn, while to Kirby she resembles a girl protecting her father. Subjugated and awkward, Selwyn helps her wind some wool into a ball, stammering amorous allusions without really daring to approach her. Borzage provides us with the image of a castrated giant, reduced to immobility, not unlike Hercules facing Omphale, as long as his problem — his alter ego Kirby — has not been resolved: "There is a thing I have yet to do before I ask anything of man or woman!" he confides to a friend. It is true that the filmmaker erects a statue to Selwyn on his steed, permanently busy scrutinizing the horizon.

The loss of Margy's spontaneous sensuality also brings about a loss: the capture of Kirby. Margy actually recognizes the fugitive's photo in Selwyn's wallet and inadvertently lets him know, under the seal of secrecy. Torn, Selwyn hesitates, then decides to go do "his duty."

Margy turns away from him in disdain. On the 7th of September, she tries in vain to precede Selwyn to warn those whose confidence she betrayed, but the cabin is empty. On the road back, the couple, now at odds, meets Kirby, who lets himself be captured without putting up any resistance: he is tired, on the point of surrendering, accompanied by his young son. Ill at ease, Selwyn resigns from the police force and gives his victim a pile of testimonies written on his behalf so that he be acquitted in court. Margy forgives her distraught lover, she catches him by the string of his whistle, authoritatively bringing him outside the police headquarters where she gives him back his revolvers, obvious phallic symbols— representative of his reinsertion in the Royal Canadian. The "capture" evoked in the very title of the film may therefore be interpreted at several levels: among its more significant qualities, *Until They Get Me* displays a poetic-picaresque illustration of the twists and turns of desire. The filmmaker will reintroduce this theme eleven years later, with the memorable *The River*. It is thus puzzling that certain critics persist in seeing Borzage as a man who painted only "disembodied" love.

"It was a mounted police picture and I was the only girl in it, but Mr. Borzage was so kind that I didn't realize I was doing my first lead, so I wasn't nervous,"[4] recalled Pauline Starke. The comedian would also star in two other Borzage films which were lost: *The Shoes That Danced* (March 1918), a romance between a small New York salesgirl and the head of some gangsters seeking to change their lives. In order to film the fighting among the gangsters, Triangle prided itself on using authentic gangs from the East Side. Another New York idyll, *Innocent's Progress* (March 1918), tells the tragic-comic difficulties of a country girl abandoned by her lover but defended from the gangsters by a seductive millionaire. In the twenties, Pauline Starke would occupy a place in the sun at Metro-Goldwyn-Mayer, before retiring with the advent of talkies.

Like *Until They Get Me*, the second Triangle western, *The Gun Woman* (January 1918), was filmed in Inceville and in the area around Chatsworth Hills in the San Fernando Valley. Nine days of intense work which often went on until after midnight. This time, Borzage was responsible for guiding the first steps of the "cowgirl" Texas (Mary Louise) Guinan, an actress of rather limited expression, but who would have a long run in a series of low-budget westerns before becoming queen of the Manhattan nightclubs during prohibition. The film opens with the strange lines of Oscar Wilde's "The Ballad of Reading Gaol" (1898):

> Some love too little, some live too long.
> Some sell and others buy.
> Some do the deed with many tears.
> And some without a sigh.
> For each man kills the thing he loves.
> Yet each man does not die.

The theme disclosed, we rapidly realize we are in an unusual world, as none of the protagonists has a first name. A bandit named the Collector robs stagecoaches in the region of La Mesa, formerly a prosperous gold mining area. The ring of the Bostonian (E.J. Brady), the tenderfoot, is stolen. The passengers of the looted stagecoach recover in a gaming saloon called "Hell's Kitchen" presided over by an energetic woman, the Tigress (T. Guinan), loved, hated, feared. She runs her business with an iron fist, expertly handles a gun, laughs in the sheriff's face when he dares utter a criticism and hates men in general; she remains glacial when, in front of her establishment, a "fool" blows his brains out because she refused to marry him. Until the night when the cold and cynical Stranger (F. McDonald) arrives. Their eyes meet: the mutual attraction is immediate. She sits down at his table, clutches his arm, and from then on, the doomed lovers remain together. The Tigress loses her claws, and cooing, lets the dark stranger understand that "A woman does get tired of doing her own protecting—even a woman like me."

In glowing colors the Stranger paints an idyllic life together in a neighboring village, in Bravos—if she manages to obtain the sum necessary to by a house together. Blinded by her passion, the Tigress takes him on as an associate in her saloon, where she cheats drunken bystanders by rigging the roulette wheels. If a customer cheats, however, the Stranger beats him up on the spot and even the Bostonian, appointed deputy sheriff, has no means to intervene. "And the Tigress is sincere in her belief that the little home will purify the money which is to be its price," an intertitle informs us. Once the sum has been amassed, the Stranger announces that he will leave first for Bravos; his fiancée will follow later. In the meantime, the Bostonian has fallen secretly for the fascinating Amazon, lost in her romantic daydreams. But the Stranger fools her: he uses the nest egg to set up a more impressive gaming room in Bravos, where prostitution and pickpocketing flourish. When he tells her the news, pointing out that he never promised to marry her, she demands he reimburse her capital within thirty days and gives him back her engagement ring—that the Bostonian recognizes as his own: it's the one stolen from him in the stagecoach! The Collector, pursued by the law, is finally exposed. The Tigress begs the deputy sheriff to grant him a month's reprieve ("My claim is greater than yours... He's mine by every law save the law made by man"), and the Bostonian yields, troubled. Once the time limit has passed, the Tigress straps on her revolvers, gallops away to Bravos, sets fire to the new saloon and kills her lover without even giving him a chance to defend himself. Before leaving, she explains to the Bostonian who then asks her to marry him, that she doesn't really feel love, only friendship for him, and that her heart has been destroyed by the fire.

At first glance, today, the plot seems rather unoriginal, although in 1918 nothing similar had yet been seen onscreen. Launched with the slogan: "Never jilt a woman who can shoot," *The Gun Woman* introduced to westerns the prototype of the trigger-happy woman that Barbara Stanwyck (*Annie Oakley*) and Joan Crawford (*Johnny Guitar*) would immortalize a few decades later. From then on Triangle would promote Texas Guinan as the "female William S. Hart." On closer examination the film is more subtle, complex and adult than it seems and we can only regret the miscasting of the star. By settling the score

"For each man kills the thing he loves": Texas Guinan shoots at Francis J. McDonald in *The Gun Woman* (1918).

in this purifying and apocalyptic way, the Tigress exorcizes her own demons (an intertitle pushes the identification with the lover to the point of presenting her as "Another Collector"). To the current themes in westerns of the time, such as revenge and justice, Borzage added romantic concepts to offer a negative vision of his usual theme. In *The Gun Woman*, all the love scenes are simultaneously scenes of betrayal, corrupted by the very nature of the lovers' pledge: dirty money against a stolen ring. Emotion overshadows the action. The filmmaker once again emphasizes matters of the heart over the code of the West, basically taking the opposing view to W.S. Hart's Calvinist ideology. It is no coincidence that, having finally killed the beast in her after the descent to hell, the heroine refuses the Bostonian's conventional love, he who represents civilization, law and morals ("Now I suppose *you* want to protect me," she hurls at him, disillusioned). The tender heart is portrayed first ironically as a scatterbrain dressed in city clothes, then sympathetically (to the surprise of everyone, he knows how to make himself respected with gun in hand) and finally touchingly, when, torn between jealousy and his love, he breaks his principles of strict legality by granting the criminal a reprieve. In the end, the woman-phoenix, who has become a murderess in the eyes of a law "made for men," is allowed to go.

Nevertheless, visually, Borzage already provides a bit of hope: each time the Tigress and her handsome associate are filmed together, the city dweller, although placed between the two, is relegated to the role of observer at the rear of the image. Subtleness is manifest in the use of signs. The spectator is immediately struck by the importance accorded to light.

The Bostonian generally moves in full daylight, but more than a simple opposition between good and evil, the double play between shadows and daylight translates the duality of human beings. The presentation of the Tigress in this context is surprising in its aesthetic audacity: Borzage does not hesitate to photograph her sauntering about in darkest night, lighting only a pan of her face or naked shoulder, in the style of German directors of the 1920s. By day, the Tigress transforms herself into a loving and timid woman; her sentimental strolls are filmed in so much sunshine that the idyll seems unreal, and her wardrobe, usually provocative, is worthy of a well-behaved upper-middle-class lady. Moreover, the presentation of the protagonists already gives us the key to the drama: at the very beginning of the film, a close-up of the Collector's face, against a black background, shows his face masked; he lifts his scarf a little and lights a cigarette, not taking his eyes off the camera. The first appearance of the Tigress is identical: she appears suddenly out of the darkness, stops and lights a cigarette. Her face, briefly lit by the flame, is then encircled by a halo of smoke. A few seconds later, a close-up of the Stranger shows him enter the saloon, slightly veiled by the smoke emanating from the cigarette between his lips. Not only does the filmmaker indicate the psychological relationship between the protagonists by these images, even their identity, but he also evokes the idea of the smoke screen, the illusion by which the heroine will become the victim. She is placed immediately between reality (the Collector) and appearance (the Stranger). By extension this illusion, which ends up a disaster, must also be consumed in smoke: in the last shots of the film, the sky has literally become invaded by the impressive black clouds of the fire, "The pyre of the past." The horizon appears to be tormented by the flames, the characters reduced to the state of shadows melting into the night.

Thanks to the director's pronounced talent for displaying the home studio stars to advantage, he was condemned to various projects. William Desmond, well into his forties, got top billing of the very first film Borzage directed for Triangle, the drama *Flying Colors* (September 1917): in it he plays a former Yale athlete who acts as a detective and arrests a crook. We find this Broadway actor in *Society for Sale* (April 1918), at the sides of a twenty-one year old starlet destined for a bright future, the extravagant and sophisticated Gloria Swanson. The screenplay is inept: a model tries to gain access to London high society, then discovers she is the illegitimate child of the aristocrat whom she has attracted. DeMille's future inspiration, who wished to prove her dramatic register after a frustrating stay at Keystone, does not cherish the memory of this film: "Mr. Borzage, a charming and gifted man, had orders to shoot endless close-ups of me in couturier dresses so if Mr. Desmond felt neglected and resentful and showed it, I couldn't blame him. He was twice my age, with a reputation and a following. I must have seemed to him a complete nobody, yet I wound up wearing more clothes than all the rest of the cast put together... I couldn't wait for it to be over."[5] In any case, it would be difficult to place together two personalities more opposed than those of Borzage and Swanson! Squarely turning his back to society dramas, the filmmaker managed to use Desmond to his advantage in *An Honest Man* (May 1918), whose theme seems to be in keeping with Borzage's preoccupations: a lively and light-fingered vagabond (Desmond) obtains work from a farmer. Believing himself to be dying, the farmer makes him promise to find his daughter, missing in the city, so that he can give her $50,000 inheritance; transformed by the blind confidence the old man shows him, the good-natured prowler proves himself as good as his word. Shortly after this film, Desmond found his niche in the western serials where his frank nature and square jaw worked wonders.

There is not much to say about *Who Is to Blame?* (May 1918) which reintroduces the clichés of the Oriental loyal to the point of servility: a Japanese rickshaw man (Jack Abbe) meekly endures his American master's temper to save him from a compromising position. The passionate drama *The Ghost Flower* (August 1918) seems more interesting; it highlights the melancholic beauty of Alma Rubens, another star with whom Borzage would work again several times in his career. Interestingly, it is set — ten years before *Street Angel*— in the seedy part of Naples. It concerns a jealous killer from Camorra who confronts a French aristocrat; they are both bewitched by Alma's almond-shaped eyes.

We would like to rediscover the two films Borzage shot with the Franco-American ex–"Ziegfeld girl" Olive Thomas in 1918–19: the comedy *Prudence on Broadway*, which tells the adventure of a daughter of Quakers who becomes the darling of New York high society, but moreover *Toton*, whose melodramatic action is set in the Latin Quarter of Paris (the "French Street" of the world's fair in San Diego serves as a backdrop). In his 1958 interview with George Pratt,[6] the filmmaker admitted that *Toton* was one of the first works that really gave him satisfaction and that showed signs of a style of his own: "I liked the feel of the story. I think from then on, I moved into a little different bracket. Directly from there I signed up with Mr. Hearst as he opened up the Cosmopolitan studios, where I made *Humoresque*." Waiting for the hypothetical copy to reappear, we can guess what in the rather fantastic adventures of the plot may have seduced him: the American painter David (Norman Kerry) marries his model Yvonne (O. Thomas), but leaves her to return to the bedside of his dying mother in the United States. David's well-off family confuses the issue; Yvonne believes herself to be forgotten and dies giving birth to a daughter, Toton (also played by O. Thomas), of whose existence David knows nothing. Disguised as a boy, the child grows up in the seedy area under the iron rule of an Apache and, as an adult, becomes the most clever pickpocket in Paris. When her father returns to France to paint with Carew, an adopted son, Toton delivers the stranger (easy prey) to her gang. But one of the crooks recognizes David and the young woman finally learns the truth about her origins. The Great War rages: the last images show Carew in uniform and his wife Toton as a French nurse — a visual constellation foreshadowing *7th Heaven*, especially as her impish little face resembles that of Janet Gaynor. According to the press, Borzage dwells on the childhood spent among the underworld, followed by the helplessness and metamorphosis of a street urchin, everything bathed in a quasi–Dickensian social climate. Life added a tragic epilogue to *Toton*: in September 1920, on honeymoon with Jack Pickford (the brother of Mary), Olive Thomas committed suicide in her Paris hotel room.

Borzage's stay at Triangle seems to have been subject to various tribulations, and the increasingly precarious situation of the firm (it closed the doors of its Culver City studios in October 1918)[7] makes the historian's work more arduous. In March 1918, while Borzage was still under contract at Triangle, his Japanese film *The Curse of Iku* was released, produced by the defunct Essanay company, whose Californian activity had ended the previous year. Curiously, the film is traced along the lines of Ince's Oriental melodramas so popular around 1914. Borzage probably directed the film shortly after his departure from American in the springtime of 1917 at the Essanay Studios in Culver City, or near San Francisco, at Niles. The hypothesis is reinforced by the fact that the filmmaker reappeared before the camera, alongside his former Japanese partner Tsuru Aoki. The plot spans three generations and tells the story of a bloodthirsty Japanese prince's grandson's vengeance on the grandson of a rival American. "Frank Borzage has done wonders in duplicating the atmosphere of Japan, both during the days when the country was in a semi-barbaric stage and during the present time of highly civilized state. He has made it a Japanese picture in every sense of the word," remarked the correspondent from the *Motion Picture News*[8]— probably sensitive to its visual elegance, though ignoring, of course, real Japanese cinema! In any case *Variety* confirms the important aesthetic qualities of the work, writing that "Locations have been selected with an artistic eye to composition and effectiveness. The handling of the Japanese tea garden bits are especially good.... The picture's principle defect is its disagreeable angle in the brutal lovemaking of a Japanese to a white girl."[9]

With *Whom the Gods Would Destroy* (April 1919), another curiosity now lost, Borzage delivered his one and only propaganda film: it deals with the First World War. Filmed at great expense for Universal studios on behalf of an independent film company (R.C. Macauley Photoplays),[10] this film was exploited outside commercial circuits, endorsed both by League of Nations societies throughout the country, and by the Leagues to Enforce Peace. (Curiously, it was banned in Sweden.) It is about a young chemist whose dangerous invention becomes the target of the German secret service. Shortly before the beginning of the war, he takes refuge in Belgium where he saves a burgomaster's daughter (Pauline Starke). The film ends by praising the idealistic pacifism of Woodrow Wilson, which ran counter to the vengeful emotions popular in the period immediately following the war; for the future filmmaker of *Little Man, What Now?* and *Three Comrades*, the Germans were also human beings.

After Triangle closed, the unemployed Borzage accepted two film projects to be undertaken during the summer of 1919. The New York theater actor Fred Stone, a former clown, acrobat and stuntman, who had just created his own production company,[11] encouraged him to film two westerns, parodies to some extent. *The Duke of Chimney Butte* (released in December 1921) shows Stone as a mischievous greenhorn, an inventive handyman who gains respect at a ranch, gets the surname of "duke" and finally neutralizes a band of cattle thieves. Belgium's Cinémathèque Royale has a copy of the second film, *Billy Jim* (released

Whom the Gods Would Destroy, a lost film with Pauline Starke and Jack Mulhall (1919).

in January 1922), an unpretentious comedy, photographed mainly in the area around Lake Louise, Alberta. Billy Jim is "the happiest and calmest guy in the area," with a vacant moon-like face and curly hair; when he is not inviting the neighborhood gang to the ice cream parlor, he is setting straight a drunkard beating his wife ("when he comes home, a man should always obey his wife!"), before getting hit over the head by the furious housewife. When he realizes he has a crush on the daughter of a rich landowner passing through town, he borrows a car, uses a friend as a chauffeur and follows her on her journey from hotel to hotel all the way to Crescent City, in the Rockies, "a city where two cars go by a year ... when the drivers have not died on the road." Feeling out of place in the luxury hotel, Billy Jim mollifies the beauty's father by feigning to be a capitalist, then plays pistol and lasso when a dubious engineer and his gang try to capture a gold mining area. Once the girl is in his arms, we learn that dumb Billy Jim is one of the wealthiest ranchers in Colorado. The gags abound, the pace is snappy, but as in later years with the Will Rogers comedies, it is hard to say who, comedian or director, is really responsible. The most hilarious moment occurs when Billy Jim's automobile is found face to face with a car going in the opposite direction on a very narrow mountain road. The cowboy calmly gets out and says to the other driver: "I'll give you 10 dollars if you allow me to move your limousine..." As the other driver is accepting the money, Billy Jim, totally calm, lifts the vehicle and sends it crashing several hundred yards away at the bottom of a ravine; he then gets back in his car and continues on his way, leaving his victim flabbergasted. Unfortunately, the Fred Stone films, released in theaters two years later, were flops; the clown did not have the desired magnetism onscreen and after his aborted attempt to break through Hollywood, he returned to the stage.

But for the young Frank Borzage, the time of probation, of trial and error, was over. Only 25 years old, he had already directed 34 films, including 17 full-length features, and the detour to Alberta bore unexpected fruit. Both Fred Stone and Olive Thomas sang his praises to Frances Marion. Active on the east coast, Marion was already one of the most sought-after screenwriters in American film. At the beginning of the fall of 1919, Borzage received a phone call from New York.

William Randolph Hearst was on the line.

4

Working for William Randolph Hearst

Immortalized onscreen by Orson Welles as caricatured in *Citizen Kane*, American press magnate William Randolph Hearst (1863–1951) entered the annals of history due mostly to his tremendous media empire, political skirmishes, his mania of collecting and his love life, which was in frequent upheaval. Hearst's filmmaking activity alone merits an in-depth study. Having always been fascinated by movies, in 1913, he launched the "Hearst International News" newsreels. In 1916, he founded International Film Services, a distribution company that financed innumerable serials and included an animation studio headed by Gregory La Cava, which produced *Krazy Cat, Katzenjammer Kids*, and a host of other series). His passion for showgirl Marion Davies—an extramarital affair that lasted 32 years—led the married man and father to seriously invest in production as a means of putting the young actress onscreen. The Marion Davies Film Corporation filmed its first features in the spring of 1918 in New York's Biograph studios.

In 1919 Hearst's mother died and he inherited a colossal fortune; construction of the legendary San Simeon castle in California began immediately. Hearst also founded Cosmopolitan Film, whose studios were located in the north of Manhattan, at the corner of 126th Street and Second Avenue; he converted the rooms of a huge German Colony brewery called "Sultzer's Harlem River Park Casino," closed due to prohibition. Paramount-Artcrafts was responsible for world distribution. From then on, they invested considerable sums, which often lost money, filming hollow and pretentious society dramas, lavishly directed by Allan Dwan or Robert Z. Leonard. Although truly talented, Marion Davies disappeared beneath the costumes and excessive decorative ornamentation so characteristic of San Simeon. Topics geared mainly toward women were inspired by serialized novels already published in Hearst publications, such as Cosmopolitan or Hearst's Magazine. One of the most popular authors of these sentimental stories was Fannie Hurst (1889–1968), whose bestsellers *Back Street* and *Imitation of Life* figure among any film buff's list of favorites. Frances Marion, on her way to becoming the favorite screenwriter of Mary Pickford, Rudolph Valentino, Lillian Gish and Greta Garbo,[1] worked occasionally for Cosmopolitan. She was a great friend of Fannie Hurst. Her skill at both novels and melodramas, as well as her influence at the studio were impressive and her choices carried weight. Bubbly and inquisitive, she knew "handsome Borzage" as of 1914, when he was under contract to Ince and she visited the set of *The Geisha*.

There are various versions as to the genesis of *Humoresque*—a Cosmopolitan production that rocketed Borzage to the top ranks of American directors. In her memoirs Frances Marion gives herself a major role by claiming she set her heart on "Humoresque—A Laugh on Life with a Tear Behind It," Fannie Hurst's novella published in March 1919 in

Cosmopolitan,[2] before selecting Borzage because of this choice. The story is about simple people with simple emotions, the humble life of Jewish families in the New York ghetto. She describes Borzage as "a stalwart, curly-headed young chap of peasant stock, with little scholastic training. He had an intuitive sense of drama, a deep sympathetic understanding of human needs, and a warm, friendly attitude toward everyone with whom he came in contact. These were attributes which made him a wise choice for a story like *Humoresque*.... Mr. Hearst could not understand my choice but he said 'go ahead,' and we started out bravely."[3] Borzage remembers having been summoned to New York, where a vice-president from Cosmopolitan handed some sophisticated topics over to him. "I don't like this type of thing, have you got any human interest stories?" The man then gave him Fannie Hurst's latest publication, a collection of several short stories: perhaps they could combine a few of them for a feature film. Borzage brought the book to the Algonquin hotel, his usual haunt, and began a very personal process that from then on would become a ritual. The first story he read, "Humoresque," immediately captured his interest. He phoned Frances Marion, then asked her to meet him and read it to him while he had his back turned to her. Intrigued, the screenwriter did so and after listening to the tone of her voice, and noticing the smallest vibration and intonation, Borzage made his decision. Frances Marion was so overcome by emotion that she stammered as she read the final paragraphs.[4] That day, the screenplay of *Humoresque* began to take shape. "Here was the story I had been looking for ever since I became a director. To me it represented the most wonderful of all human expressions—the expression of mother love. What appealed most to me in *Humoresque* was its infinite humanness, its deep pathos, and its rare rich humor."[5] The collaboration with Frances Marion was so successful that the next time Borzage worked with her, he asked her to remain on the set for the entire shoot. "It is impossible to over-estimate the value of these trifling incidents in giving color and interest to a picture story," she recalls. "In *Humoresque*, for example, the children are poking around in a garbage can and find a miserable dead kitten. You remember how the little girl says, "Somebody's throwed away a perfectly good cat!" She takes it out and hugs it in her arms. Her father, of course, won't let her keep it. So she puts it in a box and they have a funeral over it, and she sets her treasured geranium over the grave. This took only a few moments on the screen; yet it not only had a touch of comedy and pathos, but it gave you a real impression of the child's character. Later, when she reappears in the story, a grown-up young woman, I didn't have to spend time—and footage—in an attempt to show the audience that she was lovable and tender-hearted. They already knew this because of the earlier scene."[6]

Casting took place beginning in October, filming from November 1919 to February 1920. The actors were not well-known, except for delicate Alma Rubens, on her way to becoming one of the most beloved stars of Cosmopolitan and Fox Film. At Fannie Hurst's instigation, Frances Marion hired Vera Gordon, a Russian who was a staple of the New York Yiddish Theater, for the memorable role of Mama Kantor; it was her début in what was to become a long film career, devoted almost exclusively to the portrayal of Jewish mothers. "This film required 16 weeks of work, but each minute was delicious and I never felt like I was playing a part," she remembered. "You see, I know the East Side, the life of the people there. Like them, I experienced oppression, I experienced what it was to want to protect my family from it and to give them freedom."[7] Parisian swell Gaston Glass, Sarah Bernhardt's godson and protégé (he followed her last U.S. tour in 1916 and remained in the country), portrayed the young musician. Borzage's camera operator was Gilbert Warrenton, who was later to become a proponent of the German style in Hollywood (Paul Leni's *The Man Who Laughs*, Paul Fejos' *Lonesome*). With his reputation growing, the director

also introduced a member of his own family to the business: Lew Borzage. Lew left his eldest brother Dan, his former fellow accordionist (they'd performed as a duo at the Los Angeles Orpheum) to assist Frank in New York; he began as second assistant director. At the
same time Borzage moved his entire clan from Salt Lake City and set them up in a spacious
villa in the central Los Angeles, at 4227 Denker Avenue.

To capture the daily picturesqueness of ghetto life, the filmmaker used methods later
favored by Italian neorealists in the postwar and by the French New Wave in the sixties.
Forewarned by his friends, he decked himself out in old clothes to better blend into the
crowd, but mostly to ward off the pickpockets who swarmed the streets. He spent almost
four weeks scouring the dilapidated and overcrowded Lower East Side, followed discreetly
by a wagon carrying a hidden camera. Whenever possible, they replaced the wagon with a
baby carriage. The filmmaker murmured his instructions to the operator and thus managed to assemble a series of exceptional shots. As it was Warrenton's first time using
panchromatic film (sensitive to all visible radiation), the mission was a challenge. The
ghetto alleys were narrow, often too dark. They had to film behind windows, take high angle
shots from the metal platforms of emergency staircases or, in extreme cases, secretly use
incandescent lamps. For the interiors, the filmmaker innovated, using, instead of a script-
girl, a dictaphone — a modern whim! — that recorded dialogue and commentary. As Cosmopolitan's large stage sets were being used by the megaproduction *April Folly* (a Robert
Z. Leonard extravaganza starring Marion Davies), Borzage had to film what was considered an "experimental film" in the basement. The excess of electricity used on the floor
above caused incessant power outages. Disconcerted, Cosmopolitan's boss insisted several
times that Borzage include in his film a small review, costume ball or other "attraction"
conforming to the home studio's tastes. Responsive but firm, Borzage promised him a show
equally appealing to the public, although directed at ten times less the cost. Borzage granted
one concession, however: Joseph Urban (1872–1933), a Vienna architect and set designer,
a representative of the Wiener Werkstätte who would later work at the Metropolitan and
on Broadway for the Ziegfeld Follies, created elegant Jugendstil designs on the studio's
ground flour for the second half of the film as well as the stylized interior of the synagogue.
Humoresque cost $117,000, a relatively modest sum compared with the $700,000 spent by
Douglas Fairbanks and Fred Niblo on *The Three Musketeers* (1921).

The film begins with a master shot of Allen Street in 1891, swarming crowds milling
about the open-air stalls. On the ground, kids dressed in rags grab a cigarette butt thrown
away by a passer-by. In his small shop, a veritable shambles, old Abraham Kantor (playwright Dore Davidson) is busy "transforming new brasses into rare Russian antiques" with
his blowtorch, "while in the tenements above, the voice of Mama Kantor could be heard
even above the shriek and thunder of elevated traffic" (the window of the cluttered apartment looks over the El track). The housewife is energetically rounding up her children to
prepare a birthday meal for nine-year-old Leon. One kid is screeching between her legs; a
little sister of his is sliding down the fire escape into a pile of laundry; the other is playing
on an elevated platform with the neighbor's twins. Mannie, the oldest, a teenager born while
the Kantors were fleeing the Tsar's pogroms, has remained an idiot: "this living dead thing,"
paralyzed in his wheelchair, teary-eyed, staring vacantly. Sarah Kantor sighs, consoles him
and makes him laugh, tickling his nose with a feather. "One dollar for a birthday present?!"
exclaims Abraham, outraged as his wife urges him to open his purse. "I tell you, Mama,
the way you spoil our children, it will some day come back on us!" She gaily makes fun of
him while he protests with all his energy: "All right, all right, drive me crazy because he's got
a birthday." In reply, Sarah asks for a kiss and Papa Kantor grudgingly complies. During

A visit to the synagogue photographed with remarkable restraint: Vera Gordon in *Humoresque* (1920).

this time, in the street, Leon, decked out in his new striped white suit ("bought on sale," an intertitle informs us) is attacked by the smiling neighborhood kids; the suit is smeared with chalk. Then the rascals notice tiny Gina Ginsberg, "Like a little scraggy plant grown without sunlight is Gina Ginsberg, a daughter of the ghetto." The little face half buried in a scarf too big for her, a crutch under her right arm, Gina has just made a precious discovery in a garbage can: a dead cat. As she tucks the cat away beneath her coat, the children try to grab it away from her. Leon gallantly intervenes: "It's hers, and it's cold anyhow!" The kids beat him up, then he remains alone with Gina who wipes his mud-covered face with her scarf. In return, Leon shows her how to move her ears: alone in the hidden recesses of the alley, the two children wink at each other, make faces, and laugh happily.

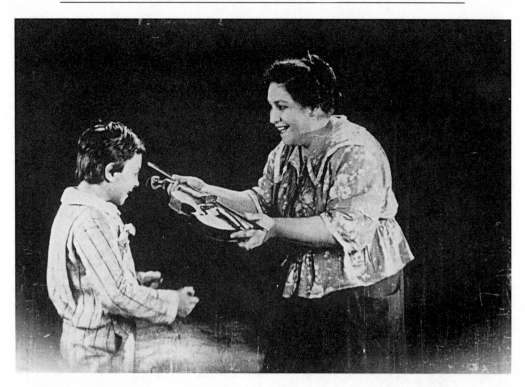

The violin of his dreams: Bobby Connelly and Vera Gordon in *Humoresque* (1920).

In these special moments, when *Humoresque* deals with the "green paradise of childhood love," Borzage demonstrates his uncanny ability to guide actors. Caught up in the joy of mutual discovery, these young actors, filmed in close-up, seem to be unaware of the camera's existence.[8] The subject could have easily become overly sentimental (as in the children's scenes in *Peter Ibbetson*), but Borzage diffuses the sentimentality, depicting natural situations comically, with lines delivered at a beautifully maintained pace. In its finest moments, *Humoresque* is the work of a delicate, discreet storyteller, already in full possession of his art. Borzage develops the subtle proportion of humor and pathos—a balance few filmmakers have mastered (Charles Chaplin, sometimes Ernst Lubitsch)—in the richly detailed scenes depicting the intimacy of family life. Whenever possible, he balances Sarah Kantor's dangerously maternal effusiveness with Abraham's comicalness, poking fun at his incorrigible stinginess with unmalicious irony. Here the little dialogue provided in the intertitles is worth its weight in gold: a recent refugee, Papa Kantor and his neighbors cheerfully massacre the English language, inverting syntax with stunning frequency, deforming words ("A dead cat she wants to plant like it was violets... Not in my home such an insanitation," "Always sacrifices are parents making!") and peppering their speech with Yiddish expressions ("nebich," "potch," "ganef"). The filmmaker respectfully captures the traditional daily life of this deeply religious Ashkenazi family, recording the rituals that mark each day. Mama Kantor's visit to the synagogue is photographed with unusual restraint for the movies. The camera stays in back, a static shot practically at the entrance of the sanctuary. The woman, seen from behind, moves to the back of the image, plunged into semidarkness. The rabbi leaves Sarah to pray in a low voice before the Torah, her hands raised. Commenting on this fleeting scene, an intertitle reads: "Forever blessed are those who have faith—and sublimest of all is the faith of a mother." This dignified and discreet approach to Judaism may be related to a key event in Borzage's life: eight months before filming *Humoresque*, he joined the Freemasons, and, as we know, the symbolic origins of this initiatory organization revert back to the construction of Solomon's Temple. This circumstance apparently sensitized the "goy" (non–Jew) to the sacred forms and practices evoked in the film.

While Mama Kantor more or less contains the rest of her brood trying to preserve the birthday cake until the meal, Papa Kantor takes Leon to a secondhand goods dealer to select a gift. A bad idea: although the father treats him harshly, the boy keeps returning to the used violin —*four* dollars!— which he noticed upon entering. He refuses a miniature cash register ("Listen, my son, to its tinkle! This is moosic!") and plugs his ears, crying when his father blows into a toy instrument ("Swell noises it makes—for only sixty-five cents!"). Furious, Papa Kantor forces his son out of the store. At home, Leon takes refuge in his mother skirts; learning the object of his desires, her face lights up. Her prayers, her life's dreams have been answered: her child will be a musician. Papa Kantor cannot believe his ears and protests ("Always a moosician! Why not you should sometimes pray for a business man — maybe in brasses like his papa!"); one of the older sons had already given them false hopes: he had run after the organ player because of the monkey! Later in the evening, when the father has gone to bed, Sarah goes to secretly buy the violin that she gives to the wide-eyed child. Leon can barely contain himself from playing it in his bed. At the same instant, in the next building, Gina's father gives his daughter a kitten. The 26-minute-long ghetto episode marks the beginning of the film, closing with the scene in the synagogue in the half-light, described above. A rich episode with the makings of a masterpiece.

However, what follows is uneven and reveals an abrupt change in style. The second part begins: dissolve to Leon, still at the violin, going from the age of 9 to 23. It shows the young virtuoso established as an artist in Venice, the final stage of a triumphant European tour where he plays for the Italian royal family. Thankfully this ellipsis spares us the details of his rise to success. From a neighboring salon, Sarah and Abraham Kantor, excited, all dressed up yet ill at ease in their evening clothes, observe their child prodigy through opera glasses. The chamberlain gives Leon a medal (Abraham, open-mouthed: "It's worth 250 dollars if it's worth a cent! Didn't I always tell you that my boy would be some day a fancy feedler!"); Mama Kantor shows the sardonic ushers a photo of the artist at age three months posing naked. In the Venetian moonlight, Leon finds Gina. Her father made a fortune and she has come to finish her education in Europe. She smoothes his face with a handkerchief and this far-off reminder of the years of poverty makes them burst out laughing. Directly cutting off any further effusion, Borzage dissolves to black at the moment Leon leans over to kiss his fiancée. To celebrate his return to the U.S., the artist plans a concert in honor of the poor neighbors from the ghetto, for whom he has reserved the best places on the dais.

Fortune smiles upon him and the Kantor clan moves to a luxurious apartment on Fifth Avenue. Silver, velvet curtains, domesticity. But the young man cannot stomach the feasts of the nouveau riche. When, at the invitation of a uniformed butler, the entire family sits down to dinner, Leon turns to the window. Europe is at war. Preoccupied, Leon observes the comings and goings around an enlistment office across the street from the building. Borzage sets up his shot in such a way that it coincides visually with the spectator's premonitions, Leon's torments and his mother's worrying. Placed outside, a few feet from the window, the camera films the musician peering into the night. The window frame is visible and creates a thick black border (premature mourning?); Leon, in evening clothes, is at the center of this tableau of death. To the left, half lying along the windowsill, the mentally retarded Mannie alternates between laughing and crying. Between the two brothers, at the back of the frame, Mama Kantor gets up from the table — and Papa Kantor, decked out in a tuxedo before a gargantuan frozen dessert, calls her to order: "Now, you eat dinner before I get mad from you!" The sequence sways back and forth between the pathetic and the hilarious.

A concert later that evening: people from the ghetto (some very colorful extra work, the extras chosen on location) madly applaud Leon. The virtuoso, whose rapid-fire ascension is seen as a credit to the entire community, sings "Kol Nidre" (the prayer of atonement) and then, after 15 curtain calls, Antonín Dvořák's Bohemian tune, "Humoresque" "that laugh on life with a tear behind it." A well-known impresario makes him a fabulous offer — but Leon has already committed to Uncle Sam: "You wouldn't want me to hide behind my violin"; he has signed up to volunteer at the front. The good-bye sequence, by far the weakest in the film, is far too long and emotional. Mama Kantor takes her uniformed son on her knee, listens once again to "Humoresque" while Gina requests he play a piece that serves as a premonition: "I Have a Rendez-Vous with Death in the Springtime." The screenplay being what it was, Borzage could not, despite restraint, avoid sentimentality — nor is he helped by Vera Gordon, whose overacting is considerably dated. Luckily, Papa Kantor reappears at the last moment to accompany his son to the station, urging the women: "No nonsense! No waterworks!" The character of Papa Kantor, a superb blend of warmth, humor and ethnicity, remains specifically Borzagian. Fannie Hurst's novella ends on the battlefields of France, where Leon is shot down. Marion and Borzage filmed a more melodramatic conclusion: Leon comes back from war, but with an artificial hand. Appalled, Hearst demanded a more optimistic ending.

In this final part of the film, as predictable as it may be, the filmmaker manages to at least somewhat rectify the film by surprising us with the theme of "love as a means of salvation" (Lucky Star, Disputed Passage); here more of a means of assistance than a transforming apotheosis. An officer (mistaken as Leon from afar) announces to the family that the musician is alive, although his arm was paralyzed as the result of an injury. Months pass. Prostrate in his chair, Leon does not heal; feeling himself now to be useless, he has lost all interest in life and is paralyzed by neurosis. In the spring, he begs Gina to seek her happiness elsewhere. Frantic, she leaves the room. When the patient sees her sway, then her shadow as she faints behind the curtain of a glassed door, he hurries to her rescue, carries her gently to a couch — and notices than he can move his arm once again. His first gesture is toward the violin... The incident is highly implausible, but the seamless direction, and the attitudes struck elegantly save it from ridicule. This remark also applies to the entire "adult" portion of Humoresque. The shifts in the film's focus throw the work off balance. Its subject, finally, is not really clear: aside from its moving social, human portrait (the sordid slice of life of the Lower East Side, zeroing in on certain emigrants) it depicts a childhood with bickering mother and father (or: how Mama imposes the violin on her child), a mother's sacrifices to raise her children out of poverty, a young man's hesitations between his art and civic duty, and finally the self-pity of an invalid whose love, barely expressed until now, will result in a happy ending. Fannie Hurst expressed no dissatisfaction with the additions nor with the evidently patched-together conclusion. Two years later she wrote a stage adaptation of her novella whose ending, this time, remained open; on the eve of his departure for France, Leon plays "A Rendez-Vous with Death" before the final curtain falls.[9] Warners supposed remake in the winter of 1945–46, directed by Jean Negulesco (followed by Delmer Daves and Irving Rapper) is radically removed from the original from the moment when the violinist grows up, and concentrates instead on the tragic passion between him (John Garfield) and his benefactress, a rich nymphomaniac (Joan Crawford).[10]

Hearst, like Adolph Zukor, president of Paramount, detested *Humoresque*, finding its portrayal of ghetto destitution too realistic. Zukor even said to Frances Marion: "If you want to show Jews, show Rothschilds, banks and beautiful things. It hurts us Jews—we don't all live in poor houses."[11] By common agreement, they decided not to release it, thinking that the mass of spectators would share their aversion to watching poverty on celluloid. On May 30, a gap in the programming of the Criterion Theater nevertheless forced them to show the film. Against all expectations, it was a sensation. *Variety* predicted it would flop at the box office—they were wrong.[12] *Humoresque* beat all records with 200,000 spectators over a 12-week exclusive run—an unprecedented film success in New York (on the average, films were shown for only one week). In Chicago (Orchestra Hall), *Humoresque* drew in 41,000 spectators in seven days. Historian Kevin Brownlow attributed this success notably to sociological factors: the post-war generation, he wrote, was rebelling against their parents; the screenplay explores young people's suppressed feelings of guilt, incidentally restoring the image of their parents.[13] But the touches of poetic realism at the heart of Allen Street are also noteworthy. The violinist Fritz Kreisler himself, who interpreted Dvořák's "Humoresque," was an ardent defender of the film in the papers. To Hearst's amazement (his flashy productions for Marion Davies did not draw crowds), *Humoresque* obtained the first artistic distinction for film ever awarded in the U.S., the "Photoplay Gold Medal" (designed by Tiffany) for the best film of 1920. This prize is generally considered the forerunner to the Oscar. Borzage would also receive that much coveted gold statuette, by fortuitous circumstance, when it was first awarded in 1929. But that's another story.

Humoresque was distributed worldwide and is one of the few Borzage films to have been shown in the Soviet Union (with the exception of *Secrets* [1924] and the hugely successful *His Butler's Sister*, during the Second World War). The great Sergei M. Eisenstein praised it highly in a 1925 essay in which he ranks Borzage along with Stroheim and Chaplin: "No one in our country knows Borzage, although his best film, *Humoresque*, shot in America, was shown here this season. Criminally, it received no publicity and passed unnoticed, although it is a rare example of sensitivity and expertise, mainly in its directing and acting…. In direct opposition (to Stroheim's films), Chaplin and Borzage, in their themes, their gentle lyricism and the femininity of their passive grief, tend to favor neurotic stimuli reminiscent of the dreamy suffering of Rousseau and Beardsley. Think of the little girl who limps, of the violinist who loses his arm in the war, of Max the kind fool, of the Jewish family's suffering and persecution, of its passive role throughout all its struggles, of the 'Muttercomplex' greatly emphasized by Borzage's direction; unfortunately, this is the only film of his I have seen."[14]

The film was influential and over the course of the decade triggered a wave of subjects glorifying—with an overdose of tears—the universality of maternal love; the most successful example remains John Ford's *Four Sons*. *Humoresque* also generated about thirty films set in the Jewish areas of New York, a series that culminated in 1927 with the first talkie, *The Jazz Singer*, where Al Jolson played the unworthy son of a rabbi.[15] The praise radically altered Borzage's status, because in one night, he had become a man sought after: in the eyes of an industry so strongly oriented to melodrama as American film, a director so talented at creating emotion, and on top of that in so much good taste to boot, was a rare gem. Cosmopolitan ensured his services for years to come; assisted by his brother Lew, the filmmaker then temporarily took up residence in New York (his California residence had been broken into during his absence).

One of Borzage's first difficulties was escaping from following Hearst's project of making Marion Davies pictures; already the press was heralding two for 1920–21, *The Love Piker* and *Enchantment*. He managed to diplomatically bypass them; Hearst would have to wait another 16 years before Borzage directed his blond muse (*Hearts Divided*). After interminable hemming and hawing with Cosmopolitan — implying several dealings and aborted departures (e.g., Fannie Hurst's story *Just Around the Corner*, which Frances Marion directed) — the director finally set his heart on material far removed from the city's hustle and bustle: the comedy *Get-Rich-Quick Wallingford*. Today this film is lost (it was only released in December 1921). It used a small town in Iowa as a set and was based on George Randolph Chester's (1869–1924) amusing "Wallingford Stories" which had already been brought to the screen many times.[16] The screenplay caused so many headaches that Borzage forgot it and improvised on the set, inspired by George Michael Cohan's 1910 stage adaptation. J. Rufus Wallingford (played by Broadway actor Sam Hardy) has become a happy charlatan who passes for a millionaire. Pretending to invest his fortune in the region, he starts a lucrative business with the money of local unscrupulous businessman, and personifying immanent justice, the rascal happily makes a fortune on their money. In this satire of capitalism, Borzage orchestrates the debut of Billie Dove, a star of Swiss origin, from Lucerne, and of Norman Kerry, who would soon become the leading man in such Lon Chaney classics as *The Hunchback of Notre Dame* and *The Phantom of the Opera*. Moreover, the film meant the crucial meeting with another of Thomas Ince's pupils: New York cinematographer Chester A. Lyons (1885–1936), a faithful collaborator as well an unjustly forgotten artist who assisted Borzage in 17 films up until 1931. Among his achievements are the fabulous twilight images of *Lucky Star* and *Liliom*.

"It is a bad story for young girls to see" concluded *Variety*'s appraisal of the "modern" melodrama *Back Pay*, brought to the screen in May–June 1921.[17] It reunited the talents of Fannie Hurst and Frances Marion. "A spicy dish for adult minds," countered *Photoplay*,[18] while the *New York Times* more appropriately perceived it as "a sentimentalized story of a woman's reclamation which makes obvious efforts to shake off sentimentality and be real, and sometimes succeeds."[19]

The film is interesting in that Borzage develops Fannie Hurst's serialized storyline by fleshing out the characters, developing their psychology and putting the inherent oversimplification in perspective. At first glance, *Back Pay* illustrates the bittersweet destiny of a victim of an "Imitation of Life" (the title of Fannie Hurst's bestseller). A young woman (Seena Owen[20]), seen from an establishing shot on the platform of a deserted train station, follows the movement of a train vanishing into the distance. (The call of the rails, a metaphor for freedom, is reminiscent of *Man's Castle* in 1933, where Spencer Tracy reacts feverishly to the slightest whistle of the train). Hester is bored to death in the little town of Demopolis, a sleepy New York suburb. On a Sunday picnic with the entire town present, Hester tells Jerry (Matt Moore), her impatient beloved, that they are too poor to consider marriage, and that she doesn't want to set up house and bury herself for life amid linens, cotton, and flannel nightshirts. She consoles him slightly, purporting to be "not yet ready" for the kind of existence he can offer her, and takes the train to New York. In a shot echoing the opening of the film, Jerry remains alone on the platform.

Manhattan, five years later. After a difficult start as a milliner, Hester has at last found the kind of luxury she had dreamed about, but at a price. A kept woman, she is the pampered mistress of Wheeler, a Wall Street banker who refuses her nothing: she has a Rolls Royce, a chinchilla coat and a second residence on Long Island. At one of her exhilarating parties, the young woman raises her glass of champagne, toasting "Here's to the wages of sin!" For at the end of her silk and satin rainbow, she is not really happy. During an excursion in the Rolls, Hester stops in Demopolis. No one recognizes her except the faithful

Jerry, still waiting for her. His salary has been raised to $50 a week. She lies to him, speaking of her career as a fashion designer and asking him to be patient. Then she resumes her life, more frenetic than ever. Cut to the trenches of the Marne, 1918: in a night rattled by explosions, Jerry collapses, crying out the name of his beloved. Hester visits him in a Brooklyn hospital: she discovers he is blind, his left lung burned by gas. He has only three weeks left to live. That very evening she begs Wheeler to let her marry the stricken Jerry. The banker, ever the gracious gentleman, agrees to this incongruous and delicate request. Although his pride is hurt, he generously offers to lodge Jerry and disappear for a month. After the marriage, Hester remains at the bedside of the man destined to die. This scene is composed allegorically: Borzage only lights the woman (in a light-colored blouse) and the fumbling hands of the blind man while he remains out of focus. The camera informs us that Jerry, on his own, has no substance; his passion has kept him alive. When he dies, the camera remains on Hester for a long time. She sits, paralyzed, as if stunned by the sudden loss; she sings the last stanza of a song she hadn't finished singing a long time ago in the forest at the farewell picnic. Fade-out. Wheeler reappears two weeks later, paternal, benevolent. Plagued by nightmares, Hester cannot return to her way of life. She breaks off with her protector, rents a modest furnished room, finds work and a kind of harmony in memory and solitude.[21]

This inner journey of this American Emma Bovary ("I guess I got a crepe-de-chine soul," she admits) is more than a portrayal of false values and the lure of capitalism to show the virtues of a modest existence. The bucolic images of Demopolis, set up like Gainsborough paintings with superb oak trees reflected in the streams, are profoundly peaceful. Jerry, the suitor, has nothing exciting to offer. Borzage describes him without malice (as already mentioned, sarcasm is fundamentally foreign to him), yet he defines this brave but conventional and sentimental boy laconically as "the most energetic clerk in The Big Store." The town's inhabitants breathe insignificance to the point of becoming invisible: coming down the stairs of the little rooming house where she lives, Hester hesitates joining the ten or so roomers chattering at the table, then sits morosely between two older men (medium shot). Cut to a close-up showing her alone at the table with a black backdrop, her neighbors to the right and left having disappeared. They reappear in the next medium shot, leaning over Hester to trade banalities (later Borzage uses this way of depicting isolation during a society party in New York: boredom is not exclusive to a particular social class). When the young woman rises from the table, her neighbors continue talking, the empty chair between them: "Hester's got an idea this town's too small for her. Notions like that don't lead to no good!" Hester's flight can be justified. As for the banker Wheeler, the alternative to the pathetic Jerry, Borzage makes him a man of discreet elegance, with no illusions regarding Hester's feelings towards him and insensitive to the distress of others. But as a lover his generosity and delicacy are beyond reproach. Hester, though, is superficial. Her "repentance" comes less from regretting not having married Jerry earlier—had she ever loved him?—than from discovering a real depth of feeling in this dull fellow. A prisoner of her own fantasies of luxury, she is unable to experience such depth. The confrontation with death awakens her. Fannie Hurst's novel (and play) repeat the moralistic stereotypes of the provincial woman blinded by the big city. Seen through Borzage's camera, *Back Pay* tells the story of a liberation, of a return to authenticity. Chester Lyons' exceptional soft focus photography of a series of flamboyant compositions encourages us to transcend the cruelty to reach a new awareness. According to Charles Chaplin's biographer, David Robinson, *Back Pay* strongly influenced Chaplin in his direction of *A Woman of Paris*, began ten months after the release of Borzage's film.

Fannie Hurst once again provided the subject for *The Good Provider*. Its plot clearly copies that of *Humoresque*, so much so that actors such as the old Vera Gordon–Dore Davidson couple and Miriam Battista, the little girl (with a kitten) were again cast. Filmed in the streets of New York in the winter of 1921/22, this tragic-comic tale of Jewish life — another film which has been lost — this time emphasizes not a mother's sacrifices, but a father's.[22] At the insistence of his adult children, the immigrant Julius Binswanger (Davidson), a peddler who made a fortune by the sweat of is brow, closes his country store. He goes to live in a luxurious city hotel where the clientele makes fun of him because he is out of place. The frenetic life, exorbitant prices and his children's bad investments lead him to bankruptcy. He contemplates suicide, but a future son-in-law steps in and saves the day. The public response of this derivation of *Humoresque* was restrained. Only the critics give us an idea of its qualities: "Borzage has come back with his direction of this. He is not a Griffith who plays upon your emotions until they shriek for mercy; he has a quieter touch."[23] "*Ciné-magazine*" in France confirmed this impression: "Those who see film as a means of expressing emotions, of depicting states of soul, as a painter reveals the secrets of nature with his brush, would do well to go see *Papa* (*The Good Provider*)."[24] Generally speaking, the American press concurred that *The Good Provider* even surpassed *Humoresque*.

Did he need to make a change after this other variation on the theme of what would become known as the nuclear family, making a kind of pilgrimage back to his roots? For his next two films, Borzage, an indefatigable athlete, rediscovers adventure, the westerns of his adolescence, the wide open spaces thousands of miles from the skyscrapers of Manhattan. To what extent were these two projects the result of his initiative or simply an order from Cosmopolitan? The first, *The Valley of Silent Men*, could well have been a personal choice because it is the result of a considerable investment in time and effort. This adaptation of a novel of the prolific James Oliver Curwood (1879–1927) — the Jack London of the poor — brought Borzage and his team to the heart of the northern Rockies, from March to July, 1922. Curwood's romantic far north, his Yukon inhabited by noble detectives of the Royal Mounted Police, was a bonanza for various producers.[25] Accompanied by his wife Rena (who improvised as set photographer), the filmmaker first shot in Banff (Alberta), where he could count on the collaboration of the Stoney Indians. The cast included Alma Rubens, Lew Cody and Joseph King (the love-struck detective of *Until They Get Me*). Then they moved to the snowy outskirts of Lake Louise, in Alberta, where *Billy Jim* had been filmed three years earlier. As the hotel was still closed, the entire cast and crew slept in the staff quarters. To film on the adjacent glacier, they had to cross the frozen lake before dawn and did not return until after dusk, when the top layer of ice had frozen over again. Later, they filmed in the province of Ontario. There, near Temiskaming, catastrophe struck: a stuntman was caught in the rapids of a river and drowned before the eyes of the technicians. An emotional man, Borzage was so profoundly moved by the accident that from then on he was less likely to use exteriors too far removed from the studios. Yet it is precisely this uninhabited landscape with its white peaks, omnipresent in the film, that give it an unexpected dimension: "Without the authenticity of backgrounds the melodrama would be stagy, but impressive vistas of awesome mountain peaks in series upon series give a commanding atmosphere that overshadows the drama and compels a sense of reality. It is a curious case of mere settings creating a real illusion for a set of theatrical situations. The romance is in the environment rather than in the occurrence or the characters who never let you forget that it is all a story," noted *Variety*, unconsciously echoing one of the lessons that Borzage had learned from Thomas Ince.[26]

Although fragmentary (in the second half), the print of the film preserved at the

Library of Congress reveals other qualities as well. As usual with Curwood, the plot revolves around a not very original mystery, here enhanced by an unusual setting. From the beginning, Borzage makes use of the unusual, orchestrating his story from what appear to be gratuitous incidents, meetings and apparitions. Minuscule figures appear amid snowy vistas and lofty faraway silhouettes; his characters seem to emerge out of nowhere, pawns of ironic destiny that inexplicably pushes them together (an impression emphasized by the many master shots). Sergeant Kent (L. Cody), a conscientious Mountie, pursues a fur stealer, gets caught in an ambush and kills the bandit. He then drags himself, now seriously wounded, to the cabin of a shady local trafficker, Barkley. Imagine his surprise when he discovers Jacques Radisson, his longtime friend who saved his life long ago. Barkley's corpse lies on the ground, strangled with a woman's hair. He is already the second person killed this way. Radisson refuses to explain his presence in the dead man's cabin. When Kent learns that he only has a few days left to live, he confesses to the murder, thus clearing his friend. A disturbed old man, suffering from hallucinations, whom the Indians nickname "the prophet," crosses paths several times with the protagonists, mumbling or fulminating words of vengeance from the Old Testament. From madness to passion: the mystery thickens when an unknown woman (A. Rubens) arrives by dogsled. Her elegant clothing is out of place and her insolence confusing. She regally settles in at Inspector Kedsty's after telling him that he is in danger of becoming the strangler's third victim; the inspector shudders and falls silent. As for the watcher, his heart begins to race with the visit of the fascinating woman at Kent's bedside, "this man who lies so beautifully for his friend." Love at first sight. Her seductive way of unbuttoning her fur coat becomes almost a strip show and on her way out, she places her lips on those of the man riveted to his chair — there is an immediate complicity, and any preliminaries or sophisticated banter would be superfluous. (The film was banned in Sweden.)

Shortly after, the doctor tells Kent some "bad" news: his wound is not mortal. As Kent has taken responsibility for the murder, Kedsty places him under arrest. In the middle of the night, the unknown woman appears at the police station with a gun, frees Kent and, with Kedsty away, hides the fugitive in her room. Her name is Marette, she tells him while in his arms: she comes from "The Valley of the Silent Men," where she wants to bring him at dawn. The following nocturnal sequence only partially exists: Kedsty comes back, drunk, lewd; Marette violently resists him. Chiaroscuro, shadows cast. Outside, a storm rages. Before dozing off, Kent sees a familiar figure outside the window. When he comes to, Marette is livid and the inspector dead. The sun has risen and the couple flees. (These fantastic adventures merely justify the admirable third and final part of the film; in fact, Marette Radisson is the daughter of the "prophet," a recluse who has lost his mind after his wife was murdered by three vagrants. Twenty years later he managed, coincidentally, to end up on their trail. Jacques Radisson, the brother of the avenger, and Marette tried in vain to warn the victims.)

By ironic destiny, the implacable Mountie, introduced by the intertitles at the beginning as "Kent the Tracker" or "The Law Bringer," becomes the man hunted by the law. The reversal of fortune is less about the motive of the falsely accused than about a code of ethics that goes beyond legality and ordinary convention (cf. *The Gun Woman*). We see a barge "on the river that flows always to the North." Kent is at the helm, Marette brings him coffee, they embrace — lyrical images of intimacy that contain in embryo all the magic of *The River*. But a police motorboat is on their trail and the rapids of "The Devil's Chute" howl downriver. Taking advantage of a bend in the river, the fugitives embrace, then jump in the water, holding hands; their barge sinks into the waves, the police believe them dead. Like the outlaw of the beginning of the film, the couple finds refuge with the Indians (a

Alma Rubens and Lew Cody, lovers on the run in *The Valley of Silent Men* (1922).

lost sequence), then attempts the mythical climb up the Grand Glacier, beyond which lies the valley of redemption. It is in *The Valley of Silent Men* that we first see Borzage deal with the symbolism of resurrection. Direction and framing clearly designate the couple's arduous journey: they are confronted by the elements, in total isolation, as if in a kind of inner odyssey, a passage that, both literally and figuratively, brings them together and liberates them (cf. climbing to the Karwendel Pass in *The Mortal Storm*). This "elsewhere" breathes eternity, seemingly escaping both time and the machinations of men. Incredibly beautiful and unusual vistas characterize this moment, which captures the photogenic with as much talent and less aesthetics than Arnold Fanck in Germany (who was only just beginning in 1922). The lovers appear to drown in an immense luminosity, full of invisible threats, but each effort brings them together. "If we fail it has been worthwhile," says Marette, out of breath after narrowly avoiding an avalanche. On a ridge, the rope breaks. Marette disappears into a crevasse, Kent glides into empty space. They catch hold of each other, seeking with the energy of despair, less anxious of losing their lives than of losing each other; wandering in a desert of ice, each one repeatedly crying out the name of the loved one. On the other side of the glacier, the couple manages to reach the cabin of the prophet at the same time as the police (who have gone around the mountain); as he is dying, the lunatic reveals the key to the enigma. Kent and Marette are freed, the refuge that is the valley majestically spread out at their feet. "They are my silent watchers—they have guarded me all my life," she says of the mountain peaks around them. "The missionary must be there with my uncle. He comes at this time every year." To sum up, *The Valley of Silent Men* is clearly more than a banal stage in Borzage's filmography.

It contrasts brutally with *The Pride of Palomar*, a potboiler the filmmaker directed the same year, in Californian's autumn sunshine (August-September) in Long Beach, at Rancho Guajone and San Diego. This strange semi-western is a barely disguised anti–Japanese propaganda film Hearst sponsored in his political campaign against Japanese immigration in California. The fantasy of the "yellow peril" had haunted America since the defeat of Russia in 1905; in 1908, Theodore Roosevelt even prohibited issuing passports to Japanese workers. In May 1922, after being insulted by a racist producer, Sessue Hayakawa sold his villa and left Hollywood. The incident reveals much about the climate of the time. In his sensationalistic press, Hearst used the so-called oriental menace as an electoral battle horse, which led to this scenario: the son of an aristocrat of Spanish origin (Forrest Stanley) returning from war in 1918 learns that his father has just died, completely broke. El Palomar, the ranch, is in the hands of a unscrupulous real estate agent trying to sell the family land to a rich Japanese who is secretly planning the Japanese colonization of the entire country. The young man obtains a one year moratoria to collect the money necessary to buy back the property. Helped by a few patriots, by the speculator's daughter (Marjorie Daw) and a racehorse winning the derby, the new Zorro manages to thwart the adverse maneuvers. The victorious bust of George Washington looks on as they throw the Oriental and his henchmen out the window! Noteworthy is the "evil invader" played by Warner Oland, a Swede who became proficient at portraying Oriental characters in the thirties (Fu Manchu, Charlie Chan).[27] There were a few typical touches in this routine work, such as the death of Don Farrel. Believing his son has perished in the trenches of France, the old man goes to a mission church. The camera remains discreetly outside the building, capturing the scene from a distance; the minute the bells ring, Don Farrel collapses in front of the altar. El Palomar's Mexican servant obstinately refuses to believe in the disappearance of her son, because "The lamp his mother lighted for him is still burning." Under the protection of this same lamp, a talisman "that will never go out," Farrel Jr. embraces his beloved.

After this foray into adventure — the last one for quite a while — Borzage reaches Thomas H. Ince's studios in Culver City in late 1922, having successfully completed his commitment to Cosmopolitan. The team of Fannie Hurst and Frances Marion collaborated on a melodrama which this time was right up his alley: *The Nth Commandment*. In it we have an early glimpse at one of the filmmaker's major themes: the young couple facing adversity. This drama depicts the daily struggle to save their union, the universe of people with modest means, employees, poverty and sickness, an ensemble of small events with a backdrop of social realism. It is part of a series of films including *Bad Girl* (1931), *After Tomorrow* (1932) and *Little Man, What Now?* (1934). Incidentally, the theme of the sick spouse foreshadows that of Sternberg's *Blonde Venus* (1932). The lead went to captivating Irish brunette Colleen Moore, the cinematographic muse of F. Scott Fitzgerald. She was a symbol of the female American athlete of the Jazz Age. The American Film Institute–Library of Congress owns a print of this precious work, although it has noticeably deteriorated and is incomplete (reels 5 and 6 are missing). What remains, however, is worth describing.

The ground floor of a department store: The drama's five protagonists are illustrated by means of a few comic vignettes, drawn with incisive observation and swarming with details reminiscent of Erich von Stroheim. In the music department, an insolent charmer named Jimmy (Eddie Phillips) is singing the latest hits, songs of spring love. Salesgirls crowd around his stand, his colleagues are jealous. But "Jimmy thinks that his pal Max holds the most enviable position in the basement," for Max is in the women's shoe department. While helping a client try on a shoe, he notices an elegant pair of ankles; he immediately changes seats to serve the newcomer. He caresses her foot, raises his head, then,

A young couple facing adversity: James Morrison and Colleen Moore in *The Nth Commandment* (1923).

finding himself face to face with a woman in her seventies, quickly returns to his first customer. In another corner of the store, Max's little friend Angie is powdering her nose and straightening her hair in a mirror while vulgarly chewing gum. In the women's department, Angie's friend Sarah (Colleen Moore) is out of breath as she tightens a well-padded customer's corset. Wrapping purchases, Harry (James Morrison), slightly built and timid, cannot take his eyes off of Sarah and surreptitiously opens packages to see if the label was written in her lovely hand. He takes a box out of his pocket and contemplates the ring he plans to give to her after closing, but his daydream is brutally interrupted when an article of clothing to be wrapped is thrown in his face. An eternal underling in an apron, Harry is the cousin of Hans in *Little Man, What Now?* Angie dissuades her friend from ruining her life with this "loser" suffering from poor health, but Sarah has already committed to the evening and Harry has promised her a surprise. She is not insensitive, however, to Jimmy's amusing courting. Jimmy stops her in passage with his cane, making advances at her. Practically the entire introduction is filmed in medium-shots with rarely more than two characters in the frame; the visual continuity operates by cuts that show dispersion, the separateness of each character. The link between protagonists is not established by a unifying camera movement, but by a logical relation (an intertitle translating a thought) and by continuity (looking off camera).

Once the characters have been presented individually, Borzage brings them together by having them meet during a brilliant nighttime sequence at an indoor skating rink. A wide angle shot filmed in contrasting tones: the skating rink garishly lit by spotlights, hundreds of onlookers on roller skates moving round the rink, and shadowy outlines passing in front of the camera in the foreground—Sarah dragging a more than slightly hesitant Harry along. Ill at ease, the young man is practically leaning on her. The camera follows their timid movements by a tracking shot. At the back of the image the dashing Jimmy suddenly appears, like a bird of prey. He pirouettes several times around the couple, finally throwing Harry off balance. Harry falls, bringing his companion down with him. We see Sarah's moral choice: remain on the ground with the sincere but clumsy guy (foreshadowing his disability) or accept the fighter's self-serving invitation. She takes the easy way out. After helping Sarah get to her feet, Jimmy shiftily holds Harry's hand, while he is still on the ground, and lifts him a few inches before letting go. His new conquest on his arm, he abandons his humiliated rival. Harry, alone in front of the camera, gets painfully to his feet; Borzage shows him trying to find his balance, overtaken on all sides by the indifferent crowd. He falls again three times, rage in his heart, and the contrast between Harry's immobility and the skaters moving freely about designate him as a pariah confined to total isolation (like the paraplegic struggling with his crutches in *Lucky Star*). Painfully he reaches a bench. Sarah and Jimmy condescend to join him, with Jimmy persisting in calling the young woman "doll." Harry hauls off and punches him, but Jimmy lures his opponent to the trail where he has the advantage of mobility. As opposed to Jerry in *Back Pay*, Harry has moral fiber: defeated once more, he sends Sarah back to her department store Casanova.

Jimmy impresses Sarah by inviting her to a Chinese restaurant; after a few magic tricks, he steps up the attack ("I'd go to hell for you, Doll. That's the kind of guy I am.") He kisses her, but his ardor wanes when Sarah speaks of marriage—and fear freezes him when she confides that Harry is stricken with tuberculosis. Panicking, he insults her and brutalizes her verbally: she must have transmitted the illness to him. Sarah runs away and what follows is basically presented in telegraphic style. "Disillusion—Remorse—Forgiveness—and Happiness again. That's Life—." The lens opens on an exquisitely tender composition: all that stands out in the dark is a pan of Sarah's luminous face—tears in her eyes—and her hand in Harry's hair (his back toward the camera). The lovers embrace on a public bench; it's night. A policeman passes, the couple rapidly separates, the policeman laughs and continues his rounds. "Before Sarah had time to change her mind." A shot of a framed wedding photo on the wall. Crouched on the ground, the young woman cleans the floor, the tiny apartment under the eaves has the smell of poverty. "She missed the noise and bustle of the store," an intertitle informs us. Angie and Max visit her, expensively dressed and accompanied by Jimmy who has made a fortune in show business. Sarah apologizes for the meagerness of the surroundings, they'll move as soon as Harry finally gets his promotion. Jimmy has made peace with Sarah—he has a kind heart, he says, he forgives her earlier behavior!—and offers to help her if need be. Unsettled by so much luxury, the young woman finds putting up with her husband difficult when he gets home from work, unaware that he has just been refused a promotion for health reasons. Prostrate, his face in a newspaper, having forgotten to remove his hat, Harry morosely declares that his apartment suits him: he feels at home. The conversation turns nasty when he discovers a cigar stubbed out in an ashtray and his jealousy explodes: "Jimmy is a real gentleman," she exclaims, "he at least would remove his hat in front of a lady! He makes $150 a week." "Why didn't you marry him?" "Because I felt sorry for you!" The couple continues in this vein: Sarah sobs, removes her apron and announces she is leaving their apartment: "I'll go where I'm not treated like a dog. I'm going away and I'm never coming back!" He smiles and replies: "Bring me a package of Camels on your way home, won't you dearie?" Sarah slams the door, the wedding photo falls to the floor and breaks. The following segment shows her alone, morose on the living room couch of Jimmy, "her consoler." The charmer is at the piano, Max and Angie are dancing. But Sarah is lost in her thoughts; a hint of a smile — cut to Harry, sitting sadly in a chair — and when Jimmy tries to approach her, she remains defensive.

Borzage treats the husband and wife scene in the naturalistic tone of *Kammerspiel* (reminiscent of the argument in Siodmak's *People on Sunday*), but in contrast to the German filmmakers, never lets himself get carried away by the cruelty of the situation: playing both dramatic and comic registers at once, he indicates that the altercation between the spouses is painful for both of them, it starts in jest and shifts involuntarily to heartbreak. The middle part of *The Nth Commandment* is lost, but sources at the time allows us to piece together what happens: Sarah brings a child into the world. They can barely survive on Harry's meager salary (his health is failing); only a prolonged cure in the sun can save the tubercular patient. It is the day before Christmas, snow is falling — a mortal menace for Harry. In despair, Sarah goes to find Jimmy; she tells her husband she is doing overtime in the store. Jimmy brings his friends to a nightclub, champagne flows freely. Clenching her teeth and swallowing her pride, Sarah listens docilely to the charmer's fantasies. For several hundred dollar bills, he orders her to perform a dance number and then bathe in a pool, completely dressed. In the meantime, Harry has discovered his wife is not in the store. He falls asleep, coughing, shivering in the freezing apartment.

The fragment of the film that has been rediscovered continues here: late in the evening, Jimmy brings Sarah home in a taxi and tries repeatedly to kiss her; she protests. He follows her to the snowy porch of her house where she defends herself with her fists and purse before slamming the door on his face. The last sequence is completely stylized. Borzage throws her into complete darkness, creating superb lighting effects with one sole source of light which emphasizes faces and hands. For the first time, it appears, the filmmaker consciously uses only the facial expressions of his actors as the landscape of the soul, and Colleen Moore's spare acting is marvelous here. In 1983 the star declared: "I enjoyed so much working with Frank — I thought he was a wonderful director,"[28] and in *Life*, writer Robert E. Sherwood placed the actress's performance among the ten best of 1923. Sarah discovers her husband fainted on the ground; she revives him, terribly distressed, and Borzage films the park bench reunion again, this time reversing the protagonists. Sarah turns her back to the camera, only a part of Harry's face and left hand (caressing his wife's hair) appear in the frame. She lies to him, saying she worked that night as a dancer in a

Facial expression as landscape of the soul: Colleen Moore in *The Nth Commandment* (1923).

restaurant. For Harry, the money she has brought back signifies salvation, California. "Baby and I will — wait!" she murmurs. Crouching in the shadows, the couple watches the child playing with a stuffed animal, a bear, brought back from the dance hall. Sarah's expression goes from tender to worried, and finally defeated. Harry: "It just don't seem fair for you to have to do it all for us." Sarah, appeased, expresses the key idea of the film: "Everythin's fair, darlin', in love. All the rules for the game o' livin' ain't written down in the ten commandments." This voyage to the end of the night winds up with a fade to black followed by a view of a villa bathed in sunshine in California; Sarah and the child welcome a regenerated Harry, returning home from work. This is the first and only totally illuminated shot in the film, the only image filmed in full daylight.

The condition of the print does not really allow us to make an overall evaluation. The twists and turns of the plot are still too full of the maudlin press dear to Fannie Hurst to entirely remove its overt sentimentality; on a title following the credits, the novelist explains that "It is the Nth Commandment you follow then, the unwritten commandment to serve, to suffer, to sacrifice for what you love and cherish." Overall Borzage manages to reduce the story's virtuousness (it appeared in 1916 in the short story collection *Every Soul Hath Its Song*) and strongly shifts the emphasis.[29] Borzage tries to answer the futile question of knowing if Sarah's strategy to obtain money can be seen as a sacrifice of love with more universal considerations, for the sacrificial devotion of the woman, as drawn by Fannie Hurst, would not lead to harmony. Besides, from a merely moral (or social) point of view the relation of self to other can only be reductive. For the filmmaker the individual is not irremediably confined to the narrowness of his self and thus condemned to solitude, abnegation or despair. Inside, he possesses the indomitable spirit to overcome. The couple's union, precisely, is the most evident symbol of this capacity. And, seen in this aspect, although still only partial, *The Nth Commandment* is the first truly Borzagian work.

5

A New Status: Producer-Director

Borzage's move to Cosmopolitan was significant because it showed he had arrived. In professional circles, some people called him "the kid"; he was youthful, dynamic and only 29. For many years the press and the public would see him as the acclaimed creator of *Humoresque*. But for the American filmmaking industry, the most tangible sign of his success appeared as of 1923. From then on, eight words would appear in the credits of all his films, in all studios: "A Frank Borzage Production — Directed by Frank Borzage."[1] The significance of this privilege enjoyed by only a rare few such as D. W. Griffith, Rex Ingram and Frank Capra (and only occasionally by John Ford and Howard Hawks) becomes clear when we realize that the large studios, especially MGM in the thirties, did not put much stock in crediting their directors. Therefore a filmmaker credited in this way (by contractual obligation) enjoyed a degree of autonomy and had greater control over his film well after shooting, even if another producer was assigned to him as general supervisor.

Borzage's start at First National in January 1923 could well have been the result of Colleen Moore's (*The Nth Commandment*) intervention. She was the reigning studio star until the end of the decade and her husband John McCormick became studio head. Associated First National was in 1917 an organization of distributors grouping together circuits of powerful movie theaters that opposed Paramount-Artcraft's monopoly. Charles Chaplin topped First National's roster with nine prestigious titles (*Shoulder Arms, The Pilgrim, The Kid*, etc.). In 1923 the company decided to produce films directly and back the directors. According to publicity, it built "the largest independent movie studio in the world," United Studios on Melrose Avenue (the future Paramount studio).[2] Borzage began there with two films, both lost, shot for magnate Arthur H. Jacobs, with whom he had been negotiating since December 1922. (A first project, *Wandering Daughters*, adapted from Dana Burnett, went to someone else). *Children of Dust* was based on the short story "Terwilliger" by Tristram Tupper, an author who fortuitously inspired Borzage five years later when he directed his masterpieces *The River* and *Lucky Star*. From March to May 1923, the filmmaker occupied three sets where he recreated the area of Manhattan around Gramercy Park: the story was set in New York, in two different time periods, a bit like *Humoresque*. Terwilliger, a little orphan caught stealing flowers in a garden for his mother's grave, takes an old gardener (Bert Woodruff) as a "father." He becomes friends with little Celia, the daughter of aristocrats. Young Harvey, from a rich family, is also in love with her. Years pass; in 1917 the two rivals leave for war. In the trenches, Terwilliger (Johnny Walker) saves Harvey's life, then disappears. At first we think him dead; the old gardener cries. But Terwilliger reappears and marries Celia (Pauline Garon). Released in August 1923, the film was quickly forgotten. While its situations lacked originality, we know that for Borzage plot is only a springboard. The stills, particularly those of the childhood scenes, carry undeniable poetic charm. The press of the time unanimously praised the exceptional newness and delicate humor of these sequences.

Frankie Lee and Josephine Adair in the lost film *Children of Dust* (1923).

The other film, *The Age of Desire* (shot in June–July), used stock melodramatic situations, halfway between *Oliver Twist* and *Toton* (1919). A widow, Janet (Myrtle Stedman), ends her first marriage and abandons her son Ranny, to marry millionaire Trask. She seeks her son out years later, full of remorse. Now an adult, Ranny (William Collier Jr.) is unaware of his origins and has become a hood following a blackmailer's orders. At his behest he passes himself off as the millionaire's lost son. He accepts Janet's money, but she finally identifies him, and after mutual vows, Trask adopts him. The production banked mostly on the name of its young star, Mary Philbin, who had just completed filming Stroheim's *Merry-Go-Round*. She would later shine in the silent film horror classics *The Phantom of the Opera* (1925) and *The Man Who Laughs* (1927). Borzage's scriptwriter, Mary O'Hara, also worked on Stroheim's film (completed by Robert Julian). We may see these lost works as a preamble to what follows.

The stars and producers of many American films of the twenties were linked in ways that were both romantic and lucrative. These associations would strongly affect both the female star and the history of Hollywood, as illustrated by the duos of W. R. Hearst and Marion Davies and Joseph M. Schenck and Norma Talmadge. In 1920 First National negotiated a fabulous contract with the independent Russian tycoon Schenck: the company had exclusivity of the films made by the star Norma Talmadge (Schenck's wife). She earned $7500 a week plus a share of the profits. Only Mary Pickford, "America's Sweetheart," surpassed Talmadge's popularity in the U.S. Talmadge began at Vitagraph in 1910; six years later she married Schenck and founded her own company, the Norma Talmadge Film Company.

Schenck set her up in a studio on East 48th Street in Manhattan where they shot movies of other Talmadge family members (her youngest sister Constance, and Buster Keaton, Nathalie Talmadge's husband). The entire company moved to Hollywood in the fall of 1921. The flamboyant and exotic romances produced for First National at the new United Studios by the team of Schenck and Talmadge were of course made to order: the melancholic velvet-eyed brunette shedding tears in sumptuous settings, playing brave heroines sacrificing themselves for love (Camille, The Duchess of Langeais, Mademoiselle Fifi), but remaining a "lady" in any circumstance — even on the sidewalk. Robert Florey wrote: "Along with charm and beauty she portrays emotions from deep within that are recorded onscreen and conveyed to us."[3] The most visible artists of the time collaborated with Schenk. Between 1922 and 1927 all of his wife's films were scripted by Frances Marion. It is not surprising, then, that in October 1923 Frank Borzage became the star's new mentor.

Things started badly. Borzage and Frances Marion began work on The Song of Love (released January 1924); the director, in charge of casting and putting the finishing touches on the script became sick (it remains unconfirmed whether or not he began shooting the picture, namely exteriors in Arizona). Chester M. Franklin took over the megaphone, but when he, too, had to take to his bed, Frances Marion completed this Saharan melodrama alone. It concerns a North African dancer (N. Talmadge) who prevents a Berber tribe uprising by falling in love with a handsome French legionnaire (Joseph Schildkraut). The film went relatively unnoticed. But the next Schenck-Talmadge project, Secrets, was a huge hit. Filming began at United Studios in October 1923. This Borzage film would skyrocket Norma Talmadge to fame, marking her biggest success in the U.S. with critics and at the box office. It grossed $55,280 its first week in New York (March 1924); eleven years later it was still on the "Highest Box Office Picture List" with global earnings of $1,5000,000. There was but one shadow on the horizon — the star mentioned condescendingly: "In Europe (aside from Great Britain), they didn't understand what the film was about."[4] As we will see, in 1933 Borzage would direct a sound remake of Secrets with Mary Pickford and Leslie Howard (cf. chap. 10).

Staged in London in 1922, Rudolf Besier and May Edginton's three-act play of the same name had been a success in New York, selling out for six months.[5] Schenk saw in it an ideal part for his wife and paid handsomely to reserve the rights. The play required masterful work by both actress and make-up artist (George Westmore), since Mary Carlton, the heroine, is shown at four different points in her life, aging from young girl to old woman. The cast also included Eugene O'Brien, one of the great silent screen lovers, who co-starred with Norma Talmadge eleven times, and femme fatale Gertrude Astor, John Ford's favored actress (she played in all his films until The Man Who Shot Liberty Valance in 1962). The play contrasts the marital code of ethics in Victorian England with the expectations of the 1920s generation (Mary's daughters are feminists revolted by the hypocrisy of their parents). Hollywood, more drawn to praise lacy romance than denounce bourgeois weaknesses, represses this aspect: the younger generation plays an insignificant role and the last episode recounting the husband's infidelity is glossed over. Aside from that, Frances Marion and Borzage replicated the narrative order of the play exactly, presenting three successive chapters in Mary's life as a dreamed flashback; the intertitles, for the most part, come directly from the script of the play on which the movie is based.

The year is 1923: in her Portchester Terrace villa in London, Lady Carlton, a bonnet-clad octogenarian has for many days watching over her critically ill husband, when the doctor tells her he is dying. Grief-stricken, the old woman retreats to the next room, gets out her diary entitled "Secrets" and writes: "If he dies, my life too is over." Then she leafs slowly through the pages, rereads the first entry, smiles and falls asleep. Dissolve to 1865: Mary,

Father insists on an explanation: Norma Talmadge with George Nichols in *Secrets* (1924).

an 18-year-old, confides to her diary her secret liaison with John Carlton (E. O'Brien), her father's secretary. Her straitlaced, haughty mother and her aunt enter the room to dress her for her first dance. Enter the maid, Mary's accomplice, with a love letter from John; as the mother questions her, she pretends the letter is addressed to her, her languid acting convincing. The delightfully meticulous ritual of dressing ensues, a sort of initiation to the froufrou refined semihumorously and semi-ironically by Borzage. Clad in a negligee, Mary plunges her hand into a basket full of corset-stays held by the servant, tries on one bouffant skirt, then another; finally, the young girl, becoming increasingly enchanted, hops into a crinoline skirt. They put a lace bodice on her, place a bouquet in one hand, a handkerchief in the other, flowers in her hair... With their hands around her waist, she holds in her breath as if immobilized by the corset, which becomes a metaphor as she transforms herself into a deliciously decorative doll, a figure to be exhibited in an appearance-conscious society. The sequence is interrupted by the furious father who bursts in, having just learned his daughter's secret. But comedy reigns supreme: vicariously experiencing her young mistress's love, the maid has a crying jag, gesturing hysterically; the father douses her with water, threatens to pour the carafe over her head and ends up pushing her out the door before double locking his daughter in her room. Filmed in master shot, the setting is theatrical: the door out of camera range, canopy bed to the left, boudoir to the right and some stairs at the back of the room leading to a great bay window. Nevertheless, Borzage considerably developed the content of the play with his delicate humorous touches and his finely-honed observations. At work is an expert rivaling Lubitsch or Cukor at his best. He defies traditional rules to break through the theatrical constraints: the first 20-minute segment, in Mary's room, is broken up into over 155 shots with extremely varied angles.

The copy of *Secrets* at Gosfilmofond (Moscow)[6] provides an accurate idea of the quality of Tony Gaudio's much-praised, fastidious photography (Gaudio later became a prestigious cameraman at Warner Bros.). Brushing away her tears, Mary discovers John's note beneath her pillow. Hearing him whistle outside she hurries to the window. On the way, she blows out the candelabras, then opens the curtains and opens the bay window; momentarily plunged into darkness, the room is illuminated by moonlight. This magical lighting promises freedom and consolation, encircling the lovers in a supernatural aura. John climbs a ladder and tells Mary they'll run away together. What follows is a sequence of undressing every bit as veiled and metaphorical as dressing, but with self-parodying fastidiousness giving way to eroticism. John stumbles over the corset that slips, revealing a part of the bust: the arrival of the father interrupts his pleasure. As John crouches to the ground, Mary hides him beneath her crinoline, turning to her father. Standing up, crushing her lover's calves, she hides the happy man's face in her skirt. The danger passed, Mary and John flee by the balcony and disappear on a large bicycle.

The third segment unfolds in Wyoming in the winter of 1870 in an isolated blockhouse where John, Mary and their baby live. The tone changes: specific Borzage touches reappear as the filmmaker returns to basics, the simple way of life, genuine relationships. The couple is never as close to one another as when they are faced with hardship. Life at the ranch is arduous; exhausted by work, Mary has blisters on her hands, the child has a fever. At nightfall a dozen robbers besiege the house to avenge the hanging of their leader, a cattle thief that John turned in to the sheriff. When John decides to go outside the law to save his small family, Mary interferes forcefully. She attacks the assailants trying to break down the door with

A romantic tableau: Norma Talmadge dreaming of the great escape, in *Secrets* (1924).

boiling water. The bullets fly across the main room, which is dramatically animated by shadows thrown off by the roaring fire in the hearth. The attack culminates in a gripping visual: while John and his hired hand are fighting at the windows, Mary runs into the child's bedroom. She leans over the crib, backs up, frightened, wants to call for help but stops at the door, hesitates, then retraces her footsteps and takes the child in her arms. Borzage captures the scene from a distance, in medium-full shot. The woman takes a mirror from the chest of drawers. Close-up of the reflection of her anxious face in the mirror; she brings it to her lips, her reflection mists over. Filmed from a distance, Mary wipes off the mirror with her skirt and places it against the baby's mouth, then examines it. A second, furtive close-up of the mirror shows the impeccably clear image of the horrified mother; the reflection wavers—she lets go of the mirror. In a second, Mary's face in the mirror seems to have aged several years. Another close-up: Mary paces in the room, hugging the dead child against her. To her husband passing by, she whispers not a word to distract him from the danger outside. Keeping her terrible "secret" until the attack has been averted, she seizes a weapon and with her own hands kills a bandit who collapses in front of the hearth. When the sheriff finally arrives and the attackers are neutralized, Mary remembers the child and returns to the death chamber.

The second to last segment, set in 1888 London, is less original. Now a successful businessman and a faithless husband, Sir John Carlton, with wife and children, has settled into the villa portrayed at the beginning of the film. One of John's mistresses (G. Astor) enters the house, causing a scandal. John intervenes, sends her away curtly, then excuses himself to his wife, who is in tears. On his knees, he begs her to forgive his infidelity. Moreover, he admits to being broke: they will have to begin anew and face adversity together. Thirty-five years later: Dissolve to Lady Carlton. The doctor awakens her to inform her that her husband's condition has improved. Her prayers have been answered: after a dreamed journey through time and space, love has triumphed over death. John calls Mary to his bedside. The old woman quickly fixes herself up in front of the mirror and enters the bedroom. The camera remains outside so as not to intrude upon their reunion, the ultimate "secrets" of those who live for each other. The End.

Secrets is a remarkably sensitive reflection focusing on the life of a couple, the passage of time and the strengthening of ties forged through challenges met together. Its very structure seems to reflect the perception of time at different ages. Cadencing the framework of the story is a slowness evocative of eternity. The episode set in 1865 possesses a lightness and undefined duration of youth (almost 35 percent of the film). The dramatic tension is at its height in the "western" episode, much more condensed, while the last episode is quite brief. The slowness of the epilogue, hovering between life and death, puts Borzage's reflections back into a perspective embracing eternity. But as opposed to the 1933 remake which places more emphasis on the couple, the silent version focused mainly on Norma Talmadge (her suitor only appears after the first half hour). "Her interpretation," wrote *Variety,* "is a work of art, deftly handled with a divine touch that makes it stand out as one of the greatest screen characterizations in years," adding that much of the success is due to Borzage: "He has taken Miss Talmadge and handled her in a manner that makes her reveal artistry such as she never displayed heretofore."[7]

In September and October 1924, Borzage began work on *The Lady,* another play that had recently been a hit on Broadway, adapted to the screen by Frances Marion.[8] As with *Secrets,* it allows Norma Talmadge to age, change outfits in each sequence and bring tears to the eyes of simple folk. In her own words she is successively a "rosebud, a flower in bloom, a wilted flower."[9] Lost for many years, this film, a copy of which has been recently uncovered at the Library of Congress, has a delightfully melodramatic storyline. Yet surprisingly, *The Lady* is almost a masterpiece.[10]

November 1918: the port of Marseilles, at the Brixton Bar, a French-English café. An ironic intertitle proclaims: "The Lady." A wrinkled hand wipes off beer spilled on the counter. Two British servicemen enter the establishment, quite drunk. The older one, noisy and uncouth, jostles the onlookers, then sprays Polly, the mistress of the place, with the contents of a bottle. She remonstrates: "That's a hell of a way to treat a lady!" While the clientele bursts out laughing, the graying manageress confides her sad story to a compatriot: "And yet once I dreamed of bein' a lady," she says with a melancholy smile. Twenty-four years ago, Polly was the queen of the London music hall, "The Girl with the Glad Eye." Flashback: courted by all the gentry, the beauty must place sentries in front of her lodge. She winds up marrying Saint-Aubyns (Wallace MacDonald), an aristocrat who is subsequently disinherited by his outraged father. The couple gamble away their reserves in Monte Carlo, and then one day Polly realizes that her husband, weary of her truck driver behavior, is openly cheating on her with a woman of the world. Polly explodes, throws her haughty rival to the ground, grabbing her by the hair and pummeling her. Scandal. "You common little trollop! Father was right!" Saint-Aubyns spits out before flying to the side of his defeated mistress. The marriage is annulled.

Months pass. After the revolt, moral decay sets in; days spent in the sunshine of the Riviera give way to nights in the taverns. A figure outline rushes into a loathsome basement dive, the café bordello run by Mme. Blanche (Emily Fitzroy). Walls peeling, sweaty with alcohol, the girls are dirty, slouching in the corners. Polly sits down at a table, hides

"I have a wonderful memory of a son like you": Norma Talmadge to George Hackathorne in *The Lady*, 1924.

her face in her hands and orders a ... cup of tea. Laughter. Realizing where she is, she takes flight, but loses her strength. She is gathered up off the pavement. Dissolve to Polly in bed, upstairs; a tiny hand emerges from beneath the sheet, clasping her index finger. Madame Blanche explains to the young mother the rates of her establishment: she will have to dance and sing. When Polly does not cooperate with the enterprising sailors, the boss wants to throw her out in the street. But Borzage's magic, even more than that of the infant, comes into play. Polly places the baby in the manageress's arms and the shrew becomes visually more humane. Shortly after, the old Marquis of Saint-Aubyns bursts in; his son has died, ruined at roulette, and he suddenly feels responsible for his grandson. Backed up by his connections, he has had Polly declared an unfit mother. Without thinking too much, she leaves the baby with the wife of an English reverend, Mrs. Cairns, providing they promise to raise him as a gentleman and never reveal his mother's identity to him.

"But hope is slow to die." For five years, Polly, a poor flower girl, haunts the streets of London in search of her son. She wanders in a fog, turning back each time she sees a little boy. (This sequence, beautifully photogenic, is also perhaps the weakest due to its mawkish sentimentality). Finally, thanks to an inheritance from Madame Blanche, Polly is able to open a café in Marseilles. The flashback ends when a fight erupts in her tavern. The English soldier of the beginning tries to pick a fight with a dancer; his young comrade intervenes, accidentally killing him. Leaning over the involuntary killer, fainted in his arms, the old woman deciphers his identification medal and pale, recognizes her own son (George Hackathorne). To save him, Polly decides to claim responsibility for the murder. But having come to, the young man refuses the sacrifice of a "stranger" "But you're not a stranger. I have a wonderful memory of a son like you." The police take him away. "Do you know why this boy is a gentleman?" concludes Polly's confidante. "Because his mother happens to be — a lady."

Told in this way, the abandoned mother's misfortunes have resonances of a dime novel. But few movies so clearly show to what degree mediocre literature can spawn the best films. *The Lady* could well be a prototype of a success that flies in the face of reason, containing the key to the Borzagian mystery, because finally, the plot contains all the unrealistic, predictable coincidences of the genre, and yet, Borzage's aimed-for alchemy of sublimation manages to escape all critical analysis. Reticently, we may observe that the filmmaker essentially proceeds by small, consecutive touches, by inserting lyrical and pathetic details amplifying the tension within the frame to its very limit. Instead of leading to overt sentimentality, the extreme dramaturgical rigor and mastery of expression bring about the alchemy of sublimation described onscreen and reflected in the theater. To sketch these opulent and decrepit portraits, Borzage draws from cinematographer Tony Gaudio's mesmerizing filters, and from the stupendous sets of William Cameron Menzies, Hollywood's most famous art director. The picturesque hovels, filthy dives and gutters of Marseilles foreshadow the much lauded poetic realism of *7th Heaven* and especially *Street Angel* (1928), of which *The Lady* is the visual predecessor.

Two sequences appear particularly stunning. Polly has just given birth. A sign at the door of the hovel announces the place will close for an hour. In the slimy basement, dark and mysteriously overproportioned (characteristic of Menzies), an Anglican pastor baptizes little Leonard; Madame Blanche acts as godmother. The "personnel" of the establishment are all there, slightly derisive at first, one whore yawning in boredom. An Asian sniggers before the strange rite, but her neighbor elbows her, calling her to order. Little by little, the cosmopolitan assembly of fallen angels is won over by emotion; in the depths of human misery, the solemnity of this strange ceremony puts a lump in people's throats, setting off tears. A quarter of a century before Max Ophuls, Borzage masterfully illustrates the "Maison Tellier" episode of Guy de Maupassant (*House of Pleasure*) in a gentler, more serious and heartbreaking tone. When the arrogant old man comes to claim his grandson, two policemen, stern doormen of institutionalized justice (like the carabinieri in *Street Angel*) accompany him. Rendered completely helpless by this monstrous situation, Polly goes through the motions of complying. She goes up to get Leonard. Once the child is in her arms, she paces, vacillating between despair and revolt: Saint-Aubyns will destroy this child as he has destroyed his own. The conspiracy of women gathers together in the room where the prostitutes scoff at the marquis, sitting on his lap, pulling his hat down over his head, etc. To make him wait and let Mrs. Cairns escape through a secret door, Polly goes on stage and sings for him, enraged, a hateful smile on her lips. Madame Blanche keeps watch by the window for when Mrs. Cairns will be out of sight with the infant. Suspense mounts. Norma Talmadge as a crucified mother, humming her tune on the verge of fainting, reveals herself adept at playing tragedy, a talent not even revealed in *Secrets*. In a few seconds, her eyes mist over her lips quiver imperceptibly, revealing herself capable of expressing the most contradictory urges. When Madame Blanche gives the signal, both fatal and liberating, Polly yields to dejection, her look falters. From triumphant, her laughter becomes hysterical. She swoops down on the old man and hits him until she is exhausted.

To sum up, *The Lady* retraces the saga of a working class girl who winds up ennobled by love, suffering and sacrifices (similar to the title character in *Lazybones*), while at the same time exposing the masks of titled nobility, depicted as despicable. Although this is not original, the purity and unexpected strength of feeling, the dignity of the actors and magnificent photography cast aside any reservations. The chorus of praise given by the press at the time for the film's qualities (coupled with excellent returns) was more than justified: upon rediscovering the film at the Pordenone Silent Film festival in Italy in October 1992, a hardened audience of film buffs was moved to tears by *The Lady*.

Nevertheless, Borzage's days at First National were numbered. As of October 1924, Schenck was in secret consultation with the independent United Artists (Chaplin-Fairbanks-Pickford). On December 5, he was elected president of the board of directors of this company and the Norma Talmadge Film Unit moved over to the competition. Shortly afterward, First National would be swallowed up by Warner Bros. Meanwhile, Borzage had already left ship to answer another call, for 1924 saw the founding of the most prestigious studio representing Hollywood's golden age, Metro-Goldwyn-Mayer.

Economically, the company with the roaring lion was only a subsidiary of the fabulously successful Loew's Inc., an empire of theaters founded by Marcus Loew and managed in New York by Nicholas M. Schenck (brother of Joseph). Buying Metro Pictures in 1919 had allowed Loew's to go from music halls to film production, but the purchase of Goldwyn Pictures, a company in serious difficulty, and the simultaneous fusion with the Louis B. Mayer Corporation on April 17, 1924, gave the company its true start.

Mayer, entrepreneurial and stubborn, eclectic, uneducated and authoritarian, took charge of the Culver City studios in the west part of Los Angeles (the former Goldwyn studios); Irving G. Thalberg, the film industry's legendary "prodigal son" (age 24) became production chief and Mayer's right hand man. Reputedly untiring and intelligent, he was also nervous and in poor health. All decisions at the young MGM were automatically submitted for approval to Mayer and Thalberg, who ruled their studio with an iron will. This new regime marked the beginning of the era of the producer-dictators, in reaction to the financially catastrophic excesses of a few autocratic directors. When this energetic duo took charge, they inherited three problematic and ruinous operations, two from Goldwyn and one from Metro. Paralyzed by the inertia of Italian administration, shooting of *Ben Hur* between Livorno and

Anzio had been stagnating for six months; Erich von Stroheim couldn't stop going through miles of exposed film for *Greed*, while Rex Ingram cheerfully went over budget on *The Arab* in Tunisia and Paris. But it was a promising beginning: the first authentic Mayer-Thalberg production in Culver City, Victor Sjöström's *He Who Gets Slapped*, was filmed in mid–June at the modest sum of $172,000 and brought in more than double its cost at the box office.

With *Humoresque* and two resounding Norma Talmadge successes to his credit, Frank Borzage entered MGM through the front door. In the fall of 1924, he moved his personal production unit, made up of cameraman Chester A. Lyons, scriptwriter Kenneth B. Clarke (his faithful collaborator at American and at Triangle), and Orville O. "Bunny" Dull and Lew Borzage as first and second assistants. At the same time, Louis B. Mayer set sail for Italy to see how work was progressing on *Ben Hur*; he returned from his European journey with an unknown Swede named Greta Garbo under contract.

In theory, Borzage was directly answerable to Thalberg. In reality, however, Thalberg was represented by a production "supervisor" in charge of reporting the smallest happenings on the set, monitoring expenses and offering profuse advice. Patriarchal and emotional, Harry Rapf specialized in tearjerkers (Vidor's *The Champ*, the Lassie series, etc.). His judgment, unsurprisingly, was rather questionable. Thus constrained, the filmmaker buckled down to his first job at MGM, the adaptation of a bitter Zoë Akins play, *Daddy's Gone A-Hunting*.[11] The six-segment marital drama was filmed in November-December 1924 under favorable auspices. Borzage obtained two fine actors who had already co-starred four times: Alice Joyce, a former recruit of Kalem whose hour of glory in 1925–26 came in Henry King's *Stella Dallas* and Herbert Brenon's *Beau Geste*. Playing opposite her was Englishman Percy Marmont, who went on to *Lord Jim*, directed by Victor Fleming. Alice Joyce was full of praise: "Frank Borzage is an ideal director. He is so sensitive. He watches his players all the time, studies their mannerisms and uses them in scenes wherever possible. It makes everything you do seem natural."[12] Visiting the sets at MGM, Margaret Reid said this about the filmmaker at work:

Mr. Borzage is a ridiculously young person with curly, red-brown hair and an ingratiating smile. There is a splendid harmony between Percy Marmont and Mr. Borzage. They both have the idealistic touch and between the two, concoct little scenes that are gems of artistry and detail. I imagine that Frank Borzage is one of the youngest directors in the business, but even at that he is far from overwhelmed by his own importance. Quite the most unassuming man I have ever worked for — and one of the easiest. He explains in detail the requirements of the scene, but if something should go wrong he does not chew the scenery as some of them do. He just looks so sorrowful and hurt that whoever is to blame feels as if he were taking advantage of a child. With hair like his there is, of course, an appropriate temper, but I have never, even in moments of greatest stress, seen him let anyone but himself suffer from it. And, next to Rex Ingram, I'd rather work for him than for any other megaphone artist in the industry. Which means, let me tell you, that Mr. Borzage is all right... A boyish, red-hair figure calling, "Goodnight, people!" Chorus, in response. "Good-night, Mr. Borzage!" with all that gratitude and affection can put into cold words.[13]

The play by poetess and novelist Zoë Akins[14] won favor with critics not because of its rather simplistic storyline (the struggle of an artist's wife, whose greatest rival is continually his work), but due to its frank dialogue and some astute psychological observations. Borzage would try to flesh out the action in this vein, a task made more difficult by the fact that Akins' central characters were inconsistent and not very lovable. He took some distance in regard to the material and the film's finest moments are those written directly for the screen (prints are in the film archives of Prague and Madrid).

The beginning of the film is original: in a New York restaurant, Edith (A. Joyce) sits down at a table across from a man hidden by a newspaper. Absorbed in reading an article, he notices too late that his cigarette is burning a hole in the page. The two protagonists discover each other (metaphorically as well) by means of a space provided by the fire. Stupefied, Julian recognizes Edith as his youthful flame, blows on the paper, gets up and takes her in his arms. Accompanying her home, he confides to her that he has left his parent's home to devote himself to painting, his passion. He says he is unstable; Edith could bring him happiness. On the porch, he kisses her. As he is a full head taller, he lifts her: Borzage shows her legs wriggling in the air. Dissolve to their daughter Janet's little legs, also wriggling, as she is kissed by her father seven years later. Julian (played by P. Marmont) says he is tired of his routine, working at a fashion magazine just to put food on the table; by common agreement with his spouse who remains in New York, he packs his bags for Paris to perfect his art. He returns to the States after a year, another man (this is where Zoë Akins' play begins). Borzage polishes up the scene of the artist's return by accentuating with poignant sobriety the child's vision: Janet, all ribbons and curls, showing her first report card to her mother, rushing to prepare a festive meal. The child runs down the stairs when the taxi pulls up. She climbs back up, perturbed: "I don't know — it seems to me it's Father," she says, sad. Julian enters, frowns as he looks around: "What horrible wall-paper!" planting a distracted kiss on Edith's lips. Then he sits down on the report card. Edith, a truly wounded doe, observes the stranger who is accompanied by two grossly inconsiderate drinking buddies brought back from Paris.

Julian openly admits to his wife that his love for her has waned and suggests he leave home to spare her further torment. Edith tries in vain to make him jealous by embracing Greenough, an aspiring suitor. In desperation, Edith and Janet move into the manor Greenough shares with his mother. Widely praised, the painter cannot find peace, his canvases are sad. Playing in the Greenough's park, Janet is crushed by the branch of an oak tree. However, in the hospital, the doctors predict a prompt recovery. A repentant Julian visits his daughter in secret in one of those heartbreaking scenes where the filmmaker's inimitable style translates the most delicate feelings. Looking lost in the room Janet doesn't recognize her father who sits down at her bedside. She stares at him, surprised, then asks: "Mommy, where is Daddy? When is he coming back?" Borzage chooses frames and gestures strangely identical to those at the end of *A Farewell to Arms*: Janet caresses her father's face; Julian takes her hand and lifts it to his mouth, kisses the little fingers — when he suddenly realizes, incredulous at first, that the fingers are no longer moving. He holds the inert child tightly against himself, lifts her from the bed and carries her in her long nightgown across the hospital room as, eight years later, Gary Cooper will carry Helen Hayes. Death comes always as a surprise in Borzage's image of reality.

"Happiness is hard to find — everyone is out for himself!" cries Julian to his rival. Dissatisfaction blinds him to the beauty that surrounds him (Edith and Janet). To find himself, he must kill within himself this egocentric infantile pipe dream that he takes for love. But he is not alone: in the drama this process brings in its wake the destruction of those dearest to him. Rare are films of the era that show with so little complacency a household's disintegration and the brutal (if not to say gratuitous) death of a child. Thalberg was against sad endings. They had changed the ending of the play, which ends with Julian and Edith permanently breaking up after losing their little girl; in spite of the tragedy the painter cannot give up his vocation and the woman mourns alone. The film, however, ends with the couple sadly getting back together: Julian and Edith are "from now on alone in the world," they "need one another." We may conjecture as to Borzage's opinion on this subject, because, welcome or not, this change does not ring true, nor does it make the storyline lighter. *Variety* observed intuitively that "In all it is a film that has more or less of a depressing effect on the audience."[15] Seeing what happened next, we have reason to believe that the filmmaker was less than enchanted by his work.

If directing *Daddy's Gone A-Hunting* seems not to have caused any major problems, *The Circle*, a rather highbrow comedy, from W. Somerset Maugham's scandalous play, "The Circle," was another story. Since the beginning of the year, the climate in Culver City gradually had become acrimonious. Thalberg was completely absorbed in saving *Ben Hur*, as Fred Niblo's team had been called back from Italy in January 1925. The chief of production personally monitored the recreation of Antioch's Circus Maximus, the largest movie set ever erected in Hollywood (at Cienega, near Venice Boulevard). At the same time MGM instigated a house policy that soon gave Culver City the nickname "Retake Valley." Mayer had under contract a series of fresh directors such as William A. Wellman, Josef von Sternberg, Monta Bell, etc., some of whom had no experience whatsoever, and whose first steps were monitored by Harry Rapf. Forcing them to slavishly follow continuity details of the scripts and giving them at most 18 to 20 days to shoot, management hoped to save considerably to reach its goal of 26 movies for the 1924–25 season. If "retakes" were necessary, these were conferred to more experienced MGM filmmakers, slower and more expensive, such as John M. Stahl or Marshall Neilan. In spite of this anonymous patch-up work, the final product was less expensive than if a high-salaried veteran had directed the film from the start. But we can also imagine, for instance, Alf Goulding's degree of frustration when his film *Don't* was subjected to 290 retakes! It also reveals the lack of creative freedom accorded by management. Even the experienced directors were subject to this new post-production strategy that considered the initial editing of the film (done by the director himself) simply as raw material, indefinitely improvable after "previews" (projection tests before a public not forewarned). This very complex production system introduced by Thalberg limited the director's role to merely filming alone and stripped him of all control over his work.

Another Broadway success—it enjoyed more than six month's exclusive run[16]—led "The Circle" to the rather ambiguous honors of the screen. This sarcastic and sophisticated tale of extramarital romps could have been a subject for Lubitsch or DeMille, whose comedies of manners filled theaters (*The Marriage Circle, Why Change Your Wife?*), but there is certainly little in common between the frivolity of Maugham's world and Borzage's romanticism. What prompted prudish MGM to buy a play that made fun of the convention of marriage, only to disfigure it upon directorial decree? Scandalized, an internal report from the scriptwriting department mentions that "the satire has been sentimentalized" and that "the direction of each scene is fundamentally misguided and unconvincing."[17] Such severity was unjustified, as we can see today thanks to the print preserved at George Eastman House (Rochester). It was produced with a great deal of care ("Old England" sets by Cedric Gibbons and James Basevi) and had a wonderful cast, featuring several rising stars, the elegant Eleanor Boardman (who married King Vidor in September 1926), the young lead Malcolm McGregor, discovered by Rex Ingram, and the talented Creighton Hale. But hidden in the credits was a small sensation, as revealed in 1974 by Stephen Harvey.[18] The beauty running away with her lover in the prologue is non other than Lucille Le Sueur, alias Joan Crawford, at age 20. Due to an error, her involvement in the film was never mentioned; Rapf was her "protector," this was her second screen role.

The title *The Circle* implies that in the Cheney clan adultery recurs from one generation to the next; however the introductory intertitle already alters the general storyline: "Man may select a wife — but he should be careful whose wife he selects!" In other words: certain husbands are easier to cheat upon than others, a statement which contradicts Maugham!

Cheney Castle, about 1890. Lady Catherine (J. Crawford) is running away with her lover,

Borzage and Joan Crawford (both sitting) discussing the prologue of *The Circle* (1924), while George Fawcett looks on. On the far left, wearing sunglasses, stands cinematographer Chester A. Lyons.

Lord Porteous, abandoning her little boy Arnold and her husband, Lord Clive Cheney. Thirty years pass. Arnold (C. Hale), now an adult, has married Elizabeth (E. Boardman) and lives in the family manor; pedantic and gruff, he is the caricature of a monocled country squire. Elizabeth prefers the company of a family friend, Teddy (M. McGregor), an athlete with whom she dreams of running away. However, she still hesitates between sacrificing position and security for her "great love." Elizabeth has invited the above-mentioned adulterous couple, living in exile abroad for many years: she wishes to see if Lady Catherine and Lord Porteous's escapade has really been worthwhile, if "secret" happiness has stood up the passing of time and social ostracism (this motive is not present in the play). The first third of the film is filled with the younger generation's impatience, if not apprehension, at facing 60-year-old visitors (that the film shows twice from the back, traveling in their limousine convertible). The suspense peaks with the unexpected arrival of cuckolded husband Lord Cheney at the manor, in hunting clothes, a rifle over his shoulder. "Never felt so keen about shooting as today!" Distraught, the young people attempt to take away his rifle, which passes from one to the other. The filmmaker defines the sides by first centering father and son together, then Teddy and Elizabeth. An ingenious geometry of shots and gestures manages to totally obliterate the theatrical structure of the plot: its transposition to a silent medium is at many moments evocative of Lubitsch's sparkling *Lady Windermere's Fan* (1925).

Elizabeth, sitting on her father-in-law's lap, distracts the old man by playing with his ears, then reveals to him why they are nervous. But Lord Cheney's pity is derisive. Although she used to be an exquisite beauty, he remembers, Lady Catherine today is probably "frail, sweet, quiet and lovely." As an aside, he lets his daughter-in-law know he has guessed her adulterous intentions. The long-awaited entrance leaves the circle aghast: Lady Catherine (Eugenie Besserer) is an intrusive creature, dolled up, extravagant, all in feathers, pearls and lorgnette. Her companion, Lord Porteous (George Fawcett) is old and grumpy, sensitive to the cold and rheumatic. The lovers of yesteryear bicker or ignore each other. "Poor Hughie!" sighs Lord Clive. Borzage maliciously sums up the situation by placing his two "love triangles" around a bridge table: Elizabeth and Teddie play against Lady Catherine and Lord Porteous, while Lord Cheney and his son, set back, watch the confrontation, ironic spectators. Borzage orchestrates a comical situation entertaining from all points of view, but miles from the "amoral" designs of Somerset Maugham. His Elizabeth, placed in the center of a vaudevillian mix-up, appears seriously troubled, insecure, watching for the least little indication that could justify her evasion, her juvenile dream of happiness. The cuckolded husband is never ridiculed, as opposed to Maugham's puppet. Finally, the emotion — and strong reminiscences of *Secrets*— surface unexpectedly in a cruel scene where Lady Catherine collapses before a photo of herself at age twenty; "You're still as beautiful," consoles her gouty husband, holding her close. In the play, the old couple helps the young couple flee in the name of passion, even if they will later regret it. The Cheneys, both father and son, are taken in. In the film, Elizabeth and Teddy flee in a car, however the chauffeur is none other than Arnold in disguise. Teddy comes out of the ensuing confrontation with two black eyes and the faithless one returns, repentant and secretly admiring, to the fold. A series of adventures that flow with both elegance and flair.

It would be pointless to seek Borzagian resonances in a plot that owes so much to compromise, especially as a short sentence in *Variety* notes incidents during the filming (February–March) worthy of "Retake Valley": "It was necessary to change the story about and have a large number of scenes retaken by other directors."[19] The Englishman Edmund Goulding was one of the filmmakers given this task, followed perhaps by John M. Stahl or Jack Conway, then MGM retake specialists. As for the film's happy ending, it is anything but an isolated case: at the same instant, at Mayer's order, Marshall Neilan had to tack on a happy end to the filming of Thomas Hardy's *Tess of the D'Ubervilles*! Outraged by such a lack of control, the director of *The Circle* drew the obvious conclusions, even if his name in the credits appears in characters as big as the title.

On April 14, Culver City announced the simultaneous departure of Frank Borzage and Erich von Stroheim. According to *Variety,* this would bring to five the number of directors who slammed the door on MGM within a few weeks. "Borzage is said to have been mainly dissatisfied by the assignments allotted him, the director wanting to make a better grade of pictures than those which had been placed in his charge."[20] As for Stroheim, he had just completed *The Merry Widow* (December 1–March 9) under nightmarish conditions; when they blocked him from entering the editing room he gave notice. On August 18, the list of defectors increased with Sternberg (who had words with Rapf during the filming of *The Masked Bride*) and Wellman, who refused the scripts imposed upon him. In his memoirs, Sternberg tells his side of the breakup: "That afternoon as I walked away from the studio, I was flanked by three other directors who had also been found wanting and were asked to leave. One was Frank Capra [sic], ... the other was William A. Wellman..., and the third was Frank Borzage who next made the beautiful film *7th Heaven*."[21] The purge was important. In the manner of veterans Rex Ingram (who chose voluntary exile in Europe), Marshall Neilan and Maurice Tourneur (they would leave the following year), Borzage firmly turned his back on the supervisor's tyranny and on the stilted, academic and bourgeois state of mind Thalberg instituted that would become the MGM's trademark. Borzage would only return to Culver City twelve years later — after the death of the famous tycoon.

6

Fox Films Spurred On by Ambition

Sought out by Fox Film in April 1925, the filmmaker had no idea it would be in this rapidly growing studio that he would reach the summit of his career. He directed eighteen films there by 1932, including his major works *Lazybones, 7th Heaven, Street Angel, The River, Lucky Star, Liliom* and *Bad Girl*. There he also rubbed shoulders with two of his most famous colleagues in the business, John Ford and Friedrich Wilhelm Murnau.

Nor did William Fox realize how important his new recruit would be for the company's future. The Fox Film Corporation officially began in 1915 and rapidly accelerated its production output thanks to the sultry Theda Bara, the first vamp of cinema, cast in made-to-measure products (a film per month between 1915 and 1919, from *Carmen* to *Salome* and *Cleopatra*); J. Gordon Edwards, the grandfather of Blake, directed her in several costumers which today have disappeared. Another goldmine for Fox was cowboy Tom Mix, under contract for ten years, and his colleague Buck Jones. They enlivened many small westerns that would become, with vaudeville, Fox's bread and butter. The most notable of these in-house directors were Raoul Walsh (as of 1915), John Ford (as of 1921), and the young Woody Van Dyke (as of 1922). Between the time it was founded and 1924, Fox saw its net profits rise from $500,000 to $2,500,000. But despite constant growth, the company was still far behind giants such as Famous Players (Paramount) and Loew's (Metro-Goldwyn-Mayer) and belonged, like Warner and Universal, to the middle echelon. The main studios (1800 acres) and the administration were in Hollywood, between Western Avenue and Sunset Boulevard.

Suddenly, the climate changed; it is no coincidence that Borzage's close and long association with Fox began in 1925. That year Fox issued new stocks for six million dollars, an increase in capital that from then on would allow it to inflate its film budgets and develop the lucrative production of newsreels, for which it held the monopoly in Hollywood. However, it was the new subsidiary, Fox Theaters, a circuit of first-run theaters on the national level, that, as of July 1925, became its decisive commercial asset and opened doors to the most daring adventures in film. To fill its theaters, the firm had to feature particularly appealing programs, aiming high. Its acquisition of the largest movie theater in the world, the Roxy Theater in Manhattan's Times Square, was indicative of things to come: this 6250-seat palace, ostentatiously luxurious, cost a mere five million dollars. William Fox also began investing in researching an optic sound system (the photographic recording of sound on the margin of the film) which would become "Movietone." The Western Avenue studios (which housed the central administration) underwent various transformations, such as adding on an enormous stage (300 × 100 feet) built for the most technically sophisticated interiors. At the same time they bought 400 acres of fallow land in Westwood (West Los Angeles), between Hollywood and Santa Monica Beach, to use as exteriors for westerns, sequences with many extras, exotic villages and oversize outdoor sets. This huge lot would be renamed Fox Hills Studio before becoming the head office of the Fox Movietone City Company (with the arrival of sound).

This change in direction was also linked to the personality of Winfield R. Sheehan (1883–1945), William Fox's right-hand man and one of the rare Hollywood producers with a university education. A delegate from the east coast (where he had been working since 1914), "Winnie" Sheehan became head of the California studios, reorganizing them from top to bottom. Temperamental, affable, sentimental, cynical and distrustful, this blue-eyed Irishman nicknamed "Little Caesar" understood that the company could not compete with Metro or Paramount's "star system" and that only the quality of its films, scripts, and direction would allow it to attain its goals. The returns from Ford's *The Iron Horse* in 1924 (the first Fox film to open on Broadway) confirmed this analysis and Sheehan immediately assigned Raoul Walsh to a big First world war epic, *What Price Glory?*; Fox paid the then-fabulous sum of $100,000 for the rights to adapt Maxwell Anderson and Laurence Stalling's anti-war play. As a result, the team of Fox directors grew to include several names already or soon to become famous: Howard Hawks, Rowland V. Lee, Allan Dwan. "Frank Borzage Productions" set up part and parcel in the offices on Western Avenue, and the filmmaker began work the same day as his former colleague at Inceville, Reginald Barker, also under contract. The work conditions differed: while at Metro, filming was generously scheduled over a sixty-day period, at 5 pm sharp the workday was over; Fox allotted on average barely 25 days for a film, but Sheehan trusted his directors totally. Once the script, budget and casting were approved, he merely supervised the final editing, without taking over.

Out of principle, Borzage had always refused to commit himself in the long term; his first contract at Fox, which was for four years, expired on December 31, 1928; he was paid $35,000 per film.[1] Far from denying his youthful stint on the stage, Borzage regularly followed the openings of all contemporary plays; as mentioned, several of them provided the impetus for his recent films. His aptitude for imagining visual equivalents to lines on stage would save him from falling into the trap of filmed theater with the advent of talkies toward the end of the decade. Borzage secretly made some trips back east so that Fox could acquire the veneer of culture it so desired. At his instigation, on May 9, 1925, the company united with influential New York producer John Golden (1874–1955), a move that allowed Fox to reserve itself the rights for the biggest Broadway successes ("The John Golden Unit of Clean American Plays"). At the same time, Borzage and Henry McRae began producing theatrical shows in New York for the "William Fox Academy of Music" and in Los Angeles for the "William Fox Vaudeville Company," troupes whose goal was to promote new talent, because Fox desperately needed stars. The shows, repurchased at extremely high prices from John Golden, were part of the "Special Productions," a category of "A" films under the general supervision of Sol M. Wurtzel. These plays included Owen Davis' "Lazybones," Frank Craven's "The First Year," Austin Strong's "Seventh Heaven," and Winchell Smith's and Frank Bacon's "Lightnin'" (filmed by John Ford). True to himself, Borzage entrusted the adaptation of the first two to his former colleague Frances Marion.

Rediscovered by Alex Gordon in the Fox vaults in 1970, *Lazybones* is the most poignant, and most finished Borzage film to precede *7th Heaven*. It translated the studio's wish to get out of a rut, because to everyone's surprise, the lead role was given to the idol of millions of teenagers: cowboy Charles "Buck" Jones. William Fox had hired him as a possible replacement for Tom Mix in 1919; *Lazybones* was his sixty-sixth film, a rare non-western and the only film in which he plays a loser. Sheehan felt Borzage would be able to guide this valiant righter of wrongs to a more "noble" register. Madge Bellamy, the young revelation from *The Iron Horse*, plays opposite him; by a strange coincidence, she had made her first screen test under Borzage's direction at Cosmopolitan studios in New York, in 1920.[2] And yet the actress, whose photo then graced the covers of *Photoplay* and *Screen Secrets*, was so preoccupied by her "glamor look" that she missed the chance of her life: "Frank and I did not get along. This was to prove a great disaster for me as he refused to have me for the role played by Janet Gaynor in *7th Heaven*, even though William Fox himself said that he had chosen me. Borzage and I quarreled over the little matter of my fingernails. In the picture, I played a poor white-trash girl. Every morning, he would inspect my nails to see if they were dirty enough. They never were, so he had mud rubbed in them. I did not think the camera was close enough to catch this detail and took it as an insult. Of course, in retrospect, I wonder how I could have been so uncooperative."[3] Due to her memorable performance in *Greed*, ZaSu Pitts was given a tragic role, one of the best of her career, a change from playing a never-ending series of comical and quarrelsome scatterbrains. Virginia Marshall, who movingly portrayed the little girl in *Daddy's Gone A-Hunting*, played Kit at age five. For his first assignment at Fox, the filmmaker pulled out all the stops: he obtained George Schneiderman, Ford's cameraman responsible for the extraordinary panoramas in *The Iron Horse*, then moved with his small unit to the settlement of Kernville (northeast of Bakersfield), where he worked from July to September, away from any interference. This was a special privilege, considering how quickly most Fox productions were filmed. Lew (second assistant) and Danny Borzage (accordion) were in the crew. As the inhabitants of Kernville stubbornly resisted working as extras, the entire team pitched in. Even the boss's wife, Rena, was made up as a village gossip. Sometimes in the evenings the three Borzage brothers would go fishing on the bank of the Kern River — John Ford's stagecoach would cross it in 1939 — and bring back fish that ZaSu Pitts and Jane Novak would prepare for the happy cast and crew.

Only the broad outlines[4] of Davis's play remained. More action was added, the end modified: the entire film pulsates with its sunny landscapes (filmed into the light), its poetic indolence. Unpredictable, like *History Is Made at Night* (1937), *Lazybones* mixes several genres, going from comedy to melodrama and ending up as a kind of tragedy. A humor tinged with irony accompanies the prologue, which unfolds in a rural setting, in Maine circa 1900: "Steve Tuttle was slow as molasses in winter, so they gave him the nickname of "Lazybones." Shot of molasses running over a cake. Steve (B. Jones), dressed like a scarecrow, is sleeping in the sunshine, his feet resting on the dilapidated garden fence, a spider web hanging from his feet. Irritated by a fly, he frowns a few times but can't find the energy to shoo it away. His old mother, a washerwoman, does it for him. A goat sniffs at his face, he murmurs "Agnes dear," opens his eyes and, furious, pushes the animal away.

The film proceeds to the first part. "And this is Agnes dear..." an intertitle specifies: the girl (Jane Novak) and her mother, Mrs. Rebecca Fanning (Emily Fitzroy), hatted and veiled, arrive together. Beneath the incensed gaze of this dragon lady, Steve timidly courts the gentle Agnes who, although charmed, reproaches him, like everyone else, for his insurmountable laziness: the garden door is stuck, the roof of the house is in sorry state ("what's the use of repairing it — it's not going to rain" Steve candidly argues); but for her, honestly, he is ready to change his ways. He invites her on board an automobile that he put together himself and drives for about twenty yards before the motor conks out. Mrs. Fanning makes a disdainful face which turns into a syrupy smile when she sees Elmer Ballister, "The Beau Brummel of the town," appear out of a carriage: she has chosen him as her future son-in-law. The fellow, affected, all dressed up and vaguely mustached, takes the two women in his vehicle. Ruth (ZaSu Pitts), Agnes' sister, who attends a school in the city, receives a missive from her mother summoning her to come back to marry Elmer. She leans sadly over the child she brought into the world after having secretly married a sailor who has since disappeared at sea...

A man lets himself slide on the side of love: Buck Jones in *Lazybones* (1925).

The second part slides into melodrama: Steve is sleeping in the hollow of a tree on the river bank, a straw hat over his eyes, a fishing rod caressing the waves. A fish escapes him; he is about to fall back asleep when he notices Ruth throwing herself into the water from atop a bridge. He dives in and saves her. In despair, Ruth tells him her story and hands over to him the infant who had remained in a basket on the shore, as she doesn't dare face her mother with her. Confronted with her pleading, Steve promises to keep her secret. Without batting an eye, he brings the baby home where his mother, Agnes and Elmer await, incredulous. Elmer, convulsed with laughter, rushes to spread the news: Steve and his "found" child, a little girl, become the laughingstock of the area. "What if people do talk — I don't care as long as *you* trust me." He cannot lie to his mother, but his speech seals her lips. Moved by her son's silent sacrifice, Mrs. Tuttle makes a tender gesture, quickly interrupted by the squealing of the infant who has rolled out of her basket. In the garden, Steve feeds the baby with the bottle, when Elmer's carriage passes by with the Fanning family. Ruth signals discreetly to her child, and Agnes signals to Steve — who answers for both. Sheltered in the four walls of their mansion, Ruth reveals the truth to her mother about her secret marriage. Mrs. Fanning — who wears a crucifix — tells the young woman she is a liar, seizes a whip and beats her savagely; she threatens to put the baby in an orphanage should her daughter reveal its existence. Learning this, Steve decides to adopt the child, named Kit, leading to a break-up with Agnes, too firmly entrenched by her bourgeois upbringing to discern her loved one's nobility of soul and the deep-hearted goodness.

Part three takes place in the summer of 1905. Ruth has married Elmer, now a bank manager: he is reading aloud an article about himself. Sitting in an armchair, she knits as she listens to him, resigned. In the street, a swarm of children tease Kit ("Lazybone's Lit-tle Moses in the bulrushes"). Ruth gets up, discovers the scene from the window, runs out-side (her husband hasn't noticed a thing) and takes the little girl in her arms; the intensity frightens the child: "Please don't look at me like that!" Elmer arrives, furious, orders his wife to go inside and chases the little girl away. Kit revolts and throws a pebble at the lout's backside. When a friend's mother also chases her away, she runs back home, with a heavy heart — framed in a long tracking shot visualizing her awareness. In the garden ("Darn that gate!") Kit finds her "Uncle Steve," sleeping of course, and rushes over. Her little face buried in his shirt, she asks him why nobody wants to play with her. He lies to her: "I guess because I'm so lazy, a good-for nothin', Kit." A tear rolls down his cheek.

Part four: spring 1915. Ruth is dying under the eyes of her fierce maternal guardian. For the first time in her life, she finds the energy to revolt, locking her mother in a room and rushing — framed like Kit, earlier — to "Lazybones'" house where she wants to kiss her child before dying. Kit has become a stunning teenager (Madge Bellamy). Borzage divides up the meeting very simply in medium-close shots and restrains the effusion by opposing Ruth's feverish, bulging eyes, her uncontrollable need to touch her child, with Kit's silent incomprehension and embarrassment, and finally to Steve's grave demeanor, his head turned away. The scene thus obtains a maximum of sobriety in the pathetic, one of the hallmarks of the filmmaker's genius. At the moment of death, Ruth grips the girl's waist (filmed from behind in close-up, so that the faces are absent); Kit looks at Steve uncomprehending, and he, very calmly, explains: "It's just a natural thing, that is — folks get weary and tired — they're just called home, Kit." Then he encourages the child to recite a prayer for the deceased, this unknown woman "who looked so sad."

Part five, introduced by the philosophical: "The sun rose at the usual hour — even though it was the year 1917, when the whole world was topsy-turvy." Mobilized, Steve goes to war: his enrollment is not explained, but it is an implicit proof of courage: "Remind me to fix that gate when I'm back," he says to console his anguished mother. Kit throws her arms around his neck, they gaze at each other a long time and kiss on the lips. Nighttime in the trenches of northern France. Steve is asleep — what else? — all dressed in the back of a shelter, holding his gun like his fishing rod: he is dreaming... Above him, a German coun-teroffensive forces his comrades to retreat. Steve wakes up, discovers the trenches empty; stunned, he goes out into the night and fires. Thinking themselves surrounded, about twenty Germans give themselves up. He is now a hero in spite of himself: his exploit makes the front page of newspapers, thrilling his relatives in the U.S. This brief episode ridicules all military vainglory, reduces heroism to a sleepwalker's reflexes, the siesta becomes the refuge of the wise man. Steve isn't even slacking off: his sleep is that of the innocent. As always with the individualistic Borzage, war appears not as a battle (the enemy is rarely visible in his films) but as a general calamity stripped of political considerations and justifications (in *Back Pay*, Jerry falls, crying the name of his beloved). "Steve was too darned lazy to write back home that he was alive — so one evening he just casually returned." But things have changed, his repair shop works, the fence has been repainted, the gate opens easily. Dick the mechanic (future director Leslie Fenton), young and dynamic, takes care of the cars. And of Kit. But Steve only has eyes for her: worried, he contemplates her, his graying temples in the mirror and hums like a teenager while playing the banjo, which he hasn't touched since Agnes left, eighteen years ago. "I'm so happy, I'm going to work" he confides to his mother, who wrinkles her brow. Steve plans on asking Kit to marry him at the large outdoor ball given in his honor; he even sports a bow tie and wears shiny shoes that are too narrow. Agnes, who has remained an old maid, has torn up her invitation to

The silent drama of several ruined lives: Buck Jones and Madge Bellamy in *Lazybones* (1925).

the ball. From her window, her heart in turmoil, she observes the jubilant people. Suddenly her mother, sitting beside her, begins rambling on, persecuted by Ruth's ghost: in her delirium of guilt, Mrs. Fanning reveals Kit's true identity. Agnes realizes, horrified, the magnitude of all that this implies. After the dance, Steve cools his sore feet in the river and observes Kit and Dick, in an embrace. Dissolve to party shoes fastened to the back of a car with the sign "just married." "At least I got rid of those shoes" observes Steve, his smile frozen. He and his mother signal broadly, while the car carrying Kit and Dick moves out of sight. Steve sniffs a bit: a hand, his mother's, enters the frame on the left and gently touches his arm.

Epilogue: summer 1925. "Lazybones" is peacefully spread out under his tree, a straw hat over his face, his good old shoes full of holes. Dragged down by a fish, his fishing rod slides into the water; Steve jumps into the waves and recovers it, his catch is so young! He gives it back its freedom (as he does Kit) after swearing. Fade to black. The End. This conclusion, lasting less than a minute, is heartbreaking by its very terseness, confirming the whole silent drama of several ruined lives. Fatalistic, he to whom nothing ever happens has accepted his lot. Steve sleeps while the river continues to flow past him. Like his life.

There are echoes of Chekhov in the cyclical trajectory of this gentle lazybones, who dreams while his whole existence of accomplishing great things is never realized, and who, without protest, meets only deception, sacrifice and suffering. (A temporal trajectory that Borzage punctuates with significant leitmotifs such as the hat, the shoes, the gate). But the acknowledgment is terrible without being bitter. In a very general way, Borzage brings his sympathy to society's rejects, because they are unproductive (Steve), weak (the Fanning sisters) or unconventional (Kit): the pariahs in *7th Heaven*, the street performers in *Street Angel*, the unemployed in *Man's Castle*, all these heroes of authentic values (who have "sad faces" when they don't find liberating love) are present. "Lazybones," the nonchalant man with little status, scorns what others say; the rare times he makes an effort, it's to help others. The people of rank — who "destroy" (Mrs. Manning Elmer) — live among them, sequestering those close to them in their repressive mansions. They are closed off, observing the street from behind their curtained windows (another visual leitmotif) and their conventions. Darkness signifies death (the trenches) or deception (the ball). The home of Steve and his mother, on the other hand, is always shown as open to the outside, therefore generous; they live in light, in the garden, behind a poorly constructed fence both dangerous and unobstructed, on the bank of a river where they save lives and find children.

With no happy ending, *Lazybones* flopped at the box office. Buck Jones's fans were unsettled by his new image, by his restrained acting, and the actor returned immediately to the usual cavalcades (Van Dyke's *Desert's Price*). American critics did not recognize the originality of the work, but in France it received excellent notices. At the Parisian opening, Albert Bonneau noted in *Cinémagazine* that *Lazybones* "carries the mark not of sadness, but of a kind of melancholy to which we are not accustomed in American films.... Buck Jones reveals excellent dramatic talent; he is very serious, subtle and some of his smiles are sad, sadder than tears or sobs would be."[5] Sixty-two years later, Dominique Rabourdin wrote: "In a 1925 film, unknown to all film historians, *Lazybones*, a man lets himself slide imperceptibly on the side of love with tenderness and sharp pain that have only their equivalent in Mizoguchi. The air they breathe in the important silent films of Borzage is extraordinarily pure, with freedom, with poetry."[6]

Taken from a recent comedy of manners by Guy Bolton and Winchell Smith, *Wages for Wives* appears to be merely a diversionary stop-gap that Borzage filmed in September–October 1925, replacing Harry Beaumont. To believe the press — the film seems to be lost — it is a light piece about married life with a touch of feminism: Nell (Jacqueline Logan) agrees to marry Danny (Creighton Hale) if he shares his pay equitably with her. But once married, Danny reneges. A modern Lysistrata, Nell goes on strike, leaving the marital home, followed by her married sister Luella (ZaSu Pitts again) and her mother Annie. The abandoned husbands go through a difficult time until the day when, tired of being separated, the three households finally reconcile.

The First Year drifts into similar waters, although its subject, treated here frankly and comically, fits more into Borzage's specific diegetic universe, focusing on the experiences and disappointments of young marrieds starting out together (*Bad Girl*, *The Nth Commandment*). Frances Marion adapted this "tragedy of married life" from a Frank Craven play that ran for two years on Broadway, with a total of 760 performances; it was the fifth most successful Broadway play in the 1917–1934 period.[7] The film sticks close to the original, with Borzage adding some occasional amusing observation or detailed characterization. Grace (Kathryn Perry) has two suitors, Tom (Matt Moore) and Dick, who hate each other cordially. Well brought up, Tom allows himself to be pressed into playing cards with his sweetheart's parents; Dick takes advantage of this to flirt with her. Tom places himself at the games table so as to be able to watch his rival's ploys, either directly or in the mirror, which allows for a diverting optical ballet as Dick tries to escape from his field of vision by diverse maneuvers. A series of humorous ellipses indicate Tom's final victory: he holds Grace in his arms, she sighs... "more than anything in the world," he gets up from the sofa, his arm cramped and his right leg asleep; a wedding ring is placed on a woman's hand, and this same hand (dissolve) wearing rubber gloves, is next seen washing dishes in soapy water... The "sudden downpours" of the young couple with their modest lifestyle accumulate and culminate in a hilarious sequence: Tom has invited Barstow, a businessman (J. Farrell MacDonald), and his intended "wife," a showgirl (Margaret Livingstone), to an impromptu dinner at home to wind up a business deal. Grace gives emergency instructions to a somewhat stereotypical simple-minded black servant, Hattie, who has never waited tables ("but I washes best"). Each couple is acting for the other. But as the aperitif bottles are empty, Hattie mixes cocktails with her old mother's contraband rotgut (Prohibition still rages), sniffs the melons in front of the guests to know to whom she should serve the "good" ones, then hands in her apron after dropping the vegetables. Grace's foot searches for the bell beneath the table, pressing against Barstow's foot, who believes she is issuing an invitation, etc. The plot itself is unpretentious, juggling between sophisticated comedy and farce: "you two are suffering from matrimonial measles— better to have them while you're young." Dick resurfaces, Grace returns to her mother, but it all works out when Tom, who has been consoling himself with 65-cent gin, gets the contract he dreamed of. The moral is summed up by the tongue-in-cheek piece of advice "don't get married until the second year!"

The two next productions seem now to have been lost. Directed between December 1925 and January 1926, *The Dixie Merchant* takes its plot from a much republished novel, *The Chicken-Wagon Family* by John Barry Benefield. Borzage took over this film, begun by Victor Schertzinger, at Sheehan's request (he was dissatisfied with the script[8]); there was every reason to believe that it would be filler-type work, illuminated by the presence of Madge Bellamy, the beautiful whimsical heroine of *Lazybones*. Borzage cast his own parents in the episodic role of an old couple. The plot is thin: an unrepentant gambler, Fippany (J. Farrell MacDonald), from the depths of Louisiana, loses his house and takes to the road in a chicken wagon like some happy hobo, accompanied by his wife and daughter. They leave him after an accident, but Fippany saves his marriage and finds a son-in-law thanks to his faithful horse, Marseillaise, who wins at the races. The critics discerned in *The Dixie Merchant* a curious mix of drama and farfetched comedy, as, in the filmmaker's hands, even the trivial acquires a human dimension. Had the film survived, it would be tempting to draw some comparisons with one of Borzage's later works, *That's My Man* (1947), in which the plot basically unfolds at the racetrack, focusing on the erring ways of an unreliable husband. The comic vignette *Early to Wed*, filmed in February-March 1926, depicts the same basic situation as *The First Year*, stressing the material difficulties encountered in married life (its subtitle is "Life and Love in 1926"). Tommy (Matt Moore) and Daphne (Kathryn Perry) get married without a cent; trying to imitate acquaintances who live beyond their means, the naive young couple falls desperately into debt. Tommy loses his job, the furniture is seized. At the last minute, they manage to con a millionaire into getting them out of their predicament. This last twist, purely conventional, manages to evade the real questions raised by the film, unless we see it as the filmmaker winking conspiratorially at the spectators, who are not taken in. In all likelihood, Borzage was practicing while awaiting a subject worthy of him. At the same time, his brother Lew finally rose to the position of first assistant director, which he would keep for the rest of his life. Frank introduced a clause in his subsequent contracts stipulating that Lew would automatically be hired to work with him.

In February 1926, Borzage busily prepared for *One Increasing Purpose*, inspired by a controversial best-seller by British novelist A. S. M. Hutchinson. This mystical drama of a survivor of World War I who despairs at the lack of love among those close to him was to be filmed mainly in London, in August, with an already completed script by Kenneth B. Clarke. But in the meantime the studio was pushing the project *7th Heaven*. *One Increasing Purpose*, which Borzage had patiently gotten off the ground, was handed over to Harry

Beaumont, who immediately left for Great Britain. In April and May, while waiting for Shee-han to finally give the go-ahead for *7th Heaven*, an "important work" whose logistics were still quite complicated, Borzage turned out a rather uneven drama, which was neverthe-less rich in subtlety: *Marriage License?*, a print of which exists in Prague. Borzage cast Alma Rubens, the heroine of *Humoresque*, for the fourth and final time. Here her femininity appears disturbingly fragile (a morphine addict, she would die four years later). Among the cast were Emily Fitzroy, the exasperating Gorgon of *Lazybones*, and a refined newcomer, Walter Pidgeon, a Canadian whom Borzage would again direct in 1940 when Pidgeon was one of MGM's top stars. The title of the play that provided the plot was more eloquent: *The Pelican* (by Fryniwyd Tennyson Jesse and Harold Marsh Harwood).[9] According to the Christian bestiary, the pelican feeds its young with its own flesh and its blood symbolizes

The aristocrat and the commoner: Emily Fitzroy and Alma Rubens in *Marriage License?* (1926).

parental (and by extension divine) love; in this case, the writers are evoking a mother's sacrifice. But whether due to the absence of Frances Marion or the magnetism of Alma Rubens, scriptwriter Bradley King's adaptation focuses more on passion than sacrifice.

Marcus Heriot (W. McGrail), a colorless descendant from a respectable line of English lords, commits himself to a commoner, the Canadian Wanda (A. Rubens). When he brings back his wife to the familial castle, the reception is glacial. Lady Heriot (E. Fitzroy), outraged by the intrusion of this "plebe" in their family tree, is determined to put an end to the scandal. The premise is similar to that of *The Lady* (1924) and many other melodramas, but Borzage quickly captivates the spectator with his intelligent eye. Visually, the characters are subordinate to the interiors of the imposing feudal domain, filmed in chiaroscuro by Ernest Palmer in a profusion of pictorial effects. Borzage systematically films the action in medium or medium-full shot to emphasize the distance between the people and the coldness of their hearts. Wanda, the only luminous spot in this haughty half-light (her dress and hat are white) is abandoned in the center of this setting, while Marcus explains his actions to his parents in the next room. The servants observe her condescendingly from the top of the stairs ("middle class!"). To announce the meal, a lackey ceremoniously rings a large gong, an instrument the filmmaker would use again as a leitmotif. The dramatic triangle of Wanda–Lady Heriot–Marcus is determined by the position of the protagonists in the frame — often, the mother places herself between the couple or blocks Wanda's way with an arm. Gestures indicate contrast: Lady Heriot, a masterful schemer, frighteningly rigid, merges with the vertical darkness of the setting (Lord Heriot remains in the shadows). Wanda, spontaneous, nerves on edge, with her slightly vulgar sensuality, is filmed sitting or lying down in a negligee, languorously wrapped around her husband. Showing aristocratic disapproval, but in reality devoured by jealousy, the mother-in-law wipes off make-up from her dear son's dressing gown. The son is sent on a military mission to India; the cruel mother takes advantage of his absence to discredit Wanda, who innocently met up with a childhood friend, by accusing her of adultery. Pregnant, Wanda is subject to the sarcasm of the court obtained by the Heriots; after a moment of hysteria, she faints before the judges. Divorce is granted without Marcus turning a hair, and Robin, the newborn, is declared illegitimate.

Repudiated, the young woman settles in the outskirts of Paris. Years pass. Robin, who knows nothing of his origins and believes his father dead, celebrates his eighteenth birthday; his mother spoils him, providing him with the finest education. For the past five years, Wanda has been seeing Paul (W. Pidgeon), who is impatient to marry her. Robin desperately wants to attend Sandhurst military academy, but only the sponsorship of the warrant officer — Marcus Heriot — can facilitate entry into this exclusive school. Therefore, the teenager gains entrance, incognito, into the castle of his ancestors, where he immediately feels at home. Lady Heriot is dead; the old Lord, paralyzed, recognizes in him the very image (and attitudes) of his son Marcus. These quite conventional twists of plot are only a preamble to the last segment, the high point of the drama, filmed almost entirely in medium close-up and close-up. Lord Heriot will have Robin accepted at Sandhurst if Wanda will return to Marcus. Successively diminished by the evil of a castrating mother (Lady Heriot) and by a spoiled teenager's selfishness, Wanda caves in a second time. In the eyes of the director, this supreme relinquishing of love, even for the child's future, is unacceptable. While he appears to respect this revolting conclusion to the letter, his direction provides diversion. Visually, Borzage captures Wanda's dilemma in a refined style reminiscent of Dreyer, pursuing her sense of despair with propriety; her way of brushing up against the walls, of bringing her hand to her mouth; Borzage focuses markedly on a shot of the powerless unhappy woman in an armchair, up against a bare wall. The break-up with Paul gives way to the most torrid embraces the filmmaker had shot to date and is prolonged by one last phone call; the receiver rolls to the carpet while Wanda, crouched down at the back of the image, buries her head in her arms. This hymn to motherhood is only a pretext for illustrating the annihilation of a woman alienated by life, too weak to react (like Ruth in *Lazybones*). There is the stench of an execution in the final scene of *Marriage License?*, an aftertaste of tragedy.

Meanwhile, development had been completed of the back lot at Westwood, in Fox Hills, with its permanent sets ("Mix Rancho" and "Buck Jones Outpost," Chinese and Hispano-Mexican villages, etc.). Raoul Walsh finished up at great expense the "French" exteriors for *What Price Glory?* For his western *Three Bad Men*, John Ford had just inaugurated a gyroscopic camera car (forerunner of the dolly) designed by Armin Fried. In short, all was ready for the happy event. For several months there had been talk of inviting to California the man Americans considered to be Europe's greatest filmmaker, Friedrich Wilhelm Murnau. The most fantastic rumors were circulating, as Murnau was reputed to be a dictator on the set; certain people in Hollywood joked that already people were practicing clicking their heels![10] Even more than *Faust* (co-financed by Paramount and Metro), *Der Letzte Mann* literally stupefied the film industry in the United States (where it was entitled *The Last Laugh*) by its technique, its syntactic audacity and its lack of intertitles. Hollywood was determined to steal the production secrets from the Germans. Fox and Sheehan's strategy was to offer Murnau a fortune for him to honor their studio with his presence, and with the film of his choice.[11] Sheehan had already gone in person to Berlin in 1925. As of November, Hermann Bing, Murnau's assistant, was a guest at Fox where, on behalf of his boss, he scrupulously observed the work methods of Ford, Borzage and Lee; in January, it was announced that Murnau would film *Down to Earth*, based on the work of Viennese novelist Julius Perutz. False alarm. The contract with Fox was signed in April 1926 and on June 23, the "German Genius" arrived finally with great ceremony in Los Angeles, accompanied by his set designer, Rochus Gliese. In his suitcases, he carried the script of his next masterpiece: *The Trip to Tilsit*, renamed *A Tale of Two Humans* before becoming the unforgettable *Sunrise*. William Fox would be the producer. The Mecca of cinema was caught up in feverish anticipation, bowled over by filming plans; old habits and convictions were shaken up, exasperating some and stimulating others. Amid this turbulence, in this electrifying environment another jewel was born: *7th Heaven*.

7

Fame Through Jacob's Ladder

There is a great deal of background leading up to the shooting of *7th Heaven*, the film to which Frank Borzage owes his worldwide reputation. It is based on a sentimental play by Robert Louis Stevenson's great nephew, Austin Strong (1881–1952), whose literary activity today has been largely forgotten.[1] Produced by John Golden, it opened in New York October 30, 1922, at the Booth Theater, with Helen Menken (Humphrey Bogart's first wife) and George Gaul in the roles of Diane and Chico. This somewhat puerile drama, which combines a sentimental look at the sordid side of life with religiosity, was a phenomenal success on Broadway, running for three seasons, with 704 performances selling out! The powers that be in Hollywood were on the lookout and took great pains to get their hands on this choice piece, set in the sordid alleyways of Montmartre, near Sacré Coeur. In March 1924, William Fox offered $200,000 to buy the play, a small fortune that John Golden refused. However, the following year he finally accepted an attractive offer from Fox. "'Seventh Heaven' to be filmed!" the press heralded in September 1925, and from that point on, show business gossip columnists were obsessed by the casting dilemmas. Borzage was not yet in the running: producer-director Emmett J. Flynn intended to keep the project for himself, and Frances Marion developed a first script for him (December). No word of the subsequent intrigues has been recorded, but Borzage's involvement appears to have been quasi-accidental. *7th Heaven* was the pet project of Sheehan, a devout Catholic. Probably concerned about Flynn's chronic alcoholism, he asked Borzage one day in late April of 1926 why he had never shown more interest in the project. "Because I understood it has been assigned to someone else" Borzage replied candidly. "But it isn't," exclaimed the head of the studio, "do you want it?" Borzage jumped at the chance.[2]

Mary Pickford, Bessie Love, Dolores Costello, Blanche Sweet and Joan Crawford were tested for the coveted role of Diane; even Helen Menken, who created the role on stage, did a screen test (March 1926). The most likely candidate was Madge Bellamy, supported on high by William Fox and Sheehan (she was his mistress); while she was in France, publicity shots of the actress were taken on the battle fields of Château-Thierry and Belleau. But, as we have seen, the heroine of *Lazybones* was rejected by Borzage, remaining inflexible in spite of pressure put on him by management. The filmmaker's mind was made up. Janet Gaynor, twenty, the delicious Cinderella of American film (Disney took her as the model for Snow White!) had begun with Fox in January, as a bit player. She was the prototype of the ingénue, a tender, touching combination of girl and woman. Borzage paid a surprise visit to the set of her fifth film, the supernatural melodrama *The Return of Peter Grimm*, directed by Victor Schertzinger.[3] He sat quietly in a corner, then left an hour later without having said a word. The same day, he announced to Sheehan that Janet Gaynor would be Diane; calling her in for testing would be superfluous. As for the role of Chico, it had been reserved in 1924 for John Gilbert, before he got angry with Fox and went back to MGM. When Borzage took over, he first thought of Bernard Nedell, who had played the Paris sewer worker in Albany, New York, but the actor backed out, not wanting to work in Hollywood. Joel McCrea was tested (nothing came of it), and George O'Brien was being seriously considered when Murnau chose him for *Sunrise*. Finally, Charles Farrell was selected. This handsome, 6'2", twenty-one year old was good-natured and possessed an almost naive candor. Farrell had gone to Borzage to intercede on behalf of a colleague, his friend Richard Arlen.[4] Borzage heard Farrell's generous plea, placed him next to Gaynor, who only went up to his shoulder (she was 5'), and hired him on the spot. This is how one of filmdom's most popular romantic couples came to be. Adulated by millions of fans, Janet Gaynor and Charles Farrell would, over the course of several years, make a fortune for Fox (12 films together, from 1927 to 1934). For the moment, however, two unknowns had been cast in *7th Heaven*.

Shooting was to start in August 1926, but the work schedule had to be completely modified after Murnau's arrival, as Fox management naturally gave priority to their illustrious guest. Concerned about promoting Janet Gaynor, Sheehan asked the German filmmaker to cast her as the country girl in *Sunrise* (Murnau had been thinking of Lois Moran). Management decided that *7th Heaven* would get the go-ahead once Murnau had finished his own film. The same fate awaited Raoul Walsh's *Loves of Carmen*, a super production with Dolores del Rio. There was nothing arbitrary about this delay: having mobilized the entire studio machinery for *Sunrise*, Sheehan wanted the people at Fox to get the most out of the newcomer's technical and artistic know-how. After much delay, shooting finally began in September in the Western Avenue studios; in November, Murnau filmed the exteriors at Lake Arrowhead (where the farmer tries to drown his wife), while, working day and night at the new Fox Hill location in Westwood, an army of workers erected the stupendous set of the big city, with its myriad of lights, planned for the following month. Due to its astronomic cost, $200,000, this set would be reused in several other films, notably *7th Heaven* and *Four Sons* (Ford).

In the meantime, Borzage's preparatory work was coming along nicely; the filmmaker spent several days in discussion with the author of the play. In the summer Frances Marion withdrew from *7th Heaven*, for reasons undisclosed (perhaps she was writing the story outline of *From Nine to Nine*, a Murnau project for Ufa-MGM that never materialized). The script was taken up by Benjamin Glazer, an Irish playwright, who was given sole credit for the Oscar-winning screenplay. Glazer's contribution was particularly apparent in the details relating to World War I: the historic context seems close to his heart, because the same scriptwriter and associate producer worked together on *A Farewell to Arms*, six years later.[5] Sheehan let Borzage know that, conscious of the magnitude of the project, Fox was not opposed to filming exteriors in Paris (pre-launch publicity was already announcing this location), should the filmmaker deem it useful. Borzage was thus invited to go to Paris to decide, while waiting for Janet Gaynor and the main studio sets to become available. Robert Florey was called in as a consultant for everything relating to French local color, and recalls: "The time frame of the film is from August-September 1914 to Armistice Day. Borzage was looking for someone who had lived in France at the time, and even though I was only thirteen at the time of Sarajevo, all the events that preceded mobilization, and especially the day of August 2, 1914, were etched forever in mind... I encouraged Borzage to go to Paris to familiarize himself with the atmosphere of the City of Light, where he had never been. He returned with the very talented French artistic director André Chotin, who would assist him in filming."[6] At that time Borzage was among the best-paid directors at Fox: in November 1926 he earned $1500 a week, the same as Raoul Walsh; only Ford earned more — $1750.

On October 6, Borzage and his brother Lew set sail for Europe aboard the Aquitaine and spent October and November in Paris; upon his return, about December 10, the filmmaker was firmly determined to recreate the atmosphere of Montmartre at the studio, where poetic interpretation of the setting (and by extension development of concepts) would not be constrained by local contingencies. After all, hadn't Murnau himself recreated Lithuania under the California sun in his *Sunrise*? A stylized reality was to be filmed, which essentially would acquire symbolic significance in light of the context. So what if Parisians didn't recognize their home! However, to maintain a degree of similarity, Borzage brought back hundreds of drawings and photographs from his trip, as well as an authentic taxi from the Marne named "Héloïse." "My idea of Chico's general characteristics and appearance I obtained from a picturesque worker I saw in Montmartre," Borzage explained. "The only trouble was, he was too picturesque. I could only suggest a very subdued version of him to Farrell when I described Chico.... I had seen many Papa Boules in Paris and they were so inimitable that I felt it would be difficult to reproduce them in life, even from photographs. Then, in a little Paris wine shop I came across a wooden statue and my problem was solved, for that was the Papa Boule I wanted to reproduce in the picture, and so I bought it and brought it back with me. And it was used as a model for his makeup."[7] Norwegian Albert Gran was cast as the voluble heavy-set taxi driver. French actor-director Emile Chautard, Sarah Bernhardt's partner who discovered Josef von Sternberg, played Chevillon, the priest. Completing the Parisian contingent, David Butler played the jovial sewage worker Gobin, but got the part due to a trick. Butler and Borzage had been friends for a long time, having shared a place together in the 1910s. The filmmaker ran into his former colleague from Inceville at a golf game. When Butler kidded that he wanted to appear in the film, Borzage suggested he not shave and hide behind a large Gallic mustache, as Sheehan wanted no part of him. Butler took his test under an assumed French-sounding name and was enthusiastically approved by the studio head! It was his last screen role, as he would be promoted to director in the following months, beginning a long career as a prolific craftsman. For the extra work, Borzage used family and friends: his elderly father played a lamplighter (a part he would play again in *Street Angel*), his mother and two sisters and former Salt Lake City neighbors played workers in the munitions factory shown at the end of the film.

Any discussion of Borzage's silent works must acknowledge Ernest Palmer (photography) and Harry Oliver (set design), both tops in their fields; their collaboration with Borzage was so successful that they worked with him again on *Street Angel* and *The River*.[8] Due to John Ford's intervention, studio manager Sol Wurtzel first assigned George Schneiderman as cinematographer of *7th Heaven*; he was a first-rate cameraman known for his contrasting outdoor photography, and his violent blacks and whites (*The Iron Horse* and other westerns). Palmer, on the other hand, had developed a technique for controlling the dazzling effects of arc lighting produced by overhead mercury lamps, modulating shading to obtain a soft, filtered light more suited to romantic settings. And luckily, Sheehan owed him a favor. Palmer, who had already worked with Borzage on three films, not only became chief cameraman, but was also sent for a few weeks to Paris at the studio's expense. Moreover, he was able to bring in his friend Oliver as the film's only set designer, freed from any other work in the studio.

The impact of Murnau's pioneering style on Borzage is noteworthy. His influence can be found in many future films: compositions emphasized by the use of chiaroscuro, stylized images and camera movements used to convey expressiveness, sets integrated to the psychological mood of the picture, etc. Above all, Murnau and Borzage's use of space is penetrated, mysteriously enhanced by inherent spirituality. Watching *Street Angel*, *The River*, *Lucky Star*, *Liliom* (1930), the night sequences of *A Farewell to Arms* (1932), the finale of *Three Comrades* (1932), the astonishing *Till We Meet Again* (1944) or even *Moonrise* (1948), we can state without exaggerating that on a strictly formal level, Borzage was the American filmmaker most strongly influenced by Murnau's aesthetics, more so than John Ford, for example. Generally speaking, the German filmmaker's presence also encouraged greater experimentation; technicians were fascinated by his ingenious tricks (use of miniatures, false perspectives), spurring them on to enrich the visual aspect by experimentation and increased camera mobility. Paul Ivano remembers good-humoredly: "Wurtzel was as blind as a bat — he always sat 50 cms from the screen. So Ernie Palmer and I could play around with filter effects as much as we liked.... Then *7th Heaven* won an Oscar, and so did *Street Angel*— so the films must have been good. But we experimented happily with Mr. Fox's money!"[9]

The use of multileveled constructions, elevators, and of the first dollies to move the cameras also affected continuity details and editing.

Officially, Murnau completed *Sunrise* about January 20, 1927, but several tricky scenes (the storm on the lake, various special effects) required an additional two weeks. The first take of *7th Heaven* was shot on Monday, January 24, and filming continued until March 12; at first, Janet Gaynor shuttled back and forth, working days for Murnau and nights for Borzage. Interviewed by Kevin Brownlow in 1976, Janet Gaynor recalled these memorable weeks: "Frank Borzage was marvelous. He was dear and he was soft and he was really a great contrast to Murnau. And yet I responded to Murnau too. But with Frank, you responded more with your heart.... He would talk to me during a scene and he loved it — which was really exciting as an actress, to have this happen to you. We would rehearse a scene up to a point and then it was supposed to be cut, but when we'd actually get into it, he would keep on talking and so instead of finishing, he'd say 'And?'— so you'd keep it going, and then he'd turn round, or you'd hear a knock on the door or whatever, and it was very exciting to do that." Comparing the tension on the set of *Sunrise* with the seductive methods favored by Borzage, Janet Gaynor continued: "for Charlie [Farrell] and for me, [the sets were] more like home than home. We just couldn't wait to be there at 9 o'clock. And we left at whatever — you know, you worked until your director dismissed you. There were no hours. Why, for me, I just went home and went to bed, I was terribly tired, but I loved it and couldn't wait to get back the next morning...." And she concludes: "The studio head [Winfield Sheehan] said that if you get the intellect of Murnau and the heart of Frank, you would have had the perfect director."[10]

Systematically comparing Strong's play, Glazer's final script (dated January 8[11]), photos from the director's personal collection, the film itself and Henry King's 1937 remake, we see Borzage's unique contribution. The considerable modifications, additions, suppressions (almost a quarter of the intertitles originally planned), and omissions due to abridging observed in the film versus the "shooting script" corroborate the studio management's frequent reproach of Borzage for his tendency to elaborate the work during shooting, working relatively independently of the script. (For convenience sake, the symbol [≠] follows passages in the film not in the script). Moreover, Borzage pared down the plot greatly, at the risk of it becoming unrealistic, which seems to be the least of his worries! He totally eliminated from the final work any expository character or episode or atmospheric element that could detract from the core of the film: the redemptive ascension of the lovers. Murnau had just composed "A Song of Two Humans" (the subtitle of *Sunrise*), a drama impregnated with a fatalistic and profoundly pessimistic *Weltanschauung*. Borzage began what can be called "A Song of Man and Woman," another tale of universal abstraction, but with a very different kind of message. For as we have said in the introduction, this last-minute reorientation manifestly lends itself, as in stories of spiritual discovery, to a transformation, much as in a "Great Work" of Freemasonry. This same symbolism would recur in all of Borzage's important films.

The fundamental theme is inscribed at the beginning of the film: "For those who will climb it, there is a ladder leading from the depths to the heights—from the sewers to the stars—the ladder of courage" [≠]. Chico works underground, in the labyrinth of the Montmartre sewers, stirring the foul waters with his pole, maintaining unflappable good humor. His workmate Rat—"the rat"—peers at the legs of passers-by through the grate. A few yards above, Gobin the street-cleaner throws a bucket of water onto the street and then spits. A street cleaner! This is Chico's dream ... to walk among people, in the sun, for isn't he "a very remarkable fellow"?[12] Cut to a medium-close shot of Nana Vulmir (Gladys Brockwell) facing the camera, her face ravaged at age twenty, whipping a body crouching on the ground: her younger sister Diane. The two orphans, who have succumbed to petty theft and occasional prostitution, live in a shabby room. Nora, an alcoholic, orders Diane to sell a stolen watch in order to buy absinth; her sister obeys, trembling, and Borzage films the shot so that Nana and her empty bottle appear in the half-shaded foreground while Diane, in the background, is in the light filtering through a barred window. The vertical division of the shot, with its light/dark, foreground/background contrasts, may reveal Murnau's influence. In a tilt shot, the camera follows the young woman as she makes her way to the bistro where she meets a receiver of stolen goods. Meanwhile, Father Chevillon arrives to tell Nana that her rich uncle is going to pay her a surprise visit tomorrow: he has just returned from the South Seas and wants to take responsibility for his two nieces.... Amid this exposition, which contains traces of melodrama (Nana is a stock type), Borzage inserts a stunning, strange short sequence [≠]: Diane comes in at night, the absinth hidden beneath a black shawl; suddenly, the street corner lights up, a lamp lighter is at work. Diane stops short and contemplates the light from the lamp (close-up); her face expresses infinite nostalgia and purity, a metaphor with Platonic resonances, and fades into black.

The next day Uncle George and Aunt Valentine, accompanied by dapper Colonel Brissac (Ben Bard), can barely hide their distaste as they enter the sisters' hovel. The uncle, very straitlaced, inquires if the girls have kept themselves "clean and decent" during their hard times, a condition he sets before helping them escape from their extreme poverty. Although Nana is secretly twisting her arm, Diane is incapable of lying. Scandalized, the snobbish relatives turn to leave, after throwing some money on the ground. Nana seizes her whip and sets herself on Diane, determined to kill her. She follows her into the street, continuing the vicious whipping. At the street corner she throws herself onto Diane in order to strangle her. Inspired by Murnau, Borzage filmed this sequence in one long tilt shot, multiplying the violence of the scene. "The movement of the camera was arrived at by having an 8 by 8 platform and eight men carrying it, upon which I could ride with my baby tripod as they ran," Palmer recalls.[13] Chico emerges from a sewer entrance, takes control of the furious shrew and chases her off. Undisturbed, he returns to a simple meal with his comrades Bud and Rat, leaving Diane unconscious in the gutter: "It wasn't worth saving, papa Boule, a creature like that is better off dead..." As she does not come round, Chico gets up unwillingly, rubs an onion under her nose and leans her against a taxi. "The trouble with you is that you won't fight. You're afraid! I'm not afraid of anything! That's why I'm a very remarkable fellow!" Returning to his comrades, he vehemently explains the reasons for his childlike atheism: the "Bon Dieu" could not have created wrecks such as Diane, Rat or himself. However, Chico "gave God a fair test"—by spending ten francs on candles, so that Heaven would grant his two dearest wishes: to become a street cleaner and find a wife—in vain. Father Chevillon, amused, overhears it all and gets Chico a job as street cleaner (thus Chico goes from dirty water to "purified" water); he then gives the amazed young man two religious medals that "may help you some day...."[14]

Diane hasn't moved. While Chico, wild with joy, announces the good news to his future colleague Gobin, she grabs a knife to kill herself. Chico grabs it from her ("With MY knife. I like that!"). She tells him she cannot continue to live without hope, and the sewer worker, pitying her, tries clumsily to lift her spirits. Nana has been arrested in a round-up of prostitutes and turns in her sister to the police; Chico, without thinking too much, saves Diane a third time by saying he is her husband. The policeman warns him that his statement will be verified.

Too late, Chico learns that a false declaration could cost him his job as street cleaner and Diane suggests she move into his place until the police have finished their inquiry: "You are a great head!" he exclaims, caressing her hair; he stands up and the weak young woman is crouched at his knees, so that his gesture inevitably recalls a benediction [≠]. "You — you have a big heart," she murmurs, kissing his hand. Diane (close-up) appears suddenly transfigured, she has gone from cute to suddenly beautiful, a surprise effect Borzage obtains by photographing his heroine's radiant face firmly turned toward heaven, lighting that creates an "idealizing" halo around her hair. (Until then, Diane had always been filmed with her face downcast, her harmonious features hidden by areas of shadow). Boule takes them to Chico's lodgings in Héloïse, his ancient taxi. Placed on a dolly, the camera follows the couple inside the building, down a dark hallway leading to a stairwell, then accompanying Diane and Chico, the camera rises to film their ascent in its entirety, up to the "paradisiacal" attic. The shot was a real technical dilemma, because no stage was high enough to go capture seven floors; especially not at the Western Avenue studios. Oliver had two stairwells built — with three and four landings respectively — then set up his camera and dolly on an elevator. The third and fourth floors were matched up using lighting effects. (According to advertising at the time, the film cost $1,300,000). Contrary to the original script, the filmmaker refused to interrupt the couple's ascent with diversionary cuts to other inhabitants. Whereas Henry King, ten years later, had his lovers walk in a zigzag up the building, Borzage insisted on absolute verticality, respecting the symbolism of this ladder up to "seventh heaven." Having reached the attic overlooking the city (the dome of Sacré-Coeur can be seen in the distance), Chico cannot hide his pride: "not bad, eh? I work in the sewer — but I live near the stars" [≠]. He owns the world because he possesses nothing. The set of the attic and the adjacent roofs were actually built at the top of the stairwell, near the very top of the stage, which meant it was possible to film into the street below. Using a simple plank to get to the neighbors in the next building, Janet Gaynor remembers that she sometimes had to fight against dizziness: "It was really quite a long way down. So the fear was sometimes a little natural."[15]

The emergence out of the shadows brought on a change of tone. The film changes levels — both literally and metaphorically. The Dickensian universe with its harsh naturalism and unwholesome neighborhoods gives way to a kind of transcendental romanticism reinforced by softer lighting and poetic stylization. From the Victorian stereotypes (the gallant simpleton, the frightened orphan), the characters are gradually transformed into atemporal archetypes as their shared intimacy transforms indifference into tenderness. Open-mouthed, Diane contemplates Chico's apartment: "It's Heaven!" The young man takes her hand to lead her across the gangway leading to the Gobin's apartment, but Diane draws back, horrified. Seated on the window sill, he sums up his existential credo while pointing to the skies: "never look down — always look up!" The sun has set, Chico yawns. Diane frowns. Before going to the neighbors, he tells her to get undressed and go to bed, which she does fearfully removing stockings, dress and petticoat in a delicately erotic scene (this shot was

The set of *7th Heaven* (1927). Frank Borzage (top left, with hat) inspects the fabulous staircases created by Harry Oliver.

censored in several states) [≠]; he returns with a nightgown borrowed from Madame Gobin and shirtless, he washes up while Diane observes him, hidden under the duvet. Then, a gentleman, he settles down to spend the night on the balcony. As night falls, Diane stands at the window, her creamy silhouette illuminated by the stars, and looks up [≠].

The next morning, Chico is awakened by the sound of coffee brewing. Hair tied back, Diane, timid and eager to cater to Chico's smallest wish, plays housewife. Chico lets himself

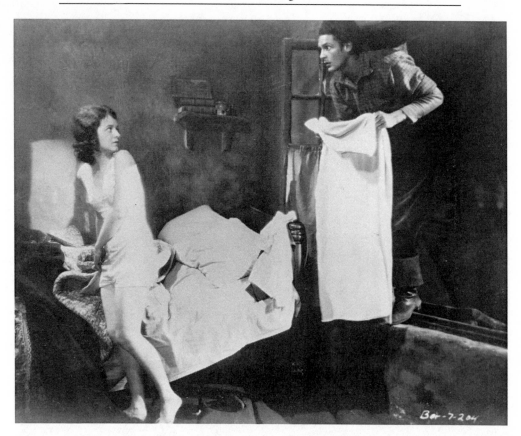

Chastity and desire: Janet Gaynor and Charles Farrell (*7th Heaven*).

be served, both pleasantly surprised and suspicious ("But you can't get around me. After the police come, you go!"). At Gobin's insistence, he furtively embraces "his wife" before leaving for work. ("I didn't mean it. Don't think you can stay," he whispers to her). Diane's face lights up, she looks on admiringly at Chico, through the round window, then steps through the open window, raises her head, screws up her courage and crosses the gangway [≠]. According to the fundamental rule of melodrama, whereby the "letter" becomes the "spirit," this domestic sequence signals the couple's intrinsic union (cf. the meal the lovers share in *Man's Castle* or in *History Is Made at Night*). In the street, Gobin teaches his new recruit how to manage the water hose, and gets liberally sprayed [≠]. Later, Chico gets his hair cut by a secretly adoring Diane. When a detective appears, Chico gets rid of him. Triumphant at having outwitted the law, he sits down, lights a pipe, but doesn't immediately realize that behind his back Diane is gathering together her few things to leave the attic. He calls her, examining his haircut in a mirror: "If you want to stay, you're not in my way." Wild with joy, she runs and picks up her scissors...[16] Another domestic vignette beautifully illustrates the feelings that are growing: Diane gathers up Chico's overcoat [≠]; she places his jacket on the back of a chair, sits down and lovingly wraps its sleeves around her as if seeking protection. Chico enters with a potted daffodil and a box containing a wedding gown. She cries, overcome. "Don't you want to marry me?" he teases her. As she wants to hear him declare his love, Chico, after much hesitation, manages to stammer: "Chico—Diane—Heaven." But no church wedding: independence above all! Having proclaimed this emphatically, he accidentally sits down on the medals given to him by Father Chevillon, and jumps up, discomfited.

Most of the admirable sequence that follows, leading up to Chico's departure for the front, does not appear in the script. With a stupefied Chico looking on, Diane cheerfully walks along the gangway ("I'll never be afraid again!") her new dress in one hand, a pot of soup for the pregnant Madame Gobin in the other. Alone, Gobin and Chico watch troops gathering in the street below: war has been declared, their regiment will be the first to leave for the front, in one hour. Chico energetically rebels [≠]; Gobin reasons with him before going to join his wife. Like an angel descended from heaven, Diane appears, framed by the window, walking on the roofs dressed in her wedding gown [≠]; Chico is mesmerized by this quasi surrealistic vision (which has overtones of the fantastic metamorphosis of Pauline Starke in *Until They Get Me*, 1917). Borzage exalts in the intoxicating sorrow of this "supreme hour" ("I'm not used to being happy. It's funny — it hurts," Diane murmurs) intercutting the scene with shots of the regiment gathered at the sound of the bugle and demonstrations of the popular enthusiasm for the war. Happiness is the most fragile of all when at its peak. The roles (and positions onscreen) are reversed: Chico breaks down, burying himself in his beloved's arms, declaring his imminent departure and his unspeakable fear of losing what he has just found [≠]. Gone are his masculine bravado and naive outbursts. "Never look down — always look up," Diane tells him, raising her index finger. "See what you've made of me. I, too, am a very remarkable fellow!" Then she begins to despair as well. Chico carries her in his arms and walks up and down the room, kissing her [≠]. They decide to get married, right on the spot. "I'm an atheist — but I'll give God one more chance," Chico declares, holding the medals given him by Father Chevillon (Borzage films the ceremony from above, from a "celestial" point of view). "Monsieur le Bon Dieu," continues the street cleaner. "If there is any truth in the idea of You, please make this a true marriage." The couple exchanges medals. As he is about to leave, Chico implores his "bride" to stand still ("let me fill my eyes with you"). A clock striking eleven fades into an image of Diane. "Every day at this hour — at eleven — I shall come to you," the lovers promise each other. But Chico has barely closed the door when a threatening Nana reappears. She sneers seeing Diane in a wedding dress and snatches away her medal. Diane throws herself upon her in a rage, seizes the whip and drives her away. "Chico I'm brave!" she cries from the window as he marches past beneath. Threats from the outside world have strengthened their bonds: Diane overcomes her fears, Chico manages to finally say "I love you." The relationship changes: from being free, he becomes dependent, while she frees herself from her sister's tyranny. He goes down to the trenches while she climbs up on the roofs. He rediscovers faith, while she is on the verge of losing it.

The first exterior shots in the film follow, as if it were necessary to insert a "reality" outside the studio, natural lighting, to weaken the lover's cocoon. The war scenes—15 minutes out of almost two hours of running time — were recorded on the Westwood property, in trenches dug several months earlier for *Havoc* (Lee) and *What Price Glory?* (Walsh). The town that appeared in *Loves of Carmen* (Walsh) became a French village west of the Marne where General Galliéni blocked the advance of Von Klück's army using about a thousand taxis requisitioned from the capital (September 7, 1914). Using a hundred vehicles, Borzage filmed the departure of the Parisian taxis loaded with soldiers, with Héloïse in the lead, on the outdoor set of the city in *Sunrise*. Models were used for the sequences showing columns of taxis bombarded by German fighter planes and Fred W. Sersen, the future head of special effects at 20th Century Fox, inaugurated his famous procedure of masking and countermasking to superimpose distinct images (taxis on the horizon). The battle scenes around the village of Senlis, which required many extras, were filmed by John Ford (who had already been second unit director for *What Price Glory?*)[17]

Chico, Rat and Gobin escape the carnage, which Borzage counterbalances with humorous touches (Rat makes off with a chicken intended for the officer's mess, Boule steals some sugar, his taxi Héloïse, destroyed by a bomb has "given her life for France!" and so on). Months, then years pass; each morning at eleven o'clock sharp, Chico, now a corporal, joins his believed in thought ("Chico—Diane—Heaven"). The two comrades religiously respect this instant of intimacy outside time and space. Diane works in a munitions factory where colonel Brissac harasses her under the pretext that "the world is upside down — ideals, beliefs, traditions, all in the discard! Each day may be our last." Along with Diane's aunt and uncle with their unforgiving morality, Borzage also focuses on Brissac, safely ensconced in Paris, away from the fighting. He represents the hedonist, materialistic temptation, a blatant opportunist. (The editing establishes a visual parallel between Brissac's maneuvers and the threat of a German soldier at the front.) Diane valiantly resists his advances, as Chico had earlier resisted flirting with a pretty, flirtatious neighbor.[18] The second war sequence is comparable to the realism of Pabst (*Westfront 1918*). Chico is involved in a night battle in which flamethrowers are used, and fire engulfs the screen. At dawn, Rat finds Chico blinded in a shell hole in the middle of no man's land. Asking his comrade the time, Chico communes one last time with his beloved. Rat is killed bringing him back to the French lines, where Father Chevillon awaits. Chico hands over his religious medal to the chaplain: "Tell Madame Chico I died looking up" [≠] he whispers, his eyes filled with tears, but a smile on his lips.

Diane is watering her daffodil when Brissac enters the attic to announce the tragic news. Diane refuses to believe him ("He's alive. I know it"). Nor will she believe the one-armed Gobin, now decorated, who joins them with his wife. But when Father Chevillon shows her the medal, she collapses: "Then he didn't come every day — he never came at all — I just imagined it?" Borzage films her seated between the colonel and the priest, worthy representatives of an established disorder. A jubilant Boule announces the armistice; people run to the windows. Outside, confetti rains down. Almost the entire last sequence, sublime in its radical pathos, in its complete defiance of rationality, is again nonexistent in Glazer's script.[19] Diane attacks the priest who tries to console her; she bursts out: "For years I have called this Heaven — I prayed — I believed He would bring Chico back to me — and Chico is dead!" At that moment Borzage cuts to Chico, who *is* alive, forcing his way through the crowd as if

Left: Chico racing up the stairs: a graphic representation of a spiral ascent. *Right*: A spiritual transfiguration (*7th Heaven*, 1927).

drawn by a magnet. The take is all the more brutal as nothing in the narration, no intertitle nor any emotional marker (dissolve, focus) prepares us for this "resurrection." It is presented as the irrefutable negation of the "truths" promulgated by the State (Brissac), the Church (Chevillon) and Society (the Gobins). Diane, in despair, is in Brissac's arms: "I'm right back at the beginning again." Chico races up the stairs calling "Diane!" (vertical tracking shot over two floors), an overhead shot of the spiral stairwell, a graphic representation of a spiral ascent. With each turn of the stairs, Chico returns into the frame, his hands groping, his distraught face turned up to the camera ("looking upwards"), shouting "DIANE!" The clock strikes eleven. The door opens. Chico runs into the attic, callings his wife's name. Diane shakes her head as if seeing a vision. They reach out to each other, she falls to her knees and he lifts her up: "Diane, I've been hit by every shell that's made! They thought I was dead, but I'll never die!" Again she falls to her knees, and he kneels opposite her. "Those big thoughts I had were the Bon Dieu after all. He is within me. Now that I am blind, I see that.—My eyes are still filled with you." Diane reassures him: she will be his eyes. "For a while perhaps. But nothing can keep Chico blind for long. I tell you, I'm a very remarkable fellow!" The lovers huddle together, embracing (to the right, in a medium-full shot), when a supernatural ray of light from the upper left envelops them. The End.

"Now that I am blind, I see ... my eyes are still filled with you" (George Farrell to Janet Gaynor in *7th Heaven*, 1927).

7th Heaven has long been acknowledged as one of the silver screen's top melodramas, but it also transcends the genre in many ways: "Some of the tender love scenes, of the enraptured duos, are among the most beautiful ever filmed," Jean Mitry wrote in 1973.[20] Like a fairy tale, *7th Heaven* functions seamlessly at the first level. Its finely honed images, carefully wrought compositions and sets, and timing alternating between drama and humor perpetuate its esthetic appeal. We marvel at the filmmaker's talent at deriving this gem of purity and inspiration from such kitsch, melodramatic, maudlin and improbable material. His ability to avoid the inherent traps in the script by constant simplicity (economy of effects, underplaying) to obtain pure emotion, in a completely authentic form, is miraculous. Viewers and critics were unanimously charmed by this naive popular idyll, as intense "as the hearts of those who are brought together by the tale."[21] The intimacy of the couple alternates harmoniously between reflections on the collective drama of war and a warm portrayal of the underprivileged. In *The Film Spectator*, Welford Beaton observes: "It is a beautiful picture because the souls of unimportant people are important, and because these souls are handled gently and tenderly by a great director."[22] But it was Janet Gaynor's face — gentle, mischievous, ultrasensitive, that provided the film's immediate appeal: an exceptional star was born. "Janet Gaynor is the great revelation of this very beautiful film," wrote *Cinéa-Ciné*. "Perhaps such lyricism has never been seen on the screen before, and such a pure and sincere flame which has nothing affected about it and is totally untroubled by the least false gesture or theatricality."[23] Realizing to what advantage Borzage's film displayed the actress's qualities, Fox decided to release *7th Heaven before* its prestige picture, *Sunrise*, which would be a more difficult picture for the average American filmgoer to grasp. *Sunrise* would also benefit from the newfound fame of its leading lady.

The film was a dazzling international triumph. It premiered May 6 at Fox's Carthay Circle Theater in Los Angeles, a kind of half–Mexican, half–Art deco palace, where it ran for 22 weeks, taking in $19,000 its first week. It opened May 25 in New York at the Sam H. Harris Theater. In 1927, only the sensational *The Jazz Singer* (the first talkie) topped it at the box office. Six years later, in 1933–34, *7th Heaven* was still ranked 31st on the "Highest Box Office Pictures List," having grossed $1,750,000. This allowed Fox to fill the gap in its finances made by *Sunrise*, which opened on September 23 meeting only with critical, not popular, success. Having already tried the process on *What Price Glory?*, the studio decided to use the Movietone–Western Electric process for the musical score. The sound version of *7th Heaven* was released on September 10. Ernö Rapée's pretty slow waltz melody: "Diane — I'm In Heaven When I See You Smile," would accompany the film around the world before it became, over the decades, the old standby played at tea dances (the theme was also used in the 1937 remake).[24] In September, to promote the film in Great Britain, Sheehan hired a theatrical company (which included Helen Menken and Godfrey Tearle) to stage Strong's play in London. The film's creators were showered with awards, including the prestigious Photoplay Gold Medal Award, previously given to Borzage's *Humoresque*.[25] But the crowning achievement came two years later. Louis B. Mayer — for not totally disinterested reasons — had pushed for the creation of an organization to encourage quality work within the film industry, and in May 1927, the Academy of Motion Picture Arts and Sciences was formed. On May 16, 1929, with Douglas Fairbanks presiding, the Academy met at the Hollywood Roosevelt Hotel and awarded the first Oscars, retroactively, for 1927–28. *7th Heaven* was nominated for best film. Frank Borzage won best director (over King Vidor for *The Crowd*), Benjamin Glazer best adaptation, and Janet Gaynor best actress for *7th Heaven*, *Sunrise* and *Street Angel*. Oliver was also nominated for his set designs.

Inevitably, the film gave rise to a number of adaptations and remakes, all of them

7th Heaven (publicity sheet).

inevitably inferior to the poetry of Borzage's film.[26] The film enjoyed great success in the Far East, and a number of remakes were made in Shanghai and Hong Kong. In *Wakaki Hi* (*Days of Youth*), released in April 1929, Japanese director Yasujiro Ozu gave Borzage a tip of the hat: two poor students are studying beneath a *7th Heaven* poster; one of them rises to go drum up some money: "I am a very remarkable fellow," he proclaims, adding "Always look up!" before making his way to *7th Heaven*, their nickname for the pawnshop.... Despite Henry King's painstaking direction, 20th Century Fox's 1937 remake with James Stewart as Chico, French actress Simone Simon as Diane and Gregory Ratoff as Boule, was an artistic disaster. (Janet Gaynor refused the part because she had fallen out with Zanuck). The film seems to be at least thirty years older than Borzage's simply because Strong's original play was somehow already obsolete when it was originally filmed. The clumsy attempts to make the dialogue convey local color destroy the message, the talky love scenes are laughable, the characters are hopelessly artificial and naïveté degenerates into silliness. The concrete realism of sound destroys the magic of the original; such a story required the archetypes and universality of silent film, with two lovers expressing themselves in a sort of exquisite mime. The few well-timed intertitles containing dialogues in the original are meant to be *read*, not heard. A final factor is noted by William K. Everson: as opposed to a Hitchcock film, where the screen is used to manipulate the spectator's emotions, a silent film, especially a melodrama, allows the public to "manipulate" the emotions of the characters by projecting their own emotions onto them. This results in an ideal harmony—between the fiction onscreen and the secret desires of the spectator—which can never be attained by a talkie.[27] As Jean-Luc Godard puts it: "The word in silent films was greater than the word in talkies."

Not surprisingly, much has been written about the second part of *7th Heaven*: it led to all sorts of philosophical-ideological conflicts within the film intelligentsia. The film's unrepentant irrationality ("I will never die"; "nothing can keep Chico blind for long"), the telepathic communion between the lovers and the final halo of light serve to illustrate the transcendental nature of Love, revealing the spiritual strength of an experience going beyond time, space, and even death. Lacanian psychoanalysis sees *7th Heaven* as nothing other than "a conflict between the Real and erotic fantasies" with Diane representing Chico's infantile fixation on his own mother, and seeing the "neurotic streetcleaner's blindness as a "punishment for broken taboos," the result of an "imaginary incest," etc.[28] This view has less to do with going "beyond" the physical world than it does with looking "beneath" the unconscious, at obscure and troubling latent desires. The spiral staircase of *7th Heaven* is not a cliché for the anguish of repression but rather suggests the overcoming of all polarities and oppositions. A more interesting view of the film was expressed by the French intellectuals of the time, in particular the surrealists. The film premiered in Paris at the Empire Cinema on November 15, 1927 and was enthusiastically received by the avant-garde writers. "In the cinema we were looking for absolute, not venal love," Georges Sadoul remembers, "and [André] Breton sent us to see Frank Borzage's *7th Heaven*, in which he claimed to have found the type of exaltation he had yet to call 'l'amour fou.'"[29] Sadoul himself suggested adding this model of "unconscious surrealism" to the list of Aragon's famous film-manifestos. In fact, we must talk of absolute love in this context, not "amour fou" or wild passion, which wrongly implies the idea of delirium and destruction.

In his key 1952 work *Le surréalisme au cinéma*, Ado Kyrou waxes lyrical about *7th Heaven*: "Separated by the course of their lives, the two lovers are united by a magnetism for which the only possible name is Love—a force which makes them aware of each other's least gesture or thought and guides their steps in a universe within which we consider ourselves to be blind."[30]

However, Kyrou's eager sympathy for the film is based on a misunderstanding because, carried away by his visceral anticlericalism, he reduces *7th Heaven* to an anti-religious treatise: "(Chico) who does not want to get married, realizes that love makes his independence, his negation of God and of social bonds, all the more solid."[31] Blinded by their own point of view, other surrealists utter similar absurdities even though the film's references to pious imagery (specific to popular melodrama) leaves them puzzled. According to Dionys Mascolo, "the populist piety is simply a vehicle for communication between the lovers.... And such communication mimics God so as to be able to destroy him all the better."[32] As for Chico's return, it is "an entirely unrealistic rendering in images of the unconscious desire of the young girl, the desire that her beloved be alive." However, this last point opens up a more intriguing interpretation, voiced by Marcel Oms in his original study of the film: "From beginning to end, [*7th Heaven*] is a dream work, the implacable unfolding of the plot following a dream logic."[33] But as Henry Agel and Michael Henry Wilson have often pointed out, we can't ignore Borzage's strong tendencies to mysticism (Christian and otherwise) which implicitly contradict overtly psychological readings of his work. Naturally, clerical circles turn away from the film's embarrassing eroticism, attempting to claim the film as their own by pointing out its Christlike iconography (the discovery of God through physical blindness). In fact, it is true that *7th Heaven* is essentially about spiritual redemption and transfiguration by love.

Philip Rosen, however, has brought up the strange dichotomy in the film between religion (i.e. its institutionalized representative, the Church) and pure spirituality resulting from an individual quest.[34] From a Masonic point of view, there is nothing contradictory about this distinction: the Ancient and Approved Scottish Rite, to which the director belonged, fully accepted the validity of Church dogma, but did not believe that it exhausted all metaphysical truths. Borzage deals with the issue by opposing faith and atheism, soon rendered irrelevant (Chico's agnosticism is seen as a temporary comic aberration). The rather puerile swaggering fellow of the beginning is "redeemed" by his genuine sincerity. The public is immediately aware of Chico's noble nature hidden within: not only does he claim to be "a very remarkable fellow" but he is. Borzage and Farrell are responsible for this interpretation; in Strong's play Chico is a selfish show-off. The Church—in the person of Father Chevillon—gives him two religious medals, the pledge of future protection (a little like the gifts or magic objects that fairies give to those they favor). From then on, there is a kind of transfer involving these medals: they seem to control the streetcleaner's blasphemy and consecrate the lovers' quasi-mystical "marriage." But the final reunion with the medals, via the priest, does not signify "physical death." Like all other characters, the priest is not conscious of the significance of his gesture, because he is one of those who "do not see," who believe Chico to be dead. In reality, the medal-object has become superfluous because it has been in some way internalized. When Chico surrenders it, he takes the final step in the "unifying" process, unbound by earthly considerations. During the final apotheosis of the lovers, the priest is the only other person present in the field, yet he is clearly excluded from the celestial light enveloping the couple. We should note that the ray of light, totally unexplained (unless used merely for decor) emanates from an off-screen source. Borzage-Sarastro, creator and master of ceremonies, thus establishes a bridge between the transcendental and the illusory world of his tale. A link may be established with the orthodox icons of St. George in which the lance (the symbol of Logos defeating the dragon) originates outside the frame of the picture.

Given these considerations, we propose (if any one decoding of the film is necessary) to bear in mind the following features, which take precedence over an excessively subjective reading of the film. As we saw earlier, Borzage fills his film with "incongruous" signs which galvanize the film narrative within (most of these signs occurred to him while shooting). More than any other of his films, *7th Heaven* presents a striking analogy with the course of Initiation as it is described in the Masonic rite. As already mentioned, intellectual honesty requires that we recognize that Borzage held deep religious beliefs (so much for Breton's followers!). A fervent Freemason, he took part in his Lodge's "Workshop of Perfection" (around 1927) and achieved the 12th level of Grand Master Mason. Having joined the Masons in 1919, the filmmaker would attain the penultimate 32nd grade, in the Ancient and Approved Scottish Rite, carrying the title of Master of the Royal Secret. However, high-sounding titles are less important than the teaching accompanying them: the logic behind this symbolism must be examined. Between 1925 and 1930, Fox's management was notoriously divided into two opposing camps: Free Masons (including Sheehan) and Orthodox Jews (including Wurtzel).[35]

We know that Masonic rites are concerned with a "new life," the passage from shadows into light. We may therefore see Chico's "benediction" of Diane on the sidewalk as the Initiation itself: in René Guénon's terminology, it is "the transmission of light," a spiritual influence that enables the individual to undertake the inner work leading by various degrees up the hierarchy, which, step by step, leads to deliverance.[36] The first steps up the staircase to Chico's celestial attic are symbolic of this "path" to enlightenment. In Masonic rites of Passage, the spiritual ascension the candidate is yet to achieve is represented by a staircase or a "Jacob's Ladder" resting on a stone or book. The staircase symbolizes the axis of the world uniting Heaven and Earth, as in the stages of Dante's *Divine Comedy*. The seven floors or levels clearly correspond to the "seven planetary heavens"—part of the alchemical vocabulary used in Masonic lodges (from whence the term "Seventh Heaven"). Finally, the spiral staircase which appears in the last part of the film is found in the Masonic symbol of the "winding stairs" leading to the "Middle Chamber," the place of death and resurrection. The night scene with Diane and Chico on the windowsill recalls the Masonic rite for the meditation of the "Flaming Star," while Diane's appearance in an immaculate white dress on the rooftops may be seen as the promise of Paradise. The vicissitudes of war (and the crossing of the gangplank over the gaping void) correspond to the trials discussed in the first chapter (in relation to *The Magic Flute*). These ordeals lead to the initiate's death by fire (the flame throwers), followed by a "resurrection" to the rank of Master. He leaves his sensual soul behind him (Rat, Chico's alter ego, dies on the battlefield). Blindness universally symbolizes a passage beyond form, the perception "by the eye of the heart." Having attained the state of Eden-like perfection, Chico now enjoys an uninterrupted beatific vision ("my eyes are full of you"). At the same time, the improvised marriage heralds the unio mystica, the total fusion of essence and soul, of Eros and Psyche which can be seen in the last shot of the film. *7th Heaven* may be seen as profession of faith by Borzage, the "three pointed Brother."

Clearly it must be recognized that this type of decoding carries the risk of over-interpretation: there is no way of knowing to what extent Borzage, at this stage in his life, had assimilated the knowledge transmitted by his initiation into Freemasonry. However, compared to the labyrinth of Freudian interpretations and the literary gymnastics of the surrealists, this approach has the modest advantage of being clearly linked to the filmmaker's real concerns. In any case, both implicitly or less explicitly, it seems clear that *7th Heaven* contains themes central to Borzage's work. All the later films, including *I've Always Loved You* (1946), *China Doll* (1958) and even the biblical epic *The Big Fisherman* (1959) contain these themes; only the circumstances, settings and degree of spirituality vary.

* * *

Borzage had many projects for the summer of 1927: *The Grand Army Man* with Alec B. Francis, *The Girl Downstairs* with Olive Borden, and *Come to My House* with Edmund Lowe and Mary Duncan. All were cancelled when *7th Heaven* struck gold. The studio spent months hunting feverishly for a subject having equal appeal, to cash in on the public's taste for the new lovebirds and their creator. *Street Angel*, filmed between September 26 and December 31, brought together previously proven ingredients: it had picturesque and sentimental appeal, and featured a European setting and marginal protagonists who were poor, farfetched, and fascinating. But Fox's criteria were not the issue. Borzage's hesitation over the summer was mostly a reflection of his difficulty in tackling a statement as evident and paradigmatic as *7th Heaven*. The starting point for the new screenplay was a four act comedy from prolific Irish writer Monckton Hoffe, *The Lady Cristilinda*, written in 1922.[37] The text underwent substantial transformation between July and when filming began: Cristilinda (renamed Angela) is initially a circus rider at the magnificent "Christopherson's Royal Circus," owned by her father. Her beloved, portrait painter Martini (Gino), is a highly talented forger. Successive screenwriters tackled the project, displacing the action from an imaginary London to Paris and finally to the sordid area of turn-of-the-century Naples. A pampered, happy-faced child is injured after falling from a horse: Cristilinda-Angela becomes a famished "street angel," a poetic euphemism for a prostitute. The Bay of Naples and the hills of Capodimonte are powerfully evoked: glass paintings and miniaturized houses on Catalina Bay, while a section of the poor area of Santa-Giovanna and the Santa-Lucia pier was built on the large Western Avenue studio set. The Los Angeles Italian community warmly provided the extra work. The cast included Alberto Rabagliati, in policeman's uniform, who became a music hall star after 1940 and was Valentino's double (this allowed him to stay in Hollywood), and Guido Trento, a very popular actor in Italy, who frequently appeared with Francesca Bertini.[38]

Borzage concentrated his efforts mainly in three areas: the pictorial aspect, the intimate asides between Gaynor and Farrell, and the sound effects. The first area was a major surprise: so strong that it made up for a good part of the film's weaknesses. Set designer Harry Oliver (who had spent the previous month studying in Naples) recalls: "I had moved the camera so many mysterious ways in *7th Heaven* that they encouraged me and in *Street Angel* I built a round set and had the whole floor moveable and a track up it and we got to everybody, moving close-ups and everything, but it wasn't easy."[39] This set revolved around a central point where technicians were posted, so that the camera could, if necessary, pivot on a 360 degree axis, continually recording the action. The viewer is immediately struck by the magnificent graphics, the boldness of the composition, the length of the shots, a visual language strongly influenced by German expressionism. However at times, during a vignette, the film evokes a fairyland reminiscent of the world of Maurice Tourneur and Ben Carré (*Prunella*). Visually, *Street Angel* is incontestably the most "German" of American silent films.[40] We almost have the impression that Borzage — whose origins, as mentioned, are German-Italian — is seeking to rival Murnau, proving to his backers that he too, is capable of excelling in the imported UFA style. (We know that Borzage studied the filming of *Sunrise* and that Murnau, reciprocally, expressed his admiration for *7th Heaven*,[41] and sometimes watched the filming of *The River*.) Murnau was so impressed by *Street Angel*'s photogenic quality that he immediately hired the cameramen responsible for it, Ernest Palmer and Paul Ivano, for his next film, *The Four Devils* (its first take was on January 3, 1928). Each shot was thought out in terms of its vanishing point, its chromatic grading, the way it conveyed mood on film. Shots were often organized around a diagonal crossing

Bor-8-120

A visual language strongly influenced by German expressionism: Janet Gaynor in *Street Angel* (1928).

the field (a balustrade, vaulted attic roof, laundry hung out, fencing) — and following Adolphe Appia's theatrical precepts (the famous "rhythmic spaces") or even Bauhaus' theories — powerful sections of murals placed at intervals around a lopsided staircase. Light shapes the space, animating surfaces with oversize projections of shadows. Yet here there are similarities with John Ford's "German" style films, *Four Sons* and *Hangman's House* (directed in the same time period): the foreign style is faultlessly assimilated, integrated into a very personal cinematographic vision. Borzage plays with the intensity without ever inserting a final gratuitous aesthetic into his narrative. This marked expressiveness, harmonious with sophisticated, fluid camera movements, this completely stylized reality manages to reduce shapes to geometric models and is limited to the depiction of adversity (first and last reels). The Pabst-like mist (reminiscent of *Pandora's Box*) enveloping Naples in sadness translates solitude, resignation, a lack of existential perspective (inasmuch as it isn't based on Transcendence) all the while at the same time erasing individual profiles.

The words placed at the beginning could easily apply to all Borzage's work: "Everywhere ... in every town, in every street ... we pass, unknowing, human souls made great by love and adversity." Two police officers in two-pointed hats appear out of the fog; fishermen are busy with their nets. A disturbance in the alley: a grocer accuses some performers of the "Circo Napolitano" who are strutting around of having stolen a salami. Gesturing, wailing, and commedia dell'arte ensue. Masetto, leader and perpetrator of the offence, is shown on the bass drum ("she was the most musical drum in Italy"). The police calm everyone down. The camera leaves the performers to dreamily explore the setting and microcosm of humanity in a descriptive tracking shot lasting over a minute, before stopping at the foot of a drab-looking building where a concierge is stirring up a group of housewives. This camera movement furtively captures an array of isolated destinies (the beggar, the priest and his congregants, etc.), impressions of a closed universe indifferent to the unhappiness of others. At the same time, however, the camera acts as guardian angel, creating canvasses, knitting together lives and places with its invisible thread.

In a tiny, shabby room, Angela (J. Gaynor) is watching over her bedridden mother. A doctor prescribes an expensive drug. The makings of a stock play... Desperate, from the window the girl watches the ploys of a prostitute being paid by a client (high angle tracking shot of the wallet). Angela ventures into the street, tries begging, then awkwardly flirts with passers by who turn away from her overly innocent face. She imitates the prostitute's affectations, hands on hips, hat at an angle, sidling up to a man eating salami who ignores her. Money has been left out on the tray of a restaurant owner: she filches it, but runs into two police officers. She is now condemned to a year in prison "for robbery while soliciting on the streets." Borzage films the entire courtroom episode by placing in the foreground the two officers, in their oversized hats with their backs to the camera; in the middle ground appears the judge, wearing a hat. In the remaining space, at the back of the image, a tiny Angela is being pushed toward the camera by a third policeman; only her eyes and forehead emerge above the desk. This impression whereby individuals are completely annihilated is carried over to the courtyard where the prisoners are parked, reduced to deformed shadows. En route to prison, Angela manages to escape: like a mouse being chased she runs, dwarfed beneath a complex of lofty archways and shifting, agitated shadows. Back home, her mother has died; the child lies down next to the body. Policemen surround the building. Angela escapes over the roofs and lands near the entertainers who gladly hide her in the big drum. Visually and spatially, we have come in a full circle: after 15 minutes the camera returns to its point of departure (even the framing coincides). The two police officers question the circus folk unsuccessfully. "Coco, salute the brave policeman!" a clown orders his little monkey, who then thumbs his nose. The circle (hostile society) has not closed in on the little fugitive. Angela conceals herself "inside."

From Angela hiding inside the torn drum, Borzage links to an image of Angela wearing a tutu, painted on the head of the repaired drum. She is now the star of the minuscule "Circo Napolitano," displaying itself in the sunny countryside. Inside a caravan, Maria is reading cards and predicts a great love for Angela. "Bah, love makes unhappy," is Angela's response. Masetto interrupts them, because a traveling painter and his goat are stealing spectators away from them. The pretty Neapolitan forcefully intervenes and when the goat knocks her down, she stamps her feet on the canvas of Gino, the painter (Charles Farrell). He puts up with this commotion, smiling, then incites the onlookers to watch the circus. Angela performs a routine on stilts (symbol of freedom and elevation as precarious as the security she thinks she has found in the "unreal" world of the acrobats). In the evening, Gino invites himself along, taking to the road with performers, because he wants to draw Angela's portrait. The young woman protests: "I don't like painters... I don't like men." In response, Gino puts her jacket on her shoulders, and takes the reigns of the caravan. The pastoral escapade leads to an idyll containing shades of Griffith. At the top of a hill overlooking Naples, Gino works at his easel whistling "O sole mio," a tune that manages to irritate Angela. He wrinkles his brow: "You make it hard to paint you, Angela — always you wear a mask — to hide the soul that is in you." She is disconcerted for a moment, hesitates to kiss him, then shoots back: "You are a painter, paint me as I am." When the canvas is completed, Angela loses her sardonic smile. Marveling at the painting's expression of purity, she exclaims: "She is lovely, Gino! But I am not like that!" "You are to me!" the painter replies. Masetto cuts short their kiss: the public awaits! From atop her stilts, Angela whistles "O sole mio" and Gino answers back lovingly. Janet Gaynor recalled in 1976: "I was told there would be a surprise and I went to the premiere and of course I couldn't imagine what it would be, because I'd seen the picture cut, but in it, Charlie and I — we whistle to each other, sort of a signal back and forth, and there we were and all of a sudden with the first whistle a real whistle came out, and of course it was a great surprise — it was not, fortunately, my whistle, because I really can't whistle, but it came out clear as a canary and that was the big surprise, that little beginning of sound."[42]

But reality reasserts itself. When two police officers blend into the spectators, the terrorized acrobat loses her balance, falls and breaks her ankle. Gino takes Angela to a doctor in Naples (as they cross the bay at night, he hums the barcarole of the film, "My Angel"). Months go by and Angela can walk again without her cane; the couple has moved into a sordid area where the prostitute Lizetta, their neighbor, is jealous of their affection. The lovers have created a world within a world (illuminated by transparent fluidity, the sfumato specific to Renaissance masters), until the day when Gino sells the painting of the "beautiful lady" for a mouthful of bread to a dishonest merchant who has recognized his exceptional talent. The swindler has the painting secretly touched up and sells it as an authentic 18th century Madonna. "It was more than a painting ... it seemed alive and understanding, like a guardian angel. Now that it is gone, I am afraid," Angela vows to her companion during a moment of mutual adoration which, with its inimitable mixture of

A shelter for outcasts: the circus in *Street Angel* (Louis Ligett, Charles Farrell, Janet Gaynor and Henry Armetta, 1928).

tenderness, freshness and poetry irresistibly evokes *7th Heaven*. Outside, strolling players are serenading, but Angela suddenly notices a policeman questioning a streetwalker. She pales, taking pity on the victim ("Perhaps it wasn't her fault"); the painter, however, is full of contempt: "You don't understand, Carissima... You are too pure at heart." Angela and Gino's union seems chaste, each one sleeping in a different place; before going to bed, the lovebirds still whistle "O sole mio" from one abode to the next. But Angela was justifiably apprehensive as Sergeant Neri, one of the two police officers from the beginning, has recognized her and followed her into the alley... The following evening, Gino comes in laden with food: he has gotten an order for a wall fresco. They are rich, can get married tomorrow. At that instant, Neri—Destiny—knocks on the door. Knowing she is lost, Angela intercepts him and in a low voice begs him to give her an hour's respite: Gino must know nothing of her past. The segment that follows is the most questionable of the film, although well directed, it is predictable and repetitive, a concession to spectators Fox publicists had promised "to transport to the Seventh Heaven of Delight"! Angela hides her imminent departure from Gino, who, tipsy from the wine, loses himself in daydreams of future happiness. The policeman gets impatient, glancing surreptitiously between the curtains. Angela implores him with her eyes—but these instants of happiness threatened by brutal separation appear to be a somewhat artificial repetition of Chico and Diane's farewell. The whistling of "O sole mio" accompanies the departure, a superfluous use of Movietone which detracts from the film, as the excess of sugary sweet Italian melodies interferes with the silent magic of their looks and renders the scene overly sentimental.

Fortunately, the image fully resurrects itself in the last reels, sprinkled with gripping compositions: scenes in the jail structured around shadows (of recluses, the pacing police officers), the staircases, huge railings, oppressive stone walls taking up three quarters of the frame, powerful, misty panoramas, etc. The next morning, Gino inquires in vain about his friend, going around to the bistros. Lizetta, the prostitute (Angela's negative "double"), who tries to take her place (by corrupting Gino's intolerable purity) receives a slap. The painter is paralyzed before the empty space on the wall where the "beautiful lady" had hung, loses all inspiration, neglects his fresco and drowns his sorrows in Chianti. In prison, Angela whistles her favorite tune, joyful because she believes that "outside, the one I love makes great things." Injustice and suffering have not managed to change her. Arrested in a round up, Lizetta ends up sharing Angela's cell. When they are both released, Lizetta eagerly tells Gino everything. "Now I am going to paint women as they really are! I shall find a girl with a face of an angel and a soul as black as hell!" he announces with a bitter laugh.

At night he roams about the red-light district (Borzage's sisters, Dolly and Susan, are noticeable) looking for a suitable model. As for Angela, she has discovered the painter's studio covered in spider webs. Famished, she wanders past stalls selling mussels, then goes down to the port, the geometrical place of despair (descending stairs, as in prison). The director films their reunion in a frame (master shot) evoking an abstract painting, divided horizontally by a patch of milk-like fog from which traces of masts in a shipyard can be distinguished. The lower part of the image, drowned in shadows, features the pier where the two shadows collide. Gino flicks his lighter and recognizes Angela. Frightened by his hateful expression, Angela flees along the parapet (followed by a long lateral tracking shot) and runs into a chapel to hide. She faints in front of the altar. Gino tries to strangle her. He upsets a Bible, realizes where he is and raises his eyes above the tabernacle. By the light of the candles, he discovers his own portrait of the pure Angela made up as a Madonna! The scene is filmed from a high-angle vertical shot, offering the point of view from the painting (focusing on Gino). The painter backs up, removes his hat, incredulous. The passage is daring, wonderfully restrained. Borzage pulls through with honors: "Look in my eyes," begs Angela at the foot of the hallucinating man so that he can "read" her innocence. Janet Gaynor's luminous beauty in close-up does the rest. Appeased, Gino takes his inspiration in his arms and carries her away from the place of worship. Two shadows emerge in the mist of dawn. The End.

Like Tom Milne, we can see *Street Angel* as merely "something of a triumph of form over content."[43] When a good 35mm copy is projected, the work offers images of breathless splendor, marking "a new peak of perfection in photography" (Mordaunt Hall).[44] The plot of *Street Angel*, on the other hand, is stripped of any truly tragic backdrop (if compared to the preceding film); its external conflicts, faithful to the tradition of the popular novel, are truly reduced to a "storm in a teacup" (Milne). The story seems too weak to merit such a powerful illustration and it does seem as if Fox were trying to artificially combine the commercial assets of *7th Heaven* with the aesthetic appeal of *Sunrise*. But how to forget that this same form, deeply anchored in the interpretative logic of Borzage, by its very nature still manages to transcend the twists and turns of the plot? On a first level, *Street Angel* tells the tale of a young girl walking the streets (or who tries to do it, but what's the difference?), loses her purity (according to criteria of the time), repents, and is forgiven by the intervention of a deus ex machina. In fact, Angela sacrificed herself heroically but uselessly to save her mother. It is a bitter young woman, disillusioned by society (controlled by prostitution in all its forms), who joins the acrobats. But her freedom there can only be short-lived, since only by confronting reality can she attain true liberation. She meets an artist with a pure heart, too idealistic and vulnerable to endure the stigmas of existence. Gino falls in love with Angela because in her he sees innate innocence. Their providential meeting leads to an interaction that Borzage ties together with everything relating to the visual: in the eyes of Gino and in spite of her, Angela becomes a virginal, ageless, inspiration of his genius. His work is that of a Master. In the eyes of Angela and in spite of her, Gino becomes a possible conveyor of hope (and of reinsertion), while embodying rehabilitated love in general, expressed by the artist's magnified vision of the young woman whom he transforms by love.

The painting expresses this interaction. Like the two medals in *7th Heaven*, it is imbued with a life of its own, with the power to transfigure and unify regardless of time and space. (From one point of view, we can see it as a metaphor of the film itself.) By revealing the pure soul of the model, the painting shows Angela, who still doesn't recognize herself in it, her chances for virtual moments of redemption: an inverse function to that of the portrait of Dorian Gray. The painting protects the couple from the animosity that surrounds them (policemen, creditors, prostitution), allowing them to maintain a sort of fortress of innocence against evil. Even after it has disappeared, the canvas maintains a presence thanks to the empty space on the wall that Borzage shows three times: it allows Gino to resist temptation (Lizetta). The forger's actions show the "true" essence of the portrait: he adds a halo the same second that Angela, this false "street angel" who has never really fallen, begins her "descent into hell" (a supreme example of arbitrary editing!). The painting of the "beautiful lady" is transformed into an icon of the Virgin. In his symbolic references, Borzage appeals to religion without involving the church. Finally, thanks to this "seeing" painting (subjective high angle shot) the lovers save each other and catharsis occurs. Angela owes her life to the painting, and it allows Gino to see beyond appearances, an understanding which encompasses all levels of reality. Referring to the painting turning up in the chapel of the port, John Belton notes: "Its unlikely presence here is less absurd coincidence than it is indicative of the mystical design of Borzage's universe."[45] At first, Gino doesn't understand how he could have drawn the angelic face of a woman he believes depraved, while she offers him her eyes so that his will open: "To think I painted you like that!" "But I am like that still..." Angela tells him, implicitly admitting the mysterious relationship existing between her and the painting. She is really inviting him to look for her "inner face," what orthodox Gnostics call the search for eikon, the archetypal icon, a timeless, immaculate model of our own face.

Preceded by a big publicity campaign, *Street Angel* opened with a great deal of fanfare on April 9, 1928 at the Globe Theater in New York, on April 10 at the Carthay Circle in Los Angeles; as a prelude, Raquel Meller warbled "Flor del Mal" (the lament of a girl of the streets...), amid a vaguely musical Mediterranean repertory. The first week in New York *Street Angel* took in $126,000, almost seven times as much as *7th Heaven*! Its overall success was slightly less than that of the preceding film: in 1933–34 *Street Angel* still placed 33rd in the list of top pictures at the box office in the U.S., having earned $1,700,000. On the artistic end, Janet Gaynor, as mentioned, won an Oscar, while Ernest Palmer (photography) and Harry Oliver (set design) were nominated. The *New York Times* and *Film Daily* both placed *Street Angel* on their list of ten best films of the year.[46] Fans wanted to see Janet Gaynor and Charles Farrell married, and Fox orchestrated a whimsical press campaign. This was to silence the conflict — the first in a long series — between Sheehan and the new star during the shooting of *Street Angel*. Janet Gaynor, who was only earning $300 a week (her starting salary), asked to be raised to $1500. Sheehan refused; threatened by a general boycott in Hollywood (all the studios joined forces against her), but defended by a formidable lawyer, the actress ended up winning her case. However, the incident forewarned of what lay ahead and explains why the next project of the Borzage-Gaynor-Farrell trio, *Blossom Time* (set to be filmed in Europe) never came to anything. In the meantime, the public flocked to theaters to see "America's Beloved Sweethearts," soothed by their touching simplicity, without looking for anything other than a delicious moment of escape. Sociologically speaking, Janet Gaynor and Charles Farrell personified the timid dreams of the masses up against the aggressive frenzy of the twenties, and perhaps the unexpressed nostalgia for a paradise lost under the assault of sex (the "It" girls), bootleggers and rampant capitalism. The conjuncture was more favorable than ever for magicians like Borzage, who knew how to capture people's hearts without closing their eyes to the bitterness of daily life, possessing the rare talent of making a fairy tale look "true." On November 14, Mussolini interrupted the film's release in Italy. The film was forbidden under the pretext that it was unrealistic, since the fascist dictatorship had "erased prostitution and destitution from the peninsula."[47] Where did reality end and fiction begin?

8

Two Forgotten Masterpieces

Aside from their underlying themes, *The River* and *Lucky Star*, the masterpieces filmed in 1928–1929, share a great deal: both are adaptations of texts by Tristram Tupper with Charles Farrell in the lead, intimate dramas focusing on two people, *Kammerspiele* set in a rural or bucolic setting recreated entirely inside a studio (another characteristic of classic German cinema). Both have synchronous musical scores and are "part-talkies," and, victims of sound, for a long time had been considered lost and are therefore practically unknown to historians, except as mythical, invisible films.

For a half-century film buffs in France have been haunted by lofty yet exalted memories of *The River* (retitled *The Woman with the Raven*); impassioned paragraphs by Sadoul, Kyrou and Mitry come to mind. At first glance, its screenplay is disconcertingly simple and contains many external similarities (such as a couple lost in untamed nature) with *The Wind* (1927–1928), a commercial fiasco. This did little to recommend the project to the Front Office. However, Borzage was considered to be "the director who had never known failure" (a ridiculous but decisive criteria); furthermore, his recent prestige rested on making films without the ordinary subjects and with an emphasis on aesthetics. Aware of their recruit's distinctive talents, Fox launched *Street Angel*, qualifying it as "Borzage's new love lyric," not exactly a selling point in the Bronx or Midwest. Borzage made "arty" films for the studio, fortunately highly successful. From then on the script department's job was to submit projects to him that were up his alley, while Ford (*Four Sons*), Walsh (*The Red Dance*), Ewan (*The Joy Girl*) and the young Hawks (*A Girl in Every Port*) shared the more obviously commercially viable high-quality films.

In June 1928 (well before *The River* was released), "The Film Daily" published a list of the "Ten Favorite Directors" of 221 film critics representing 400 American cities. The results in order were as follows: Herbert Brenon (192), King Vidor (181), Frank Borzage (159), Raoul Walsh (152), Josef von Sternberg (140), Victor Fleming (109), Fred Niblo (95), Ernst Lubitsch (74), Charles Chaplin (74), James Cruze (73). This list ruffled feathers in the artistic milieu of Hollywood due to various omissions, and 51 directors proceeded to vote on the "ten most influential directors of the profession." The results: Frank Borzage (38), King Vidor (32), Ernst Lubitsch (30), Erich von Stroheim (29), Clarence Brown (21), Cecil B. DeMille (21), F.W. Murnau (21), Henry King (20), Josef von Sternberg (16), Fred Niblo (10).[1] Incidentally, since the triumph of the Gaynor-Farrell films, the director received as much fan mail at the studio as did his stars: "Borzage has received enough presents to fill a large sized store room. These gifts come especially from the far off points of the world, including Japan, China, Persia, Arabia and India. They include rare paintings, lacquer boxes, tapestries and embroideries."[2] A theater in Rio de Janeiro already carried his name, but, as mentioned, it was in China that Borzage had the deepest impact, as attested by several local remakes of *7th Heaven*, *Street Angel* and *Man's Castle*.[3]

The River employed only a very limited number of actors; Farrell, of course, and Alfredo Sabato, the italianitá specialist for *Street Angel*, as the villain. Margaret Mann, a Scott (the pathetic Mama Bernle in *Four Sons*), portrayed the old mother of a deaf-mute played by former Lithuanian wrestler Ivan Linow. As for the enigmatic woman with the raven, on whom the whole story depends, Borzage reserved a newcomer whom he had discovered on a Chicago stage in the spring of 1927: Mary Duncan. A natural "vamp" (without a long dress), candid, cheerful, with catlike grace, Mary Duncan awoke many fantasies. In his column in the *Revue du Cinéma* (the forerunner to *Cahiers du Cinéma*), critic Jean George Auriol paid her loving homage: "Thanks to her, Frank Borzage was able to make *The River*, undoubtedly the most lyrical love film ever made.... Don't take your eyes off her: she glows, burns, trembles, her teeth are dangerous, she undulates, leaps up, escapes— passion has taken hold in Mary Duncan and drives her to madness; fear curls her lips for an instant, slides along her flesh, flames in her eyes which shed pearls, she fears that this formidable, ravishing passion she adores and that will sink her."[4] Born in Virginia in 1907, the actress studied drama at Yvette Guilbert's school in New York before making her debut at the St. James Theater in London. Borzage saw her in John Colten's *The Shanghai Gesture* (later filmed by Sternberg), where her resourceful Poppy had been the rage for two seasons. In June 1927, Sheehan hired her at Fox and took her as his new mistress. When the project Borzage had intended for her, *Come to My House*, didn't get off the ground, Murnau cast her as the "belle dame sans mercy" in *Four Devils*. They could not begin filming *The River* until Murnau (who was also using Palmer as cameraman) had finished his work.

The story of the film comes from Tristram Tupper (1886–1954), a low-profile novelist whose work Borzage, by curious coincidence, had already brought to the screen: "Terwilliger," a short story filmed as *Children of Dust* (1923). This unsociable author, former civil engineer, mercenary in Mexico, major in World War I, lawyer and journalist, lived isolated in the woods of North Carolina. He sent his prose to Philadelphia's *Saturday Evening Post*, which serialized *The River* between November 26 and December 10, 1927. At Borzage's instigation, Sheehan persuaded Tupper to act as technical advisor for the film and, simultaneously, to provide work for other productions.[5] While *Street Angel* was being edited, in March 1928 Edmund Goulding wrote a first script — refused — of *The River*, provisionally entitled *Backwash*. Filming was to take place in Banff, Alberta, Canada. But Borzage, who had directed *The Valley of Silent Men* in Canada, was reluctant, remembering the catastrophe of the stuntman drowned in the rapids (cf. chapter 4). As Tupper's story unfolded over several seasons, it was less costly to film everything in Hollywood, even if it meant recreating autumn in June, spring in July, then creating artificial snow in August (untoasted cornflakes blown about by wind machines), while making frequent use of Fred Sersen's ingenious technique of matte and counter-matte to create the illusion of unspoiled nature. With a budget of $50,000 Harry Oliver surpassed himself: in Fox Hills–Westwood, twenty minutes from the center of Los Angeles, he created a panorama of the Great North including a river with whirlpools and footbridges, hills, three rows of ten barracks on wooden piles (in false perspective). It was all surrounded by abundant forests (hundreds of pine trees imported from the High Sierra) and steep cliffs. The background — the snowy Rockies — was a combination of painted backdrop and model set on a small scale planted with dwarf trees. Oliver was jubilant when an army of squirrels adopted his set as their home, and even the two trained ravens refused to go back in their cages. In short, the general effect was captivating and fooled more than one viewer. Filming began June 11 and ended September 5. The next day Murnau brought the entire team of *The River*—Farrell, Duncan, Linow, Palmer, Oliver — to Pendleton, Oregon, to begin the unfortunate *Our Daily Bread* (alias *City Girl*), his last film in the U.S.

Set decorator Harry Oliver creates a stunning panorama of the Great North (*The River*, 1928).

To this day, only one incomplete print of *The River*—with the first and last reels missing—has been found in the 20th Century Fox vaults, by William K. Everson and Alex Gordon.[6] But the 43 minutes salvaged, out of a total of 84, contain the most widely praised sequences and confirm the film's reputation. We fully concur with Claude Beylie, in *Cahiers du Cinéma*, who remarked that it "was not only Borzage's major film (with *7th Heaven* and *Man's Castle*), but without a doubt one of the three or four high points in all silent film. As significant as *Sunrise* and *The Wind*."[7] It is therefore essential to try to restore the film: this was done with the support of the Cinémathèque Suisse (Lausanne) and the Cinémathèque Française (Paris) in 1993, by inserting a series of stills and intertitles into the excerpt that retraced all the missing parts (total running time of the restored portion: 55 minutes). A comparison between the novel, the final script (dated June 5, 1928, six days after the cameras began rolling), compared with an analysis of the sequences written under the supervision of Borzage himself (June 6, 1928), the recovered film, and various summaries in the press and illustrations from Borzage's collection is both fascinating and disturbing.[8] Fascinating because, as with *7th Heaven*, it shows that for Borzage the script was only raw material to be transmuted indefinitely en route. He appears to have recreated it from one day to the next while shooting, keeping in mind its strengths, as 80 percent of the scenes written no longer correspond exactly (sometimes not even at all) to the result on screen! This accounts for the difficulty in retracing the lost sequences.

This is notably the case for the beginning of the film. According to the script, the words at the beginning of the film universalize the theme: "There is a river called life. Its source is a hidden fountain. The sea is its goal. Upon it sail the rafts of human destinies." Images of a source, a waterfall, torrential rain, rapids (the Columbia River in Oregon), of the sea. "Summer." Allen John Pender (C. Farrell) takes leave of an old miller (B. Woodruff), who has been like a father to him, starts the barge he has spent two years building with his own hands and goes down the river. "Autumn." Allen John's boat arrives at the hydroelectric power plant in the Rockies. The water is not deep enough to continue: he must wait for the spring thaw. Allen John ties his barge in a sheltered cove and decides to take the train into the city. Getting off, he witnesses the arrest of site foreman Marsdon (A. Sabato), a brute who has just killed an engineer for lusting after Marsdon's mistress, the beautiful Rosalee (M. Duncan). Of her past, Borzage merely shows her trunk covered in labels from top international hotels, a metaphor of transient existence.[9] The woman swears to wait for him. Without a word, his features harsh, Marsdon gives her his raven: the bird will ensure her faithfulness. Police take away the prisoner, in handcuffs, before the eyes of the workers. Sam Thompson (I. Linow), a Herculean deaf-mute, intervenes as he has a score to settle with the assassin, but his old mother holds him back. Marsdon and the police leave on a boat.

This is where the recovered excerpt begins. A poster announces the closing of the site: workers are laid off until spring. A long line of men leave their barracks and climbs the steep path leading to the railroad, about a hundred yards above. The camp empties out, time stops. Seated on a rock on the edge of the river, the raven at her side, Rosalee is conscious of her solitude. She looks dejectedly at the waves. A barrel enters her field of vision, then disappears into a powerful whirlpool. She wrinkles her brow, a man, stark naked, swimming on his back, lets himself be taken away by the current to the critical spot. At the last instant he veers off and with powerful strokes heads toward the rock. Allen John is half out of the water when he suddenly realizes someone is already there and dives back into the waves. Rosalee looks at him, half-amused, half-sardonic, cheered by his modesty; he could have drowned, she says. "It's kinda fun to see how close you can come without getting pulled in ... [that whirlpool]," he replies enthusiastically, water up to his neck. "I bet a fellow would feel mighty clean if he came out of there alive!" Rosalee, bored, doesn't answer. Fascinated, Allen John tries to make conversation. He has cause to regret it. Rosalie gets up and exclaims brusquely: "I want to be lonesome! I'm sick of men. I never want to see one again!" Then she goes back to her blockhouse, followed by the inseparable bird.

Borzage develops this first, fatal encounter by means of an extreme visual contrast between the two protagonists. In their deserted camp, they are isolated from any precise context—they seem to be sub speci oeterni—and characterized immediately by their clothing. Allen John is naked—(fully at first, then partially), thus handsome, innocent, pure, savage, natural. It is the "virgin soul" of someone coming from upstream, from the source, out of primordial waters; his personality is pure and rugged like the pebbles of the mountain stream, but his inexperience with women gives him a childlike timidity. Rosalee is the complete opposite: Borzage has the audacity of showing her to us not only dressed (she is in a bathing suit in the script), but wearing an elegant jersey dress, and even more incongruously, wearing high heels! Far from being merely a Hollywood absurdity, this somewhat surrealistic provocation expresses her complete otherness (compared to Allen John, but also to Marsdon, the workers, and the simple world of the Rockies). The undulating Rosalee is sophisticated, complicated, contradictory, as unpredictable as the waves of the river, and infinitely alluring. She is an experienced woman; her clothing conceals, her silences, heavy with implications, are intriguing. Furthermore, their encounter (or opposition), in which one is naked and the other dressed, creates a strong erotic charge. The woman's relative frigidity clashes with the man's physical radiance and his contained violence. The characters

Man, Woman and ... *The River* (Charles Farrell caught by Mary Duncan, 1928).

assert themselves by their respective positions: Rosalie is static, sitting immobile on the rock, weary and bored. Allen John is dynamic, swimming in the waves, curious, audacious (he takes risks) and entrepreneurial. The setting, finally, clarifies the nature of the meeting, as well as the risks: located miles from civilization, the setting foreshadows "elemental" relationships, unleashed with all the vehemence of an untamed environment. Very generally speaking, the river symbolizes the flow of human existence, with its succession of desires, feelings, and so on. The floating rubbish at the beginning is a metaphor of Rosalee's drifting, her despair. But there is also the sexual connotation of the water with its underlying currents, and that of the whirlpool, an image of an irresistible passion, dizzying, sometimes mortal. As for the raven, it is less a symbol than a reminder or obsessive fear of the past, a remembrance of the forbidden. The juxtaposition of all these factors contributes to the action.

Allen John hears the whistle of the train at the top of the cliff; in a flash, he goes back to his barge, closes his suitcase and nails a note to the cabin door, "Back again in spring," and takes to his heels. Borzage only shows the train in miniature, with a low angle shot of it crossing a viaduct, then a quickly passing shadow of the wagons reflected on the man's breathless but joyful face: he got there too late! In the meantime, Rosalee has resigned to set the table, soon it will be evening. An undeceived smile hovers over her lips, then dreamily she sets it for two. When Allen John arrives breathlessly at the house, Rosalee is waiting nonchalantly on the porch. "I missed the train, but I'll catch the midnight," he announces sheepishly. She smiles knowingly, shrugs her shoulders, looks away and invites him in. He is concerned when he sees the table set for two: "Are you expecting somebody?" "No one but you. I knew you'd never make that train." Allen John is confused. The woman asks him to go outside and get some wood for the fireplace. He complies willingly, but coming back with his arms full, his eyes meet Rosalee's. Leaning against the table with one hand on her hips, she stares at him with disturbing intensity. As if hypnotized, Allen John kneels, obediently placing the logs at the feet of the seductress. Rosalee authoritatively points to the box where wood is stored; he puts down his load, still on all fours. She shows him the stove, and he puts in a log. This silent game of domination foreshadows a remarkable "game of blind man's bluff for two where the handkerchief goes from one person to the next" (Michel J. Arnaud)[10]: she tests her power of fascination over the "child." She doesn't know yet whether she desires him; he submits in complete innocence to show her she needs a "protector." Borzage takes his time, not placing much importance in the events, because the true conflict, unmasked with masterly precision, is found entirely in the subtleties and ambiguities of the interaction. More lyrical than dramatic in temperament, he zeroes in with insolent tranquility on the tête-à-tête of his new Perceval with this impulsive stranger, sure of her own charm and destined to experience its effects.

Intrigued and candid, Allen John ventures: "If you hate men so—why did you invite me to supper?" She thinks for a second: —"You don't count." He bites his lip and tries to smile. Later in the evening they play cards; although he is losing, Allen John finds a child-like pleasure in it; the indolent Rosalee is moderately amused. Deciding to stop playing, she suddenly lies down along the table, casting him a devastating look, as if trying to strip him of his innocence: "How many women have you known, Allen John?" "No one but you. My mother died when I was a kid." They look at each other in silence. The raven wriggles about. The young man learns that the black bird belongs to Marsdon, and that it is there to watch over her during his absence. Overcome with curiosity, he asks: "Are you Marsdon's wife?" She shakes her head. —"Related to him?" She indicates no. Finally he begins to understand. "I've learned that life is better ... alone," she adds, before marveling at his height. Rosalee stands up, and, like a child, places her back against his. But it's cheating: she is wearing high heels! She takes off her shoes and presses herself against him, her breasts against his thorax. The physical contact creates an instant of confusion interrupted by the whistle of the midnight train—missed again! Allen John is visibly shaken up; he cannot stay. On the porch, an enticing Rosalee observes him: "Oh Allen John! I believe you're afraid of me!" He smiles in answer (an admission). But he is puzzled: why doesn't he "count" in her eyes? "I meant you are a boy, and I've known only men ... like Marsdon." Allen John is annoyed: "I'm a better man than Marsdon! I'd never treat you like he did!" "Don't make me laugh! You're all alike..." Furious, he picks up his suitcase. She lights a lantern, her expression mocking him: "You may need it to find your way back..." "I'll leave it on the platform. Goodbye." "Good night." He corrects her "Goodbye." She persists: "Good night." The young man walks away, infuriated, but, climbing the path, turns back and stumbles. They both laugh good-naturedly. When he reaches the train tracks, Allen John falls asleep on the bench, awaiting the morning train.

The following brief episode is missing in the surviving print: at dawn, Allen John is awakened by the deaf-mute. He goes to the grocery store owned by the widow Thompson and stocks up with several boxes of food, reserves for the winter destined for Rosalee. The train goes by. Helped by Sam, he carries everything down to the blockhouse. When Rosalee discovers the boxes, she falls into a rage, then bursts into tears: "Do you think you can buy us body and soul with canned tomatoes, succotash, spaghetti?!" Allen John stammers that it was a misunderstanding and throws the boxes in the river. Rosalee backs down and they both wade into the water to recover the food. (End of the missing part.)

Allen John is drying his pants in front of the fire. Rosalee has changed, and now wears an exotically patterned black silk negligee. Open-mouthed in admiration, he offers her a stick of candy (bought at the store) that she brings to her mouth in a highly suggestive manner, winking meaningfully. He is getting ready to take the next train, he says, the last before spring. But while leaving he notices that the reserve of wood is almost depleted and quickly grabs an axe. Still sucking her candy, Rosalee goads him: "I don't believe you could chop enough wood to keep anybody warm!" Allen John accepts the challenge. She sits down, secretly admiring his youthful vigor. Time and the last train go by. "I knew you'd miss it," she bursts out laughing. "You *wanted* me to miss it! You think I'm a joke, don't you? I'm going back to the mill — and you can laugh alone!" In vain, she makes a gesture to hold him back.

"Winter." — The cabin is covered in snow, it is dark out. Lying on her bed, Rosalee languishes. Images fill her mind: the barrel caught in the whirlpool, the young man getting out of the water, the raven... Allen John arrives unexpectedly, on a hunting expedition; he was worried about her, and she admits: "I've been lonely, terribly lonely." They shake hands warmly: — "We'll celebrate!" Joyfully, he brings out a game of checkers and she turns away, making a face. The shadow of the raven's empty cage is seen in profile against the wall. Exasperated, the woman lights a kerosene lamp; the shadows disappear and fall on the wall above the bed, near Allen John. Rosalie throws the checkerboard to the ground, lies down provocatively on her bed and stares at the boy. "You're still thinking of Marsdon?" he asks timidly. "I'm thinking of you, Allen John." The raven spreads its wings. She takes Allen John's hand and holds it against her left breast — "Listen to my heart." But when he leans over to place his lips on her throat, the bird swoops down on the couple. Overcome with frustration, Rosalee throws herself in a rage on the raven, to kill it. Allen John interferes and is hit by the knife, but the blade has bent: a close call. Rosalee is upset, ashamed; the young man calms her down by declaring his love, but she pushes him away suddenly, violently, and throwing him out the door, without a coat. A snow storm is raging. His pride hurt, wildly inflamed, Allen John seizes an axe and attacks a pine tree, shouting: "I'll take you away from Marsdon! I'll show you I'm a better man than him. I'll cut you enough wood to keep you warm!" He removes his shirt before angrily attacking his third tree, his face whipped by the snow.

A few minutes of this extraordinary passage of sexual "transfer" in the film are missing: — Rosalee, horrified, observes this outburst from her window and goes out to try and reason with the man. He refuses to listen to her and disappears into the night after having almost completely deforested the spot. Numb with cold, shivering, delirious with fever ("I'm sinking, I'm sinking!"), he reaches his barge caught in the ice (the image of his inhibited desires) and lights the stove before losing consciousness. The fire goes out...

Returning from a bear hunt, Sam discovers Allen John inanimate on the ground. Unable to awaken him, he carries him to Rosalee's cabin where he leaves him on a couch (the enlarged shadow of Allen John, unconscious, can be seen on the wall, a veritable "mental mirror" of the woman). Sam rubs snow on the naked chest of the flushed man, to no avail. They put Allen John to bed; the deaf-mute finishes undressing him while the distraught young woman heats water and feeds him boiling liquid. But these measures are in vain. Allen John shows no sign of life. Sam lowers his arms. Rosalee gestures him imploringly to go get his mother and the giant runs off. Then comes the classic scene much praised for its "sensual chastity": nervous, agitated, the woman hovers indecisively around the bed, stops suddenly, hesitates, rapidly removes her peignoir, turns back the sheets and lies down on the naked body of her beloved. She presses herself against him, caresses his face with her hands and suffuses him with her own breath to warm him.[11] Fade-out. Medium-close shot of Rosalee, still lying over Allen John, imploring heaven: "Please, please, let him live!"

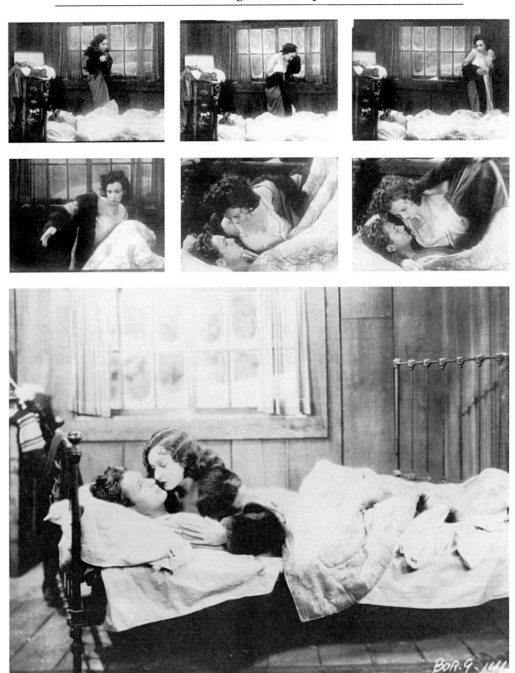

The Surrealists raved over this unforgettable scene, praised for its eroticism (Mary Duncan with Charles Farrell in *The River*, 1928).

High-angle close-up of the young man whose eyebrows move imperceptibly. Dissolve to various images: the waterfall, Marsdon in handcuffs, trains, Rosalee's smile, the raven... Allen John suddenly opens his eyes to the camera. The river, the whirlpool... He looks at Rosalee (whose face enters his field of vision), murmurs her name a few times. She swears never to leave him, because she loves him. "Enough to go down to the sea with me — in the spring?" The following close-up of Rosalee reveals a new emotion: tenderness. This is how the recovered excerpt ends.[12]

"Spring."—The glass cracks, freeing the barge. Allen John gets the boat ready for the long voyage. Rosalee goes back one last time to the blockhouse in order to give the raven its freedom. When the bird flies away, Marsdon bursts into the room; escaped from prison, he has come to reclaim his mistress and go into hiding with her. He looks cruel; the woman struggles, cries out. Allen John rushes up, but Marsdon hits him over the head with a log. While Rosalee escapes into the woods, the criminal is stopped by the enormous Sam, his mortal enemy. Terrorized by the ghost of her persecutor, Rosalee climbs onto the footbridge and jumps into the river. "When she throws herself in the torrent, her white dress, billowing in the wind from the waterfall, creates snowy curves that almost made me cry out," declared one critic.[13] The whirlpool engulfs her. Allen John dives into the heart of the maelstrom and embraces Rosalee under the water. A few seconds later, the lovers reappear on the surface, alive. Having strangled Marsdon, the deaf-mute dispenser of justice washes his hands in the river: "The river, like love, cleanses all things." The raven—the black soul of the tormentor—disappears into the horizon. The barge flows on down toward the sea. The End.

The River, whose central theme is desire, is the most erotic film of the silent era. The French press at the time, for example in "*Cinémagazine*," realized: "In all cinema, Frank Borzage's film is perhaps the one that contains the most disturbing sensuality."[14] Starting off with a situation similar to that of Daphnes and Chloe (discovering love in the solitude of the grove), the film progressively focuses on the ups and downs of seduction and refusal, ruses and inhibitions, desire constantly confronted by obstacles, until love guides the two very distinct protagonists toward a natural balance. Casting aside artificiality, love elevates both of them. Certainly Rosalee's reticence, provocation immediately followed by evasion, and her almost perverse game of hide and seek reveals her growing perplexity. First she senses her body "drift away," while still linked emotionally to Marsdon. Later she realizes she can't erase the memory of the criminal and come to terms with the Allen Spencer's idealized image of her (the dilemma of *Street Angel*, presented more concretely). But Borzage described the situation in more general terms: "It should become obvious that Rosalee is representative of all women, yet at this time she knows nothing of the tenderer emotions and, therefore, the boy is as much of a surprise and frequently as much of a delight to her as she is to him." French historian Jean Mitry noted that many viewers misunderstood the film, speaking of its "disconcerting simplicity in which it contains an ambiguity rarely seen by viewers. The game of these two people who desire, seek out and refuse each other instead of acting like everyone else in the most banal melodramas.... Rarely has the psychology of love—sensual, erotic—been rendered so exactly in its troubling, simple, complexity."[15] This fundamental dynamic between man and woman is at the very heart of the film: all the more specific psychological issues are secondary. Because at its heart, *The River* tells of the first embrace at the dawn of creation.

The synthetic nature of the ending allows us to place the narrative in a transcendental perspective. Rosalee's sudden awareness, her Metanoïa at the bedside of her frozen beloved, breaks the ice, destroys ties (the past, the raven), opens the route to the sea that the lovers will take under the providential vigilance of their guardian angel, the deaf-mute. As they both disappear into the whirlpool, Rosalee and Allen John meet the supreme, ultimate, challenge, approaching resurrection.[16] This immersion causes a rebirth, in the sense that water is both life and death; the couple is literally revived as the purifying waves have the power to both erase and reinstate them. (Perhaps there is a link between the ritualistic challenge of the Four Elements, at the end of *The Magic Flute*). If the river also symbolizes

The lovers in the heart of the maelstrom (lost scene).

man's progression on earth, the journey toward the ocean, where the waters converge, universally signifies returning to a state before creation. In short, as with *7th Heaven*, we are wary of overinterpreting, but it seems clear that the obvious symbolism of *The River* cannot be reduced to a passionate portrayal of a loss of virginity in the woods!

The film did not fare well in theaters. The world premiere was set for December 22, 1928, at the Gaiety Theater in New York, but bankers and theater owners didn't really know how to promote the unclassifiable film at a time when simple-minded, jazzy entertainment such as Warners *The Singing Fool* and *Lights of New York* ("100 percent talkie") attracted curiosity. William Fox yielded to pressure. Without the director's knowledge, Fox added a ridiculous musical Movietone prologue to the film: an obese tenor in city clothes sings the tune of the film ("I Found Happiness When I Found You") with a soprano in an evening gown! The press was furious at this sabotage and the public laughed. Welford Beaton, a well-known critic, spoke of it as "positively criminal."[17] In April 1929, Fox withdrew all its copies from circulation; naturally, the grotesque introduction was cut. The last 15 minutes were replaced by a spoken conclusion, very slightly modified. Occasional directors A. F. "Buddy" Erickson and A. H. Van Buren, a duo specially designated for this type of task, directed operations.[18] Temporarily renamed *Song of the River* and preceded by a trailer (with sound), the film was released for general viewing in the U.S. on October 6, 1929. The talkie portion of the last reel begins in the spring, with Allen John waiting for Rosalee on his barge while humming a sailor's tune, then continues with Marsdon's pursuit—the raven can be heard—Rosalee's jump into the waves and the departure of the lovers ("Clear to the sea—just you and I"). These "improvements" were not enough to draw in crowds. Practically all the American press criticized Borzage for overdeveloping the intimate scenes (to the detriment of the action), in short, of "making art." In reality, the strong sensuality of the love scenes shocked puritanical America, so much that *The River* was banned in several states and by tacit consensus its diffusion was limited; various newspapers did not review the film and important corporations even boycotted the advertising. *The New York Times* only devoted a small, embarrassed paragraph to it. Regretting Mary Duncan's too brief career, Jean George Auriol (op. cit.) denounced it retroactively: "In America, where almost all the inhabitants are still at that difficult age [!], people were shocked by its admirable freedom, its uncontrolled confidence in any kind of future. Soon a stupid, obstinate silence surrounded it, uncorrupted by the 'siren's call'; people counted to 500 and when they opened their eyes she was far away, then they could go back to being stupefied. Little by little, the film disappeared."

The reception was more positive in Europe, where the silent version, with a musical score, was released: "It is from first to last a delight to the eye... This is a picture which should convert screen enemies, if any still exist, for it is difficult to imagine any lover of the beautiful withstanding its appeal, while those endowed with imagination will delight in discovering hidden meanings in the story and its episodes," remarked *The Bioscope* (London).[19] But as with *7th Heaven*, it was in France that *The River* was so highly praised. Rationalists were of course offended that "we are spared no implausibility" and some dailies wrote nonsense about the film's style: "This mistress of an important site foreman spends the winter alone in a log cabin, without a servant, far away from the train tracks, from any habitation, in 53 degree below zero weather. She is not even informed of the outcome of her lover's trial."[20] The film was released October 31, 1929, at the Studio des Ursulines in Paris, in the Latin Quarter, where it was sold out for seven weeks. Movie fans were impassioned; but it also provoked laughter from the "reasonable" public. The American correspondent for the *New York Times* in Paris was amazed, and noted the phenomenon in a long review (January 5, 1930). And *La Revue du Cinéma* declared: "With the films of Keaton and Langdon, with *Flesh and the Devil* and *The Wind*, the River is one of the rare films in which the face of love moves us by its truth."[21] *L'Ami du Peuple* was rather laconic: "Nothing is more bothersome than a masterpiece; we really don't know in what way we admire it, but we know we love it."[22] Finally, the surrealists, not surprisingly, adored it; Ado Kyrou wrote about it at length in his *Amour-Érotisme et Cinéma* (1957) and *Le Surréalisme au Cinéma* (1963), and denouncing French cinema, the actor-poet Jacques B. Brunius (1954) includes *The River* in a list of films that possess "more real audacity and inspiration ... than the entire French avant-garde."[23] Now you know!

* * *

While Maurice Baron and Ernö Rapée were putting the finishing touches on the film's musical accompaniment, Borzage was already thinking of other projects; in November 1928 he spoke of *True Heaven* with newcomers Helen Twelvetrees and Nick Stuart, also based on a Tristram Tupper text. Meanwhile, Fox was developing a new image as Hollywood prepared for the onset of sound. In July 1927, the company had made a sensation by releasing the first sound news reels, "Fox Movietone Newsreel," which, as of October, were released weekly. Some of them are titillating, such as a message addressed to the U.S. filmed in Rome (in English), in which Mussolini announces that "talkies can bring the world together, they can prevent war."[24] This gem was shown at Times Square before *Sunrise*. Elsewhere, crowned heads of England and Spain and George Bernard Shaw speak. A special Movietone release for internal use, lasting 40 minutes and entitled *Fox Talent* (June 1928), consists of a report on studio activity: Borzage, Murnau, Walsh, Hawks and Howard introduce the actors of their films, who then say a few words. On September 15, 1928, Fox's first part-talkie full length feature was released: *Mother Knows Best* (John Blystone). Part-talkies were only an intermediary step, but from then on, to remain competitive in the face of Warners advances (Vitaphone), Fox added talking sequences to all its big features. Murnau's *Four Devils* and *Our Daily Bread* were both victims of this travesty and the angry director left Fox for Polynesia before even completing his last film.[25] However, many theaters weren't yet equipped for sound, and silent films still had a place. Since late July 1928, 1,500 workers had been working 24 hours a day, Sundays and holidays included, on "Movietone City" in Fox Hills, where they were constructing a studio with the most modern sound recording equipment of the time; it included 25 buildings, with eight soundproof stages, at a cost of $10,000,000. After 90 days of labor-intensive work, the complex was ready. The outstanding results of this activity at Fox Hills were the four buildings containing the soundproof stages for Movietone production. They were 212 feet long, 165 feet wide and 45 feet high. Each building had two stages with their own equipment, apparatus rooms, test laboratories and projection rooms. The old studio at the corner of Western Avenue and Sunset Boulevard was transformed into laboratories and management was moved to the Westwood hills.

During this reorganization — which meant a slowdown in production — the head of the company was making plans of his own. A loner, the insatiable William Fox had always dreamed of becoming king of Hollywood; his empire now consisted of 532 theaters in the U.S., plus the Gaumont chain in Great Britain. Over the years, he lost interest in filming itself — Winfield Sheehan and his second in command, Sol Wurtzel, did very well without him — and devoted himself entirely to financial transactions on the east coast (he lived in Long Island). In the winter of 1928–1929, the tycoon maneuvered to acquire control of Loew's Inc., the most powerful network of theaters on the continent, and Metro-Goldwyn-Mayer, its production subsidiary in California. On March 3, 1929, he announced to a pack of dumbfounded journalists that he had bought Loew family's shares and from then on Fox Film would be in charge of Metro, under the noses of Mayer and Thalberg! Having become the largest production and distribution enterprise in the history of film, the company owned over 1,000 theaters: it seemed as if profits would be almost unlimited. But the new giant was vulnerable and the alarmed industry on the west coast would try to put a stop to William Fox's plans of leadership.

Amid this tension Borzage began his last silent film, *Lucky Star*. On January 1, 1929, Sheehan hastened to renew his contract, eager to see him direct both Janet Gaynor and Charles Farrell in their next hit: since *Street Angel*, both stars had worked with other partners, without any resounding success. But Fox was still reluctant to place them in front of a microphone, afraid that their voices would not go over, entailing a serious loss for the studio. Borzage again based his film on work by Tristram Tupper, "Three Episodes in the Life of Timothy Osborn," a five-page short story that appeared in *The Saturday Evening Post* (April 9, 1927), which he intended to adapt with the help of Russian scriptwriter Sonya Levien. Based on memories of fighting in Flanders, the story was structured in three parts:

the hero's accident on the battlefield (October 1918); his day-to-day life after being handicapped, living with old Pop Fry, a comrade from the trenches who dies in his house; his love life shared between rich city dweller Harriet Arnold and farm girl Mary Tucker. Mary gives him the energy to overcome his disability when she tells him she is to marry Wrenn, an insignificant ladies man. Work on the script began in mid–December 1928; the characters of Wrenn, and especially Mary, were developed and the girl now had a bad-tempered mother (nonexistent in Tupper's story).

The setting was rural New England, but Borzage knew he wanted to modulate light a great deal; this excluded natural lighting, which was too unreliable. Loyal Harry Oliver was in charge of recreating on set 3 of Fox Movietone City, entirely indoors, a country-like setting, 150 × 350 feet, including two farms with neighboring fields, groves, stream, waterfall, hills, paths, in short a panorama including cows, dogs, chickens and doves! To all this was added a Village square (Easton, Massachusetts) and a small station with a railroad. Lighting this complex required 60 arc lights and 80 incandescent spotlights. However, this striking recreation of realism was only a beginning, as one critic remarked: "This story takes place in the poetic setting that belongs only to Borzage, in the landscapes reconstructed as if in a dream: the fog, the snow, the twists in the road and the fences dotted with unreal sources of light."[26] The movie poster did not feature any well-known actors beside the Gaynor-Farrell couple, around whom all the action revolves, but we should mention Guinn "Big Boy" Williams in the unsympathetic role of Wrenn; a Texas congressman and hero of innumerable westerns (until *The Alamo* and *The Comancheros* with John Wayne). The well-built man led the polo team to which Borzage and Will Rogers belonged: they'd been friends for a long time.

Filming began on February 4 under the provisional title *Timothy Osborne*, with Dan and Bill Borzage on the accordion. On March 24, there was a general commotion: William Fox decreed that as of that day, his company would stop the production of silent film for the Anglophone market; only Europe, Latin America and Asia would continue to show silent versions with intertitles, as the synchronization process was not yet developed there. Work on *Lucky Star* was suspended immediately. Gaynor and Farrell left for a few days of rest in Palm Springs; they were actually taking intensive elocution lessons with a voice specialist. Upon their return, Borzage, with some anxiety, gave them various tests on the microphone. The result was positive and Fox was relieved; filming could start again with the new sound cameras—thickly covered to stifle the noise—and dialogue finalized by New York playwright John Hunter Booth (the last take was on April 20). The "dialogue director" from Broadway instructed by Sheehan to correct the actors' diction did not remain on the set for long. Borzage recalls: "I had Gaynor and Farrell again, we did the first half in silent, and then of course talkies came in, the sound, and everybody was frightened.... Anyway, we convinced ourselves we should do the last half in sound.... These guys with the white gloves came out and put on their microphones, there was one fellow who was going to give Gaynor diction and so forth. 'What is this?' I said, 'you're a nice guy, but you've been a stage director, so have I when I was a kid, but I said you just move over around the side, will you? You're not gonna destroy the naturalness of these kids' So we finished the picture like that."[27] They remade the film as a "talkie" from the point of Mary and Tim's reunion after the war (70 percent of the action); Borzage simultaneously created a spoken and a silent version which differed on various points, particularly the ending.

The film begins in jet-black night. A weak ray of light — the suggestion of dawn — progressively reveals the outlines of a dwelling: the widow Tucker's farm. A light is lit at a small window. Mary (J. Gaynor) yawns behind the pane, takes the kerosene lamp, climbs down what seems to be a path and goes to milk the family's only cow.

Mrs. Tucker (Hedwig Reicher, transplanted from Broadway and trained by Max Reinhardt) is pumping water; four kids (including the filmmaker's nephew, Raymond Borzage) come down the stairs, half asleep, and wash their faces in a bowl. Their mother dresses them, an action barely noticeable, as the entire rustic interior exudes destitution; the place is aptly called "Poverty Hollow." Chester A. Lyons, the cinematographer of Borzage at Cosmopolitan, Norma Talmadge and MGM (12 films), resurfaced at Fox to film images inspired by Dutch masters. This series of dusk-like tableaux in which shadow and light weave their dense web is reminiscent of Rembrandt's chiaroscuro and of the Germanic style in *Zur Chronik von Grieshuus* and Murnau's *Faust*. No arbitrary contrast, no shadows artificially torn to pieces or pictural grandiloquence, but a dramatic space led by clever modulation, in which masses and values are balanced in perpetual transformation. The days are short, winter looms. The contrasts blur, the lighting softens when the day looks as if its beginning, but the sun remains disconsolately absent (except by indirect lighting, by means of a constellation of incandescent patches). The entire film is bathed in morose and photogenic grayness. In this shadowy half-light of souls will shine the "lucky star" of the title.

Martin Wrenn, an installer of power lines, drives by in his truck and asks Mary to bring his men milk. En route, he picks up Tim Osborne (C. Farrell) who lives humbly in a cottage on the road. Stopping in a small wooded area, Wrenn directs Tim to the top of a telegraph poll, gives orders to others, then sits, primping and lighting a pipe. Mary brings her pails of diluted milk and collects from each of them; Wrenn contemptuously throws a piece of silver on the ground, without even looking at Mary. She buries the coin in the ground with her foot and asks for what she's owed; Wrenn tells her off, Mary counterattacks, and atop his poll, Tim tells his boss to pay up. Annoyed, Wrenn climbs up the poll and the two fellows fight it out in the air (filmed in high-angle shots; these shots call to mind a scene between Edward G. Robinson and George Raft in Walsh's *Manpower*, in 1941). The fight is interrupted by a telegraphed message: war has been declared! Wrenn wants to volunteer, because of the French girls, who are so easy to seduce: "Promises don't cost nuthin..." Tim remains alone to finish his work and observes how Mary recovers the money hidden beneath her foot. He comes down, furious, takes the little thief over his knees and gives her a spanking; Mary digs her teeth into his thigh. They leave each other, vowing to get even and rubbing their wounds—a first physical exchange that, at this stage of the drama, can only be expressed by aggression. The poor, uncouth, filthy, wild-haired girl, the black sheep of the Tuckers, survives by pilfering and various ploys. Borzage brings her literally out of the shadows, with her features still hidden under dirt, confronting her with a pure man who works in the heights, atop a vertical (he's always the one designated to work there, an intertitle informs us), a metaphor for elevation much like the stilts in *Street Angel*. Later, Mary goes by Tim's cottage with her wagon, intending to break a window when the young man leaves to join the army. Confused, she invites him aboard her vehicle: "I got legs to walk with, thanks," he replies. She sticks out her tongue, then wipes her nose on her sleeve.

Nighttime in the trenches of France. Tim and his sergeant Wrenn have each received the same short letter from Mary, riddled with spelling mistakes ("I hope you ain't been shot dead. If you're very bored, just rite and I'll nit you some soks."). Tim is moved by this childlike burst of generosity, but Wrenn snickers. "Papa" Fry, in charge of cooking for the regiment, announces that the food intended for men in the first line is ready. An artillery fight rages. Wrenn shirks (he requisitions the only truck to "go see the girls"), after having cowardly delegated the mission to Tim and Pop Fry. Borzage shows practically nothing of the battlefield in the black night, only a flash: streaks in the horizon from a shell bursting. The canteen wagon disappears in an explosion. Other explosions show us Tim's legs caught under the vehicle and Pop Fry lying dead at his side.

Only then do we enter into the heart of the subject (the last third of Tupper's story): two years have passed. Mary notices that Tim's house is lived in; approaching it, she throws a rock at a window. At that moment the delivery man (Joe) arrives, carrying a heavy box. Tim — paralyzed, in a wheelchair — opens the door for him. The box contains broken electrical appliances, lamps, various mechanisms. A clever handyman, Tim earns his living repairing them. "I'm going to fix up that old stuff as good as new," he says with apparently unaltered good humor. Close-up of his legs. "Never thought much about busted things, till now I'm one myself." He admits feeling isolated, but Joe can't stay to chat and continues on his way. Mary approaches, wary, a rock in hand. Tim coaxes her. Flabbergasted at realizing he is disabled, she enters the room, casting aside her stone. In a flash, Tim executes a pirouette with his chair, goes to the end of the next room and brings back a chair. The girl is stupefied by the speed and agility of the maneuver. Tim repeats his trick, waltzes in the room, Mary bursts out laughing. Then, fascinated, she sits down. The room fills with charm. Borzage frames them in a lateral shot, sitting symmetrically one across from the other, the door open at the center of the image, as in a Quattrocento religious motif. Mary is serious: "What's the matter with your legs?" "Nothing... I'm just saving them." "What you savin 'em for?" "A special occasion — like a wedding, or if somebody dies." (In other words, only love and death can put an end to his "mutilated" state). Awkward silence. She tries to sell him some berries at an unfair price. Tim uncovers the ruse, and secretly seduced by her spontaneity and candor, pays her the price she asked: "For telling the truth."

The soup is boiling. Before inviting Mary to the table (she hasn't eaten all day), Tim manages to convince her to wash her hands (which are black), as "they won't melt."

In the evening, after the meal, she wipes her nose with her sleeve. Tim pulls a face. Quickly taking a pair of scissors, he makes her a handkerchief, paternally pinning to what passes for a dress. To Tim's delight, Mary is in no rush to go home (her mother will beat her anyway). "I guess you can make somethin' outta just about anythin', can't you?" she says, full of growing surprise and admiration when Tim repairs a small phonograph. They look at each other, an unambiguous allusion. After listening to a record, Tim says goodbye, threatening to call her "Baa-baa" if she doesn't wash herself better, then makes her a present of the phonograph. Mary, who has never received anything before in her life, is amazed, on the verge of tears. "Comin tomorrow? An' the next day? An' every day?" Like the attic in *7th Heaven*, Tim's cabin is an "enchanted" refuge where, although disabled, he prevails amid a colorful network of pulleys and generators, a magic port where music, gaiety and friendship are born.

Twenty-four hours later, the unkempt girl stops at Tim's with goods from the farm, including eggs. "I have a notion you'd have mighty pretty hair, if you washed it in five or six waters. I'd like to see the color anyway," says the big brother. The bet: a dozen eggs and several buckets of water later, Tim discovers—that "Baa-baa" is a blonde! But enough laughter—there is still grime around her neck and under her clothes. He has already half-unbuttoned her dress when he reconsiders and asks her age. Eighteen! Panicked, he closes her dress and orders her to go wash herself alone. The sequence — one of the most surprising of this masterpiece, is treated comically. The feigned chastity renders acceptable the particularly explicit eroticism of the operation: sexual references (eggs, hair, water), sensual physical contact (masculine hands massaging and caressing her ample hair, inspecting her neck and her bare neck and shoulders in close-up, her back partially uncovered). From this voluptuous bath emerges a woman, like Venus from the foam: beneath her curly locks,

Mary is no child anymore: Charles Farrell nearly undresses Janet Gaynor in *Lucky Star* (1929).

Mary is radiant. Simultaneously, she modifies her reflexes, instinctively hesitating when he gets ready to wash her body, although he has not yet realized the significance of his acts. A full shot then marks the new distance created by the revelation of the sexes: Mary moves away and bathes in a neighboring stream, near a waterfall. From a distance, Tim observes the way she undresses: she stretches her neck several times, then turns as if frozen by the shame of pleasure. The country bumpkin has become desirable, which signals the start of the following scene.

In town, Mary is unloading her wagon. Wrenn, in decorated soldier's uniform, arrogantly holding a riding crop, stares at her lustfully. But Flora, a local girl he had seduced by promising to marry, detains the braggart. Mary deciphers a poster announcing a dance for that same night, then stops, wide-eyed, in front of a pretty dress in a store window. When night has fallen, she runs to Tim with a package under her arms and asks him permission to change there for the ball. The cripple waits for the girl to come out of the next room, his face veiled in sadness. Her reappearance as a "lady" of course illustrates Tim's efforts, but for Mary it amounts to an unconscious declaration of love — she owes him the discovery of her femininity. He gets the first look. She naively admires herself ("Gee, that's gran"!) while Tim responds powerlessly to her gracefulness. Borzage establishes no puritanical opposition between beauty and spiritual (or other) qualities: harmonious features always express — or betray — a character's personality. It is also natural that the director mischievously again shows Mary, both cute and touching in her awkwardness, still in many ways a child rough around the edges. She has pinned Tim's handkerchief near her heart,

Nothing but Love: Janet Gaynor with Charles Farrell in *Lucky Star* (1929).

and carries her new shoes in her hands "so they won't get dirty." How has she paid for all this? By juggling some of the money that belongs to the farm, she admits contritely, adding "I'm clean all over." "You're filthy inside," explains a saddened Tim, before fixing her hair and placing a pretty ribbon in it, adding a final touch to her transformation. Enchanted, Mary stares at the mirror. She throws herself at Tim and hugs him, choking with grati-tude. Tim, face turned toward the camera, eyes half closed, is overcome. The viewer then takes part in his bitter realization. Tim slowly removes his arms, without the knowledge of the young woman. The one-sided embrace continues until it is unbearable: the atmos-phere has become poignantly uncomfortable. Mary doesn't know how to leave, torn between the joyful anticipation of her first dance and the new emotions she is experiencing. He lends her his jacket and tells her to get going: "Gee, I wish you were going with me," she sighs before fleeing into the night. Alone, dejected, Tim turns slowly around the room and closes the door. He places himself across from the crutches leaning against the wall, slides to the floor, heaves himself up, and tries to take a few steps. He falls face down. Visually, his fall hurls him out of the light, into the darkness.

At the ball, Wrenn drops Flora to lavish his attentions on Mary. He explains to her that General Pershing decorated him in person, but the townspeople whisper behind his back that he no longer has the right to wear the uniform: he was dismissed from the army long ago. Wrenn brings Mary back, first to Tim's where she changes (the rivals exchange a few caustic remarks), then to her mother's, who is ready to beat her because she's "always with that cripple." Wrenn intervenes, compliments the mother and easily wins her over:

"What you both need is a man to keep an eye on things round here." The next day the bully comes visiting, bringing his "mother-in-law" a shawl, and candy for the children. He is in civilian clothes. "The general's done promoted me to major, my new uniform is at the tailor's." They'll have an army wedding. "The general himself is coming in person." Mary is to be on the train the next morning! Mrs. Tucker remains open-mouthed. "I never expected anything for myself, but a chance of a good life for Mary." But Mary, the ingrate, is not there. Tim has prepared lunch for them; the young woman doesn't dare come in; her mother has forbidden it. No matter: Tim offers her a seat and places the table on the doorstep, so that the rather formal tête-à-tête (a kind of engagement meal) will take place without her having disobeyed! He gives her a bracelet with her name engraved inside, "just like a big wedding ring," and proposes to go to Mrs. Tucker that evening. When Mary comes home, Wrenn has left. Her mother hits her repeatedly, then sobs: "He'll make a lady out of you! We've worked so hard our whole lives, never had a red cent to call our own..." For Borzage, naive Mrs. Tucker (inside, Mary is already a "lady") has been led astray by poverty, become hardened. She personifies deluded, vacuous humanity; she wants her daughter to be happy, even making a tender gesture to console her. Mrs. Tucker "has eyes but doesn't see," like the protagonists at the end of *7th Heaven*.

Night falls, and snow flakes are falling. The landscape slowly emerges from darkness and a coat of immaculate whiteness makes for an enchanted setting. For the first time, the sky "speaks." Like the heights that serve to clarify and purify (*The River*), the snow creates—much like the mist in *Street Angel*—an enclave beyond time where the impossible becomes possible. Mary becomes impatient, her brothers and sisters are washed, but Tim still hasn't come. In vain he tried to go out, but his wheelchair had no grip in the snow. He can only wait for the storm to end. Mary surveys the road, anxiously.

Then begins what can only be called a classic scene, by its irresistible emotive impact and a sort of phenomenal poetic impudence that persists until the end. Alone at the end of his room (spatially isolated in a medium-shot), Tim lifts himself painfully off his chair, falls, and turned toward the camera, he hoists himself up to the level of his crutches. The shots that follow are linked by fade-ins, as if Borzage wanted to unsettle the notion of time, reacting against narrative convention and introducing a daydream. Tim holds himself up with his crutches. Fade-in. Close-up of his feet moving a few inches. Fade-in. Tim, standing up, approaches the camera, falls, gets up on his knees, gripping his crutches, placing them under his armpits and moves forward. Fade-in. Tim is once again at the end of the room and places one leg before the other. He sets aside the crutches and takes a few triumphant steps.

Exhausted and shaken up by her mother's words, Mary spends the night listening to the phonograph. Tim slowly leaves his house with his crutches, the snow coming down; he falls, clenches his teeth, gets back on his feet and keeps trying... In the early hours of the morning, Wrenn arrives with a wagon. Mrs. Tucker looks for her daughter upstairs. Mary lets herself be dressed, her heart sinking. Tim climbs a hill, holding on to the trees. Mary lets herself be carried off, as if to a slaughterhouse. Wrenn takes the inert young woman to his vehicle. She is half catatonic, a psychological prisoner, literally paralyzed at the very instant that her beloved begins to free himself from his infirmity. Tim moves more quickly, the camera following his frenzied strides in a lateral tracking shot from right to left, in all aspects reminiscent of Chico's reappearance after the war. The young man seems driven as if by a dynamic crescendo that he is powerless to resist. He insolently sweeps aside all rational objections. The director's unwavering candor projects the viewer into a surreal dimension transcending all melodramatic: all that counts is the fable and its profound lesson of love. Getting up the hill to the Tucker's farm, Tim notices the braggart leaving for the station

Insolently sweeping away all rational objections: Tim and his crutches in the snow (*Lucky Star*, 1929).

with his prey. He shouts, tumbles to the hollow of the small valley, and, before an astonished Mrs. Tucker and her brood, straightens up with a single crutch. Seething with rage, he grabs onto a fence and climbs up another hill. Wrenn is about to get on the train when, at the milky light of dawn Mary notices Tim's outline, alternately crawling and hobbling forward, at the crest of the hill. With its expressionistic composition, an iconic reminder of Conrad Veidt on the roofs in *Caligari*— this full shot shows Tim "simultaneously ghostlike and dreamlike, physically a giant dominating the space, while at another level, [Mary]— and she alone — sees him appear as if he were the materialization of her desires" (Joao Bénard da Costa).[28] The young woman runs up to meet him, they fall into each other's arms, but Wrenn separates them. As if delivered from his disability, Tim throws himself furiously on him and the two rivals fight it out on the ground, between the tracks. Travelers grab hold of Wrenn, half stunned, and — good riddance — set him on the passenger bridge of the train as it leaves. Mary looks at her beloved from head to foot, incredulous, falls to her knees and wraps her arms around his legs: "Tim — this was the special occasion?" "Gee, Baa-baa, I thought I was making you over and you've made me over, good as new." They stand up, embracing in front of the train tracks fading away into the horizon. The End.

In the part-talkie version, Mary ends up getting impatient waiting for Tom's visit during the blizzard. She braves the snow and joins him in his cottage, where she declares her love. Tim rebuffs her at first: "You better go home and forget me" then yields to his emotions. One passage justifies the film's new title, *Lucky Star*: "When you came like a star to light up my loneliness, you made my days bright and my nights full of hope." Mrs. Tucker

The end of *Lucky Star* (1929): a miracle in the snow.

interrupts the pair, snatches her daughter away from the cripple and takes her by force to the station in her wagon. Tim tries to stop the vehicle and gets dragged in the snow. As can be expected, the dialogue not only adds nothing; by being overexplicit it detracts from the picture, reducing the metaphoric nature of the tale. In certain contexts what it says renders the story banal, paralyzing the viewer.

In the constellation of Borzage's films, *Lucky Star* shines very brightly. No other of his films sums up with so much clarity and poetic imagination what amounts to the quintessence of his work. It contains a rare mixture of enchantment and cruelty that characterizes jewels such as Charles Laughton's *The Night of the Hunter* (1955). Refusing any spectacular diversion this time — no more taxis from the Marne, no more Neapolitan circus performers, no more rapids in the Rockies, not even any more "villains" (Wrenn is just a pitiful braggart), Borzage opts for a rough sketch: an underexposed setting, that, even more than *The River*, emphasizes two solitary people. A script built apparently on nothing other than very complex subtleties that imbue the personalities with human truth. In *Lucky Star*, his silent "swan song," Borzage combines with serenity and economy of maximum effects, themes addressed since the beginning of his career, such as the mutual taming of the sexes (*The Pitch o' Chance* in 1915) and the awakening of sensuality (*Until They Get Me* in 1917), but enriches them with an existential experience based on a profound principle of harmony. "The things we create, recreate us" the film says in substance, in such a way that *Lucky Star* is ideally part of this framework of alchemical transmutation that can be summed up as follows: two "lost" individuals, victims of the evil that surrounds them, go beyond their selfishness (or other weaknesses— disabilities) by rehabilitating themselves, by mutually stabilizing each other under the effect of their transcendent love. Ties to money are not erased, but they are looked down upon. Mary undergoes a metamorphosis that is twofold: horizontal, from girl to woman, and vertical, from daisy to rose. The outer and inner evolution is similar: before even being a love partner, Tim represents for Mary the only yardstick of truth, of integrity in what she has known until then — an existence fraught with lies, filth, and deception. If Mary illuminates this involuntary hermit's sorrow and allows him to fully realize himself (regaining use of his legs), he, on the other hand, teaches her to see beyond the veil of sorrow that stifles Poverty Hollow by awakening her to sensitivity and inner beauty. He makes a woman out of her, and she makes a man out of him: each one becomes the other's star. *Lucky Star* is a return to a verticality universally representing man's spiritual dimension. The ultimate transformation occurs by the "baptism" of the snow (both water and light) which pushes the paraplegic lover to use his legs by immobilizing his wheels. For Borzage, redemption is inseparable from embrace. This practically Tantric connection of body, soul and spirit, of physical, psychic and spiritual, and of eroticism, emotion and a form of mysticism, is fully represented in the final image, with its manifestly symbolic connotations. All Borzage shows us of Tim and Mary is the complete fusion of two bodies joined in just one dark vertical on a white background.

In the U.S., *Lucky Star* was released as Janet Gaynor and Charles Farrell's first talkie. The film opened July 21 at the enormous Roxy Theater in New York, specially equipped for Movietone. But the public's reaction was lukewarm: with its lack of sensationalism, its modesty, and perhaps a kind of sadness at its core, it was soon forgotten. Lubitsch's *Love Parade* with Maurice Chevalier and Jeanette MacDonald as the chirping lovebirds was then setting the tone. In October, Fox paired Gaynor and Farrell in a lilting comedy that was "100 percent talkie," David Butler's *Sunny Side Up*, an unpretentious farce played out in a modern New York setting and which would set new records at the box office ($3,500,000). The press totally misunderstood *Lucky Star*: the incredibly superficial opinions varied from "indifferent and poor" (*Variety*) to "a likeable mediocrity" (*New York Herald Tribune*).[29] Critics were satisfied by the quality of the sound and of the images, but they found the story itself "absurd" and "simplistic." Only Welford Beaton, the American critic of the time most attuned to Borzage, declared in Hollywood's *Film Spectator*: "It relates some chapters in the lives of some exceedingly drab people, and is set in squalid surroundings, consequently it is not a picture that will have a wide popular reception.... *Lucky Star* is not going to be one of the biggest box-office pictures that come from the Fox lot this year, but it will be one of the finest."[30] Marcel Carné, then a young critic at *Cinémagazine*, stated: "I admit that I'm partial to Borzage's films. They don't always have the necessary framework, but they are masterpieces of simplicity, imbued with purity and exquisite sensitivity. The photography is at times so smooth and pleasing to the eye, that the viewer experiences inexpressible pleasure."[31] However, like so many of his contemporaries, he remains impervious to the ending "which was probably imposed on Borzage"!

Sixty years later, *Lucky Star* is still proving its critics wrong. In 1990 the Nederlands Filmmuseum discovered in its vaults a silent print of the film, the only acceptable version, and restored it.[32] Its premiere at the Giornate del Cinema Muto in Pordenone (October 18, 1990) had an explosive effect on an international elite crowd of film buffs who gave it an enthusiastic ovation. In late January 1991, the film was scheduled as a historical curiosity at the opening of the 20th Rotterdam Film Festival. After 186 films were screened, including the latest Kaurismäki, Muratova, the complete works of Nicholas Ray, films by Losey, Godard, Kazan, Aldrich, Fuller, and Rossellini, the festival's organizers held an opinion poll to designate the best film. The public gave *Lucky Star* first place.

9

Between Glory and Disgrace

"Borzage very competently turned out a few clever dramas before becoming, thanks to the talkies, a good director." This astounding comment by Maurice Bardèche and Robert Brasillach is the only one this noted duo of historians make about Borzage in their work about silent films, initially published in 1935,[1] and would no doubt unanimously win a prize for ineptitude were it not so representative of the way Borzage was long ignored and misunderstood! Henri Agel, among many others, would set the record straight three decades later by recognizing him, on the contrary, "as one of the most marvelously lyrical souls of the silent era."[2] However, in the thirties, his career pinnacled a second time, just as gloriously.

Having opted for widespread production of talkies, Fox took on a new dimension, with some 200 artists from the theater and from radio. Among those who deserted the stage were young unknowns named Humphrey Bogart, Spencer Tracy and Paul Muni, who first took their preliminary screen tests in Fox's Manhattan studios, on 10th Avenue. The Fox ensemble of filmmakers was now diversifying: old-timers Henry King and Victor Fleming, the promising talents of Leo McCarey and William K. Howard, and a European import, Alexander Korda. The technical innovations required tighter organization, increasing the role of the producer-supervisor in charge of the infrastructure and fatally restricting directors' chances of improvising. At first, they were assisted — at least officially — by "dialogue directors" trained in the theater. The length of shooting time also decreased; circa 1926, work on a major film varied between eight and ten weeks. Now, two to four weeks were sufficient; with the cameras having temporarily lost their mobility, action was often filmed in master shot, which limited varying the camera angles.

On March 22, 1929, Winfield Sheehan scored a coup which proved beneficial for Fox in the six years to come. Forestalling rival companies, he managed to ally himself with cowboy-philosopher Will Rogers, American show business giant and veritable sociocultural phenomenon. Half Irish and half Cherokee, this rodeo veteran who then went to Broadway, began before the camera in 1919, but despite an already considerable filmography, it was the talkies that definitively established his tender honest backwoods character, timid and falsely naive, stocky, imperturbable, cheerful, with an Oklahoma drawl. Will Rogers— mayor of Beverly Hills in 1926 — was the ultimate popular hero: essentially simple and with good common sense. Unsophisticated without being superficial, he embodied the individualistic spirit in all its oddities. This American prototype of Middle America wielded considerable political influence on the radio and in the press, especially in light of Roosevelt's election and the social program of the New Deal. His first contract with Fox, provisionally for 16 months, included four films. Handsomely paid ($600,000), Rogers did not only act, but was also responsible for the stories and, at least in part, dialogue and casting. Thus began a series of 21 film comedies, brutally interrupted by the comedian's death in a plane crash in Alaska, in 1935. Meanwhile, Rogers would become not only the company's safest commercial commodity, next to Janet Gaynor and Charles Farrell (before Shirley Temple appeared on the scene), but also a kind of national symbol of integrity and optimism in a time of crisis.

Borzage was given the delicate task of directing Will Rogers in his first talkie, the light comedy *They Had to See Paris*. The choice was not fortuitous: the filmmaker and his actor were members of the same aviation club and polo team, had several friends in common, notably comic Fred Stone. Their straightforwardness brought them together. Rogers also had Fox hire his exuberant colleague, Fifi d'Orsay, a French Canadian confined to playing Parisian belles of easy virtue. The story, by Homer Croy (1926), Roger's future biographer,[3] did not aim for originality but rather introduced a type — here the placid mechanic Pike Peters from Claremore, Oklahoma, that the actor would play again in other films.[4] It allowed Borzage to improvise on a favorite theme: of "appearances vs. reality," and, a few months before the stock market crash on Wall Street, denounce the "ruinous" effects of money: the destruction of the family, prostration in the face of social success. Without searching, Pike discovers oil in his fields and becomes a millionaire. The money goes to his wife's head (Irene Rich), who demands that the Peters "become cultured" in the French capital. "I'm not used to this kind of culture," Pike mumbles when he is brought to a Pigalle night club, where singer Claudine (Fifi d'Orsay) makes eyes at him. What follows is a series of classic situations resulting from the opposition between the city and the country, snobbery and spontaneity, etc. The family is torn apart: eager for ties to nobility, Mrs. Peters pushes her daughter into the arms of a dowry-hunting marquis (Pike: "Very glaad to meet 'ya, Marc ... ee"). The son disappears with a dancer, Pike must acquire a chateau where his wife organizes evenings with crowned heads, paid by the hour. That is where the most vivid scenes occur, when Pike confronts his hosts in medieval armor — he had given his tuxedo to his valet — and fraternizes with a penniless Russian Grand Duke, a notorious scrounger. "You don't know my wife," he says to him. "Worst thing ever happened to you was the Revolution!" Borzage handles the piquant and sometimes moving asides particularly well (the "parley-vooing"), between Pike, scorned by his wife, and Claudine, the poor but caustic ambassador of "gay Paree" who teaches him the words of "Le Madelon" while pinching his nose at each nasal (she: "Aïe lovv ze Americanne!" — he: "Dat's the bes' thing ah heard sinc'ah lef Oklahoma"). In the end, the young artist, with no bitterness, acts out a scenario to convince Mrs. Peters to save her marriage by returning immediately to the U.S.

The *They Had to See Paris* project was more of an experience than an artistic challenge. To fully justify the soundtrack, the filmmaker sprinkled the dialogues, already rich in various accents, with bits of French and even Russian (without subtitles!). Borzage delegated a second unit to film the locations in Claremore (the actor's native town), while he spent July and half of August 1929 enjoying himself at Fox's Movietone City:

> It was really more of a vacation, for working with Mr. Rogers is a refreshing adventure. He has many singular characteristics, among these is one of shyness. He hates to hog the camera, and during the photographing of the action, whenever he was able, he stayed as far away from the lens as possible. When we had rushes ready at the end of a day, or the week, and tried to get him into the projection room, it was almost an impossible task.... When we were shooting the picture, he would change the lines to conform with what he thought they should be, and his version was usually better than the original script. I really never enjoyed making a picture as much before as I did this last one with Rogers.[5]

Rogers was the despair of the sound technicians, as he never acted at the same place as the scene was rehearsed: "Look, I'm not going to change Will Rogers' naturalness. Wherever he is, that's where the scene is going to be played," decreed Borzage after having microphones placed in the furthest recesses of the set.[6] The actor wore his own clothes on screen, sent away make-up artists and refused the luxurious bungalow made available to him. To the studio's amazement, Rogers did not even deign to attend the big Hollywood premiere: he went home to Oklahoma. But the film was a smash at the box office: crowds finally wanted to hear their idol's nasal voice on screen. What's more, he graced them with a mischievous song ("I Could Do It for You"). His performance, with all its hesitations, had a reserved sensitivity and was a surprise, but not to Borzage, who had won his trust. *Photoplay Magazine* named Will Rogers best actor of the month (November) and the *New York Times* placed *They Had to See Paris* on its list of the year's ten best.

On August 20, 1929, Borzage, his wife and his team headed for Ireland. The assignment, less a personal project than a prestige mission for Fox, coupled with technical experimentation — was a big-budget musical, *Song o' My Heart.* As each studio was obliged to explore this new genre, Sheehan had also plundered the world of operetta and opera.[7] This was how he managed to convince fellow Irishman John McCormack (1884–1945) — then acknowledged as the greatest tenor in the world — to perform before the cameras, for a staggering sum of $50,000 a week, and a minimum of ten weeks of shooting; the artist consented and his regal salary caused talk.[8] Janet Gaynor was considered for the female role, but was unavailable. In Dublin, researching locations, Borzage discovered her replacement: eighteen-year-old Maureen O'Sullivan. She would be the charming Jane to Johnny Weissmuller in the first sound versions of *Tarzan* (and later the mother of Mia Farrow). By chance, O'Sullivan was attending a dance when the filmmaker took note of her fragile beauty. Borzage overcame the hesitations of the girl's father and hired Maureen O'Sullivan for $15 a week. At the end of September, after exteriors in Ireland — at Moore Abbey, Erin, River Barrow and Monasterevan (County Kildare), the domain of the McCormacks — the homebound team boarded ship in Southampton, along with the new starlet.[9] From November 25 until the end of January 1930, filming continued with microphones at Fox Movietone City, where set designer Harry Oliver made in the studio an exact replica of an Irish village. To round out the casting, Borzage called on some old acquaintances: Alice Joyce, the brokenhearted woman (like in *Daddy's Gone A-Hunting*) and Emily Fitzroy, the acerbic "old maid" (cf. *Lazybones, Marriage License?*).

The third particularity of *Song o' My Heart* — besides McCormack and Sullivan — was of a technical nature: in the spring of 1929, decades before CinemaScope, Fox was already a pioneer in the development (in collaboration with Mitchell Camera Corporation and Eastman Kodak) of a wide 70mm screen system named "Grandeur." The image, in 2.13:1 format, even had a double sound track (an attempt at direct sound). This revolutionary procedure had been inaugurated in a few Fox newsreels and the musical conglomerations *Fox Movietone Follies of 1929* and *Happy Days* (1930). *Song o' My Heart*, which opened in theaters March 11, 1930, was the first dramatic film to use it. Raoul Walsh's western epic *The Big Trail* (filming began in April 1930, released in October) would be the second — and last, because theater owners were unanimously opposed to this innovation, having already sunk enough money into recent sound installations.[10]

The plot can be summarized in a few lines: The entire village is listening to Sean O'Carolan (J. McCormack) sing his melancholy laments. Several years ago, the tenor had given up an international career when Mary (A. Joyce), whom he loved, was forced by her aunt (E. Fitzroy) to marry a rich man, who later left her. Now poverty has forced Mary and her two children, teenage Eileen (M. O'Sullivan) and little Tad, to return to the village and accept the dowager's tyrannical hostility. Like her mother long ago, Eileen is forbidden to see her friend, Fergus, a poor student. Practically a prisoner, Mary has lost interest in life. To help these unfortunate people, Sean comes out of retirement and makes a triumphant tour in the U.S.

Although the film is mainly a pretext for the musical numbers (thus a hybrid product), it carries the mark of its director. We will not dwell here on the tenor's repertoire (only "A Pair of Blue Eyes" was composed specifically for the film), which consists mainly of about ten known Irish folk tunes—"Paddy Me Lad," "Ireland, Mother Ireland," etc.—that McCormack had often sung in concert or on the radio. Paralyzed by the microphones (sound quality was the main concern) the camera recorded these sentimental ballads without flourishes, placing the bard either at a church, or in his cottage, or at the end, on the stage of the Los Angeles Philharmonic (only the song "Little Boy Blue" contained action that reflected the lyrics). Yet Borzage did not stop at cleverly integrating the songs into the drama, but used the sound track to introduce a referential dimension. The lyrics of the songs comment on or complete the action: seeing Eileen and Fergus embrace in the garden, Sean goes to the piano; he sings the tale of the "prince who can't marry his princess" (and have children with her), and "their" song—"The Rose of Tralee"—lures his old flame into the house to say goodbye because "It's better to sing his sorrows than to cry it." From beginning to end, the melodies call to mind the invisible link that endures between Sean and Mary.

Borzage dilutes McCormack sugary sweetness slightly by jokes about the rural area which give the film an almost Ford-like affability. At regular intervals, two misogynous quarrelsome villagers exchange caustic remarks: ("You know, you have a lot of sense, but it's all outside your head") or show black humor ("They'll never be able to get the coffin up these stairs," he says, visiting his sick friend); the little boy Tad invents "games" that systematically cripple his friend, soon covered in bandages, etc. Borzage's characteristic touches mostly reappear in the final third: Mary, all in white, sprawled in an armchair, dies in front of a bay window overlooking the plain; at the window, a tree loses its leaves. On the other side of the Atlantic, Sean is in the midst of a recital. He confides to his accompanist, backstage "I have that strangest feeling that something has happened. During that last song, I could have sworn someone was calling my name." And although the pianist has hidden the telegram that just arrived from him (informing him of her death), Sean sings "I Hear You Calling Me" in public. A leitmotif of space and time transcended, effective by its very sobriety, going from *7th Heaven* to the musical "calls" of *Smilin' Through* (1940) or *I've Always Loved You* (1946). Obeying the deceased's last wishes, Sean returns to Ireland to take charge of his children. At the same time, Eileen rebels against her aunt "who has never known love"; her beloved returns from Dublin, demoralized: he could not successfully complete his studies in architecture, his guarantee for the future. But seeing Eileen again, the "failure" is seized with the same courageous determination, the same defiance of despair that is the psychological basis of *Man's Castle* and *Little Man, What Now?* "The failure is all on the outside—not in my heart! I still have my two hands to work for you—let's get married now!" Sean encourages them to dare what the previous generation missed. Everything remains to be done.

The American press praised *Song o' My Heart* almost unanimously, and domestically it earned $1,200,000 thanks to the film's cultural appeal in big cities such as New York, Chicago, Boston, Philadelphia, Los Angeles and San Francisco. It is difficult to judge the work in its entirety, as the version conserved and restored by the American Film Institute in 1971 is but a shadow of the original. The wide-screen 70mm prints seem lost; almost all the Irish exteriors (except for the McCormacks' cottage) have disappeared; and on the soundtrack, only the songs and a few minutes of dialogue have survived; the rest of the action is silent, with subtitles.[11] A full-dialogue version was discovered in 1974.

For Borzage, the success of both *They Had to See Paris* and *Song o' My Heart* marked an uneventful transition from silent films to talkies, with its share of trial and error, but mostly it allowed him to recover on a strictly commercial level after the slump of 1928–29, and regain the confidence of the Front Office. However, for management, the situation had shifted. After his fuming attack on Metro-Goldwyn-Mayer, William Fox had bad luck. A serious car accident had kept him away from control for too long and the new Hoover administration prosecuted him for violating the antitrust laws; the debts contracted by his enormous transactions accumulated. "Black Thursday" on Wall Street, October 24, 1929, was the final straw: Fox stocks plummeted from $119 to $1! Fox fell into the hands of the Chase National Bank in Manhattan. In April 1930, the pioneer, bankrupt, handed over the presidency to Harley C. Clarke, a Chicago industrialist, who would try to reestablish the company financially. William Fox retired from movies. On the West Coast, studio head Sheehan, more powerful than ever, remained temporarily in charge. But from then on the company was in decline.

* * *

With *Liliom*, his next production, Borzage continued the momentum marking the end of his silent period. Ignoring what was in vogue with almost suicidal pride, he undertook his most stylistically original work of the new decade. Hungarian Férenc Molnár's fantastical play, a fiasco in Budapest in December 1909, had been staged in the U.S. in a translation by the scriptwriter of *7th Heaven* and *A Farewell to Arms*, Benjamin Glazer![12] This "dramatic fantasy" has a long film history: as early as 1919, Michael Curtiz, then Kertész Mihály, filmed a version of *Liliom* in Magyar studios that remained unfinished due to political upheaval. In Hollywood in 1921, Maxwell Karger brought the play to the screen as *A Trip to Paradise*. Fritz Lang, in exile in Paris in December 1933, filmed the version best known to movie buffs, not forgetting the Technicolor-CinemaScope spectacle *Carousel* (1956), a pleasant adaptation of the Rodgers and Hammerstein musical by Henry King. Lang's film, starring Charles Boyer and Madeleine Ozeray, is the most obvious means of comparison, especially as it was financed by a subsidiary of Fox, Erich Pommer's short-lived Fox Europa.

Sheehan acquired the rights to the play on the advice of actor Paul Muni, a recruit of Chicago's Yiddish Theater newly arrived in Hollywood. Muni, still an unknown in film, humbly wanted to obtain the lead. As management only offered him the part of Fiscur, a thug (in the film: Buzzard), he broke his contract; he scored the following year in *Scarface*. As far as Sheehan was concerned, *Liliom* was a "deluxe" piece, unclassifiable, immediately reserved for Borzage and his favorite couple, Janet Gaynor and Charles Farrell. Playwright S. N. Behrman and Sonya Levien wrote the script; in charge of music was the brother of famous operetta composer, Leo Fall, Richard, whom Sheehan had expressly brought in from Vienna.[13] However, the situation became complicated when Janet Gaynor pulled out: far off in Hawaii, the star refused any more film offers unless Fox added a clause to her contract stipulating she would no longer have to appear in insipid musical comedies such as *Sunny Side Up* or *High Society Blues* (D. Butler). The studio suspended her without salary, but the actress held tight until Sheehan caved in — after seven months of "punishment."[14] Meanwhile, this unfortunate show of strength — Janet Gaynor would have been ideal as Julie!— meant that *Liliom*'s casting had to be completely reconsidered: Joel McCrea was tested for the lead, Mary Philbin and Maureen O'Sullivan were considered for Julie. Farrell, designated in a poll organized by "The Chicago Tribune" and "The New York Daily News" as "the most popular man in movies," remained at the head of the list. Management, however, did not rely on Hollywood's female candidates; Borzage decided to give a young New York actress a chance, Rose Hobart (remarked in A. Casella's *Death Takes a Holiday*, where she fell in love with Death). Farrell did not get along with her at all, in front of or behind the camera, but Rose Hobart knew Molnár's play inside out, having played the carousel barker's daughter (last act) alongside the original actors, Le Gallienne and Schildkraut.[15]

In spite of various interferences, the filmmaker claimed entire responsibility for the film; the credits are perfectly clear, beginning with "Frank Borzage's *Liliom* by Franz Molnár." Yet the more the script developed, the more the studio management worried, as the central character was disreputable (in Hungarian, "Liliom" means "tough as leather") and the intrusion of the supernatural was disconcerting. Metro's silent version, *A Trip to Paradise*, had at least adapted Molnár's story for American tastes: the innocent victim of a conspiracy, Liliom (alias Curley, the brave circus boy in Coney Island) survives his wounds after having only dreamed — under the effect of ether, on the operating table — of a stay in the great beyond. Borzage insisted on remaining very faithful to the original, in spite of negative advance warning by management. The Hays Office, Hollywood's own censorship office, had very serious reservations as the unmarried Julie becomes pregnant and the description of Heaven was "irreverent"; marriage between the lovers was imperative, the fantastic beyond had to be represented as "the delirium of the dying," and the archangel Gabriel had to disappear, etc.[16] Will H. Hays had in fact just published a new version of the moral requirements the profession set for itself to prevent local censorship, the "Motion Picture Production Code" (March 1930), approved by all the studios ... on paper. But the threat of the industry coming under their jurisdiction was real, the puritans were gaining ground. For the moment, Borzage could still turn a deaf ear. A few days before filming began, Sol Wurtzel (Murnau and Stroheim's personal enemy at Fox), who was supervising the enterprise during Sheehan's absence, convened those in charge: "I don't like a picture," he growled, "where the hero dies in the middle! Especially if he's Charlie Farrell." "In *7th Heaven*,' Borzage reminded Wurtzel, "the hero goes blind." "Yeah," the studio executive shot back, "but a blind man can still go to bed!"[17] Alas, the public proved him right.

To calm the company's apprehensions, Borzage began his film with the catchy, but provisional title of *Devil with Women*.[18] Filming, from May 19 to July 24, 1930, occurred entirely under the studio's spotlights, including "outdoor" scenes. Looking back, the aesthetic preferences of Borzage and his collaborators from *Lucky Star*, Oliver (sets), Lyons (photo) and Levien (script) were unusually bold for Hollywood; the phenomenon can only be explained by Sheehan's absence and the disorganization caused by the power struggles between Manhattan and California. Molnár's play was subtitled "Life and Death of a Gallows Bird. An Urban Legend." With this premise of extra-temporality, of legend, the filmmaker's approach, at all levels of direction, is one of resolute antirealism. Placing itself immediately in a transcendental perspective, Borzage's *Liliom* takes the opposite view of Fritz Lang's film. The Viennese director displays the picturesque side of carnival life with his incomparable editing genius, breathing life into the poetry of the urban areas, the slimy bars and the smart-alecky bad boys. But aside from a few slow-paced passages, the weakness of Lang's work lies in this realistic atmosphere of populist French drama (close to René Clair's *Under the Roofs of Paris*) which contrasts so utterly with the "afterlife sequences," when the film abruptly branches off into a kind of postcard phantasmagoria in the style of Méliès. The difference is even more noticeable among the actors, whose often excessive mimicry and light comedy numbers so characteristic of early French talkies (aside from its retro charm) clash involuntarily.

With Borzage, however, the theatricality is in large part intentional. As microphones were far away, intonations were halting and diction accentuated (involuntarily calling to mind the distancing effects sought by Brecht), the echo of the voices harmonizing naturally with

The geometrical abstraction of the sets suggests a parallel "elsewhere": Charles Farrell and Rose Hobart in *Liliom* (1930).

the elements of an abstract universe. The sets of unusual sobriety seem to be influenced by the geometrical abstraction extolled by European schools in the twenties—like Laslo Moholy-Nagy's "Machinism," Casimir Malevitch's "Suprematism" or El Lissitzky's "Constructivism." The railroad tracks, semaphore signals and embankments are concentrated, due to the lighting, in a composition of rectangles, cubes, circles, triangles, structured into rhythm and asymmetrical balancing. While suggesting space, these compositions tend to negate perceptible reality—and thus indicate a parallel "elsewhere." (At the Parisian premiere in 1923, Georges and Ludmilla Pitoëff had described the play as a kind of "geometrical enchantment," a kind of dreamlike *Caligari* set in diamond-shaped compositions.) The interiors of the houses are totally pared down: no knickknacks, and furniture reduced to only what is necessary: a couch, table, staircase, etc. The trees in the parks are just leafless branches reaching to the sky, a firmament whose only stars are thousands of flashing lights and carnival-like attractions. The lighting also conveys unrealism: in violent chiaroscuro, to create clean images stripped of ambiguity, nuance or hazy textures; characters and objects are subjected to one same luminous source, a key light. Emphasizing artificial light accentuates the night's omnipresence, as the spareness of the music draws attention to the silence, since Borzage uses Fall's melodies—and sound effects in general—with intentional parsimony. (Fall's symphonic language masterfully blends the clichés of "zingara" music, the suaveness of Emmerich Kálmán and the pomp of an Edward Elgar.) Very generally speaking, this theatricality, undertaken unwaveringly, confers an astonishingly modern aspect to the film.

The action of the drama is well known, so we will only mention aspects which differ from the play and Lang's remake. Borzage begins with the departure of the two maids, Julie (R. Hobart) and her friend Marie, who want to spend their evening off at Budapest's Luna-Park; Julie turns away an amorous carpenter (Walter Abel), as she only dreams of Liliom, the seductive carousel barker, the idol of all the women; no one can draw the ladies to the merry-go-round like him. But his jealous boss, the shapely Madame Muskát (Estelle Taylor), catches him flirting openly with Julie, whom he has just met. The filmmaker shows him whirling around on the carousel, gripping the wooden tiger his conquest has just climbed upon, then at her waist, so that the up-and-down movements between the mount and the couple unequivocally foreshadow the sexual act. Ordered to drive Julie away, Liliom stands up to his mistress and loses his job. The confrontation takes place right behind the fairground stalls — moving spots of light on a smooth wall indicate the ride's proximity — but the carousels, crowds of people, and barrel organs are silenced, as if enchanted. Liliom takes Julie for a beer at a café where music is played, where the dense crowd surrounding them seems almost static and the conversation unintelligible. For the first time, we hear Fall's music: the languorous harmonies of gypsy violins, with their syncopations in minor keys, the glissandi of the cymbal, the nostalgic laments of a choir of women invading this magical sequence where the essential is expressed between the dialogues, via a staggering shot of Julie, beautiful, serious, staring intensely at the selfish, smug man. Later, in the middle of the night, Liliom and Julie are walking in the park overlooking the rides, the fair with its Ferris wheel is all lit up — but mysteriously silent. The couple is stopped and questioned by police, threatening shadows with deep voices. A policeman warns Julie about Liliom, this notorious good-for-nothing, "a seducer of serving maids" who lives off his victims, taking their savings. Once alone, Julie swears to Liliom that if she had any money, she'd give it to him without hesitating. This declaration moves the shady character so much so that his encounter with love (which he is really incapable of sharing) leads him to go live with her. The couple lie down in the grass...

Three months go by. The lovers are living in Julie's aunt's photography studio: a bare room several feet high with an immense bay window looking over the amusement park's roller coaster, a silent, mechanical spectacle, whose thousands of lights shine in the night. Jobless, Liliom is dozing on the couch near the window while Julie busies herself with housework. "Look at him, he sleeps all day like an aristocrat!" grumbles Aunt Hulda, but, incorrigible, Julie comes to his defense: "He sleeps to forget, and when he wakes, I can see the pain in his heart." The setting has something both distressing and threatening about it. The constant presence of the rides filling the window above Liliom illustrates his desire to desert, the call of the carousels, the easy life (like the whistling of the trains for Bill, in *Man's Castle*); but this ghostly vision, rising up then going plunging to the tracks, also foreshadows the disastrous destiny which the hero cannot escape: Death awaits. "It's not like the carousel that goes round and round and gets nowhere, the train goes up and up...," he remarks later, implicitly declaring that he is, above all, trying to escape his own emptiness (expressed by the "emptiness" of the set). Waking up, Liliom is irritable, and before roaming around with Buzzard (Lee Tracy), a crook, he loses control and hits Julie. "What a dirty life I'm leading!" he vows to her, as he goes out, full of remorse but incapable of expressing it. The carpenter, in love with her, appears at the top of the stairs: "I saw him strike you!" "I'm very happy, it didn't hurt me," replies Julie, crouched on the last step and obstinately refusing his advances, which promise an ordered life such as Marie's marriage to Wolf, the simple-minded porter. Soon after, Madame Muskát resurfaces to convince Liliom to return to the carousel. He is on the point of consenting, when Julie informs him she is carrying his child.

She has barely turned her back when Liliom, overjoyed, crosses the Luna-Park announcing the good news (a tightrope walker almost loses his balance, Madame Muskát makes a face). To be able to finance his future family (whom he intends to bring to the U.S.), he agrees to take part in a job with Buzzard — robbing a cashier — and to that effect conceals a kitchen knife. Julie notices it too late.

Liliom and Buzzard await their victim at the bottom of an embankment, along the railway track. Ill at ease, Liliom has hidden his knife under his jacket ("my heart keeps jumping at the knife") and, as opposed to Molnár and Lang, Borzage multiplies the "heavenly" warnings. As for the railway tracks, "they go all the way to Vienna, and farther, to where the boats leave for America," but visually the tracks get lost in the emptiness of the night; a luxury train, appearing out of nowhere, stops for a second before them (the noise barely perceptible); comfortable travelers sprawl in deathly silence behind the windows, as if in an illusory dream. Liliom is worried, thinks he is being watched by a sparrow on a semaphore ("sparrow" is one of Julie's nicknames); his evil spirit ("the buzzard") sneers. "What about the next world? When I come up before the Lord God, and He asks me about this robbery, what am I gonna say then?" insists Liliom. The job fails: the cashier was armed. Buzzard manages to escape, but the police are on Liliom's tail and the cashier threatens him with fifteen years of prison. Wanting to save his future family from dishonor, Liliom stabs himself at the top of the embankment. Julie rushes up breathlessly and embraces his body, which lies at the feet of the indifferent policemen (discussing cigars, salaries and mosquitoes).

The singular stylistic "climate" of the film has carefully prepared the viewer for the sequences to come, which now follow without disrupting the tone. Liliom is lying on his couch — now his bier — in the studio lit only from the outside by the roller coaster, and from the inside by a single candle. The Hungarian melody resumes... Rose Hobart remembers this scene perfectly, during which Borzage taught her the difference between stage and film acting.

> He had told me the very first day that I had to remember that the camera only registered what you thought, it did not pick up emotion, which I dismissed as his having only worked with "picture" actors. When we came to the death scene with that great big head close up, Frank asked me if I wanted to rehearse it or shoot it and I answered that I'd like to just shoot it. After all, I had watched Eva Le Gallienne play that scene for months while I had been touring with her and Joseph Schildkraut when I played the daughter in the last scene with the original theater production. We shot the scene and when I got through, I looked up and saw some of the crew standing just behind the lights with tears in their eyes and I thought to myself "Wow, I've done it." Then Frank shot it 36 times more. By the third "take" I was talking to myself and the make-up man was blowing camphor in my eyes to create those perfect tears rolling down my face. When he finally said "O.K., print the 18th and the 32nd," I asked if he would print the first one too and he agreed. The next morning we went in to see the rushes and that enormous face come on screen and after about 10 seconds it became ludicrous. Absolutely nothing was happening to my face and you could hardly understand what I was saying because of my tears, it was awful! The other two takes were great. You could see what I was thinking and you could hear clearly what I said. When I thanked Frank for showing me what he had told me about the difference between theater and screen acting, he added one more thing to it. "Don't forget that you have to give that 'performance' once so that you can duplicate it." I have been eternally grateful to him ever since.[19]

From that point on, Borzage distinguishes himself from both Molnár and Lang. Julie leans over the dying man tenderly, entreating him to sleep in peace and reading the Gospel of St. John ("I am the Resurrection and the Life, said the Lord"); at these words, Liliom opens his eyes, seeks the young woman's hand and confesses his love. "I saw the trains take

Charles Farrell faces the heavenly railway in *Liliom* (1930).

us to America. I was a coward to stab myself. But maybe I'll come back on a train... The train, it's coming, do you hear it? A special train for Liliom... Julie, I'm traveling..." In the distance, a strange train moves along the luminous tracks of the roller coaster, goes down toward the studio, goes noiselessly through the bay window and into the room where it stops clean. Liliom leaves his body and climbs on board the train, accompanied by two angels of death wearing brimmed helmets. Partially transparent, the heavenly railway leaves from whence it came, crossing an interminable series of aqueducts above the clouds... The 1934 remake portrays the great beyond of children's books, full of false naïveté and veiled references: Fritz Lang, agnostic, distances himself with irony, but in doing so, undermines the logic of his story. The angels carrying his Liliom at the end, fly over Notre-Dame, pass in front of Saturn, cross the milky way, etc. At the office of heaven, the winged orderly reads "Paradise-Noon, the daily newspaper of heavenly information," answers the telephone and stamps forms. Liliom flirts with the cherubic typist, signs forbidding all sorts of activities show that, inhabited by cretinous civil servants, Heaven is just as bureaucratic and arbitrary as Earth. Finally, perpetually confronted by low-ranking police officers, Liliom denies his guilt, then gets confused by testimony filmed by celestial spies! Nothing of the sort occurs in Borzage's film, which takes Liliom's candor seriously, simply embodying his metaphorical obsession with the rails.

The heavens are strewn with railway tracks, partially buried in the clouds. Liliom walks down the train's corridor, passing sinister-looking criminals (among them, a president of a railway company who is angered by this demeaning proximity!) and ending up in the "compartment of suicides." Except for the good-natured but furtive appearance of the old archangel Gabriel, the entire last part is treated seriously; images bathe in slightly filtered monotone lighting contrasting with the darkness of existence on earth. This lighting allows real questions to be addressed, and facts to be reconsidered in the perspective of eternity; no more drama, no more music. Liliom rebels against his fate. He is taken to the end of the train where the Chief Magistrate awaits him, courteous and affable, dressed in tails (H. B. Warner). The chief meets with him in his small drawing room: "Are you really as tough as you pretend?"—and offers him a cigarette. He then explains to him that it's easy to have a big heart when you have no responsibilities: "People suppose that when they die, their difficulties are ending for them — by making your heart stop beating, you can cancel all your responsibilities—but until you have been completely forgotten, you will not be finished with the earth, even if you are dead." The Magistrate — who complains of being "surrounded by 'yes men'"— experiences secret sympathy for Liliom, whose frankness and temperament amuse him. He regretfully condemns him to ten years in "the hot place," after which he may return to earth for 24 hours to perform a "good deed" for his daughter, whom he does not yet know. Gabriel's horn announces his sentence. Gratefully, Liliom accepts. "This (condemnation) hurts you more than it does me, your Honor," he says, before climbing aboard a train to hell (which, like a Flash Gordon missile, emits sulfurous sparks); the Magistrate gives him glasses to protect his eyes. We are miles away from Lang's tragicomedy: derision gives way to compassion and social satire to a philosophical tale.

Ten years later, Liliom comes back down to Earth. Once again the setting has a theatrical aspect; the celestial train stops in front of Julie's house, which has the angular, tortuous contours of "caligarism." Liliom is pleased to surprise Julie fending off the carpenter. Passing himself off as a beggar, he approaches Louise, her little girl (Dawn O'Day, the future Ann Shirley). She tells him that her father, "the most wonderful barker in the park, everybody loved him," died in America. In vain, Liliom tries to win her affection with card tricks, then with the horn borrowed from the archangel, but its sound cannot be heard by humans! Liliom is so insistent that the girl becomes frightened; he gets angry, loses control and slaps her. Louise tells her mother about the strange episode: "He hit me, I heard the sound of it. But it didn't hurt me, it felt just like a kiss..." Julie answers her that she has also experienced this feeling, a long time ago. Repentant, the irascible fool watches the scene from the train platform and wants to intervene; the Magistrate consoles, saying he hasn't failed, but would ruin everything going back, as "the memory of you makes them much happier than ever you could make 'em." The train returns to heaven at the sound of a violin's lament. This melancholy ending differs from Molnár's text, where Liliom's repeated failure brings about his definitive damnation.

Fox's publicity department was completely perplexed as how to promote the film; theater owners were advised to insist on the "heartbreaker aspect" (alternative title: *The Loves of Liliom*) and to not publicize anything about the hero's death or his return to earth: "We strongly advise against the use of stills which show such fantastic things as the trains to the Hereafter."[20] It was a lost cause. As can be imagined, *Liliom* was a commercial flop, perhaps the most spectacular one of Borzage's entire career. Only Mordaunt Hall defended him in the *New York Times,* speaking of "a most compelling and surprising talking picture."[21] In general, newspapers refrained from mentioning its characteristic direction, unless it was to mention that "the pictorial effect of the picture is a bit affected and arty."[22] To promote the film's release in Los Angeles, Fox mobilized Will Rogers in person; his roasting of local politicians easily attracted more onlookers than the trains of Purgatory! Its original point of view went over the heads of the public and the first ravages of the Depression were hardly conducive to such a morose topic. Charles Boyer portrayed the brutish hoodlum who doesn't see the evil he does and loses himself in it with total innocence. Charles Farrell (sporting a mustache and a striped sweater) portrays the naughty boy, but one imbued with the graces—and possibilities of redemption — of childhood, as even his suicide is less of an escape than a burst of honesty. Deemed too youthful and inexperienced for the role, Farrell met with a great deal of sarcasm; in retrospect, it is his partner Rose Hobart, although a very subtle actress, who appears to be the weak link here. Although timid, humble, pure, her "victim, fulfilled by her sacrifice" displays a determination, a harshness not attenuated by her closed, Garbo-like features. While Lang's Julie (Madeleine Ozeray) is clearly a whiner, Borzage's doesn't lack emotion, but rather warmth, and perhaps also the kind of grace that Janet Gaynor would have brought to the part. In the face of the hero's apparent insensitivity and the spare setting, this radiant love is cruelly lacking. Rose Hobart does manage, however, to be deeply moving when Borzage draws out her capacity for expansiveness and total self sacrifice so characteristic of his female characters. With its stark contrasts, its flaunted unrealism and false theatricality, *Liliom* is more fascinating at first than immediately captivating. Its beauty only appears after several viewings, then never leaves. This said, the film is a veritable UFO in the Hollywood landscape and its openly experimental nature could only discourage crowds. In certain aspects, this *Liliom* was thirty years ahead of its time. Appalled by its representation of Heaven, the British Board of Censors forbad the film practically throughout the Commonwealth (October 1930); Catholic countries such as Belgium, Italy and Spain authorized it — after cutting its last half hour: "The End" appears when Liliom dies! In France and Germany, the film was never released; Austria (Molnár obliged) only showed the original version with subtitles. Which is to say that *Liliom* is practically unknown in Europe.

* * *

Overnight, it seemed Borzage was "finished" in the eyes of Hollywood. This catastrophe caused two productions already underway to be cancelled, which were to be filmed in bichrome Multicolor: *Alone with You* with Janet Gaynor and John Derrick, and *The Man Who Came Back*, a script by Behrman & Levien that describes the mutual redemption of the playboy son of an alcoholic father (Farrell) and an opium-addicted cabaret singer (Gaynor), between Shanghai and Honolulu; all Borzage's magic may have made this melodrama palatable, but Raoul Walsh, who inherited the project unenthusiastically and had Edwin Burke rewrite it (Janet Gaynor: "my worst film") did not manage to do so. To rationalize the production of talkies, Fox had just introduced the job of "associate producer" whose task was to supervise preparation, budget and direction of all studio properties; in November 1929 the company already had four of them, each in charge of four to five films, and partially responsible for six to eight others. This meant that the filmmaker's creative freedom was seriously curtailed. To make matters worse, Borzage also lost his faithful collaborator Harry Oliver. The set designer went over to MGM (*Viva Villa!*, *The Good Earth*) and retired in 1946 in the Coachvella Valley desert, where he spent the rest of his days as a hermit.

In order to compensate for the studio's losses, Borzage was obliged to agree to direct *Doctors' Wives*, a simple bread and butter film shot between December 17, 1930, and January 23, 1931. Wrongly convinced that her husband, a prominent surgeon (Warner Baxter), is cheating on her with one of his numerous patients, a haughty, young newlywed (Joan Bennett) begins assiduously visiting her husband's best friend, also a doctor (Victor Varconi). The husband now believes she is cheating on him, until he learns that his wife has been taking a nursing course to be near to him. The plot, which uses a number of hospital soap opera clichés, revolves around the anguishing question of "Is the patient the enemy of every doctor's wife?," finally decreeing that "beautiful women should never get ill" (the publicity slogans of the film). The filmmaker enhances this series of absurdities by a few deft camera movements and by judiciously inserting the leitmotif of the telephone, dreaded by the women in the title. The naked backs of the overly pretty patients were cut by the censor in a 1936 re-release.

Will Rogers animates the light comedy *Young As You Feel*. An unoriginal work, but often funny, it was filmed between March 1 and April 2 under the title *Cure for the Blues*, and did well at the box office. A skillful, dyspeptic businessman, Lemuel (Rogers), has a strict code of conduct, to which he believes he owes his millions. His two playboy sons do not emulate him: one gallivants about and the other is an avant-garde bohemian in Greenwich Village. But the golden progeny is shocked when they discover their rigid father in the arms of frivolous Fleurette (Fifi d'Orsay, of course). From then on he frequents the races and nightclubs, and Lemuel visibly rejuvenates. His epitaph will be: "Died in his infancy," he declares before heading for "gay Paree," while his sons take over the family factory. Another comedy planned for Will Rogers, *The Country Doctor (from Don Marquis' work), never went beyond the synopsis stage.

The wheel of fortune turned once again with *Bad Girl*, whose enormous success was a surprise for everyone—including Borzage! Published in 1928, *Bad Girl* was a strongly autobiographical bestseller by Viña Delmar, the Françoise Sagan of the jazz era, who was only 23, with a Louise Brooks–style hairdo and a manifest sense of self-publicity; America loved the confession of this child of the century (written in secret collaboration with her husband Eugen Delmar). Transformed into a successful play in the fall of 1930, the controversial subject would launch the career of young Sylvia Sidney on Broadway.[23] Both the novel and play paint a portrait of young wage-earners of the twenties, shown through the flirtation and the marriage of a New York typist ("Romance of the working girl") barely out of her teens and the slightly traumatic experience of her first pregnancy. They speak openly of the issues of motherhood and even of abortion. But the publicity was misleading, because aside from her premarital loss of virginity, Dot, Mrs. Delmar's "bad girl," is really very good! Speculating on the notoriousness of the title, Hollywood sensed a goldmine. Paramount, Universal, MGM, Pathé (Joe Kennedy) and Columbia successively took options on the story (1928–30); all reneged, either intimidated by the Hays Office which predicted numerous cuts, or because the "revolting" subject matter—obstetrics!—was not dramatic enough to be transposed to the screen.

When *Bad Girl*, bought on a whim, landed in Fox's offices, enthusiasm was very low. It was understood that a film carrying such a title would be conceivable only after radically purging the text, eliminating everything that had made the novel a bestseller and the play a success. At the same time, the studio organized a hypocritical publicity campaign for *Bad Girl*, claiming: "Everybody knows this girl ... there's one in every town ... tumult in her heart ... she wanted things, clothes, boy friends, fun, gayety, kisses..." Borzage, assigned to the project, at first refused it, then yielded to the management's embarrassed insistence. The studio had decided not to renew his soon-to-expire contract; *Bad Girl* would be his swan song, thought management.[24] Once acceptable in the eyes of the censor, the script was so lacking in commercial appeal that management lost interest; fortunately, the film's budget was laughable (less than $100,000), the actors were unknown, shooting lasted only 21 days (between June 1 and July 4, 1931), the affair would be a write-off. Given these circumstances, for the first time since the wild adventure that was *Liliom*, Borzage had a fairly free hand. He envisaged Spencer Tracy in the role of Eddie, but Fox's Manhattan Front Office wanted to give another beginner a chance, James Dunn, a rising star of the New York stage. Sally Eilers, who began as a child with Mack Sennett and played ingenues alongside Buster Keaton, was the "bad girl": this little brunette had the reputation of using the filthiest language in Hollywood. It was claimed that her expressions were even more scandalous than those of Carole Lombard — which was saying a lot!

Urged by the Hays Office,[25] but also out of personal inclination, Borzage discreetly circumvented everything that, in the era, was provocative, without ever losing sight of his subject. The opening "gag" was characteristic of his approach: Dot — short for Dorothy (S. Eilers) — in an elegant wedding gown, a bouquet of lilies in her arms, is nervously getting ready for the supreme moment, the "wedding march" is played; the young woman solemnly enters (dolly-out) — into a fashion show. Male clients stare at her lustfully; disillusioned, like Angela in *Street Angel* ("when it comes to women, men have only got one idea in their heads. I know all the answers, men have been insulting me for years"), but with a ready tongue, the model coolly fends off invitations from men of all ages, including her boss ("my husband is a prizefighter"). Accompanied by her friend Edna (Minna Gombell), a still-young widow, Dot then spends the evening in Coney Island where men pursue her all the more. Returning, on the boat, Edna points out an unusual creature to her: a handsome guy who isn't trying to flirt (J. Dunn)! Insulted, Dot bets she can sway him and approaches him, strumming a ukulele. She has cause to regret it: the young man (Eddie) puts her firmly in her place, pointing out her contradictory behavior ("If you don't want guys to salute you, take down your flag!"). Dot explodes: "I wouldn't be found dead with you!" Dissolve: Eddie has brought Dot home. At the foot of a stairway of a poor rental building in the Bronx, the young woman, radiant, tells him she absolutely must go in — and then sits down on a step.

The sequence that follows introduces, barely perceptibly, a change in style: the camera, which at first moved a lot, becomes more and more unobtrusive, focusing all the attention on the two protagonists, while the shots last longer to preserve their miraculous spontaneity. They both reveal their past, their dreams; Dot, who works in a clothing shop, lost her mother at birth; she lives under the rigid watch of her eldest brother Jim, who beats her when she comes in late. Eddie is a salesman and repairman in an electrical store; he has been saving for six years to open his own radio shop. The conversation is often interrupted by tenants going in and out: a drunken husband, a couple bickering noisily, a prostitute, an old woman whose mother has just died, etc. Pathetic specimens of a failed existence, each time they cut a path between the lovers on the stairs; Borzage uses this vivid commentary both as social testimony and a realistic counterpoint, a potential threat to the couple's future. "She didn't do that kid no favor, bringing him into the world," says Eddie, indignant. "What's the kid to look forward to? Born on a second floor — and probably die on the fifth." He concludes, "There's a lot of things in life besides money, but you gotta have money to find 'em." The following evening, Eddie, busy repairing a radio, forgets his date with Dot. She waits for him in the rain, then, furious, goes to him in his room. Explanations are transformed into kisses, rain continues unabated outside, and she remains near him: "let's stay here where there are ashtrays." Dot comes home at the same time as the milkman is making his rounds: "My brother will kill me," she cries. Dismissing his notions of remaining single, Eddie suggests they get married the next day, because "lots of people are married and happy" (upstairs, a couple is slamming doors, yelling). As anticipated, Jim coolly throws his sister out and Edna takes in her friend after telling the brute what she thinks of him ("See you in the cemetery").

Then begins a domestic tragicomedy fueled by misunderstandings and whose pathos is kept in check by cheerful sarcasm. As Eddie takes a long time coming to marry her, Dot believes he's ditched her; the two friends burst into tears at the kitchen table when the "fiancé" appears. "Who's dead?" he asks, dumbfounded; Edna refuses to attend the wedding

Early morning love chat: Sally Eilers and James Dunn in *Bad Girl* (1931).

ceremony (which Borzage spares us): "I hate those things, deaths, funerals, etc." The height of the misunderstanding comes with the pregnancy, as each one is convinced that the other doesn't want to hear of children. Dot has virtually an obsessional fear of giving birth since her own mother died when she was an infant; Eddie has been traumatized by his poverty-ridden adolescence. Not realizing his wife is pregnant, he secretly places his savings (intended for the shop) in a smart apartment overlooking the East River. Then he organizes a party, letting Dot believe that the place belongs to friends. Eddie gives her a tour— Dot is enchanted—before telling her the truth and making a toast: "My old lady used to scrub floors in an office building. At four o'clock in the morning she went to work, sick or well, summer or winter—and for what? To bring up a couple of kids and die, die before there was ever any comfort for her. Not for Dot! Every nickel I make, we're gonna spend it on ourselves!" Hysterical, Dot shouts for him to be quiet and reveals her state. From that point on, Eddie does household chores so as not to tire his wife (Edna, tongue in cheek: "You've got a new washerwoman, I see! Nobody knows what a husband suffers when his wife has a baby..."). But the misunderstanding persists till the end: his wife, he believes, has hidden her condition from him because she doesn't want the baby. Without Dot's knowing, Eddie finds the most renowned obstetrician in New York and, bursting into tears in his office, begs him to deliver his wife's baby: only his presence can reassure him.

So he can pay the astronomical fees of this "doctor for millionaires," Eddie deprives himself of everything and works nights. His wife thinks he is fleeing their nest; put off by the impending birth. Even the evening she enters the hospital, Eddie arrives two hours late; his face is bruised and bandaged, as if he'd been in a fight in a bar. The truth is, the "deserter" has pulled his weight and paid for it dearly: in one of the most delightful sequences in the film, the impending melodrama plunges into the comical. Eddie volunteers to fight a professional boxer in the ring, for ten dollars a round. He endures a series of blows, the viewers suffering along with him; his face swollen, he clutches onto the champion and whispers in his ear to not finish him off yet. The boxer now knows the story, and whispers to Eddie to lean on him and hold his breath. He pretends to punch him then, and, still whispering, they exchange confidences ("I got two of 'em"). Dot has resolved to leave a husband who doesn't want her baby, until the final warning sign of maternity clarifies the situation. In the taxi bringing the three of them home, Eddie instructs the chauffeur to drive carefully, because, according to the saying, he could be "driving the future president of the United States!"

There is room in the story to emphasize the characters— alert, lively, captivating — and the links forged between them. Only visually, in certain medium-close shots, or on the roof of the new apartment building, in the nocturnal compositions designed with exact symmetry between Dot and Eddie, does the intensity of their relationship appear. Because even though hopelessly in love, Eddie is incapable of admitting his love and hides his sentimental nature behind a facade of bravado. Like Bill in *Man's Castle*, he calls Dot "stupid" and "unconscious," and when she, impulsively, expresses her feelings to him, he retorts clumsily: "A guy can have a worse wife than you" or answers with a surly "okay." The dialogue, fast and furious, never theatrical, goes beyond simply imparting information. Thoughts and emotions are hidden beneath a staccato stream of sometimes overlapping wisecracks, some of which are in slang; their naturalistic crudeness diffuses the sentimentality. We find this same characteristic among the secondary characters, such as the energetic Edna. For Dot, Edna is a protective, big sister; her shrill verbal exchanges with Eddie, whom she nicknames "grouchy," are as natural as family squabbles between family members ("He doesn't like me, but I don't care. Napoleon also had some enemies"); the unexpressed respect and sympathy they have for each other are hidden behind an uninterrupted stream of invectives.

Lacking the pictorial scope of the preceding masterpieces, today *Bad Girl* remains largely ignored. Its major qualities work against it: its modesty, storyline and preoccupations are too familiar (but upheld by resolutions which are original). Directed without affectation, it is elegant in its obviousness. Although 100 percent talkie, the film never appears wordy, as the dialogue rings true and fills the images with its rhythm. Critics at the time were amazed at this piece stripped of all conventional ingredients— love triangles, jealousy, sex appeal or crimes— but buoyed by the cheerful exuberance that apparently effortlessly metamorphoses a mixture of little nothings into a gem of subtlety and charm. *Bad Girl* may be seen as a kind of forerunner to films such as François Truffaut's *Stolen Kisses* or *Bed and Board*. We can still best evaluate the filmmaker's contribution by noting that the most memorable scenes do not appear in Viña Delmar's book: the opening in the wedding gown, the surprise of the apartment bought secretly, Eddie at the obstetrician's, the boxing match, etc.

Bad Girl was considered Borzage's first "realistic" film; like the silent comedies *The First Year, Early to Wed* and the melodrama *The Nth Commandment*, this two-person *Kammerspiel* depicts the first ups and downs of married life in a working class or lower-middle class environment. But current events of the era give the picture a serious tone: the specter of the Depression haunts the streets, the threat of poverty, the lack of money condition behavior: a general phenomenon, although subtly introduced. The furtive evocation of the social conditions of these "unimportant people" is interwoven naturally into the story, and is never condescending or self-pitying. The danger first lies within: Dot's morbid torment regarding giving birth and Eddie's, no less anguished, regarding deprivation.

Fears awakened by the arrival of the child they both want without daring to admit (neither to the spouse nor to themselves). A well-known theme: a destitute couple forces themselves to create a closed universe, a romantic shelter giving them the strength to transcend the difficulties of daily life; in order to preserve this state of grace, they must first overcome ignorance and pride that block communication between them, learn to have mutual trust, respect and understanding. This fundamental process of maturation is the subject of *Bad Girl*—like that of all Borzage's important works. After all, *The Pitch o' Chance*, in 1915, was about the same subject!

Bad Girl's unexpected success—for Fox, one of the biggest of the year, taking in $1,100,000 —put Borzage back in action, commercially and artistically. James Dunn and Sally Eilers were immediately cast together in two other films. The *New York Times* spoke of "A tender and appealing shadow story, one that even takes precedence over *7th Heaven*,"[26] then included the work in its famous "Ten Best List" (1931). But Hollywood's ultimate honor would come much later, when, having left Fox, the filmmaker was in the midst of completing *A Farewell to Arms* at Paramount: on November 18, 1932, the "Academy of Motion Picture Arts and Sciences" awarded Frank Borzage, for the second time, the Oscar for best director (Sternberg, for *Shanghai Express*, lost). *Bad Girl* even won a second Oscar for Edwin Burke's script and a nomination for best film of the year (1931–32). Curiously, the film was barely distributed in Europe; perhaps its subject matter was judged too local. *Bad Girl* spawned, among others, a Spanish version for South America renamed *Marido y Mujer* (October 1931), a mediocre "sequel" concocted by Viña Delmar, *Bad Boy* (also with James Dunn, 1935) and a 20th Century Fox remake in 1940.[27] Finally, historically, *Bad Girl* was notably at the origin of Erich von Stroheim's last film, *Walking Down Broadway*. Entering Fox in September 1931, Stroheim had to shoot—adding his own vinegary twist—a very similarly inspired little story (a young couple, Manhattan, the Depression), also played by James Dunn and Minna Gombell; the growing tension between Sheehan (who favored Stroheim), his rival-enemy Wurtzel (who hated the "Hun") and the New York bankers of the Front Office jammed up everything; filming was delayed several times, the film partly returned to be "corrected" by Edwin Burke and Alfred Werker (February 1933).[28] What had promised to be a "hard" version of *Bad Girl*, ended up, under the title *Hello Sister!*, as just a sentimental hybrid. The affair was symptomatic of Fox's progressive disintegration and explains Borzage's premature departure. In July 1931, the press announced that the filmmaker had refused to renew his contract if management would not allow him to work without supervision. Fox yielded the following month; Borzage, it was claimed, would direct Janet Gaynor in *Salomey Jane. It never materialized.

Of his two last films for the studio, only the first, *After Tomorrow* is of any interest, although it was hampered by all kinds of constraints. In setting their hearts on John Golden and Hugh S. Stange's bitter play, Fox was visibly trying to draw on the ingredients of *Bad Girl* and those of another slice of life acclaimed the previous season, *Street Scene* (Elmer Rice's Pulitzer-prizewinning play, and King Vidor's film of it). The protagonists, part of the lower-middle class ruined by the economic crisis, are more than ever confronted with material difficulties and the intense selfishness of their near ones. Unfortunately, the subject was as morose as the climate in which it was filmed (December 14, 1931—January 21, 1932). The filmmaker could count on two high quality collaborators: cinematographer James Wong Howe and artistic director William Darling, but the budget was so tight— three to four sets maximum, no tracking shots—and Borzage's freedom so restricted, that nothing ever came of it. With *Bad Girl*'s returns once again stirring up the management, Borzage was invited to repeat his miracle, by saving the unsalvageable! Charles Farrell was

Lovebirds (Charles Farrell and Marian Nixon) tormented by an intrusive and hysterical mother (Josephine Hull) in *After Tomorrow* (1932).

in the cast, but Janet Gaynor remained obstinate. Still on the lookout for a replacement to remake their "ideal couple," the studio gave a chance to the gentle, dark-haired Marian Nixon, under contract since 1925 (married to director William A. Seiter).

At the center of the tale, lovebirds Peter Piper and Sidney Taylor (Farrell-Nixon) have been despairing of getting married for four years; both are humble low wage-earners in the same Manhattan skyscraper; the least bit saved disappears into a "marriage fund." But Peter must also provide for the needs of his plump, hysterical, penurious mother who manipulates and overprotects her son ("a man's best friend is his mother"), persecutes Sidney with her jealousy ("There was a time when I didn't have to ask for your kisses") and refuses to share an apartment with the couple, which would at last allow them to live together. This was a plum role, which she had already played on the stage,[29] for the hilarious Josephine Hull, one of the crackpot aunts in Capra's *Arsenic and Old Lace* (1944). Sidney has dependents of her own: each week she must contribute when her family goes over their meager budget, due to her depressive mother, Elsie (Minna Gombell), a platinum blonde who mopes, reading "True Confessions," claiming she has a migraine when she cannot escape with her lover Jarvis, a subtenant, to her sister's studio. Sidney's father, Willie (William Collier, Sr.) is a likeable oaf, an inept, underpaid insurance agent, whom Elsie, a prisoner in the cockroach-infested basement of a rental, spends long evenings reproaching for having wasted "the best years of her life." It seems an inextricable situation when a ray of hope appears: Peter gets a raise. But while preparations in the neighborhood are underway for the wedding set for the next day, and Mrs. Piper exhausts herself with emotional blackmail, Mrs.

Taylor runs away with her lover (sought by police) to Canada. Her husband has a coronary — and the young people's "marriage fund" evaporates into hospital bills. In short, their libidos must once again wait to be sated, a nagging problem that Sidney finally lays on the table, when a rival in too short a skirt (Borzage inserts two medium-close shots of her legs) harasses her husband. But Peter refuses Sidney's "daring" invitation, a refusal more indicative of a dramatic device than of reality, and one which would make the censors purr. *Variety,* however, called it "a frank, intelligent conversation about sex ... still another indication that the talking picture is more and more contending with legit as modern adult entertainment."[30]

In the end, this saga of frustration, of salaries eaten up and family neuroses, not brightened by any ray of sunshine becomes wearisome; even the song the couple strikes up at the piano to lift their spirits (appropriately called "All the World Will Smile Again — After Tomorrow") fizzles out: Sidney bursts into tears before the end! Borzage's hands are tied, like those of his heroes. We aren't accustomed to seeing so much cruelty, so little humor in his films: moments of true emotion that free us from theatrical constraint are rare here. Worth mentioning is the intimate picnic on the 102nd floor during which words of love are exchanged, with mouths full, at the same place where, the day before, a businessman jumped off. Later, Elsie leaves the marital home telling her daughter she was an unwanted child; prostrated, the young woman stares for a long time at her fiancé to determine whether he wants children... The scriptwriters get out of this trap with a ludicrouse deus ex machina: Peter surprises his hypochondriac mother in the arms of Mr. Beardsley, a pudgy widower from whom he had borrowed $100 to invest in a chewing gum factory; Peter pretends to be shocked, ordering Beardsley to legitimize his "liaison" by marrying his mother, learning at the same time that, against all odds, his modest nest egg has grown considerably! Final kiss at Niagara Falls. The Hays Office had the last word, because in the theater, the salvational windfall is an attempt at redemption on the part of Elsie, the unworthy wife, and her lover. The abandoned husband, succumbing to a heart attack, hands over the money to the young people, letting them believe it is his secret savings. On the screen, Willie refuses this "dirty money" (as required by the moral principles of the Code): no forgiveness for the unfaithful; but his rigid Puritanism, which, once again, deprives his children, seems more like personal vengeance and makes all this human muddle only more nauseating. Sidney and Peter are too colorless to transcend it.

If *After Tomorrow* transgresses by a lack of human interest, *Young America* gets mired down in convention and its singularity is due basically to the presence of Spencer Tracy. Tracy owed his beginning in film to Will Rogers, who, captivated by his natural, good boy demeanor, took him under his wing, introducing him to Borzage and Sheehan, and then to the mysteries of polo. As Larry Swindle recalls, "Borzage and Rogers were Tracy's first good friends in Hollywood. He would usually lunch with one or both at the Fox commissary, and they showed him Hollywood life outside the studio, telling him to take the part he wanted and leave the rest alone."[31] Having been out of luck with *Bad Girl,* Tracy had great hope in *Young America.* However, after this commissioned film was completed (shot between February 13 and March 10, 1932) and failed at the box office, the filmmaker consoled him by promising him a real part, made to measure, in the near future: *Man's Castle.* Another oddity: thirteen-year-old Raymond Borzage, Bill's son, obtained the important part of Nutty without his uncle's knowledge, having made application to the studio as Raymond Cortella.[32] Announced as a John Ford project,[33] the comedy in which "two adopted orphans turn a quiet home into a merry madhouse" (publicity) turns into a melodrama focusing on juvenile delinquence, in such a way that Borzage's film may be considered a forerunner to works with social resonance such as *Dead End* and *Angels with Dirty Faces.*

But the plot (probably imposed, like the preceding one) quickly becomes preachy, to the point that *Variety* accused it of being "propaganda for juvenile courts."[34] Arthur, a teen-ager condemned with a suspended sentence after a simple misdemeanor, and Nutty, his friend, break into Doray's (S. Tracy) pharmacy at night in the hopes of finding medication for Nutty's sick grandmother. Doray brings charges but his wife Edith (Doris Kenyon) takes pity, even offering to take in Arthur, an orphan, "the worst kid in town." His presence causes so much dissension between the Dorays that one evening, the youth decides to run away. He then comes across a robber in the pharmacy, whom he recklessly manages to catch after a long car chase. The Dorays eventually adopt him.

Aside from a few successful psychological scenes (the exchanges between the boys, the pharmacist's confusion), *Young America* contains all the characteristics of a run-of-the-mill film, and fades into the average, disastrously repetitive Fox productions of 1931–32; Fox was withering away artistically in tune with its sales figures. In 1931, the company was in the red to the concert of almost six million dollars. In 1932 (under the management of Sid-ney R. Kent) it even counted a negative balance of $20 million, with no film having made money. Hawks and McCarey jumped ship, John Ford was rarely seen. From strictly the point of view of salary, Borzage was at the top: for *Young America* he earned $37,000, almost a third of the production budget! For 1929, 1930 and 1931, he earned respectively $208,000, $222,416 and $171,333 (he also owned 200 shares of Fox Theater Stock).[35] As the filmmaker still owed the company one last film before his contract expired, his name was naturally associated with several projects, including an adaptation of a popular Louis Bromfield novel, *A Modern Hero*, starring Ricardo Cortez, that Fox intended to assign to "Borzage or Stro-heim" in September.[36] Other projects that didn't materialize included: *Gold Star Mothers* with Sarah Padden, *The Pilgrimage* (Jan. 1932), and *My Dear*, again starring Janet Gaynor and Charles Farrell, scripted by S. Levien and S. N. Behrman from a short story by May Edginton (February–March 1932).

But his most advanced assignment at pre-production level was the vast family chroni-cle *Cavalcade*—from the blockbuster play by Noel Coward — that Borzage was asked to pre-pare for as of March, 1932. On April 6, he left New York for London aboard the *Aquitania*, accompanied by his brother Lew and scriptwriters Sonya Levien and S. N. Behrman. In Lon-don, Borzage requisitioned the Fox Movietone news technicians and with six cameras filmed the acclaimed production by Charles B. Cochran at the Drury Lane Theater (500 extras, 25 scenes) with the goal of scrupulously studying its particularities in the company of studio dignitaries. Upon his return to Hollywood, in May, the headaches began, as the play — a series of scenes strongly evoking nostalgic and patriotic overtones of determining episodes in English history, from the Boer War up to 1930 — seemed difficult for the average Yankee to digest. Without much conviction, Borzage proposed two versions, one destined for the English mar-ket (with Herbert Marshall, Elissa Landi and Maureen O'Hara as distinguished Brits), the other, slightly more romantic, for American audiences. Pressure was exerted on all sides. On June 21, realizing he could not work without interference, he withdrew from the race to pur-sue invitations of another caliber: Mary Pickford urged him to move over to United Artists while Paramount offered him the much-coveted direction of *A Farewell to Arms*. Sheehan cau-tiously decided to preserve the British flavor of *Cavalcade* by handing over the onerous epic to Frank Lloyd, a Glasgow native. Awarded three Oscars, *Cavalcade* would make Fox's star shine one last time before the dying company merged, in the summer of 1935, with Darryl F. Zanuck's 20th Century Film Corporation. As for Borzage, he left the studio after eight years without regret; one contract film was shelved; the affair would be settled in cash.[37] Much sought after, the filmmaker was determined to pursue his career independently.

10

Freedom at the Top

A Farewell to Arms is probably Borzage's most widely known talkie, a prestigious work associated with the names of Gary Cooper, Helen Hayes and, of course, Ernest Hemingway. Hemingway, however, hated the film, even before having seen it. Feeling he was betrayed by the movies, he refused to attend a private screening preview that Paramount wanted to organize in Piggott, Arkansas, where he was staying at the time. "Use your imagination as to where to put the print, but do not send it here," he telegraphed the studio in reply...[1] This was only the first filmed version of his writing: he hadn't seen anything yet!

Today the quarrel is only of historical interest, much like the one between F. Scott Fitzgerald and those responsible for *Three Comrades*, six years later (cf. chap. 13). Much has been written about the affair, fueled by studies confirming the classic prejudices of littérrateurs against films.[2] Quite obviously, and contrary to the publicity lies, Borzage's *A Farewell to Arms* is quite removed from the best-seller, using the catchy, well-known title, the main situations, and here and there, some of the dialogue. What's more, a close looks at the 1932 film version reveals a completely personal work of Borzage ("my best picture," he said without reservation); Hemingway only provided a pretext, a framework. Hemingway's monosyllabic terseness, lean style, and existential dilemmas belong to another galaxy. "It is Mr. Borzage rather than Mr. Hemingway who prevails in this film," concluded Mordaunt Hall in the *New York Times*.[3] An artist's privilege. Who today would reproach Verdi for "falsifying" Shakespeare or for transforming *Macbeth* or *Othello* into operas inevitably more Italian than Elizabethan? We do not intend to judge the durability of Hemingway's works, but seventy years later it is apparent that the strength and brilliance of Borzage's film remains unaltered.

What can be taken to a task, however, is the publicity surrounding the film. The issue of remaining faithful to literary works had already been raised by the film industry itself, whose undisclosed goal was to obtain prestige. Starting with the first filming of fictional works, producers cultivated this misunderstanding, while in reality they were only speculating on the fame of a title or name to embellish the credits. This use of literature simply for commercial means is questionable. In the case of *A Farewell to Arms*, Paramount's publicity would swear by "the greatest American novelist of modern times," whose originality the viewer would find onscreen. The studio seems to have reveled in its use of vulgar slogans. In addition, Borzage himself probably only had a passing knowledge of the book; yet stated quite candidly that "We followed the book more closely, I venture to say, than ever has been done before in Hollywood."[4] This last remark, however, should be placed in context: looking at some of the travesties undertaken by Hollywood, such as Balzac's *Eugénie Grandet* and *La Duchesse de Langeais* (filmed as *The Conquering Power*, 1921, and *The Eternal Flame*, 1922), Tolstoï's *Anna Karenina* (*Love*, 1927) and Melville's *Moby-Dick* (1926 and 1930), Borzage was perhaps not entirely wrong.

As is known, the action of the novel is based on Hemingway's own memories. Hired as a lieutenant in a volunteer corps of ambulance drivers, he was in the Italian army's campaign on the front in Isonzo; in July 1918 his legs were riddled with shrapnel and, convalescing in Milan, he fell in love with an American nurse seven years his senior, Agnes von Kurowsky (1892–1984). The beautiful Agnes—renamed Catherine on paper—refused to marry him and, disillusioned, Hemingway had her die at the end of his book! The story was first serialized in *Scribner's Magazine* (May–October 1929), then published by Scribner's in New York. The book was a smash, selling 93,000 copies in a few weeks, because a whole "lost" generation recognized itself in young Frederic Henry's confusion. The success inspired a song and a three-act play by Laurence Stallings (author of *What Price Glory?*) and directed by Rouben Mamoulian.[5]

As can be expected, from practically the moment it appeared in print, Hollywood planned to buy the book. But the book encountered serious stumbling blocks when it came to the censor: love outside marriage, illegitimate birth, desertion, the unflattering image of the Italian army, and so on. Intimidated by pressure from various groups, first Warner, then MGM (Sept. 30), pulled out; the Italian ambassador in Washington officially protested to the Hays office, putting the studios on guard: "We have had fair warning and can expect no pity if you go ahead with this picture," threatened the censors.[6] Hemingway sold his rights for $80,000. In November 1930, Paramount announced it would go ahead, although the studio's growing difficulties due to the crash held back preparations. At the same time, Lubitsch started a film with a pacifist theme on World War I that would encounter similar difficulties, but with Germany: *Broken Lullaby*. In the winter of 1931–1932, on the verge of bankruptcy, the company decided to free up a large part of its budget, staking everything on the eagerly awaited project (the very first screen adaptation of Hemingway). As with *7th Heaven*, the roles were greatly coveted. Frederic March and Claudette Colbert were first considered, until DeMille grabbed them for his costumer *Sign of the Cross*. Gary Cooper, Nancy Carroll and director Richard Wallace, all three involved in *The Shopworn Angel* (1928), another Paramount success about World War I, took over. But Wallace was removed when the studio became aware of director John Cromwell. Transplanted from Broadway, he was at ease with literary subjects. Gary Cooper was then considered, this time alongside Ruth Chatterton. Meanwhile, the play's author, Laurence Stallings, wrote a first draft of the screenplay. Oliver H.P. Garrett scripted the definitive version, while producer-screenwriter Benjamin Glazer managed to find himself a place in the credits (Negulesco dixit).

When in June 1932 production head B. P. Schulberg had to step down—Paramount had a 16 million dollar deficit!—his successor Emanuel Cohen ignored all former options. Learning that Frank Borzage had rejected *Cavalcade*, he contacted him immediately. Furious, Cromwell went back to RKO. In spite of being in the red, Paramount Pictures was still considered the most elegant, sophisticated European studio (Sternberg, Lubitsch, Marlene Dietrich, Chevalier), where directors enjoyed a freedom unknown elsewhere. Borzage's participation was a boon all around: the studio got a talented colleague, who in turn got to work with superb material. He would later say that he was appointed director of *A Farewell to Arms* due to his family background, as Trentin, where the Borzagas were from, was one of the main theaters of action of World War I on the Italian front. Taking over the production, Borzage intended to cast Eleanor Boardman (who starred in *The Circle*) in the role of Catherine, replaced at the last minute by Helen Hayes, queen of American theater, who Paramount borrowed from MGM on Irving Thalberg's recommendation. The presence of this actress, revered from New York to San Francisco, lent the whole enterprise additional respectability. A memo from the Hays office reveals priorities: "They [the management of Paramount] intend to live or die by this picture and they are going to be as daring as possible. We feel that with Borzage directing and Helen Hayes playing the lead, they have a better chance than they might otherwise have."[7] Miss Hayes' arrival jeopardized the candidacy of Gary Cooper, who had moved heaven and earth to play Frederic; Paramount feared that his dramatic talent was not up to that of his prestigious partner. Borzage had faith in him, speculating on the dialectic between modesty and emotion that would erupt onscreen. One's discomfort would be compensated by the professional ease of the other. However, the difference in height between Gary Cooper and Helen Hayes was so pronounced (as with Charles Farrell and Janet Gaynor) that beforehand the filmmaker organized a photography session lasting several hours to put the couple at ease and see the situation humorously. He decided to limit scenes with both of them on their feet to only what was absolutely necessary. Filming required eight weeks (from July 14 to mid–September), largely in the Marathon Street studios at Devil's Gate Dam near Pasadena and on the grounds of the Paramount Ranch in San Fernando Valley, 65 kilometers from Hollywood, where famous German art director Hans Dreier (12 films with Sternberg, 10 with Lubitsch) was designing the sets for Gorizia. Cost of the negative was $799,520 and the total production cost was $900,000 (the average cost of a film at Paramount was $306,000).

For several decades the film remained invisible. Only circa 1970, when it entered the public domain, did *A Farewell to Arms* turn up in art film theaters, unfortunately often in practically unrecognizable form: overexposed 16mm prints, pallid, full of cuts that detract from a very tightly edited film. There were some explanations for this. When, in June 1938, Paramount was preparing to re-release the film in U.S. theaters, the new Legion of Decency (controlled by the Catholic church and with ties to the Production Code Administration) opposed it categorically: *A Farewell to Arms* contained "lustful love scenes," "suggestive dialogue," "illicit sex," and a lack of "compensating moral value," from then on inadmissible onscreen. After difficult negotiations between Paramount and Joseph I. Breen, the censors authorized reediting it on the condition that the "immoral" scenes be cut; this is the severely mutilated version, shortened by about ten minutes (a dozen cuts, absolutely all crucial scenes amputated) and even falsified by an addition (the wedding ring!), that for a long time seemed to be the only one to have survived in the U.S. It was bought back by Warner Bros. (who acquired the film rights in 1946[8]) and still circulates as a videocassette. Borzage's style is so economical and sober that the least cut can throw the rest of the film off balance. Furthermore, this version corrected by the Catholic church led many historians of American film to gross errors of interpretation.[9] An integral version of the film remains in the film archives of London, Brussels, and Prague. In the U.S., a nitrate print of the 1932 version was recently found in the David O. Selznick vaults and is now at last available again, after 65 years, as a DVD (Image Entertainment). Of course we refer to this version in the pages that follow: the passages cut in 1938 are indicated by the symbol [¢], the dialogue taken from Hemingway's text by [Hmy].

The original credits roll to images of an aerial attack (autumn 1916). An appropriate intertitle first coaxes the public's reaction: "Disaster as well as victory is written for every nation on the record of the World War, but high on the rolls of glory two names are inscribed — The Marne and The Piave." But what follows puts "the glory of the flag" in its proper perspective. A pan from right to left shows an idyllic Venetian landscape; then, in the foreground, what appears to be a sleeping soldier, until the camera reveals it to be a mutilated corpse; in the background, a convoy of ambulances slowly advances along a mountain road. The path is so steep it is impossible to stop the vehicles to save a wounded man who has lost a lot of blood.[10] Led by American lieutenant Frederic Henry (G. Cooper), an architecture student[11] volunteering with the Red Cross, the convoy makes its way back

Gary Cooper explains to Adolphe Menjou the "beauties of architecture" (*A Farewell to Arms*, 1932).

to Gorizia, north of Trieste, after fighting at the Austrian-Italian front. The second sequence foreshadows the complementary portion of the narrative, with its romantic implications: at the hospital. Frederic witnesses the humiliating dismissal of a British nurse impregnated by a serviceman. She wrongly confused love and duty. Catherine Barkley (H. Hayes), another British nurse, offers to help the "pariah" pack her bags. Observing this kind gesture of Catherine's, the dismissing officer points out, when speaking to the head nurse, a veritable dragon lady: "She's the only human being in the whole lot of us." In the evening, Frederic joins his roommate, Major Rinaldi (Adolphe Menjou), a boastful, pleasure-seeking surgeon ("All fire and smoke, and nothing inside," he says of himself). Borzage reduces their visit to the local bordello to a few fetishistic images: starting from behind a closed shutter, the camera frames Frederic, drunk, conversing at the table with the naked leg of a prostitute (seated on a piano); he removes the shoe from the foot that comes up to his forehead so he can explain the beauties of architecture: the woman answers him several times by wriggling her toes [¢]. An aerial attack creates panic; Frederic jumps out a window, the prostitute's shoe in hand. As for Catherine, she flees the hospital and runs toward a shelter. In the darkness, she loses a shoe, stumbling on Frederic; he catches the foot and resumes his drunken speech: "architecture is the most ancient of the arts, just as your profession is the most ancient profession" [¢]. Taken aback, the demure Catherine lets him go on. But when the lieutenant wants to place a shoe on the foot of the unknown woman, he notices that it is the wrong size... Cinderella's "wrong" slipper has let him find the "right" foot. (Of course none of this introduction appears in Hemingway's book).

Later, at a reception at the officer's mess hall, Frederic recognizes Catherine, on whom

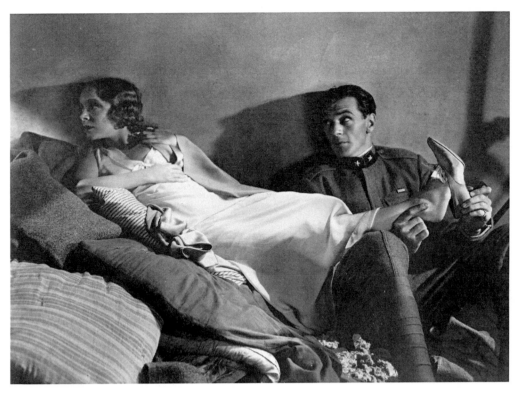

Cinderella's wrong slipper (Helen Hayes and Gary Cooper in *A Farewell to Arms*, 1932).

Rinaldi has designs. After their initial embarrassment, the American takes the nurse away from his rival; they disappear into a park. Furious, Rinaldi consoles himself with a bottle, leaving Catherine's colleague Fergie — alias Helen Ferguson (M. Philips) — whom he had intended for his comrade. They get acquainted and go for a walk. The nurse tells him that she had signed up to be near her fiancé, who died a few months earlier in the trenches at the Somme. Not realizing the implications of the war, she had not married: "I didn't know what the war was. If I had to do it all over again, I'd marry him — or anything" [Hmy—¢]. Catherine and Frederic are sequestered in a leafy oasis spangled with reflected light, at the foot of a large equestrian statue. Placed under the unusual protection of this condotiere whose mount is rising up to an enchanted unknown place, enveloped in lacy, Sternberg-like light, the two begin their flight outside time. Borzage visually indicates the isolation of his "chosen" by the downward movement of a dolly, sliding from a full shot of the stone cavalier to a close-up composition of the lovers: the dominant warrior is relegated outside the field. The emotional intensity which underscores their confidences renders any music superfluous. The entrepreneurial Frederic tries to kiss the nurse; she refuses. He insists and gets slapped. They both excuse themselves, and she says: "You're a dear. I'd be very glad to have you kiss me now if you don't mind..." [Hmy]. While Frederic does so, turning his back to the camera, Borzage focuses attention on the young woman's hand, a hand that lets go, freezes a few seconds before wrapping itself sensually, slowly, around the neck of the serviceman [¢]. This tender aside, polished in middletones, quivering with delicate eroticism, has few equivalents in the history of film, and only the wrenching embrace of Sylvia Bataille and Georges d'Arnoux in *La Partie de Campagne/A Day in the Country* (Renoir) evokes stunning passion with so much gentleness. When *A Farewell to Arms* was released, Helen Hayes, still under the charm of this enchanted collaboration (and even secretly in love with her mentor) declared she would be gratified for life if Borzage was the only director she could work with again: "He's the finest director I ever worked with! He's a genius and I've never applied that word to any director of stage or screen before."[12] Half a century later, in her memoirs, the "grande dame" of Broadway still was moved as she remembered the shoot: "Never working in film have I felt as comfortable with a director as with Frank Borzage, who had a wonderful gift for intimacy: he knew how to get inside an actor's heart and mind, and that rapport gives a special glow to his films."[13]

What follows was entirely cut by the censor in 1938: an explosion lights up the rooftops of the city, a reminder of the reality already disrupted by the sequestered lovers and the precariousness of the moment. Rinaldi, the chief nurse, and Fergie are concerned about the absence of Catherine, normally such a sensible girl. In the park, Frederic explains to the nurse that in wartime, a month of normal life becomes compressed into an hour: "What's so fine in putting it off, in draggin it out ... giving me your lips tonight and your throat tomorrow?" The soundtrack records "no"'s becoming increasingly weaker while the image fades.[14] After cutting elliptically to Fergie finding her friend's abandoned jacket, Borzage returns to the lovers lying down in a cemetery. "Why didn't you tell me?" Frederic asks, realizing that Catherine was a virgin. "There's a war on and tonight who cares, and tomorrow who knows... What did you say your name was?" Returning to her room in the early morning, the nurse pushes away the bitter reproaches of Fergie (depicted as a latent lesbian). As for Frederic, he frustrates Rinaldi with savory details of the evening and turns out the light; only his cigarette can be seen glowing in the dark.

"Suggestive dialogue and illicit sex" between Gary Cooper and Helen Hayes in *A Farewell to Arms* (1932).

This is how the first part of a three-part journey of initiation ends, as Borzage constructs his entire film around three key love scenes: in Gorizia at the beginning, in Milan, and finally in Brissago. We could even go so far as to see in them the three levels of Masonic initiation, devoted successively to "the discovery, assimilation and propagation of Light" (Oswald Wirth).[15] Hemingway depicts this initial contact in Gorizia as a simple flirtation: the officer pretends to love the nurse, she pretends to believe him; they do not yet sleep together. Removed visually from the sociopolitical context, Borzage's lovers discover the first flaw in the construction of false values (the "flag"). This led to hostility of many who detested the film: fanatics in the military, patriots and puritans. From then on, the enemy is characterized by the warring spirit that divides and confines, nihilism leading to superficiality and cynicism, and finally the repression of any kind of love (considered as threatening the established order). The head nurse does not joke about the virtue of her subordinates. In Fergie's eyes, love means only deception: fighting and death — the daily lot of the medical team — are all that is real. Along with the rationalist Rinaldi, she embodies the existential pessimism underscoring all Hemingway's prose, and that Borzage's protagonists rise up against with so much determination.

The next day the ambulances leave for the front in the Dolomites, but Frederic brusquely orders the driver to turn back. He finds Catherine at the hospital and lets her know — more by looks than by words — that he won't forget her. The nurse hangs a medal of St. Anthony around his neck. Rinaldi has discreetly observed the scene, and jealous, he has Catherine transferred to Milan. While the Italian soldiers launch an attack, the ambulance drivers gather together around a pot of spaghetti: "If nobody would attack, the war would be over!" comments the chaplain; a shell explodes in the shelter. Wounded, Frederic awakens on Rinaldi's operating table, in Gorizia. "I will see that you are decorated for bravery. Did you carry somebody on your back? Surely it was something very heroic, tell me what you did." "I was blown up eating cheese..." [Hmy]. In a burst of friendship, Rinaldi evacuates his friend to convalesce in Milan, near the "beautiful Miss Barkley."

Frederic's arrival at the Milan hospital, a converted Byzantine monastery, is shown in a series of subjective low-angle tracking shots, with the camera apparently resting on the stretcher. The faces of the stretcher bearers and nurses enter the field by addressing the camera. At first these unusual angles are unjustified, unless perhaps they are a useless and unique attempt at moving closer to the first person narration of the novel (or just an aesthetic whim). Yet, on this level of the narrative, this personalized sequence, as well as the stay in the hospital that follows, seal the radical divorce between individual adventure and collective destiny; this is where the true "desertion" begins, the awareness. Here we suggest another, more intricate, interpretation, relating both to the aspiring architect (Frederic) and the filmmaker's Masonic credo: if the entire domed building (a nonreligious building in Hemingway's book) is inevitably the image of the world, the dome itself represents the arch of Heaven, whose central opening — the "eye" — is assimilated to the Northern Star. Going beyond it amounts to leaving the conditioned world, a return to the divine unity. These are fundamental notions of the holy architecture, well known to Freemasons and explained by the symbolism and rituals of the Royal Arch Masonry.[16] Identifying with the wounded man (thus passive), the viewer may be said to enter the holy place horizontally, and making his way through long corridors, first sees arcs and vaults pass before his eyes. Suddenly the camera stops perpendicular to the eye of the dome,[17] in the precise axis formed by the face of the base and the top of the cupola, and remains in this position for several seconds. Borzage places this "narrow gate" or "Gate of the Sun" at the center of the frame, without any other flourishes, this geometrical tableau which the Masons call "the passage from square to compass," from cube to sphere, from Earth to Heaven. Horizontally (a state of profanity) Frederic is placed in the vertical axis, linking him to transcendency. This is the precise symbolic equivalent of ascending the stairs in *7th Heaven*. With this "station" beneath the dome completed, the subjective journey follows logically to the bed of the wounded man, the very place where the unio mystica will occur. Catherine runs joyously toward the camera and kisses him; she approaches until the camera frames only an extreme close-up of her eye, as if, in return for this Orphean kiss (which momentarily clouds the screen), the director was trying once again to emphasize the intrinsic relationship between the organ of amorous vision, mirror of the soul, and "the Gate of the Sun," of the dome. After introducing a sacred dimension, inherently foreign to Hemingway, Borzage breaks the subjectivity, ending the sequence in an ironic pirouette that continues the storyline: a health care aide reads the wounded man's temperature and exclaims, alarmed, that he must be delirious. Frederic reassures her: "I haven't got any fever. It's not what you think...." A statement open to interpretation...

In the evening, the chaplain from Gorizia visits him. Played by Jack La Rue (familiar from gangster movies), the priest starts off by breaking house rules and offering him alcohol. While for Hemingway the staff officer is merely a scapegoat, in Borzage's film he is a distinct, unorthodox figure. "Don't mind us, father, we're in love," Frederic tells him when Catherine enters and they speak of their future children. "I know, I've seen it in your eyes," he retorts, then realizing they are lovers: — "This too is war. Without it you would have married in God's grace, is it not so?" They nod their heads in agreement. The priest then turns his back to them — as if to maintain their mutual intimacy — and leaves the camera's field of view, murmuring a Latin liturgy. The couple observes him without a word, both moved and disoriented. "Of course you realize, father, that Army regulations prevent us from marrying," [¢] Frederic points out, while the priest, unperturbed, continues his recitation in the shadows. Then he returns and blesses the couple, placed against a pool of light at the back of the room, adding: "It was a foolish notion perhaps, I have not the right to say you are married, yet [¢] it has made me happy to do this." This highly irregular procedure[18] and its sublimation (a kind of consecration of a secret paradise) evoke the marriage with the religious medals in *7th Heaven*. The priest has barely removed himself when the head nurse comes looking for Catherine, who hides, locks the door and spends the night, "their wedding night"—near the convalescent [¢]. The camera veers off to the rooftops, swept by anti-aircraft defense searchlights. From the darkness, off-camera, Catherine whispers: "Don't I make a pretty wife? ... Feel our hearts beat?" [¢]. The spiritual purity of the union renders Borzage's lovers inseparable, but in no way excludes a physical relationship; it integrates them without conflict, as if perfectly obvious (cf. *Man's Castle*). We disagree completely with Jean-Pierre Coursodon's statement that "Borzage's attitude toward sex was a Victorian mixture of fascination and fear, of fetishistic overprizing of "purity" (i.e. chastity, virginity) and a sadistic impulse to soil it.... [He] developed his entire dramatic system on the basis of maximum sexual denial. One suspects ... that what some critics assume to be a deep religious feeling was little more than another of Borzage's devices to hold Eros at bay while keeping him sufficiently stimulated."[19] On the contrary, we believe that despite pressure from the censor, the sexual dimension is explicitly present in *A Farewell to Arms*. As Jacques Segond points out, Frederic and Catherine's relationship is "characterized by the most physical kind of passionate love, in a manner very unusual for American film at the time."[20]

July to October go by (at this point the version tampered with by the Catholic authorities in 1938 superimposes a shot of two hands exchanging wedding rings!). With Frederic recovered, the lovers can enjoy themselves and stroll around the city. But the head nurse, who doesn't hide her dislike of Frederic, discovers a stash of bottles in the officer's room and immediately has him sent back to the front. A rainy night: the camera looks through the window of a hotel used by prostitutes near the Stresa station where military convoys await (filmed in the yards of the Southern Pacific Railroad, L.A.). It moves before a painting of a nude odalisque and a few mirrors, then reveals Frederic and Catherine lying on a bed [¢]. "I wish we could do something really sinful. Everything we do seems so innocent and right," the young woman sighs [Hmy]. The goodbye sequence is punctuated by the plaintive whistling of the train; Frederic recites lines by Andrew Marvell ("To His Coy Mistress," 17th century) on the obsessive passing of time: "And always at my back I hear / Time's winged chariot hurrying near" [Hmy]. While looking outside, the nurse reveals her macabre obsession about the rain: "I hate the rain. I'm afraid of the rain because sometimes I see me dead in it, and sometimes I see you dead in it." On the doorstep, she implores him: "Say: I'll come back to Catherine." "I'll come back to Catherine. I'll always come back," a preemptive declaration much like the "I'll never die" in *7th Heaven*. Frederic has barely turned his back when Catherine takes the train for Brissago, in the Italian-speaking part of Switzerland, where she wants to give birth to have her lover's child, a secret she confides only to Fergie. Settling into a seedy little hotel, the nurse writes Frederic a letter: she speaks of a palace "fit for an empress," while the camera shows us the sordid reality. Then, in front of the camera, Catherine hides her face behind the serviceman's photograph, and sobs, murmuring words of love (excluding the viewer from her intimate sphere). In Gorizia, Frederic refrains from visiting brothels or going on drinking binges; annoyed at having lost his companion in debauchery, Rinaldi clumsily knocks over an inkpot on a letter Frederic was writing (foreshadowing disaster), then, responsible for military censure, decides to intercept all mail coming from Brissago. When Frederic, hearing nothing, has his own letters returned, he resolves to go to Milan surreptitiously to have a clean conscience, confiding only in his "godfather," the chaplain. His departure — which amounts to desertion — happens in the midst of the retreat from Caporetto, at the end of October 1917.

This terrible battle of the second army of General Capello — Italy lost 10,000 men; 30,000 were wounded and as many as 293,000 were taken prisoner — is the climactic event in Hemingway's novel, the catalyst of his story, because for the writer, the horrors of war motivate the hero's desertion. For Paramount, reconstructing the story was a real challenge, as Mussolini had threatened to forbid all of their films in Italy (where the novel was banned) if *A Farewell to Arms* insulted national honor. The studio, fearful of offending the Italian-American public, resigned itself to not mentioning the "shameful" name of Caporetto. But this precaution worked against them, because the images clearly illustrate a chaotic retreat in the mud, under driving rain and fire from Austrian fighter planes; the only geographical or demographic indication Borzage provided, a little later, is a newspaper headline proclaiming: "Italian Armies successful in great Piave offensive." In this context, the title of the newspaper appears as a sarcastic commentary on the unreliability of the press or the hypocrisy of government! After a special screening at the Italian embassy in Washington on November 25, A. H. Giannini, president of the Bank of Italy and an influential member of the Italian-American community, judged the work "acceptable," while the Fascist Independent Order Sons of Italy, rejected it. In order not to anger il Duce, Paramount refrained from distributing the film in Italy. (Borzage's film would only be shown there in 1980, on RAI television.)

Jean Negulesco was then production assistant to Benjamin Glazer. Trained as a painter, the Rumanian artist was in charge of depicting the routed army, drawing the main ideas on storyboard. Borzage's indicated that the retreat was to be "stylized rather than literal," "camera angles are to be deliberately distorted," "in lighting as well as in composition an effect of nightmare will be sought"[21]: the war seen through Frederic's eyes. The studio was so impressed by the drawings, it gave Negulesco his first chance at directing, putting him in charge of the crowd scenes for the second team. The neophyte was aiming for a "monumental" effect (his own words), applying Caligarism in the pure Germanic tradition, crossed with symbolist effects: cemeteries as far as the eye can see, panicked convoys of civilians, children and prostitutes, a staff officer's room worthy of the caves in *Metropolis*. Mischa Auer portrays an officer who kills himself beneath Mussolini-inspired graffiti: "Better to be a dead lion than a live sheep," etc.[22] Four hundred extras, most of them unemployed, were called to Paramount Ranch for five consecutive nights of filming under water jets and lights from 300 spotlights. Negulesco had erected a miniature mountain where incessant rain causes an avalanche, a metaphor of the armies in flight. But the sequence was much too long, stylistically jarring, and threatened to throw the film off balance. Borzage, who was directing the shots with Cooper, personally took over editing of the sequence and cut the retreat sequence to five minutes, reducing Negulesco's contribution to a succinct mosaic predominated by chaos and night (music: Wagner's "Valkyries Riding").[23] The difference in approach between the two directors is apparent in Negulesco's comments, which reveal a lack of understanding: "Borzage was a strange man. He'd have a scene with, say, three hundred extras, and all he'd be interested in was the way water would drip from a leaf and the way you'd see Gary Cooper passing by through this dripping water in the big retreat from Caporetto."[24] This meticulousness, in no way gratuitous, emphasizes the mysteries of intimacy over the rumblings of history, is more attuned to the fluctuations of the indescribable than to demonstrations of grandness, and dominates the photographic style of the entire film. How else to explain the unexpected trajectory of Charles B. Lang, who won an Oscar for the film's cinematography, yet, in approximately thirty unremarkable productions, had never before filmed such velvet smooth modulations of light? The master of sentimental chiaroscuro, Lang later composed the ethereal images of *Peter Ibbetson* and *The Ghost and Mrs. Muir*.

At strictly the level of the plot, the film most widely diverges from the novel as concerns Frederic's motivation. Hemingway's officer is obliged to abandon his ambulance stuck in the mud; the confusion of the retreat, the extortion and summary executions of the soldiers do the rest. In the film, the decision to desert precedes the military catastrophe: Frederic's "farewell to arms" is the result of his love, because all that matters to him is what happens to Catherine. Ever since they met, the fighting—depicted as hallucinatory, irrational, and absurdist, is only an agent of separation; atrocities on the battlefield merely serve to amplify their nostalgia for each other, seen as reality. It would be wrong to see this change as a romantic device detracting from the work, or even an alignment with Hollywood's ideology, as its logic is profoundly anchored in Borzage's vision of the world. As Tom Milne points out, "Borzage reduces this sequence to what is almost a medieval morality, a terrible pilgrim's progress as the lieutenant marches endlessly through a carnage" that borders a road strewn with allegorical compositions (faceless, mutilated people, arms crossed in misshapen doorways; three one-legged men hobbling on their crutches, a hand clenching at the sound of a burst of gunfire).[25] This may be seen as a refusal to represent that which cannot be, to attribute anything more than a stylized synthesis to horror.

Walking along the banks of the Tagliamento with the dismissed regiment, Frederic comes very close to death; the military police round up the fleeing officers and executes them forthwith. Frederic escapes by jumping in the water; he furtively climbs onto a train, reaches the hospital in Milan and enters Fergie's room by the window. Full of hatred, she rouses the building after informing the American that he will soon be a father ("I hope they shoot you! Pay you back for what you've done to her!"). Sought for desertion, Frederic hides out at a comrade's who finds civilian clothing for him; he places an ad in the newspaper in order to find Catherine. Rinaldi, concerned by his friend's disappearance, reads the newspaper and finds the anonymous placer of the ad. The comrades fall into each other arms. Realizing that his friend has not merely fallen prey to a passing fancy, that out of love he is taking incredible risks, the repentant surgeon tells him Catherine's whereabouts. Meanwhile, in Brissago, the young woman despairs ever having news of her lover. She cuts out a silhouette of herself and folds it, without a word. Some linguists[26] have pointed out "the futility of language and the importance of the image," which would tend to justify, for example, the weight of the visual message when Frederic is beneath the dome. The Caporetto episode, the description of the hotel room in Brissago, and even to some extent the final apotheosis demonstrate to what point images can refute words. So much for Hemingway.

When the mailman returns Catherine's own letters sent back by the military censor, she collapses. The shock causes her to go into premature labor. On the operating table, the former nurse comments on her own condition. (After much hemming and hawing, Paramount allowed the censor to cut all stages of the medical procedure, showing the pain of childbirth, narcosis, hemorrhaging, the dialogue between Catherine and the doctors, etc.).[27] Frederic crosses Lake Maggiore in a small boat as night falls, with the storm howling and his face whipped by a gust of wind — a premonition of death. Parallel editing alternates between close-ups of his fingers, gripping the oars, and those of Catherine, clutching the operating table. Delirious with fever, the young woman holds the doctor's hand against her face, believing it to be her lover's. Frederic rushes into the hospital, and immediately encounters Catherine sleeping on a bed. Two health care aids are talking about a Caesarian. He paces the waiting room. Seeing the torrential rain outside, he cries "Don't let her die!" A doctor tells him that the child has died. As for the health of the mother, it's out of his hands... In the early morning, the obstetrician advises Frederic to go get something to eat in a café. Exhausted, he wanders into an establishment where customers are avidly reading the newspaper: it is November 4, 1918 and the Austrian-Hungarian empire has just surrendered. Supremely indifferent to the hazards of war, Frederic orders a drink. More than any other, this moment of pathos paralyzed Gary Cooper, who, from the first day of shooting, suffered from the comparison with his too-famous partner. However, the director controls even his smallest gestures; from an upstanding officer, well turned-out and sure of himself, Frederic imperceptibly becomes vulnerable, his gait unsteady and his face ravaged with pain.

In a taped interview with George Pratt in 1958 (op. cit.), Borzage described in detail the instructions whispered to Cooper as well as the actor's reaction to them: "A scene that I wouldn't ask Barrymore, or anybody that claims he is a real fine actor to do, because he'd say 'this is impossible, I can't do this scene!' ... I wouldn't call him [Cooper] an actor, I'd call him a personality."[28] Cooper is supposed to be sitting on a table, wild-eyed, mechanically nibbling on a roll and talking to himself, sobbing a barely audible prayer, a despairing plea to Heaven ("She can't die!"). The actor rebelled until Borzage explained to him with his customary gentleness — without embarrassment — that it was the easiest scene in the whole film! Cooper didn't have to delve into or express nuances in his character, but only to feel the situation. The director's persuasion was miraculous: the actor is heartbreakingly restrained. At a preview, Leslie Howard admitted to Borzage that he would have been incapable of giving such a performance. A paradox of awkwardness and elegance, Cooper's physical uniqueness—slenderness, nonchalant gestures, innocent looks—gave him a meditative air, with a kind of seriousness that, behind an adventurous facade, foretold secretive and faraway motives. "It is a privilege to work with Frank Borzage," admitted the star a few years later. "It was he who taught me that the best acting was not acting at all, but a perfect naturalness, which comes easy when he stands behind the camera."[29]

As we approach the famous final sequence, the gulf between the movie and the novel again bears mentioning. Hemingway's couple take refuge in Switzerland and spends several months in a cottage on the shore of Lac Léman before Catherine enters the hospital; the war isn't close to ending and Rinaldi disappears after Caporetto. Borzage explained these differences to his detractors, as well as Rinaldi's transformation into Frederic's enemy, as necessary for the drama: "We could not have brought them together, the officer and the girl, as Hemingway did, in the Swiss resort, without killing our suspense. We would have had no climax." ... "As for Rinaldi, he couldn't just be there, he had to do something one way or the other."[30] Hemingway devotes barely a page to the young woman's death, a disappearance the disillusioned narrator describes: "And this was the price you paid for sleeping together. This was the end of the trap. This was what people got for loving each other." Death is merely a concrete, biological process. Catherine admits: "I'm not afraid. I just hate it." Her last words are filled with bitterness: "It's just a dirty trick." Frederic is not at her bedside when she loses consciousness; later he looks at her corpse, searching in vain for peace. "[After I had] shut the door and turned off the light it wasn't any good. It was like saying goodbye to a statue. After a while I went out and left the hospital and walked back to the hotel in the rain."

The novel thus ends with the stoic words of a man defeated, for whom existence offers no explanations: "That was what you did. You died. You did not know what it was all about. You never had time to learn." Borzage takes the opposing view of Hemingway, so to speak, as his conclusion leads to an opening, to the "eye of the dome." The love his characters experience is the result of a conscious choice, not of devastating fatality. Rhythmically, the last sequence traces the final symphonic motif of *Tristan and Isolde*, erroneously known as *Liebestod* (death through love), while Wagner had entitled it "Transfiguration" ("Verklärung"). This calls to mind Isolde's final plea, when dying: "Submerged in you, I feel my being faint in the splendor of immortal light." The Wagnerian theme is softly played when, at the bedside of the dying woman, doctor and nurses shake their heads: "We might as well let him in..." "I knew he was coming," Catherine smiles, like Tristan at the seashore, at the end of the opera. Then she asks to powder her nose and have her hair combed. A health care aide calls the American who enters the room and approaches the bed, which is under a bay window.

The scene, which lasts seven minutes, is filmed using two alternating angles in medium-close shots. One shows Frederic at Catherine's bedside, lying perpendicular to the camera axis. The other films them in oblique high-angle shots, Catherine's face turned toward the camera (Borzage visibly worked with two cameras and filmed it all at once, so as not to disturb the actors). Frederic is tearful. The couple speaks for a long time in low voices, a dialogue hovering between promises ("Tell me you'll never stop loving me — even if I die"), advice ("I want you to have other girls, though"), images of an impossible future ("When I get well, we will take a little house in the mountains"), bouts of anguish ("Don't let me go, I've been alone so much"), all of it to the sound of Wagner's nostalgic waves, from piano to forte, increasingly insistent, an uninterrupted crescendo, toward the key in B major and the feverish peak. This orgasmic sublimation—which calls to mind the endings of *7th Heaven* and *Lucky Star*—is fleshed out with corresponding replies. Frederic hypnotizes the

An offering to the light of day: the final scene of *A Farewell to Arms* (1932).

dying woman by his words, as if he were trying to prepare her for the "final journey": "You can't die, you're too brave to die! You're a fine girl, a brave girl!" "Yes, I'm a brave girl." "Whatever happens, you'll not be afraid?" "I'll not be afraid." "We've never been apart, really. Not since we met." "Not since we met." "And never can be." "Never parted." "In life and in death, say it, Catherine." "In life and in death, we'll never be parted." "I believe it and I'm not afraid." Suddenly her ecstatic expression freezes, and the arm wrapped around Frederic's neck falls. At this second, a light montage of impressions—bells, sirens, leaflets, jubilant crowds—proclaims Armistice. In unison with the last strain of the Wagnerian theme, at the music's culminating crash, Frederic lifts the body of the deceased, turns toward the bay window (medium-close shot), raises his head, holds out his beloved as an offering to the light of day, saying sorrowfully: —"Peace, peace." The image fades to white: a flock of doves majestically takes flight in the sky. The End.

The unusual exaltation and serene theatricality of this last composition threw certain viewers off, while thrilling others.[31] The bed sheet in which Frederic carries Catherine trails like a shroud — or is it a wedding gown? And do the ringing bells herald death, marriage, or victory? The flight of the birds "demonstrates Assumption of the mystical wife," writes Michael Henry Wilson pertinently[32]; in all Mediterranean civilizations, doves represent the souls of the dead, but coincidentally (or perhaps not), these birds are also associated with Venus. The final exclamation of "Peace, peace," conveys this same ambiguity; peace for men delivered from war, but peace also for those liberated from the torments of the human condition. Irrevocable death — represented by the rain — strikes Caporetto at night, in the chaos deserted by the angels; yet Catherine dies in the morning sun. Borzage's version of *A Farewell to Arms* is more of "a farewell to the world," the pure and simple negation of earthly limits;

the last shot once more excludes the spectator, as Frederic ostensibly turns his back to the camera. The oft-quoted statement by John Belton stating that Borzagian heroes "achieve spiritual gain only through physical loss"[33] seems rather oversimplified, however, and linked to an overly restrictive Cartesian opposition between body and spirit. As can be seen in several other works (*Street Angel, The River, Lucky Star, Man's Castle, Little Man, What Now?, Mannequin*, etc.), the ordeal enabling access to the dome may also be psychic. Hemingway's martyred antiheros attain a kind of virile grandeur by their endurance in the face of the absurdity of life. The characters in the film, no less tormented, find salvation in what unites them, beyond appearances. Borzage imbues these characters, who are really rather conventional—a military Don Juan, a lonely, sad nurse—with an inner flame, a nobility, and soulful inspiration that can't be found in the novel. As opposed to the novelist, the filmmaker is never interested only in Frederic (whose subjectivity leads only in one direction). In the film, Frederic experiences depth — if not existence itself — only through Catherine, and vice versa, which leads us back to the fundamental principles of all Borzage's work. Hemingway (as a latent romantic) distances himself, burying his feelings, while Borzage plunges us directly into the emotion. Hemingway communicates by action, which Borzage avoids, the way he denies any leanings toward the epic.[34] Two works fundamentally, antithetically opposed: no wonder the novelist no longer recognized his work.

When the film was released, the press made a big to-do about the alternative "happy ending" that Paramount made available to theaters. Swayed by the much more favorable reaction of women to the "conciliatory" ending of *Waterloo Bridge* (James Whale) in the winter of 1931–1932,[35] concerned about alienating viewers at a critical moment of the story, Paramount tacked on (as the shooting script ended with Catherine's death) a more ambiguous conclusion. As Borzage was already in the midst of preparations for *Secrets* and also annoyed by this messing about, it appears that the thankless task fell to Jean Negulesco (retakes November 17–19). Wagner—too lugubrious—was replaced by more all-purpose music; the first three quarters remain intact, but at the sound of the bells and sirens, Catherine opens her eyes and listens. He murmurs "Armistice"; she murmurs: "peace," and the couple embraces, cheek to cheek (mid-shot). Hemingway himself justified his animosity to the film by this concession to mass culture. Truth be told, it was much ado about nothing, because this simulated "happy ending" was never shown outside the U.S., and even there, it was mostly shown in small towns and in the suburbs. When the film was released in San Francisco and Los Angeles, the "sad" version, faithful to the novel, was shown.

If the commercial release of the film fully satisfied Paramount's public—who flocked to theaters—the reaction of critics and experts was divided. In the U.S., some of the press dwelled on the misfortunes of Hemingway while others saw the film only as "the femmes' *All Quiet on the Western Front*, the romantic side of the great holocaust,"[36] spiced up by some affronts to public decency. Censors in Ohio and Pennsylvania both made significant cuts. Germany banned the film on the spot, as its release coincided with Hitler's rise to power. Poland forbad it for two months, Australia for almost a year, but then allowed it when Paramount made five typed pages of cuts and removed the evil name of Hemingway from the credits (his novel had not appeared in Australia). It was also banned in British Columbia, and on pressure from Mussolini, in Egypt. Vienna, Prague and Paris showed this "pacifist propaganda film"[37] in the original, subtitled version, not to please movie fans, but to limit the audience! (A dubbed version was shown in Brussels, however). French censors hesitated a long time before granting permission,[38] and the reaction of certain newspapers did not augur well: "This title appears to be particularly poorly chosen, because the main character is a deserter," commented *Mon-Ciné*,[39] while fascist François Vinneuil heaped sarcasm on this work where "a chaplain assumes the glorious task of demoralizing the soldiers one by one... Americans don't appreciate physical cowardice. So they must accumulate the most horribly melodramatic circumstances to explain the desertion of a rugged guy like Gary Cooper."[40] Elsewhere, Frederic is described as a "ridiculous commie, to say the least."[41] Even novelist Francis de Croisset only saw in it "a dark melodrama, full of pretension, 'directed' by a filmmaker who, if he has seen war, has certainly forgotten it and who makes us remember it in a most disagreeable way. All of this is called *A Farewell to Arms*, which is a courteous and civil way of translating the word 'deserter.'"[42]

To sum up, in the U.S., reservations about the film were on moral grounds, whereas in the old world, they were political. This did not prevent, sporadically, recognition of its immense artistic merits. Seeking to console Hemingway, filmmaker Pare Lorentz spoke of "scenes as tender and as beautifully done as any author could ask."[43] *Le Figaro* stated that "this film is characterized by its pure lines and contains a new vision, a vertical thrust toward beauty."[44] The critic at *L'Ami du Film* exclaimed, fascinated, "With *A Farewell to Arms*, [Borzage] suddenly rises to become the greatest director in the world."[45] The opening—the world premiere took place December 8, 1932 at the Criterion in New York—benefited greatly from the Oscars, awarded a month earlier. Both Borzage and Helen Hayes were honored, for *Bad Girl* and *The Sin of Madelon Claudet*, respectively. The following year, the Academy of Motion Picture Arts and Sciences awarded Oscars to *A Farewell to Arms* for cinematography and sound recording, and nominations for best film and art direction. The film also won the prestigious National Board of Review Award in the U.S. But the last word on the film belongs to Roger Boussinot, who wrote in the *Encyclopédie du cinéma* in 1989: "It was undoubtedly the first movie in film history that we can say was superior to the original. Hemingway's novel was relatively harsh and distant. Frank Borzage gave this story about a desertion in the name of love such poetry, such a warmly conveyed element of rebellion, that *A Farewell to Arms* remains unsurpassed in the career of its author, its actors and in the genre itself."[46]

* * *

On September 3—still in the midst of Hemingway—Borzage went away for a day to United Artists' studios at the express request of Mary Pickford. Charlotte Pickford, the mother of "America's Sweetheart," was celebrating her birthday. Superstitious, she wanted this day to coincide with the first day of shooting of *Shantytown*, a romantic drama by Frances Marion set in a rundown area where victims of the tuna fishing industry lived in misery, to be co-produced by Borzage and the Pickford Corporation. Other actors approached were Karl Dane, Buddy Rogers, Blanche Frederici and Sidney Toler. The main photography was planned for October. To start things off, Borzage filmed a few shots with Mary Pickford and delegated a second unit to San Francisco for distance shots. Difficulties arose: the script wasn't completed, and the production was postponed to the following year; MGM then bought the subject for Greta Garbo, but the film was never made. In the meanwhile, Borzage had the opportunity to orchestrate a beautiful sound remake of *Secrets*.

However, this repertory melodrama was also plagued by bad luck, beginning with a spectacular false start, two years earlier. In the spring of 1930, Mary Pickford, then 38, seemed to be losing her appeal. Talkies had affected her popularity, which she desperately needed to recapture and put her company, United Artists, on firm ground after two financial disasters—*The Taming of the Shrew* and *Kiki*. The star-producer wagered her future on a movie that had made the reputation of her former rival, Norma Talmadge: *Secrets* (cf. chap. 5). Her longtime friend Marshall Neilan—formerly a reputed filmmaker, now destroyed by alcohol—began the film with the title *Forever Yours*; Benjamin Glazer wrote the script. Mary Pickford played Mara, with Kenneth MacKenna as John. But two thirds of the way through the film, and $300,000 later, the star, dissatisfied, ordered a work stoppage, and the negative destroyed![47] Reasons for abandoning the project were muddled: too talky a script, McKenna "too young" in relation to the star, she herself nervous and in the midst of a marital crisis with Douglas Fairbanks, incompetent direction, etc. Two years later, they began completely anew, under the provisional title of *Yes, John*. Prudently, Mary Pickford this time entrusted the script to Frances Marion and direction to Borzage, who had created the silent version.

This was how, with *A Farewell to Arms* barely completed, Borzage spent the winter of 1932–33 —from November 29 to January 18 (30 days of shooting)— in the former Samuel Goldwyn studios, now the domain of Associated Artists. Having just won his second Oscar, the filmmaker was paid regally and had the production firmly under control. The great Alfred Newman wrote the music and Adrian, on loan from MGM, designed the costumes. Only two small clouds appeared on the horizon: they had to abandon the idea of shooting exteriors in the Mojave desert because of bad weather, and Leslie Howard replaced Gary Cooper at the last minute (Paramount refused to loan him[48]). The Anglo-Magyar dandy had just finished *Smilin' Through* (S. Franklin), and at first may have seemed an unusual choice to play a pioneer of the West. Skinny, intellectual, fragile, at times deliciously affected, Howard had the profile of an idealistic dreamer coupled with mischievous humor. Borzage made good use of his prodigious sense of comic composition (which harmonized well with his partner's impulsive grace), so that the film, in its most moving moments, balances between a cheerful deftness and exquisite dramatic sensitivity.

A comparison between the 1924 and 1933 versions reveals the considerable skill acquired between the two. Overall, the remake follows the original plot faithfully and thus contains the same characteristics— three very different time periods and registers (comedy, western adventure, drama of the heart)— and the same flaws (overly sketchy characterizations, lack of substance in the third segment). But Borzage abandons the superfluous procedure of flashbacks and lightens the episodes by his extremely imaginative direction, moving the action at the beginning from Victorian London to the posh circles of Trenton, New Jersey, still circa 1865. The elimination of the diary (a pretext for the flashbacks), which reduced the story to a solitary daydream, shifts the balance to the couple, to life together: John becomes as important as his wife, and even appears first on screen (Howard's very original personality undoubtedly had something to do with this).

The first part is handled playfully, its predictability imposing a satirical mode: a long tracking shot of a springlike tableau catches John Carlton (L. Howard) perched on his velocipede, pedaling cheerfully. The frock coat–clad athlete meets up with the barouche of Mary Marlowe (M. Pickford), who is being subjected to her mother's chatter about her upcoming marriage to an aristocrat. While her mother dozes off, John turns rapidly around the carriage and discreetly pays his respects to the young lady, who, emerging from behind her parasol, smiles. But suddenly a bee appears, buzzing around her. John gallantly chases away the intruder, gets stung and bites the dust in a rattling crash. In the office of her father (C. Aubrey Smith), shipowner and banker, wedding preparations are discussed. Mary recognizes the enterprising cyclist among the employees; John has a black eye. He'll drown himself if he can't see her again, he writes her secretly. Aloud, Mary declines an invitation to the pastor's: "I can't Mama, I'm saving a man from drowning tonight." They meet up timidly in the moonlight, at the gate of a park. Daddy finds his daughter's behavior erratic: why is she going out, at nightfall, to pick flowers in the garden? A series of love letters, each one tenderer than the one before. The packet ends up in the hands of John's autocratic boss, who drives him away, but not before John tears up the check his ex-employer hands him. "Bravo, that's a man!" rejoices Aunt Susan, Mary's confidante, shortly before the engagement party ball.

Then follows the more tightly constructed episode that is the initiation to the froufrou in the lady's boudoir, which was one of the highlights of the silent film. When the banker announces to his guests the imminent sailing to England of his daughter and her intended lord, Mary pretends to faint, joins John in her bedroom (which he entered via a ladder) and begs him to take her to California. John: "You'll know hardship and poverty, maybe hunger." Mary: "It sounds all so beautiful." The end of the scene takes up situations from the 1924 version: Mary changes, he tries clumsily to remove her many crinoline skirts while excusing himself ("It's the first time I've ever undressed a girl"), the father bursts in, John hides beneath her skirts, etc. While the couple escapes into the night, the banker reassures his future son-in-law in the living room, tapping him on the shoulder: "You'll see, Mary is the most obedient of women."

A montage sums up the hasty marriage, then the interminable journey west in the covered wagon, braving gusts of rain, tornadoes, swamps and deserts. They near their goal: like all the other travelers, John and Mary, perched on their wagon, joyously break into "Oh Susannah! I'm Goin' to California with My Banjo on My Knee." "It's like the garden of Eden," she exclaims, admiring the surrounding greenery. He: "Well, plenty of snakes, I'm afraid, but no apples." Pan to a dozen baby blankets drying in the sun; "Sunshine," the farm boy, sings to himself while doing the laundry; a baby cries in the rudimentary thatched cottage John built for his family. During John's absence, a sadistic band of cattle thieves intrudes. The leader, with throaty laughter, commands obedience by taking the baby hostage and firing over its little head; his younger brother, a lecherous psychopath, stares at Mary, promising to come back "when I have more time." On the way home, John encounters the thieves with his cattle, but wary of their dozen or so guns, he lets them carry off the fruit of a year's labor. Borzage handles their reunion with his own flair: to protect each other, husband and wife do not speak of their trauma, putting on an act for each other every day. The truth comes out little by little, when John suggests to Mary to return to New England. But he still hesitates taking the law into his own hands, until Mary tells him the gangsters threatened her. Then, in the moonlight, we see the outline of three lynched bandits; a coyote howls and the gang leader vows vengeance. In the Carlton's blockhouse, the baby is in a state of shock; any strong emotion could kill him, the doctor has warned. The nocturnal siege of the house begins, another highlight. Mary notices that the infant is no longer reacting. Rather than capitalize on her despair, Borzage leaves the mother buried in the shadows; we only hear her murmur "no, no" while a spotlight cruelly brings out the whiteness of the baby's blankets; Mary sits down in front the camera and leans toward the small baby lying on her knees; above her, the planks explode under the impact of the bullets. The mirror pressed to the baby's mouth remains clear. These few terse shots are sufficient to sum up the tragedy. John calls Mary urgently: Sunshine is wounded. In tears, she gestures for him to be quiet as the child is sleeping, then grabs a rifle to help her husband; she saves his life by shooting down the gang leader. At the end of the siege, when the reinforcement arrives, Mary, encircled by flames as if in a painting, comes out of the burning room, the corpse of the infant on her arm. In the morning, without a word, John drives a wooden cross onto a grave and takes Mary by the shoulder, turning their backs on the smoking ruins of their home. Borzage filmed this poignant episode without a note of music for 25 minutes, the tone violent, the photography raw. Dialogue gradually decreases, the entire attack unfolds in oppressive silence, hammered only by gunfire and the whistling of ricochets. The essential is conveyed by gestures and the hypnotic images: a tour de force worthy of great German cinema.

To protect each other, husband and wife do not speak of their trauma: Leslie Howard and Mary Pick-ford in *Secrets*, 1933.

The following montage symbolically mixes ploughed fields, small planted shrubs that become trees in blossom, alternating with shots of the Carlton progeny on cradles, rocking horses and swings. 1900: John, future governor, is in the midst of an electoral campaign; his wife and four children cheer him from the balcony. At the reception following, a Mexican beauty (Mona Maris), John's latest liaison, creates a scandal and threatens to ruin her lover's career by handing over compromising letters to the press. Ashamed, John confesses everything to his wife, who tells him that she has always known about that "secret." The couple, more united than ever, faces public opinion together. John wins, becomes governor and later even senator in Washington. This third part of *Secrets* delighted gossip columnists: Leslie Howard was known to have had innumerable extramarital flings and Mary Pickford was also sending a reminder to her husband Douglas Fairbanks, notoriously unfaithful! Here, at the end, the film's weakness appears, linked to the structure of Besier and Edginton's outmoded play: the conquering of the West (*Cimarron* with a romantic tinge) serves as a backdrop to a condensed version of the American dream (a penniless young whippersnapper makes his fortune on the other shore of the continent). Mary is at the heart of the drama; the rebellious young girl transforms herself into Mother Courage and ends up as the sorrowful spouse; the overly succinct story (80 minutes) never accounts for her extraordinary perseverant marital love. But the masterful narration, with its dazzling episodes, shades of meaning and artful composition, along with the charms of the actors keep it afloat.

Borzage's conclusion contains an energetic addition that attempts to break through the straightjacket of stereotypes, and, at the last minute, anchors the film in a more personal universe. The final sequence unfolds in the present; newspaper headlines announce Senator Carlton's retirement after more than 30 years of loyal service in the Capitol. The four children, now adults, are indignantly knocking on the door of the bedroom, behind which the couple, in their seventies, is now barricaded. The progeny is shocked to learn that their parents have decided — "how childish!" — to motor back to California alone. At their age! The little old people listen, ears pressed to the door, excited like children by the turn of events. "They order us around, be in bed at nine, I'm only allowed two cigars a day!" grumbles John, taking pleasure in lighting a Havana. "Madam, your parents once frightened me, but your children terrify me!" Finally, Mary turns the key, half opens the door and explains to the younger generation: "We're tired of it. We lived with you half a century. Your father and I would like to have ourselves back again. Take our marriage to the point where it was interrupted by the birth of our children. We want to stop talking about you, we want to start talking about ourselves for a change. And besides we have secrets." As the children stare at her, stupefied, she continues: "These secrets, they are ours, we can't share them with you. Secret joys, secret sorrows, lovely and some dreadful secrets, but they all belong to us and we want to be alone with them." The old couple slams the door, escapes by the service entrance, joyfully commandeering the butler's car. "Madam, I should never have married you fifty years ago. You didn't have half the charm, the beauty and the brain you have today. I should have waited," confides John to his wife while telling off the bad drivers around him. The radio begins playing a jazzed-up version of "Oh Susannah!" and the shot of the little old couple dissolves into the radiant image of the young couple perched on their covered wagon en route to the Californian paradise.

This radiant ending is a far cry from the sad images of Leo McCarey's *Make Way for Tomorrow* (1937). Formally, it gives the story the appearance of a circular structure (replacing the flashback). The ending avoids the melodramatic pitfall of the generational conflict. With Borzage, (social) success is much more challenging than poverty. From the moment the Carltons no longer have to fight for their happiness, the lies start, and relations deteriorate. The children — in the image of their Marlowe grandparents in Trenton — become bourgeois in their luxury, and the old couple, "unworthy" like Brecht's heroine, chooses again to escape at night, fleeing the degradation of conforming to convention. After the shameless admission of the "right to have secrets" (a concept totally foreign to today's world!), the film ends with the sweethearts reappearing in a sort of eternal youth, a timeless union reflected by the music ("Oh Susannah"). "The lightness in tone reflects the light-heartedness which, in their golden years, forever recaptures a childlike beauty of spirit," concluded Henri Agel.[49] For Borzage, heartfelt reality is the only one worth capturing.

Secrets received good reviews but disappointed at the box office (it lost about $100,000 out of a total cost of $531,640). Roosevelt took office on March 1933 and launched the New Deal; the simultaneous release of the film in 25 cities — on March 15, 1933 — was handicapped by the new U.S. President's antidepression decree. On this same day, Roosevelt ordered banks closed for the entire week (the famous Bank Holidays). Several businesses panicked, reducing their salaries by half and the public, threatened by the economy, stayed away from shows. Aside from this unsuccessful film launch, United Artists owned very few theaters on the west coast. Fatalistic, but not in the least disappointed by her collaboration with Borzage, Mary Pickford said goodbye to films, from then on content to manage her companies, ensconced in her estate, Pickfair.

* * *

While examining Borzage's works and their significance, the man himself — not the high-ranking professional, but the private man, and his lifestyle — deserve some attention. As mentioned, between 1927 and 1935, Frank Borzage enjoyed considerable prestige. His public image was in keeping with this professional and social success. At that point he was still the only director in the world to hold two "Photoplay Gold Medals" and two Oscars for directing (handing out a second directorial award to a former winner gave rise to a long debate amongst the jury); moreover, four of his works had bypassed the million-dollar mark at the box office: *Secrets* (1924), *7th Heaven, Street Angel* and *Bad Girl*. In 1933, "Mister Frank" — as his collaborators respectfully called him — was in the quartet of most highly paid filmmakers ($60,000 per film) alongside Ernst Lubitsch, Josef von Sternberg and Rouben Mamoulian.

His reputation allowed him to lead a life of luxury in the time-honored Hollywood tradition, as faithfully reported by the society columnists of the era. The unmistakable signs of California-style social status nevertheless indicated radical differences in taste between the filmmaker and his wife. Rena Borzage, particularly drawn to high society, a fan of anything Polynesian (Hawaii was her second homeland), had a bustling social life and maintained an image to go with it. The couple owned two villas; one a stately domain on two floors in the center of Hollywood, located at 3974 Wilshire Boulevard; queen of the manor, Rena was responsible for the furnishings and pretentious decor (French style furniture, velvet, gold china and crystal in the style of Hearst Castle, etc.), which her husband found too lavish. "We were much happier in one small apartment," Borzage confided to his brothers and sisters (whom he supported financially until the end of his days). The other dwelling was a beach house in Las Tunas (Malibu), on the shores of the Pacific. The Borzages also owned an extravagant Hawaiian restaurant at 7566 Melrose Avenue, the Hawaiian Paradise (opened April 1936), with palm trees, live parrots, and a roof of treated bamboo. There Rena organized costume parties highly touted by Hollywood. The orchestra was flanked by two waterfalls flowing into a pond of tropical fish surrounding the dance floor![50] The ex-actress had also taken up press photography as of 1922 (during the Canadian filming of *The Valley of Silent Men*) and owned a vast collection of cameras as well as a laboratory. She also operated two clothing stores in Honolulu, the Town and Country and The Vogue Shop at Waikiki Beach. When not participating in the activities mentioned above, or at polo, aviation or amateur theater,[51] Rena traveled with women friends, telling reporters with zesty cynicism that "a planned vacation is a sure prevention of divorce."[52] She was seemingly proved right, as the longevity of the marriage defied local statistics. While her husband was busy directing a movie, Rena, covered in jewels, gaily trotted around the globe: Europe and Japan (visiting the Sessue Hayakawas, 1932), Bermuda and China (1933), Bali and Hong Kong (1936), etc. Upon her return, the filmmaker, still hopelessly in love, organized lavish receptions; in 1933 he even rented a dirigible to strew flowers over the bridge of the ship bringing his wife home!

Frank's life outside the studios and Masonic lodges mostly flourished on the playing field. Although an inveterate pipe smoker (in 1941, his collection included 876 pipes, the most precious of which came from his maternal grandfather in Switzerland), he was an accomplished athlete, lover of fresh air and unpretentiously convivial, without class consciousness. The Hollywood Athletic Club was his general headquarters, followed by the Jockey Club and the Uplifters' Club in Santa Monica Canyon. His main passions were, beyond a doubt, polo and golf. Borzage was a California polo champion ("three goaler"; handicap: one), captain of a team at the Riviera Country Club that played every Sunday,

Celebrating 20 years as a director at the Hawaian Paradise, with (L-R) Ernst Lubitsch, Rena Borzage, Richard Dix and William A. Wellman (1935).

whose members included Will Rogers, Spencer Tracy, Walt Disney, Dick Powell and Walter Wanger. He had innumerable victories and the first part of his career was affected by riding accidents (a fall in 1928 caused him to lose his sense of smell, another in 1934 fractured his collarbone), sometimes causing shooting of his films to be interrupted. His personal stable was handsomely outfitted: six to nineteen polo ponies boarded at Spencer Tracy's ranch (1937), then later at Fred MacMurray's. Bing Crosby gave him an Arabian steed for having encouraged him to persevere in his career. Borzage played golf (handicap: two) at the Lakeside Golf Club, Rancho Golf Club, Wilshire Country Club or at the Racquet Club in Palm Springs, Charles Farrell's property. He also frequently played squash and handball and skied; in 1934, he opened a professional badminton club.

On the water, Borzage owned a hydroplane for competition (for waterskiing off Catalina Island) and the yacht *Apache* (renamed *Rena B.*), given to Rena in 1927 after the triumph of *7th Heaven*. After promising her husband to stop flying her plane, in 1938 Borzage consoled her with the *Athena*, the famous 105-foot schooner bought from Tay Garnett (immortalized in *Trade Winds*). It won several regattas in Hawaii and Johnny Weismuller and Lupe Velez, still married, were frequent — and noisy — guests. Between shoots, he gladly retreated to his yacht to study scripts or fish for swordfish. (Yet he abhorred hunting.) As of August 1931, Borzage held an aviator's license and flew his "Waco F2" to visit friends (he learned to fly to combat vertigo, he said); he was president of the Hollywood Air Club, whose members included Clarence Brown, Henry King, Howard Hawks and Victor Fleming, other filmmaker-flyers. The press emotionally reported the incident that almost cost him his life, when, in the summer of 1933, he wanted to surprise Will Rogers at his Santa Monica Canyon ranch: the landing field was full of trucks of fertilizer that the pilot just barely missed. Borzage explained to columnists how he imagined his ideal vacation: to fly over the U.S. from one coast to the other in the company of Henry King (each in his own plane) and make a stopover at each golf club.

The filmmaker also had a very developed, very "Latin" sense of family. His parents lived on Ingraham St., behind the Wilshire Blvd. villa, and Frank liked to take his breakfast there, lovingly prepared for him by his mother. He bought his father — who visited him daily at the studio — a ten-acre vineyard at Riverside, so that he could make the red wine that reminded him of his native Italy; the family was mobilized for the wine harvest. The entire Borzage clan benefited from his largesse. In particular, he took care of the three children of his brother Henry (for whom he obtained work as an electrician at Fox): Frank Jr., his favorite nephew, went to military school where Rena had passed him off as the filmmaker's son; he lived for a time at his famous uncle's on Wilshire Blvd. Borzage also took care of the education of his niece Mary and provided Madeline with ballet training and about ten small parts in his films. His fondness for Henry's children was partially motivated, according to some of his family, due to the fact that they were the children of Henry's first wife, Madeline (died in 1919), for whom Frank had a notable weakness.[53]

11

The Romance of the Deprived

After *A Farewell to Arms* and *Secrets*, which took him away from Fox for more than six months, Frank Borzage was ready to take the plunge and try his luck at being an independent producer-director. This plan, eccentric as it was at a time when the majority of directors in Hollywood were tied to the major studios, and when even powerful people in the industry were feeling the effects of the recession, was not entirely new. It had begun a few months earlier. In the winter of 1931–32, Borzage and his colleagues Cecil B. DeMille, Lewis Milestone and King Vidor, all at critical points in their careers, united to form an independent production company named the Hollywood Screen Guild, whose goal was to ensure its members maximum creative freedom. Each had his own headquarters. The seat of Frank Borzage Productions was in North Hollywood (4024 Radford Avenue), but the filmmaker rarely set foot there; only his brother Lew had an office there, which he kept until his death. Borzage's manager and personal lawyer, Mike C. Levee (also co-producer of the silent and sound versions of *Secrets*) was appointed president of the Guild. According to the statutes, the four musketeers, and all their scriptwriters and actors, received only minimal salary but shared a part of the profits. At the beginning of July 1932, the company's first film was announced: the Russian drama **Chocolate*, directed by DeMille and using United Artists for studios and distribution, following the filming of *Secrets*. DeMille, returning from a long trip to the Soviet Union where he took refuge after the public disaster of *The Squaw Man*, tried to stay afloat. But the delirious biblical epic *Sign of the Cross*, begun at Paramount Ranch the same time as *A Farewell to Arms*, put him back in public favor and DeMille backed out. King Vidor developed the main outline of the script of *Our Daily Bread* for the guild, but only directed the film in 1934, in a completely different context. As for Milestone, the fourth partner, he set off for England after what he thought was Korda's invitation to direct H. G. Wells' *Things to Come*. Thus, in the spring of 1933, Borzage was the first and unique beneficiary of the Hollywood Screen Guild.

He then declined two lucrative offers, one from Paramount, *One Sunday Afternoon* with Gary Cooper and Helen Hayes, and the other from MGM/Walter Wanger, *Another Language* with Helen Hayes (March–April 1933).[1] But he needed to find a studio for technical equipment and distribution. Harry Cohn, Columbia's explosive dictator, wily and fierce, jumped at the opportunity. In the early thirties, although widely expanding, Columbia was still the poorest of the major studios. But very early on Cohn was clever enough to recognize Frank Capra's exceptional talent and gave him increasing latitude. Capra was a good investment: his films brought in millions, and he was soon recognized by the establishment, winning several Oscars. Expressly wanting for once and for all to do away with the clinkers of the Z series on Poverty Row, Cohn put his protégé on a project more artistic than commercial, the controversial *The Bitter Tea of General Yen*. These same concerns about respectability prompted him to attract Frank Borzage Productions under his roof (in

May, it would be Lewis Milestone's turn). On April 7, 1933, Borzage signed an exclusive $85,000 contract with Cohn for two films of his choice: *Man's Castle* and *The Paul Street Boys* (renamed *No Greater Glory*), difficult subjects that would have been unthinkable at Columbia two years earlier.[2] Setting up camp in the Gower Street studios, the filmmaker enjoyed the greatest freedom of his career to date. His only adversary would again be censorship.

After intense research, Borzage set his heart on an unpublished play by Lawrence S. Hazard, *Hunk o' Blue*, a morbid but highly topical subject dealing with the Depression. Beforehand, to Columbia's great relief, Borzage decided to modify the play's tragic conclusion, giving the job to scriptwriter Jo Swerling. This was an important step, because this writer of Russian origin, who later wrote the musical comedy *Guys and Dolls*, was also a close collaborator of Capra (seven films, including *It's a Wonderful Life*); he was said to be gifted at making everyday people's lives fascinating; and his characters' main traits were naturalness and individualism. Borzage also ostensibly wanted a plot that, under an updated appearance, was reminiscent of *7th Heaven*—a resemblance often emphasized by the publicity ("The Most Glorious Love Story Since *7th Heaven*"). This genesis gave birth to what may be considered the most precious gem of Borzage's sound period, the unforgettable *Man's Castle*.

Columbia managed to keep production costs low by signing very few long term contracts with actors, preferring to borrow them from the competition for a limited time. The lead role of Bill, the tramp, was written with Spencer Tracy in mind. Remember that Borzage had promised his friend a role that could propel him one day to stardom (cf. chap. 9), but for the moment, the actor was still marking time at Fox. In agreement with a press agent, the director orchestrated some publicity "suspense": for several weeks, to believe the newspapers, the coveted part was going to Gary Cooper, then James Cagney, Paul Muni or Ralph Bellamy. Tracy's casting made headlines when it was announced. The same mystery surrounded the female role: Borzage tested no less than 125 candidates, including Anita Louise, Zita Johann and Sally O'Neill, before deciding on twenty-year-old Loretta Young, a starlet at Warner who had appeared in another film about the Depression (*Heroes for Sale*) and whom Borzage had greatly admired in Rowland V. Lee's cult film *Zoo in Budapest*. Of the director and working with him on *Man's Castle* Young recalled, "That Frank Borzage had a way with actors. He made you believe your part and this intensity came over on the screen. The story was a trifle but we loved it. I proved I could really act with that one."[3] But what the camera infallibly captured (and what titillated the paparazzi) were the kinds of feelings that brought the stars together. In fact, throughout the shooting of the film, Spencer Tracy and Loretta Young were having a torrid but shameful affair: he was married, and they were Catholics to boot.

Filming took place over 30 days between July 28 and September 6. But there was an initial two-week delay in filming due to strikes that paralyzed eleven Hollywood studios, involving 27,000 employees, and setting the tone![4] Midway through filming, Helen Mackellar (Flossie) fell ill and had to be replaced by Marjorie Rambeau. As it was set in New York, where exterior costs were prohibitive, Borzage delegated a second team to shoot 180,000 feet of film on Broadway, Park Avenue, 6th and 9th Avenues, and on the banks of the East River, etc. Many of these stock shots were used for background. They reconstructed the shanty town of the unemployed ("Hoover Flats"), with 60 huts made of sheet metal and planks throughout set no. 1 on Gower Street, by using false perspectives (like Murnau did in *Sunrise*); at the back of the set, tiny shacks were inhabited by children and dwarves, and further on were miniatures of an el-train and the Manhattan skyscrapers, with windows that lit up on command. The camp was full of mud, debris, and abandoned cars. (Stephen Goosson, who sketched the Himalayan city for "Shangri-La" three years later, designed the

Lobby card of *Man's Castle* (1933).

sets). Joseph H. August was at the camera, a colleague of Borzage's from the heroic days at Inceville. He was open to experimentation, and for years had worked as John Ford's cinematographer at Fox. As was the case for Charles Lang (*A Farewell to Arms*), it seems that August's soft focus and ultraromantic backlighting, developed under Borzage, was highly influential. At the end of his career August filmed Dieterle's *The Hunchback of Notre Dame*, *All That Money Can Buy* and *Portrait of Jennie*, creating phantasmagorical compositions that totally contrasted with his earlier naturalism.

As with the sets, the film begins with an illusion, a dazzling classic sequence that calls to mind the opening of the false bride in *Bad Girl*. Pigeons peck at popcorn on the gravel in Central Park; a tilt shot shows Bill (S. Tracy) sitting on a bench, in top hat, tails, and a cape. He feeds them while curiously observing (pan right) a girl, Trina (L. Young), whose avid eyes are riveted on the pigeons. With one circular camera movement, Borzage sums up the theme of the film. The background is blurred and the focal length settles on the two protagonists. The individuals are separated from their environment; the camera angle isolates them from one another, but the pan has already established the relationship. Trina admits that she hasn't eaten for two days as she has no money. "Neither have the pigeons, but they eat regular," retorts Bill, rather abruptly, before firmly leading her into a fancy restaurant on Broadway. At desert, the couple peers at each other. Trina has been out of work for a year; Bill has never worked in his life. She had pictured becoming a streetwalker but never managed to, and is afraid of the waves of the Hudson. Bill enjoins her: "You should never skip meals," then, a big cigar in his lips, asks to speak to the manager of the establishment.

He calmly informs the boss that he doesn't have a cent. Considering the thousand of destitute people starving at his doors, the restaurant could, from time to time, provide a meal or two! As the manager, dumbfounded, tries to catch his breath, Bill threatens to harass the rich clientele and create a scandal. He quickly wins his case and, like a great gentleman, leaves the establishment with his head held high. On the sidewalk ("Nothing like a good walk after a dinner"), the bold tramp shows Trina a neon sign hidden under his jacket: he is a "sandwich man" for a brand of coffee! Laughter. The sandwich man is an allegory of a profit-based society, where the individual is worthless (cf. Vidor's *The Crowd*). But Bill disguises himself as one exploited to various ends: this occasional getup ("I don't believe in regular jobs") confers upon him authority and guarantees his freedom. The freedom of the pigeons.

It is less this joyously provocative beginning that created problems with the censors than its implications; as we will see, *Man's Castle* was cut in many places, to the extent that certain passages amputated before or soon after its release (indicated by [¢]) seem to have disappeared from most prints. Trina doesn't know where to go. Bill takes her to a large encampment of homeless people south of Park Avenue (Lower East Side, near the Brooklyn bridge); they pay no taxes and have running water — the river. Bill has no fixed address and sleeps mostly outdoors, because he hates ceilings; he can then allow himself to be lulled by the nostalgic whistling of trains, like a long distance call, and travels in his dreams. Trina meets a few of the colorful locals: Flossie (M. Rambeau), an ex-prostitute [¢], generally under the influence of gin, her former pimp Bragg (A. Hohl) and the brave Ira (W. Connelly) who used to be a minister and is now a night watchman. He got his Bible from Bill, who stole it in a hotel room since "The Good Word is free." After the introductions, Bill brings Trina to the bank of the East River and before she realizes what is happening, the tramp jumps in the water, stark naked (the shot is often censored on television). When Trina, shocked, doesn't dare join him, Bill threatens to come get her by force: "You've got a bathing suit, the one you were born in. That's the one I'm using." [¢] Bragg, a voyeur, observes Trina getting undressed. She dives in and her naked body brushes against Bill's. "Let's race." "Where to?" "To the moon." The image of the two swimmers headed for the stars fades out; the narrative begins again with Trina gaily doing laundry in a makeshift room, a few days later. "Bill is particular, everything that goes near to his skin has to be clean. I expect he's the cleanest man in the world!" It would be hard to suggest the forbidden any more delicately. As always with Borzage, elliptical continuity transmutes the censor's requirements esthetically.

Trina explains to her drunken neighbor that the rudimentary dwelling she now shares with Bill is like "a clearance in the forest." All that's missing is an oven with which she could cook better meals. Flossie warns her of her man's instability, of his unshakeable thirst for independence and his wandering (symbolized by the recurring "call" of the train). But Trina chooses to ignore her fear of being abandoned, encouraged by a domestic compromise: above the shared bed, in what passes for a roof, Bill has put together a sliding window that lets him contemplate the sky. As the saying goes, "A Man's Home is his Castle." In the street, Trina dreams, looking at an oven displayed in a store window, when Bill joins her, holding an ice cream cone. Then begins the first of the sublime asides that are the film's raison d'etre. The filmmaker has not yet shown us the couple together since their first meeting; we know that Trina, grateful to the "protector" she admires, is ready to accept anything to be able to remain in her new home (like Diane at the beginning of *7th Heaven*) and this boosts her energy and confidence. Bill speaks sharply to her, interrupting (getting an oven, even on sale, is out of the question!), but unperturbed, Trina presses herself against

The slums south of Park Avenue in *Man's Castle* (1933).

him, then responds to his harsh treatment by smiling, assenting docilely and with inflamed looks. This dialogue between people acting as though they don't hear, this antagonistic byplay rife with implications, where gestures contradict words, where sight relativizes what is heard — which recurs in all their scenes together — closes with a most characteristic "Borzage touch": the second he turns his back to go, Bill leans toward Trina's ear and murmurs something: the young woman's face lights up, but the viewer is excluded from the confidence — and will remain so (contrary to the elementary rules of dramaturgy). This byplay reveals their unique rapport whose significance escapes even initiated viewers. It is no coincidence that Bragg, the voyeur of the film, also observes the scene.

Bill earns a few dollars by taking on some risky work for Bragg: handing over a demand for payment to a music hall star protected by three gorillas, the alluring Fay LaRue (Glenda Farrell). The tramp takes advantage of the situation to watch her perform a song, then approaches her in full view of the audience, fights with her bodyguards and leaves the stage laughing, his face swollen. In the evening, while Trina is preparing dinner, Bill haphazardly opens the Bible Ira loaned him and softly reads a passage from "The Song of Songs": "Your breasts are like clusters of grapes. How fair, how pleasant thou art, O loveful delights." [¢] Then, addressing his companion brusquely: "You're a heck of a good-looking woman for a guy like me. Look at you. Skinny as a ramp, no hips, no thighs, no nothing." "I'll sort of fill up," Trina replies, in good humor, between tending to the stew she is cooking. Then Bill becomes unpleasant, aggressive: "No, you'll never look like a woman!" and she becomes affectionate, having determined correctly that his harshness is an act hiding his

Feeling discomfort at their growing love: "Don't get any funny ideas" (Spencer Tracy to Loretta Young, *Man's Castle*, 1933).

discomfort at their growing love. When he threatens to bash her teeth in, she smiles, sits down next to him and kisses him. The embrace is too intense. Bill forcibly disentangles himself: "Don't get any funny ideas," but caresses Trina's little curls with the tips of his fingers, then grumbles: "Go to work, and if that stew is burned, I'll pour it down your back!" Trina docilely returns to the cooking. Bill slips out of the room, and on tiptoe, brings in the oven she had admired in the store window. "Hey, stupid!" Trina turns back, open-mouthed, kneels, speechless, then hides her face to cry, overcome. At this point in the story, the metonymic object represents not only her desire to create a home and her desire for stability, but is also an unarticulated sign of Bill's tenderness, implying a sacrifice of nine months of freedom (nine payments). The man runs his fingers through sweetheart's hair, shaking her affectionately. Fade-out.

The sequence is an exemplary illustration of Borzage's alternating between hot and cold, which he uses to avoid sentimentality (the artificial aspect of feelings) and to stir up the viewer's emotions by simply mixing up attitudes and allusions. The viewer feels a part of the heroes' intimacy, entering into an inaccessible and fragile secret: a growing happiness. But there is also Spencer Tracy's subtlety and his broad gestures, even his outbursts are tinged with humanity, rendering this double talk credible. His disarming naturalness, the way he begins or suspends his movements, his way of simulating constant improvisation confirms that here, for the first time, the actor found a role and a director worthy of his immense talent (his career would only take off as of 1936, at MGM). There was real complicity between Tracy and Borzage, two men who resembled each other physically, with a passion for warm naturalness: "If I had to make the picture over again, I should alter hardly a line of it and certainly make no cast changes whatsoever. I consider Spencer Tracy the most unconventional leading man in pictures.... Moreover, he was in thorough sympathy with me throughout the picture—actually glad to play scenes with his back turned to the camera, his face hidden in a pillow or his hand covering his mouth—because those actions help make the situation more natural and real."[5]

Bill earns a few pennies advertising, dressed up as a clown on stilts. Borzage shows him with the children of the area who adore him, then at Fay LaRue's window where Bill reaffirms his independence ("I do anything that appeals to me"). Charmed by his glibness, the singer invites him to her couch and tries to convince him to accompany her to Europe as her bodyguard. Bragg eagerly reports the tramp's infidelity to Trina and while there he makes advances to her: "You're slim, not skinny, I've seen it." Trina rejects him violently after declaring that Bill is free to see whom he wants as long as he remains by her. When Bill comes in late to dinner, with a guilty conscience, Trina mollifies him: "You don't have to make excuses to me for anything. You're your own boss." He lies down on the bed and opens the ceiling window. Perplexed, Bill gazes at the stars in silence. His confusion increases as the days go by (he is so distracted that he even gets kicked off the local youths' baseball team) and culminates in the film's pivotal sequence.

One evening, Bill stops off at Ira's, who is watering his one and only zinnia; Flossie totters out of her shack, drunk on Eucharistic wine [¢]. "The more of that dandelion wine Flossie drinks, the less gin she'll drink," explains Ira, then, quoting "Corinthians" he formulates what could serve as an epigraph to the film: "God chose the foolish things of the world that He might put to shame those that are wise and He chose the weak things of the world that he could put to shame those that are strong" (I, 1:26). While Ira's back is turned, Bill pockets the zinnia that its owner refused to let him have: "I ain't in the flower business. God never meant for flowers to be sold." Trina throws her arms around Bill's neck. He taps her waist playfully but she doesn't let go: "Does it hurt?" "Not if you don't mean it." He takes her breath away: she clenches her teeth and clings to him. (Her body is already covered in bruises, she admits to Flossie [¢], who is continually warning her about this.) The table is set: Bill pretends to have found the zinnia in his soup and tries to start a quarrel, but Trina, not fooled, thanks him for his wonderful attentiveness and consoles even Ira when he comes to complain. During the meal we hear the whistle of a train leaving. His stomach in knots, Bill hides his face and goes to lie down. Trina opens the ceiling window. Bluebirds are flying across the sky. The man turns toward the oven (close-up), the object that ties him down, then to Trina, silent with anguish. She approaches the bed and looks up through the opening. The sky is bright, clouds scatter, the birds have gone. The landscape—like the shot—is thus subjective. The top of Trina's face is lit (close-up), which creates a visual link to the sky, which Bill speaks of to explain his obsession: "When you're alive, you wanna hang on your hunk o' blue. That's all everybody's got in the world." Then, when Trina remarks to him that there is no paradise more beautiful than the cabin they share together, Bill begins to discover his "hunk o' blue" in his companion's radiant expression, in her extraordinary doe-eyes ("No one in the movies had prettier eyes!" raved critic Jean-George Auriol[6]). But Bill scowls: "But that don't stop me from clouting you in the chin any minute!" She smiles, he entices her over to the bed, she curls up beside him. For the first time in the film, Borzage frames the protagonists so that the oblique two-shot always includes the shoulder, arm or head of the other one, thus signifying the creation of a deep tie. Bill continues to torment her ("Don't get yourself in too deep. I'm liable to be

The "hunk o' blue" in Trina's eyes (Loretta Young in *Man's Castle*).

all steam about you today and washed up tomorrow"), then consoles her somewhat dubiously: "I've known fatter ones, but not nicer." Trina cautiously announces to him that she is expecting a baby, which she is prepared to care for alone. Her voice becomes more assured, more serious: "I'm not afraid anymore. You can never leave me now, even if you go away, I've got you now. You're a prisoner inside of me." She buries herself under her lover's shoulders, crying. He leaves the shot. Fade to the railway tracks: the father-to-be determinedly climbs onto a moving freight car. In a brief montage, Borzage alternates shots of Bill escaping, and Trina lying down, staring at the ceiling window. Clutching onto the freight car, Bill looks back, and the repeated medium-close shot of Trina, out of context and quasi-magnetic, acts like a visual call transcending distance. The soundtrack is closely tied in, brimming with the following images (to express their inextricable link), the racket of the locomotive, the musical theme of the shack and the whistling of the train whose plaintive sound ends up translating not the intoxication of open spaces, but its heartbreak. "Borzage's distress, like Apollinaire's, is melodious but secretive" (H. Agel[7]). Although separated, Bill and Trina hear the same sound. The man lets go and jumps to the ground.

That same evening, Trina meets Bill while doing her shopping and repeats to him that he is "as free as a bird." "I'll remember that" retorts Bill. Cut to Ira presiding at a fleeting marriage ceremony with the poor drunken neighbor as a witness; Trina is wearing a nineteenth-century wedding gown, belonging to the night watchman's deceased wife. "Of course, it ain't the church, but the words are the same. And in the eyes of God, you are man and wife." As for the civil status, Borzage makes no bones about it: his heroes are not accountable on earth! Later, Bill awakens Bragg, as he wants to disappear after leaving Trina and the child with enough to survive. What about the "break-in" the good-for-nothing had spoken to him about? The accomplices break into a toy factory where the night watchman — Ira — is sleeping next to his revolver. While Bragg works on the safe, Bill, dreaming of his child, unconsciously gives himself away, becoming distracted by a mechanical doll whose tune awakens Ira. Gunshots. Bragg climbs through a window; Bill is trapped, a bullet in his arm. But when Bragg secretly sets off the alarm, the brave Ira takes pity on Bill and helps him to escape. Meanwhile, the crook lures Trina into his shack, tells her that her lover is lost and that she needs a new protector. Flossie appears when he tries to rape her: Bill is back, safe and sound. Trina doesn't find him right away; the mechanical doll moves forward, as Bill's messenger, as if the hobo were admitting his smallness, having too long worn the mask of a giant (the would-be millionaire, the stilts). He remains crouched behind the famous oven, the first of many links between them. She tends to his wound and

"Men-kids ... never grow up. They just keep reaching for the clouds and listen to the train whistles" (Loretta Young to Spencer Tracy in *Man's Castle*, 1933).

exclaims: "For a strong husky man, you're awfully afraid of a little thing that's not even born yet." Bill remains shamefaced. "Afraid of a baby, the most natural thing in the world, you big fool. They're born all the time. And if they happen to be men-kids, they just never grow up. They just keep reaching for the clouds and listen to the train whistles.... Even birds can't fly all the time." Like so many of Borzage's heroines, Trina reveals herself to be the strong half of the couple; however, her beautiful features and simple soul belie a singular character, because she requires of her man neither fidelity nor the certainty of a future. As Bill bursts into tears, Trina herself becomes moved, and seeing him so unhappy, says she is even ready to have an abortion [¢]. Flossie interrupts them — they have to leave the zone before Bragg turns them over to the police — and grabs Ira's gun. "This ain't murder, this is just house cleaning," she says as she calmly shoots down Bragg.

A train, heading anywhere... Bill and Trina have snuck into an empty cattle car and are lying on a bed of straw. They count the months: the child will be born in December, "Sort of a Christmas present." The cattle car foreshadows the Nativity. The locomotive whistles, but Bill tells his companion she has nothing more to fear from this sound, then presses himself against her. Trina is wearing her wedding dress with a flounced petticoat, an immaculate spot in the grimy half-light. The camera rises in a vertical dolly-out well above the platform of the freight car and frames the lovers, tenderly embracing and facing the camera. The walls of the freight car are invisible. The space expands, the protagonists seem as if suspended, magically set free from threats and material constraints, transformed into a symbolic crystallization: the apotheosis of the couple. In a flash, this last image

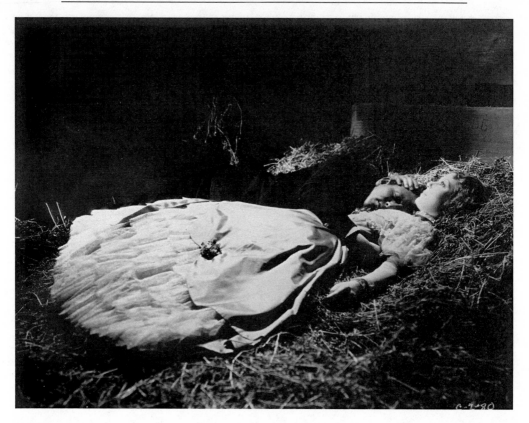

Loretta Young's wedding dress, an immaculate spot in the grimy half-light (with Spencer Tracy in *Man's Castle*).

proves that Borzage is among those who dream wide-awake, like Marc Chagall and Jean Vigo, and conjures up a picture of Bella, the bride in the air, or the newlywed perched on the barge in *L'Atalante* (1934).

People have written that *Man's Castle* was a denunciation of the economic crisis, one of the first works to attest to the tragedy of the Depression. This must be put in perspective, as when the film was released in winter 1933–34, the famous Hoovervilles were already a thing of the past. Wellman's productions for Warner, *Heroes for Sale* (July 1933) and *Wild Boys of the Road* (September 1933) first addressed the phenomenon with stark realism and violence. On the other extreme, it would be wrong to classify *Man's Castle* as a "happy hobo picture," one of the Hollywood comedies that euphemized social distress, either by praising the "joie de vivre" of tramps (Milestone's musical *Hallelujah, I'm a Bum*, February 1933), or by imposing Cinderella-like conclusions (LaCava's *My Man Godfrey*, 1936). The opening of the film unflinchingly depicts hunger and unemployment: "It'd be great to be a pigeon," murmurs Trina. "There's always someone throwing you crumbs." And although misleading, the image of the satisfied capitalist who feeds birds instead of people, and then is amazed that there are hungry people in the world, contains its share of vitriol. The same applies for the fancy restaurant, whose leftovers could feed hundreds of poor souls (Bill mentions that there are 12 million unemployed in America). But this said, *Man's Castle* branches off in a private and distinctly subjective dimension; its tragic note does not disappear, but is displaced. Extreme poverty is omnipresent, depressing, but (as far as the heroes are concerned) remains at a distance by an unreal, blissful "protective" light. As artificial as it may appear, the Hoover Flats slum area is not simply a pretext; the hoboes who are slowly dying are not simply picturesque shadows, but real characters full of pathos. Stylistically, the film juxtaposes the sordid and the idyllic, deriving its lyrical enchantment from the harshness of the dialogue and the softness of the lighting.

Like *The River*, *Lucky Star* and *Bad Girl*, *Man's Castle* is more of a character study than a story. Its great fluidity comes from a contradictory structure, linked to the ambiguity of the central character, as each scene rectifies or answers what precedes it (the alternating between hot and cold mentioned above). The appealing profile of the tramp-poet seems to be a synthesis of several of Borzage's heroes— showing to what extent the filmmaker must have contributed to the various scripts! All his characters are aristocrats of the heart. As with Trina, an innate nobility preserves them from self-destruction. These endearing characters, however, remain "incomplete" until they pass through the ordeal by fire, leading them on an inner journey which they first perceive with confusion. On various levels, Bill possesses the unshakeable optimism and charm of Chico, who lives near the stars (*7th Heaven*), the contented indolence of Steve (*Lazybones*), the resourcefulness of the unfortunate Tim (*Lucky Star*), the aplomb and energetic cynicism of Eddie (*Bad Girl*) and Frederic's obstinate integrity (*A Farewell to Arms*). But Bill most closely resembles Liliom, a selfish, unstable, and morally shaky character. Bill is to some extent Molnár's stunted adolescent who survived the hold-up and got a chance to become an adult. His multiple disguises, his need to affirm his "male" superiority with Trina, his fear of showing vulnerability, and his feigned indifference indicate immaturity and indecision. The moment of his destruction is when he finally becomes himself, which his personality proclaims by freeing itself from its egocentrism. What Bill had taken for freedom was nothing other than solitary aimless ambling, running away from others, while, far from limiting his princely independence, the stabilizing power of love reinforces it.

This journey toward self discovery does not negate or ignore the social context, but goes beyond it. In their study of American films dealing with social problems, Roffman and Purdy correctly point out that once united, neither of the lovers suffers from material deprivation; their existence is almost comfortable, their house middle class (oven, dining table, curtains).[8] Their torments are psychological (emotional security, desire for freedom). They are like the pigeons, like the birds from the Sermon on the Mountain who "neither sow nor reap" and who are fed by Heaven. Bill and Trina are never absorbed in the multitude (as opposed to the protagonists in Vidor's *The Crowd*); they detach themselves both visually by the camera angles and morally by the hope they always carry within. For Borzage's heroes are not victims. They are not humiliated and have not abandoned their dreams: their faith in happiness remains supreme. All their street scenes were clearly recreated by background projection (Broadway full of moving crowds, the night market at the end, etc.) and only rare shots mobilize more than four actors. By their technical awkwardness, the process shots emphasize the couple's otherness, their isolation in relation to their social environment. *Man's Castle* seems to address everyone; if that were the case, its moral would be simplistic. In truth, the film illustrates a meeting of two exceptional souls.

"It's funny, when people get nothing, they act like human beings," remarks Bill, consciously distancing himself from the American dream. He is not running after money. The only time the marginal character mobilizes himself for money, it isn't for himself, and the whole thing turns catastrophic: his superego voluntarily puts an end to the break-in. Trina also points out in the last reel: "It's not money I want, it's you." There is the same indolence regarding work, a value seen as both middle-class and proletarian. When the need is pressing, Bill at most engages in a few hours of easy work, but refuses any pressure and is supremely indifferent to other people's opinions of him. His way of life is his personal choice: he lives from day to day, relying only on his own resources. However, this eccentric individualist knows how to be charitable, even generous to the destitute — he does not feel a part of them. Belonging to no class, he feels he does not have to answer to society.[9] As Jean-Loup Bourget notes, *Man's Castle* contains a kind of poetic anarchism that we find in Lee's marvelous *Zoo in Budapest* (1933) and, in Europe, in Vigo's libertarian masterpieces.[10] The British magazine *Punch* remarked: "*Man's Castle* is in its own way the American counterpart of René Clair's *A nous la liberté*, showing how a man with character may keep himself outside the whole modern network of earnings and expenses, and how a life of leisure and adequate food can be lived, if only one is not too particular or conventional, on next to nothing."[11]

    Man's Castle contravened almost all the precepts of the Hays Office's Motion Picture Production Code (the list of "Don'ts and Be Carefuls") six months after the censorship become effective. Cohabitation, nude scenes, an illegitimate child, attempted rape, allusions to prostitution, suicide and even abortion, alcoholism and unpunished breaking and entering (in the case of Bill), "justified" murder (the elimination of Bragg), indecent dialogues, swearing, "blasphemous" references to religion, etc. The script was first subjected to a detailed examination at the Hays Office, led by James Wingate, before obtaining the go-ahead, not without difficulty; 23 passages were slashed from the initial script. The big shock came in November 1933, when the completed film was submitted to New York City's Censor Board. Local censorship authorities unanimously forbade screening the film, whose world premiere was set for December 29 at the Rialto. Harry Cohn was shattered. His right-hand man, Sam Briskin, personally came to New York to mollify the judges and tried to save their film. After several stormy sessions, *Man's Castle* was released with over 30 more cuts! The states of Kansas, Ohio and Pennsylvania all demanded serious modifications. Abroad, the film was judged to be "objectionable on account of confused ethical code throughout" and banned in much of the Commonwealth (Australia, South Africa, Malaya, Columbia and the British West Indies), as well as in Austria and, of course, in Hitler's Germany where, aside from *Desire*, no more Borzage films would be shown before 1946. As an epilogue, when Spencer Tracy won the Oscar in 1938, Columbia announced that the film would be re-released, to be shown at the Orpheum Theater in San Francisco. Hays opposed it, refusing to accord the purity seal to a film that celebrated cohabitation. Harry Cohn created such a fuss that the censors overturned their decisions two days later; a few dialogues were cut, and most notably, the wedding ceremony was displaced from the seventh reel to the first.[12] Morality was intact!

    Variety's alarming comments were representative of the film's reception about everywhere in the U.S.: "This is the saga of a roughneck you wouldn't put up in your stable. The horses might complain. Spencer Tracy is cast in his most distasteful role.... A picture that goes contrary to normal entertainment and appetites and tastes, its possibilities of going places looks slender at best."[13] The prediction came true: despite a few isolated laudatory voices, the first of the Screen Guild productions was a total flop. It was once again the French who first remarked the work's intrinsic value (it premiered at the Raspail 216 in its original version). The Parisian press did not mince words. For *Comedia*, *Man's Castle* was simply "one of the best films ever directed."[14] The great critic Antoine was emotional: "The birth and blossoming of such delicate, tender feelings in a rebel gives the story an unforgettable gentleness."[15] "There is not one scene that doesn't almost touch the sky, like the angels ... humor, tenderness, drama and comedy mix together, it is an enchanting circle. I know of nothing more poetic," exclaimed Pierre Wolff.[16] In retrospect, Sadoul spoke of "one of the greatest successes of this painter of loving intimacy,"[17] while Mitry, devoting several pages to this magical film, where everything is transformed by a delicate touch, concludes: "A pure jewel manages to shine through, and this sordid zone, scarcely stylized by the set, becomes a paradise of human distress."[18] The film had a galvanizing effect on French movie buffs of the time; the generation that presided in 1936 at the foundation of the Cinémathèque Française (French film archive) saw in *Man's Castle* what would later be called a film d'auteur. It is no coincidence that Jean Charles Tacchella, who began his career as a journalist at *L'Écran français* and founded the legendary film club *Objectif 49*, slips in a discreet homage to the film in *Travelling avant* (1987), a bittersweet attestation to these wondrous years. Their stomachs empty, his film lovers picture re-enacting Bill and Trina's "restaurant stunt"; alas, the tuxedo is missing.... Also, we should mention that China, although Communist, filmed in 1947 in Shanghai a distant remake of Borzage's film charmingly entitled *8000 Miles of Wind and Moon*.[19] Poetry knows no borders. Finally, the best tribute was no remake at all! George Sidney, friend and acclaimed colleague, relates in an anecdote, "We at Columbia, we owned the property and I got an idea because me and Sophia Loren, we were trying to make pictures together. And we got an idea to remake *Man's Castle* and put a little different feeling into this and that, changing the girl to an Italian lady who is fighting to get into the United States. And then we ran the picture a few times. We said forget it. We can't top this. We never touched it. And thank God no one has, because they remake things and they murder them."[20]

* * *

If, when it was released, *Man's Castle* met with a lukewarm reception, *No Greater Glory*, the Hollywood Screen Guild's last film, met with incidents that could be considered comical ... but were no laughing matter at the time. Here Borzage worked again with material by Ferenc Molnár (*Liliom*), the novel *The Children of Pál Street* (*A Pál-utcai fiúk*), published in Budapest in 1907. It was one of the most popular children's books in Hungary, translated into numerous languages, dramatized in 1936 and 1954 and filmed five times.[21] Columbia's management strongly doubted the suitability of such a subject, aside from any consideration of profit! Harry Cohn grudgingly gave his approval and Jo Swerling put the finishing touches on his script while *Man's Castle* was still in production (early September), well before it flopped at the box office. The story contained no adult parts to speak of; the main difficulty was getting about fifty teenagers to Gower Street who, according to the director's wishes, had no previous film experience. George André Breakston was cast in the central role of Ernö Nemecsek, the little carrot-haired Magyar; his mother, of French origin, was an employee in Columbia's costume department. Breakston would remain in movies (the *Andy Hardy* series), become a producer in 1948, and a director in 1954. The two leaders of the two "armies" already had experience: Frankie Darro (Feri Áts), 16, had appeared in almost 50 westerns with Tom Tyler, and Jimmy Butler (Boka), 12, had just played the military cadet in *Only Yesterday*. He had been trained at Southern California Military Academy, and was familiar with the army life.[22] In the beginning, the pack of youngsters made such a commotion in the studio that Harry Cohn in person came to the set to complain; designated "sheriff," Darro was in charge of maintaining order! In the midst of filming—which went from November 1 to December 13 (29 days), with three days of retakes in January 1934—Borzage had to be hospitalized for a week due to acute angina; Lew Borzage was then in command and directed various scenes according to his brother's instructions.

Originally, the educational interest of Molnár's novel was in the way it portrayed the symptoms of adolescence. A penetrating and painstaking observer, the writer showed the psychological dichotomy of an age torn between an aggressive need for action and romantic

Lobby Card of *No Greater Glory* (1934).

fantasizing. The adolescents become conscious of social structures after becoming responsible and assimilating into the community. But after the holocaust of 1914–18, the warlike epic of the kids from Pest took on another dimension, as it revealed nolens volens the mechanisms of manipulation leading to the conflict. Borzage and Swerling claimed the "purpose is to show futility of war, whether engaged in by adults or children."[23] This eminently pacifist intention brought about two small changes in Molnár's story: Borzage added a prologue, and had Nemescek die not in bed, but on the battlefield (the working title was *No Cannons Roar*).

The added introduction was especially important: after 25 seconds of war scenes taken from *All Quiet on the Western Front* (1930), a machine gun massacre in the trenches, the camera takes us to the packed hallway of a military hospital. Perched on his crutches, a maimed soldier harangues his comrades: "Let them shoot me, what difference does it make if the bullet comes from a comrade or an enemy! Did they ask me if I wanted to get into this war? No! They made me fight, against my wishes. Oh, I tell you, this war — any war at all is a foul and rotten thing and patriotism is a loathsome lie! Let them stand me before a firing squad if they like, oh I tell you...." Fade-out. A high school teacher exultantly addresses his students, who listen to him, electrified: "Gentlemen, there is nothing finer than patriotism, nothing nobler than war in defense of the country we like. The best service you can render your country is to take up arms when the nation is threatened, our only salvation lies in our military strength, only through war...." The juxtaposition is clearly eloquent. However, the World War I prologue, which evidently translated Borzage's point of view, was cut in almost every country (outside the U.S.) where the film was distributed!

The Pal Street boys: Jackie Searl, Donald Haines, George Breakston (whistling) and Jimmy Butler (*No Greater Glory*, 1934).

No Greater Glory tells of the confrontation between two rival gangs of high school students. We are far from the "hoodlum" wars of *Blackboard Jungle*, *West Side Story*, or more recently *Rumble Fish*. The protagonists are not maladjusted, antisocial loafers taking out their frustrations with gratuitous bloody violence, but clever schoolboys who aspire to imitate the "grownups" by mimicking their discipline, words and precepts with laughable perseverance. They reflect the "values" of the dominant ideology, translating the antagonism of the adults in miniature. Under the command of "captain" Boka, the boys of Pál Street are determined to defend their playground from a takeover by the "Red shirts"; an older, therefore stronger group, led by Feri Áts. This key area, a small fort that the enemy wants to take over, is the depot of a closed-down sawmill, surrounded by high fences and stacks of planks. Boka's army consists of twenty-three "officers" who proudly wear their kepis, and one lone soldier, the delicate fair-haired Nemecsek. They assemble to the sound of the bugle, heels clicking, lining up impeccably. The chief demonstrates the desired authority and his stereotypical harangues to rouse the gang. The ritual of the grownups is respected to the letter, from the code of honor to the punishment book. Nemecsek worships Bako; his most ardent dream is to accomplish some heroic deed, to feel fully a part of the group. But this smallest, clumsiest, sickliest and dreamiest of soldiers has an unauthorized odd habit of always wanting to whistle with his fingers in his mouth. (One "officer" is even slighter than he, only he is the owner of the bugle.) The old watchman of the grounds shakes his head when the kids yell "war!" and looks sadly at the decoration hanging from his jacket: he has only one arm.

Unquestionably, this description of the fanaticism that these misguided children apply to their "games" is meant to be critical. But Borzage eschews facility. He has enough subtlety to accept that there coexists in a child's soul a kind of combative spirit, a legitimate thirst for heroism, and chivalrous virtues. In adversity, even imaginary, these children are able to show courage and generosity, self-denial and loyalty. A gun does not a fascist make. What is denounced is the perversion of these qualities by a warlike and nationalistic upbringing. The film implicitly uncovers the arbitrariness of the stripes, the inanity of the commander's phraseology ("victory or death"), the herding instinct, the pleasure in submission, the blind idealization of the chief. By showing where alienation leads, Borzage develops his indictment. "He exalts in order to better stigmatize," Mitry points out.[24] The filmmaker-poet recognized in Nemecsek a hotheadedness and absolute candor to which he could relate. His ironic lighting becomes diffused, softened by a humane outlook. Some have criticized him for being ambiguous, while he was merely being honest.

Bako's regiment hides a traitor, Gerék; thanks to his collusion, Feri Áts has entered the coveted land and captured the flag of the "Páls." Bako seeks volunteers to recover and avenge the affront. Nemecsek volunteers: "I wanna risk my life! Maybe if I do, I'll get a promotion!" Bako, Nemecsek and a third lascar, the phlegmatic Csónakos, venture out at night into enemy territory, on an island in the Botanical Gardens. An owl screeches. The commando freezes in terror. All the enchantment of a child's imagination appears in these nocturnal compositions, between copses and streams, barely illuminated by a hesitant moon. Nemecsek falls in the water. Crouching in the thickets, the trio observes the "Red shirts";

Uniforms strangely reminiscent of Hitler's Brownshirts in *No Greater Glory* (1934).

Gerék is with them. Borzage dressed these adolescents in uniforms strangely reminiscent of Hitler's Brownshirts, and the troupe kneeling in the lantern light, with spears and banners, seems today eerily discomfiting. The intruders are discovered; and a manhunt organized. They hide in a greenhouse. Nemecsek, a water lily on his head, surrounded by croaking frogs, remains crouched in a pond. When the three intrepid boys can finally leave the place, a storm erupts... The next day, Nemecsek has caught a serious cold and is forbidden to leave his parents' poor tailor shop. But the call to "glory" is too strong: the little boy sneaks out to the Botanical Gardens at night and recovers the stolen flag on his own. Given away by his sneezing, he stands up to the enemy: Feri Áts respects this so much that he invites him to join the ranks of the "Red shirts." "I'd rather be drowned, have my brains knocked out than be a traitor!," he exclaims gallantly, facing Gerék. To punish him, the "Red shirts" dunk him several times before releasing him, chilled and shivering, under a weapon salute.

The warring parties settle the issue of territory on the battlefield; if the "Páls" take back their banner in loyal combat, they remain. Elected "general," Bako dissects a manual, "Military Tactics and Strategy in the World War." Nemecsek attends a "mobilization," spluttering, coughing, wrapped up in his scarf. As Gerék's father threatens to punish his son for his betrayal, Nemecsek publicly excuses the renegade. Impressed by the soldier's magnanimousness, Bako brings the feverish boy back to the house; on the way, the sick boy experiences hallucinations, saluting imaginary passerby. Nemecsek must take to his bed: his bronchitis is bordering on pneumonia. The doctor is concerned but merely dispenses some advice: the tailor has no money. Nemecsek despairs: he'll "miss the war!" Bako brings him the military cap he has coveted so long and the new "captain" puts it on, trembling, falling asleep happily, his forehead burning. Even Feri Áts sends his regards. Bako and his gang have dug trenches on the territory, set up catapults and traps, and made sand bombs. The attack begins and Borzage gets carried away by the action, like his heroes: he aligns the strategic high-angle shots (the position of the troupes), low-angle shots (the "tour" of command), medium-close shots (the bugle), juggling the montage brilliantly to create a series of electrifying Eisenstein-like images in which the inoffensive pitched battle is rendered aesthetic by dust and sand. The spectator follows the ins and outs of these "Indian maneuvers" with guilty pleasure. They are magnificently photographed, with a touch of humor. In the meantime, Nemescek is delirious beneath the covers; his father hears him move about, whistling, but he is stuck in his shop with a difficult customer. The cruelty of the scene is powerful: the wealthy bourgeois treats his tailor like a servant, becoming more and more agitated by the child's delirium. Shortly beforehand, the austere Gerék senior, a judge, intimidated the children since he belonged to a superior class. These touches extend the indictment to all social systems, whose inhumanity is fatal to the weak and those least adapted. Nemecsek crawls out of bed. Hurrying to the field of operations, he throws himself on big Feri Áts—whom he notices in a blur (subjective shot)—to take the flag away from him. The two boys roll to the ground. Nemecsek remains inert: he is dead. His nails are dug into the pennant, a cloth. The fighting ceases. His mother appears, breathless.

Then, against all expectations, the director achieves the unexpected: while Nemecsek's death is totally predictable and his earlier tearful gestures were irritating, Borzage, in his own inimitable way, casts our hesitations aside. The tragedy becomes palpable. When, in a suffocating silence (but backed up by music) the mother holds the boy to herself for a long time, rocking him, we are deeply moved. Fade-out: a dolly-out shot frames her carrying its body to the house (she is walking toward the camera), like a pietà, surrounded by fifty shaken-up adolescents; Madame Nemecsek looks as if she is going to faint, the children hold her up. As usual with Borzage, the scene is all the more moving by its brevity, sobriety, and silence. Standing at attention, the two armies grant honors. A tracking shot shows the faces of the comrades. The trumpet blower is crying. A pathetic kepi hangs at the end of the pole. Overview of the wasteland: in the foreground, a bulldozer is working the "sacred" ground with its shovel. "They're putting up an apartment house after all," comments the one-armed watchman with the medal. The squabble was useless.

Agel and Wilson qualify this veteran of the trenches, a witness of all that happens, as "the ancient choir of this tragedy."[25] Seen in this light, the "solemn" images of the flag ceremony reveal one last time to what extent these little soldiers were victims of illusion. Like the grownups. But we have to know how to read between the lines, uncover the symbols, distinguish the signifier from the signified. In most European countries the cumbersome prologue with its mutineer (local censorship or in tacit agreement with Columbia?) was cut, which only emphasizes the ideological misunderstanding. *No Greater Glory* was even hailed, in the same country, as a film of both the left and the right! Reactions of France under the Laval government, torn apart by faction struggles, were characteristic. The work was first forbidden by Minister Edmond Sée, under the nebulous pretext that it would be "inopportune" (December 1934). This measure led to some heated opinions in the press: "Some saw it as exaggerated nationalism, others interpreted it, we don't know how, as having communist tendencies," commented fascist François Vinneuil ironically. "The representative from 'Action française' assured: 'It has been banned as it shows children saluting the flag, obeying a code of honor.' We would answer: 'It is a patriotism which is being ridiculed.'"[26] Some applauded the ban, referring to Jean Vigo's boarding school film *Zéro de conduite*, another "odious" work because it uses children to denounce indoctrination by adults. André Antoine's commentary reveals another level of sensitivity: "Of course, we understand that this violent satire on warlike education, to which youth in almost all countries is now subjugated, may have appeared inopportune but when the minister [G. Huisman, Minister of Fine Arts] learned about the film under attack, he rightly saw in it an admirable lesson in tolerance, courage, and pity. And he gave it the go-ahead."[27] The critics' reaction ranged from praise to indignation against a "defeatist" masterpiece that was an insult to "our soldiers." The dubbed version even led one critic to remark: "This is why men have fought for four years: as Alsace, Manchuria, or a wasteland are all one and the same!" But all agreed upon the "exceptional nature" (G. Charensol)[28] of the film.

In Austria and central Europe, *No Greater Glory* was only distributed in its original version and the subtitlers were wary of translating seditious dialogue. In Vienna, the vernacular equivalent of the Hitler youth created an uproar at the screenings (November 1935), but the different National-Socialist factions were far from agreeing between themselves. The newspaper of the German colony in California, *Die Staatszeitung Kalifornien*, for example, saw the film as "a defense of heroism. All the virile virtues of the soldier, loyalty, carrying out one's duty, courage, chivalry, are glorified. If Columbia imagined it was advocating pacifism and anti-militarism, it missed its mark...: this film, which made many cry, could very well have been filmed in the New Germany."[29] The misunderstanding, carefully fueled by the right, came to a grotesque head at the 1935 Venice Biennial when *No Greater Glory* won the "Coppa del Partito Nazionale Facista per il film straniero artisticamente più riuscito."[30] "This is truly our kind of film.... In dying, the valiant young boy gives the foundation for a social structure to the living,"[31] exalted the Mussolini press, with considerable ill intent; they were pleased at seeing an adaptation of Molnár stripped of "pacifist or whining morality."[32] Harry Cohn was a fervent admirer of Mussolini, "the man who made the trains leave on time," and the studio dictator had even accepted an invitation from il Duce to Rome. In March 1933, the Columbia documentary *Mussolini Speaks* was acclaimed throughout America. But not this: the U.S. media didn't breathe a word of the questionable distinction from Venice and Columbia maintained an embarrassed silence. Il Duce's army was in the midst of invading Abyssinia. A quarter of a century later, Borzage would laughingly comment: "That was a strange thing. It was an indictment against war ... and got a citation from Mussolini!"[33]

The film won considerable critical acclaim in the U.S., including "The National Board of Review Award 1934" ("Ten Best American Films"). But the crowds stayed away; the work covered familiar territory and Columbia didn't know how to sell a product so lacking in box office appeal (short of ideas, the studio offered a bonus for the best publicity campaign). Harry Cohn consoled himself with the five Oscars and huge financial success of *It Happened One Night* (Capra). The *Los Angeles Times* felt the film's appeal was limited: "except, perhaps among the 'art' theaters or groups of individuals intent on discovering and sponsoring 'better' films. Thus it has no place in a huge Broadway first-run theater. The viewpoint is too completely European to be understood by the average American who is not imbued with the militaristic spirit inculcated in the schoolroom."[34] A recent American, Frank Capra, publicly defended *No Greater Glory*, embittered that viewers stayed away: "Sometimes when you give the people a fine, intelligent and clean, well made and interesting picture that you imagined 'clean picture shouters' will go for, they let it fail. There has not been a finer, more tender or better made motion picture turned out in some time than director Frank Borzage's *No Greater Glory*. It has everything the critics of motion pictures smut could ask for, and what does the public do? It lets a fine picture become a box-office klunk. That's one reason why the producers don't gamble on more such fine pictures. When they do, the public fails to support them."[35] Capra, Columbia's mascot director—knew of what—and of whom—he spoke. The fiasco was the Hollywood Screen Guild's swan song and at the same time put an end to Borzage's dreams of independence.

* * *

At the same time as his mishaps with the Screen Guild, the filmmaker provided for what he owed by accepting freelance engagements with other studios. His contract with Fox definitively terminated, Borzage signed with Warner Bros., and, beforehand, with Universal Pictures headed by Carl Laemmle, Jr., the founder's son. It was in Universal City's studios in North Hollywood that Borzage would create the third part in his triptych of social melodramas, *Little Man, What Now?* The story takes place at the end of the Weimar Republic, when unemployment was demoralizing the country: 4.4 million people were without work in 1930, 5.6 million in 1931, and 6 million in 1932. Making such a film in the U.S., only five years after the stock market crash, bordered on recklessness, and many events lead up to this extraordinary undertaking.

Compared to the "Major Five" (MGM, Paramount, Fox, Warner, RKO), Universal had a rough time during the Depression and was in continual financial difficulties; in 1930, it managed to pride itself on a comfortable critical and financial success with Milestone's *All Quiet on the Western Front*, but what was considered prestigious had changed, and the studio kept afloat by its remunerative cycle of fantastic films starring Boris Karloff and Bela Lugosi. Moreover, Universal was known as pro–German: not only did it make use of German talent (Leni, Freund, Ulmer, Dupont), but the Laemmle clan itself was from Wurtemberg. "Papa" Laemmle was an outrageous nepotist: he hired practically his entire family in the company—up to seventy people, rumor had it! Besides the hackers assigned to "bread and butter pictures," the studio had two high caliber directors under contract: John M. Stahl for the eighteen carat melodramas (*Back Street, Imitation of Life, Magnificent Obsession*), and young British intellectual James Whale for horror (*Frankenstein, The Invisible Man*).

Strangely, it was Whale — not Stahl — who would suffer during Borzage's temporary stay at Universal City.

In September 1933, Laemmle Junior spoke to Borzage about filming *Zest (a Charles G. Norris novel), and, more importantly, directing a spectacular remake of the musical *Show Boat*, for which William Anthony McGuire wrote the script. Borzage showed interest; he would be paid $65,000[36] for 13 weeks of work (with exteriors along the Mississippi). They had in mind Cary Grant or Russ Columbo, Estelle Taylor and Edna May Oliver; filming was to begin October 15. As problems of adaptation arose, Borzage was able to devote himself to *No Greater Glory*. But the project lagged and preparations stretched out over a whole other year. Borzage had Jo Swerling, his Screen Guild accomplice, rewrite the script and envisaged a new cast including Irene Dunne, John Boles, Charles Winniger and W. C. Fields (June–September 1934). When they finally got the go-ahead in December, the filmmaker was unavailable, already working at Warner. In winter of 1935/36, James Whale took over direction of *Show Boat* from a third shooting script by Oscar Hammerstein II. The film was so expensive that it would bring about Laemmle's downfall and the sale of the studio.

While Borzage was waiting for *Show Boat* to materialize, Laemmle gave him a choice of subjects recently acquired by the company. The filmmaker pounced on *Little Man, What Now?*, as in it he saw motifs dear to his heart. Laemmle frowned: the story of Hans and Lämmchen was so depressing, and besides, it had been promised to James Whale.... Thanks to the intervention of Margaret Sullavan, a fervent admirer of *No Greater Glory*, Whale was replaced by the newcomer (October 17, 1933); the British director consoled himself with *One More River*, the final episode in Galsworthy's *The Forsythe Saga*. *Little Man* was a "German" subject in the vein of *All Quiet on the Western Front*, and sales of the novel by Hans Fallada novel (alias Rudolf Ditzen) on which it was based almost equaled those of Remarque's story; in the U.S., the book was already in its eleventh printing. Published in Berlin in 1932, *Kleiner Mann — was nun?* met with immediate worldwide success due to its topicality; it was translated into twenty languages. On Edgar G. Ulmer's suggestion, Laemmle's agents in Berlin acquired the rights in spring of 1933.[37] Fallada's text was characterized by a keen sense of observation of the milieu and the naturalistic style specific to the New Objectivity. His novel painted the portrait of the German lower-middle class, prisoners of the inflationary spiral, reflecting the daily discouraging reality of Berlin on the eve of the Third Reich. Yet Fallada defused the vague social criticism by the apolitical attitudes of his heroes who, as representatives of their class, swept away any form of contestation with equal contempt and hope for renewal (illusory) of the country by an ethical renaissance of those in power. He backed up this political passivity by striving to maintain his own moral integrity. For this reason, the Nazis did not banish Fallada, but tried to win him over. The novelist bought a farm in the country with his royalties and survived, for better or for worse, until *1947, plagued by pressure exerted by Goebbels, marital crises, alcohol, and morphine.

Berthold Viertel began work on a Berlin version of *Kleiner Mann — was nun?* as of January 1933, but Viertel, a Jew and a leftist, fled shortly before the burning of the Reichstag. The project was taken over by Fritz Wendhausen, with a script by Herbert Selpin, with Hermann Thimig and communist Hertha Thiele in the lead roles. The result was poor: the story was misrepresented into a mystery (with songs) and the nudist Heilbutt, the young salesman who gives the couple back their hope at the end, finds happiness in the ranks of the Nazi Party![38] Universal probably knew nothing of these details. Reworking the script (McGuire, Swerling, and, incognito, writer R. C. Sherriff) delayed production by two months and illustrated the types of difficulties encountered: caution was necessary, as the company still had a subsidiary in the Reich (responsible for filming the street scenes for the background projections). Berlin monitored the work suspiciously: "We were afraid of anti–German tendencies," wrote the California correspondent of the *Film-Kurier*. "Universal realized that Germans would be offended, which is why we weren't even invited to a preview of the film." He then observed, reassured, that "the film avoids any references to the German situation of today" and that the agitators' slogans ("freedom, equality") were "taken from the French Revolution, not ours."[39] Beforehand, Will Hays' offices ranted and raved against the young couple's intent to abort and against Mia Pinneberg's dissolute life, but Universal did not cave in. Only one passage of the script was sacrificed: a French client of Mia's starts playing the "Marseillaise" on the piano. "Shut up! That's no song to sing in a German home!." The Frenchman cynically replies: "We're between wars now, aren't we?," a truth the American censors objected to, but which shows that those responsible for the film had no illusion about the new regime in Berlin and its military intentions.

Little Man, What Now? marked the providential meeting between Borzage and Margaret Sullavan, who would to some extent become his actress of choice, the muse of his sound films (she reappeared in *The Shining Hour*, *Three Comrades*, and *Mortal Storm*); not unlike Janet Gaynor in his silent films—in terms of importance and representation, not in looks. Margaret Sullavan, from an aristocratic Irish family in Virginia, was strong-willed. After four years in the theater, she was invited to Universal where John M. Stahl started her in the melodrama *Only Yesterday* (1933)—plagiarized from Stefan Zweig's *Letter from an Unknown Woman*. But seeing the rushes, the actress fled! Her agent managed, with difficulty, to keep her in Hollywood: when the film came out onscreen, Margaret Sullavan's temperament and hypersensitivity worked miracles: a star was born. The actress with the "little triangular face," "large wondrous eyes," and the "melancholy smile" (C. Viviani[40]) stayed with Laemmle on the condition — an exceptional privilege — that she could choose her parts. *Little Man* was only her second film and already her name outshone all others in the credits. It also seemed that she personally supported Borzage in his conflicts with the studio heads during filming. The distinctive collaboration between the actress, who suffered from permanent insecurity, and her director, has been described elsewhere. After two weeks of practically no direction from Frank Borzage, Margaret Sullavan turned on him and said: "You've got to help, just got to help me, you've never said a word to me, you never told me I'm rotten, I can't stand any more silence!" "If you were bad," Frank Borzage replied, "I'd tell you. You're doing it perfectly." In a lengthy tribute to the actress, the filmmaker spoke of what captured him:

> Miss Sullavan has that natural ability to grasp the essentials of a person's character. When I came to make *Little Man, What Now?*, we had the character of Lämmchen fully taped. She knew her as if she had been her intimate friend. I think I am justified in saying that Margaret Sullavan is a beautiful woman. In private life she is an exquisite, dainty little thing, as quiet as the proverbial church mouse, speaking always in a low voice. But she is not camera-proof as stars are. Many of the most famous stars are never photographed from certain angles. Margaret Sullavan doesn't mind. There are many scenes in *Little Man, What Now?* which failed to show her features at her best. To have done so would have spoiled the naturalness of the sequences. She didn't mind. She has no desire to appear as a lovely doll. [Then he adds] Please look out for the scene in which Margaret Sullavan drops from a tree into Douglass Montgomery's arms. It couldn't have been better done. Even when shooting it, there was not the slightest hint that the scene had been carefully planned. She did it so naturally that she might have been miles away from a film unit. A small point, perhaps, but a significant one. Scenes like this usually have to be shot over and over again, it is the most difficult thing in the world to look natural under such circumstances. But we shot that scene without the slightest trouble.[41]

The choice of the partner — Hans— was not as easy. Lew Ayres (the hero of Remarque's film) was first in line: in the end Borzage preferred the Canadian Douglass Montgomery, who made his screen debut in *Waterloo Bridge* (Whale) under the pseudonym Kent Douglass. Margaret Sullavan would have preferred a more "solid," virile actor than Montgomery, but Borzage always maintained that the reason they complemented each other so well on screen was due to the chemical contrast between their two personalities.[42] Filming took 36 days (from March 9 to April 25, 1934); two weeks earlier, the filmmaker began rehearsals after having instructed those playing Hans and Lämmchen to reread Fallada's novel several times; if they were imbued with the spirit of the text, the work would go faster. With some touch-ups, they reused the village and "Germanic" props from *All Quiet on the Western Front* and *Frankenstein*, on adjoining lots. The Berlin Friedrichstrasse train station necessitated sizeable construction on the Universal lot; 400 extras filled a set 360 feet long. Ulmer, half Berliner, helped out with local color. On March 16, Luigi Borzage, the filmmaker's father, died following a serious car collision in the heart of Los Angeles; Lew Borzage and his wife Pearl, who were also in the car, had to be hospitalized for two weeks.

Shooting a Hollywood film about Germany while abstaining from clichés about autocratic Prussians, and then making it profitable in the U.S. was no easy task, with resentment against the "Huns" of World War I festering. *All Quiet on the Western Front* had conquered American viewers because the former enemies were questioning the war and Milestone emphasized their humanity over their nationality. By eliminating idiosyncrasies which were too local, Borzage's work tended to be universal in the same way. The film invites a natural comparison with D. W. Griffith's *Isn't Life Wonderful?* (1924), a bitter depiction of famine and inflation, located in the Berlin suburb of Köpenick (it was a fiasco in the U.S.). But while Griffith used his penniless fiancés to represent the social landscape and elicit pity from his public, Borzage opposes innocence and perversion, beauty and ugliness, altruism and materialism in order to emphasize the "spiritual depression" which threatens his couple. We are thus in familiar territory.

An introductory intertitle carrying Carl Laemmle's signature announces that "The story of *Little Man* is the story of *Every Man*— and the question of *What Now?* is the *World's Daily Problem*... Against the tide of time and chance, *all* men are little — but in the eyes of a woman in love, a man can become bigger than the whole world." The action unfolds in Platz, in eastern Pomerania. Dolly-in: a town square, under a driving rain, with a speaker haranguing the unemployed. The dolly shot continues with a fade-in and frames Hans Pinneberg (D. Montgomery) listening distractedly to speeches about "equality" while awaiting his friend at the entrance of a building. "He says that the rich are too rich, and the poor are too poor. He's gonna fix it. He's gonna make the rich too poor, and the poor too rich," a passerby sums up ironically. This sarcasm translates less an apolitical attitude than it does distrust of the kind of simplistic revolutionary who, we know today, did not enrich the planet. The second Hans consults his watch, Lämmchen ("little lamb") appears out of "nowhere": she surreptitiously eyes the corner of the building, her face mutinous, and, facing the camera in a medium-close shot says: "What time is it, Mister?" The shot stands out from those before it by its sudden luminosity, as if the heroine's radiance chased away the flood, banished the virtually cosmic dullness. (An impression emphasized by the intrusion of a musical leitmotif and the color of the raincoats—hers is clear, his is dark.) Hans can barely contain his joy: "You are too poor having me, but I'm far too rich in having you." As usual, Borzage begins his narrative by this concise synthesis of the situation, the themes, and the characters involved. The rain establishes a psychological climate or may symbolize the night of the hearts (cf. also *A Farewell to Arms*, the mist in *Street Angel*, and the darkness in *Lucky Star* etc.); the filmmaker was thus more concerned with the metaphoric change of weather than by its material reality. The introductory camera movement has

The Romance of the Deprived: *Little Man, What Now?* with Douglass Montgomery and Margaret Sulla-van (1934).

linked Hans with the mass of unfortunates. The individual, from the beginning, has the reactions of a man unsure of himself, subordinate, basically anonymous, but who adores his companion (cf. the insignificant employee in *The Nth Commandment*, chap. 4). She, on the other hand, is identified with the source of light (his source). To restabilize the relationship, Borzage then shows Lämmchen in a high-angle shot, gripped by an irrational fear, hesitant to enter the building where the gynecologist awaits. Hans's hand enters the upper part of the frame and draws the woman up. A kind of complementarity is established.

Hans paces the waiting room, while outside, police apprehend the speaker and disperse the crowd. Old Goebbler and his sick wife (Mae Marsh), who were there before Hans and Lämmchen but had no appointment, are tired of waiting their turn and leave, angered by the "unequal treatment." Borzage looks compassionately upon the poignant Goebbler couple (described as "communists" in the script[43]), prey to bourgeois scoffing and soon victim of their unrealistic obstinance. Lämmchen is pregnant; the gynecologist declares: "Don't you worry, everything will be all right." And Hans believes he is referring to an abortion, because how could three of them live on a miserable salary of 180 marks? A misunderstanding. "It's your problem," says the doctor, coldly wishing him luck and demanding 15 marks for the consultation. Hans fumes: "There are other doctors, more understanding, more human!" A child runs and falls in the gutter; Lämmchen rushes over, consoles the child; her maternal instinct awakening, she implores Hans: "Couldn't we manage on your 180 marks a month" He assents with a kiss. This passage objected to by the censor was the object of a heated controversy between Universal and Will Hays, to the point where the film was placed on a blacklist: the lovers were living together as man and wife and wanted an abortion! On July 14, 1934 the Legion of Decency Council of the archdiocese of Chicago tried to boycott *Little Man, What Now?* by classifying it as "unsuitable entertainment." Spain, among others, eliminated this passage in its dubbed version.

Hans and his bride settle into the small town of Ducherow, but Lämmchen is soon intrigued by her husband's fearful behavior: he huddles in the back of the taxi and refuses to stop in front of where he works, for fodder and grain merchant Emil Kleinholz (DeWitt Jennings). The caricature that follows is unusually ferocious for Borzage, in the vein of German George Grosz (who designed the book cover). Kleinholz knows that there are no positions in the city and amuses himself daily by terrorizing his three young accountants— Hans, Schultz and Lautenbach — one of whom is destined to marry his unattractive and particularly foolish daughter Marie. Schultz and Lautenbach arrive a minute late in the morning, but Kleinholz already surprises them from the top of the staircase: panicked, they are on guard.[44] Borzage introduces the corpulent tyrant by a low-angle tilt shot from the bottom up: barefoot, shapeless nightshirt, a scraggly beard and bald head — the features of a brute. Shaking with throaty laughter, he utters a few threats and goes back into the kitchen where, in a composition of consummate vulgarity, the rest of the clan is devouring their breakfast. Frau Kleinholz has a piggish face, and Emil junior, 12, seems to be malevolence incarnate. Marie — "Just dumb enough to make a very good wife"— is attracted to Hans, the most appealing. "You'll have him!" promises the father. "Papa, when I get older, will you also hire a woman to help me?" the impudent brat asks, mocking. Kleinholz chokes on his coffee and bursts out laughing. (Kleinholz's grotesque anatomy and behavior did not exist in Fallada's work.) Hans had removed his wedding ring, hiding his marriage before beginning work. Kleinholz bursts into the room to announce that he is going to throw one of his "lazy bachelors" into the streets, but which one? He hesitates, sadistically scrutinizing the faces of his victims, destroying their solidarity and provoking selfishness. Alone with Hans, Kleinholz attacks: "You speak of peace and of tolerance, when the whole world is full of unrest and bigotry, to say nothing of poverty... Which one would you let go, if you were at my place? Would you fire yourself, walk the streets and starve?" the monster sneers before leaving. At a sign from her father, Marie enters; she removes a carnation from her bun and waves it under Hans's nostrils. Kleinholz observes the scene from a small circular window.

Sunday: a picnic on the banks of a stream, shielded by sunny groves. The narrative's impact depends on the emotional charge of this type of enclave, whose intense purity contrasts violently with the world's abnormality and disorder. Lämmchen, scantily dressed, barefoot, demands of her husband why he has kept their marriage secret. Hans admits to the situation at work. Relieved, the young woman bursts out in joyous laughter, flitting around the grove, climbing a tree, jumping in the arms of her bewitched husband, rolling on him and pressing him against the ground like as if she'd captured her prey (a highly erotic scene, also attacked by the censor[45]). Borzage frames his lovers first in long and sensual close-ups, then follows their frolicking in a smooth tracking shot (Lämmchen's naked legs running in the high grass). Their long kiss is interrupted by the horn of a convertible: the entire Kleinholz family is taking their Sunday outing! Emil junior sniggers. On Monday morning, the tyrant turns to his clerks, playing on their fear like a cat with a mouse: "You know why I'm laughing? This is the day I give one of you notice... You like the woods, uh, Pinneberg?" Hans doesn't flinch, but when Marie insults Lämmchen, he blurts out the truth to her. Marie sobs noisily. "Have you so much money, Herr Pinneberg?" asks the father. "I have that much pride, Herr Kleinholz," he replies, shutting the door. Enraged, Kleinholz kicks his daughter's backside. She howls. In this portion of the narrative, Borzage still mixes clowning around and nastiness in a spirit very close to the anti-bourgeois farces of Carl Sternheim, Ödön von Horváth (in the theater) and the *Kammerspiel* of silent German cinema. But he closes the Ducherow episode on a supremely refined elegiac note: three weeks have gone by; in the evening, Hans returns once more from the unemployment office with nothing. The apartment is empty. He looks for Lämmchen in the night and ends up finding her, alone and sad, sitting on a horse on a merry-go-round, lulled by the sound of a barrel organ. The rotating movement of the carousel expresses her helplessness and the distance between the couple; with each revolution it demonstrates the difficulty of contact, but also a mysterious complicity that goes beyond words. In bits, Hans learns that Lämmchen has been unable to resist hunger, she alone has eaten their food for the day and doesn't dare come home. It doesn't matter: Hans has received a letter from his stepmother in Berlin (Lämmchen had secretly contacted her): an apartment and work await them! He jumps on the merry-go-round, whose circular motion continues: dissolve to the wheels of the train, arriving in the capital. (The surprise meeting with the Kleinholzs in the country, Hans's dismissal, the unemployment, hunger and the sequence on the merry-go-round do not occur in the novel.)

In Berlin, Mia Pinneberg (Catherine Doucet) greets them on the platform, all dolled up, her dachshund on her arm. She brings the couple into a huge apartment on Spenerstrasse and assigns them a disproportionate room, with a canopy bed and period furniture. Rent: 100 marks. Lämmchen can help with the housework. As for the other details: "Holger Jachmann will attend to it." At that instant, this cheerful fifty-year-old (Alan Hale)—Mia's lover, partner and principal subtenant—is questioned in the street by a detective. He politely gets rid of the detective thanks to false identity papers and comes home, whistling. The gentleman-crook (a pimp in Fallada's work) immediately falls under Lämmchen's charm, profusely complimenting her and kissing her hand, then helps her dry the dishes. The very complex relationship between them provides one of the film's most interesting, unusual features. Jachmann (who recalls Mack the Knife in Brecht's *Threepenny Opera*) appears to be calculating and underhanded. The viewer remains on the alert, but the potential crook remains merely a disinterested protector. His first reflex is, of course, to suggest to Lämmchen she become his mistress, to shower her in gifts, but he does it so gallantly and with so much humor that she has no trouble calling him to order. From then on, he develops a friendship with her born out of admiration and respect; Lämmchen also takes secret pleasure in his company because he is all Hans is not: carelessly self-assured, imposing, ironical, colorful. He laughs heartily when he learns she is pregnant and advises her to be sure to tell her landlady nothing! But he is above all a precious ally in the conflict between son and stepmother. Mia, who personifies a class of days gone by, loves but money and her dog. Hans is both irritated by her greed (he breaks plates that his stepmother is quick to bill him for) and shocked by her amoral cohabitation; Lämmchen does not share her husband's prudery and, like Trina in *Man's Castle*, remains miraculously spared by the depravation around her.

Hans's initiation to the world's evilness continues; the promised position does not exist. Thanks to Jachmann, he obtains an interview with the head of personnel of a department store, a rigid and nervous individual who bangs on the desk with his ruler. The very stark compositions (geometrical shadows cast) document a humiliating procedure during which Hans admits he is less afraid of the street than of himself. By threatening to commit suicide, he gets a job as a salesman in the men's clothing department. In the park where Lämmchen awaits him with a picnic, Borzage reuses the opening of *Man's Castle*: the revolutionary Goebbler and his wife are huddled on a park bench; they have not eaten in 48 hours. The man notices Lämmchen throwing bread to the pigeons. He accosts her, his fists clenched: "My stomach is bigger than a pigeon's." Saddened, the young woman gives him the two remaining sandwiches: "I could say that you were kind if I didn't know you would do as much for pigeons," he grumbles, eternally dissatisfied. Window shopping with her husband, Lämmchen admires a triple-mirrored dressing table (an addition of Borzage, cf. Trina and her stove). When Hans receives his salary of 150 marks, substantially less than expected, 130 disappear immediately into the purchase of the extravagant dressing table. The acquisition both attests to his adoration for his companion, but also to his own irresponsibility. As opposed to Bill (*Man's Castle*), Hans's capacity for adapting to concrete reality is limited: his reactions are childlike, his has no fighting spirit. After the purchase, there is no more money for food or rent. The future looks grim. More than ever, Lämmchen represents the strong side of the couple, the one in control, who takes initiative and gives life. But she contributes in her own way to the "unpredictability of the grasshopper" (a mark of innocence), always refusing to know the time and sacrificing her few slices of bread to birds. Visually, Lämmchen motivates the action; Hans enters the field as an intruder "like someone sniffing a rose."[46] Now the dressing table has powers: with its three mirrors, it multiplies the presence of the positive, Lämmchen's radiance as the drama darkens. At the opening of a sequence, Borzage never films the woman standing in front of her dressing table, but the irrational object itself, delivering its triple reflection of beauty and happiness to the camera. Like the portrait of the Virgin in *Street Angel*, the mirror becomes the embodiment of a soulful quality. Jachmann is conquered: "Three beautiful ladies, one for you and two for me," he says, joking to Hans.

At night, Mia's subtenants and their "friends" celebrate with champagne, cavorting noisily. The young marrieds cannot fall asleep beneath their satin covers (it would be the last time for a long while that an American movie would show a couple, even married, sharing a bed together). Jachmann, drunk, comes into their room: "Where is my beautiful lady?" and falls asleep under the bed. Mia, looking for him, enters the room in turn and takes advantage of the situation to claim her rent. Imagine Hans and Lämmchen's stupefaction when they discover 200 marks on their covers, discreetly left by Jachmann. In the store, management introduces a minimum sales quota; the salesmen who don't reach it will be let go. Well-intentioned colleagues inform Hans of his stepmother's illicit line of work: she keeps a deluxe brothel. Hans is beside himself; Lämmchen is in the midst of preparing breakfast for the questionable clientele (not insensitive to her charms) when Hans bursts into the rooms, breaks the dishes and starts a riot. In his virtuous indignation, he even seizes a knife, but his wife calms him down. The couple pack their bags, penniless, and with a child on the way. Lämmchen bargains with the old cabinetmaker and used furniture salesman Puttbrese (Christian Rub, the one-armed man in *No Greater Glory*) who rents her his attic for a small sum: "Would you mind climbing a ladder to get to it?" The move to the Berlin working-class district of Alt-Moabit reuses the symbolic iconography of *7th Heaven*: Lämmchen joyously shows her husband the place. They enter by a trap door: "Here we have a stove. Not big enough to cook much on, but we can't afford much, so big enough... A Napoleon bed. If you look closely, you will see why Napoleon slept so often on a chair!" Finally, she shows him the access to a little garden patio on the roof, "A gateway to Heaven, directly to the sky" and where the orchestra of a neighboring restaurant can be heard. They are playing "their" waltz. But Hans is no child of the stars, is not Chico, or Bill: "I think it's horrible, it's like a stable." The melody doesn't move him, it comes from a restaurant for the rich; feeling despair overwhelm him, he begs Lämmchen to protect him from his destructive impulses.

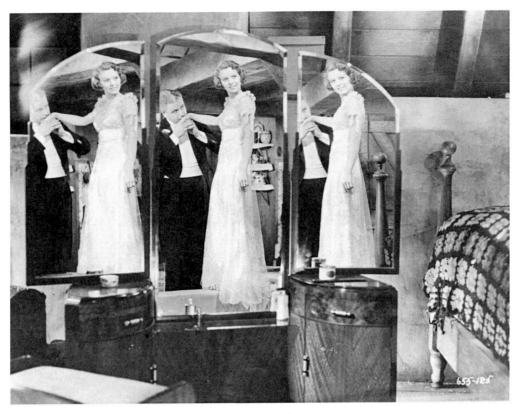

A dreamlike tableau suitable for warding off misfortune: Alan Hale and Margaret Sullavan (*Little Man, What Now?* 1934).

The film's most bitter scene involves a showy actor. Borzage addresses hypocrites in show business who recreate poverty with the sole goal of making a profit and who show the same coldness as those they pretend to criticize. Hans has been reprimanded: his sales figures are too low, his position in danger. Then appears famous screen actor Franz Schlüter (Alan Mowbray). Hans eagerly caters to his every whim. His last role? An unemployed man who broke into a cash register because "my wife was ill and my child was dying." Now the pretentious buffoon is preparing for the difficult task of playing "a poor young man from the wrong side of the town, trying his chance in society." Hans, "the voice of the people," will be able to find him adequate clothing. This veritable play within a play (which inspired Preston Sturges in *Sullivan's Travels* in 1941), leads to catastrophe. Two hours later, having tried on all the suits in the department, the showy actor gets dressed again, having bought nothing. He just wanted to rehearse his part. Hans implores him in vain to buy something, explaining his tragic situation. Outraged, the actor complains to the manager, who denies the existence of a sales quota and fires Hans. This sequence connects to another episode of "disguise," with an inverse impact. The mirror reflects Lämmchen's triple image in a superb silver ball gown, a dreamlike tableau suitable for warding off misfortune (comparable with the seraphic images of Diane and Trina in wedding gowns). Jachmann, in evening clothes, appears in the "magic" mirror, visibly enchanted. The good fairy, whose resources are definitely illegal, makes Cinderella into a fairy. He spirited the dress away from one of his former girlfriends, one of Mia's courtesans. That evening, the young Pinnebergs will be his guests at the most fashionable restaurant in Berlin! Hans, returning

home with a heavy heart, is greeted by Jachmann: "Young man, behold the gracious Queen...
Her Majesty is extremely happy tonight and in no mood for affairs of state!" Thus, the gallant crook and his destitute friends play at being rich, at society's expense. Jachmann waltzes
with Lämmchen: he is a man transformed, in contact with grace, dazzled by purity. What
does it matter if, at the end of the evening, he is uncovered by the police: en route to the
station, he sings to himself.

And truly, Lämmchen becomes "queen": her inner fantasy gives way to seriousness,
devotion, a form of nobility. Now she is bedridden: the baby is due soon, and Puttbreese
cooks her onion soup. The dressing table has fulfilled its function; the future mother barters
the favored piece of furniture for an advance on the rent, the fees for childbirth, and an
old wooden cradle, not knowing that in the meantime, Hans, still unemployed, is waiting
in line for social assistance with the same goal, encountering Kafkaesque bureaucracy. Even
his friend Heilbutt, a former men's clothing salesman, cannot help him: he has disappeared
to Holland. Hans wanders until late at night, in dark despair. In a park where people prepare for a political demonstration, he comes across his comrade Goebbler who incites him
to come listen to "a message from a great leader," (a red or a Brownshirt, it doesn't seem
to matter here). His wife? "They killed her," grumbles the extremist. "They, the ones we're
against." Eaten up by bitterness, Goebbler realized too late that his companion was slowly
dying. The crowd of discontented people increases; policemen on horseback brutally disperse them (a scene cut in Poland and Japan). Hans is thrown to the ground; he gets up,
enraged, a stone in each hand. Then he thinks again: if he goes any further, he'll never see
his wife again. This point of view saves him from easy answers offered by violence and demagogy, for which tomorrow an entire nation will pay the price.

Puttbreese notices Hans lurking in front of his shop window, too ashamed to dare enter.
The old merchant goes out to him and tells him the news: he has a son. Kneeling at the
foot of Lämmchen's bed, Hans plays with the baby's minuscule hand: "Poor little fellow,
what now?" ... "I've been a horrible failure and I don't know where to begin again," he admits
to his wife, "but I'm going to take care of our son." Lämmchen reassures him: "We created life, so why should we be afraid of it?" Heilbutt enters the attic; he is just back from
Amsterdam where he has become his own boss, he says. Hans has a place waiting, and who
knows, his son as well! Medium-close shot of the yawning infant... The End. Borzage shows
Heilbutt only for a few seconds, time for the father to announce the child's birth. The rest
of the joyful news, as well as Hans's elated chuckling, are heard on the soundtrack during
medium-close shots of Lämmchen, then of the baby, as if the filmmaker, not taken in by
this hollywoodish deus ex machina,[47] wanted to focus attention on the essential. The reversal of the final situation is so brief (and so contrived) that it doesn't manage to erase, let
alone counterbalance the climate of sadness that has descended on Germany. Hope coincides with the perspective of "escape" beyond the border, to Holland. In other words: the
Weimar Republic has no future. Hitler is waiting at the door.

Little Man, What Now? is not an immediately pleasing film; even though it was
launched with the slogan "The greatest Universal picture since *All Quiet on the Western
Front*" (released May 1931 at the Radio City Music Hall in New York), it did not meet the
company's expectations. The title was not understood everywhere: certain people expected
a document on the "career of Hitler or Dollfuss!"[48] Practically all critics praised the picture
extensively, but in the U.S. as well as in Europe, most viewers stayed away. This phenomenon was due perhaps less to the subject itself than to its male protagonist, Hans Pinneberg,
as depicted on screen. "With a sincerity which defies ridicule, this film elaborates the point
that the weakest of men may be a hero to the woman who loves him," remarked the *Times*

Unemployment and daily mortification in *Little Man, What Now ?* (Douglass Montgomery and Christian Rub, 1934).

of London,[49] The narrative is more about the man's weakness than the woman's integrity, and we never see what endears Hans to his wife. The average viewer has difficulty feeling anything other than lukewarm commiseration for this individual whose failures gradually reduce him to self-pity and hysteria. In a way, Borzage's emphasis has a counter effect: the couple's intimate feelings carry more weight than the tragedy in the streets, and Lämmchen (a lyrical counterpoint, not a dramatic one) must alone represent the couple's omnipotence.

Little Man, What Now? remains a very unusual work for its time, and caused a British journal to remark: "Film is beginning to present the truth."[50] Mordaunt Hall, in the *New York Times,* spoke of "A picture which deserves applause, for it is a relief after the tawdry, silly effusions which seem to have predominated on Broadway screens recently."[51] On the formal level, the narrative structure breaks with classical progression toward catharsis and neglects outbursts of melodrama (another unsettling factor for the public). The film presents itself as a deliberately gloomy chronicle of daily incidents, a series of events that tend to demonstrate there is no beginning, no end, so that the predominant sentiment is one of precariousness. On the other hand, Borzage imbues his "annals of poverty" with a series of colorful figures: the domestic tyrant Kleinholz, Mia and her beloved animal, the bizarre Jachmann, the actor, the fawning, exploitative head of personnel and Puttbreese, a hardened bachelor who shares his shop with his old nag and pretends to be slow to better hide his generosity. The filmmaker certainly attains Fallada's *Weltschmertz*, this poignant bitterness that remains so foreign to his nature. In Borzage's film, Hans and Lämmchen's deep bond gives them a reason to hope. But, like the novel, the film also eschews any ready-made solutions to the plethora of economic, political and moral problems suffocating the country. It imparts no lesson, preaches no moral, refuses wide-eyed optimism ("Stand Up and Cheer!") as well the satirical tone of the comedies churned out by European cinema, seeking to ward off the Depression (e.g., Siodmak's *The Crisis Is Over!,* 1934) The work simply depicts, without unduly emphasizing poverty, the difficulties encountered by a young lower-middle-class household in surviving the maelstrom; like *No Greater Glory* the accusations remain implicit. "Its atmosphere," wrote Henri Agel, "is that of Dickens sometimes crossed with a breath of Dostoevsky."[52] This makes for a story neither cheerful nor desperate, but infinitely moving, with its inimitable mixture of realism and romanticism, its delicate touch and Margaret Sullavan's magnetism. One of those "human interest stories" that Borzage was fond of. And today, a cult film.

12

The Warner Brothers Purgatory

On September 5, 1933 (while he was putting the last touches on *Man's Castle*), Frank Borzage signed a first two-year contract with Warner Brothers–First National, to make three films a year at $52,000 a film. According to the terms of the contract, the filmmaker would deliver "films of the highest type and character as is practicable, having due regard to the efficient and economic operations of Warner Brothers' business."[1] He retained the right, however, to make one film a year for another company of his choice. At the end of April 1934, "Frank Borzage Productions" settled into Warner Brothers' Burbank studios (on Sunset Boulevard). A full page in *Variety* welcomed him to his new "home," and his new boss gave him two polo ponies. Warner Brothers offered him a fortune: in 1935, Borzage could boast he was the best paid collaborator in the studio, after Mervyn LeRoy (Jack L. Warner's son-in-law): LeRoy received $198,000 a year, Borzage $156,000; he was followed by star Paul Muni ($150,000) and Michael Curtiz ($102,325). Unfortunately, it was a bad move. Since his last works had been unsuccessful at the box office, Borzage was in a position of weakness and his hands were tied, creatively speaking, until 1936!

The Burbank studio deserved its nickname "San Quentin": surrounded by a barbed wire fence, it was ruled by the iron fist of Jack "Son-of-a-Bitch" Warner, said to bark rather than speak. He supplanted his older brothers Harry and Albert in boorishness, and tension ran rife in his empire. Working conditions were exhausting and firings were final. There wasn't a set or script not profitably put to use a second or third time. The work pace was frenetic: Michael Curtiz, the Stakhanovite of the profession, churned out 35 films in seven years, and his colleague William Dieterle 17 between 1931 and 1934. But Warners legendary greed was also synonymous with efficiency and coarseness—good manners were out of place!—and influenced production: Warner films were by far the rawest, most tense and realistic in Hollywood. Gangster films, social dramas and even the Busby Berkeley musicals all translated the pushiness and thirst for power of the most plebeian of studios. Like the boss, production head Hal B. Wallis set new standards for unpleasantness and his spies reported the slightest infraction on the sets. The case of Borzage in Burbank is somewhat similar to that of Georg Wilhelm Pabst, brought to Hollywood by a contract with Warner in October 1933. Pabst was lured by a historical mega-production about Napoleon, based on Emil Ludwig's famous biography: when he arrived, the studio balked at paying his hotel costs and the promised script was far from being completed. On November 10, Pabst was assigned to *A Modern Hero* (a subject for which Borzage had been approached the preceding year at Fox). Hal Wallis, who abhorred independent spirits, had the prestigious German director monitored by a "supervisor" and bombarded him with humiliating and sometimes even threatening memos. Pabst was deemed "too slow," his camera angles were criticized (not enough close-ups, too many short cuts); he was absolutely forbidden to rewrite or alter a comma in the script approved by management, etc. "You will have to get used to our way of shooting pictures and the way we want them shot and I have explained this to you in great detail a number of times and I don't want to go over it again," fumed Wallis.[2] On March 15, 1934, with his film in the can, the "difficult" author of *The Joyless Street, Pandora's Box* and *The Threepenny Opera* was thanked; Wallis terminated his contract and sabotaged his future in the U.S. Pabst would spend two years without work in Hollywood before returning to exile in France.

Back when he was still enjoying his independence, in September 1933, Borzage had soundly criticized growing standardization and the appearance of production supervisors in the studios:

> Motion pictures are a product of mood. You can't produce them in cut-and-dried business fashion. Mass production is basically and structurally wrong. I grant that the head of a studio should be a businessman. But he should vest authority in a new type of supervisor — with definite power to accept or reject. Our present supervisory system is an indefinite control, in which glorified assistants, at exorbitant salaries, work under the mental hazard of their producer's displeasure. They veto telling scenes because they remember that six months ago the boss didn't take to that particular angle in a story. Immediately they begin bastardizing a potent situation, which might make the difference between a so-so picture and a brilliant one. There is only one man who should be in control from the moment the type of picture to be made is determined and various details about it settled — and that is the director. The present supervisory system induces a chaos comparable to that within an army without commander. ... We are spending one hundred million dollars a year in making pictures. Because of the narrow viewpoint of a handful of producers, the business has become so unwieldy that it is toppling.[3]

He realized soon enough what was in store for him with the slave drivers of Burbank!

Misery loves company, and in 1934 the principles of the Hays Code were publicly ratified. In April the Roman Catholic Legion of Decency was created, an organization strongly supported by nine million spectators and capable of boycotting any film not conforming to the ideas of the Church; since 1931, Warner Brothers had already lost $30 million following pressure from religious circles. Presbyterian Will Hays, president of the all-powerful MPPDA (Motion Picture Producers and Distributors of America), was in charge of creating the Motion Picture Production Code, begun in 1930. This federal autocensor that the film industry itself had called for to prevent federal censorship had only been loosely respected up until now. Pressured by events, Hays created its means of attack, the formidable Production Code Administration (PCA) which became effective in June; the Hollywood studios promised to no longer release movies without the PCA's official endorsement. The Code — a veritable wall of silence of Puritanism — remained in effect until 1966 to strictly regulate morality onscreen. Irishman Joseph I. Breen, a notorious anticommunist and anti–Semite, was in charge of the "cleaning" operation. From then on, films such as *A Farewell to Arms* or *Man's Castle* were no longer possible.

These preliminary remarks are essential to explain to what extent Borzage's next few years would be marked by compromise and sometimes even by outright hostility. The filmmaker began by obtaining the million-dollar project that had been promised to Pabst: on December 28, 1933, he was designated in charge of *Napoleon — His Life and Loves*, from a script by Ernest Pascal.[4] Shooting was slated to begin at the end of February 1934. Thrilled by this new challenge, Borzage immersed himself in reading, borrowing several books from Robert Florey's Napoleonic library. The prospective cast was the stuff of dreams: Edward G. Robinson (Napoleon), Kay Francis, Bette Davis or Gloria Swanson (Josephine), Ann Dvorak (Marie-Louise) and Jean Muir (Maria Walewska). But after interminable procrastination, Jack Warner halted film preparations in May 1934, frightened by the estimated costs (at the same moment he gave the go-ahead for Dieterle's *Madame Dubarry*, a film that would be butchered by the censor). The Napoleonic project would once again go through Florey (October 1935) before finally being abandoned. At this same time, Borzage announced to the press that he had joined forces with colleagues—Lewis Milestone, King Vidor, Lowell Sherman, Gregory LaCava—to create a theatrical company of quality, the Westwood Theater Guild. The enterprise, along the lines of the famous New York guild, was supervised by Zeppo Marx (who had just separated from his brothers). Borzage followed Broadway openings regularly; he hoped to stage the best plays of contemporary theater in Hollywood and let film actors perform on stage in front of a live audience. Richard Dix, Carole Lombard, Richard Barthelmess and Adolphe Menjou said they were interested, but the project fell through due to lack of funds.

Refusing to hear any talk of gangster movies, Borzage began work on *Flirtation Walk*, a musical comedy with Dick Powell and Ruby Keeler. The singing and dancing duo of Powell and Keeler was on their way to becoming one of the company's major assets after four hits in 1933–34, *42nd Street*, *Gold Diggers of 1933*, *Footlight Parade* and *Dames*; all had fabulous Busby Berkeley musical numbers, took place in the music hall milieu and used the classic situation of "putting on a show." For Borzage, Warners was prepared to modify the formula and even substantially expand the budget: *Flirtation Walk*'s action was moved to exotic locales and the filmmaker took cast and crew to Honolulu for several weeks of exteriors, followed by two weeks on the grounds of West Point Military Academy on the Hudson. The Polynesian musical number—a Native Love Dance of Tahitian women choreographed by Bobby Connolly, a disciple of Ziegfeld—was recorded on the largest set ever erected at Burbank.

Filming this festival of fluff took longer than was usual for the studio: from June 3 to September 5. As for young Delmer Daves' script, it was completely idiotic, thus conforming to the genre: Dick, alias "Canari" (D. Powell), a scatterbrained and unruly serviceman stationed in Hawaii, is pressed into chauffeuring General Pitts' daughter Kit (R. Keeler), vacationing on the island. He falls in love with her, as expected, flirting beneath palm trees to the sound of ukuleles, and decides to run away with his beloved. This is the most lively part of the film and Borzage deliciously focuses on "the war between the sexes" waged by the authoritarian and spoiled young lady, and her more than consenting victim. But the love nest is discovered and scandal threatens. In order not to compromise her "chauffeur," Kit treats him with disdain. The poor boy is devastated and throws himself into a military career as an officer and a gentleman at West Point to forget his heartbreak! Three years later, the whimsical officer is directing the musical theater group of cadets when General Pitts takes over the Academy. Kitt, accompanying her father, as if by coincidence, gets the lead in the end-of-year musical revue directed by Dick. It ends with a triumphant show, a grandiose military parade in full regalia and kisses beneath the star-spangled banner. The "Borzage Touch" resurfaces here and there: an officer is moved as he watches the procession of men he trained; instead of showing his tears, the filmmaker cuts to a little girl watching him and says: "Look Daddy, that man's crying." A credit reads: "dedicated to West Point," where the company benefited from "the full cooperation of the United States Army." Decades later we look back at it ironically, but *Flirtation Walk* topped the box office in 1934 (patriotic leagues adored it), receiving an Oscar nomination as best film and winning for best sound. To the great satisfaction of the brothers Warner, Borzage showed that he was capable of adapting to a variety of genres and styles. A certificate of eclecticism that thrilled Hollywood's business people but not movie buffs, nor, in the end, the filmmaker himself.

In July, Universal Pictures offered Borzage direction of the melodrama *Magnificent Obsession* (from the Lloyd C. Douglas novel), a far more appropriate subject than the light-hearted songs at West Point, but Jack Warner refused to free his Midas and enticed him with two "cultural subjects" programmed for 1934–35: *A Tale of Two Cities based on Dickens, with Leslie Howard as the victim at the guillotine, and *Main Street, Sinclair Lewis's social novel adapted by Casey Robinson. These projects unfortunately never materialized, but do indicate a strategic turning point in the history of the company that decided to broaden its scope with a limited number of prestigious works, costumers or literary adaptations. In November, Max Reinhardt, the genius of contemporary theatre, arrived in Burbank and with Dieterle co-directed Shakespeare's A Midsummer Night's Dream for a budget of a million dollars. Hollywood thought it was dreaming. Could Jack Warner be well-read? Two months later, the company welcomed other VIPs under its roof, press magnate William Randolph Hearst and his lady-love Marion Davies, old acquaintances of Borzage (cf. chap. 4). Cosmopolitan (Humoresque) established itself in Burbank for years to come: its first film was Captain Blood, a pirate story featuring an Australian newcomer named Errol Flynn.

Living on Velvet is without a doubt the most original and most personal film of the Warner period. At first glance it is a melodramatic vehicle for Kay Francis (the heroine of One Way Passage), the studio's femme fatale, whose elegant clothes and hairstyles graced magazines. However, Borzage gave her an unusually enthusiastic part, in a psychological drama with Fitzgeraldian overtones. Her partner, Irishman George Brent, was also a familiar face at the Burbank factory: in two years, he had appeared in 21 films! The "velvet" of the title evokes luxury, but the metaphor is ironical: it is the suave theater of desperate, misguided people defying death. The film opens to thick white clouds. Lost in the center of the image, a tiny plane battles the fog: a metonymic representation of what lies ahead. Running out of fuel between Philadelphia and Newport, the wealthy Terry C. Parker's (G. Brent) plane crashes to the ground. Terry miraculously survives, but his parents and his sister die. From then on, traumatized, the pilot seeks death above the clouds, traveling to Shanghai, Venezuela and Alaska. In Long Island, he disturbs the Aviation Day air show by taking senseless risks with the twin-engine plane of his friend Gibraltar (Warren William). As solid as a rock (thus his nickname) and steadfast, this friend gets him out of a jam with the army and takes him in. Terry admits that ever since the catastrophe, he has been living on borrowed time: "Every minute from now on is pure velvet." He has gone through his fortune and material considerations no longer interest him. "Something that tried to get me once and didn't. I'm giving him another chance, that's all. We have a lot of respect for each other, the heavens and I."

To take his mind off things, Gibraltar drags him to a party given by his beloved, Amy (K. Francis), an ultra-sophisticated New Yorker. Terry, who first only wanted to shave half his face, acts bizarrely and, scorning societal convention, greets guests without being introduced, butting into private conversations, etc., until Borzage introduces one of the most amazing film transpositions of "love at first sight" on celluloid. Terry is stoically putting up with a bore holding forth on the good weather when he notices Amy close by, subjected to a matron's reflections on monsoons. Their eyes meet and they can't look away; the meteorological diatribes continue. Their repeated two-shot (medium-close shot) is framed with exact symmetry, in front of each is one of the people creating the obstacle. Borzage sweeps the space, panning back and forth from Amy to Terry to Amy, followed by a third shot of Terry alone. Deserting his interlocutor, Terry leaves the field to follow up on the silent invitation. Amy and Terry meet face to face, in profile, looking into each other's eyes. "Could you direct me to some food? I'm hungry," stammers the man, as if hypnotized. Amy smilingly shows him a nearby table laden with food. "Sandwich?" "No thanks," he answers and the camera moves in to frame only their two faces together in one shot. The mathematical rigor of these transitions expresses both the inescapable meeting and the irresistible attraction that makes it happen. The succinct dialogue suggests the parameters of the relationship. Terry: "I'd like to say something ... something." She interrupts him: "I know. It isn't necessary." He cannot give, cannot commit himself and Amy, all senses aroused by a kind of immediate and total passion, intuitively understands the love showing through his sorrow. After a slow dance together, closely intertwined, while others around them do a lively rumba, and embarrassing silences on the terrace, they slip on their coats and escape ("It's the ideal time to leave any party: at the beginning"). It is drizzling outside and conversation is sparse and insipid⁵; only the gestures seem to count. In a café, Terry shows Amy how to stop the rain: "the ritual was entrusted to me by an old Indian chief whom I befriended as he lay dying in the Black Hills in South Dakota." Toward three o'clock in the morning, after wandering a long time, the couple stops at the foot of an equestrian statue of General Sherman (Borzage repeats the high-angle tracking shot of *A Farewell to Arms*). Then the first concrete words are uttered: their respective names. Terry freezes: "You're Gibraltar's Amy?"— and, without a word, takes her home. The sequence as a whole is explosive, especially as it breaks with Warner Brothers' usual efficient and accelerated style. Unable to create his soft, diffused lighting and insert his usual stylistic pyrotechnics, Borzage compensates with a narrative syncopation whose melodious strangeness permeates the film's very texture. Management was reportedly displeased: "One day," recalls a journalist, "a visiting supervisor, watching a scene being shot, finally walked pompously up to the director and announced: 'I don't like the way you are doing this.' Frank peered at him gently out of his blue eyes, lit his pipe deliberately and with a quiet 'Oh, you'll get used to it,' strolled away."⁶

Amy spends all the next day at her window, watching the rain fall (the medium-shot of flowing water visualizes the extent of confusion and functions as a premonition of the recklessness ahead). Terry has disappeared, Gibraltar has made inquiries; the police find him drunk, trying to start a fight in a café. Persuaded that she can help him find himself, come what may, against the advice of the man in question who describes himself as "irresponsible," a "social outcast" and a "lunatic." But Amy cannot be reasoned with: she gives up material comfort, since her Aunt Martha (who holds the purse strings) opposes the marriage. She sacrifices her social life, fancy clothes and the security and social status offered by Gibraltar. Terry: "You'll never know a minute's rest or a day's contentment." Amy: "Oh, it all sounds so wonderful!" (a line spoken by Mary Pickford in *Secrets*). Amy's total self-sacrifice makes her an almost abstract character and removes the story beyond the everyday. Amy and Gibraltar become Terry's symbolic parents, since the faithful friend also spends freely, in an amazingly disinterested way: he gives up Amy like a father giving away his daughter, finances the marriage ceremony (he is best man and the only witness) and discreetly provides for the couple. The marriage in a deserted church has a surrealistic aspect: Terry and Amy leave alone, looking in each others' eyes. Soon joined by Gibraltar, they sit on the church steps, facing the outside world. The couple deliberates, the marrieds know not where to go or what to do! Gibraltar generously lets them use his summer residence in Patchogue, Long Island ("it has a bed that Washington never slept in!") along with a car. After bargaining, the monthly rent is $4.50.

The second half of the film focuses on the tension between the charming eccentric with the sad smile and his entourage. Terry is hardly of any use in everyday living; like a child he imitates Amy, polishing a drawer handle instead of installing electricity or the telephone. Gone shopping for bread and vegetables, he returns with a box full of caviar, paté and shrimp, along with a ring for his wife. He takes the train every morning, like all his suburban neighbors, to go look for work. "Tonight I shall be a financial giant, I'll be known as Parker the Wolf of Wall Street," he promises Amy, who replies, "Parker the Job Holder is enough for me." At nightfall, she finds him on the kitchen floor feeding the dog he has just bought. He doesn't want any job "between four walls," explains a sorrowful Gibraltar. Terry rushes to his feet like a little boy, and leaves the house. We hear the sound of an airplane ("Poor devil, flying in the fog"). Amy and Gibraltar frown: it takes a lot of patience, but they must keep Terry from flying. "If only I can get that idea out of his head, that he is alone in the world—and I'll feel I got out of life everything I want." But with increasing frequency Borzage frames one of the two spouses turning their back to the camera—or to their partner. Love cannot bring redemption, cannot create a protective enclave because one side of the couple is handicapped, incapable of fitting in or opening up: he refuses the hand reaching out to save him. Only suffering brings them together; otherwise, he remains a prisoner of his destructive lucidity. Terry comes in late in the evening, with neither work nor an explanation, still prepared to give his wife her freedom. Amy grits her teeth. "Do you have any plans for the future?" asks Aunt Martha, visiting. "I don't believe in the future," he bitterly replies. "I never had a plan in my life and if I had one, I wouldn't know what to do with it."

When a stock market investment brings in a return (really a gift from Gibraltar), Amy believes in miracles and rejoices at finally being able to furnish their home. But without her knowledge, Terry spends everything, even going into debt by buying a used seaplane, as he dreams of inaugurating an aerial link between Long Island and Manhattan; workers are already creating a landing field on the adjacent land. Amy can only realize her failure and discouraged, packs her bag. "There's a void in your life, a distinct and terrible void," she confides incredulously to Terry. She had hoped to be able to fill it, but wasn't even able to make her husband happy. While Terry flies off, Amy seeks to forget, spending evenings at society parties accompanied by Gibraltar ("*I'm* living on velvet now"). Shortly thereafter, Terry resurfaces to beg his wife to come back. She refuses as long as he continues living in "this cage you built for yourself. I want *you*." Defying death, late in the evening, Terry crashes into a merry-go-round with his friend's car. He survives a second time: "When I die, I'll be in the air, it won't be on the filthy ground." In Borzage's epilogue, the survivor and Amy are found at the foot of Sherman's statue; it's dark out and snowing. "You've been a grand nurse and certainly a grand companion, but the job is over, you're free," Terry tells his wife. Amy: "Freedom's overrated." "Terry doesn't exist anymore," the young man proclaims at the spot where the spouses revealed their identities. The camera dollies out while Amy addresses the monument—or Heaven—with the whimsical verse that generates magic: "Love, general, something I learned from an old Indian chief whom I befriended as he lay dying in the Black Hills in South Dakota." Love, death and rebirth.

But there are overall defects. To its credit are several situations that appear in other Borzage films: wandering about that results in love (*Man's Castle, Three Comrades*), the "stranger on earth" who drowns his despair in gaiety (*A Farewell to Arms*), and various recurrent motifs—the call of airplanes (trains, the beyond), the reprieve, the fateful carousel, the equestrian statue, the snowy night, etc. This "light comedy against a morbid background"[7]—filmed as *Tragedy with Music* (November 6 to December 20, 1934) nevertheless suffers from a twofold handicap. As mentioned, the very "Warneresque" style of photography, its clear, rapid, functional images, never-ending medium-close shots, expeditious tempo and minimalist sets alter the tone; this monotonous tale of champagne bubbles drifts into a kind of banal psychiatric case study. Moreover, Jerry Wald and Julius Epstein's script was seriously distorted: originally, the curtain fell on a melancholy note: Terry was supposed to find peace in death in a fatal car accident and Amy consoled herself with Gibraltar.[8] This was how the

"There's a void in your life, a distinct and terrible void," says Kay Francis to George Brent in *Living on Velvet* (1934).

itinerary of a pathetic life ended, a *Lazybones* gone adrift because he thinks Heaven has "forgotten" him, the victim of an error of Providence. But a memo from Hal Wallis dated November 13 demanded two different "endings," one sad, the other happy. Then, when the studio realized that Warren William's contract was almost over and there was no reason to hone his star image, Jack Warner modified the film's conclusion — one week before the end of shooting!— and "resuscitated" Terry (George Brent, with still five years left in his contract, would have the privilege of holding Kay Francis in his arms)— without long explanations or satori. Borzage is certainly unmatched when it comes to making the unbelievable credible, but to do so he must be allowed to "prepare" the viewer, which here is not the case. This aberrant alteration, one of several the filmmaker had to endure at Burbank, simply demonstrates the management's lack of interest in this type of story (at least in the first half of the thirties).

In January–February 1935, Borzage's name appeared in connection with several Warner projects, notably *Page Miss Glory* for Marion Davies (Mervyn LeRoy undertook it). *Haircut*, a script by Sam Mintz based on a Ring Lardner short story, with George Brent and Jean Muir, and finally an ambitious project: Dickens' *The Pickwick Papers*; Lawrence Hazard would write the script for Edward G. Robinson. Nothing came of them.

The second production reuniting Kay Francis and George Brent, in spite of its promising title, *Stranded*, was even more representative of the fundamental disharmony between the filmmaker's personality and Warner Brothers' narrative stereotypes (it reused the sets of *Living on Velvet*). The film begins by a quick homage to the Traveler's Aid Society as well as a tip of the hat to its employees in charge of helping stranded travelers and abandoned children, of housing Slavic and Chinese immigrants, sustaining the unemployed, finding missing persons, etc. (Warners abandoned the original title of the film, *Lady with a Badge*, because it feared that the public would take the heroine for a lady cop). Lynn (K. Francis) dedicates herself full-time to the T.A.S. office in the San Francisco train station, but cannot prevent an old man ("I've had my fill of charity") from blowing his brains out in front of her. She has to work with a stuck-up flirtatious young woman whose rich parents finance the organization. This slice of social criticism fits easily into Borzage's universe, and Delmer Daves' script (then Kay Francis' lover) portrays the contemporary construction of the Golden Gate Bridge: *Stranded* shows several documentary images shot at Bridge Fort Point (filmed March 7–April 16, 1935). Mack Hale (G. Brent), the inflexible but fair engineer directing work on this famous bridge, calls on the Traveler's Aid Society to find one of his specialized workers and comes up against Lynn, his teenage crush. The two quarrel but fall back in love; they go out to fancy restaurants, where Kay Francis exhibits a selection of extravagant clothes. But each one has too many work obligations and the couple is rarely alone. Borzage sums up the situation by an ironic scene where Hale seeks in vain to disconnect Lynn's telephone, then inspects under the tables for immigrants! Possessive and selfish, the engineer demands Lynn to give up helping "useless" people if she wants to become his wife, which she refuses ("You build your bridge with steel, I build mine with human beings"). After the sentimental breakup, we drift into gangsters and syndicates: the racketeer Sharkey offers Hale his paid protection ("Builders' Protective Association"), without which... Hale replies with his fists. Sharkey trains some immigrants as agitators, provoking the death of a worker after having gotten him drunk, then organizes a strike on the building site. Hale is seriously wounded and the police become involved. Lynn rushes to the trade union where she faces hundreds of striking workers. She uncovers Sharkey and his acolytes; Hale delivers them to the angry masses. The couple meet again under the Golden Gate Bridge, in the moonlight. The completed bridge represents victory over oneself, the attraction of opposites. Hale has lost his cynicism; he now recognizes the enriching dimension Lynn brings to his life and accepts her conditions of marriage. A therapeutic, redeeming relationship, the way Borzage likes them, but bogged down in a lopsided, inconsistent hodgepodge.

In April 1935, Metro-Goldwyn-Mayer invited the filmmaker to direct Wallace Beery and Jackie Cooper in *O'Shaughnessy's Boy*, but Warner had other plans and William A. Wellman replaced Borzage in Culver City. The next potboiler was called *Shipmates Forever*. They began again with the same stars used earlier: Dick Powell and Ruby Keeler sing for the Navy this time. Borzage transported his cameras to the Naval Academy in Annapolis, Maryland, then hoisted them on board the U.S.S. *Pennsylvania* anchored in San Pedro, California (June 7–August 3, 1935).[9] Delmer Daves' plot is even thinner, if possible, than that of *Flirtation Walk*. The son of an admiral (D. Powell) follows in his father's footsteps to make him happy, giving up a lucrative career in radio. He falls in love with a choreographer (R. Keeler) from an old navy family, but cannot get used to life at sea until the day he distinguishes himself trying to save a comrade during a fire onboard, during naval exercises. One scene stands out where sugary sweetness is masterfully avoided: a cadet has failed his final exams at the Academy and packs his bags with his comrade looking on: he opens the door of a cabinet which chastely shields him from the camera each time he is overcome by tears, rendering the emotion all the more strong. After parades, thundering military bands and flags unfurled, the film ends on a strangely melancholy note: Powell and Keeler meet up silently in front of the sea, in front of the tomb of the sailor perished in the flames (John Arledge), a rather disturbing moment underscored by the romantic German melody that Borzage would use again in *Three Comrades*. We may see homosexual overtones in the attachment of the deceased for Powell. (Arledge would play Albert Dekker's lover in *Strange Cargo* in 1939).

* * *

"Joe, where are you?" a severely distraught Marlene Dietrich murmured into the microphone before each take of *Song of Songs*. At the insistence of both Josef von Sternberg and Paramount, the actress resigned herself to work one time only with another director. But filming with Rouben Mamoulian was difficult. There was no electricity. On January 10, 1933, a limousine burst onto the lot of United Artists where *Secrets* was being filmed. At Marlene Dietrich's personal request, Frank Borzage was urgently called to the Paramount sets to calm people down: his reputation for kindness and diplomacy was unsurpassed. The filmmaker complied, and stayed until evening directing the star in several shots of the film. Then he handed back the reigns to his colleague. Marlene did not forget him.

The association between Sternberg and Dietrich ended in 1935, after the public fiasco of *The Devil Is a Woman*. When the screen goddess's contract was renewed at Paramount, one of the clauses stipulated that Ernst Lubitsch would personally direct her in a film. A few days later, on February 4, 1935, Adolph Zukor named Lubitsch head of studio production, which meant he could no longer carry out his obligations behind the camera. To console her, the star received a salary of $500,000 for the film and got to choose his replacement: Borzage (May). Lubitsch was already sold on the subject; he wanted a Hollywood remake of a Ufa (Germany) hit from 1933, *Die schönen Tage in Aranjuez*, where the demonic Brigitte Helm succumbed to the youthful charm of Wolfgang Liebeneiner.[10] The remake was intended to correct the overly unreal image of the Sternberg fantasy, and Borzage seemed the ideal choice to render the American Dietrich more human. At the same time, Lubitsch said he wanted to study his illustrious colleague's direction of the actors of more closely. Thus Borzage was loaned out from Warners to film *Desire*.[11] Lubitsch wanted to reunite the stars of *Morocco* (1930), persuaded that Gary Cooper hid an exceptional talent for light comedy; Cooper did not at all share his enthusiasm and the "overly intelligent" lines Edwin Justus Mayer concocted for him worried him greatly. His apprehensions were finally calmed when the director of *A Farewell to Arms* was hired. The first actor pictured for the role of the bandit Carlos was John Gilbert, in free-fall since the advent of sound; Greta Garbo's old flame was then living with Marlene, who helped him overcome his alcoholism, hide his wrinkles and regain confidence. As the film was intended to be in Technicolor, Gilbert also made screen tests in color, but the stress was too great and he began drinking again. He suffered a heart attack and was replaced by John Halliday. "Marlene was incapable of resisting Gary Cooper," related Gilbert's daughter. "When my father discovered the truth he fell apart and didn't stop drinking until the day he died" (which occurred at the end of filming).[12]

Regardless of this tragic backdrop, the filming of *Desire* unfolded in virtually idyllic conditions. "The first day," said the filmmaker ironically, mischievously, "Marlene Dietrich seemed surprised when I didn't take 70 or 80 close-ups. I made one, finally I made another, I thought it would please her." Then, "Great gal, that Dietrich, it is really a pleasure to have her in a picture, what a cook! You should have been with us yesterday. We were on location. Dietrich got up at four thirty in the morning, an hour earlier than usual, to prepare lunch and take it with her on location. Three chickens, soup, delicious cake, and all kinds of cheeses." Borzage waxed ecstatic: "She made it herself and then served us. It was just Cooper, the cameraman Charlie Lang, myself and her. She hardly eats a thing but she loves to cook and wait on people. A great actress to have in a picture, huh?"[13] In September, the studio sent cameramen Eric Locke and Harry Perry to film stock shots in Europe (Paris, Mougins, San Sebastian, Toledo); filming was relatively long—from September 16 to December 21, 1935—and cost $1,400,000.[14] Jewels worth a total of two million dollars, including a $75,000 pearl necklace, were placed under permanent surveillance. Halfway through, Lubitsch changed the film's name from *The Pearl Necklace* to *Desire*, a misleading title considering the story (and which had already raised eyebrows at the Hays office in 1931 when Paramount wanted to use it for another film), but which led to a fetishist rapport among a passion for jewels, luxury and sexuality.

Almost everywhere, the direction of *Desire* raised the question of the role played by Lubitsch, and zealous historians have practically attributed the film's paternity to him (e.g., Herman G. Weinberg); Lubitsch in fact took charge of the general production of the project — although the credits included the obligatory "A Frank Borzage Production"—a project started by the Berliner himself (subject, casting). He evidently collaborated very closely on the script, but so did Borzage. As for the filming, it was the exclusive domain of the director, and the two professionals complemented each other. La Dietrich stressed this 54 years later: "Borzage was the only director of *Desire*. I was very fond of him."[15] Lubitsch's only concrete intervention on the set was on February 4–5, 1936 (a day and a half), when it was decided to do some retakes to improve the flow of the story and Borzage was already at work on *Hearts Divided*.

These statements do not belie the fact that *Desire* carries many of Lubitsch's personal, easily recognizable touches and it is particularly interesting to study the contributions of two so very different creators. Briefly, the storyline is as follows: The adventurer Madeleine de Beaupré (M. Dietrich) has stolen a magnificent pearl necklace from the Parisian jeweler Duval, passing herself off to him as the wife of psychiatrist Dr. Pauquet, and to Pauquet as the wife of the jeweler. Fleeing to Spain in her convertible, Madeleine encounters American automobile engineer Tom (G. Cooper) and hides the stolen goods in his jacket when the border guards begin their search. Dazzled by Madeleine's beauty, the vacationing Yankee is taken in. She pretends that her car has broken down and he gives her a ride, but she gives him the slip and totals his car without being able to get back the pearls. The two meet up again in San Sebastian: Madeleine has taken the identity of a countess, and her accomplice and ex-lover Carlos (J. Halliday) that of a Russian prince. Amorous looks, reconciliation. The trio spends a week in a country inn near Aranjuez where the thieves attempt to get back the necklace. But they haven't counted on the "Spanish moon"... Madeleine loses her head and admits everything to the guileless engineer. Tom beats up Carlos, returns the necklace to its owner, gets the case dismissed for his young wife (we're in Paris, after all) and sets off with her for the automobile Mecca of Detroit.[16]

The film may be divided into two parts: the first funny, cynical and airy, extremely "Lubitsch-like"; the second tenderer, more cheerful, almost a little serious, unmistakably carrying Borzage's mark. On one side style and irreverence, on the other, playful acting and delicacy. Distant sophistication vs. candid enthusiasm, or even appearance vs. reality. But this polarization is too schematic, unless one falls into the trap of pegging Borzage as a naive romantic; he is no stranger to irony. Furthermore, the work contains no distinct break or shift in tone, but maintains from one end to the other a smooth charm and visual elegance rarely surpassed: soft lighting and sparkling clear photography attest to an art at its peak. Stylistically and thematically, *Desire* belongs to Lubitsch's universe (the Europe of deluxe hotels, the high society gangsters and the amorality of *Trouble in Paradise*) and it has already been said that his "inimitable" touch crystallized mostly at the development stage (script, storyboard) and less on the set. But directing a work prepared by Lubitsch guaranteed nothing if the director hadn't a similar sensibility, as can be proved by Otto Preminger's blunders.[17] *Desire*, on the other hand, reveals a surprising complementarity between Lubitsch and Borzage, as if the second gave life and human consistency to the acrobatics of the first, sometimes even a supplementary finesse ... until the moment when the discovery of love challenges sophistication, and authentic feeling frees the actors from the decorum that is supposed to characterize them. John Belton analyzed this phenomenon remarkably, deeming that Borzage's romantic close-ups serve to oppose the "depersonalized" action, all in master shots, orchestrated by Lubitsch: "The straightforward purity of Borzage's outlook demands that his characters and their situation be taken seriously and permits him a broader range of emotional expression than cynically incredulous directors like Lubitsch allow themselves. While Lubitsch laughs at melodramatic technique and convention, Borzage sees a truth in its vision: as a narrative director, he believes in melodrama as a way of seeing the world."[18] But the singular experience of *Desire* would affect both men: "Lubitsch-like" ideas crisscross *History Is Made at Night* (1937) and Lubitsch's *The Shop Around the Corner* (1940) contains several moments that could have been created by Borzage.

From the opening, the "Lubitsch touch" can be seen in many gags and transitions: Tom is vehemently telling his boss his demands; the camera moves back—he is speaking to an empty seat; he goes decidedly to find his employer who immediately accedes to all his wishes (a holiday in Spain), using the same terms. In the street, Tom and Madeleine's cars "meet": the engineer backs up into the bumper of the limousine behind him. The seductress is wearing a white outfit in a white car (jeweler), a black outfit in a black car (psychiatrist). The entire stratagem of the theft with its confusion, doors opening and closing, risqué innuendo (the husband had exchanged his pajamas for a nightgown), sexual antagonism suggested by the choreography of the cars (Tom gets splattered, covered in dust at each overtaking, he gets revenge by jamming Madeleine's horn). The principle of the series of ironic gags focuses around an object (the necklace) whose quest will lead to a series of mishaps: Tom folds the jacket containing the jewelry in his suitcase, Madeleine is afraid the American will catch cold: "I could get closer." He complies, but takes out another jacket... While he is cleaning off the car, the adventurer starts the car and takes off violently, thinking she is carrying the suitcase—which has stayed on the road, open at Tom's feet, etc. In the grand hotel in San Sebastian, Lubitsch, Borzage and Marlene comically parody Sternberg: Madeleine plays the vamp in an extravagant setting, arousing an idiotic officer (Akim Tamiroff). "Prince" Carlos explains to Tom why his "niece" stole his car: "Wrong education. That's the trouble with our whole aristocracy. No respect for other people. Treating everyone like subjects. That's what starts revolutions."—Tom: "I guess you're right, she could start a revolution with me anytime." In Aranjuez, the thief slides her hand under the table to search the young man's pocket. He takes her hand and she doesn't dare withdraw it. Tom, delighted, exclaims to the rest of the table: "What a vacation! What a country!"[19]

But everything changes that same evening when the adventuress goes to the piano and sings for Tom, taking advantage of the situation to make eyes at him: "You're here and I'm here, with your heart and my heart, awake in a dream of romance, of delight—can it be that tonight is the night?"[20] She feigns love, then indifference, but Borzage is ready for her. Tom is completely forthright. This unyielding, simple character, gullible, good-hearted, pragmatic and a go-getter, has nothing of Lubitsch. Tom is first portrayed as a caricature of an average American lost on the continent—we hear him loudly sing "I'm driving a 'Bronson-8'" to the tune of "Cielito lindo!"—with a professional enchantress watching on. But her ingenuity no longer works along the country roads of Castille: her ruses fall flat.

While familiar with male vanity, Tom's candid and artless behavior gradually disarms her, the same way Rosalee succumbs to Allen John in *The River*. She is finally conquered not by his goodness, but by his obstinance. Travis Banton, Sternberg's incomparable costume designer, decks Marlene out in sumptuous tulle outfits while Cooper's clothes are functional; at breakfast, after the fateful night, Madeleine wears white fur (in summer, in Spain!) and Tom an ordinary bathrobe... Metaphorically, Madeleine is a victim of her reckless passion for rustling feathers and veils which serve as disguises. When Tom's car bumps into hers at the beginning, we hear Madeleine's voice, but don't see her: throughout the film, the adventuress hides behind assumed names, as she hides her true nature from herself. She is unhinged by police sirens, but not as much as by Tom's heartfelt simplicity, and the sweet nothings he whispers in her ear after a good glass of cognac, while she pretends to be dozing off in her armchair.

Joseph I. Breen (Production Code Administration) was very insistent about the time they spend in Aranjuez, speaking of a "clean love affair during the week," with "no sexual relationship." Mischievously, Lubitsch-Borzage (who submitted their script to the censor in small isolated chunks) decided to say everything by showing nothing... The couple suffer from "insomnia" and meet up on the terrace; during the kiss that fatally follows ("that Spanish moon!") from a slightly high-angle shot, Madeleine places her arms around the man who dominates her visually. Fade-out. An unmade bed, the next morning. Repeated knocking at the door. Carlos enters his accomplice's bedroom; she still doesn't budge. "Madeleine?" The woman smiles, her eyes still closed. "Yes dear?" Carlos frowns, then announces he is going into town and will take Tom Bradley to get rid of him. Madeleine murmurs something and continues sleeping. The pearls? She doesn't know where she put them. Carlos finds them on the dresser, pockets them, crosses the patio and knocks on Tom's door. No reaction. He enters: "Mr. Bradley?"—Tom smiles, keeping his eyes closed: "Yes, darling?" With difficulty he comes out of his torpor; Carlos wryly explains that they are going on a spectacular tour: he can see Spain. "I always wanted to see Spain, since I was a little boy," the American yawns. Carlos: "Well, now is your chance." "But I'm not a little boy anymore," Tom mumbles before turning over and closing his eyes. Later, Madeleine gets Tom out of bed: "My uncle wants me to persuade you to leave. Can you be persuaded?" "No." "Thank you, darling," she says, kissing him. Carlos energetically intervenes: "Now, Mr. Bradley, I don't want to be impolite, but I must insist..." Cut. Carlos goes into town alone, furious. *Time Magazine* wondered in retrospect if "the reason why the picture was approved by the Hays organization is that its agents were not sophisticated enough to understand it."[21]

These kinds of shortcuts and innuendos result from the marvelously symbiotic relationship between the two filmmakers, but the scene of psychological "unmasking," the test of authenticity and settling of accounts that follow are pure Borzage. Thus the intimate meal for two on the veranda, where Madeleine, her appetite taken away by emotion, gives her omelet to the famished Tom and observes him lovingly. Urgently brought in by Carlos, "Aunt Olga" ("I didn't smoke before I went to prison") tries to reason with the young woman, before admitting that she missed her chance of changing her existence, forty years ago, because she feared the reaction of the man she loved. The confession scene between Madeleine (blazer, skirt and scarf) and Tom is tightly constructed, beginning with his apology. He has lied to her: he doesn't earn $150 a week but $125 — he isn't a manager in Detroit, but a third assistant — his father isn't head of the local post office, but simply a mailman! "You'd better think it over... I'm neither a king nor a prince nor a count. I'm not even an elk." Madeleine explains to him that they must break off, that he doesn't know her. He

Breakfast after the fateful night: Marlene Dietrich and Gary Cooper in *Desire* (1936).

refuses: "Turn on the moon, turn out the moon." In the evening, Tom appears firm and energetic: he invites himself to sit down to eat with the two con artists and proposes a toast: "To my hostess who first stole my car and then stole my heart. My car was insured but my heart wasn't." Then he explains to "Aunt Olga" that, forty years ago, she should have admitted everything. Her friend would have been shocked: "He would have taken you over his knee and given you the spanking of your life." Tom breaks off and then turns to Madeleine: "Does it still hurt, darling?" She replies: "Just a little. Don't worry."—Tom to Olga: "He would have slapped your hands so hard that they never dreamed of taking anything that didn't belong to them," then to Madeleine, planting a kiss on her hand: "Sorry, darling, they're still a little red." To Olga: "But he would have stuck by you if he really loved you, he would have seen that you get your chance—and if anybody tries to stop you from getting your chance, I'd like to see him." These last words are addressed to Carlos. The allusive conversation continues, more tense than ever, interrupted by a dish of hollandaise sauce being passed around. They switch to European politics, very uncertain at that time. "What would America's attitude be if it really came to a war?" asks Madeleine. It's a big country, Carlos recognizes. Tom stares at him: "Six foot three..." So, after a last minute rush, the dangerous French adventuress can forget about building castles—in Spain or anywhere else—and become a good little Michigan housewife. It would, however, be absurd to blame this moral turnaround on Borzage: in 1935–36 even Lubitsch could no longer let himself defy the Hays Code with the sarcastic endings of days past.[22]

Paramount's "Operation Marlene" was a total success: the star, playing comedy for the first time, lost her stiffness, became animated, and surprised everyone with her spontaneity.

Of her work not directed by Sternberg, Dietrich said in her memoirs: "The only film I need not be ashamed of is *Desire*."[23] It was also the easiest one she ever made: "Until *Desire*, I always had to conceal my feelings and still show that I loved the man.... Sternberg never let me play love scenes."[24] But Dietrich and Cooper didn't work together again, as returns in the U.S. were slim. The film, however, was a smash in Europe. "*Desire* is the best film in which Miss Marlene Dietrich has appeared since she left Germany, and the most amusing new film to be seen in London this week," decreed Graham Greene.[25] Prague honored her with the "Filmove Listy" in 1937. In Berlin, where the film had its world premiere (even before New York!),[26] crowds lined up, surpassing the record attendance of Hathaway's *The Lives of a Bengal Lancer*. Adolf Hitler claimed he was a fervent admirer of Dietrich; in London, during the winter of 1936–37, Joachim von Ribbentrop approached the star and asked her to come "home to the Reich"; the Führer would award her the regime's highest decoration. Marlene's response is unprintable. As a result, *Desire* would be her last film shown in Germany before the end of the Nazi nightmare.

* * *

For his second-to-last Warner film, Borzage gave in to the pleas of his former boss, Hearst, finally agreeing to direct Marion Davies. The star and her powerful protector had just left MGM in anger because the much coveted role of *Marie-Antoinette* was promised to Norma Shearer. Hearst first thought about producing another film about the unfortunate queen of France, but Jack Warner, focusing on the cost, dissuaded him. Instead, he came up with another historical subject, already filmed by Warners in 1928: the "forbidden" love between Elizabeth (Betsy) Patterson and Jérôme Bonaparte,[27] Napoleon's younger brother. Borzage had been working on this subject for several months already and had intended it for Leslie Howard and Jean Muir. Alas! Marion Davies wanted to hear of no one other than singing cadet Dick Powell, her secret sweetheart, which was how *Hearts Divided* got a hilarious cast. The picture was filmed almost entirely in the studio (January 8–March 14, 1936), where a faithful replica of the aristocratic Patterson villa in Baltimore was built. Two hundred and eighty extras and 500 period costumes were used (some of which came from LeRoy's *Anthony Adverse*). All shots of Marion Davies were filmed in the afternoon, as the actress drank until late at night and refused to get up in the morning. After ten days, Hearst ordered shooting to stop and had the script rewritten, but to no avail: too many cooks had spoiled the broth. The result was an uncomfortable mixture of musical comedy and sentimental drama against a pseudo-historical background. The action takes place in 1803, when Jérôme Bonaparte is in charge of negotiating Louisiana with the Americans. The emperor's brother first passes himself off as an obscure French teacher and, incognito, wins Betsy's heart. He reveals his identity during a reception in the Patterson's manor and their engagement is announced. Furious, Napoleon intervenes, temporarily managing to separate the couple, but Jerome renounces the Wurtemberg throne his brother had intended for him, and goes to live near Betsy. The film's close is visually appealing: to symbolize overcoming the obstacle, Borzage places his camera (high-angle shot) above the Patterson's garden wall and follows (dolly-out) Betsy and Jérôme running, each on opposite sides of the wall, for about twenty yards until the gate where they can at last embrace. Rida Johnson Young's popular play, the starting point of the story was diluted so as not to offend the Code (on stage, Betsy was pregnant and her marriage with Jérôme was annulled by Paris). The central protagonists are so implausible, especially when they try to appear serious, that Borzage tries to make up for it with the secondary characters, beginning by the disturbing Napoleon portrayed by Claude Rains; after convincing Betsy to give up Jérôme "for France," Napoleon runs into Cambacérès (Halliwell Hobbes) on the bridge of

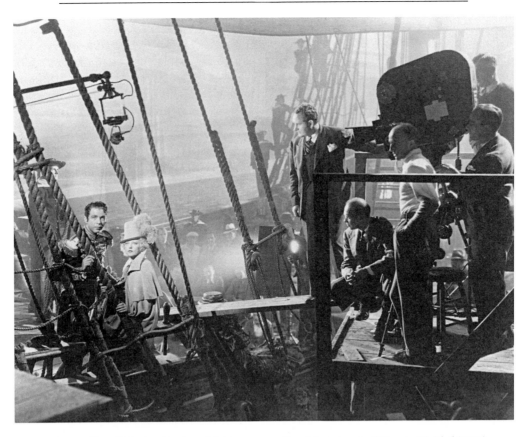

Dick Powell and Marion Davies with Borzage on the elaborate set of *Hearts Divided* (1936).

a frigate. "Success? Strategy?" asks the imperial chancellor. "Dramaturgy. An amazing good actor met an amazingly receptive audience." In other small parts we find Beulah Bondi (Laetizia, mother of Napoleon), George Irving (Jefferson) and Gaston Glass, the violinist in *Humoresque* in 1920, now Napoleon's private secretary. Not even awaiting the film premiere, Frank and Lew Borzage set sail for a two-month cruise in the Far East. They needed to take their distance...

On January 22, 1936, in the premises of the Hollywood Athletic Club (basically the filmmaker's second residence), the Film Directors Guild of America, a unionized association destined to defend the rights of directors up against the studios, held their first general assembly. King Vidor was named president. Borzage, one of the founding members, was part of the legislative committee, which was certainly not fortuitous, as he was on the verge of completing his purgatory in Burbank with a hybrid melodrama, created in the most deplorable working environment: *Green Light*. Production this time was definitely more onerous than that of *Living on Velvet* or *Stranded*, as the Cosmopolitan-Warner consortium was tackling a bestseller by the Lutheran pastor-minister Lloyd C. Douglas (1877–1951) and wanted to specially mark this event. The then very fashionable author of *Magnificent Obsession* (successfully brought to the screen the previous year), and, later, of the biblical story *The Robe*, liked to oppose the world of faith to that of scientific research to show that ideally they complement each other. In his eyes, a connection exists between the vocation of the pastor, who cares for souls, and that of the doctor, who heals bodies; in other words, the only true healing of the body must pass through that of the soul. The choice of the novel — which appeared in 1935 in Hearst's *Cosmopolitan*— was no doubt Borzage's own; he adapted two other of Douglas's books, *Disputed Passage* (1939) and *The Big Fisherman* (1958). Evidently, the subject "spoke" to him. Still, we may wonder if its transfer to the screen really conformed with what he had imagined! Hal Wallis designated Henry (Heinrich) Blanke as supervisor of *Green Light*, a mark of distinction as for a year Lubitsch's ex-assistant had been overseeing Warner Brothers' new "cultural" line, including Dieterle's *The Story of Louis Pasteur* (September 1935) or the sweeping historical films with Frederic March and Errol Flynn. But neither Wallis nor Blanke cared for Lloyd C. Douglas's story, which they deemed stupid and just good enough to fill the cash registers. Jack Warner came up with some ludicrous ideas: picturing a beginning and an end in Technicolor, with red first predominating, then green. Borzage approached Leslie Howard to play the tormented doctor, but the actor had to go back to Great Britain due to his fragile health (February 1936). Management then decided — against Borzage's wishes— to use this film as a test for Errol Flynn: it would be his first "modern" role (Flynn was finishing the exteriors for *The Charge of the Light Brigade* in Agoura). Olivia de Havilland would naturally be his partner, but the studio bypassed her at the last minute for Anita Louise, the star initially intended to play Maid Marian in *Robin Hood*. Filming began as soon as Flynn returned from the "Crimea," July 9, and was completed on September 16, 1936 in Hamilton, Montana; during this time, Wallis bombarded his supervisor with increasingly poisonous missives, cursing the director: "Frank Borzage is shooting too slow." He was "dissatisfied": "Speed it up!" He also threatened to immediately fire screenwriter Milton Krims as "Frank Borzage is starting his old tactics of calling writers down on the set at various times during the day to make changes and so forth,"[28] when it was forbidden to touch a word of the script he had read and approved of personally!

Borzage nevertheless had good reasons to want to perfect a story with overly philosophical and religious pretensions containing striking weaknesses in narration. The story itself is banal: when, destroyed by the stock market, Professor Endicott commits an error on the operating table that costs Mrs. Dexter (Spring Byington) her life, his assistant Paige (E. Flynn) takes the blame for him and nobly sacrifices a budding career; Phyllis (A. Louise), the victim's daughter, demands an inquiry and Paige is fired from the hospital. Nevertheless, she falls in love with the seductive young doctor before realizing, horrified, who he is. She flees. Paige reaches a scientific station in Montana where bacteriologist Stafford (Walter Abel) is seeking a vaccine against the spotted fever ravaging a small community; all his predecessors have failed. Paige infects himself with the vaccine. Repentant, Endicott and Phyllis (to whom Frances, a nurse, has revealed the truth) arrive terrified at his bedside. The human guinea pig survives the fever, the doctor triumphs over death and the implicated protagonists are victorious over themselves.

The semi–Christlike figure of the doctor crucifying himself for suffering humanity is a hackneyed cliché that Douglas tries to avoid (although some paragraphs on civilization and human progress today seem hopelessly outdated) by referring to an operation which is literally metaphysical. Reverend Harcourt, a graying, semi-paraplegic pastor, functions as a spokesperson for the author, a "spiritual guide" of the main characters and a sort of ancient choir. "Man's progress in life is not continual," explains the venerable clergyman. "Sometimes he is stopped by something that is bigger and stronger than he, something which he cannot understand, a red light. Sometimes a man must stop to learn through suffering before going on. For it is as inevitable as time that man progresses to a better future if not for himself then through his suffering for his fellow men. When he has learned this, the signal changes and the green light frees him to resume his inexorable march into eternity." Borzage places these explanatory words in a radio sermon that Mrs. Dexter and Paige listen to a few hours before the tragedy. But unsurprisingly, the passages in which Harcourt (Sir Cedric Hardwicke) intervenes directly are infinitely less effective than those in which the filmmaker makes the "divine plan" almost tangible by his directorial art. "There is altogether too much talk," characters in the film declare twice and, in fact, the clergyman's appearances are unbearably sententious and pontificating.[29] The preaching disposed of, Borzage finds the right tone. A gag at the beginning announces his intentions: a traffic officer is telling off drivers who have stopped (because of him): "What's the matter with you, can't you see the green light?" In other words, ordinary mortals are missing the essential point. Paige is one of those, even defining himself as "without too many scruples and not very courageous ... not a saint." For him, "religion is a kind of opiate to be used by people with hurt sensibilities to be lulled into drowsiness" and the cynic wishes his friend Stafford, who risks his life for science, "a happy burial."

The exchanges surrounding Mrs. Dexter are fundamental for introducing the parameters of Providence. The words on the radio, at the sick woman's bedside, have already established a link beyond, uniting Harcourt and Paige, for whom the speech was implicitly intended: the camera dissolves from the radio to the pastor's pulpit, inside the cathedral (St. Luke, Long Beach). Borzage captures the serenity of this smiling woman (diaphanous light, white shirt and bedclothes) and juxtaposes a two-shot with the underlying worries of Paige (dark suit, outlines of flowers and shadows on the wall) who admits, admiring his patient's complete confidence: "Things would be much simpler if we had your ... faith." When he leaves, Mrs. Dexter contemplates the photo of her daughter Phyllis. Dissolve to Phyllis, who lives in England; she is inside a church with a friend, admiring the bust of a mystic deceased in 1669: "It seems like a million years ago." But time, like space, is only a trap. When the friends leave the chapel, Borzage films a high angle shot of the gallery, moving away from the bust; this enigmatic personage, a symbol of divine imminence, observes the framework of destiny unfold from on high. Outside, Phyllis speaks of her mother who loves all creation: "birds, flowers, books, men, women, dogs," especially "Sylvia, her doctor's dog." Close-up of Sylvia, walking with her master, Paige. The animal runs alongside Harcourt who meditates alone, facing the Pacific. The big blue is a metaphor for eternity, the reverend explains to the doctor, who believes himself to be the man of a quantifiable "present" made up of chance and accidents. A simple effect of editing establishes a trans-substantial link uniting Paige, Phyllis and Harcourt beyond oceans, with the amazing Mrs. Dexter as mediator. (It is also thanks to the dog that Phyllis guesses Paige's identity and that he exiles himself.) At the moment of the operation, when the doctor in charge is delayed by banking transactions, Paige addresses Mrs. Dexter one last time. Borzage uses a subjective camera that foreshadows the fatal outcome of the operation: Paige, in medium-close shot, surrounded by menacing equipment, tries to appear reassuring: "Ready?" he asks, leaning toward the camera. The patient is framed in a very tight medium-close shot, with white as the dominant color and her barely audible "yes" expresses the acceptance of death. The surgeon then seizes the ether mask and places it over the camera; the image darkens. For Paige, the "rite of passage" has begun.

Paige is particularly struck by the intrusion of this "red light" that forces him to question the meaning of his life, by the fact that "in a split second" and "without warning" (as he repeats several times) a career can be destroyed or a future created. Obeying an irrational impulse, he has sacrificed himself to save the reputation of his mentor (which revolts his colleague Stafford, for whom "there is no room in science for either sentiments or nobility") and his gesture provokes a chain reaction around him. From then on seeking to justify his existence — or his death — he exposes himself to the disease. The melodramatic sequence (nonexistent in the novel) is developed with consummate art of lighting and timing. At the crucial moment, Paige, weak but determined to pursue his descent into hell to the end, refuses to let the bacteriologist intervene and, in a monotone, describes his condition. Borzage almost makes one realize the beneficial effect of this pushing of limits that affects all present, but immediately weakens its impact by an edifying conclusion at the clinic, then at the cathedral! Lloyd C. Douglas manages to make the reader forget the thinness of his plot because his characters live through their tormented reflections. Reduced to the events alone, the script deforms the issues brought up by *Green Light* with a selection of idealistic sacrifices (even Mrs. Dexter is "slain" for the redemption of an agnostic surgeon), during which everyone surpasses each other in magnanimousness. Finally, the film's credibility is undermined by the actors: in spite of very determined attempts to hide his natural mischievousness, Flynn's nature isn't really introspective and the colorless Anita Louise seems more preoccupied by changing costumes in each scene than making her conversion plausible. Only Margaret Lindsay (Frances) gives weight to her role of the deserted nurse.

Despite its obvious imperfections, *Green Light* marks a chapter in Borzage's filmography, as it introduces a more explicitly "mystical" leaning that would culminate in *Disputed Passage* and *Strange Cargo*. As Wallis predicted, the film was successful at the box office and the popular magazine *Modern Screen* honored this "Picture of the Month" with the "Award of Merit" (Oct.–Dec. 1936).[30]

* * *

"It would be a relief for me to get away from doing these *Flirtation Walks* and doing the same story in three different Academies. I'd like to take a crack at something different!" This was how the filmmaker answered his old friend and polo teammate Walter Wanger, when he invited him to make a picture at United Artists.[31] Hal Wallis was already threatening him: the next Borzage picture for Warner would be called *The Singing Marine*. Independent producer Wanger was of another ilk. The man that *Cahiers du Cinéma* described as "one of the most intelligent, cultured, eclectic men in Hollywood"[32] wanted to follow in Samuel Goldwyn's footsteps; he had just formed an association with United Artists to start his own company and was looking for the support of a few famous directors. To Fritz Lang he proposed *You Only Live Once*, and to Borzage *History Is Made at Night*. Obliged to release the filmmaker once a year, Warner granted him his "leave" for 1936.

Borzage was immediately captivated by the title: "It's a beautiful title, it's an intriguing title," he declared. Wanger was very proud of it. "But," inquired Borzage "where's the story?" The producer remained evasive. He had two pages of script, and two more would follow in the near future. Guaranteed. Shooting would begin in four weeks, on November 4. Borzage, Wanger and a handful of scriptwriters feverishly got down to work, not knowing exactly where they were headed. They were halfway through the story, on page 52, when they had to start shooting, as the actors, sets and studios were reserved for a specific date. For the leads, Wanger selected Charles Boyer, who had recently been acclaimed in *The Garden of Allah* with Marlene Dietrich and whom he had under exclusive contract; Colin Clive, alias Dr. Frankenstein; and the bubbly reporter from *Mr. Deeds Goes to Town*, Jean Arthur (replacing Madeleine Carroll), who here would give her most subtle performance by far. The film was created at exactly the same time as the classic *You Only Live Once*, in the same studios (Goldwyn), with the same scriptwriters (Towne, Baker), art director (Toluboff) and with Arthur Dewitt Ripley responsible for the second unit in both cases. The pages of the script dribbled in each morning. Borzage navigated on sight, and overall it began to look like a sophisticated drama punctuated with a few touches of comedy. He nevertheless shared his concern with Wanger, as he hadn't improvised that much since 1921, when he made

Get-Rich-Quick Wallingford without a script, with rather poor results! The producer begged to have faith.

One week before the end, just after Christmas (Borzage was only free until December 30), Wanger arrived with a miniature model of an ocean liner. The scriptwriters didn't know how to end their story, so why not go out with a bang? *San Francisco* had its earthquake, *The Good Earth* its locusts... The producer explained to the stupefied filmmaker that they would recreate the sinking of the Titanic, along those lines! Many people would drown. This would imply some modifications to the beginning, as Colin Clive's character would be transformed into a shipowner. Filming would be prolonged until February 9, 1937. In the end, *History Is Made at Night* required eight sets plus the neighboring studio of Educational Pictures. On the bridge of the liner in distress, constructed at great expense on a bascule, Borzage, Ripley and his assistant Joshua Logan directed 500 extras plunged into an artificial fog to hide the walls of the studio. The young Robert Parrish was one of those drowning who began singing "Closer to You, My Lord." "Our base pay was seven-fifty a day, but if we sang, we were raised to ten dollars per day," he recalled humorously. "Then Borzage decided he wanted six of the doomed passengers to cry. Another two-fifty adjustment for the lucky half-dozen." This was not an easy task: Ripley and Logan were in charge of selecting the most talented. While his colleagues toiled, "thinking about their dead mothers, the Depression, the loss of the two-fifty adjustment," Bob Parrish went discreetly to the bathroom and coated his fingers in soap which he then applied to his eyes: "The tears flowed, the cameras rolled, and Frank Borzage's reputation as a sentimental director was intact."[33] But the film's preview was a total flop. The public didn't know who to hate, as Charles Boyer, the hero, killed a chauffeur, although inadvertently, and Colin Clive, the cheated husband, was only taking revenge... So? Never short of ideas, Ripley rewrote the beginning—Clive would be the real murderer—and they got back to work one last time. Colin Clive, destroyed by alcohol, was suffering during shooting and shocked the unit by bursting into hysterical tears in a difficult scene. He died a few weeks after the premiere of the film, at the age of 37.[34]

So much for the amazing genesis of *History Is Made at Night*, which Andrew Sarris said "is not only the most romantic title in the history of the cinema, but also a profound expression of Borzage's commitment to love over probability."[35] What remains is in fact a kind of miracle: the story of its production shows that, as opposed to what some may have thought, the disconcerting mixture of genres and changes in direction were not deliberate, and that the filmmaker had only a relative role. Yet this stupendous patchwork manages not only to be very representative of Borzage's art, but to captivate his public: we don't know exactly where we're headed, but we follow each moment in delight! Even the very serious Frank S. Nugent of the *New York Times*, had to grudgingly admit that this tortuous journey resulted in an "unreasonably likeable" film.[36]

The gossip columns report that Irene (J. Arthur) has left her husband, New York multimillionaire Bruce Vail (C. Clive), an obsessively jealous, possessive man. Waiting for the judges' decision, she goes to Paris, where Vail uses a low strategy to compromise her and wipe out her chances of obtaining a divorce: their chauffeur Michael is paid to be caught in her bedroom one evening—except that history is made at night. In the next apartment, Paul Dumond (C. Boyer) is bringing back a drunken friend; he hears Irene scream, strides over to her balcony, catches the chauffeur molesting the woman and knocks him out at the moment Vail and a detective appear. Michael is unconscious. Hidden by the shadows, with his dark raincoat, lowered hat and commanding voice, Paul passes himself off as an armed robber. He grabs some jewelry, locks the men in a closet and spirits away Irene. After this

Champagne and salade chiffonade for Charles Boyer and Jean Arthur in *History Is Made at Night* (with Leo Carillo as cook, 1936).

busy, Dashiell Hammett–like aperitif, regulated like a ballet and photographed in the style of film noir (Gregg Toland), we go into an English waltz. In the taxi, the voice of the mysterious savior becomes more gentle. After giving back the jewels and explaining his actions, he invites the perplexed and fascinated young woman for a drink at the Château bleu. The restaurant is closing, but a few compliments to the chef, the "fabulous" César (Leo Carrillo) who people come from America to see, and unlimited champagne for the orchestra opens doors.

If *History Is Made at Night* represents in itself the quintessence of romantic Hollywood, the magical night at the "Château bleu" is the paradigm of sequence of seduction. As always, Borzage develops his direction from the inside, going from the intrinsic truth of characters and emotions that can be made out from the slightest batting of an eyelash. Music created by looks and by what is left unsaid create the setting, authenticate the story. Borzage knows the secret of a good sauce: everything looks delicious in the high-class restaurant, and this flavor is imparted to all that follows, even the improbable. Jean Arthur shows the true range of her talent in this classic tête-à-tête; from a fragile, frightened doe, infinitely vulnerable with her backwoods Kansas accent, she lets herself be carried away, then blossoms as time passes. Boyer too has rarely been better; refined, he orders from the chef "lobster cardinal à la César" and "salade chiffonade." Then, having made up his hand to look like a woman's face — "Coco" — he performs an indiscreet ventriloquist number that lets him ask Irene about her married life. Irene skirts the question: she wants to dance. "Beautiful, keep them warm!"

shouts Paul to poor César, who enters with his exquisite dishes as the couple starts into an interminable tango. Gastronomy and sex. Irene teeters twice on her high heels, they laugh, Cinderella throws her shoes across the room and continues dancing, barefoot... The filmmaker seasons the idyll by inserting the sequence where the husband frees himself from the closet. Vail, incarnating perversion by his worship of all-powerful money, sends the detective away; Michael comes to, his jaw sore. Vail hits him hard, calls the police and accuses the stranger (whom he takes for his wife's lover) of murder. — Tango. Paul: "There's only one thing important enough to say to you tonight." "What's that?" "Well, I don't know how it is in Kansas, but in France, it isn't considered good taste for a gentleman to say it — until he's known the lady — at least a year." Tango. The camera frames Irene's shoes, pans to her mink stole lying on the floor, and finally insistently follows the languorous steps of the dancers. The polysemy of images makes this erotic striptease — Irene is only wearing a long silk negligee — the outward expression of confidence and progressive abandonment (without saying a word, she says more to Paul than she has ever said to her husband), but also one of detachment, of breaking off: jewels, shoes and mink are signs of Bruce Vail's property. "Tonight is what I've waited for," vows Irene, going slowly, like Madeleine in *Desire*, "from sophistication to naturalness" (J.-L. Bourget[37]). When dawn appears, the "year" of waiting has passed. At the fraction of a second in which lips touch, Borzage cuts to a long shot of the violinist.

Once these premises are firmly established, everything moves quickly. Paul brings Irene back to the hotel (in a barouche, of course). Vail questions his wife who, like the police squad, believes the chauffeur was accidentally murdered by the "other man." If Irene goes back with him to the U.S., Vail concedes with a nasty smile, he will forget about the unidentified "culprit." At the end of the day, Paul reaches the Château bleu where we finally learn he is the maître d'. It wasn't money that opened doors there in the middle of the night, but his friends' affection! His formal attire and fine manners are part of his profession. Like in *Man's Castle*, the bogus robber is also a bogus wealthy man — but a true gentleman. He announces to César that he will marry the unknown American of the night before, as he's known her "forever." But Irene has left, giving in to Vail's blackmail so as to protect Paul. With Borzage, the genre of the missed opportunity, so typical of melodrama (McCarey's *Love Affair*) can have no fateful consequence, as his lovers are mutually "involved" and communicate what is essential. The very thought of betrayal is unthinkable. The truculent César swears in Italian and shows his friend a newspaper photo of "Miss America, the girl who danced with the naked feet": she is sailing for New York with her husband. Paul immediately picks up the phone and asks to be connected with the liner; Irene sobs "goodbye" into the receiver, but explains nothing. Vail is sadistically enjoying his triumph and prepares to celebrate a second honeymoon: "Wouldn't it be wonderful, Irene, if you were a magician and could change me into him? Just think, you two alone, right now, in this room, on this boat, in the middle of the sea. What would you give, Irene?" She immediately replies: "I'd give my *soul!*" It is he, she cries, who has created this other man, who has literally called him forth with his jealousy. Vail swears he'll kill her. Paul and César take the next liner. But how to find Irene who has left her marital home, and trailed by the multimillionaire's detectives, earns her life as a model under her maiden name? Nothing could be simpler: Paul and César open a fancy French restaurant in Manhattan, "Victor's." Everyone, sooner or later, tries out a famous spot, so one day she'll end up coming there...

A new turn of events: the French police have arrested the murderer, they say, and ask Vail and his wife to testify. Irene believes that Paul is imprisoned. If Vail manages to free him, she promises in despair, she'll come back to him. Before sailing for Paris aboard the

Hindenburg (!), the couple dines at Victor's. Irene bursts out laughing uncontrollably when she recognizes Paul, but forces herself to not betray him. Paul is at first offended, thinking she laughed because the "prince" is only a maitre d' (he is unaware that the "princess" is really a model). However, Irene goes to meet him in the restaurant after the closing; the young woman celebrates their reunion by playing the bourgeois couple and by preparing him "eggs à la Kansas," a way of showing her true nature. The next morning (where were the censors?) she reveals why they cannot return to France. But Paul cannot abide the idea of an innocent man taking the blame for him, even if, as Irene insists, that signifies "two lives versus one."

In order to clear the falsely accused man, the lovers sail for Cherbourg aboard Vail's new liner, the S.S. *Princess Irene*, making its inaugural crossing. Midway, the ship's captain gets a call from New York: Vail orders the maximum speed to beat the record for crossing the Atlantic, despite fog and icebergs; his true intention is to sink the ship, as he fears that the lovers will make French justice relent. In the luxury cabin of the lovers, a tango of bare feet and "lobster cardinal à la César," but the threatening moaning of the fog horn punctuates the sound track, foreshadowing the couple's separation in Paris, and a catastrophe at sea for the viewer. Borzage makes the "blind" boat a microcosm of the world, a universe ruled by money, now at the mercy of a vicious paranoiac assuming the right to control destinies. The shock of the collision with the iceberg is masterfully filmed; the scenes of panic are in no way inferior to those of Dupont, Selpin, Baker or Negulesco dealing with the tragedy of the Titanic. In a few images, Borzage captures the range of human emotions: a hysterical man fights to gain access to the lifeboats for women and children; old couples say

The *Titanic* revisited: Jean Arthur on the sinking ship in *History Is Made at Night* (1936).

goodbye to each other, etc. Irene categorically refuses to leave the bridge without Paul, holds on to him with all her might and almost falls into the ocean. The ship sinks slowly. According to the radio, only a handful of passengers were able to save themselves in the lifeboats. The scuttling of the *Princess Irene* metaphorically represents the end of the shipowner's hold over his wife, now freed from her false status of "aristocrat." In Manhattan, Vail holes up in his office; the camera (now subjective) frames his letter of confession to the police, then zooms without transition toward a large portrait of Irene while a gunshot is heard. The oil painting presides above a model of a ship in distress; the "powerless" shipowner could only possess his wife except by means of this sort of altar (cf. *Street Angel*) with fetishist connotations; Irene appears in it in a black dress, which brings us back to a first painting of the young woman in a light-colored dress, hanging significantly on board the ship.

The last scene is of a virtually unreal whiteness. A heavy silence, the diaphanous fog of dawn, faraway snatches of a hymn. Sitting on a walkway, isolated by the fog, Paul and Irene look lovingly at each other; their conversation is disjointed, senseless: they have no words left and have so much to ask each other: "Did you always look like this?" "Where did you go to school?" "When did you fall in love with me?" "We have nothing to fear now," murmurs Paul, "everything now seems so little, so unimportant." They are at peace; miracles are now possible. A loudspeaker announces to the shipwrecked that the watertight rooms of the ship are intact and have managed to keep it afloat. A succession of close-ups of faces, cries of joy, tears, silent prayers. The End.

Between the Château bleu and the *Princess Irene*, the two pillars of this fairy tale, Borzage moves effortlessly from distress to comedy, then from drama to tragedy. A series of coincidences leads us from a frivolous scene to morbid psychodrama, accumulating blackmail, shipwreck, miscarriage of justice and suicide, also having us cross the Atlantic as if we were taking the subway. Of course the story seen in its totality is incredible and borders on pastiche to the point of becoming improbable. But it is made of remarkably filmed compositions, crackles with directorial ideas and is acted to perfection. We don't believe in the story, but in the characters and the emotions that motivate them. Borzage's intimacy literally frees us from confining stereotypes in such a way that, in the face of so much conviction and exquisite sensitivity, this unusual melodrama manages to overcome the viewer's last defenses.

Before undertaking *Green Light*, Borzage had signed, for the sake of form, a second five-year contract with Jack Warner (July 8, 1936) that was supposed to begin upon the completion of *History Is Made at Night*. The events surrounding the script of the film left him time to try his hand at radio. To help out Cecil B. DeMille, ensconced in Montana filming the battle scenes of *The Plainsman* (Jean Arthur as Calamity Jane!), Borzage quickly replaced him at the microphone of the traditional DeMille Radio Lux Theater and broadcast a play by Margaret Mayon, *Polly of the Circus* (CBS November 30, 1936) that featured the voices of Loretta Young, James Gleason and Lionel Barrymore. At the same time, David O. Selznick was seeking to negotiate with Jack Warner, as he wanted to have Borzage direct *The Prisoner of Zenda* with Ronald Colman (scheduled for February 1937); Warner said no: the director had already been assigned to a musical-military comedy with Dick Powell, *The Singing Marine*, to be filmed at the San Diego naval base![38] Borzage practically lost his legendary calm and when filming of *History Is Made at Night* had to be prolonged beyond his granted leave, he seized the opportunity to definitively leave Burbank, a year before his option expired. A press release explained that "Frank Borzage felt he did not fit into the Warner type of film and has been anxious to leave the studio." An understatement.

13

At MGM: Stars and Real Life

In a note dated May 1933, David O. Selznick fought for creators to gain relative independence. Soon to become wealthy and powerful, he advised MGM's New York office (Nicholas M. Schenck) to ensure "the permanent addition of men like Frank Borzage, King Vidor and Victor Fleming, for I think we should be a lot better off with fewer supervisors and more producer-directors, increasing our chances of getting an ever greater number of outstanding pictures."[1] Fleming began at Culver City that same year and became a kind of institution. As for the two others, they still resisted the lure of temptation; Borzage had not forgotten his humiliating stay at MGM in 1924 (cf. chap. 5) and preferred to devote himself to the Hollywood Screen Guild. Vidor also cherished his temporary freedom (until 1938).

In the meanwhile, MGM underwent serious changes. With the extreme care it gave its products, its abundance of stars, filmmakers and technicians under contract, the studio became the Rolls-Royce or Tiffany's of the film industry. It counted 4,000 employees, 23 sound stages and extended over 117 acres. Its earnings—14.5 million dollars in 1937—were unsurpassed. The pace of filming was comfortable—from four to five weeks for an average film—and budgets were generous: from one million for a Jeanette MacDonald operetta, to 2.8 million for *The Wizard of Oz*. The producer was king and the star system was at its peak: Greta Garbo, Norma Shearer and Joan Crawford, Clark Gable, Spencer Tracy and Mickey Rooney were the most scintillating names in the studio of superlatives claiming to have "More Stars Than There Are in Heaven." But the main change resulted from the death of Irving Thalberg; the expert of the studio's first decade died in 1936 in the prime of life, leaving Louis B. Mayer alone in charge. As a cynical pragmatist, Thalberg had naturally molded the company's style in a way that was moderate, solemn and outwardly attractive; intermittently, though, his taste for financial risk and innovation betrayed a romantic temperament (*Freaks, Romeo and Juliet, The Good Earth*). More of an administrator than an innovator, Mayer was outrageously sentimental; he loved the most predictable, conventional products: operetta, family films, inexpensive but lucrative series (*Tarzan, The Thin Man, Andy Hardy, Dr. Kildare*). His studio was also the most respectful of the taboos and restrictions imposed by the Code, whose values Mayer embraced.

Creatively speaking, the restructuring had both advantages and drawbacks. With Thalberg's death, the days of the studio head's constant, central presence at all levels of production were over; Mayer had neither the time, nor the desire, let alone the competence, for such an activity. This work was delegated to a committee of supervisors (renamed "executive producers"), where each had full responsibility for current projects, specializing in a genre or linked to a specific star. They chose the subjects, designated scriptwriters, cast the films and also named the director. From then on, quality of films at MGM varied considerably, depending on the talent of the new supervisory administrators. Alongside Harry Rapf, Hunt Stromberg or Bernie Hyman, Mayer also placed people capable of more artistic undertakings, including Mervyn LeRoy (a renegade from Warner), pioneer Sidney A. Franklin and above all, young ex-scriptwriter Joseph L. Mankiewicz, 28, who had not yet tried his hand at directing and was in charge of high caliber "women's pictures" and specifically managed Joan Crawford's career.

Among the many categories comprising the big MGM "family," Frank Borzage, King Vidor and Victor Fleming belonged to a privileged set, as they benefited from the loose status of producer-director, which gave them, if not more autonomy, at least more authority during the creative process. Tay Garnett related how "Victor Fleming was once visited by a producer on his set. He asked the producer how long he planned to stay on the set. The producer said he wasn't sure, so Fleming went home and said: 'call me when you leave the set....'"[2] And James Stewart stated: "And this stuff 'bout no freedom! Nobody told Lubitsch what to do, or Frank Borzage!"[3] Only two days after the last take of *History Is Made at Night*, February 11, 1937, vice-president Eddie Mannix invited Borzage to his bungalow. The director signed a lucrative contract linking him (along with his brother Lew as always) to Culver City for five years; in 1940 his annual salary was $169,000, or $3250 a week. During this time he worked on twelve films, including such key works as *Three Comrades* and *The Mortal Storm*, before running into serious setbacks in relation to his private life. Borzage began by refusing the first project MGM submitted to him, the melodrama par excellence *Madame X*, based on Alexandre Bisson's play (Sam Wood took charge). Instead, he set his heart on *Marry for Money*, a subject reserved for the Crawford-Mankiewicz duo that would be renamed — after much procrastinating —*Mannequin*. But the storyline was still too stereotypical, and the filmmaker wanted more human consistency and less glamour (March 1937); the script had to be reworked so extensively that shooting was delayed until the fall. To clear his name with the Front Office and show goodwill, Borzage agreed in the meantime to a bread and butter picture that would let him work again with his friend Spencer Tracy.

Fate had it that the filmmaker and Fritz Lang crossed paths again in *Big City*, as Borzage inherited the team from *Fury*: Tracy (who hated Lang), author Norman Krasna and cinematographer Joseph Ruttenberg. At 28, Krasna was the prodigal son on the lot; his plays and scripts were already selling like hot cakes, and initiator and associate producer, he was mainly responsible for *Big City* (filmed between mid–June and July 28, 1937). Casting was interesting: Tracy (Oscar 1937) played opposite Austrian phenomenon Luise Rainer (Oscars 1936 and 1937 and the New York Critics Best Actress Award). Called in 1934 to replace Greta Garbo, the Viennese actress had a meteoric career in Hollywood, consciously sabotaged by Louis B. Mayer; the big boss did not approve of her "anti-publicity" marriage to communist writer Clifford Odets and the fiery actress had the gall to stand up to him at the slightest provocation. A few names from the silent era appear in supporting roles: Hungarian Victor Varconi, Alice White and Guinn Williams (*Lucky Star*).

In the small world of New York cabdrivers, a war is raging between the independents, mostly emigrés, and the unionized "Comet Cab Company." Joe Benton (S. Tracy), a fierce independent, is married to Anna (L. Rainer), a Rumanian who landed three years earlier in the U.S. with her brother Paul (V. Varconi); in six weeks, she will finally be entitled to an American passport. To hurt the competition, Comet's boss hires thugs belonging to Beecher, a gangster, to provoke a series of pileups and fistfights. Comet sends them away, but Beecher knows how to make himself indispensable: he places a bomb in a box of clothing that Anna had sent her brother (who is working secretly in a Comet garage to spy on the enemy). The explosion kills Paul and destroys the premises where the gangsters then let loose a few rounds of gunfire. The bloody attack is blamed on the independents; the state prosecutor is looking for someone to blame. The municipality finds a scapegoat to save the incriminated drivers: Anna, the foreigner. Hadn't the booby-trapped parcel come from her? To satisfy the prosecutor, the mayor orders the young woman — who is pregnant — repatriated to Europe. But the taxi drivers, in a show of solidarity, each take turns hiding Anna; the police tail and intimidate them, but to no avail. In the evening, Joe joins his wife by climbing over roofs. Anna, however, gives herself over when federal authorities attack the drivers who have wives and children. An hour before the ocean liner sails, Joe is allowed to visit his wife, cooped up with six other unfortunates in an unsanitary cabin in steerage; very weak, she is about to give birth. "Maybe I'll be back in some years," she murmurs, not really believing it. Joe wants to follow her to Rumania; she shakes her head: "In a village where they walk without shoes," with unemployment everywhere? Victims of an error of justice, the couple is being crushed by the state machinery and Borzage frames his faces very tightly, as if suffocating in the dimness of sadness. Then, without warning, forgetting social commentary, criticism of unrestrained capitalism and the characters' feelings of helplessness, the story veers off into the most superficial, artificial ending imaginable.

In Borzage's defense, the last twelve minutes, filmed on location in New York, are not his work, but that of hack George B. Seitz (the *Andy Hardy* series) and his cameraman Clyde De Vinna. By coincidence, Joe discovers the written confession of one of the gangsters' accomplices. Flanked by his colleagues, he urgently seeks the mayor whom he ends up tracking down in Jack Dempsey's famous restaurant on Broadway (Brill Building), where the politician is presiding at a banquet with all the old champions of the ring. Boxer Jack Dempsey was a world heavyweight champion from 1919 to 1926,[4] and in the film he is surrounded by other sports idols such as James J. Jeffries, Big Jim Thorpe, Man Mountain Dean, Louis "Bull" Montana, Don Sugai Matsuda and Maxie Rosenbloom. They all appeared out of friendship for Borzage, whose passion for sports is legendary. This gymnasium of athletes in evening clothes listens to Joe's poignant recriminations and decides to lend him a hand! The ship is sailing in seven minutes? They commandeer the taxis, set off sirens and suddenly the streets of Manhattan are transformed into the Grand Prix. On the docks, an ambulance attends to Anna. Beecher and the Comet drivers hurry to teach the competition a good lesson. They are met with the top fighters from the ring, and even the mayor himself rolls up his sleeves. Anna gives birth during the carnage. Later, an Orthodox priest baptizes the baby who receives about fifty names, those of his fighting godfathers. This noisy finale, with its Keystone Cop race and its fight scene worthy of Tay Garnett, distills a kind of wide-eyed Capraesque optimism: the entire community of "good guys" stands behind the persecuted couple. This virtuoso display is funny, at times hilarious, but we are in another film.

At times, we can't help but have the impression that this "big city symphony" (with only James Cagney missing) is a Warner subject that found its way onto a desk at the very conservative MGM — were it not for Spencer Tracy's humanity and Luise Rainer's feverish hypersensitivity. Cinematographer Ruttenberg, reputed in Culver City for his somber tones, designed the camera work in close collaboration with Borzage: "I made a film for him no one ever talks about, and it's really too bad because *Big City* is a marvelous film.... He was a great filmmaker and a very pleasant collaborator. He liked details, the kind of things that no one notices reading a script. People like Borzage, Boleslawski and Lubitsch liked to work on the details of a character and that is perhaps why their films still hold up. You never notice Borzage's technique — which is partly what makes it so special."[5] The lighting of shots with Luise Rainier brings out her big, expressive eyes, dreamy smile, and one has only to watch again the scene of Anna's birthday, in the first third of the film, where the actress' face is lit as much by the candles from the cake in the darkness as by the mysterious music coming from a radio (a surprise gift from Joe), to understand Ruttenberg's words.

In order to sensitize the spectator to the drama that lies ahead, Borzage also gives us a dazzling ten-minute introduction. First a sight gag. Joe is driving when he notices a ravishing brunette wearing a beret waiting on the sidewalk with a shopping bag. He stops and addresses her: "Taxi, lady?" "No, thank you." "Free ride, sister." She turns and ignores him, haughtily outraged. He gets out of the vehicle and takes her by the arm: "My name is Joe Benton, what's yours?" "Please, take your hand away." "Come on, relax, you're only young once." She gets mad: "Take your hand away!"—A zealous policeman runs to the rescue ("Spring fever?") and suddenly, the young beauty throws her arms around Joe's neck: they were joking, they're married. The policeman's face. The bantering continues in the taxi. Joe inquires where Anna has spent the afternoon. She teases him, then serious: "Well, if you must know, I have a second husband in the Bronx." "I hope you're telling the truth, honey, because if there's one thing I can't stand, it's a liar!" She comes up from behind and bites his ear. He barely avoids an accident. The flirting continues in the stairway (she pretends to faint, he wants to throw her over the banister, etc.), then in their pathetic two rooms on the East Side where Joe has a go at speaking Rumanian while Anna bursts out laughing. At the top of his form, the filmmaker draws a portrait of marital happiness, naughtily euphoric, bringing out what is unique and precious in their relationship. Sentimental without sentimentality, served up by visibly ecstatic actors: "Working for Borzage was a perpetual joy," Luise Rainer remembers, who at the time was going through a difficult period in her life, already contemplating divorcing Clifford Odets.[6] It was probably the quality of its acting and directing that earned *Big City* the distinction of *Photoplay*'s "Best Picture of the Month" in November 1937. In other respects *Big City* resembles so many other MGM products of the post–Thalberg era: a lot of great talent wasted on a script that was only a pretext.

Luise Rainer teases Spencer Tracy, her amourous taxi driver (*Big City*, 1937).

With this first job over, Borzage linked forces with Mankiewicz for the three films to come. He began personally working on the script of *Mannequin* in April, in close collaboration with Mankiewicz and Lawrence Hazard, author of *Man's Castle*. Only the skeleton remained of Katherine Brush's unpublished story "Marry for Money," destined for *Cosmopolitan* and bought by MGM in 1936 specifically for Joan Crawford. The oft-told tale of a Cinderella from the slums who, to escape poverty, marries the first man who comes along, combined with the typical Depression-era motif of the destroyed millionaire who rebuilds his fortune, is reminiscent of too many earlier Joan Crawford vehicles (*Dancing Lady*, *Sadie McKee*) to be satisfactory on its own. The studio tried to flesh out the image of the actress, no longer in the bloom of youth, uncomfortable in screwball comedy and too modern for costume roles. So Mayer threw her in the arms of his greatest male star, Spencer Tracy. Crawford asked for newcomer Alan Curtis (noticed in a screen test) for her other partner and Mankiewicz even allowed her to attend script conferences. As mentioned, Joan Crawford had already played a tiny part in Borzage's *The Circle* (1925) and tested for *7th Heaven*.

Filming of *Mannequin* (September 7–October 25, 1937) led to many rumors of dissension between Tracy and Crawford; a hardworking, ambitious perfectionist, she had difficulty putting up with Tracy's nonchalance and even indifference toward his profession, transformed by the camera into a fascinating naturalness he found effortless. In her autobiography, she denied the facts: "(Tracy) walks through a scene just as he walks through life. He makes it seem so easy, and working with him I had to learn to underplay... We never had a moment's disharmony."[7] In her desultory conversations with Roy Newquist, however, a different story comes out: "He turned out to be a real bastard. When he drank he was mean, and he drank all through production. He'd do cute things like step on my toes when we were doing a love scene — after he chewed on some garlic...."[8] Obviously, the actress did not have Katharine Hepburn's playful sense of humor and taste for witty repartee, and the two stars never worked together again.[9] Finally, the film's title was a real headache; for over a year, management bombarded itself with memos on the topic, suggesting various titles such as *Class* (Mankiewicz), *Saint or Sinner*, *Shop Girl* or *Three Rooms in Heaven* (Borzage). As Adrian had designed 28 dresses specifically for Miss Crawford, they opted for *Mannequin*, lacking anything better, yet aware that the title was misleading.

MGM had rarely portrayed poverty and the daily life of the working class in such a somber light. Jessie Cassidy (J. Crawford) leaves the factory with hundreds of other workers, punching her time card, crosses through the congested squalor of Hester Street (in Manhattan's Lower East Side) and enters a tenement house. Borzage follows her up three floors of dirty stairways, barely lit by a flickering naked lightbulb; the cries of an infant can be heard throughout the building. Jessie screws the light bulb back in before continuing — a mechanical gesture she will repeat each time, symbolizing her desire to escape this existential dead end (like Janet Gaynor and the streetlamp in *7th Heaven*). "During the making of *Mannequin*," recalls cinematographer George Folsey, "the director kept the camera continually on the move. In one scene, he placed the camera on a 75 foot boom to follow Miss Crawford as she walked on three flights of stairs of a tenement house. 'Miss Crawford,' Borzage declared, 'has the type of vivid personality that demands movement, she is the ideal photographic subject because she is equally lovely from any angle.'"[10] As it happens, the camera movements at the beginning reflect her inner nervousness, made up of frustration and the need to escape, while the duration of the shots exposes the surrounding filth. The same tone pervades in the Cassidy's apartment, where all behavior seems to have been frozen over time: the father, incorrigibly lazy, only leaves his armchair and his newspaper for meals, served on time; ravaged by work, the mother toils in a foul-smelling kitchen, with dripping taps; the brother, Cliff, a sixteen-year-old good-for-nothing, finds, like his father, any excuse not to look for work.[11] The men let themselves be served, grumbling; the clan lives off Jessie's meager salary, and who lives on her dreams: "Eddie and Saturday night." Eddie (Alan Curtis), the local show-off, is her lifeline. An evening under the neon lights of the amusement park, moonlight on the beach. Returning home, shouting is heard in the stairway; a couple is bickering; Jessie screws back in the flickering lightbulb once too often, and it blows. The stairwell is in darkness. At first paralyzed, the young woman gets control of herself, runs after Eddie and implores him to marry her.

In a room full of sailors, shipowner John L. Hennessey (S. Tracy) tells his workers about the flourishing state of his company; good humor and openness reign; the workers adore their model boss who, after leaving Hester Street—in other words nothing—built up his enterprise with his own hands. The self-made man takes a friend out to eat in a dive in the neighborhood where he grew up: the boss of the so-called Chinese restaurant is named Horowitz! Here Jessie and Eddie are celebrating their wedding. The shipowner offers champagne to the table. When Jessie expresses the wish that her relatives be as happy as she, Borzage inserts a cruel shot of her mother that speaks volumes about the disillusions ahead. In a surge of excitement fraught with repercussions, Eddie introduces his wife to the "famous Mr. Hennessey"—it could always be useful—then strongly insists she act friendly and dance with him. "You've got everything?" inquires the wealthy industrialist, intrigued by her radiant expression. Jessie: "Well, everything we'll ever need: each other." The shipowner appears troubled at meeting a person capable of loving so intensely and selflessly: "I just didn't think things like that happen outside of books." But the jukebox strikes up "Always and Always,"[12] Jessie excuses herself from her gentleman and persuades her reluctant husband to dance to "their" song. The scene, singularly incongruous in such a realistic setting, synthesizes the various levels of the action. Pressing up against the ear of her indifferent (although flattered) guy, Jessie, in close-up, her eyes luminous, sings the words of the song aloud. A cruel moment in the arms of a potential pimp and blackmailer, with the undeceived mother looking on. A sublime moment, as well, unnoticed by others on the dance floor, that reveals this "gift of the gods" mysteriously received by a vulnerable young girl at birth: the power to attain what is essential by total self-sacrifice. Eddie is intrinsically impervious to it; Hennessey is haunted by it, for Jessie imbues him with love at a distance. In the hands of another director, the sequence would be ridiculous; Borzage-Sarastro uses it to release an alchemical process that, like in *History Is Made at Night*, transcends the clichéd situations of an eminently predictable plot.

Eddie brings Jessie to a stylish apartment with a view of the East River; the husband sleeps late, while the wife leaves him money and runs to work, first at the factory, later on stage at a music hall. In the evening, Eddie pushes her to go to the parties Hennessey organizes in the secret hope of seeing her again. The shipowner invites her out on the terrace, tries to dazzle her with his assets, but Jessie, still blind, waxes enthusiastically about her own "love nest." Deeply moved, he kisses her. She lets him, then slaps him and leaves. Hennessy catches her and challenges her to show him her "paradise" that surpasses anything money can buy: "I wanna see those three rooms. I've been wondering what makes them mean so much more to you than anything I've got means to me." When they arrive at the apartment, Eddie is in the midst of handing back the place to its true owners, home from vacation! Jessie pays the damages caused by cigarette burns on the table. The couple moves to Hester Street, to a lugubrious hotel room, and things go from bad to worse: the show Jessie worked in closes, Eddie loses at gambling, incurs debts and ends up in prison. Hennessey pays his bail. One evening, the good-for-nothing reveals to his wife his plan "that will send us on the right side of the street." All Jessie has to do is marry Hennessey, divorce him six months later and return with substantial alimony! Revolted by his baseness, Jessie leaves him. She is earning her living as a model on Park Avenue when Hennessey, more and more taken with her, asks her to marry him. Unknowingly, Jessie has transmitted her luminosity to him. He wants to give her everything with nothing in return; he says, "I have enough love for two." ("Always" is playing on the radio, but Jessie no longer hears it.) Finally she gives in, divorcing Eddie and marrying the industrialist on a trip to Europe, not really loving him at first. Honeymoon in an Irish cottage (the film reuses blocking from *Street Angel*, with the couple close to the fireplace). Jessie realizes that they are made for each other, but fears going home; if she doesn't pay him, Eddie has threatened to make the shipowner believe the marriage was only a ploy. Hennessey is urgently called home as his shipyards are on strike, his empire crumbling. The ruined man comes across Eddie with Jessie and thinks he knows everything. He sends her away. At the last minute, Borzage short-circuits the mechanics of melodrama, sweeping away the conventional mishaps come before. As in *Man's Castle*, the power relationship is reversed: serene, steadied by love, the woman takes the initiative. Jessie lets herself be insulted but categorically refuses to leave. She gives him her jewels so he may begin anew, in a three-room apartment, with her. As he is still in shock and doesn't react, she slaps his face. "There you go slapping me again," says he, surprised. Jessie: "That worked the last time."

Mannequin is not the most satisfying Joan Crawford film, but is perhaps the most honest because, as Christian Viviani remarks, Borzage manages to capture her "inner suffering, her vulnerability, the anguish of a malnourished teenager" that would torment her entire life.[13] The first half, on Hester Street, firmly anchors the personalities and story in reality, finally revealing the passionate flames smoldering beneath the misery, which gives the film a lyrical strength, a conviction that later evaporates. Borzage paints a Sunday portrait of the Cassidy's worthy of the anguished snapshots of *After Tomorrow* (1932); slumped in their armchairs across the room, father, brother and husband smoke in shirt-sleeves and spit on the system that favors the rich, while this pathetic trio unscrupulously let themselves be supported by women and social assistance. In the background, Jessie and her mother toil under a mountain of dishes (Borzage films them framed by the pipes). "Your future is gonna be the past," says the mother to her daughter in a resigned tone. "Live your life for yourself... Your father was the spitting image of Eddie." Not having the strength to react, Jessie is doomed to domestic slavery, as Eddie and Cliff are to live by their wits on the street. Implicitly, the filmmaker shows it is not easy to escape one's condition, family or social environment. At the same time, he refrains from facile endings, and from the simplistic explanations favored by MGM to address juvenile delinquency in urban areas. For once, the Pollyanna-ish mind-set and conciliatory tone of *The Devil Is a Sissy* (Van Dyke, 1936) and *Boys Town* (Taurog, 1938) are not tolerated. The same goes for the working class milieu: in *Riff-Raff* (Ruben, 1936), Spencer Tracy faced a "personalized" strike, as union disturbances were the work of ill-intentioned agitators. Having experienced extreme poverty himself, the filmmaker was far too aware of the complexity of social mechanisms and their psychological effects to be satisfied with a dialectic illustration. In *Mannequin*, he does not dwell on facile contrasts between the rich and the Hennessey passes effortlessly from one world to the other, as fortune has not altered his fundamental qualities and he is prouder of getting along with his men than of his possessions. With Borzage, strikes, like wars, may be summed up as a kind of fatality beyond people's control: linked by their solidarity towards other paralyzed shipyards, Hennessey's workers are genuinely saddened at their powerlessness to support their boss. They lose their jobs the same time he loses his.

Hardly an American-style "success story": Alan Curtis with Joan Crawford in *Mannequin* (1937).

Mannequin is not an American style "success story." While we see familiar elements in it, Jessie's revolt is more spiritual than material. She is not looking for money — as opposed to those surrounding her — but a goal, hope, affection. A "three-room" apartment. She makes the initial mistake, understandable in her condition, of crystallizing her emotional impulses on illusions (even the three-room apartment on the water is a trap), then in Hennessey meets a man who knows the value of beings and things. He intuitively perceives her profound identity ("beautiful" but not "helpless," as opposed to the violets she holds in her hand). To be truly free, Jessie must first become herself, which she does by abandoning her husband to live alone, then by paying back the debt to the shipowner (Eddie's bail). As for Hennessey, he places the incarnation of his fantasies on a pedestal (the mannequin), neglects his shipyards, and the precarious "three-room" apartment he offers her in the Irish moors (the temptation of a retreat) is far from reality. The industrialist loses his fortune in time to save his marriage. His bankruptcy allows him to start anew, to dissipate misunderstandings and illusions, to wipe out the past. The soul mates are now ready to submit equally to the "ordeal by fire" of poverty, catharsis in a real three-room apartment that seals their union. This solar itinerary needs to occur beyond, or in spite of, moral convention — all the more emphasized by its realistic setting. Belgium, Ireland and Lithuania thus forbad the film in 1938 due to its "immorality" and its disregard for the "values of marriage" (Hennessey and Jessie's extramarital relations, the calculated marriage, etc.); Quebec and Great Britain cut Eddie's dialogue concerning the ploy for divorce.

* * *

Between takes on the set of *History Is Made at Night*, Charles Boyer spoke to Borzage for the first time of his friend Erich Maria Remarque, the German, anti–Fascist novelist whose writings had been burned and who was now in golden exile in Switzerland.[14] He had him read his last book, *Drei Kameraden*, published the preceding year in Amsterdam, then in Boston and in London in English translation.[15] The author of *All Quiet on the Western Front* was of course not unknown in Hollywood and James Whale had just brought his war story *The Road Back* to the screen (Universal City, February-April 1937). Remarque tells of a group of German soldiers returning to life after four years of coming close to death. R. C. Sherriff adapted the text very faithfully, conscious, like Whale, that their film would be banned in several European countries for its pacifism. Georg Gyssling, the German consul in Los Angeles, warned Universal about Berlin's reaction and sent threatening letters to about twenty actors, which provoked a demonstration by the Hollywood Anti-Nazi League (created in July 1936). A few weeks before the premiere, the new heads of Universal got scared, hacked up the film in the editing room and had the obscure Edward Sloman reshoot what was liable to offend Goebbels' sensibility.[16] *The Road Back* was only a shell of a film. These tribulations (which would hurt Whale's career) also shook up management at MGM; the Republican Mayer didn't want to be at war with anyone, especially if the company's capital was at stake, and famous though he was, Remarque spelled trouble. Nevertheless, the project of *Three Comrades* was already programmed by Culver City well before the novel appeared in bookstores.[17] It dealt with the friendship of three survivors of the trenches, Erich, Otto and Gottfried, and their difficulty adapting to peace. It also portrayed love for a tuberculosis sufferer, the political and social troubles of a Germany in ruins and the death of one comrade, killed by a rioter.

Borzage's role at the preparatory stage is difficult to determine, but it is reasonable to assume he was interested in the project from the time he began at MGM. The first actors approached (June 1937) were Spencer Tracy and Luise Rainer, the stars of *The Big City*, plus Robert Taylor and James Stewart, but this casting never materialized. Rigidly patriotic, Robert Taylor balked at the idea of playing a sympathetic German and it took all Louis B. Mayer's authority for him to comply with the studio's wishes (Alan Curtis and Dennis O'Keefe also tested for the role of Erich). Joan Crawford replaced Luise Rainer in July, Franchot Tone replaced Spencer Tracy in December. After serious reflection, Joan Crawford gave up the role of Patricia, erroneously believing she would only be a foil for the three comrades and not the star of the film! Loretta Young was approached (*Man's Castle*) but she wasn't available; the key role thus went to the marvelous Margaret Sullavan, who then began a six-film contract for Metro (January 1938). The presence of this fervent admirer of Borzage would reinforce the filmmaker's position on the set if need be. For there are three aspects in the saga of the making of *Three Comrades*: the problems arising from seven successive drafts of the script (mainly Mankiewicz's domain), those involving the film's political content (Front Office and censorship), and finally Borzage's own work.

"Can't producers ever be wrong? Oh Joe! I'm a good writer, honest!"— Francis Scott Fitzgerald's cry of distress to Mankiewicz, executive producer of *Three Comrades,* has remained famous in American literary history.[18] "I personally have been attacked [by the literary world] as if I had spat on the flag," commented the ever-sarcastic Mankiewicz,[19] saying elsewhere "If I go down at all in literary history, in a footnote, it will be as the swine who rewrote F. Scott Fitzgerald."[20] Here is not the place to go into the details of the turbulent collaboration between the great novelist and the no less great filmmaker; three generations of literature students have examined the pathetic case of Fitzgerald in Hollywood; the slightest variations of the script have been recorded step by step, Fitzgerald's initial screenplay has even been the object of a separate publication. Yet amazingly, looking through this vast amount of writing we see Borzage was practically ignored, as if this film, very representative of the director, were the exclusive work between the co-producer and his scriptwriter![21]

Mankiewicz, who spoke German and was very familiar with Germany of the twenties,[22] supervised the progress of the script. The first script was by British playwright R. C. Sherriff, already familiar with Remarque's style, procedures and preoccupations (*The Road Back*); but Sherriff eliminated Gottfried's murder and the political background, believing that these elements didn't gel with the story of Patricia, suffering from tuberculosis (February–May 1937). Dissatisfied, Mankiewicz turned then to F. Scott Fitzgerald: who better to capture the disenchantment of the postwar "lost generation" and capture the ethereal character of Patricia? The novelist, who suffered from chronic alcoholism, fought to maintain his salaried status at MGM: he was in debt and the bills from the sanatorium for his wife Zelda were prohibitive. "Scott was one of my idols," recalled Mankiewicz. "I hired him personally for this film, and had to fight, while everyone in the studio said he was finished; why take a risk with him?" The producer promised himself he would be sole author of the script (at $1000 a week, he was by far the best paid scriptwriter in Hollywood).[23] Fitzgerald gave up drinking temporarily and began work on a first draft in August (script dated August 1). To his credit, he succeeds quite well in structuring and concentrating a particularly long-winded novel, eliminating a number of secondary characters, inversing roles and introducing some good ideas (Erich's stammering on the phone, the piano at Pat's, etc.). But he doesn't take into account the requirements of film narration, nor — more seriously — those of the censor. When Fitzgerald allows himself to introduce a farfetched sequence in which Saint Peter plays the "heavenly operator" connecting the lovers, a rumor spread round the entire studio; Eddie Mannix, Mayer's right-hand man, had an Irish temper and forced Mankiewicz to go back on his word by imposing Edward E. Paramore as co-scriptwriter (October). This didn't help matters; Fitzgerald despised his colleague, an honest worker, and the two rivals got in each other's way. Mankiewicz himself reworked passages and put other writers, incognito, to the task, such as Waldo Salt, Lawrence Hazard (*Man's Castle*) and young poet David Hertz, author of some of the film's best lines ("Is that the road home?"). A comparison between Fitzgerald's very literary text and the final script clearly shows that Mankiewicz's worries were justified: the writer did not have dramatic flair; his scenes lack verve, vividness, and his dialogues, while perhaps beautiful to read, are artificial when spoken. Margaret Sullavan and Franchot Tone rebelled against his verbal tirades that destroyed naturalness and slowed down the action. His characterizations abound in interesting details emphasizing psychological motivations and subtleties, but which an inventive camera could express infinitely more effectively. In accord with Borzage, the actors skipped several passages of the dialogue, so that only a third of Fitzgerald's script appears in the completed film.

The other significant complaint against the author of *The Great Gatsby* was his inability to detach himself from Remarque's script on precise issues, a necessity, given that the novel touches on subjects taboo in Hollywood. Regarding morality, Fitzgerald was against the lovers marrying (they just live together in the novel) and introduced "sympathetic" prostitutes, inadmissible in the eyes of the Hays code. But it was politics that poisoned everything: Mankiewicz feared Mayer would hear of this and pushed the Front Office to intervene, with consequences similar to those of Whale's film. The novel opens in Berlin around 1928; Remarque implicitly portrays the rise of the dictatorship and the profiteers in favor of it. Fitzgerald, who abhorred Hitler and anti–Semitism, wanted to "unmask" Remarque's anonymous terrorists; in his script he retained the portrayal of Blumenthal, the Jew who fought for Germany in World War I, then developed a bloody confrontation scene in the streets. The democratic speaker harangues the crowd — "Madness is about to steal away your honor, and your liberty. It speaks with the voice of liberty, but..." — when about 300 men in SA uniforms intervene, preceded by a brass band. This passage does not exist in Remarque's novel, nor does the portrait of the ideologist Becker, Gottfried's activism or the scene at the end. In the epilogue, Fitzgerald, Paramore and Hertz wanted to specify that Erich and Otto go back to the city to carry the torch of their assassinated comrade and fight against Hitler's mobs, "enter the struggle against the evil force that is now engulfing their fatherland, Germany."[24] These few allusions were enough to make Louis B. Mayer swoon. The studio was already embarrassed enough by the visit of Vittorio Mussolini, the son of the dictator, personally invited to Hollywood by Hal Roach (September 1937), then a business associate at MGM; il Duce had even named Roach president of a branch of MGM in Rome. When Vittorio Mussolini began glorifying the bombings of Abyssinia, scriptwriter Donald Ogden Stewart organized resistance throughout Los Angeles; the reception of people in the film industry was glacial and il Duce's son packed his bags after two weeks. But the episode created a lot of bad blood.

Since the fall of 1936, German consul Georg Gyssling had written Joseph I. Breen (Production Code Administration) on three occasions to share his serious concerns regarding the *Three Comrades* project. The chief censor warned Mayer of "the considerable difficulties American companies could encounter in Europe" should he persist. "It is almost certain that a film based on this story would provoke huge protests on the part of Germans and German-Americans, and it would definitely be banned in Germany and Italy" (letter of January 22, 1938, and in Austria, as of March). As mentioned, MGM, Paramount and 20th Century Fox continued to sell films in Germany; in 1937 their Berlin subsidiary even acceded to anti–Semitic decrees and fired all their Jewish employees (the head of Paramount in Germany, Paul Thiefes, was a notorious anti–Semite). Finally, to recover their profits in reichsmarks, MGM invested in 1938 in the German armament industry and then sold its shares to American banks established in the country, all with Washington's blessing.[25] At a conference of top MGM management, January 26, 1938,[26] Breen summed up the obligatory changes to the script as follows: the film's action would unfold between November 1918 and December 1920, at a moment when the Nazi Party (founded August 8, 1920) was still in its infancy; this meant eliminating passages relating to inflation, anti–Semitism (Blumenthal) and the burning of books banned by Goebbels, as well as images of swastikas and brown uniforms. They also agreed to conceal the fact that Patricia was a kept woman. Mankiewicz protested vigorously against eliminating a political backdrop indissociable from the story, but, fearing the entire production would be boycotted in the Reich, Mayer took Breen's side. "At this point," the Communist *New Masses* reported, "the brilliant Breen made a suggestion which he insisted would please everyone, including the Nazis: make the young thugs Communists instead of storm troopers. Mankiewicz slammed his script on the table and stormed out, threatening to tear up his contract if any such thing were done... An honest book, and honest film artists have little chance against capitalist greed, guarded in the name of decency, by the vulgarians of the Hays Office."[27] An irrefutable observation. Mankiewicz (who also threatened to reveal these tactics to the *New York Times*) at least had his way on this point, which won him Fitzgerald's public acclaim. Facing the press alerted by the indiscreet remarks, Mankiewicz took refuge behind Remarque: "There is no political propaganda in the book and there is none in the picture, there is not a single mention of Hitler or Nazism in the book as there is none in the picture" (which is correct)[28]. Invited by Mayer to a private screening of the working print, Gyssling nevertheless rejected the entire enterprise, as it was based on a novel held in contempt. A few final facts regarding the political aspect of the film: *Three Comrades* was banned in Rumania due to its "pacifistic tendencies and communist ideas"! The rioting scenes were cut in Poland, Greece and Japan. In the eyes of the extreme right in France (François Vinneuil), not taken in, the film showed that "the Judeo-Marxists, the rioters of Berlin and Hamburg, the assassins of Munich are apostles as white as snow, killed cowardly by bullets in their backs."[29]

Actual filming began only once Breen's last reservations had been swept aside, the day Hitler became commander in chief of the Wehrmacht, February 4, 1938; shooting required 52 days, until April 2. They also had to wait for a rainy day, as "Maggie" Sullavan was superstitious and refused to begin a film without the blessing of the clouds![30] Everything was filmed inside the studio. Great German cinematographer Karl Freund, the right-hand man of Murnau (*Der Letzte Mann, Faust*) and Lang (*Metropolis*) was at the camera for two weeks, then replaced by Joseph Ruttenberg. On the adjacent lots, 4.5 acres of urban areas were constructed, with brick houses and paved streets (which would be reused in several later films, from *Above Suspicion* to *The Mortal Storm*); Freund, who had an aversion to natural light, had the entire complex covered with a tarpaulin. But European politics took care of darkening the horizon and the news didn't brighten the shoot: on March 11, Austrian Chancellor Schuschnigg stepped down and on the 13th, Hitler entered Vienna triumphantly. After that, how not to label the anonymous ideologies confronting each other in the film?

While the complex genealogy of *Three Comrades* does not make evaluating it an easy task, it does lead to certain observations. The novel — of rather mediocre literary quality — takes its journalistic tone and certain themes from Hemingway's *A Farewell to Arms* (Remarque reused the motif of condemned love at the heart of the socio-political torment in *The Night in Lisbon* (1962) where Hélène, suffering from cancer, replaces the tubercular Pat). Fitzgerald established a link between Pat and Nicole, his sick heroine of *Tender Is the Night*, but we may also interpret it as a projection of his own situation with Zelda; the writer openly emphasized depicting the emotional bond among "comrades toward and in spite of everything," this alcohol-induced friendship against despair that runs through his work (and is not as strong in Remarque's). On the other hand, all metaphysical references in the film enraged him; finally, the contrast in social status of the lovers was reminiscent of the Gatsby-Daisy liaison, or even that between Scott and Zelda. Mankiewicz ("Monkeybitch" or Joe Manowizf, as Fitzgerald mischievously called him), seems mostly to have just polished things up (the joking between the comrades, for example), because the author of *All About Eve*'s contribution to the film remains virtually imperceptible. There is no doubt, however, that Borzage was not only kept informed by Mankiewicz of the slightest developments in the script, but that he had his own (final) say in things. According to George Sidney, then a young assistant at Metro, filmmakers of the stature of "Mister Frank" decided alone about continuity, could make substantial changes without consulting the scriptwriters and even reinvent entire scenes on the set.[31] In conclusion, *Three Comrades* profited from Fitzgerald's sensitivity and from Borzage's tenderness, distilling a "feeling of precarious grace"[32] where their respective universes commingled. But the completed film's vision is more than eloquent: Borzage not only confers upon the work a stylistic unity, but also imbues it, esthetically and thematically, with a personal touch all his own.

After credits sustained by the popular German march "Nun ade, Du mein lieb Heimatland" dating from 1850 (the "Comrade Song"[33]), the camera enters a pilots' mess hall. A young aviator stands at attention before a senior one: "Major, now that the war is over, may I call you father again?" An officer proposes a toast to the comrades of all humanity, living or dead. At the bar, Erich (R. Taylor), Otto (F. Tone) and Gottfried (Robert Young) drink to their own health: "To us. Not from day to day now, from year to year. To us." Learning that his Fokker "Baby" will undergo the dishonor of being dismantled, Otto finishes it off with a grenade.[34] The years pass... 1918, 1919, 1920. A fanatical crowd throws stones, breaking a store window; violence and terrorism rage. "Too many people are closing their doors and windows and whistle in the dark," remarks Gottfried, the only one of the three friends sensitized to the political threat: "What are the new heroes of the Fatherland doing today? Poisoning the drinking water?" Despite all precautions of the wary censors, the terminology and tactics of the extremists, the type of confrontation and the situations are much more evocative of Germany in 1930 than that of the postwar period, which could explain why *Three Comrades* has the (slightly misleading) reputation of being "anti–Hitler."

The trio keeps a small garage in the city because mechanics are needed: "There'll be all sorts of things to repair: souls, consciences, hearts broken by the thousands." The will to "repair" will become the motor of the action. To celebrate Erich's birthday, the comrades go for a drive in the country with their car-mascot "Baby," and effortlessly overtake faster racing cars (Otto drives it like a plane). The car intrigues the powerful Breuer (Lionel Atwill), a war profiteer who stops at the same inn, accompanied by his mistress, Pat (M. Sullavan). As in *Little Man, What Now?*, Borzage has her appear out of the car like a wood-nymph from the trunk of a tree, while a melody gently begins playing: Erich seems paralyzed, his comrades wish him happy birthday! During the meal together, Breuer invites the trio to join the ranks of his "organization" and states his autocratic credo: "Too many people think they

Franchot Tone, Margaret Sullavan, Robert Taylor, Robert Young and Lionel Atwill in *Three Comrades* (1938).

have a right to opinions nowadays. What Germany needs is order, discipline!"[35] The temptation of totalitarianism lies in wait. Gottfried gets worked up; Otto calms him. Erich cannot take his eyes off Pat; her family was comfortably off, she tells him. Her father, a German, was killed in the war; she herself feels "we're neither dead nor alive," like so many others of her generation.

Soon afterward, Erich telephones Pat (a split screen shows them both at once) and goes to get her; the young woman only occupies two rooms of the huge family villa; the rest no longer belongs to her. Erich brings her to his favorite café, Alfons' (Guy Kibbee), but Pat's behavior remains mysterious. She must be home by ten o'clock, says "I'm a very superficial and frivolous person," then confides "when I learned I was going completely broke, I decided to live as I like." The two friends join them at the table, but Gottfried, who "is fighting for reason in a madhouse," stays away, noticing a stranger. If Erich is in love with Pat ("Erich's alive, he's got something to live for"), Otto is her brother, her confidant, someone who says "My life is something of the past." With two pairs of eyes watching, she whispers to him that she has been seriously ill. She comes home at the time set by Breuer, her protector, but no longer accepts his financial assistance from him. As for Erich, he has been unable to hide his jealousy and wants to be excused. "Send flowers, they cover everything. Even graves..." Gottfried advises him, without realizing that clouds are gathering above his own head. Strangers destroy "Baby"'s engine; after sneaking his way into a clandestine printing plant to explain to his political mentor, Dr. Becker, that he can no longer follow him without placing his two comrades in danger, Gottfried barely escapes an attack.

Breuer invites Pat and her new friend to an elegant evening in a nightclub, but Erich, a proletarian trained in the trenches, has no suit and doesn't know how to dance. Mobilizing thread and safety pins, Otto and Gottfried patch up a suitable tail coat for their male Cinderella. Pat wears a splendid silver gown; her knight is so impressed that he stammers and barely dares to approach her. His tail coat is far too narrow and tears on the dance floor. Breuer's questionable guests howl in laughter. Humiliated, Erich flees and gets drunk at Alfons', trying to forget this "rich man's girl," but when he returns back home, he discovers Pat dozing on his doorstep. She is shivering and coughing; he warms her. Their declaration of love has dawn-like overtones. Pat: "This is a lovely time of day." Erich: "It isn't day, it isn't night." "The edge of eternity, let's stay right here forever." "Between day and night?" "That's what we were born into, that's where we belong." Gottfried encourages Erich to marry Pat, while Otto does the same with the young woman. Pat is reluctant, her future uncertain; Otto begs her to forget her tuberculosis: "Aim at the stars!" (a metaphor we are tempted to take literally, cf. *7th Heaven*). Then, in Alfons' café, Borzage introduces one of those marriages of the heart, fairy tale-like in its unusualness, between comicalness and pure poetry. A gathering place for those traumatized in the war, the restaurant is beyond time: "No clocks here" Otto explains, and for certain regulars "the dates of battles are the only calendar." The owner plays Schubert's "Ave Maria" on his record player, then Mendelssohn's "Wedding March," when Pat enters the room on Otto's arm and they join Erich and Gottfried. The four stand in a silent row facing the record player and the filmmaker removes the viewer from the premises: a passerby in the street observes that the café is closed, peers through the shutter and notices four figures at the end of the room turning their backs to him (foreshadowing the famous final shot). The record player slows down; Mendelssohn peters out at the most moving moment. Alfons wipes away a tear and pronounces the solemn "I declare you man and wife." Everyone kisses. The ceremony is notable in that it is without words, presided only by the music ("We can't talk about you, we'd have to sing," Erich says to his wife). The melody is an immaterial link between the beings; the music introduced in the film the moment Pat appears is here a kind of spiritual support. The director gives it the power to express an essential indivisibility, sealing the total union of the couple and the comrades. Otto says to Pat: "Where you walk, we three walk beside you, now." The piano is one of the instruments that celebrate this "communion": it condemns entry into Pat's room until Erich, the pianist, "forces" the barricade; later, surrounded by strangers and deprived of his comrades, Erich can no longer play.

The young marrieds leave for their honeymoon at the seashore (the Baltic?). Pat doesn't dare tell her husband she is in pain ("Maybe you're just in love with a fragment"), but reckless exertion on the beach sets off the drama: she is afflicted by internal hemorrhaging. At this moment the filmmaker inserts the film's only master shot (except for the final one), showing Erich from an extremely high angle, tiny, carrying Pat, fainted, to the hotel, and the sudden distancing introduces the perspective of eternity, an irreversible break in the texture of the story (in tune with the tearing of the lung tissue). A few seconds earlier, Pat had been counting the cries of a cuckoo to know how many years she had left; from then on, the countdown begins. Braving night and fog, and driving at breakneck speed, Otto brings Professor Jaffé to the bedside of the sick woman; Borzage mostly focuses on her eyes (foreshadowing the last moments of *The Shining Hour*). In October at the latest, the doctor decrees, Pat should enter the sanatorium in the Alps. Back in the city, the three comrades live in fear. Gottfried: "I saw the sun coming up and I thought about Pat." Fall arrives. Erich still can't find work and the competition with another body shop degenerates into a fistfight on the street. The young woman goes to her mountain retreat only on October 20, a week late, seven "stolen" days during which Erich constantly repeats to her "I thank God for you," like a mantra. The city is in turmoil; a counter-demonstration of irregular military forces with brass bands, knouts and rifles has interrupted Dr. Becker's humanitarian speech. Gottfried is caught up in the melee, due to his political consciousness. While helping his mentor get away, he is shot down in front of his two friends by a gunman lying in ambush. Not a word to the police. Winter comes, as cold as death. Every night, Erich and Otto crisscross the snowy city looking for the assassin. On Christmas Eve, Otto finally tracks him down, follows him with "Baby"'s headlights and then follows on foot through the alleyways (a series of compositions focused on the depth of the field). Borzage had the insolent idea of transforming this manhunt into vengeance from Above: the panic-stricken killer climbs over the cathedral wall but the doors are locked; inside we hear the "hallelujah"'s from Handel's *Messiah* which serve as a musical background for the entire sequence. Otto confronts the terrorist along the nave and empties his gun into him; an illuminated gothic stained glass window behind the dispenser of justice supports the sentence. Amazingly, the Hays Code let such audacity pass! Christmas, snow and the oratorio evidently don't appear in Remarque's book (where Alfons takes revenge upon Gottfried), nor in Fitzgerald's script.

Otto and Erich go up to the sanatorium, as Pat is to undergo a delicate operation that will require absolute immobility for two weeks. "We love each other beyond time and space now," she murmurs to Erich, then dons her silver lamé dress one last time to go to a dance. For the sequence that follows, which required seven days of shooting, Borzage blocked all access to the set. The thoracoplasty[36] has succeeded. When the patient comes out of her anesthesia, Otto, her alter ego, is at her bedside. She immediately guesses what no one has dared tell her: he has sold "Baby" to cover the astronomical cost of the operation, and Gottfried will never return. "If you starve yourselves, perhaps I might live a few months longer," she calculates. "If you sold the repair shop, that might add a few more weeks..." What has she left to offer now, besides worries, old age and ugliness? Otto explains to her that she gave life to Erich, and to him, a happiness he never knew existed. Alone with her husband,

Pat pulls the wool over his eyes; they dream of going to South America, the recurrent utopia of the four. But she says to Erich: "It ticks so loud, your watch, it's so threatening." He pulls it off angrily and breaks it. "Now time is standing still," she breathes. Erich goes out for a moment with his friend, who is taking the train back. He has barely closed the door when the music reproduces the ticking of the watch; Pat gathers together her remaining energy, pushes back the sheets. The camera, in a high-angle shot, rises strangely from a medium-close shot to a full shot and, identifying itself with the point of view of the Angel, follows Pat's hesitating steps toward the balcony. Stiff, delicate in her white nightgown, her beauty slips into a state of grace, almost weightless on a white carpet, clings onto a white chair and opens the doors. On the balcony, the encompassing luminosity of the snow already foreshadows the Beyond. With one hand, Pat weakly holds onto the balustrade, with the other, she calls to her spouse. Erich notices her. Letting go of any earthly mooring, she extends both arms out into the open. We hear the wind blow. Pat collapses on an angle, carried away like a dead leaf. Erich hurries up the stairs. Spread out on the ground, she finds just enough strength to murmur: "It's right for me to die, darling, it isn't hard and I'm so full of love." The spareness of the effects, the concision of the gestures and editing border on the miraculous: Borzage captures the most beautiful death in film history.

Erich and Otto gather at the cemetery. Erich: "South America is so very far away. I wish they were going with us!" A machine gun rattles, Otto frowns: "There's fighting in the city." While the two friends sadly turn their backs on the graves, Pat and Gottfried appear, translucent, and flank them as they walk away. The four figures disappear into a stylized horizon, unreal like a twilight by Caspar David Friedrich. It has been said that this last scene was one of the controversial cases between Fitzgerald and his employers. The writer wanted to illustrate the everlasting spirit of resistance, showing "the march of four people, living and dead, heroic and unconquerable, side by side back into the fight."[37] From a Borzagian perspective, such a return would mean denying what had been acquired, taking an inconceivable step backward. His heroes are not "strictly individualistic,"[38] because the nature of their respective sacrifices calls for the elimination of the principle of individuation ("so full of love") while the community is only the sum of individuals, not their negation. All Borzage's tragic endings possess this same sadness without despair, for his characters, so horribly afflicted, are not abandoned to Fitzgeraldian excess: "We'll never be afraid of anything," Erich promises his beloved. No trace of morbidity, nor of "venerating death as an escape from unsolvable social problems,"[39] as it is not about an escape from chaos, but once again, going beyond it. On two occasions, Borzage introduces the first measures of Wagner's "Liebestod," in reference to A Farewell to Arms. His four comrades who move into a "no man's land suspended between heaven and earth" (M. Henry Wilson[40]) celebrate the victory of spirit over matter.

The successive transfer from text to image—from Remarque to Borzage—provoked many semantic shifts; the most singular results from the role of space (as an illusion linked to corporeality) in relation to that of time (superior because it is more immediately linked to the subtle, psychic world) perceived as a spiritual journey. Everything in *Three Comrades* tends to obliterate well-defined space inasmuch as a geometrical place of the action. The very first shot relativizes spatial reality by its expressionistic quality and establishes a kind of cosmic hierarchy, because above the military camps, huge fiery letters appear in the sky: "November 11, 1918." We are perhaps no matter where but not no matter when. No geographic names situate the events. We guess that we are in Germany because the uniforms and names are Germanic and Erich says "I'm gonna spill champagne from Hamburg to Munich." But the action unfolds "in the city," "at the seashore" or "in the mountains";

A no-man's-land suspended between heaven and earth: the final scene of *Three Comrades* (1938).

the city (too provincial to be Berlin) is 120 miles from the sea and only a few hours from the Alps; the geography is thus imaginary. South America represents "elsewhere," both literally and figuratively. Borzage eliminates everything foreign to his characters' preoccupations, and unabashedly uses as backgrounds painted scenery, rear projections, studio stucco bathed in improbable lighting, in short, artifices which render the situation theatrical (while still maintaining a minimum of plausibility, as opposed to *Liliom*); what is visible is only a facade which becomes less and less of a physical obstacle. Spatial distance doesn't really exist, it is no coincidence if the telephone conversations between Pat and Erich always occur on a split screen. The fade-in going from Pat on the right of the Christmas tree in the sanitarium, to Erich on the right of the tree at Alfons' suggests that the protagonists are united by something beyond physical distance. At the other extreme, everything works to recall the passing of time, as we are dealing with reprieve from death (cf. the aviator in *Living on Velvet*). The watch, the cries of the cuckoo, the short, fervent prayer, "I thank God for you" repeated "every ten seconds" point to the sand sifting through the hourglass. "Summer is so short!" Pat exclaims. A true romantic, Borzage imbues time with a "mystical" force: the seasons fly by, the wind blows through the trees, carrying away leaves, the camera follows a newspaper blowing away to focus on a date with lethal precision: "October 20, 1920"— (the departure for the sanatorium).

The trio as a specific entity is visually isolated from the moment they appear in the mess hall — the camera focuses on three backs— then turning toward the camera, each one in profile proposes an individual toast. Gottfried dreams of universal brotherhood through political action; Erich, the youngest, wants to get drunk and go gallivanting ("you're a baby," Pat tells him); Otto, the most thoughtful and perhaps the most wounded (Franchot Tone in his best performance prior to *Phantom Lady*), simply fights to ensure the happiness of the two others. This indestructibly pure friendship is what gives them the strength to continue living; rum and songs keep the bitterness at bay. Pat's arrival does not affect the balance, except that the three musketeers now become four. Her ethereal nature illuminates their daily lives without a cloud of jealousy, and firmly places Erich "among the living." In return, the exceptional friendship among the trio saves Pat from Breuer's corrupted hold; Otto teaches the young woman courage (to dare marry), Erich removes her fears. The wedding ceremony is held among the four of them because the filmmaker enlarges his unit, going from the love of the couple to love per se.

These creations of Borzage's poetic idealism are necessarily imperishable, but the greatness of sacrifices required is proportionate to the threat. Bloody totalitarianism, poverty or sickness, the threat weighs on all the action with apocalyptic overtones. The Evil is abstract; it is a cosmic force whose proto–Nazi terrorists are but accidental instruments (the killer lying in ambush seems almost horrified of his crime). Gottfried temporarily renounces his militancy to preserve his friends, and they compel him to ignore the deteriorating social climate to maintain the balance of their unit; Borzage assimilates politics with death, even though Gottfried gives his life for a good cause ("It took me a long time, but I finally made up my mind"). Erich and Otto lose Pat. As for Pat, her disappearance resembles a suicide while it is really the supreme act of generosity and freedom toward those she loves; by opening the doors and going out on the balcony, Pat seems to be waking up. (In Remarque's novel, Pat dies of tuberculosis in her bed, convulsing horribly; in Fitzgerald's script, she gets up and holds her arms toward the ceiling to tear at her scars.) The film benefits here from Margaret Sullavan's extraordinary presence. "I have always had very high regard for Frank Borzage as a director," Joseph L. Mankiewicz declared to us. "As far back as *A Farewell to Arms* I was impressed by the sensitivity he demanded from his actors, in very sharp contrast to the exaggerated emotional displays of early dramatic films in Hollywood. Margaret Sullavan's performances in both *Three Comrades* and *Shining Hour* were not at all surprising."[41] The actress (who has never been more ravishing than in this film) had nothing of the usual tubercular patients appearing on film, portrayed melodramatically. She is consumed in silence, conscious of her time running out and the fragility of happiness. Her art, her nervous delicacy and choked voice contribute significantly to create the climate of unbearable melancholy where each second of love-friendship takes on vital importance. "'The time to learn how to live comes too late': this line from a poem by Aragon could serve as an introduction to all Frank Borzage's work," concluded Claude Beylie. "We are constantly amazed by his grasp of the ephemeral, which requires an irrepressible thirst for eternity."[42]

Douglas Sirk mentioned that in film: "The angles are the director's thoughts. The lighting is his philosophy."[43] Fitzgerald broke down when he saw the film in the theater; apparently he no longer recognized his script and, impervious to cinematographic subtlety, became indignant at Borzage's work, "that glorified cameraman."[44] But the mortified novelist's dire predictions did not come to pass: "I think you now have a flop on your hands," he threatened in his letter of January 20 to Mankiewicz. "The little fluttering life of what's left of my lines and situations won't save the picture ... there were tears in my eyes, but not for Pat — for Margaret Sullavan" (op. cit.). *Three Comrades* did more than respectably at the box office, considering the moroseness of the subject. The National Board of Review placed it on their top ten list for 1938 and awarded Margaret Sullavan for her performance. In addition, the actress was nominated by the Academy for Best Actress (1938), and won two prizes in Great Britain, the "British National Award" and "Picturegoer's Gold Medal."

The names of Borzage and Fitzgerald crossed one last time, in relation with a common project called *Infidelity,* under the leadership of Hunt Stromberg (February 1938). The film was to be a vehicle for Joan Crawford. Officially, Fitzgerald was adapting an Ursula Parrot novel of the same name published in *Cosmopolitan,* and that the studio had just acquired. But he actually was given the green light to concoct whatever he pleased. The novelist threw himself into this new task and developed a storyline in tune with the title, full of autobiographical annotations (he tried to justify in it, among other things, his own liaison with Sheilah Graham). Nicolas Gilbert, a Long Island millionaire (Gary Cooper), is cheating on his wife Althea (Crawford) when he runs into his childhood sweetheart, a secretary (Myrna Loy); his friends avoid him, his wife packs her bags and Nicolas drowns his sorrow in surprise parties with the Broadway crowd until, matured, he finds a way to reconcile with his wife.[45] At the end of March, production submitted Fitzgerald's uncompleted script to the Hays Office, who refused to even discuss the matter! The studio had had enough headaches with *Mannequin* and the comedy *Wife Vs. Secretary* (Clarence Brown) and did not insist. As an alternative for Borzage, MGM entered into negotiations with Hearst-Cosmopolitan to try to buy back the rights for *Humoresque* to make a sound remake (April); but Hearst had already sold them to Jack Warner, who seven years later would make a flamboyant melodrama — with Joan Crawford.

14

The Mystical Dimension

Toward the end of the decade, Borzage seemed to have reached a turning point in his inner life. The man always remained extremely discreet on this subject, as mentioned, and we can only express hypotheses based on the theme and content of the works in question. While the director unquestionably continued to exalt passionate lovers, from one film to the next, love took on a more openly mystical dimension. MGM itself declared in 1940: "With pictures such as *A Farewell to Arms*, *Little Man, What Now?*, *Three Comrades* and *Disputed Passage* to his credit, Borzage has achieved a reputation of being somewhat of a mystic. The underlying spiritual values in these stories are what have attracted him most."[1] It was as if Borzage now, in a kind of profession of faith, wanted to remove a mask and openly recognize what seemed implicit as of *7th Heaven*. *Green Light* in 1937 and *Three Comrades* in 1938 already foretold what lay ahead. In them, love is no longer a goal in itself—was it ever—but a means, a vehicle to accede to a transcendental state by renouncing the self. At a higher level, it is the supreme spiritual act, implying the fusion with the loved one. Surprising as it may seem, these concepts—very far removed from Hollywood and the modern world in general!—appear strongly in the three next works, so restrained in appearance: *The Shining Hour*, *Disputed Passage* and *Strange Cargo*.

The initial idea for the first film came this time from Joan Crawford herself. In February 1934, the actress and her husband Franchot Tone had both been very moved by a hit play at New York's Booth Theater, entitled *The Shining Hour*, written by a young Welshman, John Keith Winter.[2] MGM was aware of it as Edmund Goulding had already thought of making it into a film with Norma Shearer in 1935, and Mayer immediately bought the rights to this "romantic tragedy" for Joan Crawford when she made her wish known. The star wasn't shy this time (perhaps she had learned her lesson after missing her chance with *Three Comrades*), as she asked to be partnered with two formidable actresses, both with solid stage experience: Margaret Sullavan, her main rival at Culver City, and Fay Bainter. "I'd rather be a supporting player in a good picture than the star of a bad one," she declared to the boss.[3] Crawford and Sullavan on the same set: Mayer had serious apprehensions. With such an explosive cast, it was naturally Mankiewicz and Borzage who inherited *The Shining Hour*, as the two enjoyed the confidence of these ladies. Borzage wanted to include Charles Boyer, but the Frenchman, who had just played Napoleon in the arms of Greta Garbo, imitated his Corsican model, and chose to flee! His part went to Robert Young. "I always expected a big blowup anytime," remembered Fay Bainter.[4] But surprise: shooting went off without a hitch (August 22–October 3, 1938) and the two prima donnas got along fine; nervous and anxious by nature, Joan Crawford passionately admired her rival who seemed perfectly at ease under the spotlights, despite her advanced state of pregnancy. "In one scene I had to carry Maggie out of a burning house," Crawford recalled. "Maggie was pregnant, I thought three months, but just before the fire scene, they told me *seven* months.

I'd never have guessed. Now that I knew, I was urgently concerned. I carried this girl out of the burning house, trying to watch for falling timbers, trying not to slip on the gravel. I'm strong, heaven knows, but I wasn't strong enough. I fell on the gravel, on my elbows and knees to break the fall, so Maggie wouldn't get hurt. My elbows and knees were bloody, but I didn't know. I was hysterical over Maggie. She had her eyes closed, and they didn't open. 'Maggie, dear, are you all right? Maggie!' I screamed. She waited until I was frantic. Then she opened those wide eyes of hers and grinned. She was just fine. She never played jokes unless she adored you, but what a time to show it!"[5]

Overall, the drama focuses on the trouble a beautiful stranger spreads when she enters an old established British family, hardly an original point of departure in itself. Winter's play unfolds in a Yorkshire manor where daily life revolves around family ties and secular traditions. MGM appointed Jane Murfin ("Smilin' Through") and humorist Ogden Nash to Americanize this worldly melodrama and tailor it for Joan Crawford. The action was thus moved to rural Wisconsin and a fifteen minute prologue in Manhattan was tacked on to situate the "bewitching" character of Olivia Riley, an inveterate city dweller from Tenth Avenue and — in keeping with the Crawford image — a dance star in a popular nightclub. Tired of her bohemian life, Olivia finally yields to the advances of Henry (Melvyn Douglas), a member of the influential landowning Linden family, and marries him without really loving him. The news saddens a cohort of ex-lovers and suitors (the piano strikes up a funeral march); some sarcastic remarks exchanged between guests at the engagement party belie the Mankiewicz touch. David Linden (R. Young) is at the celebration, delegated by the sour-tempered Hannah (F. Bainter), the eldest sister of the clan, to prevent such a shameful marriage. David insults Olivia, gets slapped in the face, and precedes the new marrieds to their property far off in the Midwest. Olivia is welcomed with genuine kindness by Judy (M. Sullavan), David's wife, and with equally genuine hostility by Hannah, an old maid harboring incestuous jealousy. Everything about the intruder is subject to criticism, from dresses to drinks and her taste for luxury. For the first time in years, David sits down at the piano and plays Chopin's "Waltz in C flat minor," transformed by Waxman into a leitmotif for adulterous desire (Olivia has already danced a jazz version of it in the nightclub).

David's ploy does not escape Hannah and, in vain, she warns Judy of the peril her sister-in-law represents. David in fact takes advantage of the slightest occasion to be alone with Olivia ("I want what I haven't got and I'm bored with what I have"). The drama relegates Henry to the sidelines — the trusting gentleman-farmer, smoking his pipe, surveying the construction of his future residence, across the lake — while the venomous Hannah intervenes only periodically to fan the flames. Borzage is mainly interested in Olivia's torment, more and more obsessed by and physically attracted to her brother-in-law, and Judy's silent suffering. Gone riding with David, Olivia betrays herself — while the man places his hands on her shoulders, she continues to speak as if nothing had happened — but resists his passionate declarations with the strength of despair (stripped of her sophistication, Joan Crawford responds beautifully here): she recognizes the situations that have trapped her in the past and hesitates, torn between sensual longing and loyalty, cold lucidity and self-respect: "I look like a lady sometimes, that's my trouble..." Elsewhere, the filmmaker shows her torn between the desire to dance and systematically refusing her husband's lips.

But it is the singular character of Judy, the Borzagian heroine par excellence, far removed from all the female archetypes in the genre, that dominates *The Shining Hour*. With vibrant charm and astounding simplicity, Margaret Sullavan expresses the modesty and self-sacrifice of this neglected woman passionately in love with her husband; in comparison, Joan Crawford's Olivia appears artificial. Judy has been friends with David since childhood and knows that he has never loved her, she confides to her new friend (whom she refuses to consider as a rival). Like Henry, Judy loves for two, ready to accept everything, give everything, without a trace of bitterness and even less jealousy (a unique phenomenon in a "women's picture"); all that matters to her is her husband's happiness. Although sometimes she dreams that David finds her "exciting." The harmony between these two "rejected" women is one of the bigger surprises of the film; it stems no doubt from the fact that Judy loves too much to subjugate her loved one, while Olivia doesn't love enough.

Once the villa is completed, the Linden clan throws a barbeque dance for the whole area, a long evening during which conflicts erupt. Olivia is molested by a drunken trumpet player whom she unwittingly led on, then, in a moment of helplessness, David kisses her. "What do you think happens next, David?"—David of course has not thought of that, guided solely by his own pleasure. Ashamed, Olivia begs her husband to go away with her for six months. Henry is not taken in and agrees, which infuriates Hannah. Late in the night, Judy wipes the suspicious lipstick from her unfaithful husband's lips, then, alone with Olivia, eyes moist, suggests she marry David: "Sometimes two people are made for each other... Go away with David. You're going to do what I would do!" Olivia doesn't understand that Judy is leading her to question her marriage to Henry to fully pursue her desire, for she is incapable of experiencing such determination. Meanwhile, driven by rage, Hannah sets fire to their new home. In tears, Olivia contemplates the annihilation of her "false" refuge, based on artificial feelings and values. Suddenly, Judy runs into the inferno... João Bénard da Costa has aptly remarked that with Borzage, the more a script becomes disjointed with a series of improbabilities, the more the characters seem to develop, gaining in human credibility, "as if they found in this improbability a deeper justification for their singular existence."[6] From this point on, the play and film diverge. Keith Winter has Judy perish in the accidental fire of some barn, a suicide which frees the lovers; the last act shows how Olivia and David overcome their shock and obey the wishes of the deceased by leaving the premises together. The film takes us elsewhere, partially because of the Hays Code (Breen threatened a ban), but also because the "shining hour" takes on a significance of a whole other magnitude. Borzage puts the compromise to work for him.

The veil lifts: Olivia unhesitatingly runs toward the fire and saves Judy, risking her own life. In the early morning, Olivia, her hand burnt, asks to see David, moping in the living room, deathly worried about his wife: "Judy was going to free us—and she has," she tells him. "A world full of us wouldn't make one of Judy." Then she leads David to his wife's bedside. Judy's last appearance shocks the viewer as the image (in close up) is bizarre and unexpected. The young woman's face is entirely covered in bandages, a large white oval leaving just enough space for her eyes. We hear a smothered voice: "David!" He kneels, silent, and buries his head in the bed sheets. "Hello, David!" Then, without a word, she looks at Olivia, eyes shining, nodding that all is well; Olivia tiptoes out. This dialogue of "faceless eyes" has more emotional impact than any verbal exchange; the composition formally attests to Judy's fundamental otherness while creating a feeling of unknown (the spectator won't know if and to what extent she is disfigured): "A magnificent visual idea," noted Christian Viviani, "that is an attempt to isolate the character from the reality of the context, while letting her exert an irrational power of those on the same level."[7]

As it deals with a confined situation between five people, the groupings in the field define the nature of their relationships; the compositions indicate isolation or more or less conscious associations, hypothetical bonds or rejection. A continual counterpoint is established between the full shots (which externalize the separation) and tighter frames; the rapid alternating of medium-close shots between Judy and her new sister-in-law immediately

Catharsis through fire: Joan Crawford saves Margaret Sullavan in *The Shining Hour* (1938).

suggests spontaneous friendship and the growing emotional bond between them, even before anything is explained by words or action. When Olivia and Henry dream in front of the model of their cottage, Judy watches over them like a guardian angel, while Hannah and David, factors of dissension, remain outside the field, or set back. When Olivia dances, Borzage brings out both her solitude and egocentric nature by framing her from a distance, in a full shot at the cabaret, or having her dance alone among the Lindens. The character of Olivia is also shown in perpetual movement, her face turned away, escaping her husband, David, Hannah, and above all her own contradictions that frighten her. The camera finds ingenious ways to capture the various interactions, translating the fundamental interdependence of the five. All are transformed by one aspect or nuance of love, tying them together. The various ways these feelings are manifested permanently affect the behavior of the other characters, setting off a cascade of reactions. The group is divided into those who have attained a degree of harmony between themselves and the events (Judy, Henry) and those who remain puppets of their selfishness (David, Olivia, Hannah). Among the latter, desire — perfectly legitimate in itself — is only desire for its own sake, a kind of self-gratification. Throughout all the idylls of his filmography, Borzage continuously denounces the sterility of individualism. According to him, the "shining hour" synthesizes the only truly worthwhile experience a human being can know: forgetting oneself by giving oneself completely. Judy is not the one sacrificed, but triumphant. Her immolation (or willingness to do so) is a catharsis by fire that dissipates the fog of subjectivism and narcissism, finally allowing characters to see a naked reflection of themselves — which explains why the filmmaker does not dwell on the spectacle of the fire, but focuses on capturing the reflection of the flames on the faces of his heroes: depending on which one, the revelation has undertones of hell.

Until present, Borzage expressed these ideas via the couple; *Three Comrades* and *Shining Hour* extend them to the group. The happiness of a Linden is only possible if shared by all Lindens. By her emotional handicap, one of them paralyzes the four others. At the end, Olivia leads David to Judy and Hannah and pushes Henry toward Olivia. When Olivia leaves the room of the wounded, Borzage places her in one of the rare consciously "constructed" shots of the film: the camera films her from a high angle, descending a large spiral staircase leading to an entrance hall where Henry and Hannah await her. This polysemous image expresses both Olivia's reintegration following her awareness, awakening a feeling of altruism, and by the sudden depth of the field, the scope of the journey. The wide angle conveys not only a feeling of isolation, but relief and peace. Fred Camper comments on the unexpectedness of the shot — a direct echo to the unexpected one of Judy in bandages: "The sharp high angle can be nothing but a force beyond the power of the individual characters, a force which is bringing them together."[8] The desire of a brother-in-law, the jealousy of an aging sister-in-law and the torment of a wife have been transformed into love by the fire that destroyed their home. From a worldly melodrama with stereotypical conflicts, Borzage manages once more to produce a drama of transfiguration and redemption, even if, at first glance, this development is translated in psychological and not metaphysical terms.

The above remarks are the result of a detailed study. Contemporary critics and viewers saw *The Shining Hour* only as a rather highbrow product, too literary for the Saturday night crowd, stylishly constructed with stars according to proven formulas. The film's career was dim.

During a stay in London in the summer of 1938, Louis B. Mayer took Hedy Kiesler under contract, a dazzlingly beautiful Austrian actress who had just been seen — naked — in Gustav Machaty's scandalous film *Extase*. Mayer lost all judgment. Greta Garbo was forgotten! He returned to Hollywood with "his" discovery, changing her name to Hedy Lamarr, and instructing playwright Charles MacArthur to come up with a script worthy of the event. MacArthur did so half-heartedly. The drama of the decade shaped up as follows: aboard an ocean liner sailing from Europe, Doctor Decker prevents the model Georgi from killing herself after an unhappy love affair with a rich, married New Yorker. Decker offers the woman a job in his clinic in a poor area, then marries her. But Georgi cannot forget her millionaire... Two hundred pages later, she realizes her place is still beside her valiant husband. Spencer Tracy played the doctor, Walter Pidgeon his rival. And as Sternberg had made miracles with Marlene Dietrich, here he was in charge of what was titled, for the moment, *A New York Cinderella* (shooting began October 18). But Mayer could not sit still in his huge office and interfered at every step in the direction — of something that was never seen. After fifteen days of shouting, Sternberg quit. On November 21, Borzage was assigned to the task: he had three films with Margaret Sullavan to his credit and perhaps his presence would calm an angry Spencer Tracy. The title was changed to *I Take This Woman*. Borzage worked on this chore until January 1939, at which date Spencer Tracy had to leave for *Stanley and Livingstone* (Henry King) at 20th Century Fox. Work stopped. Everyone was relieved; even Mayer had begun to realize that the screenplay was unappealing and that his new starlet was no Sarah Bernhardt. But the boss was stubborn: he retained two of Borzage's sequences, had the script rewritten by a dozen anonymous workers and replaced Pidgeon with Kent Taylor. Between December 1939 and January 1940, the tough as nails Woody S. Van Dyke, the house "film doctor," bungled the job in 23 days. His comment: "The funniest thing in Hollywood since Jean Harlow died." The film was reworked so many times over its eighteen months in production ($700,000 in losses) that it was ironically dubbed "I Re-Take This Woman" or "Mayer's Folly." It bombed at the box office. *I Take This Woman* was not an isolated case at Culver City, but was perhaps the most grotesque, representative example of a studio where directors were replaced one after another. With some luck, this resulted in impersonal but luxurious products such as *The Wizard of Oz*, worked on by such diverse talents as King Vidor, Richard Thorpe, George Cukor, Mervyn LeRoy and Victor Fleming. Rumor, still unverifiable today, had it that in 1938 Borzage also collaborated on a film about Richard Strauss, *The Great Waltz*, officially signed by Julien Duvivier, but which we know was seriously reworked by Victor Fleming and Josef von Sternberg.

With these misadventures barely over, Borzage followed up on an invitation from Paramount to direct *Disputed Passage*.[9] This latest Lloyd C. Douglas marathon novel had been serialized in *Cosmopolitan* and published in New York the following year with 200,000 copies sold. Douglas had the wind in his sails, in bookstores as on screen; after *Green Light*, Warner released *White Banners* (Edmund Goulding). At Paramount, where he had not returned since *Desire*, Borzage was put in charge of directing the first "A" film of two little-known actors, craggy-featured John Howard (who usually played the amateur detective Bulldog Drummond in the series of the same name) and ex–Miss New Orleans, Dorothy Lamour; the sarong-clad brunette had just greatly increased her fan mail by portraying a Polynesian in *Hurricane* (John Ford). Condemned for life to semi-exotic dress, Dorothy Lamour played the impassive Oriental, which helped conceal her limited talent. The roles of the opposing surgeons were played by the wonderful Akim Tamiroff (future accomplice of Orson Welles), who spent a month studying beforehand in various Los Angeles hospitals, and William Collier, Sr., the unstable father in *After Tomorrow*.

Lloyd C. Douglas was invited with great ceremony to the studio and formally approved the venture (in the credits he is seen signing a letter thanking Paramount). Borzage was, however, unhappy about changes to the end of the story[10] in the novel, the hero is attacked and seriously wounded during a fight in New York's Chinatown. Scriptwriter Bayard Veiller[11] made use of the news to introduce more spectacular sequences, as the action was displaced to China, in the midst of the Sino-Japanese conflict. On December 13, 1938, the people of Nanking were massacred by the invader; the last quarter of the film takes place in the region of Chungking, occupied by the troops of the Kuo-min-tang, which would become the main target for Japanese invasion in early May 1939. *Disputed Passage* was filmed at that moment, from April 17 to June 5; the rocky landscape of Lone Pine was used to portray the Far East, and the U.C.L.A. campus served as the university setting. The film was authorized in Shanghai in 1940 after all bombing scenes were eliminated, rendering the ending incomprehensible.

Beaven (J. Howard), a first-year medical student, is attending the introductory course of surgeon "Tubby" Forster (A. Tamiroff), a worldwide celebrity venerated for his science but also feared as he is caustic and tough ("Statistics prove that at least 60 percent of you are so completely dumb that you will be forced to leave"). After having vaunted the merits of pure science, Forster reviews this batch of students; full of vitriol, he humiliates them, picking on Beaven, who comes from a religious school where they believe in a "soul" and in a "beyond." "Brother Beaven" stands up to him very articulately and wins those laughing over to his side. Borzage emphasizes the separation between great expert and his flock by very marked high- and low-angle shots (which explains the difference in level of the audience) and even by panning rapidly, subjectively zigzagging back and forth, when Forster tries to find the unique female student in the group: early on, the nervous camera movement translates the misogyny of the surgeon, for whom women haven't the right to exist (in his courses) and represent a threat. Beaven studies with determination, sacrificing flirtation,

Science versus faith: Akim Tamiroff and John Howard in *Disputed Passage* (1939).

evenings out and vacations for medical research. At the graduation ceremony, Forster names him his unique assistant, proof of intellectual honesty as their points of view on life diverge radically. Beaven accepts for the sake of his work: "Like you, I recognize that the ship is more important than the crew." Old professor Cunningham (W. Collier) who presides over the ceremony is the complete opposite of Forster. "In the years you've been here, your minds were all you had to use. You have worshiped one shrine: science, and that is as it should be," he tells the graduates. "But now you will have to use your hearts, and through them you will find an even holier shrine... You cannot cure a body and leave a soul in torment." He then addresses medical ethics and describes the soul as "a part of man no anatomist has ever found." To denote Beaven's indecisive stance, who hasn't the hardheartedness of his professor, Borzage places a sardonic comrade on his left ("He's not a doctor, he's a missionary, and a dull one") and on his right, a medium-close shot of the still unknown face of Audrey, alias Lan Ying (D. Lamour); the young Oriental says nothing, just looks at him intensely, as if Borzage wanted to indicate the implicit identity between the iconic message represented by the beautiful stranger and Cunningham's spoken message.

Five years go by. Beaven (now sporting a moustache, and Forster a beard) is even harder on his own students than his mentor, whose idea of "pure science" he admires; the man has become grossly insensitive. When the professor is beaten up by a student he failed, Beaven replaces him and operates on Audrey, an American orphan whose arm was wounded in the war, in China, where she was born and raised. There her adoptive parents, Mandarins, were massacred by the Japanese; the Cunninghams are her parents of choice. But she is philosophical: "My name, my face, they do not matter. It is inside that a person is what he is." Beaven listens to her, fascinated by this mix of suave beauty and serenity, and treats the hospital patients more humanely. He spends a fishing weekend (Christlike symbolism) at the Cunningham's and watches a sunset with Audrey. Forster sees his "transgressing" disciple slide between his fingers and secretly persuades Audrey to give up the idea of a marriage that would annihilate Beaven's scientific works. The young woman leaves secretly for China to join the troops of Chiang Kaï-shek. When he discovers what really happened, Beaven leaves the U.S. to look for her — but he may as well look for a needle in a haystack! Wherever he goes, the inhabitants are suffering terribly from the "enemy" bombs (the word "Japanese" is never uttered).

Spending an evening in a destroyed village, Beaven gives in, forgets his individual quest and cares for the numerous mutilated civilians a French missionary doctor (Victor Varconi), himself wounded, had packed into a makeshift hospital. He realizes that he has arrived at the theater of his own jihâd, the holy war of the soul against itself. Borzage plunges the entire last part of this "descent into hell" into darkness: the village is a strange place, nameless, without recognizable dimensions, invaded by noxious fumes, a veritable no man's land between life and death. We make out human forms, notice groans and tears (laudable photography with expressionistic overtones by William C. Mellor). Suddenly, airplanes are heard. Trying to save a child he has just operated on, Beaven is buried under the rubble; he is found unconscious, a piece of shrapnel in his head. Forster, alerted by a telegram, runs to his bedside and desperately tries to operate by the flickering light of the lanterns. To the tension, Borzage adds the progressive deformation of images, oblique camera angles, silent shadows of the villagers. A transfusion is required, the missionary gives his blood... The operation is successful, but Beaven remains in a coma. "Nothing can help, except something inside the patient, something we call the will to live," explains the Frenchman to Forster, skeptical: "I speak of nothing strange, Monsieur, I speak only of his soul." Beaven's guide spots Audrey in a Red Cross camp and the young woman jumps on a monoplane.

As can be guessed, these twists and turns lead to a miraculous recovery and the discomfit of the empirical villain; once the problem of "soulless" medicine is exposed, Lloyd C. Douglas, champion of breaking down open doors, destroys his entire argument and proves absolutely nothing except the agelessness of melodramatic clichés. This led Graham Greene to write that "the film exhales a nauseating blend of iodine and glucose."[12] But what cinema! If Greene had focused less on the story, he would have discovered an admittedly uneven, bizarre work, but one that is fascinating in every respect.

In a study on *Disputed Passage* that made quite a stir in English-speaking countries,[13] American critic Fred Camper set out to demonstrate how Borzage's visual style, far from being a simple illustration, already exhaustively expresses his metaphysical conceptions. Starting from a raw image, Camper concludes that Borzage displays an overall "immateriality" of objects and characters, an effect obtained by lighting that diminishes their physical presence and density in the field: "All the characters have presence only in two dimensions; as real beings they seem almost weightless, floating in abstracted surroundings. By filming all of his characters in this way, Borzage denies any of them a position in the world which would make real their assertion of their own egos: thus he makes their conversion and transcendence inevitable. In a sense they have "transcended" everything from the opening of the film." This point of view may be defended, but Camper pushes his argument even further when he states that by including then excluding them from the field or even by displacing in the space certain secondary objects (or characters) by a simple change of camera angle, the filmmaker wants to convey that they have no specific geographic presence or permanence in themselves. "One never feels that the specific positions of objects has any significance or exerts any influence ... [this] has the effect of integrating all the objects with each other.... In Borzage's universe, all things are inseparable from each other; no person or object can have any independent casual effect.... All objects are abstract non-representational entities of light and dark which are connected not by any spatial mechanics but by the generalized spiritual sense which seems to pervade the whole frame. Objects have no meaning outside of the general spirituality.... Love is not an end: only an agent which helps to dissolve the distinction between things." Tempting though they may be, these observations are clearly over-interpretive, at least in the very general framework established by Camper. As such, they appear unfortunately applicable to an incalculable number of films with strongly "profane" preoccupations, and the rare examples the author quotes to back up his thesis are not very convincing. Yet this doesn't mean that Borzage's films don't contain a "unifying" metaphysical vision reminiscent of Meister Eckhart, Muhyiddin Ibn 'Arabi or Hildegard von Bingen. Symbols clearly inserted in the narrative texture show it, and often, on a more palpable level, the direction itself—which brings us to the final sequence.

As usual, Borzage dresses it up in his own way, combining editing and composition with mathematical rigor. Entering the dimly lit room, Audrey kneels before the body of her beloved; we see only his head buried under bandages (cf. *The Shining Hour*). As soon as Audrey, in medium-close shot, her eyes lit by a spotlight, addresses Beaven (and the camera) gently—"I am here to stay. Don't leave me now"—Borzage reveals the wounded man's face: the woman's presence gives him back his identity. Audrey's luminous look and tender voice are symbols of Life. He moves imperceptibly. "Please come back to me," she implores him. "It's only a little way." He opens his eyelids and closes them again. (Audrey is filmed subjectively through a veil that is lifted and then replaced.) Night falls. Audrey refuses to go to bed: he could come to. Borzage films her in close-up, as she lifts her eyes, then pans to the ceiling, riddled with holes, through which we see a stormy sky and rays of moonlight. The camera remains focused on the celestial opening, the music swells, dissolve: day is breaking, the camera comes back down to reveal a master shot of Audrey, Forster, the Frenchman and Beaven. Medium-close shot of Beaven opening his eyes and weakly murmuring: "Audrey, darling, don't go." The maneuver is extremely perilous and borders on the kitsch, but is saved by the incredible sincerity and concision harmonizing form and content. The tension arises from the contrast between the almost statue-like immobility of the characters and the uninterrupted division of space. Defeated, haggard-looking, Forster undergoes a "second birth": "I guess you could call it a miracle," he sobs. Audrey places a hand on his arm and gives Beaven the other. Camera angles and gestures indicate integration, such that the physical regeneration of one leads to the spiritual regeneration of them all: frozen in their attitudes, the characters transmit a salvational energy to each other by a kind of human link. But it is Audrey's loving face and eyes that made the pan to the heavens possible: "The pan here not only integrates the characters into their setting but also associates Beaven's recovery with a divinely regenerative force as mysterious as the dawning of a new day" (J. Belton).[14]

To sum up, Borzage becomes disinterested in the sterile debate of the beginning to focus on the following main themes: Forster has lost the concept of love due to a personal tragedy (his fiancée died of an undiagnosed case of appendicitis) and recaptures it via the wife of his assistant. Beaven imitates his professor, using science and withdrawing into himself to protect himself from life and emotions. Without realizing, Forster himself starts the mechanism which inevitably leads to the conversion of all. Lloyd C. Douglas's intentionally nebulous discourse (he doesn't mention God or one religion in particular, nor are we confined to agnostic humanism) seems to suit Borzage; while respecting the novelist's strict meaning, he imbues the allegorical tale to his more universal vision of things, in which he clearly concludes that man, in the West as in the East, is not self-sufficient and that the love that allows him to surpass himself is not psychic or the result of chemistry!

If *Disputed Passage* is at times disconcerting, *Strange Cargo* beats all records for the unusual and today has equal numbers of detractors and supporters. Impenitent nonbelievers grind their teeth; embarrassed exegetes shake their heads, while fans of Hollywood eccentricities delight in this curious mix in which religious parable is disguised in an adventure film.

Returning to Culver City, Borzage once again joined forces with Mankiewicz for a production bringing together the top stars at MGM, Joan Crawford and Clark Gable (appearing together onscreen for their eighth and final time); Gable, at the height of his popularity, had just finished *Gone with the Wind* with Selznick. Many years later, Joan Crawford remembered with emotion: "Clark and I did our best work together in *Strange Cargo*. We always had been close, sometimes too close, but now we knew each other as mature persons and the chemistry was still there and it added to the fire. The screenplay was splendid and Frank Borzage let us take it and run. And, baby, we ran!"[15] Here the star departed dramatically from her usual roles and appeared practically without makeup, for the first time since *Paid* (Sam Wood) in 1930. "For *The Women* I'd had a $40,000 wardrobe, for *Strange Cargo* I had three dresses, worth less than $40 all together!"[16] Peter Lorre played an oily toad-like man and Melvyn Douglas started out as the enigmatic Cambreau, before an inspired Borzage replaced him with Ian Hunter. The film, begun as *Not Too Narrow ... Not Too Deep*, was based on a story of the same name by New York novelist Richard Sale,[17] dramatized by his wife Anita Loos and adapted for the screen by Lawrence Hazard (*Man's Castle*). The book appeared in New York and London in 1936, Borzage had had an option on the material since March 1938 and the script was improved over an 18-month period — which meant they were enthusiastic about it and that the original storyline was only a vague point of departure! Since the action unfolds in French Guyana, in the fictional prison of Santa Margola, then in the surrounding tropical jungle, a penal colony was reconstructed on a four-acre surface. The famous "Lot 2," kingdom of Tarzan, was the tropical rainforest and the sequences on the shoreline were filmed in Laguna and Pico Beach (shooting from December 6–28, 1939, with retakes on January 9, 1940). Preparations for the film took place in an almost surrealistic environment: the war had just erupted in Europe, but the sole event preoccupying people at MGM was the world premiere of *Gone with the Wind* in Atlanta — who was invited, who was left out, would there be enough seats? We can legitimately wonder if, at the moment when the planet was on the point of being thrown into a state of turmoil, Borzage didn't conceive *Strange Cargo* as a kind of protest against the phenomenal futility of the Mecca of moviedom.

The story, disordered and fantastic, begins like a classic adventure film. The first part: a prison on Devil's Island (the name is never mentioned so as not to irritate the French government). Verne (C. Gable) is an indomitable, previously convicted criminal, with a record of 16 months in solitary confinement, 90 lashes of the whip and five attempts to escape in three years: "I'm a thief by profession. There's nothing worth stealing around here except liberty." They don't come any tougher. Grideau, the warden, sends him to work on the docks where Verne casts his eye upon Julie (J. Crawford), a prostitute from Marseille; she throws away what remains of a cigarette; Verne walks over the hands of his friends, picks up the butt, sniffs it, licks around it and brings it voluptuously to his lips: he's been missing more than nicotine! Julie has barely gotten rid of the clinging "M'sieur Pig" (Peter

The convict and the prostitute: Clark Gable and Joan Crawford in *Strange Cargo* (1940).

Lorre), a lecherous informer, when Verne, hiding, begins flirting with her. Crouched on the ground among barrels on the unloading dock, the convict grabs the prostitute by the ankle. Julie, furious: "What do you want?"—Verne: "Guess." "Why, you crummy convict!" Prisoners are not allowed to speak to women, who risk being deported from the colony if they are caught in the act. But Verne gives the guards the slip and joins Julie in her room. In prison, nothing untoward is noted: the number of convicts returning is correct, for an unknown by the name of Cambreau (I. Hunter) has snuck into the line and surreptitiously taken Verne's place. Pig notices Verne at night and denounces him to the authorities; to save her skin, Julie hands over Verne to the police, but they order her to leave the island within twelve hours. In the dormitory, Verne learns that his old enemy Moll (Albert Dekker) is planning an escape with six other convicts. Cambreau and he join the group (the stranger pays for both of them). Moll knocks out Verne while he is sleeping. When Verne wakes up, the others have fled; in the Bible Cambreau left next to him, he discovers, however, a note of encouragement and the map of their itinerary to the sea where a boat is waiting for them. *Strange Cargo* displays a bunch of cynical, vicious people, the underbelly of humanity, "Men to whom the present, the future and the past are one." All that subsists are the crudest physical relationships, sex and fighting. Telez, a religious fundamentalist, holds his companions in misfortune up to public disgrace; the intellectual Hessler (Paul Lukas), a killer of women who quotes Marcus Aurelius, complacently displays his evil nature; Moll is a thickheaded brute. Verne, finally, exudes a raw energy, his innate independence giving him vitality and insolence that favor him (like Bill in *Man's*

Castle); the plan of escape transmitted in a Bible may seem a funny idea, but it already indicates the nature of his "liberation."

Second part: Verne disappears in turn. The suicidal crossing of the jungle — marsh fever, quicksand, Indian arrows, crocodiles, snakes, downpours — has two victims. On his path, Verne delivers Julie from the claws of the adventurer Marfeux, who has been keeping her prisoner with false promises. Stiletto heels get stuck in the mud, her large hat catches in the trees, and her dress is soon in tatters. The couple spends the night around a campfire. Disheveled, sticky, scratched, Julie tries to recognize herself in the reflection of a tin of food. It is to a woman without makeup, metaphorically denuded, that Verne reads the "Song of Songs"; Julie is shaken up by this homage to the divine loved one, hides her face, and for the first time, shows real emotion, bursting into tears. Mankiewicz in 1978: "It was almost a good film. I wish it could have been made later.... Christ, you couldn't even indicate that Clark Gable screwed Joan Crawford in their trek through the jungle on the way to the beach!"[18]

The five other fugitives have reached the shores of the Atlantic and on their forced march, Cambreau has exerted an increasingly stronger influence over them. Calm, seeing things clearly and speaking rarely, he is familiar with the identities of the whole brood, knows who is armed, shows the right direction, finds food, sets an example. Telez, still plunged into the holy scriptures, and whom the others had stoned because he refused to share his bread, reaches the beach crawling; he has been bitten by a deadly snake. "I'll kill 'em, they stole my crucifix," he gasps. The crucifix is merely a piece of wood, retorts Cambreau, it's in his heart that he must seek God. "If sometimes things are said against me,

A journey between life and death: Ian Hunter and Joan Crawford in *Strange Cargo* (1940).

you'll speak for me?" the dying man asks, appeased. Cambreau makes the promise, closing Telez's eyes. Verne and Julie arrive at dawn, at the end of their strength. The other convicts have finally located the cutter meant to bring them back to civilization. As Moll wants food and the woman to be shared, Verne confronts him, victoriously, and takes charge of the little sailboat. In the high seas, Julie amuses herself by provoking the crew, languidly pressing up against the captain and kissing him four times. Cambreau predicts that the wind will die down. Becalmed for five days under a torrid sun, the weakest lose their nerve: "The wind should come soon," announces Cambreau. "But before the wind comes, some of us will die." In fact, when during a brawl, the keg of drinking water falls into the ocean, a runaway sacrifices himself to fetch it and is devoured by sharks; Moll accidentally kills his lover Dufond. Someone must drink from the cask and risk his life to see if saltwater has gotten into it. They draw lots. Julie bravely insisted on participating in the draw and she and Verne remain as the two final candidates. Verne throws himself on the beaker, but Moll, in an unexpected gesture of nobility, forestalls him, swallows the contaminated liquid and dies in the night. The brute does not sacrifice himself for his enemy (Verne), but to save Julie from what he has just gone through: the loss of a loved one. Before dying, the runaways have found peace in their souls. "They found the way themselves," Cambreau explains to Julie, who is dreaming of a new life — if only Verne would open his eyes. But the prostitute cannot help her rebellious convict: "I can't do anything for Verne, I don't even know how to pray." "You've been doing nothing else all this time," replies Cambreau, implying that her desire to be with the man she loves amounts to a prayer.

Third part: land is in sight. The four survivors debark at night, as Grideau and his policeman are watching the port. Hessler refuses Cambreau's "spiritual saccharine," calling him a "leader of sheep" and heads off to look for "a lonely lady with money." For this unrepentant Bluebeard, there is no salvation. "We won't see each other anymore," announces the stranger to him. (It would be a mistake to see Hessler as an equal of Cambreau, a negative image: the monster loses himself and does not escape his destiny.) Verne and Julie remain, hidden in the hut of a fisherman (Victor Varconi). Verne wants to reach Cuba and take up his former life, with Julie in tow. She refuses: "I've seen men die, they were thieves like you and as rotten as me, but when their time came, they suddenly got hold of something, something I've never had, something worth having or whatever it is. I don't wanna wait that long for mine. I want it now." She leaves the cabin, but runs into Pig who offers her a deal: if she marries him, he'll let her lover escape. Verne surprises them and thinks he has been betrayed. Thanks to Cambreau's intervention, Julie prevents Verne from murdering the informer; she then leaves with him.—A terrible storm erupts: the sea rages. Cambreau follows Verne on board the fishing boat that is to bring him to Cuba, then, confronted with the incorrigible selfishness and blindness of the convict, decides to retrace his steps. But he knows too much. He lets himself be thrown out to sea without resisting. "Relax and wait for the water to dry up," Verne tells him sardonically. "In Heaven and on Earth, in the whole world nobody can save you but me. So when you say your prayers, say them to me. You were right when you said God is in me... I am God!" The Satanic equation remains in his throat as lightning tears through the darkness: seeing Cambreau sink, he dives and brings the body onboard. Too late, the horrified fisherman realizes the man is dead. Verne despairs at this sacrifice, but Cambreau opens up his eyes again as if he had heard him and the prisoner presses against him, overcome with gratitude. In the morning, Verne meets up with Julie and delivers himself to the authorities. He has three years left. "So you found something stronger than you, after all?" jokes Grideau, not realizing that his remarks identify the love for a woman with spiritual teaching. Cambreau watches the scene from afar and goes away; the fisherman beside him discovers himself and makes the sign of the cross.

It has been said that *Strange Cargo* was perhaps a Christian variant of Luis Buñuel's *La Mort en ce jardin* (*Death in This Garden*), into which Sadie Thompson, the "fallen woman" in *Rain* (another role of Joan Crawford) had wandered. An accumulation of gritty naturalism, sex and religious discourse that J.-P. Coursodon qualified as "stupefying," "heavy" and "confusing."[19] Undeniably, the film is overly obvious at times, and has talky passages. We believe its singularity is also its main weakness: this is perhaps Borzage's least elliptical, by far most explicit work.[20] But at its level, it is perhaps also the most audacious (some would say pretentious). What limited the segment in the Chinese village in *Disputed Passage* can be extended here to the entire film and includes a community of individuals. In the image of *The Odyssey* or of *Mahâbhârata*, the place of the action is a vast battlefield of the soul. The long crossing contains all the characteristics of a journey of initiation and the hostile nature surrounding the runaways, is, literally and figuratively, an obstacle to "liberation," because it is only the reflection of their congenital savageness. But, like in Jacob's struggle with the Angel, the opponent is a catalyst. Cambreau, who seems in cahoots with these elements, creates the battleground, so to speak, foresees the flat calm or the storms, lets himself be thrown overboard so that Verne can experience the double baptism by water (the sea) and fire (lightning). The sound of his voice prevents Julie from stabbing Marfeux. We notice that Cambreau's message is never moral, but one of redemption and forgiveness. The condemned all meet their end with a serenity they derive from the omniscience of this mysterious companion. John Belton notes that this "presence enables them to accept their own mortality and to understand their own divinity."[21] For once, Sarastro himself leaves his "Solar Temple," enters in the game of ordeals and officiates as enlightener. Aside from the passionate violence of the exchanges between Gable and Crawford, *Strange Cargo* possesses Borzagian qualities which preserve it perpetually from ridicule: unwavering sincerity, absence of simplistic views and solutions, and emphasis (poignant restraint, often without musical background).

Given the go-ahead by the Hays Office, *Strange Cargo* opened in theaters in New York on April 25, 1940. The studio took precautions, heeding various preliminary warnings: Joseph I. Breen had characterized a first script dated April 26, 1939, as "unacceptable" and demanded a total of eight pages be eliminated, due to "unnecessary brutality and gruesomeness," "perverted sexual relationship" (homosexuality between Moll and Dufond) and "sacrilegious dialogue." MGM retorted that the film illustrated in fact the fate of a group of violent, blasphemous individuals and that these factors were in part indispensable to the story. On October 23, Breen came back fighting, advising Louis B. Mayer: "We urge and recommend that you cover yourselves with protection shots, in order that the elimination of such scenes may not completely destroy your story continuity." One month before the premiere, on March 28, the Legion of Decency classified this "amalgam of religion and licentiousness" with the moral code of "C" ("condemned"), but the studio did not think they would encounter serious opposition. An error: religious and family institutions across the country organized a boycott. After two weeks of showing it, police authorities in Detroit and in Providence forbad the film at the request of Catholic institutions. Boston and other cities followed suit. For the first time in years, local censorship was enforced, a phenomenon that perplexed the Hays Office. The warning shot was like a thunderbolt in Culver City, as MGM was not used to being treated this way! *Strange Cargo* had the honor of being one of the very rare major productions in Hollywood that the Legion fully condemned, for its "irreverent use of Scripture" as much as for its "suggestive dialogue and sequences." They anathematized, among others, a scene in which one of the fugitives reads the prostitute a passage from the Old Testament used in Catholic Liturgy in reference to the Virgin (the "Song of Songs"), and the incongruous role played by the Bible as incidental. Finally, "there is more physical contact between Crawford and the men in the picture than in any film I can recall in a long while."[22] MGM took all prints out of circulation, made the changes demanded and on October 10, the Legion of Decency revised its decision: *Strange Cargo* obtained an A-II rating ("Unobjectionable for adults"). Only a few sexual connotations remain in the dialogue.

However, Joan Crawford's thighs, the recitation of the book of Solomon and even the "naturalistic concept of religion contrary to the teachings of Christ" cited by the Legion of Decency were only pretexts. The diversity of opinions within the commission reflected widespread confusion, with some reproaching the film for "the irrational character of the 'religious' experience portrayed in the story" and others for its "suggestion of pantheism, which denies the transcendence of God"! But what fundamentally disturbed censors the most, was the enigmatic character of Cambreau. Who was he, where did he come from, was he human or divine? Members of the committee saw in him a personification of God, others a Christ figure (but the name of Christ is never uttered in the film). To what corresponds, in this case, "a subjective emotional experience without relation to dogma, faith or grace" (which must have been enticing to someone as virulently anticlerical as Mankiewicz)? On this subject, Borzage could quote Joseph de Maistre, his famous Masonic Brother who wrote in 1782: "True religion is much older than eighteen centuries, it was born the day that days were born." In reworking the film, MGM tried to make Cambreau a bit more human. But the question remains, the "holy man" disappears as he came and Borzage clearly refrains from providing an answer. Visually, however, the filmmaker establishes a singular relationship between the two main male protagonists. Verne becomes visible at the beginning of the film when he emerges from black night (he was in solitary confinement) while Cambreau finds himself without warning among the convicts under the burning sun. For Verne, rising up out of the night foreshadows his evolution; his grimaces and hesitations illustrate his difficulty at confronting the light which is his inevitable destiny. Cambreau has come to help the others die, and help Verne live; he takes his place by slipping into the prison. The ending reverses the relationships. Verne is on the bridge of the ship, in the morning sun, and Cambreau evaporates against a black background. According to the traditional laws of symbolism, light, like night, may have double meaning; brightness may signify the created world (as an illusory "externalization" of the Divine) and darkness, on the contrary, the unconditioned state beyond Creation into which Cambreau reintegrates after having, according to the Masonic adage, brought the "Light out of the Shadows" and "Order out of the Chaos." In this case, we are tempted to see a parallel between those mysterious spiritual masters who appear and disappear throughout History, and that eighteenth-century Free-Masons designated as "Superiores Incogniti."[23] A very strange cargo, indeed!

15

The Mortal Storm

The third part of the famous "German triptych," after *Little Man, What Now?* and *Three Comrades, The Mortal Storm* is, along with *Till We Meet Again* in 1944, one of Borzage's last masterpieces. Here his lovers are subjected to the ultimate, most pitiless ordeal — the one which, during filming, the director himself would have to face, and the greatest crisis of his life.

Hollywood studios always first sought to make a profit, experience having shown that pure entertainment got the best returns. They avoided politically complex or delicate subjects susceptible of offending the average viewer; under the pretext of free competition, film companies produced works that upheld the status quo. We have already seen that the Hays Office specifically ensured that American film, as a whole, was free from any explicit propaganda. However, with the advent of dictatorships in Europe and the progressive arrival of refugees, the Californian film community found itself in a difficult situation. Until that time, Congress's political isolationism had stifled any thoughts, in the private or public sectors, of making antifascist propaganda films, and ideological convictions had to be camouflaged (e.g., Dieterle's biopics for Warner). The Anschluss and the Czechoslovakian crisis were followed by a new influx of outcasts; the Hollywood Anti-Nazi League soon included 5000 members. Leni Riefenstahl arrived in Hollywood to study American cinema technique; the studios refused to admit her: "American films are barred from Germany, so we have nothing to show Miss Riefenstahl that would interest her."[1] Only Walt Disney opened his doors to her.

The American novelist Phyllis Bottome, who had studied psychoanalysis with Alfred Adler in Vienna, had earned a solid reputation for her books dealing with psychopathological cases, and some had been filmed: *Private Worlds* (1935), set in a psychiatric clinic, directed by Gregory La Cava, with Claudette Colbert and Charles Boyer. *Danger Signal*, a study of a psychopathic homicide, bought by Hollywood as soon as it came out in 1939, was refused across the board by the Hays Office and, after being worked on by 21 scriptwriters (!), fell into the hands of Robert Florey in 1944–45. Bottome was living in Germany when Hitler came to power. Witnessing the atrocities of the new regime, she devoted her novel *The Mortal Storm* to the progressive transformation of "a people of poets and philosophers" into a fanatical mob. The book was published in London in 1937 by Faber & Faber, and in New York by Little, Brown & Co. in April 1938. One month earlier, antifascists William M. Dozier and Kenneth MacKenna, in charge of MGM's Story Department, submitted a synopsis of the novel to Louis B. Mayer's office. Mayer was still quite reluctant to tackle such an openly ideological subject, just having dealt with the problems caused by *Three Comrades*. He no longer feared losing the German market: the number of American films sold each year to the Reich had decreased from 64 to 36 since 1933, so this area of profit had become insignificant and pessimists in Hollywood resigned themselves to forgetting about the whole European market (which had represented 30 percent of foreign profits), not including Great Britain. But like the competing companies, MGM had some difficulty pinpointing the mood of its native public and feared the devastating effects of a rash political mobilization. Isolationist currents were still very strong and the average American was not yet concerned by what was going on in Europe (in September 1939, despite the annihilation of Poland, 96 percent of the population questioned by Gallup was against entering into war). This was reflected in MGM's ideological and commercial hesitations. For example, Clarence Brown's film *Idiot's Delight* (released in January 1939), was originally a pacifist play by Robert E. Sherwood whose action also took place under Mussolini; on screen, any reference to real countries disappeared! Seized by a kind of schizophrenia, between 1936 and 1939 the ultraconservative studio scheduled and unscheduled several times the adaptation of *It Can't Happen Here*, Sinclair Lewis's famous novel describing the establishment of a fascist dictatorship in the U.S. But they lacked courage; the company also acquired the rights to *I Had a Comrade* by Vincent Casselrose, a former prisoner of the Nazis, and John Gunther's bestseller *Inside Europe*. MGM even spent $55,000 on Erich Maria Remarque's *The Heroes*, a story of the exodus of German Jews after 1933: it was to star Spencer Tracy, Robert Taylor and Margaret Sullavan and be directed by Borzage. But Phyllis Bottome's work won out. While the novelist was on an extensive U.S. conference tour on the Nazi peril, Dozier and MacKenna feverishly besieged the studio heads with their synopsis of *The Mortal Storm*. The Munich Crisis helped, and the team finally won their case. On December 27, 1938, finally, Phyllis Bottome was invited to Culver City to discuss a possible adaptation.

The Mortal Storm project was facilitated by another event: since December, the *New York Post* had a huge hit publishing the series *Confessions of a Nazi Spy*, the true story of a former FBI agent, Leon G. Turrou, who had recently uncovered a German spy ring in the U.S. Warner Bros. pounced on the subject (Jack Warner had closed his subsidiary in Berlin in May 1933, when one of his Jewish employees was forced to resign). On December 22, in Burbank, Anatole Litvak began filming *Confessions of a Nazi Spy*, a rather lackluster feature, but with the historical merit of being the first to mention Hitler's name and unequivocally denounce his dangerous politics, specifically in American territory. Its filming was somewhat nervously followed by Hollywood; armed men discreetly monitored access to the set. Warner Bros. thus opened hostilities (with Roosevelt's secret blessing), although the film was above all an inquiry into the "fifth column," containing news excerpts, and fared poorly in the U.S.; in Milwaukee, Nazi sympathizers set fire to the movie theater! It triumphed in London and Paris, but following protests from Minister Ribbentrop, *Confessions* was forbidden in six European and eight Latin American countries. (All theater owners who showed the film in Warsaw were later executed by the SS.) The tiny independent company PRC was bold enough to address the Nazi terror in Germany itself, with the low-budget film *Hitler, the Beast of Berlin* (dir.: Sam Newfield, under the pseudonym of Sherman Scott) which Hays refused to approve. Diplomatically renamed *Beasts of Berlin*, the film was released, virtually unnoticed, in November 1939 and was banned in New York and New Jersey. Finally, in January the same year, Chaplin began work on *The Great Dictator*, but only started filming September 9: the Hays Office and London informed him that his work would not pass the censors because it was unacceptable for an officially neutral country to ridicule a foreign head of state, no matter how "grotesque"! Filming of the misadventures of dictator Adenoid Hynkel and his Jewish double would continue until October 1940, four months after the release of *The Mortal Storm*. To sum up, even if a degree of caution was still required, a reversal was underway: the industry was prepared to respect the Rooseveltian principles of "defensive neutrality" and not make warmongering movies, but it no longer felt obliged to hide its sympathies.

Like Mankiewicz and LeRoy, Sidney A. Franklin was a creative talent Mayer had just thrust into the position of producer. A sensitive, delicate filmmaker, very romantic, but overly modest, he had, starting in the 1910s, been responsible for some impressive successes (*The Good Earth*, based on Pearl Buck's novel and the two first versions of *Smilin' Through*).[2] Franklin and his faithful collaborator, English scriptwriter Claudine West (Oscar for *Mrs. Miniver*), had been working for several weeks on the script of *Ninotchka*. Replaced by Lubitsch on April 20, 1939, the team began working on *The Mortal Storm*. The studios arranged for Hollywood producers and directors to privately view the Ufa newsreels which depicted the power of Hitler's armies, and well before MGM chose to get involved, Franklin and a few colleagues from Culver City (including Bernard Hyman), shocked by what they saw, decided to pave the way. Two emigrants, George Froeschel and Paul Hans Rameau, were put in charge of the general structure of the story and verifying accuracy; Claudine West mainly developed the dialogue. Franklin hired Viennese reporter and novelist Froeschel for $150 a week (he had been living in California without work since 1937 and was contemplating suicide) at the insistence of agent Paul Kohner, who helped many Germans emigrate. It paid off: Froeschel later authored several prestigious films at MGM (*Waterloo Bridge, Random Harvest*). Rameau, the son of a Max Reinhardt actor, wrote several scripts from 1919 on, notably Willi Forst's *Mazurka*; in the credits he used the pseudonym Anderson Ellis, fearing the Nazis would take revenge on his mother, living in Berlin. He admitted never having read Phyllis Bottome's novel and worked uniquely from a synopsis written in German and from reports on the Third Reich published in *Der Aufbau* (New York).[3] And yet, Froeschel and Rameau's contributions were still a watered-down version of reality: "Had we put in what they told me, no one would have believed it," Franklin wrote thirty years later.[4] The scriptwriter was probably also inspired by the play *Professor Mamlock* by communist Friedrich Wolf; this drama describes the progressive boycott of a great Berlin professor of surgery, a Jew finally driven to suicide by the SA. The play was very well known by emigrants and the Soviet film based on it was shown in art houses and experimental theaters in the U.S. (in New York as of November 11, 1938.)[5]

Although immersed in *Strange Cargo*, Borzage was designated to direct the operation, thanks to his filming of Remarque and to Margaret Sullavan, the main star of *The Mortal Storm*. She appeared with James Stewart and Frank Morgan, her two partners from the delightful *The Shop Around the Corner*, which Lubitsch had just wrapped up in Culver City. James Stewart never hid that he owed his career to Margaret Sullavan (the love of his life), and, having attended the same drama school in Massachusetts, they were on their fourth film together since 1936. Robert Young, for the third time with the Borzage-Sullavan team, and Maria Ouspenskaya, the impressive dowager with Mongol features (she had just moved her acting school from New York to Hollywood), completed the cast.[6]

During numerous story conferences, Franklin and Borzage decided to somewhat distance themselves from the literary source, for motives involving dramatization, censorship and political opportunism. In Phyllis Bottome's novel, Freya Roth, half–Jewish, has a communist lover, Hans (Martin, in the film) Breitner; he is persecuted after the burning of the Reichstag and — halfway through the story — is shot down by Otto von Rohn (Freya's half-brother) and Fritz Marberg, two SA members. Freya is pregnant by Hans and Fritz wants to marry her, but his mother, an anti–Semitic aristocrat, tells Freya the name of her lover's assassin. While her father perishes in a concentration camp, Freya secretly gives birth at Hans's mother's place in Munich, then flees with the baby via Austria to California and freedom, leaving behind "The Mortal Storm of the dictatorship." As we will see, the storyline was completely changed. In the final script, dated October 1939, there was no more

The Mortal Storm (1940), publicity sheet.

unmarried mother, and above all, no communist: the recent German-Soviet pact had destroyed whatever sympathy the public may have felt for him! The role of the professor was developed and a boycott of university courses added (cf. *Professor Mamlock*); Mrs. Roth now escapes with her youngest son. The burning of the Reichstag was replaced by a book burning (as the film was not set in Berlin) and, according to the codes of the time, the word "Jew" was replaced by "non–Aryan": Hollywood feared the emotional charge of the word "Jew," as anti–Semitism was still virulent in various regions of the U.S. In the movie, Professor Roth no longer wears a Star of David, but simply a "J" on the sleeve of his prisoner's uniform (an inaccuracy as the "J" only appeared in passports).[7] At the end, Freya is killed in the massif of the Karwendel (Margaret Sullavan knew how to die so well...), her friend Martin Breitner is arrested by Fritz and the SA. But at the express request of Phyllis Bottome, Martin is able to escape the Nazi henchmen so that the film could at least end with a tiny note of hope[8] (although the scene of Martin's arrest had been photographed for preliminary publicity). It was very unlike Hollywood to have a film end more sadly than the novel on which it was based!

After much hesitation, the Front Office gave the go-ahead and filming began on February 7, 1940. In Europe, the Battle of Karelia had been raging for a few days; a Gallup poll the same month indicated that 83 percent of American citizens favored France and Great Britain over Hitler. Swiss set designer Henry S. Noerdlinger, DeMille's former right-hand man and MGM's specialist on "European subjects," settled problems of local color and props, not always an easy task: 29 companies categorically refused to make the hundred or so flags showing the swastika, and a studio department had to take care of it! The second unit, directed by Richard Rosson, filmed the ski-runs and sequences at the Karwendel Pass in Sun Valley, Idaho (April 5–10) and above Salt Lake City, Utah; Olympic champions John Litchfield and Beth Crookes doubled for Stewart and Sullavan. Jack Arnold, from the special effects department, designed a vehicle on three sliders that allowed them to follow the skiers very rapidly without the camera trembling.

Questioned about his actors fifteen years later, Borzage told Lawrence J. Quirk: "(Margaret Sullavan) was one of the most generous and unselfish people I ever knew when it came to other actors; she boosted them, encouraged them, always wanted them to give their best. She had great respect for Frank Morgan, and she and Stewart opined that he was giving the best performance in the film, which I, too, felt he did. 'Frank has played so many dithering idiots and damned fools and dunces and dolts in so many pictures that people forget how wonderful he can be in a straight, serious role,' Maggie told me at the end of shooting— and truer words were never spoken." As for the phlegmatic Robert Young, he "always seemed to come alive when he found himself in a picture with her. In a Sullavan picture he didn't just walk through his role like he did in so many things. I never saw him more intense than in *The Mortal Storm*. The part was a strong one, but he did ample justice to it. 'I don't want to let Maggie down,' he told me once, after a particularly tough day on the set."[9] Judith Anderson and Scotty Beckett were first cast as Mrs. Roth and her youngest son Rudi, but Borzage replaced them after two weeks by Irene Rich (whom he had directed in *They Had to See Paris*) and Gene Reynolds.[10] The subject matter soon influenced the mood on the set, which became intense, quiet, serious: gone were the familiar horseplay and practical jokes. "But picking up a paper and scanning headlines in the evening, then coming to the studio the next day to enact events which occurred only yesterday, is another story," commented Borzage.[11] Over the course of the weeks, the climate on the set became more tense. Berlin let it be known via the Swiss Embassy in Washington that all collaborators on the film, like those of *Confessions of a Nazi Spy*, would be "punished" when "Hitler has won the war"; according to Robert Stack, members of the German-American Bund had even infiltrated the studio and tried to sabotage the book burning sequence by starting a fistfight.[12] The end of filming was impatiently awaited; it too was enlivened by some strangely amusing moments: at meals, the Brownshirts and the "tommies" from *Waterloo Bridge* (on the next set) shared the same table.

The film was completed on April 19 — ten days after the Germans landed in Norway — and cost $900,000. It is interesting to see what motivated Borzage the first weeks, even though no one yet knew the extent of the nightmare: "We're filming a human interest story of a family's disintegration. It just happens to have Nazi Germany as its background. Our picture won't have any 'heavies' and it's not an attack on Germany. It's just a picture of what happens when a force like that arises. There are not heavies because the storm troopers are shown believing in what they do. We don't condone the brutality, naturally. We try to show the fanatic fervor that motivates it, but we don't excuse it."[13] Franklin confirmed this approach: "All I wanted to do was tell the story of a family in Germany today and what happened to it. I bent over backwards to avoid making villains of the men in order to show that the system is the real heavy. Robert Young, for instance, is one of the leading Nazis. Yet he isn't a heavy; he merely believes that way. When you see the souls of people destroyed by their beliefs, you merely feel sorry for the people, but you hate the system."[14]

Here begins what can only be called the "case" of *The Mortal Storm*. Various recent publications credit the major part of the film not to Borzage, but to producer-director Victor Saville, according to his own statements. The affair is so unbelievable that it necessitated a thorough investigation. Some preliminary information: Born in Birmingham, Victor

Saville, a pioneer, had been working since 1923 in British cinema; he made handsome but outdated costumers such as *The Iron Duke* (Wellington at Waterloo, in 1934), and *The Dictator* (the Struensee affair, 1935), and later *Kim* with Errol Flynn (1950); a pleasant although unmemorable filmography. In June 1938, Louis B. Mayer named the prolific Saville, an incomparable organizer, as head of MGM's British branch.[15] When this department closed due to the war, Saville joined the ranks of producers in Culver City. In his unpublished memoirs, Sidney A. Franklin sums up this introductory stage:

> The more terrible the war news from abroad, and the atrocities that were being committed, the more difficult my participation became. Every time I went on the set, it was like a private Germany of our own. I loathed the very sight of the swastika and all it stood for, and as production proceeded, I became increasingly disturbed. We were about half way through, when I went down on the set; stormtroopers were singing the Horst Wessel song, and some of them jumped a Jewish character and beat him into insensibility. It made me ill. The scene on the stage was like seeing the real thing that I'd been reading about in the newspapers. I went straight to Eddie Mannix and told him that, believe it or not, I wanted to be relieved of the *Mortal Storm* picture. "I don't know whether you understand why," I said, "but I can't act impartially towards the picture and I think my value as a producer has gone. The subject matter makes me quite ill." What excuse have I got? None. I loved the picture—particularly the escape, and the marriage in the mountains—yet the whole thing became repulsive to me. From a certain point on I realized I couldn't do the picture justice. The production was handed over to Victor Saville.[16]

The transfer of powers remained an internal affair, as the British Saville could not appear in the credits of an MGM anti–Hitler film without infringing upon the Neutrality Act, as the U.S. was not yet at war (aside from Borzage, no producer was mentioned in the official sources). Management merely announced on March 2, after almost a month of filming: "Victor Saville has been assigned to assist producer Franklin in order to relieve him of some of the burden and allow him to devote more time to preparations for *Waterloo Bridge*." Franklin nominally remained producer until mid–March.

At this point in our investigation, we must introduce some facts of a private nature that would have no place here, had they not strongly influenced the filming of *The Mortal Story*, and, even more so, Borzage's subsequent career. Since Christmas 1939, relations between the filmmaker and his wife Rena had been rapidly deteriorating. As explained earlier, the couple had very different lifestyles. Rena, upper middle-class and cultured, liked a lot of company, parties (perhaps a little too much, insinuated caustic Louella Parsons), luxury, and trips. Conscientious, hardworking, from a proletarian background, Frank was less inclined to social life, aside from his athletic activities. Their feelings for each other were not evenly matched. "Frank did anything to make Rena happy, paid for everything, all her fancies. She spent money like water, there always had to be something happening when she was around. He spoiled her, he put her on a pedestal," described his sisters Dolly and Sue. "The thing he loved most in his early life was Rena, he idolized her. Look at Janet Gaynor and Helen Hayes: they had the same body as Rena, it's not a coincidence! He probably never stopped loving her, but a man can just take so much, I guess..." Rena considered her marriage with more equanimity: "I respect him, but I don't love him," she even admitted to her sister-in-law. On this point, the filmmaker melds with the heroes of his stories: he loves for two. Daily reality, however, was less romantic and the couple's private life was increasingly strained. About five years after their marriage, Rena had an abortion without her husband's knowledge (he adored children), because she wanted to resurrect her flagging career as an actress, and didn't want children anyway. Rena soon discovered she was bisexual. She took numerous trips around the world with lesbian friends or young lovers, whom she purportedly collected quite freely. The couple had separate rooms, but throughout the thirties, their affection for each other kept them together.[17] According to certain family members, Borzage consoled himself elsewhere sexually, and was said to have had discreet affairs with several actresses, including Lupe Velez, Mary Pickford, Marion Davies, Joan Crawford and Hedy Lamarr.[18] But during the first months of 1940, the disintegration of their marriage came to a point of no return: *The Mortal Storm* became the filmmaker's own storm. It seems that its somber tone was related to its creator's frame of mind. Borzage withdrew into silence, distancing himself from Rena's perpetual guests and drowning his sorrows in alcohol. His behavior was puzzling; the marriage fell apart in a few weeks. On June 7, 1940, at a double celebration for Rena's birthday and their 24th anniversary, Frank got up without a word of explanation, left his Wilshire Boulevard mansion with the party in full swing and moved into the Hollywood Athletic Club; an employee moved his personal belongings. According to witnesses, Rena had gone beyond the limit by publicly toasting a man he didn't approve of (probably one of the two gay men with whom she lived). On July 30, Frank demanded a divorce on grounds of mental cruelty. On August 7, Rena in turn demanded a divorce, for the same motives. Gallantly, Borzage gave in; on Christmas, he even surprised his wife by giving her a car. On January 22, 1941, the divorce was granted in favor of Rena, who obtained $250,000 in damages and interests, despite her disastrous management of their joint account: four months earlier, the press had discovered the Borzages were $155,600 in debt![19] Frank then moved in with his brother Lew and sister-in-law Pearl on Chiselhurst Drive, where he remained for four years; they had a hard time stopping him from drinking. The former couple still maintained contact: Rena continued to read all books and scripts susceptible for filming by Frank. She died of cancer five years after Frank, on February 19, 1966, in the Pacific Palisades mansion Borzage had given her after their separation, the former residence of his mentor, Thomas H. Ince.

Returning to the filming of *The Mortal Storm*, in an interview given to John Kobal in 1969, Victor Saville gave his version of what happened after Franklin's departure:

> Mayer called me in to read over the script, and look at what they'd shot so far. I told him "these boys haven't got the ideas of the Nazis at all — they're not polite and there's just something wrong with it" — so he said "What are you going to do?" and I said: "Stop all production. Give me time to read the script and let me talk to the director and stars," which I did. They were all intelligent people, they saw what I was after. Then I went down on stage when we'd re-started shooting and I found Borzage was obviously in great difficulties. I think he was having personal problems at the time. I walked on the set and he was so glad to see me, he sat down in a chair while I sketched out and rehearsed the first sequence. I don't remember what it was — anyway I did it, then I said, "alright — shoot it," and walked off the stage and came back down when they told me they'd got it. Borzage was fine, because he recovered afterwards." (John Kobal): "How much of the film did you direct?" (Saville): All but a week... Borzage was not a Jew. I was. I had much more feeling for the Jewish doctor and his dilemma.[20]

On December 4, 1972, during a tribute organized by the National Film Theater in London, Saville repeated to Kevin Brownlow: "Mayer called me in after four days shooting. Said they were in trouble. I looked at it and you know what a nice man Sidney [Franklin] was. They weren't Nazis — they were far too nice. So I took it over — directed it, because Borzage was having wife trouble and was drinking a lot." MGM could not hide Saville's participation much longer: in September 1941 a Senate subcommittee named "America First Committee" (presided by Charles Lindbergh) attacked Hollywood's anti–Nazi films and accused the "Anglo-Jewish lobby" of trying to lead the U.S. into war. The founder of the movement, Senator Gerald P. Nye (who we know was in contact with the Germans and belonged to the committee of inquiry into Roosevelt initiated in Congress six months earlier) mostly attacked MGM's film, for which a British subject was responsible. Borzage responded publicly via the press: "Senator Nye's statement is incorrect, as I started and finished direction of *The Mortal Storm*, and at no time was I ever removed from my directorial duties."[21]

According to George Sidney, then in charge of screen tests for *The Mortal Storm*, and unaware of any supposed replacement of Borzage, Victor Saville was "pompous, abrasive and arrogant"[22]; his remarks, it is true, are not exactly overly modest! Joseph L. Mankiewicz's observations continue in the same vein: "I know very little about Victor Saville—none of it very reassuring."[23] Borzage's two sisters and his niece, all doing extra work, never saw Saville. Asked about this affair, Robert Stack (who played Otto von Rohn) clarified: "I was only in about ⅓ of the movie, and I don't remember Victor Saville being on the set, let alone directing. I met him once or twice, but certainly Frank Borzage was the director of *The Mortal Storm* when I was around. It's always depressing to me when people take credit for someone else's talents after they're gone."[24] Gene Reynolds (who played Rudi) openly confirms these statements: "Mr. Borzage shot all the scenes I worked on in *Mortal Storm*. I was on the picture six or seven weeks and he was to my knowledge the only director. Mr. Saville was the producer. There is no question that Frank Borzage directed all of *Mortal Storm*. I remember Mr. Saville visiting the set, talking to the actors (something few producers did in those days) and communicating some good ideas very well."[25] Finally, James Stewart briefly but incontestably refuted Saville's bragging: "Frank Borzage directed all of the picture *Mortal Storm*. No one but Frank Borzage directed *Mortal Storm*."[26] What's more, the complete set of shooting stills from the MGM archives (on file at the Academy of Motion Picture Arts and Sciences) shows Borzage working on all the important sequences in the film. What is clear is that Saville seems to have wrongly taken all the credit. Better acquainted with the political climate, he may well have directed a few crowd shots (perhaps the book burning, the master shot of the concentration camp); his correspondence on file at the University of Southern California mostly reveals preoccupation with historical or geographical details.[27] In conclusion, should any doubt subsist as to the film's paternity, one has only to glance at Victor Saville's own films—and then watch *The Mortal Storm*!

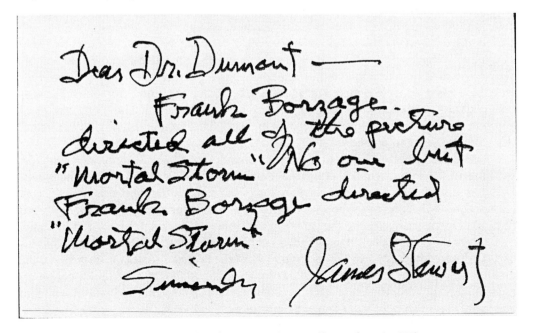

Letter to the author from James Stewart (September 12, 1990).

The film begins with menacing storm clouds gathering. Off screen, a commentator speaks of the hidden, homicidal instincts of human nature and asks "How soon will man find wisdom in his heart and build a lasting shelter against his ignorance and fears?" Like *Lucky Star* ten years earlier, *The Mortal Storm* links sky and snow. It all begins on a sunny morning, January 30, 1933, in a small university town at the foot of the Bavarian Alps (the camera pans, revealing its whiteness).[28] What will become a chronicle of complete destruction is constructed around a series of scenes that echo one another, the second ones negatively mirroring the first.—At the entrance of a large, comfortable home, the mailman delivers a mountain of mail for Professor Roth (F. Morgan), celebrating his 60th birthday. The entire household is in commotion, preparing for the great day. Holding a chair in physiology at the university, Roth, a Jew,[29] is married to an aristocrat (I. Rich); he receives presents from Erich and Otto, his wife's sons whom he considers as his own, from Freya (M. Sullavan), and from the youngest son, fourteen-year-old Rudi. The camera follows the professor in a long tracking shot as he approaches the venerable university where everyone greets him respectfully. The caretaker and his university colleagues exchange mischievous winks, greeting him as though nothing were out of the ordinary. Roth hides his disappointment. The second he enters the auditorium, Borzage amplifies the thunder of applause and stomping of feet by a rapid circular camera movement that reveals a room filled to the gallery (where Freya, Rudi, and their mother are sitting). Roth brushes away a tear. A student introduces two speakers in Latin, friends of the family who are rivals in love (for Freya) and in politics. They enter the field at the bottom of the image, standing up, literally emerging from the crowd as paragons of the old and new Germany: medical students Martin Breitner (J. Stewart), future veterinarian, and Fritz Marberg (R. Young). Fritz, the most talented disciple, makes an impeccable speech. Martin, who has lost his notes, improvises and gives the professor a trophy representing the flame of science, a gift from his students, at which point the entire assembly sings "Gaudeamus igitur." In the evening, the celebration continues among the family, eight of them seated around a large oval table (filmed in a slightly high-angle shot). Freya is flanked by Fritz and Martin. "We are a very united family—we pride ourselves on our tolerance and our sense of humor," Roth toasts. "May our happiness continue as long as we live." Fritz takes advantage of the occasion to announce his engagement to Freya (whom he has not really consulted). Martin is saddened, but joins in the congratulations. A rare kind of harmony permeates these first fifteen minutes: there is a state of communion (the table) and of human warmth with no trace of sentimentality or affectation, as if Borzage wanted to emphasize the intrinsic qualities of all his characters one last time before "fleeing Paradise." This excludes facile condemnation: all, without exception, will be victims.

Amidst the general jubilation, Martha, the maid, announces: "Something wonderful has happened, they have made Adolf Hitler Reichskanzler of Germany." When the bombshell falls, differences and schisms carry over into the composition of the shots. The camera descends to the level of the people. Carried away by enthusiasm, Fritz, Otto, Erich and Rudi rush to the radio, becoming intoxicated by the appalling landslide of "Sieg heil!" shouted by the SS and SA legions standing at attention. The four others observe from a distance, overcome: seated to the right and left of the deserted table (medium shot), the professor and his wife frame Freya and Martin, standing up in the background; a close-up isolates Freya and Martin to indicate this "new alliance of souls" (J. Belton) which from then on replaces that of blood. All expressions freeze, the lines are drawn. Returning to the table, Fritz, Otto and Erich paint a portrait of a powerful Germany, soon to become master of Europe and the world: "Who is not for us is against us." The conversation becomes

Adolf Hitler is Germany's new ruler: the sudden ideological schism carries over into the composition of the shot (*The Mortal Storm*, 1940).

acrimonious when Martin vows he prefers peace to war and refuses to rally to the ranks of the Nazi Party. Fritz calls him a communist ("red fish"). After the radio broadcast, a second outside intrusion provides the coup de grace: a phone call from the district chief, the SA Mann Holl, mobilizes the three party members. Martin turns a deaf ear, he will not go with them: "Peasants have no politics, they keep cows." Fritz leaves, threatening: "If they want to keep their cows, they better have the right politics." The older generation remain at the table, along with Freya ("No woman's business," they have told her), the peasant-veterinarian Martin (representing common sense and nature) and the young Rudi who repeats but doesn't understand what he has been taught in school: "the individual must be sacrificed to the welfare of the state." The fade-out is metaphoric.

Weeks have passed. At the Breitner's isolated farm, in the Alps, Martin, his elderly mother (Ouspenskaya) and the servant Elsa, a teenager hopelessly in love with Martin, are caring for a newborn foal. The mountain is identified with perpetual values; ideology and demagogy have no hold over its inhabitants. Since the political upheaval and Freya's engagement, Martin has interrupted his studies and retreated into a kind of "inner exile." Freya pays him a surprise visit, reproaches Martin for living like a hermit and persuades him to join her brothers at the inn, in the name of a "Pact of eternal friendship we all wrote and signed with our own blood." Isn't he "the sanest person" she knows? Martin and Freya side by side ski down to the town, to meet their first ordeal, after a joyous descent sadly echoed by the film's final images. The beer hall is full of students shouting themselves hoarse and swaying to the lighthearted melody of "Ergo bibamus," filmed in a tracking shot from right

A few against many: James Stewart and Margaret Sullavan in *The Mortal Storm* (1940).

to left across the length of the room. Martin sits down, joining Erich, Otto and Fritz; they have agreed not to discuss politics. (In his book, Frederic Lamster astutely noted that the order at the table calls to mind that at Roth's birthday party: seated at the head of the table, Martin in a sense becomes the keeper of the professor's flame[30]). Martin congenially greets his former instructor Werner, a man in his seventies; Fritz disapproves: the teacher is an incorrigible democrat. Holl, in party uniform, enters the room. Fritz surreptitiously removes his arm from his half–Jewish fiancée's shoulder. Arrogantly, Holl gives Werner the Nazi salute; he answers by "good evening." At the instigation of the noisy SA, the whole restaurant in unison breaks out into the "Horst Wessel Song,"[31] standing up, right arms raised in a Hitlerite salute, facing a handful of Brownshirts on stage. The scene is both symbolic and terrifying: Freya stands slowly, invites Martin to do the same so as not to attract attention, but the couple turn their backs on the SA and, horrified, observes around them the ardor of a nation suddenly seized with fanatical fervor. (Bob Fosse would remember this scene for the Biergarten in *Cabaret* in 1972). Borzage isolates Freya and Martin in a sea of extended arms which he examines, slowly panning from left to right, then in a fade-out, enough time to be subjected to three verses of the cursed hymn. The couple, standing up, calm (they represent verticality, the solidity of the mountain), contrasts with the sound and sight of the surrounding aggressiveness; only Fritz, staring disapprovingly at the rebels, is framed in a different angle from his comrades, as if to indicate his ambiguous position as both activist and lover. Between the opening tracking shot and the second inverse camera movement, each associated with specific music, the camera resumes with the transformation of Germany.

Brusquely, Holl gives the order to stop, addressing Werner, "Are you dumb, or don't you like our glorious song?" Eight brutes encircle the elderly man, forcing him to sing. It is too much for Martin, who cuts himself a path through the menacing crowd, coming to the defense of the teacher and helping him leave the place unharmed. There follows a violent altercation between Martin and his childhood friends ("We want to know where you stand"); for the third and last time, Fritz asks him if he will join their ranks—a moment with biblical resonances, interrupted by shouting in the street. The teacher is being pummeled by a hoard of the SA. Martin and Freya go out and get him back on his feet. Borzage later reuses this contrast between gemütlichkeit and inhumanity in a brief train sequence, amid an assorted crowd, still singing meekly. Fritz reproaches his fiancée: her behavior will not make her father's life any easier. Things may soon change for him...

A long tracking shot shows Professor Roth approaching the university (completely identical to that at the beginning); people avoid him, students lower their heads. The old caretaker, devoted and friendly, tells him about the new instructions from the administration: the "Heil Hitler!" is now obligatory, but he will continue to greet him in the usual way—when there are no witnesses. Cut brusquely to Roth in front of his audience: all, without exception, are wearing the SA uniform. Ready to pounce should he make a false move, the students wait silently, the camera immobile and their expressions rigid. When Roth, during an experiment involving biochemical analysis, maintains that "science has been unable to discover any difference in the blood of the various races," Holl accuses him of being a liar and orders his fellow students to boycott the course in the name of Aryan purity. Borzage continues with a visual ellipsis: Fritz, the model student, leaves the auditorium last; Roth turns out the light (morning has suddenly become night) and the room appears lit by the flames of an enormous blaze in the courtyard. From a balcony, Roth watches the burning (high-angle shot); hundreds of students are publicly burning the works of Heinrich Heine, Albert Einstein, Stefan Zweig, Thomas Mann, etc. The sequence is thus the negative counterpoint of the first: the initial camera movement implies that the professor has remained true to himself while those around him topple; the acclamations are past, the auditorium a wall, the birthday candles and flame from the trophy are transformed into the fire of inquisition that Roth contemplates "from above."

From then on, the drama speeds up. Freya breaks up with Fritz: "I know now I couldn't live in your world. You belong to this new Germany that persecutes my people." Borzage frames them symbolically: Fritz, tormented, in the dark and Freya facing the lit window, watching the snow fall. In the evening, the young woman is taken home by Martin. An outcast (even his helpers have left the farm), he thinks it would be better if they don't see each other anymore, but Freya begs him to not leave her alone. As Erich, Otto and a few Brownshirts surround them, Martin defends himself alone against six of them until Mrs. Roth intervenes. Rebuffed by their chief, Erich and Otto leave the family home for good. The next day, Freya goes to the Alps. The couple is embracing when Werner, the teacher, appears, pursued by the Gestapo. Martin offers to take him to Innsbruck by secretly crossing the Austrian border at the Karwendel pass, a little-known entry point. Mrs. Breitner promises to look after Freya. Soon after, the farm is searched. "You don't choose your friends very carefully, Miss Roth, do you? You know your name doesn't sound very well to German ears." The servant Elsa (Bonita Granville), haunted by rumors of torture, loses her nerve and her panic alerts the executioners; if Martin wants to live, he can no longer return. We recognize the Borzage touch in the relationship between Elsa and her rival, devoid of jealousy: contrary to the usual scheme of things, the beautiful girl never thinks of revenge ("if I should say something that might harm Martin, I'd kill myself") and both Freya and Mrs.

Breitner choose to ignore her fateful weakness. Elsa is brutalized twice for a man who considers her no more than a child.[32]

Late August, 1933. Freya assists her father who, not allowed to teach, is writing a physiology tract, awaiting a posting in Vienna. But the Gestapo strikes: Roth disappears. The administration remains silent, fearing reprisals: an SS officer tells Erich and Otto: "I suggest that you cease these tactless inquiries." In despair, Freya turns to Fritz, in the name of their old romance, and he secretly manages to obtain a five-minute nighttime interview in a concentration camp (probably Dachau). On Lot 3 of Culver City, art director Wade B. Rubottom constructed—for the first time in the movies—as exact a replica as possible of such a camp (six weeks of work, 150 workers). Documentation about them was practically nonexistent, and it was put together from precious information from second unit director Richard Rosson, who had been interned for a month in a Nazi camp in Graz, Austria (April–May 1939).[33] Two hundred and fifty extras played the prisoners who struggled, heads shaved, under torrential rain, surrounded by high voltage barbed wire fences; the SS flag flies from the top of the security tower. Studio reports mention a sequence much longer than that of the release print (which would justify the first working title of the film, *Concentration Camp*), as 18,000 feet of film were printed for a giant tracking shot around the perimeter. Mrs. Roth finds her husband in a dark visiting room (a confidential document informs us that he is imprisoned for life); the prisoner emerges from the darkness, stooped, his hands covered in bruises, his beard and hair white. The SS guards remain invisible in the shadows; a single glaring lightbulb isolates the couple in the center of the image. The expressionistic composition of the shot confers upon the couple a universal dimension:

The very first replica of a Nazi concentration camp in motion pictures (*The Mortal Storm*, 1940).

suffering humanity is symbolized here, without throbbing violins or seething anger. Roth makes light of his condition, then urges his wife to leave the country. But she won't leave without him: "You will be free soon." "Yes, I shall be free, my dear," the old man confirms before returning to his darkness.

Winter is approaching. Freya is going over Rudi's lessons with him. Martha, the maid, has just given her notice when an SA officer enters, filmed from the back. It is Otto who announces: "Mother, be brave, he is free at last." The official version: a heart attack. (Otto's presence establishes an indirect link between the sons.) Mrs. Roth, Freya and Rudi get on the train for Austria. At the border, the Gestapo finds the professor's "seditious" manuscript in Freya's belongings, declaring: "You've shown yourself unworthy to represent the German race abroad." Mrs. Roth and Rudi continue on to Innsbruck. Placed behind Mrs. Roth, who has been waving goodbye to her daughter since the train started again, the camera follows Freya and the Gestapo agent to the steps, until they are hidden by a wall, which serves as a premonition. Returning to the family home, Freya discovers an enigmatic message from Mrs. Breitner. She goes to the Alps where Martin is waiting for her: he has secretly come back to help her escape. They thank Elsa for "her courageous help" and send her back to the city so she will have an alibi. Time is of the essence: climbing to the pass will be difficult. "We have had no time for the little things lovers say or do," Freya laments, as if they had found each other too late, while Martin consoles her: "We'll have our whole lives to say them. Nothing will ever separate us again." Because the couple in *The Mortal Storm* was "born out of adversity more so than into adversity"(C. Viviani)[34]: each sign that destroys family harmony (the collective balance) invisibly reinforces their union. While giving her children their leave, Mrs. Breitner opens a glass cabinet and removes a "wedding cup," before conducting a vernacular wedding ceremony: for centuries, the family has married by inscribing the names of the spouses on a new cup. The old mother takes the cup reserved for her son and pours brandy into it which comes from Martin's apple tree, the one under which she expected, cradled and pampered him. "I hope you'll marry in the church, but since it cannot be, for me, this is the moment of your wedding." While Freya and Martin drink in turn, Mrs. Breitner closes her eyes and invokes upon each a heavenly blessing. The couple says "Amen" and Borzage zooms onto the talismanic cup, held by the three protagonists. The rustic ritual synthesizes into a kind of communion all that is threatened by the "Mortal Storm": the union of the couple (and by extension, family unity, the heritage of the ancestors), but also access to what is sacred. The vertical dimension is symbolized by the primordial tree and by the sap of fruit preciously transmitted from generation to generation. A fade-out establishes the passage from the cup of love to the powers of evil, located at the inn. In a horizontal tracking shot from right to left, the filmmaker frames an accordionist (cheerful music) which tries to cover the cries of terror coming from the next room, showing a few uncomfortable clients, a coatrack soiled by Nazi symbols, a door opening brusquely: Elsa has talked. The Gestapo has expressly designated Fritz to head a patrol in charge of intercepting his childhood friends atop the mountains: "In the service of your country there are no human relationships!" Only Otto and Erich are exempt.

The marriage and communion are followed by the ascent. It has taken all night to climb the Karwendel and Freya's strength is gone. "Every time I look back you seem to be smaller. You're so very tired. Your face is so small and white," Martin observes, climbing this "ladder of courage" praised in the prologue of *7th Heaven*. "We're not lost, are we?" Freya asks, at the end of her journey. The sun comes up, Austria, salvation, is only a few miles away. When Fritz's patrol appears behind a ridge, the fugitives begin their descent at high speed. Borzage films them in a master shot, as if they have melted into the immaculate landscape,

as if swallowed by a luminous sphere in which physical laws no longer exist. The long austere ascent has led "to the fields of the virgin snow, in reach of the rising sun, there where
the transfigured being finally meets his Creator" (M. Henry Wilson).[35] The soldiers open fire
(medium-close shot); Freya falls. Martin, his shoulder has been grazed, continues his escape
on skis, after having gathered Freya in his arms, with no apparent effort. Fritz orders them
to stop fire, skis down about thirty feet and, horrified, notices that the snow (a symbolic
shroud) is stained red. Martin reaches friendly soil, carrying his wife almost ceremonially.
Freya regains consciousness: "We made it, didn't we, we're free," she breathes, before closing her eyes. Martin: "Yes, we're free. Listen, you can hear the church bells from the village." "I'm tired now, yes, very, very tired." She snuggles up against his shoulder and breathes
her last breath. The bells chime (as in *A Farewell to Arms*). Martin shakes his head, distraught
(and the camera focuses on him, not Freya who has just died surreptitiously). Never in the
director's earlier work is the word "freedom" so unequivocally assimilated with the liberation from the human condition on earth. The night that darkens the world in *The Mortal
Storm* leaves Borzage's heroes no place, no alternative aside from refuge in transcendent
light. We could speak of Borzage's darkest, most somber film, if the whiteness that visually
marks the film from the very first images did not carry a message of eternity.

The nocturnal epilogue opens with a full shot of the Roth's deserted home. A magical place, the kingdom of shadows. Oppressive silence. In the darkness of an empty room,
standing wordlessly at the window, Erich and Otto watch large flakes of snow fall. Fritz
enters, not daring to approach his comrades; he makes his report in the doorway, hesitant,
out of breath, then shouts: "I had no choice! It was my duty!" He then leaves. The snow
intensifies. Erich: "Freya killed, it doesn't make sense. And Breitner goes free." Otto: "Yes,
free to think as he believes, wasn't that what he said?" Erich, enraged: "Free to fight against
all we stand for." Otto stares at his brother: "Yes. Thank God for that." Erich slaps him
and leaves. Otto slowly walks through the rooms, the voices of the past rise up in the night,
as if awakened by objects and furniture from days gone by that a subjective camera brushes
past. They speak of a very united family, of peace preferable to war, of the flame of knowledge. The film closes with this "second" birthday, a surreal moment of memory and judgment. The camera stops at the foot of the big staircase. We hear Otto quickly leave, haunted
by memories. Outside, the snow erases his footsteps; the front door to the Roth's home
appears in the background, as at the beginning of the film.

We will not dwell on the repetitive quotation that Saville boasts having added to the
final shot.[36] However, in this conclusion as in what precedes it, it would be impossible to
ignore the ties between this work and *A Farewell to Arms* and *Three Comrades*. The last third
of the film has no noticeable link to Phyllis Bottome's book, even though the novelist
claimed: "The new incidents invented by the scriptwriter are not alien incidents. They
could have happened in the book itself without violating its contents. In the one or two
radical changes in the film, I think that the greater success sometimes lies with the script."[37]
The final polysemy clearly translates Otto's conversion, a purifying form of rebirth at the
cost of everything dearest to him (the family home also has a white exterior, its door leading to happiness) and foreshadows a secret resistance, like that of Martin. But the symbolic
burial of Nazism (or of what this represents on the cosmic level) first and foremost attests
to the inevitable victory of the snow, of the immortality of the spirit.

Of course these considerations take nothing away from the more concrete, more
restrained level of the work, once placed in its historical context. But it would be pointless
to reproach *The Mortal Storm* for never trying to analyze the how and why of the National-
Socialist phenomenon. The film is consciously emotional and its conflicts more ethical than

ideological in nature. The film is a metaphor for man's inner struggle, and, like unemployment in *Little Man, What Now?* or the social chaos in *Three Comrades*, the calamity here is much more spiritual than simply political or economic (naturally an unacceptable interpretation for a committed Marxist). Its Germany is thus more mythical than real, although in certain aspects, it manifestly attempts to give as faithful an image as permitted by the conditions of the time. Some have accused *The Mortal Storm* of "cowardice" for taking refuge in the past of Nazism instead of confronting the then current reality, which is doubly ridiculous: how then to describe the spread of Nazism (one of the story's merits) and in what way could Hitler's terror be less paralyzing in 1933 than in 1940? Klaus Mann (Thomas Mann's son) wrote that he felt the film "makes us feel sorry for a group of honest and cultured people, but does not shake us up. We do not perceive the horrible cries of millions of tortured human beings in the stifled groaning of a few suffering individuals."[38] This was not the opinion of his companions in exile who exclaimed in *Der Aufbau*: "An overwhelming, captivating film. We, who have lived through a part of the same experience, can confirm to what extent it is authentic."[39] Noted exiled publisher Kurt Pinthus even thought that "this profoundly moving film, nevertheless objective, translates that terror of Nazi Germany in terms of its calm oppression; it is all the more effective for its lack of emphasis on propaganda."[40] To strike the public full force, *The Mortal Storm* shows the Hitler regime's impact on only a few individuals, set in the countryside (cf. Edgar Reitz's *Heimat*). These people must be at once close and credible: an upper-middle-class family (here bourgeois liberals), prosperous, without too many Teutonic idiosyncrasies. The presence of James Stewart, the democratic idealist of Capra's comedies, is in no way accidental. Roth is an "assimilated" Jew, with no choice but to have a hopeful attitude toward the new Reichskanzler. The disintegration of the nation is thus illustrated by the more dramatic one of the family microcosm: the attack on the family assimilates the "innovators" with the barbarians (as did Minnelli in *The Four Horseman of the Apocalypse*). It is the betrayal of an abused childhood which accepted Hitler as a father substitute and rejected the integrity of the family.

The Mortal Storm begins andante, deliciously lingering on the professor's funny little ways (his absentmindedness, his touch of vanity, his fondness for his rubbers). The process leading to a totalitarian hell, then to desolation, appears only gradually and is summed up in four representative phases: the birthday meal on January 30, the SA chant at the inn, the *Gleichschaltung* of knowledge at the university, and the logical conclusion at Dachau: the number of uniforms increases from one phase to the next. As for the possibilities of action in a fascist state, they crystallize around Martin and Fritz. One speaks little, the other a lot; one listens to his heart, the other learns by heart. The first enters into the clandestine almost in spite of himself (by rescuing Werner), his credo is simple and refers to nature: "A man's right to speak is as important as food or drink"; his political activism is a result of his ethical convictions. Fritz, on the other hand, sacrifices ethics for his role in the party. His choice entangles him in contradictions, because he is one of the ambitious opportunists who become assassins in spite of themselves; as the supposed future son-in-law of the professor, at first he is unaware of the brutality of the new regime; he agrees with Otto who says that "men like father are an honor to Germany." At the same time, someone who reasons differently than he is guilty of high treason. Although Roth's best student, he will go as far as to deny scientific evidence (the absurdity of the racial theory), then give up Freya — less out of loyalty to the Führer than to further his career in the Party. His aberration will lead him to kill the woman he loves, but he will rescue his rival. Claudine West said: "It's a picture without a bully. We have done our best to picture him, not as an unscrupulous bully, but as a boy who becomes the tool of a machine too great for him to stop."[41] That is one important aspect of *The Mortal Storm*'s originality: it responds to the horrors imposed by the state not by calling for vengeance (which would be easy), but by praising the generosity of spirit and tolerance of a few isolated people; it even elicits a kind of compassion toward those gone astray who scorn this sentiment. We find a similar approach in *Till We Meet Again* (1944) where — unheard of for an anti–Nazi film at the time!— a Wehrmacht soldier makes the sign of the cross after inadvertently killing someone. Here some of Roth's wisdom is quite fitting: "I never prized safety, either for myself or my children. I've prized courage." Borzage rejects spectacular window dressing and gaudy sensationalism here, evoking the Nazi monstrosity by disarmingly simple means. Roth's arrest is indicated by his rubbers, brought back by the university caretaker; no scenes of sadism are shown in the concentration camp (the dialogue that unfolds there is, on the contrary, heartbreakingly gentle), and even the elimination of the professor isn't shown, but related orally by a biological fact: his heart stopped. However, if the violence often remains indirect, the power of the film language renders it practically unbearable: "What is outstanding about Frank Borzage's direction is its restraint," noted John Mosher. "The cruel story is told without any of the highlights of horror. We feel that what lies behind is worse than what we are shown."[42] In other words: great art.

The film opened at the Capitol in New York on June 20, 1940, the moment that France fell. It was accompanied by an appropriate MGM short feature, *The Flag Speaks* (David Miller) which tells the story of the Star-Spangled Banner and the birth of American democracy. With its characteristic tastefulness, *Variety* remarked: "With the devastating directness of a Stukas diver, *The Mortal Storm* is a film bomb which is about to explode in American theaters. It is as timely as the latest news broadcasts from European capitals, and even more exciting."[43] Bosley Crowther, king of the New York critics, did not lack tact, writing in the *New York Times*: "One of the most harrowing and inflammatory fictions ever placed upon the screen. ... [A] passionate drama, struck out of the deepest tragedy, which is comforting at this time only in its exposition of heroic stoicism.... The most distressing thing about this heartrending picture — aside, of course, from the deep and bitter tragedy contained in its story — is that it reaches the screen so late, so unforgivably late. It is the sort of picture we should have seen about five years ago."[44] However, we have seen what difficulties the project encountered until then, in Hollywood and in Washington. Without wishing to overly praise MGM (which has often been accused of pusillanimity and reactionary conservatism) we should acknowledge that the company pulled all stops to make *The Mortal Storm* a definitive, formidable indictment against the Third Reich, without a lot of fanfare. It was the first of its kind to come out of a major studio, and what's more, did so in peacetime. Frightened by its own boldness, MGM launched the film on the domestic market with astounding slogans such as "A great book becomes a great movie..." or even better, "A Love Story of Today — with the loveable stars of *The Shop Around the Corner!*"

But the film achieved its goal and mobilized people. "What matters now," concluded the *New York World Telegram*, "is not so much the national tragedy of Germany when Hitler and his hordes took over, but how we can combat such things here."[45] *The Mortal Storm* won several distinctions including *The New York Times* Annual "Ten Best" List 1940, The Blue Ribbon Award Badge of Merit (Best Picture of the Month, June 1940), *Film Daily*'s Ten Best Pictures 1940, and the "Canadian Critics Best Selection of 1939–40."

The German ambassador to Washington was very worried: "This film, which is now playing in all cities in the U.S., is one of the best anti–German pieces of propaganda created by Hollywood."[46] On July 9, Goebbels responded by banning all American films in occupied

Europe. MGM closed its Berlin office on August 14, and on the 18th, Hollywood production was definitively forbidden in the Reich. Fritz Hippler, head of the ministry's Film Section, justified these measures by referring directly to *The Mortal Storm*, *The Great Dictator* and *The Beast of Berlin*.[47] In the meantime, each California studio conducted its own little contribution to the news, in general by means of a spy thriller or adventure story: since February 26, Walter Wanger and Hitchcock were working on *Foreign Correspondent*, a work that encouraged Washington to enter the war (United Artists, released in August). At 20th Century Fox, Darryl F. Zanuck produced a remake of *Four Sons* (Archie Mayo) that was released in theaters in May: the action was displaced to Sudetenland, among the German and Czech peoples. On June 23, shooting began on *Arise My Love* (Mitchell Leisen) at Paramount, the adventures of two reporters at the beginning of the war. MGM began *Escape* (Mervyn LeRoy) on July 16, and the same month, spectators could see *The Man I Married* (formerly *I Married a Nazi*) by Irving Pichel. *The Mortal Storm*, however, remains one of the rare productions with Nazism as its core subject. We should also mention that none of these films were financially profitable. Middle America, especially, shunned this Borzage work, judging it far too depressing; in total, *The Mortal Storm* took in only $4,000,000 (a fifth of what *Gone with the Wind* grossed in 1939–40).

Brazil, Venezuela, Peru, Guatemala and Costa Rica rejected the film after injunctions from Berlin. Distribution in Europe was limited to Great Britain, because the rare neutral nations spared such as Switzerland forbad the film for reasons of propaganda. England was openly enthusiastic, and was the only country in which *The Mortal Storm* made money. London critic Colin Whitebait exclaimed: "But this film of Borzage's is so moving, and shows so realistic an understanding of the growth of the Nazi 'new world' ... For eighty minutes [sic] it succeeds in making an air raid or two seem irrelevant."[48] Although not much drawn to Hollywood productions, filmmaker Basil Wright, one of the fathers of the legendary British documentary school, went as far as to admit: "The curious thing is that with all its bogus trappings it almost comes near to genuine tragedy. This is largely due to Frank Borzage's brilliance as a director. Famed for years as Hollywood's greatest tear-compeller, he here uses his powers, and indeed, all his sincerity, in an effort to give a purely emotional picture of one aspect of the Nazi regime ... but within the restricted area chosen the film has an unexpected integrity.... Borzage can direct this type of stuff better than anyone; to the most hackneyed scenes he brings a freshness of eye and a great mastery of technique."[49]

Coming from such an austere, intransigent artist, this is indeed a compliment! Naturally, the film only reached the European continent after the Holocaust. But eclipsed by the ravages of the war and the revelations of Auschwitz, its qualities appeared puerile. *The Mortal Storm* was released in Belgium in 1948, at the worst possible moment, and was judged, inevitably, in light of the recent suffering. On a political level, the war was still too close, and on the artistic level, neo-realism was the criterion. The reaction of the public and the press in Brussels was so disastrous that MGM decided not to release it in France. Ten years later, however, the film was widely acclaimed in West Germany and Austria. It has been aired since then on French television (Patrick Brion's "Le cinéma de minuit," on FR3) with much publicity, allowing the film to be reevaluated in France. *The Mortal Storm* has the painful authenticity of heartbreaking testimony," wrote André Moreau (alias Patrick Brion) in 1976. "Borzage did not want to make this a film with a social message, but we have rarely felt with so much exactitude the disintegration of a nation and the abolition of its human principles."[50]

16

Wandering Downwards with Highlights

As of 1940–41, MGM became bogged down in an unfortunate routine. Management increasingly avoided thought-provoking subjects, which remained the result of specific, isolated endeavors: Fleming's *Dr. Jekyll and Mr. Hyde* (1941), Wyler's *Mrs. Miniver*, Cukor's *Keeper of the Flame* and LeRoy's *Random Harvest* (1942). These were exceptions. From then on, the U.S. economy was focused on the war effort, and Louis B. Mayer oriented studio production to pure entertainment, obligatorily accessible to the entire family (such as the teenage comedies starring Mickey Rooney and Judy Garland), or patriotic and/or anti–Nazi films; after Pearl Harbor, war films exalting the heroism of American combatants were popular. Borzage categorically refused to make films of this genre, or gangster movies. The studio also lost several of the stars who had made its reputation: James Stewart enlisted in the army in 1941, Clark Gable in 1942, followed by Robert Montgomery and Robert Taylor. Greta Garbo retired after the semi-failure of *Two-Faced Woman* (1941), Joan Crawford left Culver City in 1943, Margaret Sullavan only made one more film there. The type of films Borzage made after *The Mortal Storm* reflects this hybrid situation. Romantic elegies were no longer acceptable at MGM.

In the summer of 1940, Borzage was assigned to direct *Flight Command*. The film was begun at the request of the government. Washington considered it urgent to sensitize the country to the preparations of national defense and the honor fell to the most powerful Hollywood studio, for which they received the support of the army. In this very specific framework, the work was no less prestigious than *The Mortal Storm*, at least in the eyes of the Front Office. Robert Taylor and Walter Pidgeon (the future "Mr. Miniver" whom Borzage hadn't directed since *Marriage License*? in 1926) were the valiant pilots; comic Red Skelton made a conspicuous debut. At first glance, film buffs may be amazed to see such military propaganda, hardly favorable for lyrical inspiration, follow the masterpieces mentioned above. However, that would be forgetting that Borzage was still a passionate aviator, and that, also, some distance was vital after the evils of Hitler. Finally, perhaps the previous experience led him to react more strongly to the world menace that was looming. "When altruistic service is the keynote of life today," he said, "when all of us are responding to appeals to stick by our ideals and if necessary to fight in support of them, boy-meets-girl seems far less important. I believe we can afford to take time out from affairs of the heart for a while, even in motion pictures."[1] Who was Borzage trying to convince, as *Flight Command* was far from neglecting the question?

The story was written by a retired Navy commander, Harvey Haislip; the script was reworked by veteran Wells Root (Hawks' *Tiger Shark*), who in turn was discreetly assisted by R. C. Sherriff. A war film for men, which Borzage at times almost manages to transform into a "women's picture." The "Hell Cats," the elite aviators of Fighting Squadron Eight of the U.S. Navy, based in San Diego under the command of Bill Gary (W. Pidgeon) dislike newcomer Alan (R. Taylor), a cadet from the air school in Pensacola called in to replace one of their own killed during exercises. But to this classic situation — an overly confident newcomer learning to fit into the group — the script adds the ups and downs of a marital crisis. Lorna (elegant brunette Ruth Hussey), the commandant's wife, suffers from her overworked husband's noticeable severity, who demands from her what he requires of himself: courage and sacrifice. She escapes her solitude in the hangar of her brother Jerry, an officer secretly perfecting an anti-fog radar. One evening, Alan helps Jerry try out the radar, but the device gives out and Jerry crashes (Borzage always had him hum "Old Sailors Never Die, They Just Sail Away"). Bill, far from realizing the depth of his wife's sorrow ("Hang on to yourself, darling, tight — you've shown the rest how to take it!") leaves for two weeks in Washington. She bursts into tears in front of Alan who finds the right words to console her, and later, to teach her to smile again. The filmmaker develops this platonic relationship by small touches, with his customary finesse and sensitivity; Lorna, now the center of interest of the film, finds in Alan an unhoped-for kindred spirit ("You're so much like Jerry"), while he, either innocent or too much of a gentleman, doesn't realize she's falling in love. Completely distraught, Lorna packs her bags when her husband returns from his mission. The Hell Cats find their commander dejected and blame the breakup on Alan. Outraged, the cadet hands in his resignation. The ending is predictable, but is both sure-handed and suspenseful: during perilous maneuvers (searching for shipwrecks, running out of gas, crash landings, fog, etc.), Alan saves Bill's life, proves the reliability of Jerry's radar and regains his comrades' confidence. Bill emerges from the coma when Lorna, who rushed to his bedside, prays silently, pressing her husband's hand to her forehead. Familiar elements (although ... Robert Taylor without a woman!) packed into a solid action film.

The public appeal of *Flight Command* resided in its rather spectacular air exercises over the Pacific. It was filmed (August 19 to October 11) mainly on the grounds of the Naval Air Station (NAS) North Island in San Diego, with 18 VF-6 biplane bombers; the shots above Coronado Island were the work of the well-known Paul Albert Mantz, an unmatched air stunt champion.[2] Robert Taylor was so impressed he obtained his aviator's license shortly after. Landings and takeoffs were programmed aboard the aircraft carrier USS *Enterprise*, but due to increasingly alarming world news, the ship had to return unexpectedly to Pearl Harbor for maneuvers (it barely escaped the Japanese attack, one year later). Borzage thus delegated a second unit headed by Richard Rosson who worked for six weeks aboard the aircraft off the coast of Hawaii.[3] The various shots are so skillfully incorporated into the scenes filmed in Culver City that *Flight Command* was nominated for an Oscar in 1941 for its special effects. The film premiered in Washington on December 17, at the Pan American Aviation Day, with many uniformed servicemen in the audience. The successive surrenders of Belgium, the Netherlands and France were in everyone's minds. The *Los Angeles Times* sensed the film's topicality: "It is probably the first feature of its type ... and has exceptional news value in the light of events today."[4] In plain words, MGM's tip of the hat to the Hell Cats is intended as a general homage to the U.S. Navy, renamed here "The Maginot Line of America." Hopefully, this shield would be harder to bypass than the French one, should it ever come under fire. By recreating the dramatic conditions of a conflict, with all its clichés, *Flight Command* tried, in fact, to do more than simply glorify the country's defense. Like the White House, it spoke of peace, but was already thinking of war.[5]

Borzage's next venture was a genre he hadn't touched since the twenties, the western. A big-budget western, filmed in Technicolor, *Billy the Kid* was considered a novelty. Designed specifically for Robert Taylor, it nevertheless departed considerably from the biography of the unfortunate William Bonney, and even the name of his legendary opponent was changed from Pat Garrett to Jim Sherwood (Brian Donlevy). The plot is simple: having become an outlaw for avenging his father, whose killer was acquitted, the Kid joins up again with Hickey's band. However, he meets up with his childhood friend Jim, now sheriff, and falls under the kindly influence of farmer Keating, Hickey's enemy, and of his daughter Edith (Mary Howard), Jim's fiancée. When Keating is killed by Hickey's men, "left-handed" Billy is transformed into a merciless killer. Having avenged himself, he refuses to give himself in to the authorities and pushes his friend Jim into a suicidal duel. "But you fired with your right hand!" exclaims the sheriff, to the dying man. "I won't do it anymore...," promises the Kid before closing his eyes.[6] This production, which shows a sympathetic killer, seriously disturbed the Hays Office; a first script was even rejected because it contained too many deaths and drinking binges (September 28, 1940). Borzage's Kid, dressed entirely in black like an angel of death, is a simple, hot-tempered man, unhinged by the fact that his protector (Ian Hunter, the good mystic from *Strange Cargo*) plays the piano and refuses to carry a gun.

Billy the Kid was the first color film to show the fabulous scenery of the Monument Valley.[7] Borzage took a team of 150 to Arizona where he began filming December 16, 1940, mainly in the region of Flagstaff and at Manning Ranch in Tucson (with interruptions due to snow). On the evening of January 12, 1941, after approximately four weeks of work, Borzage, for the first time in his career, had to be replaced. As we mentioned in the previous chapter, the filmmaker then found himself in the midst of divorce proceedings—the divorce was finalized on January 22, 1941—and the emotional stress (probably drowned in scotch) exhausted him. This was a great opportunity for David Miller, until then confined to short features, whom MGM designated as his replacement, under Norman Taurog's discreet supervision; Miller completed the film on March 26, after having directed all studio scenes in Culver City and numerous matching shots with the background projections. It is thus very difficult to assess Borzage's actual contribution to the film, but we can probably credit him with the nighttime stampede, a good many of the corral scenes at the Keating's, the discovery of the bodies of Pedro and Keating and the impressive cavalcades across Monument Valley (in pursuit of the killers). Attributing the remainder of the film is more difficult, which is perhaps for the best, as the film leaves no lasting memory.

At first glance, this professional breakdown did not appear significant; it is difficult to determine whether it affected the aborted project *Bombay Nights, with Joan Crawford, that Borzage was working on in January 1941. For his next MGM production, the filmmaker received a large budget as it was a musical version, in color, of *Smilin' Through*, enlivened by Jeanette MacDonald, the indefatigable singing nightingale. However, this new assignment was not initially destined for Borzage; the production was begun by Robert Z. Leonard, the usual creator of Miss MacDonald's kitsch operettas. The role of the inconsolable Sir John initially went to Robert Taylor, but he chose to leave on vacation. James Stewart was then considered, but in a fit of patriotism (or as an escape?), the actor enlisted in the Army Air Corps in March and had to be replaced by Brian Aherne. The bubbly red-haired, green-eyed soprano acted for the one and only time with her husband Gene Raymond (the roles of Kenneth/Jeremy Wayne). *Smilin' Through* was a meeting ground for old acquaintances such as Sidney A. Franklin and Victor Saville, the successive producers of *Mortal Storm*. The sentimental play by Jane Cowl and Jane Murfin (1190 performances, as of 1919!)[8] had already been filmed twice by Franklin: a silent picture in 1922 with Norma Talmadge (star of Borzage's *Secrets* and *The Lady*), and again in 1932, with Norma Shearer, Leslie Howard and Fredric March. The terrible blitzkrieg that ravaged London occasioned the reprogramming of *Smilin' Through*, a Hollywood daydream about "Ye Olde England," this time enlivened by British, Scottish and Irish ballads, and even by Kipling's patriotic hymn "Recessional." Englishman Victor Saville produced this "third reincarnation" (B. Crowther), which benefited from Technicolor by Natalie Kalmus and an abundance of romantic-pastoral sets in true MGM style. The garden with the weeping willow, constructed on an entire set, was alone worth its weight in roses (filming from May 8 to July 5, 1941). The first week, all scenes were filmed both in black and white and in color, in order to compare the results. Borzage didn't hesitate: "With Technicolor, the feelings are stronger, and the human beings warmer and more lively." Artistically, *Smilin' Through* is successful as the director cultivates its palette: "The interiors as well only benefit from the process [Technicolor]. We have chosen colors with the utmost care, limiting ourselves to the most subtle and delicate pastels. The most important thing is to not make the public conscious of the fact that the film is in color."[9]

The melodrama in petticoats, set in an idyllic cottage in Kent, spans a half a century. It begins in 1897, the year of Queen Victoria's Diamond jubilee, when the old aristocrat Sir John, against his will, takes in his late wife's niece, Irish orphan Kathleen, age five. For decades, Sir John has been living as a recluse, conversing with the ghost of his wife and only love, Moonyean, killed in 1868 by a jealous rival, Jeremy Wayne, in the midst of their wedding ceremony (seen in flashback). But over the years, Sir John is delighted to find Moonyean's features in those of his adoptive daughter. On a stormy afternoon in 1914, American Kenneth Wayne, son of the killer, meets Kathleen in the family manor (deserted since the tragedy), and immediately falls in love with the young woman. Sir John recognizes Kenneth and vehemently opposes their union; his tenacity fueled by hatred stands in the way of his daily contact with Moonyean's spirit. Brokenhearted, the lovers separate. Kenneth leaves for war and returns in 1918, his legs injured. Sir John becomes aware of his selfishness and sends Kathleen to meet him at the station. He dies during her absence, playing chess with his old friend, the reverend. His ghost finally rejoins Moonyean's, who brings him to the Beyond.

Critics have thought they discerned in this work countless motifs favored by the filmmaker, such as absolute love overcoming temporal barriers, the rebirth of Moonyean through Kathleen, etc., and have determinedly integrated these factors in their interpretive designs. This is perhaps a little over zealous, forgetting Cowl and Murfin's play and especially Franklin's sound film of which this version is an extremely faithful copy, going sometimes as far as to reproduce the camera movements and some of the film's sets (the 1932 version was also filmed at MGM). The dialogues are 85 percent identical, although often shortened, no doubt to render the scenes more natural and make way for the movie's ten or so musical numbers. A comparison with Franklin's film is also instructive; globally, the 1932 version is more successful, more alert and inventive, imbued with mischievous humor. Unfortunately, five films prior to the end of her career, Jeanette MacDonald had neither the self-irony nor the youthfulness of the thirty-two-year-old Norma Shearer. Borzage's version is less talky, dramatically tighter, but as if doubly paralyzed by the extra-cinematographic constraint of the play (quite outdated in 1940) and too many singing numbers, the filmmaker contents himself with an honest, heavy-handed illustration, occasionally marred by sliding into decorative sentimentality. A few sequences attest to great talent, although frozen in a kind of lassitude. First, when as if pushed by destiny, Katherine and her imbecilic companion take refuge in the dusty Wayne estate, light a fire in the chimney, discovering beneath spider webs the portrait of the long-ago murderer and are surprised by the enigmatic master of the house; then, when he, having shared a glass of old port with Kathleen, listens fascinated by candlelight, as the young woman plays the piano; and finally when Kenneth returns from the front and desperately hides his infirmity from his beloved, feigning indifference, Borzage surpasses Franklin's version. Franklin seduces by his rather detached elegance, Borzage by his absolute mastery of emotions. The final shots are inventive: on the road from the station to the manor, Kathleen and Wayne's car passes, of course without seeing them, the ghosts of Moonyean and Sir John in their nuptial carriage. A way of symbolizing everlasting love. But the old man lost in his memories of vanished happiness and the ectoplasmic recurrences of his Irishwoman belong to another world. Indeed, *Smilin' Through* is in the vaguely spiritualist literary vein[10] of *Peter Ibbetson*, *Portrait of Jennie* and *The Ghost and Mrs. Muir*, which remains, in spite of its tempting appearances, quite removed from Borzage's universe. The shadows of Pat and Gottfried at the end of *Three Comrades* are not really ghosts intervening in the lives of their friends. We are far from Allan Kardec or Kübler-Ross, for with Borzage, the spiritual is not fantastic or phantasmagorical; it is reality beyond form. *Smilin' Through* opened in theaters December 5, 1941. Two days later, Pearl Harbor was bombed and America entered the war. Aside from the unconditional coterie of Jeanette MacDonald fans, who was still interested in the apparitions of Moonyean?

The Vanishing Virginian is the story of captain, prosecutor and politician Robert Davis Yancey (1855–1931), a citizen and model father of his family although very impetuous, a fiery patriot working tirelessly for the community, whose granddaughter Rebecca Yancey Williams, had just recounted his idiosyncrasies in an amusing biographical novel (1940). The nostalgic, sentimental comedy that Borzage derived from it (filming: September 3–November 13, 1941) may be classified somewhere between an MGM family film, cherished by the studio boss, and Americana, a genre that sang the obsolete charms of backwoods America and whose inspired artisans included such lyrical temperaments as Henry King or John Ford. Evidently this film with its slightly patriotic emphasis was apropos (it often deals with the Bill of Rights), and more or less reserved for the domestic market. The task of bringing this humorous incarnation of national virtue to life fell to the delightful Frank Morgan (the martyred professor of *The Mortal Storm*), while Spring Byington (the unfortunate patient operated on in *Green Light*) played his wife, the continually absent-minded Rosebud, lost in her reading. But after Morgan, the star of the show was Mayer's recent discovery, coloratura soprano Kathryn Grayson (Rebecca Yancey), a rather cold beauty making her second film. Borzage pleaded in vain to Mayer to replace her with Judy Garland, whom he admired intensely. The family chronicle extends from 1913 to 1929, enough time for Mr. Yancey (as his family calls him) to complete his second mandate in the service of the small city of Lynchburg. The film warmly alines vignette after vignette, from the "captain's" bursts of temper, which impress no one, to the vague suffragette leanings of his two daughters (one wants to become a lawyer, the other a soprano), dramas and daily loves, local elections, a trial to save a Black from hanging and the fight against those awful prohibitionists! Particularly noteworthy are the improvised banjo playing on the porch, when the clan reunites, grandmother included, and start singing "Won't You Come Home, Bill Bailey?," and the homily delivered by the patriarch for his black friend and employee, who died of a coronary after having saved a Yancey child from the horns of a bull. Borzage succeeds in serving this up with naturalness, and were it not for his characteristic kindness, we could see vague ties to Ford's *The Sun Shines Bright* (1953). (Francis Ford was, incidentally, in the cast.)

Borzage's next film, *Seven Sweethearts*, was also a musical comedy with Kathryn Grayson, who was on the verge of becoming a star of MGM musicals. A producer of Hungarian origin, Joseph Pasternak, emigrated to the U.S. in 1921, but manager of Deutsche Universal in Berlin between 1926 and 1933, initiated this indirect homage to old Europe. Turning his back on Nazism, Pasternak brought back with him to Hollywood director Heinrich Kosterlitz (who became Henry Koster) and in 1939 launched his brother-in-law, a great comic of German-speaking cinema, the chubby Szöke Szakall (anglicized to S.Z.

Sakall), with his pince-nez. Pasternak made finding European plays and films susceptible of being snatched up by Hollywood industry his specialty. While his ambitions were limited: "never make an audience think," and he wanted "no true villains in my films,"[11] the man had a knack for crowd-pleasers and a weakness for anything dealing with music. At Universal he "made" Deanna Durbin and saved the company from bankruptcy by making use of the teenager's soprano voice and syrupy charm. Mayer therefore drew Pasternak to MGM in 1941 to have him sponsor Kathryn Grayson's recordings. The story of *Seven Sweethearts* was written by Walter Reisch, another emigrant from Central Europe, but Pasternak "neglected" to indicate the true origin of his script: in 1949, Hungarian playwright Ferenc Herczeg would sue MGM for plagiarism, demanding $200,000 for having used his play *Sieben Schwestern* (1903) while he was rotting in a concentration camp. MGM was obliged to pay him a substantial amount.

Dedicated to Holland who "produced New York and the Roosevelts," *Seven Sweethearts* takes place in Little Delft, Michigan. Borzage therefore had a picturesque village reconstructed, with facades right out of *Kermesse héroique* (*Carnival in Flanders*) for $75,000 and filled it with 200 extras in folkloric costume. Shooting was from March 31 to May 11, 1942 (with exteriors filmed at Playa Del Rey). All of MGM's ingénues were brought together (even Kathryn Grayson's own sister, Frances Raeburn) to romance beneath the windmills and gather tulips around Van Heflin, one of Culver City's young male hopes during the absence of Gable, Taylor and Stewart. The plot can be summed up in a few lines: New York journalist Henry (V. Heflin) is reporting on the tulip festival in Little Delft, a place beyond time not appearing on any map; the inhabitants play chamber music in the town square, preferring Mozart to boogie-woogie. The Seven Tulips Hotel where the reporter is staying is owned by the comical Van Maaster (S. Szakall) and his seven pretty daughters. The owner only accepts nice clients, and the establishment has neither telephone, nor room keys and no one stoops to asking for payment. Henry is soon at the end of his rope: "Drifting through the tulips when everywhere else in the world History is being made! What a life!." Billie, the second oldest, replies to him, very aptly: "Maybe life would be better with a little less History?" The reporter falls in love with the oldest of the "seven tulips," Regina (Marsha Hunt), infatuated with the theater; the other sisters all have men's names and wear men's clothing, as their parents wanted boys. But when Billie (K. Grayson), the second, begins to sing, Henry falls for her. According to custom, the Van Maaster girls can only marry if the eldest already has a husband. But Regina does not want to give up Henry, whom she considers her ticket to Broadway. After a free-for-all, tears and some agitated trips back and forth between "New Amsterdam" (alias New York, where the fanciful Regina has enrolled in courses in dramatic art) and Michigan, Papa Van Maaster is finally able to organize the collective wedding of his seven daughters. The poor pastor stammers and perspires a great deal as he enumerates the names of the fourteen spouses: Martin marries Victor, Paul marries George, Theodore marries Albert, etc.!

It would be absurd to see *Seven Sweethearts* as anything other than a pretty but insignificant diversion, served up gracefully and refreshingly. But Borzage understandably was trying to extricate himself from this rut into which he may have been pushed by setbacks, both professional (*Billy the Kid*) and private. Evidently, MGM had nothing else to offer him, or at least nothing tempted him, and in the fall of 1942 the filmmaker regained his freedom.

* * *

A freelancer once again, Borzage agreed to begin a work on a project more technical than artistic and which should be considered as a kind of contribution to the war effort.

Sol Lesser (future producer of the *Tarzan* series) asked him to help with a huge patriotic undertaking: showing the activities of the Stage Door Canteens, cabarets exclusively reserved for American servicemen on leave, who could eat there free and spend an unforgettable evening, hosted by stars of show business. Borzage was a significant asset, as his name opened doors and attracted a multitude of celebrities on the set of *Stage Door Canteen*. Aside from Helen Hayes (*A Farewell to Arms*) and Tallulah Bankhead, another star of the American theater, Katharine Cornell, accepted for the first — and last — time to appear before a camera; Lesser paid the exorbitant sum of $50,000 to the American Theater Wing (which sponsored the Stage Door Canteens) to use Miss Cornell's name in the credits. As he wanted to use artists from both the east and the west coast, Borzage recorded some performances at Fox's New York Movietone studios (West 44th Street), and others at Samuel Goldwyn in Hollywood, an exhausting task requiring 60 days of shooting (November 30, 1942–April 10, 1943). Approximately eighty stars of screen, radio and theater appeared for free; Lesser kept 8.5 percent of the profits for himself, with the remainder of the film's considerable intake — $4,500,000, including two million in 1943 alone!— going to the American Theater Wing.

Delmer Daves (Borzage's accomplice at Warner) designed a vague pretext of a structure linking the appearances and justifying the subtitle *A Soldier's Love Story*. On the eve of departing the U.S. to go to war, four young GIs, nicknamed Dakota, California, Texas and Sunset, spend three nights leave in New York. The small-town soldiers have some time to start up romances that have no future with hostesses of the Stage Door Canteen, even escaping to rooftops after midnight to dream of marriage, despite the strict rules of the establishment forbidding personnel to meet the servicemen outside work hours. The ultimate rendezvous never takes place as the soldiers have to sail hurriedly to Europe. In a final bittersweet scene, Katharine Hepburn consoles one of the girls who was supposed to get married that day (Cheryl Walker) and encourages her to return to work because "he's fighting for the kind of world in which you and he can live together in happiness, in peace, in love. Don't even think about quitting." Aside from its sociological aspect, *Stage Door Canteen*'s major asset is its constellation of well-known faces. Katharine Cornell, in charge of handing out desserts, recites the balcony scene from "Romeo and Juliet" with a theater student in uniform; stripper Gypsy Rose Lee carries meat pies, Lynn Fontanne and Alfred Lunt serve sandwiches, Ray Bolger and Alan Mowbray are the wine stewards, Sam Jaffe interprets for Soviet sailors, Johnny Weissmuller washes dishes, bare-chested. Harpo Marx spies on his female prey by holing up in a phone booth, Merle Oberon, Paul Muni and George Raft haunt the kitchens, etc. On stage, the orchestras of Benny Goodman, Count Basie and Xavier Cugat make the crowd swing, while Yehudi Menuhin plays Rimsky-Korsakoff's "Flight of the Bumble Bee" and Schubert's "Ave Maria." This work was rewarded with two Oscar nominations, for best song ("We Mustn't Say Goodbye") and best scoring of a musical picture. The work is undeniably a curiosity, beat all box-office records for 1943[12] and led several studios to try their luck with All Star Productions. Warner (David Butler's *Thank Your Lucky Stars* 1943), Universal (Edward Sutherland's *Follow the Boys*, 1944), Columbia (Lew Landers' *Cowboy Canteen*, 1944). Delmer Daves wrote and directed himself *Hollywood Canteen* (1944) for Warner Brothers. None of these star-studded features, a rather tedious genre in itself — managed to harmonize the "numbers" and the story (slight as it may be) as successfully as *Stage Door Canteen*.

Borzage kept his volunteer activities going by filming a short feature with the same set in New York for the *American Red Cross* (February 6, 1943). Then he followed up on an invitation from screenwriter-producer Felix Jackson at Universal City, where he hadn't worked since *Little Man, What Now?* Jackson (his real name was Joachimson) was one of Joe Pasternak's German collaborators, brought over from Europe in 1937. He conceived *Destry Rides Again* (a parody of a western with Marlene Dietrich and James Stewart) and was the mentor of Deanna Durbin, whom he married in 1945. Jackson began by following Pasternak to MGM; realizing that the honchos at Culver City "would let six to eight months go by before casting a first glance at a completed script,"[13] he returned to Universal where the work climate was probably less luxurious but incomparably more dynamic. Jackson appreciated what Borzage had done for Kathryn Grayson at MGM and also wanted to show off the vocal talents of his own protégé. Borzage's mission was to style the new Deanna Durbin, now twenty-one, designing an adult profile for her. The change of scenery, in a less rigid studio, was beneficial. While far removed from his masterpieces of the thirties, *His Butler's Sister* is more worthwhile than its title indicates. On the level of cinematographic inventiveness, it's the only one of Deanna Durbin's twenty-one films worthy of attention (aside perhaps from Siodmak's *Christmas Holiday*, a half-successful foray into a dramatic register that she made immediately after). Borzage surrounded the young star with three of his acquaintances, Franchot Tone (*Three Comrades*), Pat O'Brien (*Flirtation Walk*) and Akim Tamiroff (*Disputed Passage*). Begun June 28, 1943, with a comfortable budget (the final scene featured 800 extras), the comedy was completed in September, after sixty days of work without incident.

This deliberately fairy tale-like anecdote ("A Fable of the Day Before Yesterday," warn the credits) is often irresistibly funny. Ann (D. Durbin), a young girl from backwoods Indiana, goes to New York in pursuit of a singing career; an audience with the famous composer Charles Gerard (F. Tone) would open all doors for her. She wants to live on Park Avenue in the sumptuous apartment of her half-brother Martin (P. O'Brien), whom she believes to be a millionaire while he is really only the very privileged butler of, great coincidence, the same Charles Gerard! One of the butler's tasks actually consists of keeping at bay the horde of teenage girls who want to have their voices heard. Against his will, Martin hires Ann as a servant at Gerard's, prevents her from singing (he wants to keep his own job), then tries to keep her away when his boss begins flirting with her. All ends well after a series of farcical misunderstandings and a few songs. The script's inventiveness consists of course in delaying as long as possible the moment when Gerard will hear his pretty maid sing (which occurs five minutes before the end). Incidentally, the two scriptwriters of the film, Lithuanian poet Samuel Hoffenstein and Elizabeth Reinhardt, wrote Lubitsch's *Cluny Brown* (1946), another comedy that mischievously juxtaposes the life of the rich with that of their domestics (Hoffenstein had previously worked on *Desire*[14]).

His Butler's Sister fits into Borzage's universe less by its conventional plot than by its direction. The "Lubitsch-like" presentation of the characters is original: the camera follows Ann from behind down corridors and through the restaurant car of a train, recording the admiring reaction of all the men that the heroine passes. Martin is also shown from behind, in a silk dressing gown, a Havana in hand, a snifter of brandy to his left, ensconced in a stately armchair—but his telephone conversation is punctuated with "No sir. Is there any message, sir? I'll make a note of it, sir." The natural seduction of Ann will be a source of much heartbreak, not only among the servants in the building where Gerard lives—five of the most stylish butlers ("gentlemen's gentlemen") are at her feet—but also among the composer's guests who desert their spouses in the living room to busy themselves in the kitchen! Her most fervent admirer, a butler named Popoff (A. Tamiroff) will unwittingly become the catalyst for the happy ending, lamenting: "I'm nine years in America. Seven of them I spent waiting for a woman. Is this your democracy?" As for Martin's expropriated comfort (he even wears his boss's clothes), it explains why the little brother ends up plotting against

A "Fable of the Day Before Yesterday": Deanna Durbin (left), Franchot Tone and Evelyn Ankers in *His Butler's Sister* (1943).

his bothersome sister. The film takes off from the moment Ann is invited to Popoff's birthday party in a Russian cabaret. Earlier, she had begged Gerard, who was suffering from a lack of inspiration, to not abandon show business. Her dress (similar to that of Trina in *Man's Castle*) reveals her in all her femininity; silence settles around the composer and his maid, foreshadowing the birth of a passion that will blossom at the cabaret. Courted one by one by the five lovelorn butlers, Ann begins to sing at length a nostalgic Russian melody, to the sound of the balalaikas. The softly lit medium-close shots are full of sensuality; the languorous melody reveals her talent to the public and proclaims her love for Gerard. The message is perceived mysteriously: that night Gerard decides not to join his mistress (Evelyn Ankers) in Maine and makes a surprise appearance when the song is barely over. Without a word of explanation, he takes Ann to the dance floor, a bewitching dance that Borzage, decidedly inspired, prolongs with an unusually beautiful nighttime walk. A high-angle tracking shot shows the couple walking hand in hand in the dim light of the lampposts, the camera accompanies them and descends progressively to their level. We realize they've been walking like this for hours; when they aren't silent, they converse about their past and what they have always looked for, a melody, a theme, always the same: "I love you." Excluding the viewer from their sphere of intimacy, Borzage has them walk through patches of enveloping darkness. The couple is at times barely perceptible. They enter the elevator of the building (the camera remains outside), the doors open on the 32nd floor; the couple is embracing.

The lovers walk into the apartment (Borzage follows them from a distance, from behind) and they murmur, walking down the hallway. Once in the bedroom, Ann flops down on her bed; the camera films her from above, reversed in the frame, marking her upheaval. The rich photography is due to the phenomenally talented Woody Bredell, the man whom they said was capable of lighting a football stadium with a match (that same year, he photographed Siodmak's *Phantom Lady*).

Even more interesting is the role played by the music, an integral part of the action: at the beginning, in the train compartment, Ann sings Gerard's tune to a women's lingerie salesman because she mistakes him for the composer, who hears her pretty voice from the platform and searches in vain to find out where it's coming from; dramaturgically, the scene informs the viewer of the young woman's real talent, but at the same time the editing establishes an ineffable link between the future lovers by means of the notes. Back home, Gerard dreamily plays this tune on the piano, secretly observed by Ann (who doesn't suspect why he is playing it). She will sing the tune at this same piano and Gerard, in the next room, believes he's hearing a radio program; the misunderstanding between the two is "visualized." The same melody brings them together, however, on the dance floor of the Russian cabaret, during the course of an evening. An ephemeral meeting, as Gerard has never consciously heard Ann sing (he doesn't notice her own "melody"), is unaware of her talent and flees from auditions, so that music is both the link and the "vertical" obstacle. The two picture abandoning all music when they break up, following a maneuver of Martin who personifies another barrier, of a social nature.[15] Ann enters Gerard's hierarchal universe as a servant and it is up to the composer to establish the "horizontal" equilibrium. This is what happens during the final "Butler's Ball," the servants' big gala where Popoff and his colleagues want to launch their protégé by having her publicly sing an aria from *Turandot*. Gerard has given up leaving New York a second time, but (like Ann earlier, to remain at Gerard's) he must use cunning to gain access to the ballroom which is forbidden to the employers; he passes himself off as the cousin of his own cook. On stage, Ann breaks into "Nessun Dorma," her eyes staring at the ceiling; her invocation of the "prince who'll be her own" is heard. As if magnetically drawn to her, little by little Gerard makes his way through the crowd; she "feels" him as he approaches and lowers her eyes at the last notes of Puccini. Like Gerard descending from his pedestal, she runs down the steps of the stage to meet him, through a human corridor that has inexplicably formed. Borzage films her mad race in a dolly-out shot for almost 20 yards, and the dynamic of the movement gives the impression of sweeping away all obstacles from what the music has just expressed.

It would be pointless to see in *His Butler's Sister* anything other than a charming comedy which the few elements mentioned occasionally transform into a rough outline of *I've Always Loved You* (1946). Nothing dishonorable and certainly nothing to get offended about as did Georges Sadoul in France. "A sinister bomb," he fumed. "Or moreover a ratatouille made and reheated a hundred times, good to turn the most cast-iron stomach. A film to avoid."[16] Was the Communist historian irritated by the light treatment of the social context, or was he perhaps simply in a bad mood that day? In any case, viewers in his ideological homeland did not share his opinion, as in the Soviet Union *His Butler's Sister* was one of the greatest popular successes of the war years!

* * *

It was at Paramount, the studio where *A Farewell to Arms* and *Disputed Passage* came to life, that Borzage finally found a subject near to his heart, one that somehow synthesized his spiritual inclinations and his love films. Associate producer David Lewis submitted to him an unpublished anti–Nazi play by Alfred Maury, *Tomorrow's Harvest*, for which Lenore

Coffee, purveyor of melodrama for the female public, wrote the script.[17] This is how *Till We Meet Again* was born, the most underrated work along with *Living on Velvet* and *China Doll*, but also the most underestimated jewel in Borzage's filmography.

David Lewis first promised the film to Irving Pichel, with Ingrid Bergman in the lead, but negotiations broke down. When Borzage took over the project from scratch, the initial casting included two big stars at Paramount, flamboyant Maureen O'Hara and elegant British seducer Ray Milland; as the drama takes place in France during the Occupation, the rest of the cast was fairly cosmopolitan. The Russian Sokoloff played a French gardener, Russian stage actor Konstantin Shayne (Akim Tamiroff's brother-in-law) a German major, a role he had just portrayed in *Five Graves to Cairo* (B. Wilder). Czech Walter Slezak once again played a mayor-collaborator (after Renoir's *This Land Is Mine*), Viennese Johann E. Wenngraft (alias John Wengraf) was head of the Gestapo, and Marguerite D'Alvarez repeated before the camera a role she played in the French Maquis, a worker in the Resistance. Filming went from October 28, 1943 to January 18, 1944. After six days, Maureen O'Hara left them in the lurch: she was pregnant and her doctor forbad her to continue. Borzage was unruffled and daringly gave the part to a relative unknown, starlet Barbara Britton, whom he had already tested for a previous film.[18] A providential replacement, as the delicate freshness and ingenuity of this quasi debutante (filmed virtually without makeup) contributed enormously to the film's general credibility.

A pan, during which the credits roll, shows the roofs of an old convent, on the edge of a French village in 1943 (the images were shot at the mission in San Juan Capistrano); the day is peaceful and sunny, doves fly around a bell tower, a row of little girls in white crosses the courtyard and garden, led by Sister Clothilde, a pretty novice, barely twenty. The nun stops across from the camera and a master shot shows her reciting a Marian litany that her pupils repeat in unison behind her. Suddenly there are shouts, orders, several gunshots beyond the walls. A few children are startled (medium-close shots) and continue to pray, following the example of their elder who doesn't show her distress but, on the contrary, prays even harder. The war savagely intrudes into an idyllic landscape (the opening of *A Farewell to Arms*), opposing noise to calm, shouting to invocation, dark uniforms to the whiteness of the veil and the garden path. Outside, three villagers destined for forced labor in Germany have managed to escape the brutal soldiers. Questioned by the children, sister Clothilde knows nothing and, moreover, doesn't want to know anything. She entered the convent at the age of eight (after a family tragedy that she has suppressed) and never left. She is the one in charge of the orphans: "I like getting these little ones, they haven't been hurt. At least if they have, they're young enough to forget." Cabeau the gardener, a member of the Resistance, informs the Mother Superior (Lucille Watson[19]) of the three men refusing to work in Germany, hiding in the chapel, outside the convent, when Major Krupp announces himself at the door, accompanied by Mayor Vitrey, an obese collaborator, fearful and obsequious. It's "a mere matter of form" explains the Mother Superior to the gardener, a kind of a game between the Major and herself: he always excuses himself for having to question her, she excuses herself for wasting his time — as only the diocese can grant authorization to search the premises. The interview unfolds exactly as expected; the Mother Superior gives her word that she is hiding no one inside the convent and the officer, who nevertheless suspects some secret activity, courteously departs. Borzage renders the antagonisms subtle: born in 1871, during the Franco-Prussian war, the nun has the courage of her convictions ("I was born to the sound of German boots tramping over France") and the military man, as threatening as he is, does not hide the admiration he feels for this formidable opponent ("One is never through with the Germans," he jokes).

The sun has set. In the crypt beneath the chapel, Sister Clothilde scours the floor on her hands and knees—when from a trapdoor in the ceiling an American aviator, John (R. Milland) appears. From the top of the ladder, Borzage introduces a subjective high-angle shot of the kneeling novice, "chosen" this way by the eye of destiny. Disconcerted, she lowers her eyes. The man must find Cabeau in order to reach London with information about the Resistance concerning "the wall of the Atlantic" (to prepare for the invasion); Clothilde rises, ignoring his questions—"Perhaps I have been rude. Just how does one speak to a nun?"—and ends up responding "as little as possible," still openly turning her back to him. Nevertheless, she complies. Accompanied by Vitrey, Major Krupp returns to the cloister the next day unbeknownst to the Mother Superior and advances toward Clothilde, surrounded by doves. Terror-stricken (like Elsa in *Mortal Storm*), she drops her ball of wool: her inexperience and fear of men make her a perfect victim. One of the novice's pupils is playing hide-and-seek and throws herself on the officer. Krupp stares at her suggestively, suavely praising her fifteen-year-old beauty in the language of Goethe. Clothilde is horrified. If the aviator is not found within 24 hours, threatens Krupp derisively, three of these charming teenagers will be deported: "There's always room in the Reich for healthy young girls." Losing all control, Clothilde runs after him: "And if someone knew where he was ... the girls ... you wouldn't take them?" One "if" too many; even Vitrey is uncomfortable. Although the novice is silent afterward, her silence is a vow, as she is forbidden to lie. When evening comes, the Mother Superior reproaches her this moment of weakness: "My child, what, are you afraid? You know so little of that world outside and yet you find it so terrifying." The

Clothilde (Barbara Britton) leans over the murdered Mother Superior (Lucille Watson) in *Till We Meet Again*, 1944).

convent is the only world she wants to know, answers Clothilde. The nun reprimands her: "You have the inclination to pride. You're proud that you're safe, proud that life can never touch you," then reminds her that in the image of Christ, nuns must also experience suffering. A patrol knocks on the door of the convent. As the Mother Superior refuses to open it, the Germans shoot out the lock, hitting the nun full force. Clothilde takes her in her arms. A soldier crosses himself, appalled. Krupp arrives, furious, places the men who have contravened his orders under arrest, removes his hat and excuses himself to the woman dying on the ground: "A mere matter of form," she retorts, a double-edged reply, as it may also apply to death itself. Then she taps the head of the novice as a sign of consolation — but also of transmission (the composition designates Clothilde as carrying on the struggle) — and murmurs a prayer. Clothilde leans over the deceased to the sound of Gregorian chants; the camera frames the pietà and rises in a dolly-out, in a highly metonymic ascending movement.

On a visual level, *Till We Meet Again* is a memorable osmosis between the filmmaker and his Germanic cinematographer Theodor Sparkuhl, who had long been working with minimalist lighting and expressionistic chiaroscuro. In Berlin in the twenties he was responsible for photography for twelve Lubitsch masterpieces (*Sumurun, Das Weib des Pharaoh, Anna Boleyn, Die Bergkatze*, etc.) and collaborated with Lupu Pick, Dupont, Oswald, Gliese and Robison. From then on (with one brief exception), the entire film takes place at night, with studio scenery, painting and model sets whose poetic potential is maximized by the duo. What originally may have been a response to budgetary necessity is cleverly transmuted into a dramaturgic factor: the night enveloping the action casts a veil of intimacy on the couple in question, isolating them without really separating them from their environment, like the forest in *The River*. The interest doesn't reside in the usual suspense mechanisms, but in the psychological development. This wish for intimacy, focusing on the human beings and the inexpressible is already discernable in the succession of the film's working titles: *Tomorrow's Harvest*, with its activist connotations, to the more biblical *Give Us This Day* to settle on *Till We Meet Again*. These shifts are revealing: seen by Borzage, *Till We Meet Again* is no more a film about the French Resistance than *7th Heaven* is a film about France at war!

The partisan supposed to accompany the American aviator to the coast, passing for his wife, has been arrested. Donning civilian clothing, Clothilde replaces her and joins John under her maiden name, Louise Duprez; he doesn't recognize her, but her face intrigues him. Borzage mobilized Paramount Studio's highest set ("stage 18") for the inside of the 35 foot-high mill, with three flights of stairs; an enormous crane filmed the ascent and descent, which takes on a symbolic dimension. Before taking an identification photo, the Resistance worker asks the young woman quickly wash her face and do her hair (like Janet Gaynor in *Lucky Star*). He removes her shawl and coat; Clothilde contemplates her face in the mirror, disoriented, surprised and fascinated, gradually discovering (and we along with her) her woman's features so long hidden. This reflection in the mirror marks her entry into the world, the confrontation of reality with her own nature (like Joan Crawford's image in a tin of food in *Strange Cargo*). Her turmoil increases when she has to put on a wedding band and at first extends the wrong hand, the right. Now she is a soldier, leaving an ecclesiastic order for a secular one, the "bride of Christ" becoming the wife of an aviator, the guardian angel of the orphans transformed into the protectress of an allied spy. The couple climbs into a cattle wagon and for part of the night is transported through the countryside. Faraway, bells ring for Matins; mechanically Clothilde crosses herself, still half asleep. She opens an eye, discovers the wedding band on her ring finger, sees the aviator sleeping beside her and is wide awake. When a German patrol vehicle conducts an inspection, Clothilde simulates the wife to perfection (John plays dumb). In the early morning, the unusual couple enters a forest. Crossing through the woods—the ultimate daylight sequence—represents the "external" reminder of the convent garden (a reminder that necessarily functions as a commentary). By saving a little bird fallen from its nest, John echoes the care given to the children by the novice. The state of grace she seeks also exists beyond the clergy's jurisdiction, and the groves provide the conditions for a "shared calling"; John opens up to his traveling companion, speaking proudly of his little boy in the United States. Clothilde, who is used to the dim light of the chapel, gets a slight sunburn. Waiting for nightfall, sheltered in the bushes, the American begins to confide in her, and, after months of solitude, speaks at length about his wife Peggy ("the girl next door"): their classes together, their marriage against their parents' wishes, the lipstick she always wore, the warmth of her body. "I miss her. I miss waking up beside her ... miss her head on my shoulder ... the scent of her hair..." Clothilde becomes more and more dreamy, then abruptly refuses to hear more.

Once the sun sets, the couple ventures forth into open territory, alongside an aerodrome allied bombers are using as a target. Amid raging fires, wailing sirens and shooting by the Anti-Aircraft Artillery, John firmly embraces Clothilde to protect her with his body; thrown to the ground, he covers the young woman's head with his hand. The novice is visibly shaken, less by the bombs than by this brusque physical contact. But John is wounded in the chest; she helps him to an isolated farm, a Resistance safe house. She bares the American's chest to dress his wound and spends the rest of the night caring for him. Borzage carves images of incandescent poetry, veritable reminiscences of Murnau, when the young woman fetches water at the well, her hair loose, washes her face and then sits at the wounded man's bedside. In a delirium, John takes her for his wife, holds her hand and begs her not to leave him anymore. She spends a tormented night. At the first light of dawn, Clothilde kneels on the ground, her shawl drawn forward like a wimple. John opens his eyes, finds the tableau of their first meeting and calls: "Sister?" Clothilde reacts immediately, unveils herself, loses her nerve and bursts into tears. The American indicates to her, laughing, that this isn't the time, she has an invalid to care for, and primly puts back on his shirt. "I don't remember a thing," he says, "I hope I was polite to you." "You didn't know who I was," replies Clothilde enigmatically. Now it's her turn to open up (the dawn outdoors is metaphoric): she admits having been traumatized by her father's liaison while her mother was seriously ill (which explains her entering the convent and her reaction to Major Krupp, a father figure). She didn't know a man could be as kind as John; she also feels responsible for the death of the Mother Superior, whose confidence she betrayed by only thinking of her own comfort, and has left the place she held dearest to atone for her error. Could she return? She feels so lost... Regrets are useless, replies John with the same pragmatism as the Mother Superior. He then drifts into a surprising testimonial to married life, which, celebrating the inseparability of holy and profane love, synthesizes all of Borzage's *Weltanschauung*: "You shouldn't [feel lost]," explains the aviator. "God is everywhere. And everything outside the convent isn't ugly and frightening and sinful. Marriage can be the most beautiful thing in the world. It's like finding your other self. Once you've found her, you're only half a person without her." He describes the emptiness he feels when his wife is away, speaks of shared sorrows (the death of a child), the various trivial details that make up life together. "Someone to make you feel masculine and superior and protecting. Although you know all the time that without her, you're not so much... Someone who makes an empty house a home and a home, a haven." Clothilde (medium-close shot) absorbs these words intensely, this revelation of an unsuspected dimension, her voice tight with emotion: "You say it like a litany." "What's that?" "A kind of prayer." Her childhood trauma disappears. The speech is made with so much conviction and commitment on either side that it amounts to an invisible union sealing their new intimacy, which Borzage indicates by an ironical ellipsis: the sun is setting, they're preparing to leave, the aviator drops the ash from his cigarette on the ground: "Oh John!" protests Clothilde, "just after I swept!" John leaves the farm first. "It's a nice little house. I never realized before how cosy a little house could be," sighs Clothilde — and remains back to snuff out the candle. The smoke from the candle disappears into the night; Clothilde returns for a few seconds to the doorstep of her lost "haven," dreaming in the shadows about what cannot be.

The action resumes. Clothilde has gained assurance and initiative. John tires quickly; the couple gets into a bus full of soldiers. But the aviator's dressing comes loose and a bloodstain appears on his coat, at the level of his heart. Clothilde places her head there for the remainder of the journey, her hands in those of the wounded man. The soldiers snicker. "You were frightened. Your heart, it pounded so, that's how I knew you were frightened," she says, innocently, when the bus finally arrives at its destination. The novice has blood on her cheek: Eros and death. The small coastal town is engulfed in fog; there are no more trains; the tracks have been destroyed. The station master, a collaborator, tells Vitrey of a suspicious couple in the restaurant. Vitrey (of whom the Mother Superior had said "our poor mayor stands twisting his hat — and his conscience") risks his neck if the fugitives are not found. Inside the restaurant, a German soldier demands out loud, "A girl who talks!" "They're all the same, those Nazis," comments the waiter. "They try to act like conquerors, but they know that they have conquered nothing. They are lonely, homesick and hated." Losing his patience, the soldier grabs hold of Clothilde and John knocks him out. Vitrey bursts in, escorts the couple to his office and alerts Major Krupp by telephone. John threatens to blow himself up with a grenade, along with his precious documents, but his companion refuses to move away, thus revealing her unexpressed attachment to the aviator, who immobilizes the mayor. The couple takes refuge in Madame Sarroux's laundry, the headquarters of the local resistance. But they have been discreetly followed by Krupp, the head of the local Gestapo and the SS; the Nazis do not want to attack before ensuring they'll be able to get hold of the documents. Sanction of an established fact: "You're no longer a couple," decrees Madame Sarroux, making Clothilde a waitress in the boarding house of the workers building the fortifications of the "wall of the Atlantic," and John one of these workers. Melancholy, Clothilde has changed upstairs, and again wears her shawl like a wimple. John goes into her room, sits down near her, pulls down the shawl and tenderly places the palm of his hand against her cheek. Separation is imminent; each gesture, each look, each word implicitly conveys the inadmissible. The gardener, Cabeau, enters by a window: at midnight, he will wait for the American with a motorboat just below the boarding house and transport him on board an allied submarine. Sister Clothilde cannot return to the convent; the Gestapo has her description. "She's going with me!" decrees John, on sudden impulse. To England or somewhere else, he hasn't thought about it, but she cannot remain here! Cabeau is taken aback and Clothilde replies, radiant: "This time we have spent together, the dangers we have shared, it has made us friends. And its natural for a man to be anxious about his ... friend." While the couple goes away, the Gestapo arrests Madame Sarroux and makes her speak under torture.

Spotted by Vitrey in the canteen, Clothilde decides to warn the American hidden in one of the numerous rooms of the establishment. The corridor is gloomy, winding. A wisp of smoke appears from a dark corner. She runs. "John, be careful!" she murmurs. As the image of the snuffed-out candle signified the end of a symbolic marriage (at the farm), Major

Krupp's cigarette smoke announces the end of a life. (The image itself already indicated danger in *Gun Woman* in 1917). "So our American is right here. Once more, let me thank you!" says the German ironically. By committing this second but fatal error, Clothilde recovers the meaning of her profound vocation, and what follows is less of a sacrifice for sentimental reasons than the refusal to betray her reason for living. Confronted by the Gestapo, she states she can obtain the documents sought in exchange for the aviator's life — if they let her do it herself. "I promise on the vows I hope to make as a nun that I will come back," she adds. Krupp vouches for her: "I know this girl, she does not lie." Clothilde finds John and tells him of her decision to stay. Where will she go? "Where I am going I shall be safe." Then she gives him the ring she had forgotten to remove: "Take this to your wife. She will put it on your finger, you'll wear it always," thus sealing the "alliance of souls" portrayed in *The Mortal Storm*. The second they are about to fall into each other's arms, the signal for departure sounds. Midnight. Clothilde opens the trap door leading to the boat and John disappears from her life as he came into it, except that Borzage inverses the position of the "lovers": now, she is above him, having undergone, within herself, a rite of passage. Going down the ladder, John kisses his companion's hands; the boat pulls away. The novice calmly returns to Krupp, ready to face the firing squad. The officer, having been tricked, is furious. Shot? Martyred? No, that would be too simple: "You're a woman, and quite a lovely one. You can be much more useful to us alive than dead." The thought of seeing her deported to a military brothel in Poland revolts even Vitrey, who threatens the major with his pistol. The men fight, a shot is fired — accidentally or on purpose? — and sister Clothilde, hit in the back like the Mother Superior earlier, collapses on the landing. The visual reminder of the water links her to John: *Till We Meet Again*. Spread out on the ground and lit in a state of transfiguration (the camera rises in a high-angle shot), the dying novice murmurs a prayer of thanks in the night. The camera slides from her face to her right fist which opens in an ultimate reflex, revealing the small crucifix of her rosary. The End.

In spite of its title which implies the presence of a couple, *Till We Meet Again* first translates the specific journey of Sister Clothilde, focusing on the fate of a woman who, in the course of her travels, actualizes qualities inherent to other female models: Peggy (the wife), Madame Sarroux (the Resistance worker) and the Mother Superior (the nun). Borzage doesn't simply illustrate the opposition between a "contemplative" faith (the novice) and an "active" one (the Mother Superior), should these terms really be opposed, but that between a false and a true vocation. Clothilde goes from repression, from blindly fleeing from the world (which often prevents her from perceiving dangers prudently) to accepting it and finally surpassing it. Acquiring this maturity, existential as much as spiritual, is at the heart of the film. Like for Angelina, the scorned orphan in *Street Angel*, blossoming can only occur at the cost of real life and its ordeals. At the beginning, Clothilde closes up like a shell, reciting her litany, when she notices the gunfire, but it is the confrontation (a consequence of her first refusal) with external reality that reveals all her tension and gives way to a painful metamorphoses. Her meeting the aviator — which can also be seen as that of the soul and its physical shell — allows her to recognize and experience love, exposing her to a more universal vision of her journey. A perilous meeting for the two of them (inasmuch as each is "married") because physical attraction is never excluded and Borzage, with the delicacy we know him for, sprinkles their chaste exchanges with subtle ambiguity; John falls unconsciously in love with Clothilde from the moment he discovers the nun in her, and not the unknown Resistance worker. Similarly, his praising his married life with Peggy makes the young woman reel! Their respective paths had been simultaneously designed at the age of eight: she takes refuge in the convent, he meets his future wife. Caught between

A nun that had the American clergy all worked up: Barbara Britton in *Till We Meet Again*, 1944.

identification and transfer, the two protagonists reveal themselves to each other, to definitively realize that their paths on earth diverge. Their relationship nevertheless remains imbued with purity, expressed ideally by Bernard F. Dick: "A purity that never descends to naiveté because the individuals are too intelligent for regression and too serious for passion."[20] Neither is shamed by their shared experience, but, on the contrary, they feel wonder and profound gratitude (Clothilde's ultimate prayer may be understood in this sense). The Hays Office and the Legion of Decency were naturally appalled when the project was announced (March 1943), judging beforehand that it constituted a "great and serious offense to Catholic patrons." And "details suggesting the possibility of some kind of physical love" between the protagonists got the American clergy all worked up. In September, church authorities tried to put pressure on Paramount to block the production. In a stormy correspondence between Breen and the studio, Paramount yielded on a few points: Sister Clothilde was transformed from a nun into a novice, some dialogue disappeared (John: "Life without you — I can't imagine it"; Clothilde: "Goodbye, my love") and the aviator was given a wife and a child whom he loved.[21] Borzage, we have seen, transformed this constraint by magnifying it according to his own criteria.

Considered superficially, the subject could deter anyone not fond of nuns, and we shudder to think of what Leo McCarey would have done with it! The film had "critics" (we hesitate to use this word) who compared it to contemporary films dealing with religion such as *The Song of Bernadette* (Henry King) or the amusing *Going My Way* (Leo McCarey), but with Borzage, the religious never degenerates into religiosity. There is nothing pious or preachy about *Till We Meet Again*, no ecstatic affectations; its character-accomplices follow their convictions to the end, for themselves, without seeking from the viewer anything other than understanding (the same they show to others) or possibly sympathy. We can see how a such story could be a risky venture, but Borzage — as we've come to expect — sweeps aside reservations by his warm sincerity and simplicity, free from any dogmatism or cliquishness. The word "love" is never used directly, and yet this unclassifiable film speaks only of it. We are far from the both humorous and tender duel between the nun and the marine in *Heaven Knows, Mr. Allison* (Huston), at the opposite spectrum of Bresson's tormented asceticism. If pressed, we could consider a simultaneous link to Rossellini and Murnau, with the intelligent, innocent eye of the first and the lyrical-romantic "Kammerspiel" of the second.

The multiple subtleties of *Till We Meet Again* were hardly accessible to the average filmgoer, as demonstrated by the rather cool reception to the film. Inopportunely, Paramount decided to delay release until August 29, 1944; in the meantime, the Allies had landed and a part of France was already liberated. The work was thus reproached for its lack of originality (as of the winter of 1941–42, films about the Resistance were legion), its "reflective moments" that made the action flag and above all its flagrant irrelevance to the present day. Wags spoke of a subject as modern as that of *Marie-Antoinette*. "This film has neither significance nor conviction," concluded the *Los Angeles Times*,[22] a just opinion ... if the viewer is incapable of seeing that it is precisely the film's reflective moments (with all they convey) and its immateriality that give it its true meaning. Some even were irritated by its lack of aggression. In this vein, the Canadian province of Ontario censured the scenes in which Major Krupp showed respect, even sympathy for the Mother Superior: a true German would not be capable of such feeling. Already an indication that *Till We Meet Again* leaves the beaten path.

* * *

After missing the opportunity of working together in *Till We Meet Again*, Borzage directed the resplendent Maureen O'Hara in — who would have believed?— a pirate film in color, entitled *The Spanish Main*. Plunderers of the seven seas decidedly had the wind in their sails: Curtiz's big success at Warner, *The Sea Hawk* in 1940 gave rise to a flotilla of films about buccaneers whose appeal was enhanced by "glorious Technicolor." Two years later, *The Black Swan* (Henry King) at 20th Century Fox paved the way and MGM had been preparing *The Pirate* since 1942[23]; in the summer of 1944, Paramount filled its theaters with Mitchell Leisen's *Frenchman's Creek*, as did RKO with the wacky *The Princess and the Pirate* (David Butler), tailored for Bob Hope.

Originally, production got underway due to the efforts of Austrian-Hungarian émigré, Baron Paul Georg Julius von Henried, Ritter von Wasel-Waldingau, better known to movie fans by his screen name, Paul Henreid. The actor was then anxious to modify his image of the suave ladies' man fighting the Nazis that clung to him after his role as a Resistance publisher in *Casablanca*. Before giving RKO a try, he had submitted a synopsis of *The Spanish Main* to Jack Warner, who refused it ("we already have Errol Flynn"). The head of RKO, Charles Koerner, accepted enthusiastically, as he saw it as an opportunity to celebrate Maureen O'Hara's return to the screen after a long maternity leave. The actress, whose red tresses made the Technicolor explosive, was well-versed in the genre (she co-starred with Tyrone Power in *The Black Swan*) and asked for Borzage to direct her. It was once again Henreid, a close friend of Bertolt Brecht, who introduced musician Hanns Eisler to RKO, cast Germans Fritz Leiber and Curt Bois and demanded that the script of his saga on the seas be rewritten by Herman J. Mankiewicz (the brother of Joe) after the official scriptwriter was fired. Mankiewicz's politicized text emphasized "the pirate's struggle for

freedom" and ended spectacularly with the revolt of the slaves and the burning of Cartagena (the ancient term "Spanish Main" designates the area of the Caribbean under Spanish rule in the seventeenth century); at the last minute the ending had to be modified for
financial reasons, to the great dismay of Henreid and Mankiewicz.[24] The names of Henreid, O'Hara and Borzage still allowed for a comfortable budget; the film cost $1,669,260,
of which $35,000 was for special effects; the shots of the fortress of Cartagena as well as the
naval battle between the superb miniature galleons *Barracuda* and *Santa Madre* were filmed
at the RKO ranch in Encino, in a tank of water constructed expressly for Alexander Korda's
Lady Hamilton. Borzage entrusted the second unit responsible for the fighting to a very old
acquaintance, the famous "Breezy" Reeves Eason whom he had rubbed shoulders with on
the sets of the American Film Co. in 1916. The scenes in the garden of the fortress were
filmed on the sets of *The Enchanted Cottage* (completed three months earlier); the bridge,
the interiors of the cabins and the miniature galleons were immediately used again for
Rowland V. Lee's *Captain Kidd* (alias Charles Laughton).

The plot is classic: The pilgrim ship of Dutch captain Van Horn (P. Henreid), destined
for the Carolinas, is run aground in Cartagena, in New Granada. The cruel Spanish viceroy
Don Alvarado (W. Slezak) has the survivors thrown in prison. Van Horn escapes and, now
a pirate going by the name of *Barracuda*, begins tracking down Spanish vessels in the
Antilles. He kidnaps Francisca (M. O'Hara), the daughter of the viceroy of Mexico and Don
Alvarado's fiancée, and marries her by force. Fearing reprisals from the Spanish, the "Council of Pirates" of the isle of Tortuga traitorously delivers Francisca to Don Alvarado, but he

Prisoner of the Pirate! Maureen O'Hara and Paul Henreid in *The Spanish Main*, 1945.

Women dueling over a dashing pirate: Paul Henreid, Binnie Barnes (foreground) and Maureen O'Hara in *The Spanish Main* (1945).

wants to capture his enemy and has the pirates imprisoned. Van Horn enters the fortress to recapture Francisca who has now fallen in love with her abductor. She helps him thwart Don Alvarado's trap and free the crew. Thanks to a ruse, the couple reaches the high seas, beyond the reach of Spanish canons. With Borzage in charge of the ship, the film's profile was slightly modified: certain characters became more human, others border on self-parody; the fleshy Walter Slezak again played a treacherous, corrupted potentate, a role he had already enacted, but more grotesquely, in *The Princess and the Pirate* and that he would repeat in Minnelli's *The Pirate* three years later. His portrayal is truly regal: cynical, sly, smug and lewd, his tyrant's vices are myriad. Learning of the shipwreck of the Dutchmen, he smiles: "Most inconsiderate of my rocks. I shall have them reprimanded," then drives a dagger into Van Horn's hand. The romantic side is emphasized: Binnie Barnes plays the famous Anne Bonney, an Irish woman-pirate much talked about on the seas,[25] and here rivals with Maureen O'Hara: "A favorite part," the actress remembers. "I trained for several months with a sword-master... I could have beaten Errol Flynn. I did all my own stunts and I went at it so hard, the boys were afraid I'd nick them. I played her repressed hunger for Paul Henreid and her hatred of Maureen O'Hara as something real, gritty, forceful."[26] The erotic component of the story was stressed. Anne Bonney removes her rival's nightgown with the tip of her sword (we hear only the beauty's cry) and suspends this "white flag" from the main mast.

During filming (77 days, from November 20, 1944 to February 22, 1945) Borzage and Henreid took cunning pleasure shocking observers from the Hays Office in charge of timing the length of the kisses. The pirate married the aristocrat in order to humiliate the viceroy. "I've been taught never to mind dogs or peasants," she hurls at him in the ship's cabin. Henreid promises to sell his red-haired prey as a slave in Algiers, then orders her: "Undress! If you don't, I'll tear your clothes off and throw you to the crew." The individual timing it all was horrified and reported the details of this alcove scene to his superiors, "the rankest and most openly suggestive I have ever seen!" With the chaperone gone, it was shot again with its true dialogue: "Put that on! Or I'll throw you to the crew without it" (a line incidentally cut in several states).[27] In the press, Maureen O'Hara attested to an even further state of undress.[28] In total, seven "daring" minutes of the film were sacrificed by the censor, but Borzage included a few master shots of the actress—the pirate has spread her out on his couch, she awaits the supreme outrage—which says a lot more than all the bared flesh. Then, to her great disappointment, the hot-blooded princess spends her wedding night alone... As an aside: it was during an impromptu visit to the set of *The Spanish Main* that John Ford chose Maureen O'Hara to star in *The Quiet Man*. Overall, Borzage emphasizes the couple's ambivalent relationship and insists on the metamorphoses undergone by Francisca, impassioned, to the point where one reporter complained; "There are some fights between ships and several hand-to hand combats, but they are simply used to decorate the love story."[29] What else could we expect from Borzage, whose conclusion is decidedly dreamlike? At nightfall, Van Horn and his followers attack the bishop's suite, disguised as monks and climbing onto the galleon where Don Alvarado wants to claim Francisca. The sequence is bathed in an unreal "Prussian blue," creating an ambiance reminiscent of De Chirico. When the viceroy discovers the hoax, he calls for help, but the bridge of his ship is deserted, like a phantom vessel. He runs toward the bell of the forecastle to alert the fortress which overhangs the creek, when a dagger appears in the night and is plunged into his side; the man totters, rings the bell—the death-knell—and three hooded outlines rise up before him. Paralyzed at the sight of these messengers of death (in truth, the pirates decked out in cowls), he lets himself be tied up without resisting. The commander of the fort observes from a distance how Don Alvarado and Francisca, on the poop deck, are blessed by a priest (in reality Van Horn) and relenting, lets the ship sail. While fireworks streak the sky in celebration of the wedding, the tyrant agonizes, tied to his armchair.

A stylistic exercise or a work obligation? Both, no doubt. Behind the panache, irony and various twists and turns of this delightful swashbuckler, we can nevertheless discern certain familiar strengths. Like Madeleine (*Desire*) and Julie (*Strange Cargo*), Francisca is brought (first against her will) to recognize her true nature and discover her feelings, a process that finally brings about the salvation of the Dutchman, saved by her (literally and figuratively) from Spanish jails on one side, and Anne Bonney's traps on the other. In both cases he escapes the piracy (of all the pirates, the viceroy is incontestably the most fearsome). The disguise allows Francisca to approach the handsome stranger of the beginning (she passes for her lady's companion) and this same strategy will allow the "stranger" to free her in turn. For the theme of the film is liberation: from chains (slavery, enforced marriage), from degradation (corruption, life of plunder). Having arrived peacefully, as a pilgrim, Van Horn leaves covered in a cowl which, by its very symbolism, absolves him of past violence and confirms the permanence of his profound options, glorified by love. But it wasn't these characteristics that attracted the public at large and the critics. Captivated by the infectious enthusiasm of the actors,[30] by the liveliness and the shimmering colors of the adventure, they gave *The Spanish Main* an impressive welcome. Highly praised, the film earned $1,485,000, an amount that rose to $14,000,000 over the years and temporarily saved a faltering RKO. Borzage was once again in the saddle.

17

Republic Studios in Sublime Mode

Republic Pictures was synonymous with "B" pictures. For any nostalgic movie buff, it was the Mecca of low-budget, interchangeable westerns (John Wayne, Gene Autry, Roy Rogers) completed in one week, fantastic thrillers and serials thrown together with marvelously "camp" titles: *Mysterious Dr. Satan, G. Men Vs. the Black Dragon, King of the Rocket Men, Zorro's Black Whip, Drums of Fu Manchu, Captain America,* etc. The company was founded in 1935 by Herbert J. Yates, president of Consolidated Film Laboratories, and its rapid, efficient production, bearing the insignia of the eagle, was highly profitable in the back country. With the boom of World War II, Republic's profits exceeded a million dollars. Actress Vera Hruba Ralston, involved with Yates since 1941, encouraged her lover to finance one or two prestige productions a year, projects designated under the "Premiere" label that would allow Republic to compete with the major studios. To do so, the company sought to associate with veterans who had international reputations, making considerable concessions to do so.

On June 16, 1944 Yates sought out Borzage. At first, Borzage was difficult (in Hollywood, working for Republic was not exactly seen as a promotion) and demanded a three-film-a-year contract with a salary of $100,000 a film plus 30 percent of the profits—at the time, the most exorbitant salary ever demanded by a director in the U.S.! Yates hesitated, then reopened negotiations a few months later. On February 1, 1945 (Republic was celebrating its tenth anniversary), Borzage signed a contract for "semi-autonomous profit-participation." The five-year agreement entailed one film a year, chosen, conceived in complete artistic freedom, with a maximum budget of $1,500,000. Lew Borzage was abruptly appointed associate producer. The filmmaker, whose name in the credits was required to prominently appear with the film's title, possessed his own unit of technicians and actors (unit manger: Gene Anderson); furthermore, he alone could extend the annual option binding him to the studio, and Republic couldn't fire him! Borzage hadn't enjoyed so much independence since the glorious days at the Hollywood Screen Guild in 1933–34. He was now, with Alfred Santell, the company's unique producer-director. Allan Dwan arrived in the fall of 1945 (and remained nine years). Hopes were high and the galaxy of talent recalled the world triumph of *7th Heaven* in 1927 that skyrocketed Fox to new heights. "That's what we're hoping for," Borzage admitted quite openly. "That's what Herbert Yates wants. And I'll tell you another good omen. John Ford, who turned out so many of the early Fox hits, is to be here on the lot too. We're to have a double bungalow together."[1] But Ford changed his mind for the moment; Orson Welles would work at Republic in June 1947 (*Macbeth*), Lewis Milestone and Fritz Lang (*Secret Beyond the Door*) in 1949, John Ford, finally as of 1950 (*Rio Grande, The Quiet Man, The Sun Shines Bright*).

In February 1945, the press announced a first Borzage film, the Technicolor mega-western *Dakota*, with John Wayne. A disagreement between Wayne and his partner Vera

Ralston put a halt to the project, which was then entrusted to Joseph Kane who completed the film in black and white. At the same time, Borzage and Yates agreed on a truly melodramatic subject; the public was saturated with war stories and Republic speculated on renewed interest in films about classical music such as *Fantasia*, *Intermezzo* (Ratoff), and especially the highly fanciful biography of Frederic Chopin produced a few months earlier at Columbia, *A Song to Remember* by Charles Vidor. A sensation at the box office, this film contained long musical passages during which José Iturbi "dubbed" Cornel Wilde at the piano. The invisible virtuoso: here was an idea to explore. Wilde was so convincing that he received many concert offers after the film's release! But Borzage wasn't interested in making a costume picture: too costly, too many constraints. Oddly enough, Borden Chase, a former Brooklyn taxi driver, whose name today is inseparable from the classic westerns of Hawks (*Red River*), Mann (*Winchester '73*) and Aldrich (*Vera Cruz*), came up with the story of *I've Always Loved You*. His short story "Concerto" (written in 1937 for *American Magazine*) was inspired by the career of his wife, pianist Leah Keith, a prodigy who played the illustrious Carnegie Hall at the age of eight. Magnanimously, Borzage bought his short story for $42,500 and hired him as screenwriter, telling him "make me cry." Then, on the advice of musical director Walter Schwartz, he came up with a masterful publicity stunt by drawing Arthur Rubinstein, "The World's Greatest Pianist," to Hollywood. It was precisely *A Song to Remember* that convinced Rubinstein of the opportunities movies offered for disseminating the classical repertory. Republic — the same studio that had made a fortune with the tunes of singing cowboy Gene Autry!— offered him $40,000 for twenty-eight minutes of piano playing on screen, and the famous virtuoso agreed for the first time to work in movies, stipulating that only great music would be used. Borzage asked him to choose the pieces to insert in the film, and even to determine the length: Chopin, Beethoven, Mendelssohn, Wagner, Bach, Schubert, Brahms, Villa-Lobos, with Rachmaninoff's *Concerto in C Minor* for piano and orchestra as the highpoint. Backed up by a studio orchestra with 110 musicians, Rubinstein recorded the entire concerto, then reduced it from 34 to 12 minutes for the playback. Moreover, the pianist "dubbed" the playing of the characters of Myra, Goronoff and Hassman.

The main problem was choosing the actors. The secondary roles would go to experienced actors such as Maria Ouspenskaya (*The Mortal Storm*), irresistible German comedian Felix Bressart (*Ninotchka, To Be or Not to Be*)[2] and his Berlin colleague Fritz Feld, longtime assistant of Max Reinhardt. The key role of the orchestra leader under whose mesmerizing influence the heroine would fall was first offered to José Iturbi (who had some acting experience), but he was unavailable. Finally the coveted role of the musical Svengali went to Philip Dorn, featured in many anti–Nazi films and who was under contract to MGM; practically unknown in the U.S., he was a star of pre–World War II German films under the name Frits van Dongen (his real name was Hein van der Niet). A native of Schweningen (Holland), Dorn had been active in Berlin starting in 1935, appearing opposite Kristina Söderbaum as the young lead in films by Veit Harlan, *Verwehte Spuren* and *Die Reise nach Tilsit* (1938–39). He also played the fascinating Maharajah in the Hindu diptych *Der Tiger von Eschnapur/Das indische Grabmal* (R. Eichberg version): a charismatic male presence indeed! The heroine and her husband were discovered a week before shooting began, after almost seventy tests. Anglo-American William Carter had practically no acting experience and had just been demobilized following an injury in Tobrouk, then taken prisoner by the Germans. But Borzage's proudest discovery was twenty-two-year-old Catherine McLeod. This California brunette, a former extra at MGM, had a Jennifer Jones–like figure and a shy but headstrong nature that corresponded remarkably to her part. Furthermore, Miss McLeod had been practicing piano for eight years. While the hands of Goronoff on the keyboard were really those of Rubinstein, the lead actress, in whom Borzage placed great hopes (her contract linked her as much to him as to Republic), did her own fingering. After Gaynor-Farrell, then Eilers-Dunn (*Bad Girl*), the filmmaker fervently believed he was launching a new couple of lovebirds in the Hollywood firmament. Unfortunately, times had changed and his discovery was no more than a passing phenomenon. Despite approximately twenty films and much work in television, Catherine McLeod was never again as convincing as here, and William Carter retired from show business abruptly in the mid 1940's to go into real estate.

To the dismay of Herbert J. Yates, Borzage erected the most luxurious spacious sets ever conceived in Republic's studios (North Hollywood), rivaling MGM itself in velvet, satin and plushness. The film was budgeted at $1,553,623, but ended up costing close to $2,000,000; shooting required 65 days—from August 6 (a terrible omen: the day the atomic bomb exploded on Hiroshima) to October 25, 1945. This was a far cry from the $30,000 budgets and seven days of shooting allocated to the company's usual serials.[3] Exteriors were filmed at Farmlake, on the private ranch of Rowland V. Lee, near Chatsworth: this friend from the 1910s, who had just taken early retirement (after the failure of *Captain Kidd*), had recently made his land available to colleagues.[4] There Borzage constructed the Hassman's idyllic Dutch cottage and farm. A place to settle down, after the film, he joked! The cost was also driven up by the use of trichromatic Technicolor. *I've Always Loved You*, as mentioned, was the first — and last — intrusion of Republic into the ruinous domain of Natalie Kalmus (afterward, the studio limited its ambitions to the bichromatic process of Trucolor or Magnacolor). To that effect, the filmmaker surrounded himself with two handpicked collaborators: his former cinematographer Tony Gaudio (*Secrets* and *The Lady*, 1924) who received an Oscar nomination for his Technicolor cinematography in *A Song to Remember* and Hamburg art director Ernst Fegté, who had just won an Oscar for his sparkling colors in *Frenchman's Creek* (Leisen). Borzage wanted to emphasize his chromatic tonalities as the drama takes shape. "The color overshadows the plot," he declared. "The use of color is intensified as the picture reaches the climax. In early sequences, the color is delicate. As the action builds, the color itself becomes more dramatic and intense, so that finally the color, action and music rise to one dramatic crescendo."[5] The images of the concert at Carnegie Hall were dominated by purple and black. (The Technicolor laboratories could not deliver copies due to a shortage of film, so the film's release would be postponed from February to August 1946.)

The strange chromatic symphony is part of the attraction of this extraordinary work and for which, we repeat, Borzage assumes entire responsibility. At first glance a pretext for a classical music recital, the film is in reality a visual manifestation of the "concert" of two souls (in its etymological sense of "accord"), magnified by music and color. Due to pressure from distributors and theater-owners, the film's working title, *Concerto*, judged too highbrow, had to be changed to *I've Always Loved You*— a concession to fluff.— Philadelphia, circa 1925. In a posh high society drawing room, illustrious pianist and orchestra leader Leopold Goronoff (P. Dorn) is auditioning young talents susceptible of obtaining a four-year bursary under his direction.[6] The camera moves into this cold decor (stucco, columns, marble busts), full of parents smiling hypocritically and model children performing pieces they've learned too well (among them, a young André Previn). Sipping his whisky, Goronoff coarsely shows his boredom, when he notices his old Viennese friend Fredrick Hassman (F. Bressart) and his protégé Myra (C. McLeod).[7] Accolades and reproaches: long ago, Hassman's career had been "ruined" by a woman, for he married and settled in the

I've Always Loved You, the delirious concerto of two souls (Catherine McLeod, Felix Bressart and Philip Dorn, 1946).

U.S. Although very intimidated, Hassman's young student is not only dazzling (an incorrigible skirt-chaser, Goronoff gazes at her ankles on the pedal), she has spirit to boot! When she launches into Beethoven's "Appassionata" on the piano, the master, like the rest of the listeners, is taken aback and makes an exceptional admission: "You have a great talent!" "She's my daughter," replies Hassman. Dissolve. The Hassman cottage, surrounded by flowers in the Pennsylvania countryside, some time later. We hear a piano (Rachmaninoff's "Prelude in C Minor"); the music is integrated into the environment. Paying a surprise visit, Goronoff has to enter by the window: the doors of the countryside are closed to him. The natural universe of the Hassman's is not his. In fact, father and daughter are playing a duet and have not heard the doorbell; the moment the maestro makes his entrance, Myra is recalling his boorishness. But "Goronoff is Goronoff," his unmatched genius and his musical intransigence make up for his character defects, and the first part of the film above all strives to bring out this scintillating individuality that a slew of adjectives wouldn't be enough to describe. Dictatorial and egocentric, charming, generous, flighty and infantile, this unpredictable, arrogant, absent-minded, cowardly, vain liar is all of the above — in spades. However, when he sits down at a Steinway, nothing stands in his way; as an extremely demanding mentor, nothing escapes him. Music is his ideal. Here we recognize all the romanticism of a certain kind of literature, but Borzage is less interested in this rather familiar basic situation (*The Red Shoes, The Seventh Veil*) than in the conflict in personalities, and even more remarkably, in their means of communication.

The filmmaker sketches his musician with humor: when he boasts of his female conquests, a parrot interrupts him and makes him laugh at himself; Myra is in charge of keeping away his former mistresses (with her fists if necessary) while her Casanova concert player hides. (Philip Dorn delights in emphasizing the self-parody!) Barely having arrived at the Hassmans', Goronoff asks for hospitality for an undetermined time period and cancels his concert of that evening and the European tour of the next day. He sits down at one piano, and Myra at the other, and sleep or mealtimes no longer exist (Chopin: "Prelude in C Major" and "Nocturne"). The only reminder of reality: the noisy tractor of a neighboring farmer, George Sampter (W. Carter), the girl's childhood friend and secret suitor. Four weeks of intensive lessons with the maestro and Myra falls passionately in love, a most submissive lover. "She's mine. I discovered her..." are the terms Goronoff uses to introduce his pupil to "Babushka," his grandmother (M. Ouspenskaya), who lives in a luxurious suite in New York. Myra ("Butterball") is warmly received and immediately adopted by the dowager; the concertos continue on even more intensely until dawn. Other customers of the establishment should be pleased, decrees Nicholas (F. Feld), the private secretary: the music of the divine Goronoff is free, and what's more, they get listen to him in bed! The four tour the capitals of Europe, from Prague to London, then sail for Rio de Janeiro (to the music of Villa-Lobos); George, who remains in constant correspondence with Myra, reads old Hassman about the successes garnered by master and pupil. "Now, the main theme. I am the man," announces Goronoff during a lesson; Myra, her face ecstatic, thinks to herself (voice-over): "And I'm the woman, I love you." But he continues authoritatively, as if he had heard her: "There is no woman in music." Thus begins a cumbersome dialogue about love, constantly referring to music. In Rio, Goronoff's boorishness reaches a new low: Myra is in charge of playing for atmosphere in the salon, while he pays court to a local beauty on the balcony, beneath the starlight. Lost at the back of the image, Myra massacres Wagner's "Liebestod," thus ruining the seducer's maneuvers. Later, she dismisses the stuck-up young woman to whom Goronoff had promised marriage (Goronoff: "Why do they always believe me?") by showing her the ring on her finger, in reality a ring given to her by George and that she removes only when she plays. "That's magnificent!" the musician congratulates her, "Why didn't I think of that before! Now we can get rid of them all that way!" The scene sums up the paradoxes of the drama: Goronoff does not consider Myra as his lover and equal, but as an extension of himself, subjected to his will, one he can exploit like a pretend wife. His hold is such that Myra uses the gift of her longtime friend (a sign of real love) to feign a liaison resulting from her fantasies. Soon after the news of Hassman's death, Myra feels ready to give her first solo concert; Goronoff has her debut at Carnegie Hall in New York, where he directs the orchestra. Not for her, but to show to the world that he, the genius, can "create out of nothing." Her program includes Rachmaninoff's "Concerto no.2 opus 18."

Borzage presents this first ordeal in its entirety (14 minutes), first capturing the nervousness in the flower-laden loge, the arrival of the music critics and the colorful reactions in the balcony where George is sitting; not much of a music-lover, he arrives late. Goronoff warms up the audience with the overture of *The Magic Flute*. After an overview of the room, the first notes of Rachmaninoff at the piano give way to a dolly-in (full-shot of the podium) to focus on Myra and Goronoff, the latter standing facing the musicians (medium-close shot), at the second the orchestra joins in. The dynamics of the continuity and the visual glissandi are organized parallel to that of the musical segments (a technique Alain Resnais would develop), but during the course of the performance, Borzage captures Myra several time in high angle shots, as if perceived by the conductor to whom she seems to reveal all the sensuality and palpitations that sustain her playing. The metaphorical act of love (the piano, whose lid reflects Goronoff's "phallic" verticality, becomes the place of their games) is commented on from the outside; in particular by stagehands in the wings, who notice progressively that the pupil is about to surpass the master. "She's taking over, stealing the show from Goronoff," murmurs one listener, electrified. Goronoff stiffens, his face tenses, as if paralyzed by the passionate playing emanating from the keyboard and incapable of equally matching it to direct the entire symphony. Increasingly concerned, the pianist scrutinizes the maestro who angrily tries to drown out her playing. "Why is he fighting her? She plays well," a critic wonders. "Too well," sighs Babushka. At the climax of the score, Borzage violently juxtaposes subjective shots of Goronoff (low-angle shot) and Myra (high-angle), one in the grips of a deaf fury, trying to impose his masculinity, the other on the verge of tears (she, voice-over: "Don't be angry with me, maestro, don't fight against me please, I love you!"). The stagehands observe that "he's taking a beating from a gal." The battle of the sexes finishes in coitus interruptus, at the end of the piece: while the audience applauds madly, Myra flees. The couple meet up at the hotel; Myra makes herself small: "I know I played very badly too ... you were magnificent ... whatever I am, you've made it"—but the humiliated male chases her away, shouting: "How dare you try to imitate me at the piano? My style, my technique!" Babushka consoles her downcast grandson. Blinded by self-love, cloaked in his own theatricality, he cannot see, let alone accept this kind of crazy one-way love that inflames Myra.

However, the true frenzy has only just begun, for if Myra has fled the hold he has over her, she hasn't broken free. In her native home in Pennsylvania, the young woman sits down at the piano, removes her ring and launches into Rachmaninoff's "Ballad in G Minor." It is dark out. George is sitting on the veranda when Babushka Goronoff arrives in a taxi. She stares at the "nice boy" who welcomes her in the garden and who asks her news of her grandson. Leopold? At that very moment, he is playing Carnegie Hall. Myra, seen through the window, is playing, her eyes closed; she seems absent, like a sleepwalker. In the New York concert hall, Goronoff, just as concentrated, plays the exact same notes at the same second. "Yes, she talks with him," comments Babushka. "Talks?" "Her voice is the piano. She says: I'm here master, I sit beside you, I play as you play, the things you play..." "I don't understand," says George, dazed. "No, you could not understand, nice boy. Maybe Leopold will not understand either. But he will hear her." The rival protests: "Goronoff is in New York." "What difference? A hundred miles, a thousand miles. Walls cannot stop that voice, distance, time, nothing." Impossible to not think of the lovers in *7th Heaven* communicating beyond the battlefield, or the telepathic call of *Song o' My Heart*. But observing that George has deep affection for Myra, Babushka climbs back into her taxi after a final piece of advice: "You want her, nice boy? Then fight for her." George enters the living room and authoritatively places himself between Myra and her piano, breaking the charm. Myra leaves the room, furious. At the same moment in New York, Goronoff, playing passionately, stops clean; he gets up, frantic, announces to the audience that he will no longer play, and then leaves. In the garden, George says to Myra: "You're in love with a dream," then asks her to marry him; he knows of her ties to the musician and that should Goronoff give her the slightest indication, she would run to him. Moved by George's declarations, this "good, fine, clean man," Myra agrees to marry without really loving him... The "blind lovers" retreat into isolation, one in a self-imposed retirement, the other in a marriage of convenience.

After these far-reaching 75 minutes (out of a total of 117), there is a break in the story which recalls the schizoid conflict the heroine faces: from now on, two irreconcilable stories are superimposed. We will not pursue the banal refrain of Republic's publicity ("Can a woman give her lips to one man and her longing to another?"), but we guess in which direction Borzage wanted to orient his work. By tracing George from a Charles Farrell–like character (big and strong, natural, frank, solid), he opposes the healthy equilibrium of a man near to the earth with the destructive instability of the egomaniacal artist. *I've Always Loved You* became the perturbed itinerary of a woman seeking inner harmony, torn between contradictory attractions (a bit like Joan Crawford in *The Shining Hour*). But basically, Borzage does not believe in the fundamental elements of the script and we have the impression that, trapped in a dead end, the artist in him accumulates paradoxes intentionally. Actress Catherine McLeod has confirmed to us that on a psychological level, the filmmaker showed characteristics of both male temperaments represented, at times dominating and unpredictable, at others, disconcertingly kind.[8] The calculations of the screenwriters cannot succeed, first because the downright surreal nature of the Myra-Goronoff relationship has nothing diabolical initially (on the contrary, it blossoms in the most marvelous of music). For the viewer, the eccentricity of the musicians is naturally more captivating than the rationality of a sentimental middle-class colorless character like George, even if we know that Goronoff couldn't satisfy his ex-pupil's aspirations—without giving up himself— and that their union is doomed. (Van Hesling had to triumph over Dracula, but what woman hasn't dreamed of being carried away by the prince of darkness?) Besides, as the man playing George has no acting experience and absolutely no appeal, he is a poor match for his radiant partner. The actress playing his daughter, Porgy, is scarcely better off; her silly simpering airs are so off-putting that we wonder if the filmmaker didn't do it intentionally! In short, the counterbalance made up of Goronoff's personality and appeal is simply too powerful, the comparison too crushing for the film not to founder at the end.

After the frenzied romantic story, there follows a slice of family life. Time has passed. Myra is sewing, while "nice boy" George plays with their little six-year-old girl, Porgy. Lightning flashes, they turn off the radio. At the prodding of the child and her father, Myra goes back to the piano that she hasn't touched since her marriage (but George has had it tuned behind her back). A few chords of Brahms, Schubert, Mozart. A flash of lightning illuminates her window—but also that of Goronoff in New York. "Strange, tonight I feel like playing," he says to his grandmother, and carries on with "their" concerto. Babushka interrupts him, as the woman he loves to madness is married. Impossible, fumes the musician: "She's mine, I created her!" The dowager sets him straight. His only mistress, she tells him, is his music: "Men, women, children all come and go. Pretty faces grow old, pretty hands grow thin, soon one is nothing but a name on a stone. Music goes on forever, Leopold, it has no pretty face to grow old, no pretty hands to grow thin, always it is sweet and fresh and kindly to the ears." This surprising speech makes music at once the symbol of spirituality and the vehicle of love, a rapport that Mozart would have agreed with (cf. the role of music in *Three Comrades*); it also establishes the complementarity between the protagonists, as Goronoff is driven by the music, and Myra, by love. After promising his grandmother that he will not try to see Myra again, Goronoff takes up Rachmaninoff. Babushka dies discreetly, reading the score. Thousands of miles away, Myra brusquely breaks off playing the same piece and declares she'll never play again. George guesses the nature of the interference and reproaches his wife of having given everything to their life together— except herself: "If a man can't have all of a woman, he might as well have none." Then he asks her to continue playing, but this time for him. At the piano, Myra struggles with her obsession and prays to heaven to prevent her from seeing Goronoff again.

Fifteen years later, improbability attains new heights with a totally artificial situation. Encouraged by her father, Porgy has secretly taken lessons with the young professor Severin, an ex-student of Goronoff. Now she is ready for her first concert—at Carnegie Hall, no less! But is Porgy truly qualified? Only Goronoff could answer that. George, who wants to provoke exorcism by confrontation, asks his wife to get Porgy to play before the maestro. Myra, after much hesitation, does so. The magical couple sees each other again: age has no hold on them (as music is spared by time and they "are" their music, to some extent). Myra has become more resplendent, her Svengali even more seductive, and the thrill of their reunion enlivens the film. Porgy's case is settled in under a minute: she does not feel the notes; the master holds out his gloves and his stole, reassures her politely and escorts her to the door, to remain alone with the mother—who refuses his advances but is overcome nonetheless. A change in the concert program: Myra plays under Goronoff's baton. Porgy sits down without a word to her father and gives him her arm. "You say I'm not your master, then play," Goronoff defies Myra, and once again the melody bewitches; but as Borzage no longer has recourse to the division of the first concerto he translates the harmony of its execution by sweeping camera movements. At the hotel, the faithful Nicholas is listening to the radio, identifies Myra's playing immediately and announces the great news to Babushka (medium-close shot of a photo of the departed), whose satisfied expression passes (dissolve) to Myra's radiant face (extreme close-up), like a transmission of powers. Myra can finally see herself clearly. Now it is she who directs the conductor, or as F. Lamster says, "Myra plays *with*, rather than *for* Goronoff"[9]; full of admiration, he capitulates admitting (voice-over) "I was wrong, Myra, there *is* a woman in music."[10] The words are liberating. Meanwhile, Porgy has brought her father backstage. Noticing him, Myra seems to be emerging from a dream, rises in the middle of a movement (Goronoff stares at her, wide-eyed), majestically leaves the stage and falls into George's arms: "I've always loved you!" "And I've always known," replies her husband. This "awakening" itself is completely dreamlike. While the viewer grimaces, strangled by unspeakable frustration, Borzage returns to Goronoff and his musicians, who are filmed until the end of the concerto (the everlasting spirit of music), despite the absence of the soloist, as if he were seeking to deny figuratively what he has just shown literally.

In a well-known essay on "The Spiritualization of Decor and Editing," Belton conceives this ending as "a final victory of feeling over environment," and sees Myra's rising from the piano to walk toward George and Porgy as an "absurdly triumphant gesture": it is as if for the first time she is awakening to the world and her family's affection.[11] This intention, as stated above, seems however to be contradicted by the portrait itself, virtually caricatured in its insipidness, that the filmmaker paints of the little family; George's move to exorcism may also be seen as perverse: the father uses his daughter to force Myra to see the maestro again. But he, like his wife, has serious doubts as to Porgy's artistic abilities and consciously pushes her to catastrophe (Myra speaks of a similar case that ended up in suicide).[12] Finally, the use of the title *I've Always Loved You* is paradoxical: it appears in the final dialogue in relation to George, but during the entire film, it can only refer to the sole liaison truly shown, between Myra and Goronoff! (In the script, it is he who utters the words, at the hotel before the concert.) The publicity of the film also ignores George entirely. The ending thus places the final exaltation at the level of the work's latent content. Fully conscious of the improbability of his story (which Catherine McLeod confirmed to us), Borzage extends the unreality to matching colors, tastefully lush interiors and painted backdrops that betray themselves as sets. Whatever the reasons for the psychological-dramaturgical imbroglio of the script, the film "functions" essentially at the level of fantasy and the violent frustration it provokes at the end is similar to what happens when any fantasy collides with reality. But all these paradoxes are swept aside if we look at *I've Always*

Loved You for what it really is: a film not about music, of course, but a visual symphony dedicated to love, to love in all its forms—its surges of melodic fancy, its vehemence, its states of subordination or possessiveness, its games of complicity and cruelty, its expectations and its fantasies that sometimes collide with a fundamental quest for harmony, refuge and trust.

Compared to the company's usual products, the presence of *I've Always Loved You* among Republic's other productions seems positively surrealistic! The phenomenon is so incredible that R. M. Hurst simply left it out of his otherwise very conscientious book devoted to the studio's history[13]; the film is not even mentioned, while it was the most expensive, and artistically speaking, the most ambitious ever produced by the company (it was shown at the International Festival in Locarno in 1948). The public at large flocked to theaters, but critics in both the U.S. and Europe outdid each other in sarcasm. "So much beauty, and such violent insults to the intelligence have seldom been mixed together in a modern-day picture," wrote the *Los Angeles Times*, for example,[14] and *Harvard Lampoon* gave the film its "Worst Movie Award 1946" (small consolation: it shared the honor with Fritz Lang's *Scarlet Street*). Completely unreceptive to the work's originality, the press of the time, in the best of cases, merely praised Rubinstein's musical contribution to the film.[15] Despite excellent returns (especially in urban areas), the film —which was too expensive— did not cover its cost. Over the years, however, the giggles of reporters and proponents of Kultur gradually were replaced by more subtle evaluations, first in France (the film opened in Paris in July 1950). Luc Moullet wrote in 1962 in one of the rare pieces that *Cahiers du Cinéma* devoted to the filmmaker: "*I've Always Loved You* is perhaps Borzage's masterpiece... The excess of insipidness and sentimentality exceeds all allowable limits and annihilates the power of criticism and reflection, giving way to pure beauty."[16] One year later, in his book *American Romance*, then in 1967 in *Les Grands Cinéastes que je propose*, historian Henri Agel speaks of a film "which by the very excess of its outrageous sentimentality, heralds certain of Minnelli's flights. ... In Borzage's emotivity and the doctrine of the value of suffering, throughout this melodiously dramatic odyssey, there is something so disturbing that we become dizzy."[17] Recent screenings of the film have increased the coterie of fans of "an amazing work, disconcerting at times, with marvelous charm" through which breathes "a wind of madness" (Olivier Gamble),[18] of which João Bénard da Costa, director of the Portuguese Film Archive, is the most ardent admirer: "Truly, truly, I tell you that it's the most hallucinating, most beautiful of Borzage's films, ... the most outrageous ever conceived in Hollywood," in short, the director's "most intense, insane artistic accomplishment"![19] Certain people resist this disarming excess of kitsch coloring, heightened emotions and ultra-romantic music, where Borzage compensates for the lack of strong actors and the triviality of the story by the audaciousness of his creation. *I've Always Loved You* is not destined for a public unaware of Borzage's particularities, but his uncompromising jubilation has something irresistible for the aficionado. We are tempted here to reiterate the assessment of Tavernier and Coursodon, analyzing Nicholas Ray's marvelous *Johnny Guitar*, speaking of one those films "that cannot really be appreciated unless we recognize their ambiguity, the uncomfortable proximity of the ridiculous and the sublime that characterizes them."[20]

The direction of *I've Always Loved You* corresponds to a sunny period in the life of Borzage who remarried a month, practically to the day, after the end of shooting. Even his closest colleagues were unaware of his decision as he kept his private life so secret. On November 26, in Las Vegas, Borzage married Edna Marie Stillwell (1915–1982), ex-wife of comedian Red Skelton whose onscreen debut he had directed (*Flight Command*). Divorced from the actor in 1943, Edna wrote several short radio plays and remained Skelton's business manager. Witnessing the marriage was Ward Bond. But like his idyll at Republic Pictures, matrimonial happiness would be short-lived. Edna did not get over her separation from Red — who had remarried shortly before — just as Frank could still not forget Rena. The couple divorced on July 18, 1949.

* * *

The filmmaker had reserved himself the right to direct one film a year outside Republic; in December 1945, Lucille Ball's independent company submitted to him the Technicolor project *Love's Young Dream, based on a short story by Stanley Corvin. Borzage preferred a freelance project of Ginger Rogers, who wanted to set herself up as a producer in Hollywood after her contract expired at RKO. Her first foray was Magnificent Doll, resulting from an association between the star, Hallmark Productions (Skirball-Manning)[21] and Universal. Novelist Irving Stone wrote the story for the historical melodrama. Stone was the well-known author of several biographies of artists such as Van Gogh (Lust for Life) and Jack London (Sailor on a Horseback), but also of American historical personalities: Lincoln, Rachel Jackson (The President's Lady), Jessie Benton Fremont (Immortal Wife), etc. As its working title indicated — The Life of Dolly Madison — the film had the pretense of illustrating a few episodes of the life of Dorothea "Dolley" Payne Todd Madison (1768–1849), the wife of the fourth U.S. president James Madison. Pretense — for rarely has a script so badly mistreated historical fact. In fact, the film and reviews spell the heroine's name as "Dolly," when the correct spelling was "Dolley." The filmmaker was not taken in, hence Ginger Rogers' remark in her memoirs: "Frank Borzage was a nice man; however, his drinking interfered with his attention to the script."[22] The production itself was sumptuous, gleaming with imposing costumes and sets (cost: $1, 796,000). Borzage filmed from June 5 to August 14, 1946, at Universal City with exteriors at Chatsworth, at the ranch of his friend Rowland V. Lee. Ginger Rogers "borrowed" from Sam Goldwyn the debonair David Niven, her partner in Bachelor Mother; the British actor, mobilized in 1939, returned here to American screens. Burgess Meredith, who played opposite Ginger Rogers in Tom, Dick and Harry, portrayed the other man in the life of the "magnificent doll." While making the picture, the actress was supposedly kissed 361 times by her partners, according to an inauspicious publicity gimmick!

The film begins in Virginia in 1783, at the end of the War of Independence, when landowner Payne becomes a Quaker and compels his daughter Dolly to marry a coreligionist and live in austere Philadelphia. An epidemic of yellow fever puts an end to the gloomy marriage: Dolly loses her father, husband and child. Opening a rooming house (small hotel) with her mother, she is courted by Senator Aaron Burr (D. Niven), a charming but unscrupulous politician, and by Congressman Madison (B. Meredith), a timid, idealistic bachelor. Dolly lets herself be seduced by Burr, but abandons him when he reveals his ambition of becoming dictator of the "so-called United States." She marries Madison and supports his political career all the way to the White House, where he becomes Secretary of State under Jefferson, Burr's arch enemy. In 1814, Burr incites a coup d'état with a private army. He is imprisoned, but the court pardons him and Dolly prevents the impenitent man from being lynched by the furious crowd, which actually violates the laws as the conspirator encourages... Magnificent Doll's major flaw is its disjointed, unappealing plot, strewn with historical characters (Jefferson, Alexander Hamilton, Lafayette) uttering patriotic speeches for or against the rights of citizens, filmed diligently but unemotionally by a tired or powerless Borzage. Many of his tableaux are superbly composed (the nighttime exodus of the people during the epidemic, the pastoral landscapes in the style of eighteenth-century painting) and the filmmaker gives his characters an undeniably human aspect, but the narration becomes bogged down, academic. Strangely, the heroine's sentimental ups and downs pervade not only the film's tone, but also its style: heavy and poignant in the Quaker episode, unimaginatively illustrative with the wise Madison, finally tormented, elegant and inventive when Burr appears. "You have a very odd way of making danger attractive," confides Dolly, both frightened and bewitched, to her concerned cavalier for whom "all the world's a stage." Burr takes Dolly to seedy taverns where his political friends are headquartered, has her watch duels and helps her escape police raids. The couple's embraces are bathed in a diffused, sensual light. The vibrant images translate the power of an attraction which the script can only counter with courageous democratic convictions. Aaron Burr (1756–1836), a complex figure whose true life would have resulted in an infinitely more fascinating film, is misrepresented as a Fascist dandy, promoting an American-style totalitarianism. Perhaps even more topically, Ginger Rogers was a member of the militant right-wing organization The Motion Picture Alliance for the Preservation of American Ideals (February 1944), which organized the anti–Communist crusade in the country and encouraged the McCarthy investigations. Perhaps the Burr of *Magnificent Doll* was the unavowed incarnation of the Stalin-like spirit? In any case, the film lost money. This costumer was a complete waste of time.

Borzage's artistic reverses clearly indicate a slump. The reasons were multiple: first, the director had still not completely recovered from the breakup in his private life in 1940–41. His former confidence was shaken up by his disappointments at MGM; during the filming of *I've Always Loved You*, Borzage, plagued by uncertainty, filmed certain shots up to a hundred times from all sorts of angles. A common practice of William Wyler, but totally unexpected of Borzage. The casting of the film revealed similar hesitations. Furthermore, the filmmaker found it increasingly difficult to uncover motivating scripts that awakened his creativity and were in sync with his sensitivity. Republic was anxious to compensate for losses incurred by the recent musical extravaganza and Borzage feverishly sought a subject to placate the studio. In November 1945, he contemplated *That Man Malone* with John Wayne, in Technicolor; Catherine McLeod and William Carter would round out the cast. The project fell through. They got out of the predicament temporarily, settling on a rather modest black and white film entitled *That's My Man*. The work, a mixture of sports comedy, sentimental sketch and conjugal melodrama, unfolds around the racetrack, a universe familiar to Borzage, a great horse lover. It was filmed mostly in Hollywood Park and at the local hippodrome where Yakima Canutt set the races (October 22–December 19, 1946). Catherine McLeod, still under contract to Frank Borzage Productions, was onboard. She played opposite Don Ameche, the irresponsible charmer from *Heaven Can Wait* (Lubitsch), hired to replace Henry Fonda.

That's My Man begins on Christmas Eve, in teeming rain. Taking pity, a taxi driver picks up Joe Grange (D. Ameche) and his three-week-old colt, "Gallant Man." In vain, Grange seeks a hotel for the night in Los Angeles ("That's the trouble with the world," he complains, "it's full of strangers!"). He has left his accounting job in order to train a horse, his longtime dream, and his landlady has thrown him out. Captivated by his eccentricity, Connie (C. McLeod), a salesclerk in a drugstore, puts him up for the night. The colt destroys the apartment, but the two fall in love and marry. Gallant Man brings them luck: he wins all the races and soon makes his owners a fortune. However, Grange is an inveterate gambler, incapable of resisting a bet or a game of poker, which gradually makes his wife feel an increasing lack of security: she longs for stability. When she gives birth to a son, Grange gives her a sumptuous villa in Bel Air, won at cards. He increasingly frequents the gaming tables at night, forgetting his own parties, New Years and even Christmas. Her nerves frazzled, Connie asks him to leave. Grange retires Gallant Man — and his luck turns. He loses everything at poker.

He runs, however, to the bedside of his son suffering from pneumonia, and watches over him until he is cured. He then disappears to Florida where he begins working again as an accountant. Connie realizes that her husband, eccentric though he may be, has eminent qualities, and sees only one way to welcome him back to the conjugal home: bringing Gallant Man out of retirement, attempting a return to the racetrack. The horse wins the "Hollywood Gold Cup Race," a surprise victory that seals the couple's reunion.

We immediately recognize all the ingredients of a genre whose best-known gems remain Frank Capra's *Broadway Bill* (1934) and its 1950 remake *Riding High*. But like its ambiguous title, *That's My Man* refers as much to the husband as to the horse. As with *Living on Velvet* (1935), Borzage focuses on the disintegration of the couple (what *Variety* unabashedly called "Too much dead weight between races"![23]); Gallant Man is the catalyst of the idyll; his retirement brings about Grange's regeneration, and his final victory saves (?) the marriage. On the other hand, luxury brings about alienation — embodied by the disproportionately huge living room in Bel Air — and separation (as in *Secrets*). A few memorable moments are noteworthy, such as the wedding night in a seedy hotel overlooking an amusement park; distraught as she observes how much her husband is consumed by his desire to gamble, Connie closes the door to the balcony, from where flashing lights of the carousels beckon to the easy life (*Liliom*) and the voices of the poker players on the next floor, to temptation. Grange is suffocating; he opens the window and his wife tries to drown out the call of the outside world by making as much noise as possible. Also notable is the shot of Connie abandoned, asleep among the presents at the foot of the Christmas tree, and the scene where Grange, in a monotone, recites to his feverish son the sad poem "Little Boy Blue" (by Eugene Field). But overall, the film is disappointing.[24]

The next Republic project, planned in co-production with Famous Artists Corporation, created quite a bit of bad blood. For close to a year and a half—from February 1946 to the fall of 1947—Borzage tried to get off the ground a kind of mystical mega-western entitled *Crosswinds. The screenplay by Steve Fisher and Bradley King was based on a Martha Cheavers novel, *Fall on Your Knees* (published previously in *The Ladies' Home Journal* and that Borzage acquired for $60,000); it told of a priest from a lost village of the Far West who was as comfortable with a Colt as with the Good Word. Philip "Goronoff" Dorn was considered for the role of the gun-toting reverend, alongside Catherine McLeod (August 1946); six months later, Borzage entered into negotiations with Gary Cooper and the very young Natalie Wood. A few weeks before shooting, studio boss Herbert J. Yates vetoed the project, arguing that the theme bore too many similarities to *The Miracle of the Bells* that Irving Pichel was directing. Borzage became stubborn and the affair degenerated; lawyers were called in. At this juncture, the filmmaker decided to break off with Republic as soon as he completed his following film. *Crosswinds was urgently replaced with *Moonrise*.

* * *

Moonrise, for the movie buff, is Borzage's best-known work of the postwar period. Although atypical, it was also the director's final big artistic success. A cult film that at the time fared very badly in its country of origin, barely noticed by the newspapers (that called it "slow, mannered and repetitive") and far too morose for the Saturday night crowd! It was mainly in London, where it opened only in suburban areas away from mainstream theaters, that *Moonrise* caught the attention of the new school of critics such as Gavin Lambert, future editor-in-chief of *Sight and Sound* and one of the chief proponents of the "Free Cinema" of the sixties. *Moonrise* "shows that Borzage as a creative personality is still very much alive," he proclaimed in *The New Statesman*,[25] praising the poetic, melancholic and sardonically humorous qualities of a film as "damned" as its hero.

Immediately following its publication (first serialized in *Collier's Magazine* in 1945, then the next year at Viking Press, New York), the novel *Moonrise* became much in demand as the subject for a film. John Steinbeck probably influenced author Theodore Strauss, former *New York Times* drama critic, who in it paints a somber character study against a background of acerbic social criticism. Several companies competed to bring the book to the screen, beginning with Paramount (December 1945), then Garson Kanin for actor John Garfield ("the Jean Gabin of the Bronx"), and finally John Farrow for his protégé Alan Ladd (November 1946). But the tribulations had only just begun and the complete list of the film's originators ("production credits") is enough to throw off the most discerning of historians.[26] The legal-financial imbroglio attests to the new working conditions of Hollywood in the forties, characterized by the irremediable decline of the big studios (antitrust law, television) and the thirst for independence of many filmmakers and stars such as Frank Capra–William Wyler–George Stevens (Liberty Films, 1945), Leo McCarey (Rainbow Prod., 1945), William Dozier–Joan Fontaine (Rampart Prod., 1947), John Wayne (Batjac Prod., 1947), John Ford–Merian C. Cooper (Argosy Pict., 1940; 1947) Fritz Lang–Walter Wanger–Joan Bennett–Dudley Nichols (Diana Prod., 1945), Douglas Fairbanks, Jr. (The Fairbanks Company, 1947), William Dieterle (Pandora Films, 1947), [Elliott] Nugent, [Robert] Montgomery Inc. (1946), etc.

It finally went to young independent producer Marshall Grant, who paid Strauss $50,000 for the rights, then offered $335,000 (plus a say in the distribution and choice of director) to James Stewart should he accept the lead. The star declined and Burt Lancaster was considered as a replacement. The deal was firmed up in January-March 1947, budgeted at $1,315,000 (distribution: United-Artists), bringing together the following artists: John Garfield would play the lead (the son of a hanged man) and William A. Wellman would direct (in the tradition of *The Ox-Bow Incident*). Communist writer Vladimir Pozner, a 1946 Oscar nominee for Siodmak's psychoanalytic drama *The Dark Mirror*, would develop the script; at the request of the censor, long passages of "illicit sex" between the characters of Danny and Gilly had to be eliminated.[27] Pre-production work began March 19, but when the Bank of America (who was advancing most of the money) began demanding supplementary guarantees, the young company could no longer meet its obligations; after having paid Wellman $40,000 for eight weeks of preparations, Grant was ruined. Garfield jumped ship. With a good subject for a film and a mountain of debts, Grant changed gears and sought to entice small studios such as Republic. In October, he found a savior in the person of Charles K. Feldman, a much sought-after agent who had also become an independent producer by inaugurating the "one picture deal." Feldman, an enemy of old Louis B. Mayer and the reactionary tenants of the Hays Office, had organized several successful projects, for Howard Hawks (*To Have and Have Not*, *The Big Sleep*, *Red River*), and later for Elia Kazan (*A Streetcar Named Desire*). Feldman, not afraid to speak his mind, joined forces with Grant and Republic (for operations), then suggested the project to Borzage. This is how *Moonrise* came to be, costing $849,425, the most expensive film made at Republic since the exorbitant *I've Always Loved You*.

As soon as Charles Haas' script was ready[28] (November 6, 1947), Borzage and Feldman worked at reducing cost as much as possible. No stars. Casting included a virtual unknown, Dane Clark,[29] and Republic's prettiest star, the fragile Gail Russel (*Angel and the Badman*, *Wake of the Red Witch*); experienced black actor Rex Ingram — the unforgettable genius in *Thief of Bagdad*, the Good Lord in *Green Pastures*— and the "First Lady of the American Theater" Ethel Barrymore had episodic roles (she makes a brief six-minute appearance at the end). But the main savings occurred with the sets, where art director Lionel Banks accomplished miracles. The action of the film unfolds in thirty different places, 85 percent of which are exteriors. They decided to reconstruct everything in the studio, on only two shooting sets, calculating the slightest camera movements and shooting angles from a very precise storyboard. A first set, 120 × 200 feet, contained a swamp (with a lake and a pond), a fairground, the interior of a manor and an area of the city; a second housed a forest and various interiors. Estimated initially at $125,000, the set, incidentally quite remarkable, cost only $28,000 and the film was completed in 34 days (from December 29, 1947 to February 5, 1948). The role of a carnival barker went to big brother Bill Borzage.

A village in the South, in Virginia, 1932. After the credits, photographed against a background of a puddle of water in which centrifugal circles form, the camera films a dolly-out shot (close-up) of the legs of three men walking. It is dark out, raining. The legs climb a wooden staircase — of a scaffold — and the camera turns away to focus on about ten witnesses with their umbrellas, then above them, shadow figures against a prison wall, the execution. The executioner places the rope around the neck of the condemned man, then the camera pans to the assistant at left who opens the hatch. Cut to: the shadow of the hanged man hovering above the crib of a crying baby, little Danny, the hanged man's son; the camera backs up to reveal that it's only the shadow of a doll swaying, already insinuating that this macabre "inheritance" is tied more closely to obsessive fear than to reality. The soundtrack reproduces, like a leitmotif, the steps of the condemned man, mixed with a mocking nursery rhyme chanted by a chorus of children: "Danny Hawkin's Dad was hanged! Danny Hawkin's Dad was hanged!" Danny, seven years old, in a high, wide-angle shot, is seen crossing a playground, still to the rhythm of the fateful footsteps; the image of his father's legs reappears periodically, so that Danny really seems to "walk in his footsteps." Jerry, one of the kids, mimics a man strangling himself with a rope; a crowd of children surrounds and torments the orphan who rolls in the mud with his enemy, while the camera swoops down on them like an eagle on its prey. Six years have passed; teenagers — still led by Jerry — throw Danny against a tree and smear his face with mud... An execution in shadow figures (this time foretelling the "execution" to come).

Nighttime, drizzle, legs move toward the right in the high grass — those of the adult Danny (D. Clark). The camera follows them a moment, to the recurrent rhythm of the steps of the hanged man, then forks off to the left, revealing an isolated dance hall in the middle of the forest. Behind the bushes, we hear Jerry (Lloyd Bridges) shouting violently at Danny, forbidding him to dance with Gilly: "she's out of your class..." This two-minute introductory montage, with highly stylized images (and sound[30] and optic distortions) translates very compactly the extent of the trauma that will condition Danny's incoherent behavior. Borzage thus chose an "obsessional" language of shadows and light directly stemming from his own silent films (mainly *Street Angel*, 1928), to depict this unreality that situates the prologue in the realm of psychosis.

The tone of voices rises, the camera enters the bushes where a drunken Jerry, dressed in white (the upstanding middle class), continues to taunt Danny, dressed in black (the social misfit, the black sheep): "Did your old man have time to tell you how it feels to drop six feet at the end of a rope?" A vicious fight ensues. Jerry takes a big rock to kill his opponent; Danny grabs it from him and bashes in his head. Even though he acted in self-defense, he doesn't contemplate giving himself up to the police, and hides the body in the thickets, so great his alienation (he believes his past has condemned him in advance) and his unconscious desire for death. Returning to the dance hall, the young man sides with Billy, a mentally retarded deaf-mute, another social outcast also persecuted by the local youth. In the washroom, Danny notices, alarmed, that he has lost his pocketknife in the woods. He joins

Manslaughter: fate or heredity? (Dane Clark, Lloyd Bridges, *Moonrise*, 1948).

again pretty schoolteacher Gilly (G. Russell) on the dance floor, where his brusqueness, authoritarianism and unpredictability draw attention. He then gets behind the wheel of the car to bring Gilly and some friends back to town, unleashing his contained violence on the gas pedal; the image of Jerry, rock in hand, appears to him in the windshield. Increasingly worried, Gilly compares him to an overly lonely child breaking his toys. Danny accelerates. The vehicle rolls over twice (subjective camera), but the passengers escape with a few contusions. Gilly regains consciousness in the arms of the horrified reckless driver: the accident makes him realize the ambivalence of his act — it almost put an end to his own torment, but could have also caused the loss of his loved one.

The script consciously watered down the evilness in the novel: it is less man's "intrinsic cruelty" (in which Borzage doesn't believe) than the memory of adolescent razing that feed his hatred. The ostracism toward Danny is manifested in his sharp retorts to everyone and in the attitude of the girls (moreover, he is poor). Yet his isolation is also partly imaginary, as several characters in the drama are sincerely fond of him: his Aunt Jessie (with whom he lives), the bartender, the crooner, the sheriff and Mose (Rex Ingram), an old eccentric solitary man living in the marshland where he raises hunting dogs. It is said he has read all the books; Danny owes his carefully chosen vocabulary to this black hermit philosopher. Gilly manages to overcome the fear she feels at Danny's mood swings and his aggressiveness— at first she fiddles with her handkerchief (close-up) when he approaches— and her pity is gradually transformed into attraction. When he clings to her in despair, declaring his love, she forgets the boy who asked her to marry him and who has mysteriously disappeared: playboy Jerry Sykes, son of the local banker. Borzage gives no explanation for this sentimental turnaround. However, the obsession that he can never escape from a kind of inherited fatality destining him for the gallows paralyzes Danny's efforts to communicate; he can really only express himself by furtive gestures, away from people looking on, his jaw tense. "Why are we hiding? You make me feel guilty when I've done nothing," Gilly declares to him, intrigued. By dint of patience and psychology, the young teacher manages to "free" him for a few minutes during a magnificent, intimate sequence: the couple meets secretly in the old abandoned Blackwater Mansion, on the edge of the swamp. Night has fallen; the place has neither electricity nor candles. Danny, withdrawn, his movements abrupt, approaches Gilly to satisfy his urges. The young woman fends him off with jokes, by pretending they're at a great ball, addressing the august owner of the premises whose portrait graces a wall and inviting her disoriented cavalier to waltz silently in the shadows. The balm works: to the notes of a faraway violin, the camera rises to the height of the chandelier; the lovers, barely perceptible, whirl in silence in the dusty room; the camera slowly descends again, capturing the dark silhouette of the couple embracing before the window, the unique source of light. Danny's spirits have lifted, and he laughs good-naturedly. "I've never seen you like this before!" exclaims Danny. "I've never been like this before!" Gilly replies. Although fleeting, this is a key moment: Danny, for the first times, sees the possibility of escaping what he takes for fatality, and it is his beloved who shows him this "opening," this alternative to self-destructiveness.

Danny's other haven is with his childhood confidant, Mose, and his dogs, who have an impact on him. For Mose, everything, everyone, is entitled to be called "Mister"—from "Mister Dog" to "Mister Guitar"—for, as he observes with Borzage, "there isn't enough dignity in

The excluded, a recurrent theme in Borzage's work: Rex Ingram, Dane Clark, Harry Morgan in *Moonrise*, 1948.

the world." Along with his great compassion, Mose possesses a caustic wisdom. "What if there's bad blood in me, makes me do bad things?" Danny asks him, prey to his obsessive fantasies. "Blood keeps you alive, it doesn't tell you what you have to do," retorts the wise black man. Once, he took in a tramp dying of solitude. The man had raped a woman and the police were after him: "When I think he got fifteen years for being lonesome, not for having bad blood!" In other words, Mose is trying, indirectly, to explain to him that he is using his "curse" as an excuse; he must go beyond it or else "resign from the human race. And that's about the worst crime there is." But the warmth of those close to him provides only temporary relief; Danny lives in his own prison and he alone holds the keys to free himself. Yet the tighter the noose of justice becomes, the more the "child of the swamps" withdraws into a neurotic silence that betrays him. He always shudders at the kindly voice of the sheriff, and is terror-stricken when a private detective shows up at the banker's.

Moonrise has the singularity of being a profoundly subjective work; Borzage places the viewer in the tormented man's state of mind, seeking to let him share the man's feeling of suffocation. The filmmaker reserves the artifices of the subjective camera for the suicidal moments (the car accident, the fall at the fun fair). He obtains his claustrophobic effects by employing the techniques and values of silent films that the film noir in general, and Orson Welles' masterpieces in particular, were then reviving: angular photography, diagonal composition, marked high- and low-angle shots, depth of field (violent interaction between a face or object in the foreground and background of the image), etc. Danny is trapped, isolated inside the camera's field of view, pursued by objects (mirrors, aquarium) or else confused in an opaque grayness, conveying melancholy. The choice of cinematographer John L. Russell was key to this success: he had just photographed Welles' *Macbeth*. His name appears in the credits of *Psycho* (1960) and in 17 Hitchcock television features. Borzage applies masterfully the strange quality he had always used sparingly and which now must have seemed to him a fashionable phenomenon. However, a double-edged malaise arises from his compositions: while it makes us share in the protagonist's anxiety, it also translates the filmmaker's discomfort with this genre — the psychological crime film, whose morbidity is foreign to him. According to his widow,[31] Borzage had very mixed feelings about *Moonrise*; he considered it a work filmed out of obligation (to free himself from his contract with Republic). He spoke little about it in the press, except to describe it as a stylistic exercise: "a moving picture in sound as opposed to a talking film."[32] As early as June 1945, the filmmaker publicly expressed his indignation at the outbreak of gangster films, attacking, among others, Max Nosseck's *Dillinger*, a Monogram production. His call to reintroduce more vigilant self-censorship regarding criminal violence had caused quite a stir in Hollywood circles.[33] The unwholesome, somewhat macabre atmosphere of *Moonrise* disturbed him, much more so than Danny's pathology, which was close to Terry's in *Living on Velvet* (1935). These reflections explain the strange dichotomy of the work, halfway between the dark romanticism of film noir and drama of regeneration, a watershed of a vision of the world inherently at odds with despair.

Danny, Mose, his bloodhounds and a few hunters track down a raccoon in the swamp; they come dangerously close to the place where Jerry was killed. One raccoon is hiding at the top of a tree; the dogs bark furiously. Danny climbs up and finds himself face to face with the terrorized animal, in reality, himself: Borzage films a close-up of the face of one and dissolves to the snout of the other. Danny gets his bearings, hesitates, then glances toward the roof of the dance hall, visible behind the thickets. Afraid the dogs will look further, but also out of a desire to punish himself, Danny frenetically shakes the branch; the poor animal falls and is torn apart. The diversionary tactic is in vain as the dogs discover the course and the mentally retarded Billy now carries Danny's knife, which has been found. "There's no reason to kick the dog. *She* didn't kill Jerry," Mose pipes up when his friend kicks the animal responsible. From then on, the net closes in, the sheriff (like Mose) guesses everything. Poor Danny loses control and later even tries to strangle Billy to get back his pocketknife. This last explosion of violence conceals another call to death: Billy is not only his brother in terms of harassment; his infantilism and his aphasia reflect his own emotional infirmity, this dark side of himself that he wants to kill (the scene is lit by a flickering lightbulb swaying in the room). Borzage synthesizes the drama of the boy in the film's most oppressing scene, at the fairground where Danny and Gilly go out together in public for the first time. His minimalist sets, his unpleasantly tight compositions, the tragic, monotonous cadence of a refrain of the local dance band recall the nightmarish, dreamlike atmosphere of *Liliom*. Having spotted the sheriff and his wife in the crowd, Danny, without thinking, jumps on board a Ferris wheel where, very quickly, he feels even more trapped. The camera (on a dolly) follows his seat as it rises in the air and stops at the very edge of the field while other onlookers gather. Gilly examines her friend: "You keep trying to tell me something..." Danny finally tells her about his birth in the hills of Chinamook; his mother was weakening before their eyes, but the city doctor refused to go see her and she died. His father took a gun: "It took three bullets to kill him, took 'em three weeks to hang Pa." But imagine Danny's terror when, once again immobilized in the air, he notices the sheriff sitting in the carriage above him. The policeman cannot catch him; the murderer cannot escape. They observe each other, glued to this metaphoric wheel, uncontrollable, and pitiless, like time. This "static pursuit"—which masterfully embodies the fugitive's powerlessness and his persecution complex (for the sheriff is also the image of the father)—for a second time (following the car accident) sets off a reaction of suicidal panic: Danny hurls himself into the emptiness. The subjective camera jumps in his place. The night of bewilderment dissipates; Gilly leans toward the camera. Danny (voice-over) begs her to bring him to a safe place.

"Sometimes murder is like love. It takes two to commit it," sighs the sheriff in discussion with the medical examiner, who says ironically: "You should have been a preacher, not a bloodhound!" "All I know is that a human being and what's made him is a lot more than you cut out of him at the autopsy table!" With these words, Borzage distances himself from the leanings of film noir and indicates his own conclusion (which is not at all "a final morality to satisfy the censor," as some have thought[34]). As opposed to the film noir, for which the descent into hell is a given, its exposition serving as its own justification, *Moonrise* is conceived entirely around a potential "healing," of a mythical journey involving a return to roots.

To say Danny is saved by Gilly's love would be an oversimplification, as the young woman appears to be more of a "reward" than exclusively inspiring his salvation; in fact, her role remains ambiguous, as she is both his reason for hope and the indirect source of his torment, as it is by fear of losing her that the outcast hushes up the facts. Danny takes refuge at Mose's, but his arguments ("You'll have to tell someone ... or else you'll go on killing a dead man over and over"), nor those of Gilly can make him give himself in: "Ain't nobody gonna shake me out of the tree like a coon! I gotta get answers!" Danny escapes through the swamp and reaches the hills of his native Chinamook, pursued by the sheriff's men and Mose's bloodhounds ("I wish they were dead!" Mose sighs). From the swamps, the camera pans to the room with the crib where Danny was born. The grandmother (E. Barrymore) comforts her grandson; realizing the hatred and bitterness he still harbors against his genitor (which prevents him from accepting himself), she speaks to him at length about his father, his goodness, his zest for life, but also about his concern for the baby's future. Despite the tragedy, she always refused to change Danny's family name, because she is proud of it. Her son took responsibility for his actions, found his own answers. Danny spends the night in the blockhouse; at dawn he comes out with a gun. The sun is shining. "The coward blames what he does on other folks," his grandmother reminds him. Danny stops before his father's gravestone; the camera markedly focuses on the inscription "May he rest in Peace." The young man leans his gun against the stone and walks down, unarmed, to meet the sheriff. Smiling, almost radiant, he pets one of Mose's dogs. Gilly emerges from the woods. The sheriff forbids them to handcuff the fugitive: "Let him walk back like a man." Danny and Gilly walk away, in each other's arms, "to rejoin the human race" (says Mose). The last composition is a master shot: the space has expanded, showing a horizon of sunny plains and valleys; the depth of the image conveys a feeling of freedom and serenity.

Formally this ending is the exact "positive" reflection of the prologue. The aspect of the bizarre gives way to clarity both in tone and narration. The repetitive mental images, division of time, surprise effects and misleading clues (the doll) have vanished and are replaced by a visual language, extremely simple and clear: as with Griffith or King Vidor, obviousness is transformed into lyricism. (A process completely at odds with the fastidious psychoanalytic explanations that forties' films adored.) From the unidirectional shots at the beginning (walking in front of the "dead end" of the camera) the movements become varied at the end, the characters disperse in the field. The couple goes away, the sheriff and his men have preceded them and are no longer visible, and Mose stays behind with his dogs. From the initial "oppressive" high-angle shots with the camera focused on feet, stagnant water and mud (symbols of a contaminated soul), Borzage responds by low-angle shots revealing Danny's moral value (the "dignity" Mose holds dear) and showing the sky for the first time. The swamps disappear from the field; the forest opens. The night of execution at the prison walls is replaced by the morning illuminated in unspoiled nature. This brightening of images corresponds to the essence itself of the process of identification; from an anonymous shadow on a slimy wall, the "damned" father has finally become the human being whose photo Danny contemplates in a newspaper clipping at his grandmother's. By reintegrating into society (by turning himself into the authorities whom we sense will be indulgent), the touchy, evasive boy becomes a man; he performs his first voluntary act. In *Moonrise*, the anti-hero's inner journey is strictly psychological. But the intelligence and concision of the direction broaden its scope considerably, to such an extent that David Kehr (in a remarkable essay on the film) declares: "Borzage makes the clearest statement of his career, his testament so to speak." In fact, the structure and visual style of *Moonrise* meld together to constitute "a formal assault against all naturalistic philosophy,"[35] thus negating the narrow determinism resulting from it. This point of view was foreign, if not indifferent, to viewers in the postwar era, but proves to what extent the filmmaker remains true to himself.

At an era when Borzage's reputation had noticeably diminished, *Moonrise* (released in March 1949) shows him once again in top form. At that moment the director chose to retire from the movies for close to ten years.

18

In Semi-Retirement

In 1948, Borzage ended his association with Republic Pictures and, without further explanation, retired from movies until 1957. Much has been speculated about this long absence from the screen, and the lack of information helped foster the most farfetched hypotheses. After *Moonrise* was screened in Paris, Ado Kyrou, carried away by his own romantic imagination, wrote: "Borzage's usual melancholy here is tinged with pessimism. The couple is still caressed by poetry, but his heroes bear the mark of failure. I watched this film with tears in my eyes. It is the protest of a proud man betrayed both by the movies and life itself."[1] The legend of the "cursed filmmaker" was born. Drinking, which plagued the sets of Hollywood, was wrongly suspected as having played a role in the director's stopping work. According to his close relations, this may have been a paralyzing factor between 1940 and 1942, but Borzage recovered eventually at the end of the decade. Others, in the U.S., have gone as far as to find political reasons: "*Moonrise* is the last film Frank Borzage completed before the blacklist forced him into a ten-year period of inactivity," wrote David Kehr, an aberrant claim reiterated in several British and American works.[2] It is plausible that the paranoid climate instituted by the anti–Communist inquiries of the House UnAmerican Activities Committee as of May 1947 did not encourage him to remain in the studios. But Borzage, politically a Republican (like Ford and Wellman), could not have been worried by any of his films or associations. We do know that he distanced himself from the "witch-hunt" and was one of the eight courageous directors[3] who refused to sign Cecil B. DeMille's petition aiming to strip "leftist" Joseph L. Mankiewicz of the presidency of the Screen Directors Guild of America, during the stormy meeting of October 22, 1950. While fundamentally conservative, Borzage was intelligent and honest enough to differentiate between generosity, social commitment and Joseph Stalin!

The truth about Borzage's inactivity is much more prosaic: the filmmaker was completely at odds with postwar Hollywood, whose production methods and fashionable themes he considered pointlessly depressing and cynical. Moreover, the slow disappearance of the studio system made for a more aggressive work climate, and Borzage's personality was not combative. On March 24, 1949, he took part in the Oscar ceremony and personally presented the golden trophy to John Huston for *Treasure of the Sierra Madre*—a way of passing on the flame to the next generation. Borzage was fortunate in that he could afford not to work. He had gotten rid of his status symbols of yesteryear: the airplane had been sold at the beginning of the war, John Wayne bought the yacht *Athena* and in 1948, the famous 19 Arabian polo horses found shelter at Fred MacMurray's ranch in northern California. The filmmaker invested a great deal in real estate and with Red Skelton owned the luxurious rental building *Wilshire Palms* (on Wilshire Blvd.), at one time occupied by Ava Gardner and Mickey Rooney. He was president and co-owner of the *California Club Cabana* in Santa Monica (along with Johnny Weissmuller, Fred MacMurray, Ann Dvorak and Robert

Walker). Borzage thus devoted himself to his favorite sports and hobbies, mainly golf on the links of the Lakeside Golf Club, in Palm Springs at Charles Farrell's, and at the California Country Club in Culver City, which he also owned with Fred MacMurray, John Wayne, Mitchell Leisen and Bo Roos. His passion for golf would occupy him full-time. In 1947 he launched the "Frank Borzage Annual Movie Golf Tournament" at the Rolling Hills Country Club, a tournament for charity in which all of moviedom took part; for a dollar entry fee, the public could watch Linda Darnell, Fred Astaire and Adolphe Menjou on the fairways. A short feature in Technicolor, *Rough But Hopeful* (Courneya Hyde Productions), attests to the event. Among other philanthropic activities—as part of the Masonic Shriners—Borzage financed the wing of a pediatric clinic. Borzage's active affiliation with the Shriners—a charitable organization devoted to helping burned or disabled children, and unhappy childhood in general, in retrospect sheds light on one of the filmmaker's less well-known concerns. We mentioned his regret at not having children (one of the issues with Rena), as well as his commitment to his nieces and nephews. We now better understand the marked intensity of numerous sequences in his filmography dealing with misunderstood children (*Humoresque, Daddy's Gone-a-Hunting*), orphans (*Lazybones, Children of Dust*), delinquents (*Toton, Young America*) and those scandalously manipulated by adults (*No Greater Glory, The Day I Met Caruso*).

His circle of faithful friends (and naturally, golf partners) of this last decade was made up of Mary and Tay Garnett, Ozayda and Rouben Mamoulian, Dolly and William A. Wellman, Molly and Joe Youngerman, Lillian and George Sidney, Pilar and John Wayne, and cinematographer William Daniels. The postwar period also brought happy changes to his private life. In 1948, at the California Country Club, while he and Edna Stillwell were in the midst of divorce proceedings, Borzage met Juanita ("Nita") Scott, a young accountant of Germanic-Irish descent working in television. She exerted a positive influence: he gradually gave up drinking following a few stays at a San Diego detoxification clinic. Finally, on June 16, 1953 in Las Vegas, Borzage married the woman who would be the companion of his last years. Witnesses included Mr. and Mrs. Johnny Weissmuller. The couple settled into a comfortable villa at 1206 Malcolm Avenue, in West Los Angeles (they moved to 10827 Wilshire Boulevard later in the fifties).

However, the filmmaker did not consider himself retired for good. "But there was quite a spell there," he told George Pratt in 1958 (op. cit.), "where all it seemed that the industry wanted was these psychological dramas and the gangster pictures I don't really like, I don't believe in. So I turned down one script after another and finally started playing golf—and you know how time flies when you play golf! And this goes from day to day, week to week, six years, seven years." Interviewed by the *New York Times* in September 1957, he elaborated: "I won't say that golf is a substitute for directing, but I did get in a lot of time on the links. The main reason for my inactivity, however, has been that I haven't been able to find a suitable story. The motion picture industry is a frightened industry. I don't know why it's frightened, but the product reflects fear. There are just too many psychological pictures, too many mysteries and pictures consisting solely of sentimental goo."[4] Each morning, the director stopped by his office at "Frank Borzage Productions" in North Hollywood to discuss possible subjects for movies and offers from various studios with Lew. In May 1952, he told the press of a project originally named *California Quartet*, an adaptation of four American short stories whose author-scriptwriters, including William Saroyan ("The Pheasant Hunter"), Joseph Petracca ("Adios Muchachos") and John Fante ("The Dreamer")—wanted a share in the profits.[5] But financing never materialized.

Borzage was in Argentina in March 1954, where, along with Mary Pickford, he was

part of the jury of the Gran Festival Internacional Cinematografico in Buenos Aires. Returning from a tour as a representative of the movies in several Latin American capitals, he
observed that "Hollywood motion pictures still are the free world's greatest weapon in the
cold war against international Communism. The high standards of living, the sacred heritage of freedom and the happiness and high spirits of people living under a democratic
rule, which our movies reflect, are doing a remarkable job in turning misguided masses
away from the brainwashing tactics of Soviet foreign agents."[6] The same year in May, Nita
and Frank Borzage were the guests of honor at the "Film Festival in Southeast Asia," held
in Tokyo; they stayed in Japan three months and notably toured the film studios of Kyoto.
Ceremonial awards arrived later in life: in October 1955, the Festival of Film Artists organized by the Film Archives of George Eastman House in Rochester, N.Y., held a small retrospective and honored Borzage for the first decade of his career with the George Eastman
Award for 1915–1925. The George Eastman Award for 1926–1930 followed two years later.

Television also came his way, after a false start in 1950: NBC had proposed he direct
the program Masterpiece Playhouse, specializing in dramas by Shakespeare, Wilde,
Chekhov, etc. Poorly advised by his administrator, Bo Roos, Borzage had refused. In 1955
another deal surfaced, when NBC began working on a series of 35 25-minute television
dramas brought together under the label of Screen Directors Playhouse, to be aired between
May 1955 and December 1956. This exceptional series, sponsored by Eastman Kodak, was
produced by the Screen Directors Guild of America in association with Hal Roach with the
goal of creating a contingency fund for colleagues. It stands out from other televised
anthologies of the time as its episodes were all selected and directed on a volunteer basis
by film directors (and important ones): for some, it was their only foray into television.
Leo McCarey, John Brahm and George Waggner directed two episodes; John Ford, Raoul
Walsh, Allan Dwan, Fred Zinnemann, William Dieterle, Henry C. Potter, William Seiter,
Norman Z. McLeod, George Marshall, Ted Tetzlaff, Ida Lupino, David Butler, George Sherman, Byron Haskin, Claude Binyon, Frank Tuttle, Hugo Haas, Lewis Allen, Gower Cham-
pion, John Rich and Ted Post each directed one; Tay Garnett and Borzage directed three.
Almost all were filmed in the Hal Roach's Culver City studios, on a budget of approximately
$50,000 each.

Borzage's first episode is the least interesting of the three. Day Is Done (filming: August
23–26, 1955) takes place during the Korean War, in the spring of 1951. The morale of the
American troops is low. Zane (Bobby Driscoll), a young recruit, finds a bugle on a corpse
during a nighttime mission behind enemy lines. Sergeant Norris (Rory Calhoun), a fervent fan of the instrument, encourages him to play to raise servicemen's spirits and befriends
the rookie. During a massive attack by the Chinese, the GIs remain paralyzed in their
trenches until Norris sounds the charge of the bugle, as did Custer's 7th Cavalry long ago.
The enemy is driven away and Norris killed. Zane searches for his body on the battlefield
and plays in his honor. Two friends linked by a talismanic bugle; a subject better suited
for Raoul Walsh.

Borzage took over shooting of the much more successful A Ticket for Thaddeus (April
10–14, 1956) after Ray Milland backed out. Tay Garnett photographed the filmmaker on
his director's chair in the sequence before the credits. A. I. Bezzerides (Kiss Me Deadly)
wrote the script and Paul Ivano (Street Angel) did the cinematography. The nights of Polish cabinet maker Thaddeus Kubaczik (Edmund O'Brien), a Nazi concentration camp survivor recently settled in Los Angeles, are fraught with nightmares; the SS is breaking down
his door. His fear of uniforms renders him paranoid: he even fears the postman. Returning from work in his van, in Calabassas, he crashes into the car of wealthy Ralph Bowen

(Alan Hale Jr.), who was driving over the speed limit. Thaddeus blames himself without thinking, and appears terrorized before the judge. Bowen's lawyer is on the verge of winning the case when an eyewitness reveals the truth. Thaddeus, who expected to be deported to a camp and had packed his bags, realizes that as a U.S. citizen he has nothing to fear from the law if he is innocent. Moving in private (the intimate scene between the Kubaczik couple), poignant in the courtroom scenes.

The most personal television drama, however, is the third (the penultimate of the series), a little gem entitled *The Day I Met Caruso*. Apparently it was the only one distributed before its broadcast, to movie theaters in Europe. Zoë Akins (*Daddy's Gone a-Hunting*) wrote the script, evangelical in its simplicity: Elizabeth (Sandy Descher), a very wise little girl from an austere Quaker family, takes a train trip in the company of Enrico Caruso (Lotfi Mansouri), while he is on a U.S. tour.[7] She enters his compartment "to upbraid thee," describing him as "worldly and extravagant." He has "too much fine fur on thy coat, kisses too many ladies for no reason" (on the platform) and occupies "this room for thyself, which only a large family should travel in." She advises him: "Be worthy of thy gift, Mr. Caruso." "Do you come often to the opera?" he inquires. "No. Father would never even think of taking a child to the opera!" But "on rainy afternoons" she is allowed to listen to Mr. Caruso's records on the gramophone. Captivated by the child's gracefulness, he invites her to stay. In the five hours that separate Boston from New York, the famous tenor teaches her how to play cards (sinful!), and then begins to sing operatic arias, explaining to her the plots of *La Bohème*, *Rigoletto* and *I Pagliacci*. Elizabeth, who has led a sheltered existence, now discovers diversity: "I thought it would be wicked to have such thoughts before I met

Love is equated with music and music with heaven: little Sandy Descher in the television short *The Day I Met Caruso* (1956).

thee." Her face lights up; she can't take her eyes off the tenor, and Borzage renders her intense engagement almost palpable. Caruso makes her laugh loudly, shouting and joking so much that the child, entranced by the fine singer's melodious generosity, opens herself up to fantasy, learning to love life by casting aside the restrictions of her sect, seeing "what you love bloom, like the garden. The flowers, they're not afraid to be fancy." Upon arrival, the child reflects that she is "not afraid to wish for what I wish for." A transfigured Elizabeth is greeted by her father, he who refused to kiss her because "a child is not to be petted like a kitten." Contaminated by Caruso, he ends up hugging his daughter in his arms. During the impromptu concert, Borzage twice captures Elizabeth's glowing features superimposed against the clouds in the sky (a dreamlike shot as the clouds are not visible from the window). Once again, love is equated with music and music with heaven (*Three Comrades, I've Always Loved You*, etc.), a spiritual link that Borzage emphasizes by comparing the silent prayer of the "Quaker signorina" to the tenor's performance: "I like your way of giving thanks" (to heaven), the little girl declares to him. Both thanks and a blessing: when the train stops due to a military convoy (it is 1917–18), Caruso sings "Over There" for the unfortunate men departing for the front. "We can't help but see an opposing, troubling relationship between these two trains, one transmitting the essential qualities of life, the other rolling toward death," Pascal Pernod astutely remarked.[8] Rather than ignore the war (like the Quakers), Elizabeth learns that we must comfort its victims, if only with the magic of music. Taking leave of her on the station platform, Caruso exclaims: "Arrivederci, till we meet again!" And in fact, this philosophical jewel in the form of a poem recalls *Till We Meet Again* portraying the blossoming and maturing of Sister Clothilde.

Borzage summed up conclusively the overall experience of these three television films: "I must say it was a lot of fun to direct (them). I'd like to do more television. They make films more like we used to make pictures in the old days: a tight schedule and a fast pace."[9] It was again a kind of return to the golden age of silent films that he made thanks to his old friend George Sidney (assistant on *The Mortal Storm*). At Columbia in the spring of 1957, Sidney filmed *Jeanne Eagels*, the tragic life of the stage and screen actress. Kim Novak played the fallen star (1894–1929), with Jeff Chandler as her lover and partner. The script had been written, among others, by Sonya Levien (*Lucky Star, Song o' My Heart, Liliom*) and old acquaintances also appeared before the camera, such as Virginia Grey (*Secrets*, 1933) and Gene Lockhart (*Billy the Kid*). Accompanied by his inseparable brother Lew, Frank Borzage played himself directing Jeanne Eagels under the spotlights at Paramount, evidently a historical misrepresentation (as the two never worked together), but a rare occasion for viewers to see the filmmaker "in a real-life situation"! This episodic role must have made him nostalgic for the set, as he returned to movies shortly thereafter.

In fact, the *China Doll* project had long lingered on Borzage's desk: it was mentioned in the press as early as 1953, under the title *The China Story*. The action centered on Air Force aviators who replenished the Chinese guerrillas fighting the Japanese in Burma, during the war (a context found again in Robert Parrish's *The Purple Plain*, the following year). In June 1955, Pat Kelly and James Benson Nablo, the authors of the short story, completed a first script judged unsatisfactory. In the meantime, Borzage could leisurely arrange financing for his film "comeback," backed mainly by John Wayne. The "Duke," as mentioned, was part of the filmmaker's circle of friends and *China Doll* was implemented as part of his company, Batjac Enterprises.[10] Wayne's brother, Robert E. Morrison, was the film's associate producer, and the cinematographer, veteran William H. Clothier, was under personal, permanent contract to the star. Victor Mature, "the Hunk" of innumerable adventure flicks, accepted the lead for a salary of $125,000. The female star, Li Li Hua, with more than sixty films to her credit, was a very popular actress in Asia and had her own Hong Kong production company.[11] With a modest budget, *China Doll* was filmed in five weeks (August 15–September 20, 1957), with "Chinese" scenery between Saugus and Newhall, at the Los Angeles International Airport and with interiors at Samuel Goldwyn's studios. But the posters and publicity conceived for *China Doll* appear deliberately misleading; both Mature's presence and John Wayne's backing seem to promise a war extravaganza. The film released furtively in the summer of 1958 is nothing of the kind. On the contrary, it is such a personal film that to be truly appreciated, it must be placed in the context of Borzage's entire work. Its working title, modified because it wasn't commercial enough, was *Time Is a Memory*—a subject ripe for analysis.

As with *Living on Velvet* (1935) and *The Shining Hour* (1938), the film begins with the image of an airplane above the clouds, an iconic message conveying (beneath the surface) a feeling of wandering, floating, indecision. The unrealistic drowning out of the noise of motors by the music reinforces the emblematic nature of the shot. In 1943, the American military aircraft—a C-47—is returning from Calcutta and flying over the Himalayan massif toward the airbase in Kunming, China, with supplies and men on board. In command is Captain Cliff Brandon (V. Mature), one of the officers in charge of the base, rendered morose and sullen by incessant war and rain. On the ground he behaves disagreeably with his subordinates, gets drunk alone at Sadie's Place (half nightclub, half brothel) or he plays chess with Father Cairns (Ward Bond), from the local mission. "You're in danger of losing your knight," jokes the priest, alluding to their interrupted game. "I'm looking forward to losing my (k)night, but not over chess!" But a familiar prostitute no longer interests him: he gives her money so as not to see her. An old Chinaman attempts to sell his daughter to a Yankee serviceman who retorts with a scowl: "Buy his daughter? I don't even drink their water!" At nightfall, this same old man accosts Brandon, staggering as he leaves Sadie's. Brandon mechanically gives him a fistful of dollars, murmuring "no thank you" after having illuminated the young woman's face with his lighter, and disappearing into the night, unaware that he has just bought a servant for three months. The very beautiful shot of the Chinese girl's features in the glow of the flame is of course metaphoric; this stranger will be the aviator's "light in the dark." The next day, Father Cairns explains to the furious serviceman that he cannot send Shu-Jen (Li Li Hua) or "Precious Jewel" back home without condemning her honorable family to misery. At Sadie's, where she almost ended up, Shu-Jen dons a woman's outfit and is transformed: her coming down the stairs to the admiring looks of the opposite sex recalls similar moments, from *Until They Get Me* (1917) to *Little Man, What Now?* (1934). From then on, Borzage again uses the situation developed in *7th Heaven* (1927) and *Man's Castle* (1933): the woman, grudgingly tolerated, progressively transforms the soldier's hovel into an intimate home full of flowers; she removes his shoes, washes his shirts, amorously serves him coffee and scrubs the floors; when the American tells her to "scram!," she bursts out laughing. But he learns to adapt to her ministrations. His men notice a change: "That's the second time he smiled this week!" one of them exclaims. Brandon takes in a second tenant, a little Chinese boy named Ellington, a war orphan who serves as his interpreter. Little by little, the small family breaks through his isolation. However, he conspicuously continues to refuse the food the Chinese woman prepares for him, going to Sadie's to get drunk.

Returning one evening from a routine mission in Calcutta, Brandon must take to his bed, afflicted with malaria. He lies down, shivering with fever. Shu-Jen covers him with warm blankets while he deliriously murmurs "Precious Jewel, every day lovelier..." Like Mary Duncan in *The River* (1928), the woman lies down on top of him in order to transmit her warmth. The game of quotations continues: from the couple in bed, the camera rises, panning toward

A Confucian wedding ceremony in *China Doll*: Ward Bond, Li Li Hua and Victor Mature.

a window beneath the sky lit up by flashes of lightning. Dissolve. In the morning, the window shows a sunny landscape, the camera backs up, revealing Brandon awakening in his bed, then Shu-Jen at the other end of the room, cleaning off his shoes. Shu-Jen approaches him tenderly and notices that the fever has gone down, after a symbolic ellipsis strictly identical to that of the miraculous recovery in *Disputed Passage* (1939). Except for one important detail: Brandon is naked beneath the sheets and excuses himself to the Chinese girl for what he did during the night. For the first time, Borzage is truly explicit as he combines the outpouring of love, the power of heaven and the bodies coming together, three factors inseparable in the regenerative process. But Shu-Jen's abnegation frightens Brandon ("All she wants to do is give. I don't understand someone like that"), who takes refuge in whisky. She awaits him at night, putting on his military jacket, like Janet Gaynor (*7th Heaven*). Learning she is pregnant, he persuades her to marry him. There follows an exotic variation on the "marriage of hearts" illustrated so many times: Shu-Jen wants a Chinese wedding, complete with traditional costumes, palanquin and paper dragons, which allows Borzage to perfect a scene both original and discreet, without an ounce of gratuitous folklore and only a drum to give it rhythm. Father Cairns explains the Confucian ceremony in a low voice while guiding the gestures of the ignorant suitor; two aviators and their nurses symbolically represent the parents of bride and groom. The traditional kiss of the newlyweds is replaced by a triple bow.[12] In an unexpected phenomenon for American film of the era, the Catholic priest doesn't whisper a word of the Christian benediction and abstains from the least bit of proselytizing (as does the saxophone-playing nun who, bizarrely, takes part in the ceremony).[13]

Brandon and Shu-Jen are barely married when they are separated by war—as were Chico and Diane thirty years earlier. Aside from the uniforms and the airplanes, nothing until now has given any indication of a conflict, whose *raison d'être* is purely dramaturgical. Brandon's squadron is transferred to Lufeng, at the Burmese border, in order to replenish General Stilwell's army (spring 1944). Months go by. When Shu-Jen gives birth to a little girl, Shiao-Mee, Brandon obtains a transfer for his family. But returning from a parachute drop in Burma, he finds Lufeng under fire from Japanese aircraft. Covered by the Flying Tigers, the captain manages to land his C-47 to save the survivors at the base. In its last twelve minutes, *China Doll* comes to life, offering superb action scenes as well as inspired visualization. The entire base is devastated; the Japanese Zeros will return at any moment. Shu-Jen is dead, buried in the rubble of the control tower. While the survivors clamber on board the aircraft, Brandon carries his wife outside, lays her on the ground and covers her one last time with his jacket. He then orders the pilots of the C-47 to fly off without him (these are his last words in the film). Returning to Shu-Jen, he makes out the cries of an infant, his daughter. He ends up discovering her beneath the corpse of young Ellington, killed shielding her body. At that very moment, the Japanese fighter planes swoop down and Borzage films them from/on an incline, increasing the savagery of the attack tenfold, transforming the Zeros into hideously ferocious birds of prey. The American runs from the burst of gun fire and brings the baby to shelter. He hangs his dog tags around the infant's neck, murmurs something inaudible to her (goodbye, forgiveness), hugs her, lingering, and goes out to position himself behind an automatic cannon, clearly a futile, suicidal

Victor Mature and Li Li Hua, victims of World War II in *China Doll* (1957).

action. The sequence alternates between the virtually unreal attack of the birds of death, accompanied by the roar of machine guns on either side — Brandon is firing relentlessly — and shots of the baby playing with her father's dog tags: the only sound we hear is Shu-Jen's leitmotif playing softly. Borzage emphasizes the interaction between images of death and life, in such a way that his scene takes on a cosmic dimension. The attacker's anonymity is finally answered by that of the one attacked: Brandon literally falls apart when a bomb explodes. The camera backs up as quickly as the wind blowing about the smoke from the explosion, revealing a full shot of the ruins, to the sound of the crying infant.[14] — Epilogue: 1957, at Los Angeles International Airport. The ex-aviators and nurses who were the "parents" of the young marrieds of Kunming await the arrival of their "granddaughter" Shiao-Mee, age 13, found by Father Cairns in a Hong Kong orphanage. When the young girl appears at the top of the passageway, a mysterious silence falls (even the exclamations of the "grandparents" are no longer audible). Shu-Jen's melody softly begins playing; Shiao-Mee walks down the stairs, radiant, and wordlessly displays her father's dog tags that she is wearing around her neck. One of those magical moments only Borzage can capture, one that conveys to us that his lovers "live again" through their daughter.[15]

"The Greeks say that no one really knows happiness until after he's dead," says Sergeant Foster in the film (Dan Barry), a former student of ancient philosophy nicknamed "Plato" by his comrades. As Belton has observed, the shortened quotation is from the dialogue between Solon and Croesus as reported by Herodotus.[16] Deformed as it may be in relation to the original, the passage prepares for death of the couple and lets us catch a glimpse of their happiness after death. This transcendental conclusion is aspired to by works such as *A Farewell to Arms*, *Three Comrades* and *The Mortal Storm*, but for the first time, Borzage's lovers live their "Liebestod" together. Belton and Lamster (op. cit.), are wrong to see the aviator's death as a "sacrifice," for Brandon does not remain in Lufeng to save his daughter (he believes her dead) and even less to protect her, weapons in hand (he would better protect her by hiding with her, not drawing the attention of the enemy)! A lone wolf, disillusioned, he only recognized too late the happiness before him, a bit like Liliom, Terry (*Living on Velvet*), David (*The Shining Hour*), Myra and Goronoff (*I've Always Loved You*) and many others (perhaps even as far back as the hero of *Nugget Jim's Pardner*, in 1916). That Father Cairns is his only friend indicates the potential lying within him. War is at the origin of his self-destructiveness; through it he will be able to join his "Precious Jewel." Her physical weakness (Brandon always covers her with his raincoat, a symbol of protection) corresponds to his great moral strength and equilibrium. Here the most typical ingredients of the Borzagian narrative are present: if only the entire film had the quality, emotion and furor of this final third! Unfortunately, *China Doll* is a captivating mishmash hampered by some banal scenes, at times draggy (the chatting in the bar) and underdeveloped characters (Brandon's various subordinates). Nor is Victor Mature always up to par as the pilot touched by grace, so that certain domestic sequences with Li Li Hua fall flat. It remains an end-of-career film for Borzage, strangely familiar, strewn with self-quotations (a bit like Lang's Hindu diptych, Hawks' *Rio Lobo* or Chaplin's *The Countess from Hong Kong*). A film that recapitulates, provocative as it embraces a theme deemed old-fashioned, out of sync with the concerns of 1958, but also unapologetic and straightforward in its description of an interracial union. The openness with which all the characters accept this supposedly "problematic" love is rather surprising, whereas a film as recent as Joshua Logan's *Sayonara* still depicts the racist reprobation, tragedy, even suicide that American-Asian relationships could cause. Here, intolerance is simply unknown. A bit on the defensive with the skeptical reporter of the *New York Times,* Borzage described *China Doll* as "the greatest love story

I have found since *7th Heaven*.... This is no sticky sweet, sentimental bit of hogwash!"[17] And he confided to George Pratt (op. cit.) in April 1958: "It's a good human interest story, it's a love story, it has a tragic finish but the audience liked it when I previewed it. I personally like it and I hope it goes and maybe a lot of it won't, but I think it's my kind of picture."

The release of *China Doll* was limited. However, critical response in the U.S. was rather positive, and the American press good-naturedly heralded the return of a former giant. "*China Doll* is the kind of story you used to find in the women's magazines back in 1912," remarked *The Hollywood Reporter*. "The amazing thing about it is that much of it seemed to delight the women in the preview audience of 1958."[18] *Los Angeles Examiner* noted that "(The film) was produced and directed by Frank Borzage, a veteran among the masters of movie-making, which was a lucky thing indeed for the picture. Without Borzage's famed skill..., the fallacious story would have been like unto a dud rocket at Cape Canaveral."[19] As for the severe *New York Times*, it admitted that "Mr. Mature and Miss Hua are a far cry from *7th Heaven*'s Chico and Diane. But Mr. Borzage — and welcome back — still has what it takes."[20]

The Big Fisherman, Borzage's 99th and last film, was also his third encounter with Lloyd C. Douglas (*Green Light* and *Disputed Passage*). Not an entirely fortuitous one, however. After the worldwide triumph of the biblical epic in CinemaScope *The Robe* (1953), from Douglas's novel of the same name, and of its sequel, *Demetrius and the Gladiators* (1954), several producers were interested in *The Big Fisherman*, the final work of the writer-pastor, written shortly before his death (published in 1948) and this time devoted to St. Peter the Apostle. As of June 1954, Brian Foy and Edward Small procured the rights; producer and reverend James K. Friedrich, the VIP of religious films destined to the parallel circuits of Lutheran churches (Cathedral Films and Century Films, Inc.) took up the option for himself in May 1955, still with no concrete results. In October 1957, Rowland V. Lee, a religious man well-versed in the Holy Scriptures and a personal friend of Lloyd C. Douglas, came out of retirement with the firm intention of producing *The Big Fisherman*, in return for the support of Buena Vista/Walt Disney. However, he felt he hadn't either the energy or the caliber of expertise to direct the picture himself. When approached to direct, King Vidor declined; the subject didn't inspire him. Michael Curtiz accepted (July 1958), but busy filming *The Hangman* for Paramount, was unavailable in time, fortunately, as religious themes were not his forte. Lee finally approached his friend from the pioneer days at Inceville, and on September 2, Borzage took charge of this $4,000,000 mega-production that would require four months of shooting (October 1, 1958–January 23, 1959), 73 sets and 3,740 extras. The casting was original, and Howard Keel, the singing star of MGM musicals, got the title role; Borzage selected him for his masculine performance, his humor and his great simplicity. The young heroine was played by Susan Kohner (the daughter of agent Paul Kohner and Mexican actress Lupita Tovar) who had just portrayed the rebellious black-white girl in Sirk's *Imitation of Life*. Herod was acted by anglicized Czech Herbert Lom, who specialized in villains: he was one of Mackendrick's "Ladykillers," Napoleon in *War and Peace* (Vidor) and would even play the phantom of the opera for Terence Fisher before finishing up as a paranoid police chief in *The Pink Panther Strikes Again*. The extra work contained some unusual features: Francis J. McDonald, who introduced the filmmaker to Hollywood in 1912–13, played a scribe. And for the first time, the five Borzage brothers all worked together, Frank, Lew and Henry behind the camera, Danny and Bill in front of it, made up as Pharisees.

The start of production on *The Big Fisherman* coincided with the filming of the most spectacular epics in the history of Hollywood, the genre then making a dramatic return to the screen: in the fall of 1958, William Wyler was shooting *Ben Hur* at Cinecittà and King

The Borzage Brothers on the set of *The Big Fisherman* (1959): Lew, Dan, Frank and Bill.

Vidor *Solomon and Sheba* at Valdespartera, in Spain; at the end of January 1959, Anthony Mann began shooting *Spartacus* (later taken over by Stanley Kubrick) in Death Valley, while in October, Liz Taylor and Rouben Mamoulian signed a contract for *Cleopatra* in London, and in November, Nicholas Ray was hired for *King of Kings* in Madrid. *The Big Fisherman* immediately stood apart from these sweeping, "exported" epics in that it was filmed entirely in California. John De Cuir, one of the top set designers, erected magnificent interiors of Herod's palace in the Universal City studios; all the Middle Eastern exteriors were filmed at Rowland V. Lee's ranch in Chatsworth, West San Fernando Valley (the city of Tiberias, Capernaum, the sea of Galilee), then in the neighboring desert of La Quinta, near Palm Springs (the Bedouin camp). The result was more authentic than nature itself.

The rather convoluted plot — it runs three hours — unfolds in Roman Arabia (today Jordan), in Galilee, in Judea and in Rome. Deran, the moody son of the King of Arabia, covets princess Fara (S. Kohner), but she prefers Prince Voldi (John Saxon). Her mother Arnon, a noble of Arab blood,[21] reveals to her before dying the secret of her birth: Fara is half–Jewish, the daughter of Herod Antipas (H. Lom); the tetrarch of Galilee then abandoned his wife for his depraved sister-in-law Herodias (Martha Hyer). Since this affront, the tribes of Arabia have sworn merciless hatred upon the Judeans. Like many others before her, Fara swears to avenge her mother by killing the despot; she disguises herself as a boy and leaves for Galilee. En route, she is robbed by bandits, meets John the Baptist and finds shelter at the home of Hannah (Beulah Bondi) and her robust stepson, Simon the fisherman (H. Keel). He only believes in God from afar and is angry at the Nazarean whose teachings led his

Simon-Peter shattered by the Sermon on the Mount: Howard Keel in *The Big Fisherman*, 1959.

helpers astray — John, James and Andrew. Hired to translate Greek at the palace, Fara waits for an opportune moment to act. However, she attends the Sermon on the Mount and is perturbed by the injunction to "love thine enemy": she flees, covering her ears. Simon directly witnesses a miracle and converts; in the evening, he goes as far as to "turn the other cheek" to men who ridicule and hit him, but the fiery fisherman slips up, loses his patience and beats them up! Fara is present when John the Baptist is beheaded and the palace is ravaged by anger from Above. Supported by Simon, she abandons the idea of stabbing her father, a pitiful puppet fallen into disgrace in Rome and placed under the jurisdiction of Pontius Pilate. Prince Voldi, who has joined his princess in Galilee, must return to Arabia where Deran has ascended to the throne. Fara follows her beloved, accompanied by "the big fisherman." The treacherous Deran has become a paraplegic; Fara prevents him from having Voldi whipped to death and the apostle miraculously heals the sick man, who in return promises to free the lovers. But Deran goes back on his word and is struck dead. Proclaimed king, Voldi can no longer marry Fara, as she is of mixed race. She sacrifices her love and returns to Judea on Simon's boat to work at reconciling the Arab and Hebrew peoples. "It's a wonderful day for fishing," the holy man announces to her. Sailing up the coast of the Dead Sea, they hear Christ preach at the summit of a mountain.

Contrary to what the title implies, the film's central character is not the "big fisherman." The filmmaker's attention focuses on Fara and Voldi, the two lovers, and Simon-Peter's influence on them (through the message of the Beatitudes). In this regard, Lloyd C. Douglas's plot seems almost custom-made for Borzage. Truth be told, the script is quite far removed from the book, a mediocre, long-winded novel with often absurd situations.[22]

Borzage shifted emphasis by abstaining from illustrating the multiple episodes dealing with the last days of Christ, from Easter to Pentecost, and the martyring of St. Peter in Rome (the end of the novel). He spares us the biblical clichés and enlivens the plot with a few more original reflections. Like the pariah in *Moonrise*, Fara undertakes a journey that exorcizes her inner turmoil at its source; Simon is a substitute for her natural father and helps her find her identity. Dagger in hand, facing Herod, she realizes that Esther (her pseudonym) is now dead within her: "I am free. I am no longer an outcast... I am Judean, Galilean, Egyptian, Roman, Greek, all of them," she sobs. "And I am only what I have always been," retorts the despot bitterly, signifying "infernal" suffocation within the shackles of his own limitations. Nevertheless, critics on both sides of the Atlantic greeted the film with a slew of stupidities, not unlike those used, for instance, to describe Mankiewicz's magnificent *Cleopatra*. Only a few proponents of the French New Wave resisted facile disdain, occasionally venturing to take the work seriously. Jean Douchet concluded in *Arts* that, given the genre, the film was "superior to *Ben Hur*. At least it is never ugly nor vulgar."[23] But the most fitting remarks by far appeared in *Cahiers du Cinéma*: "In his return to the movies," wrote Jacques Joly, "Frank Borzage doesn't produce his finest work, but, aside from a few absurdities, certain concessions to history, we find the filmmaker's visual genius intact: classical direction, linear storyline... The film, from one end to the other, is extremely beautiful to look at. When Susan Kohner cuts her long black hair in front of her mirror, when Borzage lingers, portraying her joy at finding women's clothing again, when Simon's mother dies a simple, happy death, so rare in the movies, poetry truly appears on screen and gives the impression of happiness. When Susan Kohner and John Saxon meet up on horseback in the dust of the desert, when the wind destroys Herod's palace at the moment John the Baptist is beheaded, all conventions are swept aside; what remains is a love poem of death, joy and sorrow."[24]

The film has weaknesses, is at times ponderous and contains uneven performances. But aside from its surface curiosities (the appearance of Arab tribes with reference to the Ka'bah in a biblical tale, allusions to the Israeli-Arab conflict, repeated use of flashbacks in an epic film, etc.), *The Big Fisherman* is as noteworthy for what it refuses to convey as for what it does. Borzage rejects—almost categorically—the usual ingredients of the genre, the battles, clashing of cymbals, unrestrained orgies and sadomasochism favored by Cecil B. DeMille and Samuel Bronston. Cavalcades are rare, the spectacular is often sacrificed to characterization (Herod's opportunism and paranoia, Fara's hesitations). Salomé, that degenerate teenager, isn't even mentioned. The beheading of John the Baptist is only suggested by shadow figures against the wall of the palace, as is the inevitable Roman orgy going on behind reddish wall coverings; we distinguish cries and, outlines of dancers cavorting in all directions when a slave presents the head of the saint on a platter. A rather surprising, artistically innovative sequence, captured by long camera movements (we are struck by the supreme, almost majestic use of space) resulting in "divine intervention" of undeniable power: a supernatural wind rises and sweeps through the palace, reversing the throne, taking with it curtains and ornaments. The flapping fabrics that streak the screen and the panic of the revelers create an unforgettable ballet. The portrayal of religious scenes and miracles is low-key: no heavenly rays, no Bach fugues or violins à la Miklos Rozsa, no wild ecstacy. The Sermon is delivered in concentrated silence. Of Christ, only approached in reverse-angle shots, we see not even the outline (as in *Ben Hur*), just a furtive panning of an immaculate robe or a hand framed as an introduction; as the film progresses he is less visible, while his voice grows stronger, for all that counts is his Word. Of course, this absence of dramatization, this archaic imagery may disconcert, even irritate the viewer, but the film is infused with a singular serenity, the work of a man at peace with himself.

A supernatural wind sweeps through Herod's palace: Herbert Lom in *The Big Fisherman*, 1959.

Various shots refer back to the symbolic esthetic of silent films. When Christ calls his apostle-fishermen at the seashore, Borzage films them in a phantasmagorical twilight, drowned in fog (a still troubled vision to which the crystal-clear limpidity of the final images responds). Technically, the film inaugurates the UltraPanavision 70mm process, allowing for clean, intense, exceptional hues in the depth of field. Like Borzage and Lee, cinematographer Lee Garmes had learned his craft with Thomas Ince, and the filmmaker (his first foray onto the wide screen) obtained exceptional support from him. Garmes had worked for Hitchcock, Hawks, Ophüls, photographed the most beautiful of Sternberg's productions (*Morocco*, Oscar for *Shanghai Express*) and demonstrated his mastery with color in Vidor's *Duel in the Sun*. Yet he claims: "The finest thing I ever did on the screen was *The Big Fisherman*. It was very lovely. Everything in that film was magnificent.... The whole film glowed like a series of Rembrandts. I believe that picture will one day be acknowledged to be a visual masterpiece."[25] Starting out with stylized sets, Borzage and Garmes actually worked as colorists; the royal library is composed of vermillion, Veronese green and yellow ocher, and the enormous banquet room provides a fascinating ensemble of cobalt blue (the sky), crimson (the wall coverings) and gold. At times, the richness of the chromatic spectrum and the formal, quasi-geometric simplification of the frames identifies the film's style with the Florentine Mannerism of Bronzino or Pontormo. Cinematography, set decoration and costumes were all nominated for Oscars in 1959.[26] In short, *The Big Fisherman* deserved better than the irony of the pulp writers on duty. The film, however, paid for its lack of theatricality with mediocre returns ($3,000,000 in 1960); only by frequent, truncated panscan screenings on television did it recoup its cost. A paradox!

The period of 1959–1960 was again rich in future plans. Frank and Lew, for example, were working on *Papa*, an NBC television movie conceived by writer John Fante; *Feer & Mrs.* was destined for 20th Century Fox. The most advanced of these projects was entitled *The Pearl King*, an Italian-American co-production (Frank Clemente International Co.). The script — uncompleted — was inspired by the novels *Kokichi Mikimoto and His Pearls* by Iwazo Ototake and *The Pearl King* by Robert Eunson. It dealt with the exploits of Kokichi Mikimoto (1858–1954), who was the first to cultivate artificial pearls. Borzage had visited the then 96-year-old Mikimoto on the island of Tatokujima ("Pearl Island") during his trip to Japan, and had obtained authorization to bring his life to the screen. He would work on this final project until his strength abandoned him, in October 1961.

On the eve of his death, Borzage still had to undergo the ordeal of *L'Atlantide/Journey Beneath the Desert*. Pierre Benoit's best-seller (1919) was well-known, translated into fifteen languages and had sold over two million copies to date. The member of L'Académie française situates his lost continent within northern Hoggar, where the summit of the ancient kingdom of Neptune survived the cataclysm of the "Sahara Sea." This inviolable retreat is inhabited by the sublime Antinéa, the last descendant of Atlantis, and her faithful Touaregs. A fantastical creature par excellence, a metaphor of the fascination of the desert incarnating the duality of death and desire, Antinéa attracts travelers and white servicemen to make them literally perish of love. The bodies of her lovers undergo an orichalque bath (the legendary auriferous metal described by Plato) and are placed, duly numbered, in a room of "conquests" in the heart of the underground palace. One day, a guest resists the spells of the queen... In all, this exotic tale has been brought to the screen seven times[27]; the Franco-Italian initiators of the present blend — Fides, Paris (Gérard Ducaux-Rupp) and C.C.M. Film, Rome, in association with Edgar G. Ulmer — speculated on the name of a world-renowned director to help finance and cast the film, to be shot in Technicolor and Super-Technirama 70. Several Hollywood veterans such as Raoul Walsh, Jacques Tourneur and Robert Aldrich had already been drawn to Rome, where Ulmer himself had just completed the American version of *Hannibal* with Victor Mature. When approached, Borzage agreed (his personal copy of the script, preserved at the Margaret Herrick Library, bears the title *Atlantis, City Beneath the Desert* and the obligatory mention "A Frank Borzage Production"), which convinced the young Jean-Louis Trintignant to accept the male lead, on the advice of film-buff friends.[28] Alongside him were Georges Rivière, Rad Fulton, Amedeo Nazzari and Gian-Maria Volonté; some of them had to memorize the English dialogue of the cosmopolitan mishmash without understanding a single word!

Frank and Nita Borzage arrived in Rome on August 19, 1960, where the paparazzi made a great to-do over the director's partly Italian origin. They had planned to film at Cinecittà, in Madrid and in North Africa, but once the director was on location, the producers' ambitions melted away. The exteriors, Borzage learned, would be limited to Ostia and Colomb-Béchard. The role of the Lorelei of the Sahara — played in the past by Stacia Napierkowska, Brigitte Helm, Maria Montez and Ludmilla Tchérina — had been offered to the radiant black actress Dorothy Dandridge (*Carmen Jones*). But her fees were high, and Swedish Anita Ekberg was approached. In the end, the producers chose Israeli starlet Haya Harareet, discovered in the recent *Ben Hur* (and the future Mrs. Jack Clayton), who wouldn't strain the budget. Getting the project off the ground was so chaotic that filming in the Titanus-Farnesina studios began only on November 1. Forty-eight hours later, Borzage left the set, never to return. The *Hollywood Reporter* announced tersely: "After two days of shooting, director Frank Borzage was replaced by producer Edgar Ulmer. Inability to surmount the language barrier was given as reason for the amicable parting."[29] Ulmer offered other reasons, the first being the one given to the actors in the film: "This film was conceived by another director and not by me. When, due to the illness [sic] of poor Borzage, I had to take over the film, I found myself up against a slew of difficulties. When a director is obliged to rewrite at night what he's going to shoot the next day, certain dangerous situations develop."[30] In an interview with *Cahiers du Cinéma*, Ulmer did admit, however: "It was an entirely normal production that I took over during filming (and I had to reshoot what had already been done), as Borzage wasn't able to direct a film abroad. In Hollywood there are some very good directors who work in the studios and press a button each time something goes wrong. But in Italy you have to improvise, and Borzage, who was nevertheless one of our great directors, didn't have the Latin temperament and wasn't aggressive—both necessary if you want to work in this country."[31] In his own words, Borzage left the film because the production company could not guarantee him a solid financial base; he found the working conditions disgraceful, unworthy of him. It is true that the filmmaker detested raising his voice. "Ulmer was a horrible man, so crude," Borzage's widow confided to us. "He always shouted at Frank." Used to Z series and makeshift budgets, Ulmer saw the project to completion after having entirely modified the script (by modernizing it, including a nuclear explosion), altering Benoit's plot from start to finish. Edmond T. Gréville and Giuseppe Masini helped direct this *Atlantide* which was released after interminable fussing about and cuts. In hindsight, the result justifies Borzage's departure (even if the prints released in West Germany and Austria misleadingly displayed his name): even Ulmer's ardent admirers have to admit it is a major flop, featuring a ridiculous script, unimaginative direction and supremely ugly sets (designed by Ulmer himself). Compared to this onslaught of kitsch, *Siren of Atlantis*, the version patched together in Hollywood in 1948 with Maria Montez, is a masterpiece! Borzage, the bard of love, filming Benoit's strange erotic extravaganza with Dorothy Dandridge... We can dream.

However, a serious blow had been dealt. Humiliated and discouraged, the filmmaker returned to the U.S. He had no idea that he had only nineteen months to live. During his stay in Rome, accompanied by his friend Joe Youngerman, he had gone to the hospital where a biopsy was taken of a suspicious swelling on the neck. He remained on the operating table four hours, but a benign tumor was diagnosed. Six months later, however, in May 1961, he returned to hospital in Los Angeles due to generalized weakness. New tests contradicted the diagnosis made in Rome: the tumor was malignant and now inoperable. Borzage knew he was doomed, but didn't speak of it, following the adage by which he had lived: "Be like the sun dial—report only when the sun is out." In February 1962, he again received the David Wark Griffith Award (today the Lifetime Achievement Award) presented in Santa Monica by the Directors Guild of America "for outstanding contributions in the field of film directing." George Sidney, president of the Directors Guild, bestowed the distinction upon the filmmaker, then bedridden, barely able to speak, struck down by horribly painful throat cancer. On June 8, Borzage left Cedars of Lebanon Hospital after six months of futile treatment. He died June 19 at nine o'clock in the morning at his villa on Wilshire Boulevard. He was sixty-eight.

The funeral took place on June 21 at the Church of the Recessional in Glendale, alongside Forest Lawn Memorial Park cemetery. Several hundred people attended the ceremony. The remains were carried by William A. Wellman, David Butler, Rouben Mamoulian, Tay Garnett, Joe Youngerman, William Daniels, John Ford, Delmer Daves, Willis Goldbeck, Josef von Sternberg, George Stevens, Frank Sennes and Clarence Brown. Also present at the burial (aside from the entire Borzage clan) were Janet Gaynor, Spencer Tracy, Jeanette MacDonald, Charles Ruggles, Antonio Moreno, Gilbert Roland, Mervyn LeRoy, Henry

King, Eddie Mannix, Arthur Lubin, Sol Lesser, Andrew McLaglen, Sally Eilers and Virginia Grey. "In a final tribute to his friend, Borzage," reported the *Los Angeles Herald-Examiner*, "George Sidney described the Italian-Swiss director as 'a fine sportsman, a wonderful and understanding director, and a great friend. Success,' he added, 'never changed this quiet, kind, thoughtful, loving man.'"[32] According to Sidney, Borzage's last words to his wife were: "Nita, we found our own *7th Heaven*."

Filmography

Precise sources for the years leading up to 1920 are lacking; the dates of the reviews in *Moving Picture World* or those of the official release determine the chronology. As of 1920, all films follow in *the order in which they were shot* as opposed to when they opened in theaters. Borzage films followed by the sign [‡] appear to be lost.

```
┌─────────────────────────────────────────────────────────────────────┐
│                         ABBREVIATIONS                                 │
│                                                                       │
│  adapt.= adaptation / art dir. = art director / assoc. = associated   │
│  / asst. = assistant / chor. = choregraphy / cost. = costumes /       │
│  dial. = dialogues / d. = distribution / edit. = editor / exec.       │
│  prod. = executive producer / lyr. = lyrics / mus. = music / mus.     │
│  dir. = musical direction / photo = cinematographer / prod. =         │
│  production / dir. = direction / rel. = release / spec. eff. =        │
│  special effects / supervis. = supervision / techn. advis. =          │
│  technical advisor                                                    │
└─────────────────────────────────────────────────────────────────────┘
```

Borzage as Actor

The current state of research does not allow us to claim that the list that follows is exhaustive; for more details concerning the films featuring Borzage as actor only, we refer the reader to Davide Turconi's extensive research in *Griffithiana* no. 45, December 1992, from which we borrow the shooting dates of Thomas H. Ince productions.

1912

On Secret Service, 2 reels—Kay-Bee (Thomas H. Ince)/d. Mutual—dir.: Walter Edwards, cast: Nick Cogley, Anna Little, Francis Ford, Walter Edwards (11–1-12).

When Lee Surrenders, 2 reels—Kay-Bee (Thomas H. Ince)/d. Mutual—dir.: Thomas H. Ince, cast: Charles K. French, Robert Edeson, Anna Little (11–8-12).

Blood Will Tell, 2 reels—Kay-Bee (Thomas H. Ince)/d. Mutual—dir.: Walter Edwards, cast: J. Barney Sherry, Ray Myers, Ethel Grandin (12–13–12).

1913

The Pride of the South, 3 reels—Broncho (Thomas H. Ince)/d. Mutual—dir.: Burton L. King, cast: Francis Ford, J. Barney Sherry, Charles Edler (3–19-13).

The First Stone, 1 reel—American Film Co., Beauty—dir.: Frank Cooley, cast: Virginia Kirtley, Irving Cummings (3–27-13).

Youth and Jealousy, 1 reel—American Film Co./d. Mutual—dir.: Allan Dwan, cast: Wallace Reid, Vivian Rich (5–3-13).

Drummer of the Eighth, 2 reels—Broncho (Thomas H. Ince)/d. Mutual—dir.: Jay Hunt, cast: Mildred Harris, Cyril Gottlieb (5–28-13).

The Battle of Gettysburg, 5 reels—New York Motion Picture Corp. (Ince)/d. Mutual—dir.: Thomas H. Ince, cast: Willard Mack, Charles K. French (6–1-13).

A Dixie Mother, 2 reels— Broncho (Thomas H. Ince)/d. Mutual — dir.: Jay Hunt, cast: Gertruby-Claire, Richard Stanton (6–4-13).

The Pride of Lonesome, 1 reel— American Film Co./d. Mutual — dir.: Hal Reid, cast: Wallace Reid, Vivian Rich (6–28–13).

The Crimson Stain, 3 reels— Kay-Bee (Thomas H. Ince)/d. Mutual — dir.: Jay Hunt, cast: Leona Hutton, Frank Newberg, Ed Coxen (7–4-13).

The Foreign Spy, 1 reel— American Film Co./d. Mutual — dir.: Hal Reid, cast: Wallace Reid, Vivian Rich (7–5-13).

When the Prince Arrived, 1 reel— Rex Motion Picture Co./d. Universal —cast: Margarita Fisher, Joseph Singleton, John Dalton, Robert Z. Leonard (8–7-13).

The Mystery of the Yellow Aster Mine, 2 reels— Bison-Universal Film Mfg. Prod./d. Universal — dir.: Wallace Reid, cast: Wallace Reid, Pauline Bush (8–23-13).

A Woman's Stratagem, 1 reel— Rex Motion Picture Co./d. Universal —cast: Margaret Fisher, Robert Z. Leonard, F. B. (=Frank Harvey) (8–23-13).

The Gratitude of Wanda, 2 reels— Bison-Universal Film Mfg. Prod./d. Universal — dir.: Wallace Reid, cast: Wallace Reid, Pauline Bush, Jessalyn Van Trump, Arthur Rosson (8–30-13).

In the Twilight, 2 reels— Sigmund Lubin Film Mfg. Co.— dir.: George Terwilliger, cast: Lionel Adams, Marion Barney, Maidel Turner (8–30-13).

Silent Heroes, 2 reels— Broncho (Thomas H. Ince)/d. Mutual — dir.: Jay Hunt & Walter Edwards, cast: Estelle Allen, Thomas Chatterton (9–24-13).

Loaded Dice, 1 reel— Kay-Bee (Thomas H. Ince)/d. Mutual — dir.: Burton L. King, cast: Louise Glaum, Walter Edwards (10–3-13).

The War Correspondent, 2 reels— Broncho (Thomas H. Ince)/d. Mutual — dir.: Jay Hunt (or Walter Edwards), cast: Alfred Vosburgh (11–19-13).

The Days Of '49, 1 reel— Kay-Bee (Thomas H. Ince)/d. Mutual — dir.: Jay Hunt, cast: Estelle Allen, Thomas Chatterton, Herschel Mayall (11–21-13).

Retribution, 2 reels— Nestor-Universal Film Mfg. Prod./d. Universal — dir.: Wallace Reid & Willis Lobards, cast: Wallace Reid, Dorothy Davenport, Phil Dunham, Ed Brady (12–6-13).

A Cracksman Santa Claus, 1 reel— Powers Co.-Universal Film Mfg. Prod./d. Universal — dir.: Wallace Reid & Willis Lobards, cast: Wallace Reid, Dorothy Davenport, Edward Brady (12–13-13).

A Hopi Legend/A Pueblo Romance, 1 reel— Nestor-Universal Film Mfg. Prod./d. Universal — dir.: Wallace Reid, cast: Wallace Reid, Dorothy Davenport, Phil Dunham (12–27-13).

1914

The Wheel of Life, 2 reels— Nestor-Universal Film Mfg. Prod./d. Universal — dir.: Wallace Reid, cast: Wallace Reid, Dorothy Davenport, Edward Brady (1–24-14).

A New England Idyll, 2 reels— Broncho (Thomas H. Ince)/d. Mutual — dir.: Reginald Barker (or Walter Edwards), cast: Rhea Mitchell, F.B. (=John Brown), Fanny Midgley (2–4-14, shooting: Nov 2–11, 1913).

A Romance of the Sea, 2 reels— Broncho (Thomas H. Ince)/d. Mutual — dir.: Walter Edwards, cast: Robyn Adair, Romona Radcliffe, Walter Edwards (2–11-14, shooting: Nov 15-Dec 1, 1913).

A Flash in the Dark, 1 reel— Nestor-Universal Film Mfg. Prod./d. Universal — dir.: Wallace Reid, cast: Wallace Reid, Dorothy Davenport, Edward Brady (2–14-14).

The Silent Messenger, 2 reels— Domino (Thomas H. Ince)/d. Mutual — dir.: Charles Giblyn (or Gilbert P. Hamilton), cast: Anna Little, Herschel Mayall (3–12-14).

Desert Gold, 2 reels— Kay-Bee (Thomas H. Ince)/d. Mutual — dir.: Scott Sidney, cast: Charles Ray, F.B. (=John Carson), Clare William, Frank Norris (3–13-14, shooting: Dec 12–17, 1913).

The Geisha, 2 reels— Kay-Bee (Thomas H. Ince)/d. Mutual — dir.: Reginald Barker, cast: Ramona Radcliffe, Tsuru Aoki, Sessue Hayakawa, F.B. (=John Carver) (4–10-14, shooting: Jan 5–23, 1914).

Samson, 6 reels— Universal Film Mfg. Prod./d. Universal — dir.: J. Farrell Macdonald, cast: J. Warren Kerrigan, Kathleen Kerrigan, George Periolat e.a., F. B., Harold Lloyd, Hal Roach (=extras) (4–30-14).

In the Purple Hills, 2 reels— American Film Co.— dir.: Gilbert P. Hamilton (5–24-14).

The Ambassador's Envoy, 2 reels— Domino (Thomas H. Ince)/d. Mutual — dir.: Reginald Barker, cast: Sessue Hayakawa, F.B. (=Richard Hastins), Gladys Brockwell (5–28-14, shooting: Mar 23-Apr. 8, 1914).

Children of Fate/Love's Western Flight, short—Nestor-Universal Film Mfg. Prod./d. Universal—dir.: Wallace Reid, cast: Wallace Reid, Dorothy Davenport (5–30–14).

Love's Western Flight, 2 reels—Universal Film Mfg. Prod., Nestor/d. Universal—dir.: Wallace Reid, cast: Wallace Reid, Dorothy Davenport, Phil Dunham, William Wolbert (6–3-14).

Claim Number Three, 1 reel—Sigmund Lubin Film Mfg. Co.—cast: Dolly Larkin, George Routh (6–6-14).

The Wrath of the Gods. The Destruction of Sakura Jima, 6 reels—New York Motion Picture Corp., Domino-Special (Thomas H. Ince)/d. Mutual—dir.: Reginald Barker, Raymond B. West, Thomas H. Ince, cast: Sessue Hayakawa, Tsuru Aoki, F. B. (=Tom Wilson) (6–8-14, shooting: Jan. 27-Feb 13, 1914).

A Relic of Old Japan, 2 reels—Domino (Thomas H. Ince)/d. Mutual—dir.: Reginald Barker, cast: Tsuru Aoki, Sessue Hayakawa, F.B. (=Jim Wendell), Gladys Brockwell (6–11–14, shooting: Mar 7–21, 1914).

A Tragedy of the Orient, 2 reels—Broncho (Thomas H. Ince)/d. Mutual—dir.: Reginald Barker, cast: Tsuru Aoki, Sessue Hayakawa, F.B. (=Thomas Arnold) (6–13–14, shooting: Feb 14-Mar 18, 1914).

The Romance of the Sawdust Ring, 2 reels—Domino (Thomas H. Ince)/d. Mutual—dir.: Raymond B. West, cast: F.B. (=Jack Dorn), Gladys Brockwell, Charles Swickard (8–13–14, shooting: Jun 8–22, 1914).

Stacked Cards, 2 reels—Kay-Bee (Thomas H. Ince)/d. Mutual—dir.: Scott Sidney, cast: Gladys Brockwell, Thomas Chatterton, F.B. (=Travers) (9–5-14, shooting: Jun 27-Jul 2, 1914).

Parson Larkin's Wife, 2 reels—Broncho (Thomas H. Ince)/d. Mutual—dir.: Scott F. Sidney, cast: Leona Hutton, F.B. (=James Larkin), Webster Campbell (9–23–14, shooting: Jul 17–27, 1914).

The Right to Die, 2 reels—Broncho (Thomas H. Ince)/d. Mutual—dir.: Raymond B. West, cast: Enid Markey, Herschel Mayall, Gertrude Claire (9–30–14).

The Typhoon, 5 reels—New York Motion Picture Corp. (Thomas H. Ince)/d. Paramount—dir.: Reginald Barker, cast: Sessue Hayakawa, Gladys Brockwell, F. B. (=Renard Bernisky), Tsuru Aoki (10–10–14, shooting: Apr 20-May 1, 1914).

The Desperado, 2 reels—Broncho (Thomas H. Ince)/d. Mutual—dir.: G. P. Hamilton, cast: Richard Stanton, Leona Hutton (11–4-14).

Nipped, 2 reels—Domino (Thomas H. Ince)/d. Mutual—dir.: George Osborne, cast: Tsuru Aoki, Sessue Hayakawa, F.B. (=Tom Wright) (11–19–14, shooting: Aug 15–26, 1914).

A Crook's Sweetheart, 2 reels—Kay-Bee (Thomas H. Ince)/d. Mutual—dir.: Scott F. Sidney, cast: Lewis Durham, Leona Hutton, F.B. (=the Dip) (11–27–14, shooting: Sep 23-Oct 5, 1914).

A Romance of Old Holland, 2 reels—Domino (Thomas H. Ince)/d. Mutual—dir.: Jay Hunt, cast: Elizabeth Burbridge, Joseph J. Dowling, F.B. (=Peter Veldt) (12.-2–14, shooting: Sep 14–23, 1914).

The Panther, 2 reels—Broncho (Thomas H. Ince)/d. Mutual—dir.: Walter Edwards, cast: Louise Glaum, Walter Edwards, F.B. (=David Brandt) (12–16–14, shooting: Oct 16–24, 1914).

In the Sage Bush Country/Mr. Nobody, 2 reels—Kay-Bee (Thomas H. Ince)/d. Mutual—dir.: William S. Hart, cast: William S. Hart, Rhea Mitchell, Herschel Mayall (12–25–14).

1915

In the Land of the Otter, 2 reels—Domino (Thomas H. Ince)/d. Mutual—dir.: Walter Edwards, cast: Louise Glaum, F.B. (=Joe Eagle), Jerome Stern (1–14–15, shooting: Oct 7–15, 1914).

The Girl Who Might Have Seen, 2 reels—Kay-Bee (Thomas H. Ince)/d. Mutual—dir.: Raymond B. West, cast: Leona Hutton, F.B. (=George Fowler), Edward Brennan (3–12–15, shooting: Dec 12, 1914-Jan 3.1, 1915).

The Mill By the Zuyder Zee, 2 reels—Domino (Thomas H. Ince)/d. Mutual—dir.: Jay Hunt, cast: F.B. (=Dirk Brandt), Herschel Mayall, Margaret Thomson (3–18–15, shooting: Nov 4–22, 1914).

In the Switch Tower, 2 reels—Broncho (Thomas H. Ince)/d. Mutual—dir.: Walter Edwards, cast: Walter Edwards, F.B. (=Joel Wharton), Gertrude Claire (3–24–15, shooting: Dec 29, 1914-Jan 5. 1915).

The Fakir, 2 reels—Domino (Thomas H. Ince)/d. Mutual—dir.: Walter Edwards, cast: Walter Edwards, Rhea Mitchell, F.B. (=Tom Waldron) (4–1-15, shooting: Jan 6–15, 1915).

Molly of the Mountains, 2 reels—Broncho (Thomas H. Ince)/d. Mutual—dir.: Charles Swickard, cast: F.B. (=John Harlow), Rhea Mitchell, Alfred Hollingsworth (4–7-15, shooting: Dec 6–14, 1914).

The Disillusionment of Jane, 2 reels—Broncho (Thomas H. Ince)/d. Mutual—dir.: Jay Hunt, cast:

F.B. (=Jim Norton), Elizabeth Burbridge, J. Barney-Sherry (4–21–15, shooting: Jan 28-Feb 11, 1915).

The Cup of Life, 5 reels— New York Motion Picture Corp. (Thomas H. Ince)/d. Mutual — dir.: Raymond B. West, Thomas H. Ince, cast: Bessie Barriscale, Enid Markey, Charles Ray, F. B. (=Dick Ralston) (4–26–15, shooting: Oct 29-Dec 21, 1914).

The Spark from the Embers, 2 reels— Broncho (Thomas H. Ince)/d. Mutual — dir.: Jay Hunt, cast: F.B. (=Hal Choate), Elizabeth Burbridge, Walter Edwards (5–5-15, shooting: Feb 12–21, 1915).

Her Alibi, 2 reels— Domino (Thomas H. Ince)/d. Mutual — dir.: Jay Hunt, cast: Elizabeth Burbridge, F.B. (=Joe Bailey), C. N. Mortenson, Harry Keenan (5–20–15, shooting: Feb 22-Mar 2, 1915).

The Scales of Justice, 2 reels— Domino (Thomas H. Ince)/d. Mutual — dir.: Walter Edwards, cast: Walter Edwards, Clara Williams, F.B. (=Paul Armstrong) (5–29–15, shooting: Jan 16–26, 1915).

The Tavern Keeper's Son, 2 reels— Broncho (Thomas H. Ince)/d. Mutual — dir.: Jay Hunt, cast: F.B. (=Juan Capella), Gertrude Claire, J. P. Lockney (6–9-15, shooting: Mar 10–20, 1915).

The Secret of Lost River, 2 reels— Kay-Bee (Thomas H. Ince)/d. Mutual — dir.: Jay Hunt, cast: F.B. (=Tom Hornby), Louise Glaum, Jack Davidson, Estelle Arlen (6–18–15, shooting: Mar 1-Apr. 9, 1915).

His Mother's Portrait, 2 reels— Kay-Bee (Thomas H. Ince)/d. Mutual — dir.: Howard Hickman, cast: F.B. (=Burt Hamilton), Margaret Gibson, Lewis J. Cody (7–2-15, shooting: Apr 25-May 8, 1915).

The Tools of Providence/Dakota Dan/Every Inch a Man/The Struggle in the Steeple, 2 reels— Broncho (Thomas H. Ince)/d. Mutual — dir.: William S. Hart, cast: William S. Hart, Rhea Mitchell, F. B. (="Ace" Farrell) (7–7-15, shooting: Mar 19–30, 1915).

The Hammer, 2 reels— Kay-Bee (Thomas H. Ince)/d. Mutual — dir.: Richard Stanton, cast: F.B. (=Donald Barstow), Margaret Gibson, Leona Hutton, Arthur Maude (7–9-15, shooting: Apr 6–20, 1915).

A Knight of the Trails/Prowlers of the Plains, 2 reels— Kay-Bee (Thomas H. Ince)/d. Mutual — dir.: William S. Hart, cast: William S. Hart, Leona Hutton, F. B. (=Bill Carey) (8–20–15, shooting: May 17–26, 1915).

Farewell to Thee, 1 reel — Reliance-Majestic Co. (David Wark Griffith)/d. Mutual —cast: Willard Mack, Enid Markey, Margaret Thompson, J. Frank Burke (8–21–15).

A Child of the Surf, 2 reels— Reliance-Majestic Co. (David Wark Griffith)/d. Mutual — dir.: John B. O'Brien (or James Douglass), cast: Teddy Sampson, Spottiswoode Aitken, F.B. (=Robert) (8–21–15).

A Friend in Need, 1 reel — American Film Co., Beauty/d. Mutual — dir.: James Douglass, cast: John Sheehan, Beatrice Van (=Frank) (9–18–15, shooting: August).

Mixed Males, 2 reels— American Film Co., Beauty/d. Mutual — dir.: James Douglass, cast: John Sheehan, Beatrice Van, Nellie Belle Widen (9–25–15).

Alias James, Chauffeur, 2 reels— American Film Co., Beauty/d. Mutual — dir.: James Douglass, cast: Neva Gerber, F.B. (=Frank Burton), Jimsey Maye (10–16–15).

Touring with Tillie, 2 reels— American Film Co., Beauty/d. Mutual — dir.: Archer MacMackin, cast: F. B. (=Cliff Burridge), Neva Gerber, Lucille Ward (10.23.15).

One to the Minute, 2 reels— American Film Co., Beauty/d. Mutual — dir.: John T. Dillon, cast: Neva Gerber, William Carroll, Rae Berger (10–30–15).

Almost a Widow, 2 reels— American Film Co., Beauty/d. Mutual — dir.: John T. Dillon, cast: Neva Gerber, Beatrice Van, Lucille Ward (11–6-15).

Her Adopted Father, 2 reels— American Film Co., Beauty/d. Mutual — dir.: Archer MacMackin, cast: F.B. (=Edward Hart), Estelle Allen, Lucille Ward, Rosemary MacMackin (11–6-15).

Anita's Butterfly, 2 reels— American Film Co., Beauty/d. Mutual — dir.: John Dillon, cast: Neva Gerber, F.B. (=Jack), Charles Bennett (11–13–15).

Aloha Oe, 5 reels— New York Motion Picture Corp., Kay-Bee (Thomas H. Ince)/d. Triangle — dir.: Richard Stanton, Charles Swickard, cast: Willard Mack, Enid Markey, Margaret Thompson, F.B. (=Dr. John Hawley) (11–18–15, shooting: Jun 7-Aug 11, 1915).

Cupid Beats Father, 2 reels— American Film Co., Beauty/d. Mutual — dir.: James Douglass, cast: Neva Gerber, F.B. (=Frank), William Carroll (11–20–15).

Nobody's Home, 2 reels— American Film Co., Beauty/d. Mutual — dir.: James Douglass, cast: Neva Gerber, William Carroll, F.B. (=Dick), Mollie Shafer (12–4-15).

Making Over Father, 2 reels— American Film Co., Beauty/d. Mutual — dir.: Archer MacMackin, cast: Neva Gerber, F.B. (=Aubert Haines), William Carroll (12–11–15).

Two Hearts and a Thief, 2 reels— American Film Co., Beauty/d. Mutual — dir.: John Dillon, cast: Neva Gerber, F.B. (=Jack Nelson), Lucille Ward, Rae Berger (12–11–15).

The Clean-Up, 2 reels—American Film Co./d. Mutual—dir.: Charles Bartlett, cast: Winnifred Greenwood, F.B. (=George Prescott), George Field (12–18–15).

Settled Out of Court, 2 reels—American Film Co., Beauty/d. Mutual—dir.: Archer MacMackin, cast: Lucille Ward, William Carroll, F.B. (=the son), (12–25–15).

The Cactus Blossom, 2 reels—American Film Co., Mustang/d. Mutual—dir.: Thomas Chatterton, cast: F.B. (=Reed Avery), Anna Little, Dick LaReno, Chief Big Tree (12–25–15).

1916

Mammy's Rose, 1 reel—American Film Co./d. Mutual—dir.: James Douglass, cast: Neva Gerber, F.B. (=Frank), Antrim Short (2-4-16, shooting: 1915).

Two Bits, 2 reels—American Film Co., Mustang/d. Mutual—dir.: Thomas Chatterton, cast: Anna Little, Thomas Chatterton, Mary Thorne, Jack Richardson (4-7-16).

The Awakening, 2 reels—American Film Co., Mustang/d. Mutual—cast: Anna Little, Jack Richardson, Nita Davis, Art Acord (4–14–16).

Realization, 3 reels—American Film Co./d. Mutual—dir.: Thomas Ricketts—cast: Alfred D. Vosburgh, Vivian Rich, George Periolat, Louise Lester (4–29–16).

Enchantment, 2 reels—American Film Co./d. Mutual—*script: Frank Borzage*—cast: Vivian Rich, Albert Vosburgh, George Periolat, Laura Sears (8–21–16).

1917

A Mormon Maid, 5 reels—Jesse L. Lasky Feature Play Co./d. Freedman Enterprises (Paramount)—dir.: Robert Z. Leonard, cast: Mae Murray, F. B. (=Tom Rigdon), Hobard Bosworth (12-2-17).

A School for Husbands, 5 reels—Jesse L. Lasky Feature Play Co./d. Lasky (Paramount)—dir.: George H. Melford, cast: Fannie Ward, Jack Dean, Edythe Chapman, F. B. (=Hugh Aslam) (19-3-17).

Fear Not/The Twisted Soul, 5 reels—Butterfly-Universal Film Mfg. Prod./d. Universal—dir.: Allan J. Holubar, cast: Brownie Vernon, Myles McCarthy, Murdock MacQuarrie, F. B. (=Franklin Shirley) (17–11–17).

Wee Lady Betty, 5 reels—Triangle Film Corp., Kay-Bee (Thomas H. Ince)/d. Triangle—dir.: Charles Miller, cast: Bessie Love, F. B. (=Roger O'Reilly), Charles K. French (19–8-17).

Borzage as Director.

1915

The Pitch o' Chance. Prod.: American Film Company, Inc., Mustang Features/d. Mutual Film Corp.—script: [Frank Borzage]—photo: L. Guy Wilky—asst.-dir.: Park Frame—release: 24 Dec 1915—length: 2 reels; 1671 ft.; 26 minutes (18 fps).

Cast: Helen Rosson (Nan), Frank Borzage (Rocky Scott), Jack Richardson (Kentuck, the Gambler), Lizette Thorne (Kate).

1916

Life's Harmony. Prod.: American Film Company, Inc. (Flying A)/d. Mutual Film Corp.—co-dir. & script: Lorimer Johnston—photo: L. Guy Wilky—asst.-dir.: Park Frame—release: 22 Feb 1916—length: 3 reels; 2820 ft., 46 minutes (17 fps).

Cast: Vivian Rich (Faith Pringle), George Periolat (Josiah Pringle), Alfred Vosburgh (Gordon Howard), Louise Lester (Letitia Pringle).

The Silken Spider [‡]. Prod.: American Film Company, Inc. (Flying A)/d. Mutual Film Corp.—script: William Parker—photo: L. Guy Wilky—asst.-dir.: Park Frame—release: 7 Mar 1916—length: 3 reels

Cast: Vivian Rich (Bona Leonard), Alfred Vosburgh (Reverend Lewis Dunstan), George Periolat (Brian Leonard), Louise Lester (Ursula Jacques), King Clark (Neal Jacques), Warren Ellsworth (Caleb Giles), Lillian Knight (Mrs. Dunstan).

The Code of Honor [‡]. working title: *Derelicts*. Prod.: American Film Company, Inc. (Flying A)/d.

Mutual Film Corp.— script: William Parker — photo: L. Guy Wilky — asst.-dir.: Park Frame — release: 21 Mar 1916 — length: 3 reels

Cast: Alfred Vosburgh (Cpt. Frank Marvin), Vivian Rich (Zena, Valpar's niece), Estelle Allen (Ruth Chase), Frank Borzage (Ltn. Bob Chase), George Periolat (Molne Valpar), Ward McAllister (Monte).

Two Bits [‡]. Prod.: American Film Company, Inc., Mustang Features/d. Mutual Film Corp.— dir.: Frank Borzage (started by Tom Chatterton) — release: 7 Apr 1916 — length: 2 reels

Cast: Frank Borzage (James Hardeman), Anna Little (Two Bits), Jack Richardson (Jed Silmpson), Mark Thorne (Al Morley).

A Flickering Light [‡]. working title: *The Awakening.* Prod.: American Film Company, Inc., Mustang Features/d. Mutual Film Corp.—co-dir.: C. Rea Berger — script: Karl Coolidge — photo: L. Guy Wilky — asst.-dir.: Park Frame — release: 14 Apr 1916 — length: 2 reels

Cast: Frank Borzage (Jim), Jack Richardson (Hardy Anderson), Anna Little (Madge).

Unlucky Luke [‡]. Prod.: American Film Company, Inc., Mustang Features/d. Mutual Film Corp.— script: [Frank Borzage] — photo: L. Guy Wilky — asst.-dir.: Park Frame — release: 28 Apr 1916 — length: 2 reels

Cast: Frank Borzage (Luke Drummond), Jack Richardson (Seth Powers), Anna Little (Lucy Manners), John Gough (Ezra Smead).

Jack [‡]. Prod.: American Film Company, Inc., Mustang Features/d. Mutual Film Corp.— script: Karl Coolidge — photo: L. Guy Wilky — asst.-dir.: Park Frame — release: 26 May 1916 — length: 2 reels

Cast: Frank Borzage (Jack), Dick La Reno (Gilman), Anna Little (Frances), Margaret Nichols (Eva, Gilman's Daughter), Jack Richardson (Raymond Welton).

The Pilgrim. Prod.: American Film Company, Inc., Mustang Features/d. Mutual Film Corp.— script: Edward A. Kaufman — photo: L. Guy Wilky — asst.-dir.: Park Frame — release: 9 Jun 1916 — length: 2 reels, 1888 ft., 29 minutes (17 fps).

Cast: Frank Borzage (the Pilgrim), Anna Little (Nita Dudley), Jack Richardson (Joe Mex), Dick La Reno (Jim Niles), Mary Gladding (Little Eva).

The Demon of Fear [‡] Prod.: American Film Company, Inc., Mustang Features/d. Mutual Film Corp.— script: [Frank Borzage] — photo: L. Guy Wilky — asst.-dir.: Park Frame — release: 30 Jun 1916 — length: 2 reels

Cast: Frank Borzage (Thomas Marsh), Anna Little (Anna), Jack Richardson (James Oliver), Queenie Rosson (Rebecca Oliver).

Quicksands of Deceit [‡]. Prod.: American Film Company, Inc. (Flying A)/d. Mutual Film Corp.— script: [Frank Borzage] — photo: L. Guy Wilky — asst.-dir.: Park Frame — release: 13 Jul 1916 — length: 3 reels

Cast: Vivian Rich (Ida Allen), Alfred Vosburgh (Hugh Conway), George Periolat (John Hardy), Queenie Rosson (Eleanor Hardy).

Nugget Jim's Pardner/The Calibre of Man. working title: *That Good for Nothing Kid.* Prod.: American Film Company, Inc., Mustang Features/d. Mutual Film Corp., Supreme Film Corp.— script: [Frank Borzage] — photo: L. Guy Wilky — asst.-dir.: Park Frame — release: 14 Jul 1916 — length: 2 reels, 1569 ft., 26 minutes (16 fps).

Cast: Anna Little (Madge Keith), Frank Borzage (Hal), Dick La Reno (Nugget Jim" Keith), Jack Farrell.

That Gal of Burke's/Daughter of the Ranch [‡]. Prod.: American Film Company, Inc., Mustang Features/d. Mutual Film Co.— script: Lawrence Payson — photo: L. Guy Wilky — asst.-dir.: Park Frame — release: 28 Jul 1916 — length: 2 reels

Cast: Frank Borzage (Charles Percival), Anna Little (Tommie Burke), Jack Richardson (Arnold Blake), Dick La Reno (Mr. Burke), Gordona Bennett (Mr. Burke's New York Sister), Queenie Rosson (Mabel).

The Courtin' of Calliope Clew [‡]. Prod.: American Film Company, Inc., Mustang Features/d. Mutual Film Corp.— script: [Frank Borzage] — photo: L. Guy Wilky — asst.-dir.: Park Frame — release: 11 Aug 1916 (shooting: June) — length: 2 reels

Cast: Frank Borzage (Calliope Clew), Anna Little (Prudence Matthews), Charles Newton (Dr. Matthews).

Nell Dale's Men Folks [‡]. Prod.: American Film Company, Inc., Mustang Features/d. Mutual Film Corp.— script: Kenneth B. Clarke, Frank Borzage — photo: L. Guy Wilky — asst.-dir.: Park Frame — release: 25 Aug 1916 (shooting: June-July)—length: 2 reels
    Cast: Anna Little (Nell Dale), Frank Borzage (Zeb Dale), Webb Parker (John Dale), Harvey Clark (Bart Trevis), Oscar Gerard (Dick Remson), Chick Morrison (Bill Remson).

The Forgotten Prayer [‡]. working title: *The Man Who Forgot*. Prod.: American Film Company, Inc., Mustang Features/d. Mutual Film Corp.— script: Kenneth B. Clarke — photo: L. Guy Wilky — asst.-dir.: Park Frame — release: 31 Aug 1916 (shooting: April-May)—length: 3 reels
    Cast: Anna Little (Alice Page), Frank Borzage (Dan Page), Perry Banks (Mojave" Matt), Jack Richardson (Arthur Sandford).

Matchin' Jim [‡]. Prod.: American Film Company, Inc., Mustang Features/d. Mutual Film Corp.— script: [Frank Borzage] — photo: L. Guy Wilky — asst.-dir.: Park Frame — release: 8 Sep 1916 — length: 2 reels
    Cast: Frank Borzage (Matchin' Jim), Chick Morrison (Murphy), Anna Little (Phyllis Ellings), Dick La Reno (Ellings), Harvey Clark (Hawkins), Queenie Rosson (Marg).

First feature film: Land o' Lizards [incomplete]. Prod.: American Film Company, Inc./d. Mutual Film Corp., Masterpictures ByLuxe Edition — script: Kenneth B. Clarke — photo: L. Guy Wilky — asst.-dir.: Park Frame — release: 21 Sep 1916 — length: 5 reels
    Cast: Frank Borzage (the Stranger), Harvey Clark (Ward Curtis), Laura Sears (Wynne Curtis), Perry Banks (Dave Moore), Anna Little (Bobbie Moore), Jack Richardson (Buck Moran).

Immediate Lee [‡]. new release title (1922): *Hair Trigger Casey*. Prod.: American Film Company, Inc./d. Mutual Film Corp., Masterpieces ByLuxe Edition — script: Kenneth B. Clarke, from his novel *Immediate Lee* published in *The Saturday Evening Post*—photo: L. Guy Wilky — asst.-dir.: Park Frame — release: 16. Nov 1916 (shooting: August-September)—length: 5 reels/4600 ft.
    Cast: Frank Borzage (Immediate Lee [1922: Casey]), Anna Little (Beulah), Jack Richardson (Kentuck Hurley), Chick Morrison (John Masters), William Stowell (King), Harry McCabe, George Clark, John Smith, Charles Newton.

1917

Flying Colors [incomplete]. Prod.: Triangle Film Corp./d. Triangle — script: John Lynch, from story by R. Cecil Smith — release: 23 Sep 1917 — length: 5 reels
    Cast: William Desmond (Brent Brewster), Golda Madden (Ann), Jack Livingston (captain Drake), Laura Sears (Ruth Lansing), J. Barney Sherry (Craig Lansing), George W. Chase (Jimmy McMahon), John P. Lockney (Brewster, Sr.), Bert Offerd (Cockney), Mary McIvor (Stenograph), Ray Jackson (Manager's Son).

Until They Get Me. Prod.: Triangle Film Corp./d. Triangle — prod. supervision: Allan Dwan — script: Kenneth B. Clarke — photo: Claude H. "Bud" Wales— release: 23 Dec 1917 (New York 2 Dec 1917)—length: 5 reels, 4187 ft., 63 minutes (17 fps).
    Cast: Pauline Starke (Margy), Jack Curtis (Kirby), Joe King (Selwyn, RNMP), Wilbur Higde (Cd. Draper, RNMP), Anna Dodge (Mrs. Draper), Walter Perry (Sergeant Blaney, RNMP).

1918

The Gun Woman. Prod.: Triangle Film Corp., Kay-Bee/d. Triangle — prod. supervision: Allan Dwan — script: Alvin J. Neitz — photo: Claude H. "Bud" Wales, Pliny Horne — release: 27.1.18 — length: 5 reels/4523 ft./60 minutes.
    Cast: Texas Guinan (the Tigress), Edward Joseph Brady (the Bostonian), Francis J. McDonald (the Stranger [the Gent]/the Collector), Walter Perkins (Sheriff Joe Harper), Thornton Edwards (the Vulture), George Chase (the Vulture).

The Curse of Iku [‡]. new release title (1919): *Ashes of Desire*. Prod.: Essanay Film Mfg.Co. (Verne R. Day); Perfection Pictures/d. George Kleine System — prod. supervision: M. Blair Coan —

script: Catherine Carr, from story by Sam Small Jr.— release: 1 Mar 1918 (©1 Aug 1919)— length: 7 reels

   Cast: Frank Borzage (Allan Carroll/Allan Carroll III), Tsuru Aoki (Omi San).

The Shoes That Danced [‡]. Prod.: Triangle Film Corp./d. Triangle— prod. supervision: Allan Dwan— script: Jack Cunningham, from story "The Shoes That Danced" by John A. Moroso published in *Metropolitan Magazine* (Dec. 1917)— photo: Pliny Horne— release: 3 Mar 1918— length: 5 reels

   Cast: Pauline Starke (Rhoda Regan), Wallace MacDonald (Harmony Lad), Richard Rosson (Stumpy Darcy), Anna Dodge (Mrs. Regan), Lydia Yeamans Titus (Mother Carey), Anne Knovel (Mamie Conlon), Edward Brady (Wedge Barker), William Dyer (Hogan).

Innocent's Progress [‡]. Prod.: Triangle Film Corp./d. Triangle— prod. supervision: Allan Dwan— script: Frank S. Beresford, from story by Frances Quillan— photo: Pliny Horne— release: 24 Mar 1918— length: 5 reels

   Cast: Pauline Starke (Tessa Fayne), Lillian West (Madeline Carson), Alice Knowland (Aunt Lottie), Jack Livingston (Carey Larned), Charles Dorian (Olin Humphreys), Graham Pette (Masters).

Society for Sale [‡]. working title: *The Honorable Billy.* Prod.: Roy Aitken, Triangle Film Corp./d. Triangle— prod. supervision: Allan Dwan— script: Charles J. Wilson, from story by Ruby Mildred Ayres— photo: Pliny Horne, asst.: William H. Daniels—cost.: Peggy Hamilton— release: 21 Apr 1918— length: 5 reels

   Cast: William Desmond (Honorable Billy), Gloria Swanson (Phyllis Clyne), Herbert Prior (Lord Sheldon), Charles Dorian (Furnival), Lillian West (Vi Challoner), Lillian Langdon (Lady Mary).

An Honest Man [‡]. Prod.: Triangle Film Corp./d. Triangle— supervision: Allan Dwan— script: George Elwood, George E. Jenks, from story by Henry Payson Dowst— photo: Pliny Horne— release: 5 May 1918— length: 5 reels

   Cast: William Desmond (Benny Boggs), Mary Warren (Beatrice Burnett), Ann Knovel (Ruby Cushing), Graham Pette (Old Man Cushing), William Franey.

Who Is to Blame? [‡]. working titles: *The Loyalty of Taro San; The Honor of Taro San.* Prod.: Triangle Film Corp./d. Triangle— story: E. Magnus Ingleton— photo: Pliny Horne— release: 19 May 1918— length: 5 reels

   Cast: Jack Abbe (Taro San), Jack Livingston (Grant Barton), Maude Wayne (Marion Craig), Lillian West (Tonia Marsh), Lillian Langdon (Mrs. Craig).

The Ghost Flower [‡]. Prod.: Triangle Film Corp./d. Triangle— script: Catherine Carr, from story by Madeline Matzen— photo: Jack McKenzie— asst.-dir.: Amy E. Sacker (Naples sequences)— release: 18 Aug 1918— length: 5 reels

   Cast: Alma Rubens (Giulia), Charles West (La Farge), Francis J. McDonald (Tony Cafarelli), Richard Rosson (Paola), Emory Johnson (Duke of Chaumont), Naida Lessing (La Serena), Tote Ducrow (Ercolano).

1919

Toton [‡]. UK: *The Vital Spark* (*A Romance of Montmartre*). Prod.: Triangle Film Corp./d. Triangle (Special Presentation)— story: Catherine Carr— photo: Jack MacKenzie— release: 30 Mar 1919 (shooting: August-Sept. 1918)— length: 6 reels

   Cast: Olive Thomas (Toton/Yvonne), Norman Kerry (David Lane), Francis J. McDonald (Pierre), Jack Perrin (Carew).

Whom the Gods Would Destroy [‡] aka: *Whom the Gods Destroy.* working title: *Humanity.* Prod.: Ollie L. Sellers, for C.R. Macauley Photoplays, Inc./d. First National —from short story "Humanity" by Charles R. Macauley and Nan Blair— photo: Jack MacKenzie— asst.-dir.: Justin H. McClosky— asst. edit.: Tom Logan— techn. staff: Nan Blair, Milton Menasco, Jack Mackenzie, Sidney R. Flower— laboratories: Rothacker Film Mfg.— hand color work: Watterson Rothacker— release: 15 Apr 1919— length: 7 reels

   Cast: Jack Mulhall (Jack Randall), Pauline Starke (Julie), Kathryn Adams (Elsa Klaw), Harvey Clarke (Wolf von Schwartz), Charles French (Herr Klaw), Walter Whitman (Matthieu), Jean Hersholt, Wilton Taylor, Millard Wilson, Eddie Hearne, Nanine Wright, George Pierce, Alberta Lee,

Betty Schade, Utahna La Reno, Walter Perkins, William Dyer, William V. Meinke, John Cossar, Frank Newburg.

Prudence on Broadway [‡]. Prod.: Triangle Film Corp./d. Triangle — story: Catherine Carr — photo: Pliny Horne — release: 6 Jul 1919 — length: 5 reels

Cast: Olive Thomas (Prudence), Francis McDonald (Grayson Mills), Harvey Clark (John Melbourne), John P. Wild (John Ogilvie), Alberta Lee (Mrs. Ogilvie), Lillian West (Mrs. Allen Wentworth), Edward Peil (Mr. Wentworth), Mary Warren (Kitty), Lillian Langdon (Mrs. Melbourne), Claire McDowell (Miss Grayson).

The Duke of Chimney Butte [‡]. Prod.: Andrew J. Callaghan, for Fred Stone Productions/d. Robertson-Cole Pictures — script: Marian Ainslee, from story by George Washington Ogden (Chicago 1920) — photo: Jack MacKenzie — release: 4. Dec 1921 (also ©) — length: 5 reels; 4600 ft.

Cast: Fred Stone (Jeremeah Lambert, "the Duke), Vola Vale (Vesta Philbrook), Josie Sedgwick (Grace Kerr), Chick Morrison (Kerr, the Son), Buck Connors (Taters), Harry Dunkinson (Jedlick).

Billy Jim. Prod.: Andrew J. Callaghan, for Fred Stone Productions/d. Robertson-Cole Pictures — script: Frank Howard Clark, from story by Jackson Gregory — photo: Gus Peterson — release: 29 Jan 1922 (©19 Jan 1922) — length: 5 reels; 4080 ft./1239 m.; 55 minutes (20 fps).

Cast: Fred Stone (William James, known as "Billy Jim), Millicent Fisher (Marsha Dunforth), George Hernandez (Dudley Dunforth), William Bletcher (Jimmy), Marian Skinner (Mrs. Dunforth), Frank Thorne (Roy Forsythe).

1919–1920

Humoresque. Prod.: Cosmopolitan Productions, New York (William Randolph Hearst); International Film Service Co./d. Famous Players-Lasky Corp.; Paramount Artcraft Pictures — script: Frances Marion, from *Humoresque: A Laugh on Life with a Tear Behind It* by Fannie Hurst (published in *Cosmopolitan Magazine*, March 1919; Harper & Brothers, New York 1918) — photo: Gilbert Warrenton — art dir.: Joseph Urban — 2nd asst.-dir.: Lew Borzage — mus. arrang. : Hugo Riesenfeld (and "Humoresque" by Antonín Dvořák) — release: 30 May 1920 New York (Criterion Theatre) [private screening: 4 May 1920 New York; ©23.Jun 1920] — length: 6 reels ; 5631 ft.; 76 minutes (20 fps).

Cast: Alma Rubens (Gina Berg [Minnie Ginsberg]), Vera Gordon (Mama Kantor), Dore Davidson (Abraham Kantor), Bobby Connelly (Leon Kantor, child), Gaston Glass (Leon Kantor, adult), Helen Connelly (Esther Kantor, child), Ann Wallick (Esther Kantor, adult), Sidney Carlyle (Mannie Kantor), Joseph Cooper (Isadore Kantor, child), Maurice Levigne (Isadore Kantor, adult), Alfred Goldberg (Rudolph Kantor, child), Edward Stanton (Rudolph Kantor, adult), Louis Stearns (Sol Ginsberg), Maurice Peckre (Boris Kantor), Ruth Sabin (Mrs. Isadore Kantor), Frank Mitchell (Baby Kantor), Miriam Battista (Minnie Ginsberg, child).

1921

Get-Rich-Quick Wallingford [‡] aka *Wallingford.* Prod.: Cosmopolitan Productions, New York (William Randolph Hearst)/d. Paramount — script: Luther Reed, from play by George Michael Cohan (New York 1910), inspired by *Get-Rich-Quick Wallingford: A Cheerful Account of the Rise and Fall of an American Business Buccaneer,* by George Randolph Chester (A. L. Burt, New York 1908) — photo: Chester A. Lyons — art dir.: Joseph Urban — release: 4 Dec 1921 New York (Rivoli) (also ©) — length: 7 reels; 7381 ft.

Cast: Sam Hardy (J. Rufus Wallingford), Norman Kerry (Blackie" Daw), Doris Kenyon (Fannie Jasper), Diana Allen (Gertrude Dempsey), Edgar Nelson (Eddie Lamb), Billie Dove (Dorothy Wells), Mac Barnes (Andrea Dempsey), William T. Hayes (G. W. Battles), Horace James (Timothy Battles), John Woodford (Mr. Wells), Mrs. Charles Willard (Mrs. Dempsey), Eugene Keith (Harkins), William Carr (Quigg), William Robyns (Abe Gunther), Theodore Westman, Jr. (Groom), Patterson Dial (Bessie), Jerry Sinclair (Judge Lampton), Benny One (Wallingford's Valet).

1921–1922

Back Pay. Prod.: Cosmopolitan Productions, New York (William Randolph Hearst)/d. Paramount — script: Frances Marion, from story by Fannie Hurst (in *The Vertical City*, Harper & Brothers, New York-London 1922); Art titles: Grace Walter—photo: Chester A. Lyons—art dir.: Joseph Urban—release: 8 Jan 1922 (also ©); Feb 1922 New York (Rivoli)—length: 7 reels; 6460 ft.; existing print: 5505 ft., 84 minutes (19 fps).

Cast: Seena Owen (Hester Bevins), Matt Moore (Jerry Newcombe), J. Barney Sherry (Charles G. Wheeler), Ethel Duray (Kitty), Charles Craig (Speed), Jerry Sinclair (Thomas Craig).

The Good Provider [‡— except a 7 minute fragment]. Prod.: Cosmopolitan Productions, New York (William Randolph Hearst)/d. Paramount — script: John Lynch, from story by Fannie Hurst (in *Saturday Evening Post*, 15 Aug 1914)—photo: Chester A. Lyons—release: 2 Apr 1922 New York (Rivoli) (©19 Apr 1922)—length: 8 reels; 7753 ft.

Cast: Vera Gordon (Becky Binswanger), Dore Davidson (Julius Binswanger), Miriam Battista (Pearl Binswanger), Vivienne Osborne (Pearl Binswanger), William [Buster] Collier, Jr. (Izzy Binswanger), John Roche (Max Teitlebaum), Ora Jones (Mrs. Teitlebaum), Edward Phillips (Man in Broadway), Muriel Martin (Girl), James Devine (Mr. Boggs), Blanche Craig (Mrs. Boggs), Margaret Severn (Dancer).

1922

The Valley of Silent Men [incomplete]. Prod.: Cosmopolitan Productions, New York (William Randolph Hearst)/d. Paramount — script: John Lynch, from *The Valley of Silent Men: A Story of the Three River Country* by James Oliver Curwood (Cosmopolitan Books Corp. and Grosset & Dunlap, New York 1920); titles: Grace Waller—photo: Chester A. Lyons—asst.-dir.: Lew Borzage—prod. manager: John Lynch—release: 28 Aug 1922 New York (Rialto) (©6 Sep 1922)—length: 7 reels, 6500 ft.; existing print: 4148 ft., 47 minutes (22 fps).

Cast: Alma Rubens (Marette Radisson), Lew Cody (Sgt. James Kent, RNMP), Joseph King (Buck" O'Connor), Mario Majeroni (Pierre Radisson, the Father), George Nash (Inspector Kedsty, RNMP), J. W. Johnston (Jacques Radisson, the brother, aka "the prophet), John Powderface (Indian Chief), High Mucky-Muck (Papoose, his son).

The Pride of Palomar working title: *Homeward Bound*. Prod.: Cosmopolitan Productions, New York (William Randolph Hearst)/d. Paramount — script: Grant Carpenter and John Lynch, from story by Peter Bernard Kyne (New York, 1921); titles: Grace Waller—photo: Chester A. Lyons—release: 19 Nov 1922 New York (Rivoli) (©15 Nov 1922)—length: 8 reels, 7596 ft., 104 minutes (21 fps).

Cast: Forrest Stanley (Don Mike Farrel), Marjorie Daw (Kay Parker), Tote Du Crow (Pablo), James Barrows (Father Dominic), Joseph Dowling (Don Miguel Farrel), Alfred Allen (John Parker), George Nichols (Bill Conway), Warner Oland (Fuji Okada), Mrs. Jessie Hebbard (Mrs. Parker), Percy Williams (Butler), Mrs. George Hernandez (Caroline), Edward Joseph Brady (André Loustalot), Carmen Arselle (Mrs. Supaldio), Eagle Eye (Nogi), Most Mattoe (Anita Supaldio).

1923

The Nth Commandment [incomplete]. UK: *The Higher Law*. Prod.: Cosmopolitan Productions, New York (William Randolph Hearst)/d. Paramount — script and supervision: Frances Marion, from story by Fannie Hurst (in *Every Soul Hath Its Song*, Harper & Brothers, New York-London 1916)— photo: Chester A. Lyons—release: 8 Apr 1923 New York (Rivoli) (©3 Apr 1923)—length: 8 reels, 7339 ft., 80 minutes; existing print: 4010 ft., 58 minutes (22 fps).

Cast: Colleen Moore (Sarah Juke), James Morrison (Harry Smith), Eddie Phillips (Jimmie Fitzgibbons), Charlotte Merriam (Angine Sprunt), George Cooper (Max Plute).

Children of Dust [‡] working titles: *Terwilliger; Sands of Time*. Prod.: Frank Borzage, for Arthur H. Jacobs Corp./d. Associated First National Pictures— script: Agnes Christine Johnston, adapt.: Frank Dazey, from "Terwilliger" by Tristram Tupper (in *Lucky Star*, Grosset & Dunlap, New York 1929)—photo: Chester A. Lyons—art dir.: Frank Ormston—edit.: Howard P. Bretherton—release: 28 Aug 1923 New York (Proctor's 58th Street) (©1 Jun 1923)—length: 7 reels; 6228 ft.

Cast: Bert Woodruff (Old Archer), Johnnie Walker (Terwilliger), Frankie Lee (Terwilliger child), Pauline Garon (Celia Van Houghton [or: Helen Raymond]), Josephine Adair (Celia Van Houghton child), Lloyd Hugues (Harvey Livermore), Newton Hall (Harvey Livermore child), George Nichols (Terwilliger's father-in-law).

The Age of Desire [‡] working titles: *Dust of the Doorway; Against the Grain.* Prod.: Frank Borzage, for Arthur H. Jacobs Corp./d. Associated First National Pictures — script: Mary O'Hara, adapt.: Dixie Willson, titles: Lenore J. Coffee — photo: Chester A. Lyons — art dir.: Frank Ormston — release and ©: 20 Sep 1923 — length: 6 reels; 5174 ft.

Cast: Joseph Swickard (Marcio), William Collier, Jr. (Ranny 21 years old), Frank Truesdell (Malcolm Trask, Millionaire Husband), Bruce Guerin (Ranny 3 years old), Frankie Lee (Ranny 13 years old), J. Farrell McDonald (Dan Reagan), Mary Jane Irving (Margy 10 years old), Myrtle Stedman (Janet Loring), Aggie Herring (Ann Reagan), Mary Philbin (Margy 18 years old), Edithe Yorke (Grandmother).

The Song of Love [‡] working title: *Dust of Desire.* Prod.: Norma Talmadge Productions (pres. by Joseph M. Schenck)/d. Associated First National Pictures — dir.: [Frank Borzage], Chester M. Franklin, Frances Marion — script: Frances Marion, from novel *Dust of Desire* by Margaret Peterson (New York 1922) — photo: Tony Gaudio — release: 24 Feb 1924 New York (Rivoli) (©13 Dec 1923) — length: 8 reels; 8000 ft; 79 minutes.

Cast: Norma Talmadge (Noorma-hal, the Dancer), Joseph Schildkraut (Ramon Valverde), Arthur Edmund Carewe (Ramlika), Laurence Wheat (Dick Jones), Maude Wayne (Maureen Desmard), Earl Schenck (Commissionar Desmard), Hector V. Sarno (Chandra-lal), Albert Prisco (Chamba), Mario Carillo (Captain Fregonne), James Cooley (Dr. Humbert).

1923–1924

Secrets. Prod.: Frank Borzage, for Norma Talmadge Productions (pres. by Joseph M. Schenck); assoc. prod.: John W. Considine, Jr./d. Associated First National Pictures — script: Frances Marion, from the play *Secrets: A Play in a Prologue, Three Acts and an Epilogue* by Rudolf Besier & May [=Helen Marion] Edginton (1922; publ. Simon French, New York-London 1930), and the novel *Secrets* by M. Edginton (publ. in *Harper's Bazaar*, Dec. 1918) — photo: Tony [Gaetano] Gaudio — art dir.: Stephen Goosson — cost.: Clare West — makeup: George Westmore — musical arr.: Samuel L. Rothafel (NYC); theme song: "Memory Lane" — release: 24 Mar 1924 New York (Astor) (©11 Feb 1924) — length: 8 reels; 8363 ft./2550 m., 91 minutes; existing print: 6400 ft./1920 m, 83 minutes (20 fps).

Cast: Norma Talmadge (Mary Marlowe-Carlton), Eugene O'Brien (John Carlton), Patterson Dial (Susan, the Maid 1865), Emily Fitzroy (Mrs. Marlowe 1865), Claire McDowell (Aunt Elizabeth Channing 1865), George Nichols (William Marlowe 1865), Harvey Clark (Bob 1870), Charles Ogle (Dr. McGovern 1870), Francis Feeney (John Carlton Jr. 1888), Alice Day (Blanche Carlton 1888), Winston Miller (Robert Carlton 1888), May Giraci (Audrey Carlton 1888), Gertrude Astor (Mrs. Eustace Mainwaring 1888), Winter Hall (Dr. Arbuthnot 1923), Frank Elliott (Robert Carlton 1923), George Cowl (John Carlton Jr. 1923), Clarissa Selwynne (Audrey Carlton 1923), Florence Wix (Lady Lessington 1923), Frank Westmore (the Baby).

The Lady [incomplete]. Prod.: Frank Borzage, for Norma Talmadge Productions (pres. by Joseph M. Schenck)/d. First National Pictures — script: Frances Marion, from play by Martin Brown (New York 1923) — photo: Tony Gaudio — art dir.: William Cameron Menzies — cost.: Claire West — edit.: Hal C. Kern — release: 25 Jan 1925 New York (Colony) (©15 Jan 1925) — length: 8 reels, 7357 ft.; existing print: 5950 ft., 86 minutes (18 fps).

Cast: Norma Taldmadge (Polly Pearl), Wallace MacDonald (Leonard Saint-Aubyns), Brandon Hurst (Saint-Aubyns, Sr.), Alf Goulding (Tom Robinson), Doris Lloyd (Fannie St. Clair), Walter Long (Blackie), George Hackathorn (Leonard Cairns), Marc MacDermott (Mr. Wendover), Paulette Duval (Countess Adrienne Catellier), John Fox, Jr. (Freckles), Emily Fitzroy (Madame Blanche), John Herdman (John Cairns), Margaret Seddon (Mrs. Cairns), Edwin Hubbell (Kid in London), Miles McCarthy (Mr. Graves).

1924–1925

Daddy's Gone A-Hunting. UK and working title: *A Man's World.* Prod.: Frank Borzage (pres. by Louis B. Mayer), Metro-Goldwyn Pictures — script: Kenneth B. Clarke, from play in 3 acts by Zoë Akins (Boni & Liveright, New York 1923) — photo: Chester A. Lyons — art dir.: Cedric Gibbons — edit.: Frank Sullivan — asst.-dir.: Orville O. "Bunny" Dull — release: 22 Feb 1925 New York (Capitol) (©9 Mar 1925) — length: 6 reels; 5851 ft.; existing print: 1710 m., 60 minutes (24 fps).

Cast: Alice Joyce (Edith), Percy Marmont (Julian), Virginia Marshall (Janet), Helena D'Algy (Olga), Ford Sterling (Oscar), Holmes Herbert (Greenough), Edythe Chapman (Mrs. Greenough), James Barrows (Col. Orth), James Macelhern (Bensen), Martha Mattox (Mrs. Wethers), Margaret Reid (Reporter), Charles Crockett, Kate Toncray, Barbara Tennant.

1925

The Circle. Prod.: Frank Borzage, Metro-Goldwyn-Mayer Pictures—dir.: Frank Borzage, [and Edmund Goulding (retakes)]—script: Kenneth B. Clarke, from the comedy in 3 acts by William Somerset Maugham (W. Heinemann, London 1921)—photo: Chester A. Lyons—art dir.: Cedric Gibbons, James Basevi—cost.: Ethel P. Chaffin—asst.-dir.: Orville O. "Bunny" Dunn—release: 20 Sep 1925 New York (Capitol) (©14 Sep 1925)—length: 6 reels, 5511 ft.; existing print: 5324 ft, 75 minutes (21 fps).
Cast: Eleanor Boardman (Elizabeth), Malcolm McGregor (Edward Lutton), Alec B. Francis (Lord Clive Champion-Cheney), Joan Crawford (young Lady Catherine), Eugenie Besserer (old Lady Catherine), George Fawcett (Lord Hugh Porteous), Creighton Hale (Arnold Champion-Cheney), Otto Hoffman (Dorker), Eulalie Jensen (Mrs. Shenstone), Frank Braidwood (young Lord Hugh), Derek Glynne, Buddy Smith.

MGM Studio Tour aka: *City of Stars; 1925 Studio Tour*—Prod.: Metro-Goldwyn-Mayer—dir.: Bruce Humberstone—length: 30 minutes—Studio tour in Culver City. (Frank Borzage directs Eleanor Boardman during the shooting of *The Circle.*)

Lazybones. Prod.: Frank Borzage (presented by William Fox), Fox Film Corp.—script: Frances Marion, from play by Owen Davis (New York 1924)—photo: Glenn MacWilliams, George Schneiderman—asst.-dir.: Orville O. "Bunny" Dull—song: "Lazybones" by Frank Silver—release: 4 Dec 1925 New York (Loew's) (©30 Aug 1925)—length: 8 reels, 7234 ft.; existing print: 6395 ft., 78 minutes (22 fps).
Cast: Charles "Buck" Jones (Steve "Lazybones" Tuttle), Madge Bellamy (Kit), Edythe Chapman (Mrs. Tuttle), Leslie Fenton (Dick Ritchie), Jane Novak (Agnes Fanning), Emily Fitzroy (Mrs. Rebecca Fanning), ZaSu Pitts (Ruth Fanning), William Norton Bailey (Elmer Ballister), Virginia Marshall (Baby Kit), Danny Borzage, Rena Rogers-Borzage, Lew Borzage (extras).

Wages for Wives [‡] working title: *The Family Upstairs.* Prod.: Frank Borzage (presented by William Fox), Fox Film Corp. (Golden Series)—script: Kenneth B. Clarke, [Eve Unsell], from play *Chicken Feed: or Wages for Wives; a Comedy in Three Acts* by Guy Bolton & Winchell Smith (New York, 1924)—photo: Ernest G. Palmer—asst.-dir.: Orville O. "Bunny" Dunn—release: 18 Jan 1926 New York (Loew's Circle) (©29 Nov 1925)—length: 7 reels; 6650 ft.; 72 minutes.
Cast: Jacqueline Logan (Nell Bailey), Creighton Hale (Danny Kester), Earle Foxe (Hughie Logan), ZaSu Pitts (Luella Logan), Claude Gillingwater (Jim Bailey), David Butler (Chester Logan), Margaret Seddon (Annie Bailey), Margaret Livingston (Carol Bixby), Dan Mason (Mr. Tevis), Tom Ricketts (Judge McLean).

The First Year. Prod.: Frank Borzage (presented by William Fox), Fox Film Corp.- script: Frances Marion, from a comedy in 3 acts by Frank Craven, *The First Year: A Comic Tragedy of Married Life* (New York 1920—The John Golden Unit of Clean American Productions)—photo: Chester A. Lyons—asst.-dir.: Orville O. "Bunny" Dunn—release: 7 Mar 1926 New York (Rialto) (©10 Jan 1926)—length: 6 reels, 6038 ft., 75 minutes.
Cast: Matt Moore (Tom Tucker), Kathryn Perry (Grace Livingston), John Patrick (Dick Loring), Frank Currier (Dr. Myron Livingston), Carolynne Snowden (Hattie, the Maid), J. Farrell MacDonald (Mr. Barstow), Frank Cooley (Mr. Livingston), Virginia Madison (Mrs. Livingston), Margaret Livingston (Mrs. Barstow).

1925–1926

The Dixie Merchant [‡]. Prod.: Frank Borzage (presented by William Fox), Fox Film Corp.—script: Kenneth B. Clarke, [Edfrid Bingham], from the novel *The Chicken-Wagon Family* by John Barry Benefield (Grosset & Dunlap, New York 1925)—photo: Frank B. Good, asst.: Irving Rosenberg—asst.-dir.: Orville O. "Bunny" Dull—release: 7.3.26 (also ©)—length: 6 reels; 5126 ft.

Cast: J. Farrell MacDonald (Jean Paul Fippany), Madge Bellamy (Aida Fippany), Jack Mulhall (Jimmy Pickett), Claire McDowell (Josephine Fippany), Harvey Clark (Baptiste), Edward Martindel (John Pickett), Evelyn Arden (Minnie Jordan), Onest Conly (Eph), Paul Panzer (Whitcomb), Mary Borzage, Lew Borzage Sr. (an Old Couple).

1926

Early to Wed [‡] [under-title: *Life and Love in 1926*] — working title: *Separate Rooms*. Prod.: Frank Borzage (presented by William Fox), Fox Film Corp. — script: Kenneth B. Clarke, from story "The Splurge" by Evelyn Campbell (publ. in: *McCall's Magazine*, November 1924) — photo: Ernest G. Palmer — asst.-dir.: Lew Borzage — release: 17 Jun 1926 New York (Stanley Theater) (©18 Apr 1926) — length: 6 reels; 5912 ft.; 75 minutes.
Cast: Matt Moore (Tommy Carter), Kathryn Perry (Daphne Carter), Albert Gran (Cassius Hayden), Julia Swayne Gordon (Mrs. Hayden), Arthur Housman (Art Nevers), Rodney Hildebrand (Mike Dugan), ZaSu Pitts (Mrs. Dugan), Belva McKay (Mrs. Nevers), Ross McCutcheon (Bill Dugan), Harry Bailey (Pelton Jones).

"Marriage License"? UK and working title: *The Pelican*. Prod.: Frank Borzage (presented by William Fox), Fox Film Corp. — script: Bradley King, [Eve Unsell], titles: Elizabeth Pickett, from the play in 4 acts *The Pelican* by Fryniwyd Tennyson Jesse & Harold Marsh Harwood (New York 1925; publ. E. Benn Ltd., London 1926) — photo: Ernest Palmer — asst.-dir.: Lew Borzage. — release: 17 Oct 1926 New York (New Academy) (©22 Aug 1926) — length: 8 reels; 7168 ft.; existing print: 2060 m., 70 minutes (24 fps).
Cast: Alma Rubens (Wanda Ross-Heriot), Walter McGrail (Marcus Heriot), Richard Walling (Robin), Walter Pidgeon (Paul Lauzun), Charles Lane (Gen. Sir John Heriot), Emily Fitzroy (Lady Heriot), Langhorne Burton (Cheriton), Edgar Norton (Beadon), George Cowl (Bruce Abercrombie), Lon Poff (Footman), Olaf Hytten (Detective).

1927

7th Heaven. Prod.: Frank Borzage, supervis.prod.: Sol M. Wurtzel (presented by William Fox), Fox Film Corp. — script: Benjamin [Barney] Glazer, [revisions: Philip Klein], [first version: Frances Marion], titles: Katharine Hilliker, H. H. Caldwell, from the play in 3 acts by Austin Strong (S. French, New York-London, 1922); research: Judith Ann Gilbert — photo: Ernest Palmer, asst.: Stanley Little, Harold Schuster — assoc. camera: Joseph A. Valentine, asst.: Julian Robinson — lights: David Anderson. — art dir.: Harry Oliver, asst.: Fred C. Stoos — edit.: Barney Wolf, supervis. edit. : Philip Klein — mus.: William Perry (piano); songs: "Diane (I'm In Heaven When I See You Smile)" by Ernö Rapée, lyrics: Lew Pollack (waltz); "Seventh Heaven" by William Perry, Ronn Carroll; orchestration: Samuel L. Rothafel (NYC); studio orchestra on set: Eddie Frazier, George Ewing, Leslie Moe, William Markowitz — asst-dir.: Lew Borzage, Park Frame — French advisor: André Chotin, [Robert Florey] — cost.: Kathleen Kay, uniforms: Bert Offord — makeup: Charles Dudley, hairdresser: Kitty Thompson, Peggy Chrisman — script: Ralph Kaufman — matte paintings: Max Borch, supervis.: Fred W. Sersen — miniatures: Walter Pallman, asst.: Fred Morck, Jack Tolkin — special war effects: Louis Witte — portraits: Max Autrey, production portraits: Frank Powolny — electricians: Charles Erlund, asst.: J. L. Sigler — props: Mack Elliott, asst.: Eddie Radus — stage carpenter: Frank Pierson — construction: Lester J. Shaw, special wood effects: Joe Les Coulie; special stone work: Bush Baldridge — special props: William Jones, Ike Rosen — plastic art: Archie Jett, asst.: George Young — publicity: Peggy McCall — release: 6 May 1927 Los Angeles (Carthay Circle Theatre); 25 May 1927 New York (Sam H. Harris Theatre); sound version: 10 Sep 1927 (©19 Jun 1927) — length: 12 reels, 10807 ft., 120 minutes (24 fps).
Cast: Janet Gaynor (Diane Vulmir), Charles Farrell (Chico Robas), Ben Bard (Col. Brissac), David Butler (Gobin), Albert Gran (Papa Boule), Gladys Brockwell (Nana Vulmir), Emile Chautard (Father Chevillon), George Stone (Rat), Jessie Haslett (Aunt Valentine), Lillian West (Arlette), Marie Mosquini (Madame Gobin), Brandon Hurst (Uncle George), Lewis Borzage Sr. (Streetlighter), Dolly Borzage (Street Girl), Sue Borzage (Street Girl), Mary Borzage Sr. (Woman in bullet factory), Lois Hardwick.

Street Angel working titles: *The Lady Cristilinda; Naples; The Painted Lady*. Prod.: Frank Borzage;

supervis. prod.: Sol M. Wurtzel (presented by William Fox), Fox Film Corp.— script: Marion Orth, titles: Katherine Hilliker, H. H. Caldwell, adapt.: Philip Klein, Henry Roberts Symonds, [Frances Agnew, Lilian Ducey], from the comedy in 4 acts *The Lady Cristilinda* by Monckton Hoffe [1922] (S. French, New York-London 1926)— photo: Ernest Palmer, Paul Ivano— asst.: Harold Schuster— art dir.: Harry Oliver— cost.: Kathleen Kay— edit.: Barney Wolf, supervis.: Philip Klein— asst.-dir.: Lew Borzage, Ralph Kaufman— mus.: Ernö Rapée; theme song "My Angel (Angelo mio)" by Ernö Rapée, lyr. Lew Pollack (Movietone -Western Electric); mus. score (NYC): Samuel L. Rothafel— matte paintings: Fred W. Sersen— spec. eff.: Louis Witte— techn. advis.: Dr. Alfredo Sabato— release: 9 Apr 1928 New York (Globe Theatre); 10 Apr 1928 Los Angeles (Carthay Circle Theater) (©3 Apr 1928)— length: 10 reels, 9221 ft., 117 minutes.

Cast: Janet Gaynor (Angela), Charles Farrell (Gino), Guido Trento (Neri, Police Sergeant), Henry Armetta (Masetto), Natalie Kingston (Lisetta), Alberto Rabagliati (Policeman), Louis Liggett (Beppo), Milton Dickinson (Bimbo), Helene Her (Maria), David Kashner (Strongman), Jennie Bruno (Landlady), Gino Conti (Policeman), Hector V. Sarno (Spaghetti Cook), Dickie Dickinson (Acrobat), Lew Borzage Sr. Mary Borzage Sr., Sue Borzage, Madeline Borzage (extras).

1928

Fox Talent. Prod.: Fox Film Corp. (William Fox), "Fox Movietone Special" (without number)— length: 3 reels, 40 minutes— release: June 1928 New York (Gaiety Theater)— Frank Borzage, F. W. Murnau, Raoul Walsh, Howard Hawks and William K. Howard introduce the stars of their films.

Fox Movietone News (no. 0282A)— release: 27 Jan 1928 — Frank Borzage introducing *Street Angel* (Dedication of Park Row, new home to Fox writers and directors).

Fox Movietone News (no. C8126–8128)— release: 1 Dec 1928 — Presentation of the *Photoplay* Gold Medal Award for *7th Heaven* to Frank Borzage by Winfield Sheehan and Sol Wurtzel, in the presence of Charles Farrell and Janet Gaynor.

The River [incomplete] working titles: *Backwash; Song of the River.* Prod.: Frank Borzage; supervis. prod.: Sol M. Wurtzel (presented by William Fox), Fox Film Corp. (Fox Movietone Talking Picture)— talking sequences: A. H. Van Buren, A. F. "Buddy" Erickson— script: Philip Klein, Dwight Cummins, [Edmund Goulding], [sound version: dial.: John Hunter Booth], from the novel by Tristram Tupper (Grosset & Dunlap, New York 1928; prepublished in: *The Saturday Evening Post*, 26 Nov-10 Dec 1927)— photo: Ernest Palmer— spec. eff. (matte paintings): Fred W. Sersen— art dir.: Harry Oliver— edit.: Barney Wolf— mus.: Maurice Baron, [Hugo Riesenfeld]; mus. dir.: Ernö Rapée (song: "I Found Happiness (When I Found You)" by E. Rapée, lyrics: Lew Pollack)— Technical and Story Advisor: Tristram Tupper— asst.-dir.: Lew Borzage— release: 22 Dec 1928 New York (Gaiety Theatre) (©23 Jan 1929; general rel. 6 Oct 1929 [talking part.]; 8 Dec 1929 [silent]).— length: 7 reels; 6536 ft.; 84 minutes silent vers.: 8 reels; 7704 ft.); 16mm fragment: 1583 ft., 49 minutes (22 fps).

Cast: Charles Farrell (Allen John Pender), Mary Duncan (Rosalee), Ivan Linow (Sam Thompson, the Deaf Mute), Margaret Mann (Widow Thompson), Alfred Sabato (Marsdon, Foreman), Bert Woodruff (the Miller).

1929

Lucky Star working titles: *Timothy Osborn; The Lucky Star.* Prod.: Frank Borzage; supervis. prod.: Sol M. Wurtzel (presented by William Fox), Fox Film Corp.— script: Sonya Levien, dial.: John Hunter Booth, titles: Katherine Hilliker, H. H. Caldwell, from story by Tristram Tupper, in *Lucky Star; or, Three Episodes in the Life of Timothy Osborn, and Other Stories* (Grosset & Dunlap, New York 1929, prepublished in: *Saturday Evening Post*, 9 Apr 1927)— photo: Chester A. Lyons, William Cooper Smith— art dir.: Harry Oliver— edit.: Katherine Hilliker, H. H. Caldwell; sound edit.: Margaret Clancey— sound: Joseph Aiken (Western Electric-Movietone)— asst.-dir.: Lew Borzage— release: 21 Jul 1929 New York (Roxy," part-talkie version); 21 Aug 1929 Los Angeles (Criterion) (©5 Aug 1929)— length: 10 reels, 8784 ft., 85 minutes (silent version: 8725 ft.); restored silent version: 7879 ft./2623m., 106 minutes (20 fps).

Cast: Charles Farrell (Timothy Osborn), Janet Gaynor (Mary Tucker), Guinn "Big Boy" Williams (Martin Wrenn), Paul Fix (Joe), Hedwig Reicher (Mrs. Tucker), Gloria Grey (Milly), Hector V. Sarno (Pop Fry), Raymond Borzage (John Tucker, the Kid), Jack Pennick (Military Driver).

First talking feature:
They Had to See Paris. Prod.: Frank Borzage (presented by William Fox), Fox Film Corp. (Fox Movietone) — script: Sonya Levien, dial.: Owen Davis Sr., [Will Rogers], titles: Wilbur J. Morse, Jr., from story by Homer Croy (Grosset & Dunlap, New York 1926) — photo: Chester A. Lyons, Al Brick — art dir.: Harry Oliver — edit.: Margaret V. Clancey — cost.: Sophie Wachner — sound: George P. Costello (Movietone) — mus.: Sidney Mitchell, Archie Gottler, Con Conrad (song: "I Could Do It For You) — asst.-dir.: Lew Borzage — dial. dir.: Bernard Steele — 2nd unit dir.: J. W. Kaufman (locations) — length: 10 reels; 8,620 ft. (also silent version); 93 minutes — release: 18 Sep 1929 Los Angeles (Fox-Carthay Circle Theatre); 11 Oct 1929 New York (Roxy) (©11 Sep 1929).

Cast: Will Rogers (Pike Peters), Irene Rich (Mrs. Ida Peters), Owen Davis, Jr. (Ross Peters), Marguerite Churchill (Opal Peters), Fifi D'Orsay (Claudine), Rex Bell (Clark McCurdy), Ivan Lebedeff (Marquis of Brissac), Edgar Kennedy (Ed Eggers), Bob Kerr (Tupper), Christiane Yves (Fleuril), Marcelle Corday (Marquise of Brissac), Theodore Lodi (Grand Duke Makiall), Marcia Manon (Miss Mason), André Cheron (Valet), Gregory Gay (Prince Ordinsky), Frances Rich.

1929–1930

Song o' My Heart. Prod.: Frank Borzage, supervision: Joseph Jefferson McCarthy (presented by William Fox), Fox Film Corp. (Fox Movietone) — script: Sonya Levien, dial. & story: Tom Barry; titles: Kerry Clarke — photo: Chester A. Lyons, Al Brick (35mm); John O. Taylor (70mm *Grandeur*) — art dir.: Harry Oliver — cost.: Sophie Wachner — edit.: Jack Murray, supervision: John Stone — sound: Edmund H. Hansen, George P. Costello (Western Electric Movietone) — asst.-dir.: Lew Borzage — mus.: George Lipschultz; songs: "Little Boy Blue" (Ethelbert Nevin), "Paddy Me Lad" (Albert Hay Malotte), "I Hear You Calling Me" (Harold Herford, Charles Marshall), "A Fair Story by the Fireside," "Just for a Day," "Kitty My Love," "The Rose of Tralee" (Charles Glover, C. Mordaunt Spencer), "A Pair of Blue Eyes," "I Feel You Near Me," "Song o' My Heart" (Charles Glover, William Kernell, James Hanley), "Then You'll Remember Me" (Alfred Burns, William Michael Balfe), "Loughi Sereni E-Cari," "Ireland, Mother Ireland"; McCormack's songs are accompagned by Edwin Schneider (piano) — dial. dir.: Tom Barry. — length: 9 reels; 7,740 ft.; 85 minutes — release: 11 Mar 1930 New York (44th Street Theatre); 19 Apr 1930 Los Angeles (Grauman's Chinese Theater) (©11 Feb 1930).

Cast: John McCormack (Sean O'Carolan), Alice Joyce (Mary O'Brien), Maureen O'Sullivan (Eileen O'Brien), Tom Clifford (Tad O'Brien), J. M. Kerrigan (Peter Conlon), John Garrick (Fergus O'Donnell), Edwin Schneider (Vincent Glennon, the Pianist), J. Farrell MacDonald (Joe Rafferty), Effie Ellsler (Mona Glennon), Emily Fitzroy (Elizabeth Kennedy, the Aunt), Andres De Segurola (Guido), Edward Martindel (Fullerton, the Impresario).

1930

Liliom aka *The Loves of Liliom.* — working title: *Devil with Women.* Prod.: Frank Borzage (presented by William Fox), Fox Film Corp. — script & dial.: Samuel Nathaniel Behrman, continuity: Sonya Levien, from the play *Liliom, egy csirkefogó élete és halála* by Ferenc Molnár (Budapest 1909) — photo: Chester A. Lyons — art dir.: Harry Oliver — edit.: Margaret V. Clancey — mus.: Richard Fall; songs: "Dream of Romance," "Thief Song" (Richard Fall, Marcella Gardner) — sound: George P. Costello (Movietone) — cost.: Sophie Wachner — asst.-dir.: Lew Borzage — length: 11 reels; 8,472 ft.; 89 minutes — release: 3 Oct 1930 New York (Roxy Theatre); 30 Oct 1930 Los Angeles (Loews's State Theater) (©2 Sep 1930).

Cast: Charles Farrell (Liliom), Rose Hobart (Julie), Estelle Taylor (Madame Muskat), Lee Tracy (Buzzard), James Marcus (Linzman), Walter Abel (Carpenter), Mildred Van Dorn (Marie), Guinn Williams (Hollinger), Lillian Elliott (Aunt Hulda), Bert Roach (Wolf), H. B. Warner (Chief Magistrate), Dawn O'Day [=Anne Shirley] (Louise), Gino Conti (Policeman).

1930–1931

Doctors' Wives. Prod.: Frank Borzage, assoc. prod.: John W. Considine, Jr. (presented by William Fox), Fox Film Corp. — script: Maurice Watkins, from the novel by Sylvia and Henry Lieferant (Little Brown & Co., New York 1930) — photo: Arthur Edeson — edit.: Jack Dennis — art dir.: Joseph Urban, William Darling — sound: George Leverett — cost.: Sophie Wachner — techn. advis.: Harry

W. Martin, M.D.— asst.-dir.: Lew Borzage.— length: 79 minutes; 7'354 ft.— release: 24 Apr 1931 New York (Roxy Theatre) (©28 Feb 1931).

Cast: Warner Baxter (Dr. Judson Penning), Joan Bennett (Nina Penning-Wyndram), Victor Varconi (Dr. Kane Ruyter), Helene Millard (Vivian Crosby), Paul Porcasi (Dr. Calucci), Nancy Gardner (Julia Wyndram), John St. Polis (Dr. Mark Wyndram), Cecilia Loftus (Aunt Amelia), George Chandler (Dr. Roberts), Violet Dunn (Lou Roberts), Ruth Warren (Charlotte), Louise MacKintosh (Mrs. Kent), William Maddox (Rudie), Marion Lessing.

1931

Young as You Feel working titles: *Father and the Boys; Cure for the Blues.* Prod.: Frank Borzage (presented by William Fox), Fox Film Corp.— script: Edwin Burke [Don Marquis, Philip Klein, Barry Conners], from the play *Father and the Boys* by George Ade (New York, 2 Mar 1908)— photo: Chester A. Lyons, Don Anderson, asst.: John Van Wormer, Robert Mack— art dir.: Jack Schultze— edit.: Margaret V. Clancey— song: "The Cute Little Things You Do," sung by Fifi D'Orsay (mus.: James F. Hanley)— sound: George P. Costello— cost.: Sophie Wachner— asst.-dir.: Lew Borzage— length: 78 minutes; 9 reels, 7'000 ft.— release: 7 Aug 1931 New York (Roxy Theatre) (©14 Apr 1931).

Cast: Will Rogers (Lemuel Morehouse), Fifi D'Orsay (Fleurette), Lucien Littlefield (Noah Marley), Donald Dillaway (Billy Morehouse), Terrance Ray (Tom Morehouse), Lucille Browne (Dorothy Gregson), Rosalie Roy (Rose Gregson), John T. Murray (Col. Stanhope), C. Henry Gordon (Harry Lamson), Marcia Harris (Mrs. Denton), Joan Standing (Lemuel's Secretary), Gregory Gaye (Pierre).

Bad Girl. Prod.: Frank Borzage (presented by William Fox), Fox Film Corp.— script: Edwin Burke, from the novel by Viña Delmar [and Eugene Delmar] (Harcourt Brace & Co., New York 1928) and the play by Viña Delmar and Brian Marlowe (1930)— photo: Chester A. Lyons; 2nd camera: David Ragin, asst.: J. P. Van Wormer, Harry Gant, Harry Dawe; stills: Raymond G. Nolan— edit.: Margaret V. Clancey— art dir.: William Darling— cost.: Dolly Tree— sound: George P. Costello— asst.-dir.: Lew Borzage— length: 8,046 ft.; 89 minutes— release: 14 Aug 1931 New York (Roxy Theatre); 25 Aug 1931 Los Angeles (Grauman's Chinese Theater, Criterion) (©18 Jul 1931).

Cast: Sally Eilers (Dorothy "Dot" Haley), James Dunn (Eddie Collins), Minna Gombell (Edna Driggs), William Pawley (Jim Haley), Frank Darien (Lathrop), George Irving (Dr. Burgess, the Obstetrician), Sue Borzage (extra).

1931–1932

After Tomorrow. Prod.: Frank Borzage (presented by William Fox), Fox Film Corp.— script: Sonya Levien, [William Collier, Sr.] from the play in 3 acts by John Golden & Hugh S. Stange (Samuel French, New York 1930)— photo: James Wong Howe, 2nd camera: Dave Ragin; asst.: Paul Lockwood, H. C. Smith; stills: Bert Lynch— edit.: Margaret V. Clancey— sound: George Leverett— art dir.: William Darling— cost.: Guy S. Duty— mus.: James Hanley (song: "All the World Will Smile Again After Tomorrow")— asst.-dir.: Lew Borzage— length: 79 minutes— release: 4 Mar 1932 New York (Roxy Theatre) (©12 Feb 1932).

Cast: Charles Farrell (Peter Piper), Marian Nixon (Sidney Taylor), Minna Gombell (Elsie Taylor), William Collier, Sr. (Willie Taylor), Josephine Hull (Mrs. Piper), William Pawley (Malcolm Jarvis), Greta Granstedt (Betty), Ferdinand Munier (Mr. Beardsley), Nora Lane (Florence Blandy).

1932

Young America. UK: *We Humans.* Prod.: Frank Borzage (presented by William Fox), Fox Film Corp.— script: William Conselman, [William Rankin, Maurine Watkins], from the play by John Frederick Ballard (New York, 28 Aug 1915), inspired by the stories "Mrs. Doray Stops Talking" and "Mrs. Doray Starts Talking Again" by Pearl Franklin— photo: George Schneiderman— art dir.: Duncan Cramer— asst.-dir.: Lew Borzage, Ad Schaumer— mus.dir.: George Lipschultz— sound: Eugene Grossman— edit.: Margaret V. Clancey— cost.: Guy Duty— length: 6,423 ft.; 71 minutes— release: 6 May 1932 New York (Roxy Theatre) (©25 Mar 1932).

Cast: Spencer Tracy (Jack Doray), Doris Kenyon (Edith Doray), Tommy Conlon (Arthur Simpson), Ralph Bellamy (Judge Blake), Beryl Mercer (Grandma Beamish), Sarah Padden (Mrs. Taylor), Robert Homans (Patrolman Weems), Raymond Borzage (Edward "Nutty" Beamish), Dawn O'Day

[=Anne Shirley] (Mabel Wells), Betty Jane Graham (Cassie Taylor), Louise Beavers (Maid), Spec O'Donnell (Bull Butler), William Pawley (Bandit), Eddie Sturgis (Bandit), Dave Kashner.

A Farewell to Arms. Prod.: Frank Borzage, assoc. prod.: Benjamin Glazer, Edward A. Blatt, Paramount Pictures [1949 distrib.: Warner Bros.]—script: Oliver H. P. Garrett, Benjamin Glazer, [Laurence Stallings], from novel by Ernest Hemingway (Scribner; Grosset & Dunlap, New York-London 1929) and the play by Laurence Stallings (1930)—photo: Charles Bryant Lang, Jr. ASC; process photogr.: Farciot Edouart; asst.-photo: Robert Pittack, Cliff Shirpser; stills: Sherman Clark—art dir.: Hans Dreier, Roland Anderson—cost.: Travis Banton—mus.: Ralph Rainger, John Leipold, Bernhard Kaun, Paul Marquardt, Herman Hand, W. Franke Harling—edit.: Otho Lovering, George Nicholls—sound: Harold C. Lewis—techn. advis.: Charles Griffin (war scenes), Dr. Jardini (hospital scenes)—2nd unit dir. and asst. prod.: Jean Negulesco—asst.-dir.: Arthur Jacobson, Lew Borzage, Charles Griffin—script-girl: Grace Dubrae—props: Joe Robbins, Joe Thompson, Clem Jones—length: 96 minutes [censored version 1938: 86 minutes]—release: 8 Dec 1932 New York (Criterion); 5 Jan 1933 Los Angeles (United Artists Theater) (©5 Jan 1933).
Cast: Helen Hayes (Catherine Barkley), Gary Cooper (Ltn Frederic Henry), Adolphe Menjou (Major Alessandro Rinaldi), Mary Philips (Helen Ferguson), Jack LaRue (the Priest), Blanche Frederici (Head Nurse), Henry Armetta (Bonello), George Humbert (Piani), Fred Malatesta (Manera), Mary Forbes (Miss Van Campen), Tom Ricketts (Count Greffi), Robert Cauterio (Gordoni), Misha Auer (Italian Officer), Gilbert Emery (British Major), Peggy Cunningham (Molly), Agostino Borgato (Giulio), Paul Porcasi (Inn Keeper), Alice Adair (Prostitute), John Davidson, Doris Lloyd, Georges Regas.

1932–1933

Secrets working title: *Yes, John.* Prod.: Frank Borzage; assoc. prod.: Mike C. Levee [Mary Pickford, Pickford Company Prod.]/d. United Artists (Joseph Schenck)—script: Frances Marion, from the play by Rudolf Besier and May Edginton (as produced by Sam Harris); addit. dial.: Salisbury Field, Leonard Praskins—photo: Ray June ASC—edit.: Hugh Bennett, John Hoffmann (transitions)—cost.: Adrian—mus.: Alfred Newman—sound: Frank Maher—art dir.: Richard Day (decorations: Julia Heron)—prod. manager: Ed Ralph—asst.-dir.: Lew Borzage—technical & story advisor: Elsie Janis—length: 85 minutes—release: 15 Mar 1933 New York (Rivoli) (©15 Mar 1933).
Cast: Mary Pickford (Mary Carlton-Marlowe), Leslie Howard (John Carlton), C. Aubrey Smith (Mr. Marlowe), Blanche Frederici (Mrs. Marlowe), Doris Lloyd (Susan Channing), Herbert Evans (Lord Hurley), Ned Sparks (Sunshine), Allan Sears (Jake Houser), Mona Maris (Señorita Lolita Martinez), Lyman Williams (William Carlton child), Huntley Gordon (William Carlton adult), Virginia Grey (Audrey Carlton child), Ethel Clayton (Audrey Carlton adult), Ellen Johnson (Susan Carlton child), Bessie Barriscale (Susan Carlton adult), Randolph Connelly (Robert Carlton child), Theodore Von Eltz (Robert Carlton adult), Jerry Stewart, King Baggott, Florence Lawrence, Francis Ford, Paul Panzer.

1933

Man's Castle working titles: *Hunk o' Blue; A Man's Castle.* Prod.: Frank Borzage, Hollywood Screen Guild (Mike C. Levee), Columbia Pictures Corp.—script: Jo Swerling, [Frank Borzage], from the play by Lawrence S. Hazard—photo: Joseph H. August A.S.C.—art dir.: Stephen Goosson—mus.: Frank Harling, mus. dir.: Constantin Bakaleinikoff; song: "Surprises" by Harry Akst, Edward Eliscu (sung by Glenda Farrell)—edit.: Viola Lawrence—asst.-dir.: Lew Borzage—sound: Wilbur Brown—length: 79 minutes—release: 29 Dec 1933 New York (Rialto) (©18 Nov 1933).
Cast: Spencer Tracy (Bill), Loretta Young (Trina), Glenda Farrell (Fay LaRue), Walter Connolly (Ira), Arthur Hohl (Bragg), Marjorie Rambeau (Flossie), Dickie Moore (Joie, the Crippled Boy), Harvey Clark (Café Manager), Henry Roquemore (Roue), Hector V. Sarno (Grocer), Helen Jerome Eddy (Mother), Robert Grey (Head Waiter), Tony Merlo (Waiter), Kendall McComas (Slacks), Harry Watson (captain of base-ball team).

1933–1934

No Greater Glory working titles: *The Paul Street Boys; Men of Tomorrow; No Cannons Roar.* Prod.: Frank Borzage, Hollywood Screen Guild (Mike C. Levee); Columbia Pictures Corp. (Harry Cohn);

prod. supervis.: Samuel Briskin — script: Jo Swerling, from the novel *A Pál-utcai fiúk* (The Kids from Pál Street) by Ferenc Molnár (Budapest 1907) — photo: Joseph H. August A.S.C. — art dir.: Stephen Goosson — edit.: Viola Lawrence — asst.-dir.: Lew Borzage — mus. & mus. dir.: Louis Silvers — sound: Glenn Rominger — length: 78 minutes — release: 4 May 1934 New York (Roxy Theatre); 6 Jun 1934 Los Angeles (Filmarte Theater) (©3 Mar 1934).

Cast: George Breakston (Ernö Nemecsek), Jimmy Butler (Boka), Jackie Searl (Geréb), Frankie Darro (Feri Áts), Donald Haines (Csónakos), Rolf Ernest (Ferdie Pasztor), Julius Molnar (Henry Pasztor), Wesley Giraud (Kolnay), Beaudine Anderson (Csele), Bruce Line (Richter), Samuel S. Hinds (Geréb's Father), Ralph Morgan (Andros Nemecsek, the Father), Lois Wilson (Mme Nemecsek, the Mother), Egon Brecher (Racz), Frank Reicher (Doctor), Tom Ricketts (Janitor), Christian Rub (Gardian), Harvey Clark (Client), Howard Leeds, Basil Bookasta, Bob Wagner (Red Shirts), Eddie Buzzard, Douglas Greer (Pál Street Boys).

Little Man, What Now? Prod.: Frank Borzage, assoc. prod.: Henry Henigson, Universal Pictures (Carl Laemmle, Jr.) — script: William Anthony McGuire, [Robert Cedric Sherriff, James Atherton; scenario continuity: Jo Swerling] from the novel *Kleiner Mann — was nun?* by Hans Fallada [=Rudolf Ditzen] (Berlin 1932) — photo: Norbert Brodine A.S.C., asst.-photo: William Dodds — art dir.: Charles Danny Hall, [Edgar George Ulmer] — edit.: Milton Carruth; supervis.: Maurice Pivar — mus. & mus. dir.: Arthur Kay — makeup: William Ely, Jack P. Pierce — script-girl: Cora Palmatier — asst.-dir.: Lew Borzage, John Gates, Sergei Petschnikoff — prod. manager: M. F. Murphy — sound: C. Roy Hunter, supervis.: Gilbert Kurland — length: 98 minutes — release: 31 May 1934 New York (Radio City Music Hall) (also ©).

Cast: Margaret Sullavan (Lämmchen [Emma] Pinneberg-Mörschel), Douglass Montgomery (Hans [Johannes] Pinneberg), Alan Hale (Holger Jachmann, alias Hermann Kranz), Catherine Doucet (Mia [Maria] Pinneberg), Fred Kohler (Karl Goebbler, the Communist), Mae Marsh (Frau Goebbler), DeWitt C. Jennings (Emil Kleinholz), Alan Mowbray (Franz Schlüter, the Actor), Muriel Kirkland (Marie Kleinholz), Hedda Hopper (Nurse), Sarah Padden (Widow Scharrenhofer), Earl A. Foxe (Frenchman), George Meeker (Schultz), Bodil Rosing (Frau Emilie Kleinholz), Donald Haines (Emil Kleinholz Jr.), Monroe Owsley (Kessler), G. P. Huntley Jr. (Joachim Heilbutt), Paul Fix (Lauterbach), Carlos de Valdez (Dr. Sesam), Thomas Ricketts (Mr. Sesam), Frank Reicher (Lehmann), Christian Rub (Karl Puttbreese), Etienne Girardot (Spannfuss), Max Asher (Chauffeur), William Augustin (Detective), Torben Meyer (Headwaiter), Bert Roach (Robust Man), Fritzi Ridgeway (Girl), Roger Cluett (Student), Al Taylor (Cashier), John Ince (Man), Robert Graves (2nd Headwaiter), William Norton Railey (Insurance Clerk), Helen Dickson (Heavy Woman), Lowell Drew (Meek Husband), Anders Van Haden (Soap Box Orator), Max Asher (Chauffeur), Russ Powell (Man), Jeanee Hart (Girl), Ed Hart (Porter), George Rosing.

Flirtation Walk. Prod.: Frank Borzage, supervis. prod.: Robert Lord, First National-Warner Bros. — script: Delmer Daves, from story "Eyes right!" by Delmer Daves and Lou Edelman — photo: Sol Polito A.S.C., George Barnes A.S.C.; 2nd camera: Al Green; asst.: Frank Evans; stills: Mac Julian — edit.: William Holmes, asst.: William Phelan — art dir.: Jack Okey — cost.: Orry-Kelly — choregr.: Bobby Connolly — mus. dir.: Leo F. Forbstein (Vitaphone Orchestra); songs: Mort Dixon, Allie Wrubel (Flirtation Walk," "I See Two Lovers," "Mr. and Mrs. Is the Name," "When Do We Eat?," "Smoking in the Dark," "No Horse, No Wife, No Mustache) — sound: E. A. Brown — asst.-dir.: Bill Cannon, Lew Borzage — cost.: Orrry-Kelly — techn. advis.: col. Timothy J. Lonergan, Lt. M.P. Echols — spec. eff.: Bert Longworth — length: 97 minutes — release: 28 Nov 1934 New York (Strand Theatre) and Los Angeles (Hollywood Theater) (©16 Nov 1934).

Cast: Dick Powell (Dick "Canary" Dorcy), Ruby Keeler (Kit Fitts), Pat O'Brien (Sgt. Scrapper Thornhill), Ross Alexander (Oskie), John Arledge (Spike), John Eldredge (Ltn. Robert Biddle), Henry O'Neill (General Jack Fitts), Guinn Williams (Sleepy), Frederick Burton (General Paul Landacre), John Darrow (Chase), Glen Boles (Eight Ball), ltn. Joe Cummins (Cadet), Gertrude Keeler (Dancer), Col. Tim Lonergan (General), Tyrone Power, Carlyle Blackwell Jr., Dick Winslow (Cadets), Maude Turner Gordon (Dowager), Frances Lee (Blonde), Avis Johnson (Redhead), Mary Russell (Girl), William J. Worthington (Civilian), Cliff Saum, Paul Fix (Soldiers), Sol Bright (Native Leader), Emmett Vogan (Officer), Frank Dawson (Butler), Madeline Borzage (Dancer), Sol Hoopii and his Native Orchestra, University of Southern California and Army Polo Teams.

1935

Living on Velvet working title: *Tragedy with Music*. Prod.: Frank Borzage, Jerry Wald (supervis. Edward Chodorov), First National-Warner Bros.— script and story: "Tragedy with Music" by Jerry Wald, Julius Epstein — photo: Sid Hickox ASC — art dir.: Robert M. Haas—cost.: Orry-Kelly — edit.: William Holmes— dir. mus. Leo F. Forbstein (The Vitaphone Orchestra); song: "Living on Velvet" (mus. Al Dubin, lyr. Harry Warren)— asst.-dir.: Lee Katz, John Gates, Lew Borzage—length: 77 minutes— release: 7 Mar 1935 New York (Strand) (also ©).

Cast: Kay Francis (Amy Prentiss), Warren William (Walter "Gibraltar" Pritcham), George Brent (Terrence Clarence Parker), Helen Lowell (Aunt Martha Prentiss), Henry O'Neill (Thornton), Samuel S. Hinds (Henry L. Parker), Russell Hicks (Major), Maude Turner Gordon (Mrs. Parker), Martha Merrill (Cynthia Parker), Edgar Kennedy (Counterman), Lee Shumway (Officer), Sam Hayes (Announcer), Walter Miller (Leader), Emmett Vogan (Officer), May Beatty, Mrs. Wilfrid North (Dowagers), Frank Dodd (Reverend), David Newell (Smalley), Bud Geary (Aunt Martha's Chauffeur), William Wayne (Butler), Gordon "Bill" Elliott (Commuter), Stanley King (Private), Niles Welch (Major's Aid), Selmer Jackson (Captain), Harry Bradley (Party Guest), Grace Hayle (Woman), Harry Holman (Bartender), Wade Boteler (Desk Sergeant), Eric Wilton (Travis, Pritcham's Butler), Harold Nelson (Sexton), William Norton Bailey (Drew), John Cooper (Messenger Boy), Jack Richardson (Taxi Driver), Jay Eaton, Lloyd Whitlock (Men), Eddy Chandler (Policeman), Paul Fix (Intern), Frank Fanning (Doorman), Eddie Phillips (Eddie at Party), Austa (Max, the Dachshund).

Stranded working title: *Lady with a Badge*. Prod.: Frank Borzage, Sam Bischoff (supervisor), Warner Bros.— script: Delmer Daves, add. dialogue: Carl Erickson, from story "Lady with a Badge" by Frank Wead, Ferdinand Reyher— photo: Sid Hickox ASC— art dir.: Anton Grot, Hugh Reticker —cost.: Orry-Kelly — mus. dir.: Leo F. Forbstein (Vitaphone Orchestra)— edit.: William Holmes— asst.-dir.: Lew Borzage — length: 73 minutes— release: 19 Jun 1935 New York (Strand) (©17 Jun 1935).

Cast: Kay Francis (Lynn Palmer), George Brent (Mack Hale), Patricia Ellis (Velma Tuthill), Donald Woods (John Wesley), Barton MacLane (Sharkey), Robert Barrat (Stanislaus Januschek), June Travis (Jennie Holden [Mary Rand]), Henry O'Neill (Mr. Tuthill), Ann Shoemaker (Mrs. Tuthill), Frankie Darry (Jimmy Rivers), William Harrigan (Updyke), Joseph Crehan (Johnny Quinn), John Wray (Mike Gibbons), Edward McWade (Tim Powers), Gavin Gordon (Jack), Mary Forbes (Grace Dean), Florence Fair (Miss Walsh), Burr Carruth (Old Man), Emmett Vogan (Officer on Ferry), Samuel R. McDaniel (Porter), Harry C. Bradley (Conductor), Eily Malyon (Old Maid), John Kelly (Sailor), Mae Busch (Lizzie), Joan Gay (Diane Nichols), Edwin Mordant (Surgeon), Harrison Greene (Blustery Man), Eleanor Wesselhoeft (Mrs. Young), Wally Wales (Peterson), Wilfred Lucas (Pat, a Worker), Glen Cavender (Kolchak), Joe King (Dan Archer), Frank Sheridan (Boone), Emma Young (Chinese Girl), Mia Liu (Japanese Girl), Rita Rozelle (Polish Girl), Louise Seidel (Danish Girl), Frank LaRue (Doctor), Lillian Harmer (Desk Attendant), Zeffie Tilbury (Old Hag), Lillian Worth (Blonde), Georgia Cooper (Floor Nurse), Spencer Charters (Sailor), Tom Wilson (Immigrant), Philo McCullough (Immigration Officer), Adrian Morris (Rivet Boss), Milton Kibbee (Pat), Vesey O'Davoren (Butler), Adrian Rosley (Headwaiter), Junior Coghlan (Page), Jack Richardson, Stan Cavanagh (Taxi Drivers), Edwin Stanley (Police Surgeon), Edward Keane (Doctor), Niles Welch (Safety Engineer), Walter Clyde (Assistant), Marbeth Wright (Pat, the Timekeeper), Donald Downen (Operator), Claudia Coleman (Madame), Patrick Moriarity (Steve Brodie), Sarah Padden (Workman's Wife), Dick French (Clerk), Jessie Arnold (Scrubwoman), Henry Otho (Worker), Vesey O'Davoren (Butler), Tom Wilson (Immigrant), Richard Loo (Groom), Frank Marlowe (Rollins, an Agitator), Leo White (Haines, a drunken Worker).

Shipmates Forever working titles: *Anchors Aweigh*; *Classmates*; *Dress Parade*; *Navy Sweethearts*. Prod.: Frank Borzage, Cosmopolitan Productions (W.R. Hearst), prod. supervis.: Lou Edelman/d. First National-Warner Bros.— script and story: Delmer Daves— photo: Sol Polito ASC— mus. dir.: Leo F. Forbstein, songs: Harry Warren, Al Dubin (Don't Give Up the Ship," "I'd Rather Listen to Your Eyes," "All Aboard the Navy," "I'd Love to Take Orders from You," "Do I Love My Teacher), Frank Crumit (Abdul Abulbul Emir," lyr. et mus.)—chor.: Bobby Connolly—art dir.: Robert M. Haas—cost.: Orry-Kelly— edit.: William Holmes— techn. advis.: Com. M. S. Tisdale, U.S.N., Ltn. W. J. Beecher, U.S.N., Edward L. Adams— asst.-dir.: Lew Borzage, Bill Cannon—length: 109 minutes— release: 17 Oct 1935 New York (Strand Theatre) (rel. 12 Oct 1935).

Cast: Dick Powell (Richard John Melville III), Ruby Keeler (June Blackburn), Lewis Stone (Admiral Richard Melville), Ross Alexander (Sparks), Eddie Acuff (Cowboy), Dick Foran (Gifford), John Arledge (Coxswain Johnny Lawrence), Robert Light (Ted Sterling), Joseph King (Commander Douglas), Frederick Burton (Admiral Fred Graves), Henry Kolker (Doctor), Joseph Crehan (Spike), Mary Treen (Cowboy's Girl), Martha Merrill (Sparks's Girl), Carlyle Moore, Jr. (Second Classman), Harry Seymour (Harry), Ernie Alexander, Victor Potel (Radio Fans), Emmett Vogan (Officer), James Flavin (Instructor), Guy Usher (Captain), Frank Marlowe (Seaman), Peter Potter (Upper Classman), Ed Keane (Doctor), Dennis O'Keefe (Trainee), Meglin Kiddies (Children), Madeline Borzage, Frank Borzage Jr. (extras).

1935–1936

Desire working title: *The Pearl Necklace.* Prod. & artistic supervision: Ernst Lubitsch (presented by Adolph Zukor), Paramount Pictures (A Frank Borzage Production); execut. prod.: Henry Herzbrun — script: Edwin Justus Mayer, Waldemar Young, Samuel Hoffenstein, [Vincent Lawrence, Benn W. Levy], from the play *Die schönen Tage in Aranjuez* by Hans Székely and Robert A. Stemmle — photo: Charles B. Lang Jr., ASC, Victor Milner ASC; Eric Locke (locations in Europe) — mus.: Friedrich Hollaender, song "Awake in a Dream": F. Hollaender, Leo Robin (lyr.) — art dir.: Hans Dreier, Robert Usher, A. E. Freudeman — edit.: William Shea — cost.: Travis Banton — sound: Harry D. Mills, Don Johnson — spec. eff. .: Farciot Edouart, Harry Perry — asst.-dir.: Lew Borzage — length: 2'613 m./99 minutes — release: 11 Apr 1936 New York (Paramount Theatre); (©28 Feb 1936).

Cast: Marlene Dietrich (Madeleine de Beaupré), Gary Cooper (Tom Bradley), John Halliday (Carlos Margoli), William Frawley (Mr. Gibson), Ernest Cossart (Aristide Duval, Jeweler), Akim Tamiroff (Police Official), Alan Mowbray (Dr. Maurice Pauquet), Zeffie Tilbury (Aunt Olga), Harry Depp (Clerk), Marc Lawrence (Valet), Henry Antrim (Chauffeur), Armand Kaliz, Gaston Glass (Jewelry Clerk), Albert Pollet (French Policeman), George Davis (Garage Man), Constant Franke (Border Official), Robert O'Connor (Customs Official), Stanley Andrews (Customs Inspector), Rafael Blanco (Haywagon Driver), Alden [Stephen] Chase (Hotel Clerk), Tony Merlo (Waiter), Anna Delinsky (Servant), Alice Feliz (Pepi), Enrique Acosta (Pedro), George MacQuarrie (Clerk with gun), Isabel La Mal (Nurse), Oliver Eckhardt (Husband), Blanche Craig (Wife), Rollo Lloyd (Clerk in Mayor's Office), Alfonso Pedroza (Oxcart Driver).

1936

Hearts Divided working title: *Glorious.* Prod.: Frank Borzage, Harry Joe Brown (supervis.), Cosmopolitan Productions (W.R.Hearst); executive prod.: Jack L. Warner, Hal B. Wallis/d. First National-Warner Bros. — script: Laird Doyle, Casey Robinson, [James K. McGuiness, Charles Lederer, Jean Negulesco], from the play *Glorious Betsy* by Rida Johnson Young (New York, 7 Sep 1908) — photo: George Folsey, ASC — edit.: William Holmes — art dir.: Robert M. Haas — cost.: Orry-Kelly, L. L. Burns — mus.: Harry Warren, Al Dubin, [and Erich Wolfgang Korngold, uncred.] (songs: "My Kingdom for a Kiss," "Two Hearts Divided," and Negro Spirituals "Nobody Knows the Trouble I Seen," "Rise Up Children and Shine" sung by The Hall Johnson Choir); mus. dir.: Leo F. Forbstein (Vitaphone Orchestra) — asst.-dir.: Lew Borzage, Johnny Gates — length: 76 minutes — release: 12 Jun 1936 New York (Strand Theatre) (©29 Jun 1936).

Cast: Marion Davies (Elizabeth [Betsy] Patterson), Dick Powell (Jérôme Bonaparte), Claude Rains (Napoléon I), Charles Ruggles (Henry Ruggles), Edward Everett Horton (John Horton), Arthur Treacher (Sir Harry Treacher), Henry Stephenson (William Patterson), Clara Blandick (Aunt Ellen Massenbird), John Larkin (Isham), Walter Kingsford (Pichon), Etienne Girardot (Du Fresne), Halliwell Hobbes (Jean-Jacques de Cambacérès), Hobart Cavanaugh (Innkeeper), George Irving (Thomas Jefferson), Hattie McDaniel (Mammy), Sam McDaniel (Servant), Freddie Archibald (Gabriel), Beulah Bondi (Laetizia Bonaparte), Philip [Lucky] Hurlic (Pippin), John Elliott (Monroe), Granville Bates (Livingston), Clinton Rosemond (Darkey), George André Béranger (Jefferson's Secretary), Gaston Glass (Claude-François de Méneval, Napoléon's Secretary), Wilfred Lucas (Valet), Louise Bates (Woman), Stuart Holmes (Man at Ball), Florence Fair, Ethyl Sykes (Women at Ball), Leigh De Lacy (Dowager), Libby Taylor (Black Mammy), George Davis (French Sailor) and The Hall Johnson Choir.

Green Light. Prod.: Frank Borzage, Henry Blanke (surpervis. prod.); execut. prod.: Jack L. Warner, Hal B. Wallis, Cosmopolitan Prod.-First National/d. Warner Bros. — script: Milton Krims, [Paul Green, Mary C. McCall, Jr.], from the novel by Lloyd Cassel Douglas (Boston 1935) — photo: Byron

Haskin ASC, 2nd camera: Alan Roberts, asst.: J. Koffman; stills: John Ellis— art dir.: Max Parker— asst.-dir.: Lew Borzage, Max Parker, Frank Heath— mus.: Max Steiner; dir.mus.: Leo F. Forbstein (orchestration: Hugo Friedhofer)—cost.: Orry-Kelly— sound: Robert E. Lee— spec. eff.: Fred Jackman Jr., H. F. Koenekamp, Willard Van Enger— edit.: James Gibbons—props: Oren Haglund— length: 85 minutes— release: 12 Feb 1937 New York (Strand Theatre) (©25 Jan 1937).

Cast: Errol Flynn (Dr. Newell Paige), Anita Louise (Phyllis Dexter), Margaret Lindsay (Frances Ogilvie), Sir Cedric Hardwicke (Dean Harcourt), Walter Abel (Dr. John Stafford), Henry O'Neill (Dr. Endicott), Spring Byington (Mrs. Dexter), Erin O'Brien-Moore (Pat Arlen), Henry Kolker (Dr. Lane), Pierre Watkin (Dr. Booth), Granville Bates (Sheriff), Russell Simpson (Sheepman), Myrtle Stedman, Shirley Lloyd (Nurses), Wade Boteler (Traffic Cop), Jim Pierce (Harcourt's Chauffeur), Jim Thorpe (Indian), Milton Kibbee (Other Man), John Butler (Driver), Bess Flowers (Mrs. Dexter's Nurse), Noel Kennedy (English Messenger Boy), Louise Stanley (Switchboard Girl), Douglas Wood (Chairman), Miki Morita (Japanese Boy), Lillian Elliott (Mrs. Crandall), Lyle Moraine (Chauffeur), Sibyl Harris (Mrs. Crowder), James Farley (Man), Sam Rice (Storekeeper), Lowden Adams (Butler), Harvey Clark (Man), Ed Chandler (Policeman) and The St. Luke's Choristers.

Radio: CBS 30 Nov 1936 (Radio Lux Theatre): *Polly of the Circus*, from the play by Margaret Mayo, hosting, production and direction by Frank Borzage, with the voices of Loretta Young (Polly Fisher), James Gleason (Rev. John Hartley) and Lionel Barrymore (Rev. James Northcott).

1936–1937

History Is Made at Night. Prod.: Walter Wanger Productions/d. United Artists— script & story: Gene Towne, Graham Baker, [Frank Borzage, Arthur Ripley]; addit. dial.: Vincent Lawrence, David Hertz— photo: Gregg Toland ASC, David Abel ASC— art dir.: Alexander Toluboff— sound: Paul Neal— edit.: Margaret Clancey— mus.: Alfred Newman —cost.: Bernard Newman— spec. eff.: James Basevi— ass.-dir.: Lew Borzage— dial.dir.: Joshua Logan— 2nd Unit dir.: Arthur Ripley— ventriloquist: Señor Wences— length: 97 minutes— release: 27 Mar 1937 New York (Rivoli) (©26 Mar 1937).

Cast: Charles Boyer (Paul Dumond), Jean Arthur (Irene Vail), Leo Carrillo (Cesare), Colin Clive (Bruce Vail), Ivan Lebedeff (Michael, the Chauffeur), George Meeker (Norton), Lucien Prival (Private Detective), Georges Renavent (Inspector Millard), George Davies (Maestro), Adele St. Mauer (Hotel Maid), Jack Mulhall (Waiter), Robert Parrish (Ship Passenger), Barry Norton, Harvey Clarke, Phyllis Barry, Helene Millard, Edward Earle, George Humbert, [cut from final print: Maurice Cass (Librarian), Oscar Apfel (Writer)].

Radio: CBS 5 Apr 1937 (Radio Lux Theater): Frank Borzage is a guest interviewed by Cecil B. DeMille (prod. & direction) before the broadcast of *A Farewell to Arms* starring Clark Gable (Frederic), Josephine Hutchinson (Catherine) and Adolphe Menjou (Major Rinaldi).

1937

Big City title on television: *Skyscraper Wilderness*. Prod.: Frank Borzage, Norman Krasna (dir. prod.), Metro-Goldwyn-Mayer Pictures—co-director: George B. Seitz (New York locations)— script: Dore Schary, Hugo Butler, from story "Mary Christmas" by Norman Krasna— photo: Joseph Ruttenberg ASC, Clyde De Vinna ASC (New York)— edit.: Frederick Y. Smith— mus.: William Axt— art dir.: Cedric Gibbons, asst.: Stan Rogers, Edwin B. Willis—cost.: Dolly Tree— asst.-dir.: Lew Borzage— length: 80 minutes— release: 10 Sep 1937 Los Angeles (Uptown Theatre, preview); 16 Sep 1937 New York (Capitol Theater) (©27 Aug 1937).

Cast: Spencer Tracy (Joe Benton), Luise Rainer (Anna Benton), Charley Grapewin (Mayor of New York City), Janet Beecher (Sophie Sloane), Eddie Quillan (Mike Edwards), Victor Varconi (Paul Roya), Oscar O'Shea (John C. Andrews), Helen Troy (Lola Johnson), William Demarest (Beecher), John Arledge (Buddy), Irving Bacon (Jim Sloane), Guinn Williams (Danny Devlin), Regis Toomey (Fred Hawkins), Edgar Dearing (Tom Reilly), Paul Harvey (District Attorney Gilbert), Andrew J. Tombes (Inspector Matthews), Clem Bevans (Grandpa Sloane), Grace Ford (Mary Reilly), Alice White (Peggy Devlin), Ruth Hussey (Mayor's Secretary), Danny Borzage (Taxi Driver) and, playing themselves, Jack Dempsey, James J. Jeffries, Jimmy McLarnin, Maxie Rosenbloom, Jim Thorpe, Frank Wykoff, Jackie Fields, Man Mountain Dean, Gus Sonnenberg, George Godfrey, Joe Rivers, Cotton Warburton, Bull Montana, Snowy Baker, Taski Hagio, Don Sugai Matsuda.

Mannequin working titles: *Three Rooms in Heaven; Class; Marry for Money; Shop Girl; Saint or Sinner.* Prod.: Joseph L. Mankiewicz (A Frank Borzage Production), Metro-Goldwyn-Mayer Pictures—script: Lawrence Hazard, [Frank Borzage], from story "Marry for Money" by Katherine Brush—photo: George Folsey ASC—mus.: Edward Ward (song: "Always and Always" by E. Ward, lyr.: Robert Wright, Chet Forrest)—edit.: Frederick Y. Smith—art dir.: Cedric Gibbons, Paul Groesse (art dir.), Edwin B. Willis (set dec.)—cost.: Adrian—asst.-dir.: Lew Borzage—sound: Douglas Shearer—length: 92 minutes—release: 14 Dec 1937 Los Angeles [preview]; 20 Jan 1938 New York (Capitol) (©11 Jan 1938).

Cast: Joan Crawford (Jessie Cassidy), Spencer Tracy (John L. Hennessey), Alan Curtis (Eddie Miller), Ralph Morgan (Briggs), Mary Phillips (Beryl), Oscar O'Shea (Pa Cassidy), Elizabeth Risdon (Mrs. Cassidy), Leo Gorcey (Clifford Cassidy), George Chandler (Swing Magoo), Bert Roach (Schwartz), Marie Blake (Mrs. Schwartz), Matt McHugh (Mike), Paul Fix (Smooch), Helen Troy (Bubbles Adair), Philip Terry (Man at Stage Door), Gwen Lee (Girl Worker), Donald Kirke (Dave McIntyre), Virginia Blair, Jim Baker, Ruth Dwyer (Wedding Guests), Jimmy Conlin (Elevator Operator), Frank Jaquet (Stage Doorman), Viola Callahan (Mrs. Williams), Eddie Gribbon (Policeman), Mitchell Ingraham (Man on Ship), James Flavin (Burly Man), Francis Ford (Tim O'Rourke), Frank Puglia (Rocco), Joe E. Marks (Horrowitz), Douglas Wood (Rogers), Harvey Clark (Clark), Kathrin Claire Ward, Kathryn Sheldon (Women), Maurice Samuels (Abe), Jack Kennedy (Sandy), Mary Gordon (Mrs. O'Rourke), Hal Le Seuer (Tout), Jessie Graves (Servant), Bonnie Bannon (Young Girl), James Blaine (Cop), Orville Caldwell (Theatre Manager), Granville Bates (Gebhart), WabyBoteler (Turnkey), Frank Shannon (Sergeant), Edith Trivers (Secretary), Nino Bellini (Trinet), Chester Gan (Chinese Waiter), Russ Clark (Trainer).

1938

Three Comrades. Prod.: Joseph L. Mankiewicz (A Frank Borzage Production), assoc. prod.: William Levanway, Metro-Goldwyn-Mayer Pictures—script: Francis Scott Fitzgerald, Edward E. Paramore, [Joseph L. Mankiewicz, David Hertz, Waldo Salt, Lawrence Hazard, Robert Cedric Sherriff], from the novel *Drei Kameraden* by Erich Maria Remarque (Querido Verlag, Amsterdam 1937)—photo: [Karl Freund], Joseph Ruttenberg ASC—mus.: Franz Waxman (songs "Ragtime College Jazz," "Mighty Forest," "Comrade Song," "How Can I Leave Thee?" by F. Waxman, lyr.: Chet Forrest, Bob Wright)—art dir.: Cedric Gibbons, Paul Groesse (art dir.), Edwin B. Willis (set dec.)—edit.: Slavko Vorkapich, Frank Sullivan, Laslo Benedek—sound: Douglas Shearer—asst.-dir.: Lew Borzage—length: 98 minutes—release: 2 Jun 1938 New York (Capitol Theatre); 20 May 1938 Los Angeles (preview); (©26 May 1938).

Cast: Robert Taylor (Erich Lohkamp), Margaret Sullavan (Pat Hollmann), Franchot Tone (Otto Koster), Robert Young (Gottfried Lenz), Guy Kibbee (Alfons), Lionel Atwill (Franz Breuer), Henry Hull (Dr. Heinrich Becker), George Zucco (Dr. Plauten), Charley Grapewin (Local Doctor), Monty Woolley (Dr. Jaffe), Spencer Charters (Herr Schultz), Sarah Padden (Frau Schultz), Ferdinand Munier (Burgomaster), Morgan Wallace (Owner of Wrecked Car), Priscilla Lawson (Frau Brunner), Esther Muir (Frau Schmidt), Walter Bonn (Adjudant), Edward McWade (Majordomo), Henry Brandon (Man with Patch), George Chandler, Ralph Bushman (Comics), Donald Haines (Kid), Claire McDowell (Frau Zalewska), Marjorie Main (Old Woman), Mitchell Lewis (Boris), E. Alyn Warren (Bookstore Owner), Ricca Allen (Housekeeper), Roger Converse (Becker's Assistant), Jessie Arnold (Nurse), Barbara Redford (Rita), Alva Kellogg (Singer), Norman Willis, William Haade (Vogt Men), Leonard Penn (Tony), Harvey Clark (Bald-Headed Man), George Offerman, Jr. (Adolph), Madeline Borzage (extra).

The Shining Hour. Prod.: Joseph L. Mankiewicz (A Frank Borzage Production), Metro-Goldwyn-Mayer Pictures—script: Jane Murfin, Ogden Nash, [Joseph L. Mankiewicz], from a play in 3 acts by John Keith Winter (Doran & Co., Garden City, N.Y. 1934)—photo: George Folsey ASC—mus.: Franz Waxman—edit.: Frank E. Hull—art dir.: Cedric Gibbons, Paul Groesse (art dir.), Edwin B. Willis (set dec.)—cost.: Adrian—chor.: Tony DeMarco—sound: Douglas Shearer—hair stylist: Sydney Guilaroff—asst.-dir.: Lew Borzage—length: 76 minutes—release: 10 Nov 1938 Hollywood (Westwood Village, preview); 19 Jan 1939 New York (Capitol) (©14 Nov 1938).

Cast: Joan Crawford (Olivia [Maggie] Riley), Margaret Sullavan (Judy Linden), Melvyn Douglas (Henry Linden), Robert Young (David Linden), Fay Bainter (Hannah Linden), Allyn Joslyn (Roger

Q. Franklin), Hattie McDaniel (Belvedere), Frank Albertson (Benny Collins), Oscar O'Shea (Charlie Collins), Harry Barris (Bertie), Tony DeMarco (Van Stillman, Olivia's Dance Partner), Claire Owen (Stewardess), Jim Conlin, Granville Bates (Men), Roger Converse (Clerk), Francis X. Bushman, Jr. (Doorman), Frank Puglia (Headwaiter), George Chandler (Press Agent), Sarah Edwards (Woman), Buddy Messinger (Elevator Boy), Charles C. Coleman (Butler), Edwin Stanley (Minister), E. Allyn Warren (Leonard), Grace Hayle (Mrs. Briggs), Jacques Vanaire (Waiter), Cyril Ring (Candid Cameraman), Bess Flowers (Nurse), Grace Goodall (Mrs. Smart), Jack Raymond (Farmer), Madeleine Borzage (extra).

1938–1939

A *New York Cinderella* release title: *I Take This Woman* (1940). Prod.: [Lawrence Weingarten, Louis B. Mayer, James K. McGuiness], Bernard H. Hyman, Metro-Goldwyn-Mayer — dir. [Josef von Sternberg, Frank Borzage], Woodbridge Strong Van Dyke II — script: James Kevin McGuiness, [Charles MacArthur e.a.], from story by Charles MacArthur — photo: Harold Rosson ASC, [Bud Lawton, ASC] — mus.: Bronislau Kaper, Arthur Guttman — art dir.: Cedric Gibbons, Paul Groesse — cost.: Adrian — sound: Douglas Shearer — edit.: George Boemler — [asst.-dir.: Dick Green/Lew Borzage] — length: 96 minutes — release: 26 Jan 1940 Hollywood (Westwood Village," preview) (©23 Jan 1940).

Cast: Spencer Tracy (Dr. Karl Decker), Hedy Lamarr (Georgi Gragore), Verree Teasdale (Madame Maresca), Kent Taylor (Phil Mayberry), Mona Barrie (Sandra Mayberry), Paul Cavanaugh (Bill Rodgers), Jack Carson (Joe), Louis Calhern (Dr. Duveen), Laraine Day (Linda Rodgers), Reed Hadley (Bob Hampton), Frances Drake (Lola Estermonte), Marjorie Main (Gertie), George E. Stone (Katz), Willie Best (Sambo), Leon Belasco (Pancho), Don Castle (Ted Fenton), Charles Trowbridge (Dr. Morris), Charles D. Brown (Police Officer), Gayne Whitman (Dr. Phelps), John Shelton, Tom Collins (Interns), Florence Shirley (Mrs. Bettincourt), Rafael Storm (Raoul Cedro), Natalie Moorhead (Saleslady), Syd Saylor (Taxi Driver), David Clyde (Steward), Nell Craig (Nurse on Ship), Lee Phelps (Policeman), Matt McHugh, Polly Bailey, George Humbert, Rosina Galli, Esther Michelson (People at Clinic), Peggy Leon (Georgi's Maid), Edward Keane (Dr. Harrison), Jack Chefe (Waiter), Jean ByBriac (Headwaiter), Florence Wix (Mrs. Winterhalter), Jimmie Lucas (Taxi Driver), Charles Sherlock (Steward), William Cartledge (Newsboy), Dalies Frantz (Joe Barnes), Lowden Adams (Butler). — *Josef von Sternberg's cast (1938):* Fanny Brice (Madame Maresca), Walter Pidgeon (Phil Mayberry). — *Frank Borzage's cast (1938/39):* Ina Claire (Madame Maresca), Walter Pidgeon (Phil Mayberry), Adrienne Ames (Linda Rodgers), Leonard Penn (Bob Hampton).

Radio : KNX 27 May 1939 — *Revue for Screen Guild Show.* Directed by Frank Borzage, with the voices of Nelson Eddy, Douglas Fairbanks Jr., Fibber McGee and Molly, Ann Sheridan, Roland Young and Oscar Bradley's Orchestra.

1939

Disputed Passage. Prod.: Frank Borzage, assoc. prod.: Harlan Thompson (execut. prod.: William LeBaron), Paramount Pictures — script: Anthony Veiller, Sheridan Gibney, from the novel by Lloyd Cassel Douglas (Grosset & Dunlap, New York 1939) — photo: William C. Mellor ASC — mus.: Friedrich Hollaender, John Leipold — art dir.: Hans Dreier, Roland Anderson; set dec.: A. E. Freudeman — edit.: James Smith — asst.-dir.: Stanley Goldsmith — cost.: Edith Head — sound: Hugo Grenzbach, Richard Olson — length: 89 minutes — release: 11 Oct 1939 Los Angeles (Westwood Village, preview); 25 Oct 1939 New York (Paramount) (©27 Oct 1939).

Cast: Dorothy Lamour (Audrey Hilton [Lan Ying]), Akim Tamiroff (Dr. "Tubby" Forster), John Howard (John Wesley Beaven), Judith Barrett (Winifred Bane), William Collier, Sr. (Dr. William Cunningham), Victor Varconi (Dr. LaFerrière), Gordon Jones (Bill Anderson), Keye Luke (Andrew Abbott), Elisabeth Risdon (Mrs. Cunningham), Gaylord Pendleton (Lawrence Carpenter), Billy Cook (Johnny Merkle), William Pawley (Mr. Merkle), Renie Riano (Landlady), Z. T. Nyi (Chinese Ambassador), Philson Ahn (Kai), Dr. E. Y. Chung (Dr. Ling), Philip Ahn (Dr. Fung), Lee Ya-Ching (Aviatrix), Roger Gray (Gibson), Jack Chapin (Terrence Shane), Dave Alison (Intern), Mary Shalek (Dirty Nurse), Alma Eidnea (Scrub Nurse), Paul M. MacWilliams (Doctor), Charles Trowbridge (Dean), Dorothy Adams, Joleen King, Henrietta Kaye, Hortense Arbogast, Edith Cagnon, Patsy Mace, Fay McKenzie, Gloria Williams (Nurses), Jimmy F. Hogan (Messenger Boy), Kitty McHugh (Telephone Operator), James B. Carson (Hotel Clerk), Paul England (Britisher), Richard Denning (Student).

1939–1940

Strange Cargo working title: *Not Too Narrow, Not Too Deep*. Prod.: Joseph L. Mankiewicz, Metro-Goldwyn-Mayer Pictures (A Frank Borzage Production) — script: Lawrence Hazard, Lesser Samuels, from the novel *Not Too Narrow . . . Not Too Deep* by Richard Bernard Sale, adapted by Anita Loos (Simon & Schuster, New York/Cassell & Co. London, 1936) — photo: Robert Planck A.S.C. — mus.: Franz Waxman — edit.: Robert J. Kern — art dir.: Cedric Gibbons; assoc.: Daniel B. Cathcart, Edwin B. Willis (set dec.) — makeup: Jack Dawn — sound: Douglas Shearer — asst.-dir.: Apr 1940 New York (Capitol); (©27 Feb 1940).

Cast: Clark Gable (André Verne), Joan Crawford (Julie), Ian Hunter (Cambreau), Peter Lorre (Cochon ["Mr. Pig"]), Paul Lukas (Hessler), Albert Dekker (Moll), J. Edward Bromberg (Flaubert), Eduardo Ciannelli (Telez), Victor Varconi (Fisherman), John Arledge (Dufond), Frederic Worlock (Grideau, head of Penal Colony), Paul Fix (Benet), Bernard Nedell (Marfeu), Francis MacDonald (Moussenq), Betty Compson (Suzanne), Charles Judels (Renard), Jack Mulhall (Dunning), Dewey Robinson (Georges), Harry Cording, Richard Alexander, Bud Fine, James Pierce, Hal Wynants, Christian Frank, Mitchell Lewis, Stanley Andrews, Dick Cramer, Ray Teal, Jack Adair (Guards), Gene Coogan, Eddie Foster, Frank Lackteen, Harry Semels (Convicts), Art Dupuis (Orderly), Stanley Andrews (Constable), William Edmunds (Watchman).

1940

The Mortal Storm. Prod.: [Sidney Franklin, Victor Saville], (A Frank Borzage Production), Metro-Goldwyn-Mayer Pictures — script: Claudine West, Andersen Ellis [=Paul Hans Rameau], George Froeschel, [John Goulder], from the novel by Phyllis Bottome (Faber & Faber, London 1937) — photo: William Daniels ASC, operat.: Al Lane ASC, asst.-photo: Bill Reilly — mus.: Edward Kane, Eugene Zador, [Bronislau Kaper]; mus. dir.: Nat W. Finston — art dir.: Cedric Gibbons, Wade B. Rubottom (art dir.), Edwin B. Willis (set dec.) — cost.: Adrian, Gile Steele — makeup: Jack Dawn, Lillian Rosine; hair stylist: Sydney Guilaroff — edit.: Elmo Veron, asst.: Marshall Neilan III — sound: Douglas Shearer — asst.-dir.: Lew Borzage, Sandy Roth, Dolph Zimmer, Walter Strohm, Al Shenberg — script-girl: Willie Calihan — techn. advisor: Henry S. Noerdlinger — stills: Jim Manett — 2nd Unit dir.: Richard Rosson (photo: Leonard Smith, Lloyd Knechtel) — length: 100 minutes — release: 20 Jun 1940 New York (Capitol); 17 Aug 1940 Los Angeles (Four Star) (©25 Jun 1940).

Cast: Margaret Sullavan (Freya Roth), James Stewart (Martin Breitner), Robert Young (Fritz Marberg), Frank Morgan (Professor Dr. Viktor Roth), Robert Stack (Otto von Rohn), Bonita Granville (Elsa), Irene Rich (Emilia Roth-von Rohn), William T. Orr (Erich von Rohn), Maria Ouspenskaya (Hilda Breitner), Gene Reynolds (Rudi Roth), Russell Hicks (Rector), William Edmunds (Lehman, the Caretaker), Esther Dale (Marta, the Maid), Dan Dailey Jr. (SA-Führer Holl), Granville Bates (Berg), Thomas Ross (Schoolteacher Werner), Ward Bond (Franz), Sue Moore (Theresa), Harry Depp (2nd Colleague), Julius Tännen (3rd Colleague), Gus Glassmire (4th Colleague), Dick Rich, Ted Oliver (SS Guards), Howard Lang (Man), Bodil Rosing (Woman), Lucien Prival, Dick Elliott (Passport Officials), Henry Victor (Gestapo Official), William Irving (Waiter), Bert Roach (Fat Man in Café), Bob Stevenson (Gestapo Guard), Max Davidson (Old Man), John Stark (Gestapo Official), Fritz Leiber (Oppenheim), Robert O. Davis [=Rudolf Amendt-Anders] (Hartmann), [Ski Understudy: John Litchfield, Beth Crookes].

Flight Command working title: *Hell Cats*. Prod.: J. Walter Ruben (A Frank Borzage Production), Metro-Goldwyn-Mayer Pictures — script: Wells Root, Cdr. Harvey Haislip, [R. C. Sheriff], from story by H. Haislip, John Sutherland — photo: Harold Rosson ASC — mus.: Franz Waxman; song: "Eyes of the Fleet" (Ltn. Cdr. J. V.McElduff, U.S.N.) — edit.: Robert J. Kern — art dir.: Cedric Gibbons, Urie McCleary (art dir.), Edwin B. Willis (set dec.) — cost.: Dolly Tree, Giles Steele — spec. eff.: A. Arnold Gillespie — sound: Douglas Shearer — techn. advis.: Cdr. Morton Seligman U.S.N. — 2nd unit dir. (aerial photo): Richard Rosson, Elmer Dyer; airial operators: Paul Mantz, Laura Ingalls, Frank Clarke — asst.-dir.: Lew Borzage, Walter Strohm — length: 113 minutes — release: 17 Dec 1940 Washington, D.C.; 16 Mar 1941 New York (Capitol) (16 Dec 1940 Los Angeles preview) ©12 Dec 1940).

Cast: Robert Taylor (Ensign Alan "Pensacola" Drake), Ruth Hussey (Lorna Gary), Walter Pidgeon (Squadron Cdr. Bill Gary), Paul Kelly (Ltn. Cdr. Dusty Rhodes), Shepperd Strudwick (Ltn. Jerry Banning), Red Skelton (Ltn. "Mugger" Martin), Nat Pendleton (C.P.O. "Spike" Knowles), Dick Purcell (Ltn. "Stitchy" Payne), William Tannen (Ltn. Freddy Townsend), William Stelling (Ltn. Bush), Stanley Smith (Ltn. Frost), Addison Richards (Vice-Admiral), Donald Douglas (First Duty Officer), Pat Flaherty (Second Duty Officer), Forbes Murray (Captain), Marsha Hunt (Claire), Lee Tung-Foo (Jung), John Hamilton (Pensacola Commander), Gaylord [Steve] Pendleton, Jimmy Millican (Enlisted Men), Jack Luden (Hell Cat), Dick Wessel (Big Sailor), Reed Hadley (Admiral's Aide), John Sheehan (Mechanic), Otto Han (Gogo), Irving Bacon (Taxi Driver), Pat Flaherty (2nd Duty Officer), Albert Morin (Waiter), Claire Owen (Mrs. Frost), Forbes Murray (Naval Captain), George Offerman, Jr. (Small Sailor), James Seay, Walter Sande (Officers), Gayne Whitman (Doctor), John Raitt, Ed Smith, Cliff Danielson, Howard Wilson, Hal Le Seur, Gilbert Wilson, Bob Davis (Hell Cats).

1940–1941

Billy the Kid. Prod.: Irving Asher, Metro-Goldwyn-Mayer Pictures—dir.: [started by Frank Borzage], David Miller, [Norman Taurog, supervision]—script: Gene Fowler, from story by Howard Emmett Rogers and Bradbury Foote, inspired by the book *The Saga of Billy the Kid* by Walter Noble Burns (Doubleday, Page & Co., Garden City, N.Y. 1926)—photo: Leonard Smith ASC, William V. Skall ASC; 2nd unit (locations): Sid Wagner, Charles Boyle (Technicolor)—edit.: Robert J. Kern—mus.: David Snell (songs: Ormond B. Ruthven, Albert Mannheimer)—art dir.: Edwin B. Willis—asst.-dir.: [Lew Borzage], Al Shenberg—length: 94 minutes; 10 reels—release: 19 Jun 1941 New York (Capitol); Preview: 22 May 1941 Hollywood (©28 May 1941).
   Cast: Robert Taylor (William Bonney, alias Billy the Kid), Brian Donlevy (Jim Sherwood [=Pat Garrett]), Ian Hunter (Eric Keating), Mary Howard (Edith Keating), Gene Lockhart (Dan Hickey), Henry O'Neill (Tim Ward), Frank Puglia (Pedro Gonzales), Cass McAndrews (Sheriff), Cy Kendall (Cowboy), Connie Gilchrist (Mildred), Ethel Griffies (Mrs. Hanky), Chill Wills (Tom Patterson), Guinn Williams (Ed Bronson), Olive Blakeney (Mrs. Patterson), Lon Chaney Jr. (Spike Hudson), Frank Conlon (Judge Blake), Mitchell Lewis (Bart Hodges), Dick Curtis (Kirby Claxton), Ted Adams (Bill Cobb), Earl Gunn (Jesse Martin), Eddie Dunn (Pat Shanahan), Grant Withers (Ed Shanahan), Joe Yule (Milton), Carl Pitti (Bat" Smithers), Arthur Housman (Drunk), Lew Harney (The Duke), Priscilla Lawson (Bessie), Kermit Maynard (Thad Decker), Slim Whitaker (Butch), Ray Teal (Axel), Wesley White (Bud), Ben Pitti, George Chesebro, Jack L. King (Hickey Gang), Jules Cowles, Edwin J. Brady (Vagrants), Frank Hagney (Man in Saloon), Buck Mack (Gambler), Tom London (Leader).

1941

Smilin' Through. Prod.: Victor Saville (A Frank Borzage Production), Metro-Goldwyn-Mayer Pictures—script: Donald Ogden Stewart, John Balderston, from the play in a prologue and 3 acts by Jane Cowl and Jane Murfin [pseud.: Allan Langdon Martin] (New York 1919) and the script by Claudine West and Ernest Wajda (1932)—photo: Leonard Smith A.S.C. (Technicolor, consultant: Natalie Kalmus, Henri Jaffa)—art dir.: Cedric Gibbons (art dir.), assoc.: Daniel B. Cathcart; Edwin B. Willis (set dir.)—cost.: Adrian, Gile Steele—spec. eff.: Warren Newcombe—makeup: Jack Dawn—sound: Douglas Shearer—edit.: Frank Sullivan, Peter Ballbusch—mus. dir.: Herbert Stothart, mus. & songs: "The Kerry Dance" (L.J. Molloy), "Drink to Me Only with Thine Eyes" (lyr. Ben Johnson), "Just a Little Love, a Little Kiss" (Un peu d'amour" by Leo Silèsu, English lyr.: Adrian Ross), "Rose of Tralee" (Charles W. Glower), "Ouvre ton coeur" (George Bizet), "Smilin' Through" (Arthur A. Penn), "There's a Long, Long Trail A-Winding" (Alonzo Elliott, lyr. Stoddard King), "Smiles" (Lee S. Roberts, lyr. J. Will Callahan), "Land of Hope and Glory" (based on "Pomp and Circumstance" by Sir Edward Elgar, lyr. A. C. Benson), "Recessional" (Reginald de Koven, lyr. Rudyard Kipling)—asst.-dir.: Lew Borzage—length: 100 minutes—release: 5 Dec 1941 New York (Capitol); New York Preview: 5 Sep 1941 (©4 Sep 1941).
   Cast: Jeanette MacDonald (Kathleen Dungannon/Moonyean Clare), Brian Aherne (Sir John Carteret), Gene Raymond (Kenneth Wayne/Jeremy Wayne), Ian Hunter (Reverend Owen Harding), Jackie Horner (Kathleen as a child), Frances Robinson (Ellen), Patrick O'Moore (Willie Ainley), Eric Lonsdale (Charles), Frances Carson (Dowager), Ruth Rickaby (Woman), David Clyde (Sexton), Wyndham Standing (Doctor), Emily West (Chorus Singer ["Land of Milk and Honey"]).

The Vanishing Virginian working title: *Mr. Yancey of Virginia.* Prod.: Edwin Knopf (A Frank Borzage Production), Metro-Goldwyn-Mayer Pictures—script: Jan Fortune, from the novel by Rebecca Yancey Williams (E. P. Dutton, New York 1940)—photo: Charles Lawton ASC—mus.: David

Snell, dir.mus.: Lennie Hayton, songs: "The World Was Made for You" (Johann Strauss), "Evening by the Moonlight," "Bill Bailey" (trad.); mus. adapt.: Earl Brent, Spiritual arranged by Jester Hairston — edit.: James E. Newcom, Peter Ballbush — art dir.: Cedric Gibbons, assoc.: William Ferrari, set dec.: Edwin B. Willis — cost.: Robert Kalloch, Gile Steele — makeup: Jack Dawn — sound: Douglas Shearer — historical advis.: Louis Noerdlinger — asst.-dir.: Lew Borzage — length: 101 minutes — release: 27 May 1942 New York (Criterion) (2 Dec 1941 Los Angeles preview); ©2 Dec 1941.

Cast: Frank Morgan (Capt. Robert Davis Yancey), Kathryn Grayson (Rebecca Yancey), Spring Byington (Rosa Yancey), Natalie Thompson (Margaret Yancey), Douglass Newland (Jim Shirley), Mark Daniels (Jack Holden), Elizabeth Patterson (Grandma), Juanita Quigley (Caroline Yancey), Scotty Beckett (Joel Yancey), Dickie Jones (Robert Yancey, Jr.), Leigh Whipper (Uncle Josh), Louise Beavers (Aunt Emmeline), J. M. Kerrigan (John Phelps), Harlan Briggs (Mr. Rogard), Katharine Alexander (Marcia Marshall), Dolores Hurlic (Sugar), Marcella Moreland (Baby), Cleo Desmond (Aunt Mandy Brown), Barbara Bedford (Mildred Simpson), Dudley Dickerson (Alexander), Howard Hickman (Dr. Edwards), Alfred Grant (Jeff Brown), Arie Lee Branche (Edith Brown), Erville Alderson (Judge Fred Stuart), Edward Hearn, Hooper Atchley (Members of the Jury), Francis Ford (Mountaineer), William Forrest (Wm. Harrison Jordon), Matt Moore (Charles Inglestadt), George Irving (Roger Payson), Clinton Rosemond (Negro Minister), Kieth Copland, Charles Bates, Margaret Campbell, Dickie McCoy (Grandchildren), Lee Bennett (Joe adult), Rita Quigley (Caroline adult), Anelle McCarthy (Grandchild), Cliff Danielson (Robert adult), Jester Hairston (Mover), Rex Downing (Newsboy), Helen Blizzard (Robert Sr.'s Wife), Myrtle Anderson (Maid).

1942

Seven Sweethearts working titles: *Tulip Time; Tulip Time in Michigan; Seven Sisters; House of Seven Sisters*. Prod.: Joe Pasternak (A Frank Borzage Production), Metro-Goldwyn-Mayer Pictures — script: Walter Reisch, Leo Townsend [from the play *Sieben Schwestern* by Ferenc Herczeg, Vienna 1903] — photo: George Folsey ASC — mus.: Franz Waxman (songs: "You and the Waltz and I," "Little Tingle Tangle Shoes" by Walter Jurmann and Paul Francis Webster; "Tulip Time" by Burton Lane and Ralph Freed) — edit.: Blanche Sewell — art dir.: Cedric Gibbons, assoc.: Paul Groesse, Jack Moore; set dec.: Edwin B. Willis — cost.: Howard Shoup — makeup: Jack Dawn, Sydney Guilaroff (hair stylist) — sound: Douglas Shearer — chor.: Ernst Matray — asst.-dir.: Lew Borzage — length: 98 minutes — release: 5 Aug 1942 New York (Lexington) (©11 Aug 1942).

Cast: Kathryn Grayson (Billie Van Maaster), Van Heflin (Henry Taggart), Marsha Hunt (Regina Van Maaster), Cecilia Parker (Victor Van Maaster), Peggy Moran (Albert Van Maaster), Diana Lewis (Mrs. Nugent), S. Z. Sakall [=Szöke Szakall] (Mr. Van Maaster), Isobel Elsom (Miss Robbins), Carl Esmond (Jan Randall), Louise Beavers (Petunia), Donald Meek (Minister), Lewis Howard (Mr. Nugent), Dorothy Morris (Peter Van Maaster), Frances Rafferty (George Van Maaster), Frances Raeburn (Cornelius Van Maaster), Michael Butler (Bernard Groton), Cliff Danielson (Martin Leyden), William Roberts (Anthony Vreeland), James Warren (Theodore Vaney), Dick Simmons (Paul Brandt), Cecil Stewart (Organist), John Maxwell (City Editor), Gladys Blake (Telephone Operator).

1942–1943

Stage Door Canteen (A Soldier's Love Story). Prod.: Sol Lesser, assoc.prod.: Barnett Briskin (A Frank Borzage Production), American Theatre Wing/d. United Artist — script: Delmer Daves — photo: Harry J. Wild ASC — art dir.: Hans Peters, Victor Gangelin (set dec.); prod. designer: Harry Horner — sound: Franz Maher, Hugh McDowell — cost.: Albert Deano — edit.: Hal C. Kern — asst.-dir.: Lew Borzage, Virgil Hart — makeup: Irving Berns — talent coordinator: Radie Harris — mus. supervis.: Freddie Rich; music dir.: C. Bakaleinikoff; songs & musical numbers: "We Mustn't Say Goodbye," "The Machine Gun Song," "Sleep, Baby, Sleep," "You're Pretty Terrific Yourself," "Don't Worry Island," "Quick Sands," "We Meet in the Funniest Places," "American Boy," "A Rookie and His Rhythm" (Al Dubin, James V. Monaco), "She's a Bombshell from Brooklyn" (Sol Lesser, Dubin, Monaco), "The Girl I Love to Leave Behind" (Richard Rodgers, Lorenz Hart), "Why Don't You Do Right?" (Joe McCoy), "Bugle Call Rag" (Jack Pettis, Billy Meyers, Elmer Schoebel), "Marching Through Berlin" (adapt. from "Deutschland über alles" by Belford Hendricks), "The Lord's Prayer" (Albert Hay Malotte) — length: 12,034 ft.; 134 minutes — release: 24 Jun 1943 New York (Capitol) (©14 Jun 1943).

Cast: Cheryl Walker (Eileen), William Terry (Ed "Dakota" Smith, GI), Marjorie Riordan (Jean), Lon McCallister (Jack "California" Gillman, GI), Margaret Early (Ella Sue), Michael (Sunset) Carson, GI), Harrison ("Texas," GI), Dorothea Kent (Mamie), Fred Brady (Jersey), Marion Shockley (Lillian), Patrick O'Moore (Australian), Ruth Novel, Francis Pierlot, Madeleine Matthey-Borzage, Sue Williams-Borzage (extras)—and the "Guest Stars": Judith Anderson, Henry Armetta, Kenny Baker, Tallulah Bankhead, Ralph Bellamy, Edgar Bergen, Ray Bolger, Helen Broderick, Ina Claire, Katharine Cornell, Lloyd Corrigan, Jane Cowl, Jane Darwell, William Demarest, Virginia Field, Dorothy Fields, Gracie Fields, Arlene Francis, Vinton Freedley, Billy Gilbert, Lucile Gleason, Vera Gordon, Virginia Grey, Helen Hayes, Katharine Hepburn, Hugh Herbert, Jean Hersholt, Sam Jaffe, Allen Jenkins, George Jessel, Roscoe Karns, Virginia Kaye, Tom Kennedy, Otto Kruger, June Lang, Betty Lawford, Gertrude Lawrence, Gypsy Rose Lee, Alfred Lunt and Lynn Fontanne, Bert Lytell, Aline MacMahon, Harpo Marx, Elsa Maxwell, Helen Menken, Yehudi Menuhin, Ethel Merman, Ralph Morgan, Alan Mowbray, Paul Muni, Elliott Nugent, Merle Oberon, Franklin Pangborn, Helen Parrish, Brock Pemberton, George Raft, Lanny Ross, Selena Royle, Martha Scott, Cornelia Otis Skinner, Ned Sparks, Bill Stern, Ethel Waters, Johnny Weissmuller, Arleen Whelan, Dame May Whitty, Ed Wynn—and the Orchestras of Count Basie, Xavier Cugat (with Lina Romay), Benny Goodman (with Peggy Lee), Kay Kyser, Guy Lombardo, Freddy Martin.

American Red Cross (short)—Prod.: Sol Lesser, for American Red Cross—photo: Harry J. Wild ASC—cast: Capt. Eddie Rickenbacker.

His Butler's Sister working title: *My Girl Godfrey*. Prod.: Felix Jackson, assoc. prod.: Frank Shaw (A Frank Borzage Production), Universal Pictures—script: Samuel Hoffenstein, Elizabeth Reinhardt—photo: Woody Bredell ASC—edit.: Ted Kent—art dir.: John B. Goodman, Martin Obzina (art dir.), Russell A. Gausman, T. F. Offenbecker (set dec.)—cost.: Vera West, Adrian—sound: Bernard B. Brown, Joseph Lapis, E. Wetzel—spec. eff.: John P. Fulton—asst-dir.: Lew Borzage—mus.: Hans J. Salter, mus. dir.: Charles Previn, arr. mus.: Max Rabinovich; songs: "In the Spirit of a Moment" (Bernie Grosman, Walter Jurman), "When You're Away" (Victor Herbert, Henry Blossom), "Turandot" (Puccini, sung by Deanna Durbin), "Is It True What They Say About Dixie?" (Irving Caesar, Sammy Lerner, Gerald Marks, sung by Iris Adrian, Robin Raymond), vocal coach: Andres de Segurola—length: 94 minutes/8430 ft.—release: 29 Dec 1943 New York (Loew's Criterion Theater) (8 Nov 1943 Los Angeles preview); ©17 Nov 1943.

Cast: Deanna Durbin (Ann Carter), Franchot Tone (Charles Gerard), Pat O'Brien (Martin Murphy), Evelyn Ankers (Elizabeth Campbell), Akim Tamiroff (Sergejevitch Popoff), Alan Mowbray (Jenkins), Walter Catlett (Kaleb), Elsa Janssen (Saverena), Frank Jenks (Emmett), Sig Arno (Moreno), Hans Conreid (Reeves), Florence Bates (Lady Sloughberry), Andrew Tombes (Brophy), Iris Adrian (Girl on Train), Robin Raymond (Blonde on Train), Stephanie Bachelor (Dot Stanley), Franklin Pangborn, Roscoe Karns (Fields), Russell Hicks (Sanderson), Marion Pierce (Margaret Howard), Madeleine Matthey-Borzage (Dancer), Sue Williams-Borzage (extra).

1943–1944

Till We Meet Again working titles: *Tomorrow's Harvest; Give Us This Day*. Prod.: Frank Borzage, assoc. David Lewis, (exec. prod.: B.G. De Sylva), Paramount Pictures -script: Lenore Coffee, from the play *Tomorrow's Harvest* by Alfred Maury—photo: Theodor Sparkuhl ASC, Farciot Edouart ASC (process camera)—mus.: David Buttolph—edit.: Elmo Veron—art dir.: Hans Dreier, Robert Usher (art dir.), Ray Moyer (set dec.)—spec. eff.: Gordon Jennings ASC—asst.-dir.: Lew Borzage, Harry Caplan—sound: Max Hutchinson, John Cope—makeup: Wally Westmore—technical advisor: Father Jo Van Schulenberg—length: 88 minutes—release: 29 Aug 1944 New York (Rivoli) (©29 Aug 1944).

Cast: Ray Milland (John), Barbara Britton (Sister Clothilde [Louise Duprez]), Walter Slezak (Marcel Vitrey, the Mayor), Lucile Watson (Mother Superior), Konstantin Shayne (Major Krupp), Vladimir Sokoloff (Pierre Cabeau, Gardener), Marguerite D'Alvarez (Madame Sarroux, Laundry Woman), Mona Freeman (Elise, an Orphan), William Edmunds (Henri Maret, the Forger), George Davis (Gaston, Waiter), Peter Helmers (Examiner), John Wengraf (Gestapo Chief), Mira McKinney (Portress), Tala Birell (Madame Bouchard), Buddy Gorman (Messenger), Dawn Bender (Françoise), Eilene Janssen (Yvonne), Henry Sharp (André), Alfred Païx, Eugene Borden (Refugees), Muni Seroff (Jacques), Philip Van Zandt (Lieutenant), Georges Renavent (Gabriel), Diane Dubois, Janet Gallow,

Nils Rich, Sharon McManus, Mary Thomas, Diana Martin, Yvette Duguay (Orphans), Byron Nelson, Don Cadell, Hans Furberg, Robert Stevenson (German Soldiers), Frances Sandford, Iris Lancaster (Girls in Restaurant), Nina Borget (Jeanette), George Sorel (Gendarme), Marcelle Corday (Elderly Waitress), Francis McDonald (Driver of the Cart), Crane Whitley (Man with Silver).

1944–1945

The Spanish Main. Prod.: Frank Borzage, exec. prod.: Robert Fellows, assoc.prod.: Stephen Ames, RKO Pictures—script: George Worthington Yates, Herman J. Mankiewicz, from story by Aeneas MacKenzie—photo: George Barnes ASC (Technicolor), [Frank Redmond]; color consultant: Natalie Kalmus, advisor: Morgan Padelford—mus.: Hanns Eisler; mus. dir.: Constantin Bakaleinikoff—art dir.: Albert S. D'Agostino, Carroll Clark (art dir.), Darrell Silvera, Claude Carpenter (set dec.)—sound: John E. Tribby—2nd unit dir.: "Breezy" Reeves Eason—spec. eff.: Vernon L. Walker ASC—asst.-dir.: Lew Borzage, Lloyd Richards—edit.: Ralph Dawson—cost.: Edward Stevenson, Joe De Yong, Dwight Franklin—Naval techn. advisor: Capt. Fred Ellis—sound: Phil Mitchel, James G. Stewart—length: 110 minutes—release: 20 Sep 1945 Hollywood preview; 6 Nov 1945 New York (Palace) (©29 Sep 1945).

Cast: Paul Henreid (Capt. Laurent Van Horn), Maureen O'Hara (Doña Francisca de Guzman y Argandora), Walter Slezak (Don Juan Alvarado de Soto, the Viceroy), Binnie Barnes (Anne Bonney), John Emery (Mario Da Bilar), Barton MacLane (Captain Black), J. M. Kerrigan (Pillory), Fritz Leiber (Bishop), Nany Gates (Lupita), Jack LaRue (Lieutenant Escobar), Mike Mazurki (Swaine), Ian Keith (Captain Lussan), Victor Kilian (Captain of the "Santa Madre"), Curt Bois (Paree), Antonio Moreno (Commandante), Alfredo Sabato (Sailor), Brandon Hurst (Captain Salter), Bob O'Connor (Master at Arms), Tom Kennedy (Captain McLeon), Marcelle Corday (Señora Perez), Norma Drury (Señora Montalvo), Abe Dinovich (Singer), Max Wagner, Ray Spiker (Bullies), Juan De La Cruz (Majordomo), Leo White (Hairdresser), Cosmo Sardo, Leo Schlessinger (Spanish Guards), Jack Wise (Manicurist), Dan Seymour (Jailer), Ray Cooper, Jamiel Hasson, Alf Haugan, Al Haskell, George Bruggerman, Chuck Hamilton, Jean Valjean, Demetrius Alexis, Carl Deloro (Officers), Don Avalier (Pirate).

1945

I've Always Loved You. UK and working title: *Concerto.* Prod.: Frank Borzage, assoc.-prod.: Lew Borzage, Republic Pictures (Herbert J. Yates)—script: Borden Chase, from his novel *Concerto* (published in *American Magazine*)—photo: Tony Gaudio ASC (Technicolor); color consultant: Natalie Kalmus, asst.: Francisco Cugat—mus.: Sergei Vassilievich Rachmaninoff (2nd Piano Concerto," "Prelude in C# Minor), Frederic Chopin (G Minor Ballade," "Prelude in C Major," "Nocturne," "Prelude No. 1 Opus 28), Ludwig van Beethoven (Appassionata Sonata 23), Felix Mendelssohn (Rondo Capriccioso), Richard Wagner (Liebestod), Johann Sebastian Bach (Toccata and Fugue), W. A. Mozart (Die Zauberflöte," "Sonata No.1), Franz Schubert (Moment Musicale), Johannes Brahms (Lullaby), Heitor Villa-Lobos (Brazilian Folk Song) ; mus. dir.: Walter Scharf, piano: Arthur Rubinstein—edit.: Richard L. Van Enger—spec. eff.: Howard and Theodore Lydecker—art dir.: Ernst Fegté (prod. designed in color); set dec.: John McCarthy Jr., Leonora Pierotti; architecture: Howard E. Johnson—makeup: Bob Mark, Peggy Gray (hair stylist)—cost.: Eleanor Behm—sound: Earl Crain Sr., Howard Wilson, John Stransky Jr.—asst.-dir.: Jam Nelson—length: 117 minutes—release: 29 Aug 1946 New York preview (Criterion); 6 Sep 1946 New York (©21 Jun 1946).

Cast: Philip Dorn [=Frits van Dongen] (Leopold Goronoff), Catherine McLeod (Myra Hassman), William Carter (George Sampter), Maria Ouspenskaya (Mama Goronoff ["Babouchka"]), Felix Bressart (Fredrick Hassman), Fritz Feld (Nicholas Kavlun, Goronoff's Private Secretary), Elizabeth Patterson (Mrs. Sampter, the Cook), Vanessa Brown (Georgette ["Porgy"] Sampter, 17 years old), Lewis Howard (Prof. Michael Severin), Adele Mara (Señorita Fortaleza), Gloria Donovan (Georgette ["Porgy"] Sampter, 5 years old), Stephanie Bachelor (Redhead), Cora Witherspoon (Edwina Blythe), John Sheehan, Al Hill Sr. (Stagehands), Maurice Cass, Lillian Bronson, Mira McKinney (Music Teachers), Charles Coleman (Butler), Pauline Carter (Girl of 12), Natalie Kosches (Niece), André Previn (Long Hair), Gordon Dumont, Edgar Caldwell, James R. Linn (Call Boys), James Kirkwood (Murphy), Forbes Murray (Music Critic), John Mylong (Impresario), Junius Matthews (Little Man), Heater Sarno (Man with Lasket), Harry Depp (Neighbour), Madeline Matthey-Borzage (Woman in Public).

1946

Magnificent Doll. Australia: *Magnificent Lady* working titles: *Dolly Madison; The Life of Dolly Madison.* Prod.: Jack H. Skirball, Bruce Manning, Hallmark Productions Inc./d. Universal-International— script & story: Irving Stone—photo: Joseph Valentine ASC—mus.: Hans J. Salter; mus. dir.: David Tamkin—asst.-dir.: John F. Sherwood, Joe Kenny—art dir.: Alexander Golitzen (art dir.), Russell A. Gausman, Ted Offenbecker (set dec.); set dec. supervis.: Jack Otterson—cost.: Travis Banton, Vera West (hats: Lily Dache)—sound: Charles Felstead, Robert Felstead—edit.: Ted J. Kent—makeup: Jack P. Pierce; hair stylist: Carmen Dirigo, Anna Malin—set continuity: Adele Cannon—prod. manager: Arthur Siteman—length: 8,710 ft.; 96 minutes—release: 15 Nov 1946 New York (Loew's Criterion) (©9 Dec 1946).

Cast: Ginger Rogers (Dolly Payne), David Niven (Aaron Burr), Burgess Meredith (James Madison), Stephen McNally (John Todd), Peggy Wood (Mrs. Payne), Frances Williams (Amy), Robert H. Barrat (Mr. Payne), Grandon Rhodes (Thomas Jefferson), Henri Letondal (Count D'Arignon), Joe Forte (Senator Ainsworth), Erville Alderson (Darcy), George Barrows (Jedson), Francis J. McDonald (Barber Jenks), Emmett Vogan (Mr. Gallentine), Arthur Space (Alexander Hamilton), Byron Foulger (Servant), Joseph Crehan (Williams), Larry Blake (Charles), Pierre Watkin (Harper), John Sheehan (Doorman), Ruth Lee (Mrs. Gallentine), George Carleton (Howard), Jack Ingram (Lane, the Courier), Olaf Hytten (Blennerhassett), Sam Flint (Waters), Boyd Irvin (Hathaway), Lee Phelps (Hatch, a Better), Lois Austin (Grace Phillips), Harlan Briggs (Quinn), John Hines (Dr. Ellis), Ferris Taylor (Mr. Phillips), Eddy Waller (Arthur), Stanley Blystone (Bailiff), Stanley Price (Man at Platform), Victor Zimmerman (Martin), Ja George (Governor Stanley), Ethan Laidlaw (Sanders, Soldier), Mary Emery (Woman), Carey Hamilton (Senator Mason), Dick Dickinson (Man Who Falls), Larry Steers (Lafayette), Frank Erickson (Captain White), Grace Cunard (Woman with Baby), Tom Coleman (Mr. Carroll), Pietro Sosso (Mr. Anthony), Jack Curtis (Edmund), Harry Denny (Mr. Calot), Garnett Marks (Justice Drake), Jerry Jerome (Thomas), John Michael (Ned), John Hamilton (Mr. Witherspoon), Harlan Tucker (Ralston), Vivien Oakland (Mrs. Witherspoon), Al Hill (Man), Joe King (Jailer), Brandon Hurst (Brown), Madeleine Matthey-Borzage (Woman in Courtroom).—Narrated by Ginger Rogers.

That's My Man new release title (1953): *King of the Race Track*—UK: *Will Tomorrow Ever Come?* working titles: *Gallant Man; Turf Café; That Man of Mine.* Prod.: Frank Borzage, associate prod.: Lew Borzage, Republic Pictures (Herbert J. Yates)—script: Steve Fisher, Bradley King, from their story—photo: Tony Gaudio ASC, Bud Thackery—mus.: Hans J. Salter; mus. dir.: Cy Feuer—edit.: Richard L. Van Enger—art dir.: James Sullivan, Frank Arrigo (art dir.), John McCarthy Jr. (set dec.)— spec. eff.: Howard Lydecker, Theodore Lydecker—2nd unit dir.: Yakima Canutt—sound: Richard Tyler—cost.: Marie Hermann—makeup: Bob Mark, Peggy Gray (hair stylist)—techn. advisor: Jack Smith—asst.-dir.: Dick Moder—length: 104 minutes—release: 3 Apr 47 New York preview (Globe) (©7 Apr 1947).

Cast: Don Ameche (Joe Grange), Catherine McLeod (Ronnie), Roscoe Karns (Toby Gleeton), John Ridgely (Ramsey), Kitty Irish (Kitty), Joe Frisco (Willie Wagonstatter), Gregory Marshall (Richard), Dorothy Adams (Millie), Frankie Darro (Jockey), Hampton J. Scott (Sam), John Miljan (Secretary), William B. Davidson (Monte), Joe Hernandez (Race Track Announcer), Dorothy Christy (Woman), Matt Moore (Bowler's Owner), John Arledge (Thunder's Owner), Renee Carson (Nurse), Robert Riordan (Doctor), Michael Branden (Man), Lynne Lyons (Woman), Billy Henry (Richard age 3), Lois Austin (Nurse), Ray Walker (Stranger), John Sheehan (Pharmacist), Sarah Selby (Woman), Frank Scannell (Husband), Al Hill (Man at Window), Earle S. Dewey (Deaf Man), Frank Darien (Hotel Clerk), Francis McDonald, James Kirkwood, Charles Miller (Men), Lorin Rakter (Reporter), Rodney Bell, George Pembroke (Owners), Bill Neff (Weights Man), Torchy Rand (Girl Spieler), John Montague (Ramsey's Friend), Mary Bye (Hat Check Girl), Marshall Reed (Reporter), Garry Owen (Worker), Bill Borzage (Stewart)—and "Gallant Man" the Horse.

Rough But Hopeful (Scenes from the Frank Borzage Movie Golf Tournament)—Prod. & dir.: Courneya Hyde Productions, Los Angeles—length: 8 minutes, Technicolor (16mm).—with Red Skelton, Charlie Kemper, Bob Hope, Bing Crosby, William Bendix, Wayne Morris, Dennis O'Keefe, Randolph Scott, Guy Kibbee, Mickey Rooney, Buddy Rogers, Don Ameche, Johnny Weissmuller, Jack L. Warner.

1947–1948

Moonrise. Prod.: Charles F. Haas (Marshall Grant Pictures Prod.), Charles K. Feldman Group Prod. (A Frank Borzage Production)/d. Republic Pictures (Deluxe" Prod., Herbert J. Yates) — script: Charles F. Haas, [Vladimir Pozner], from the novel by Theodore Strauss (published in *Collier's Magazine*, 1945; The Viking Press, New York 1946) — photo: John L. Russell ASC — mus.: William Lava; songs: "It Just Dawned on Me That There's Magic in the Moonrise (The Moonrise Song)" (W. Lava, Harry Tobias) sung by David Street, "Lonesome" (W. Lava, Theodore Strauss) sung by Rex Ingram — edit.: Harry Keller — art dir.: Lionel Banks (art dir.), John McCarthy Jr., George Sawley (set dec.) — cost.: Adele Palmer — makeup: Bob Mark, Peggy Gray (hair stylist) — asst.-dir.: Lee Lukather — spec. eff.: Howard and Theodore Lydecker (Consolidated Film Industries) — sound: Earl Cain Sr., Howard Wilson — edit.: Harry Keller — length: 90 minutes — release: 9 Sep 1948 Hollywood tradeshow (Paramount); 6 Mar 1949 New York (Globe) (©9 Sep 1948).

Cast: Dane Clark (Danny Hawkins), Gail Russell (Gilly Johnson), Ethel Barrymore (Grandma Hawkins), Allyn Joslyn (Clem Otis, the Sheriff), Rex Ingram (Mose Jackson), Henry [Harry] Morgan (Billy Scripture, the Halfwit), David Street (Ken Williams, Musician), Selena Royle (Aunt Jessie Hawkins), Harry Carey Jr. (Jimmy Biff), Irving Bacon (Judd Jenkins), Lloyd Bridges (Jerry Sykes), Houseley Stevenson (Uncle Joe Jingle, the Old-Timer), Phil Brown (Elmer), Harry V. Cheshire (J. B. Sykes), Lila Leeds (Julie), Virginia Mullen (Miss Simpkins), Oliver Blake (Ed Conlon), Tom Fadden (Homer Blackstone), Charles Lane (Man in Black), Clem Bevans (Jake), Helen Wallace (Martha Otis), Michael Branden, Bill Borzage, Tiny Jimmie Kelly, Ed Rees, Casey MacGregor (Barkers), John Harmon (Baseball Attendant), Monte Lowell (Man), Jimmie Hawkins, Gary Armstrong, Buzzy Henry, Jimmy Crane, Harry Lauter, Bob Hoffman, Joel McGinnis (Boys), Timmie Hawkins (Alfie), Dorren McCann, Candy Toxton (Girls), Steven Peck (Danny, age 7), Johnny Calkins (Danny, age 13), Tommy Ivo (Jerry, age 7), Michael Dill (Jerry, age 13), Linda Lombard, Stelita Ravel (Dancers), Renee Donatt (Ticket Seller), George Backus, Monte Montague (Hunters).

1955

Fox Movietone News (no. 113–928) — release: 19 Nov 1955 — Frank Borzage receiving the George Eastman Award at the Festival of Film Artists in Rochester (NY), together with Mae Marsh, Marshall Nolan, Mary Pickford, Buster Keaton, Harold Lloyd, Lillian Gish and Cecil B. DeMille.

Day Is Done (television). Prod.: Willis Goldbeck, Hal Roach Studios Production (prod. supervis.: Sidney Van Keuren; prod. coordinat.: William M. Sterling), for Screen Directors' Guild, presented by Eastman Kodak Co. — script: William Tunberg — photo: Hal Mohr ASC — asst.-dir.: Lew Borzage — art dir.: Charley Pyke (art dir.), Charles Thompson (set dec.) — edit.: Bruce Schoengarth — spec. eff.: Jack R. Glass — sound: Willard Starr, Joel Moss — story editor: James J. Geller — casting: Ruth Burch — length: 25 minutes — premiere: 12 Oct 1955 NBC-Television (Screen Director's Playhouse No. 2).

Cast: Rory Calhoun (Sergeant Sam Norris), Bobby Driscoll (Private Eddie Zane), Richard Crane (Private Archer), Douglas Dick (Cpt. Carlson), Michael Emmet (Cpt. Harris), James Goodwin (Jones), Robert Arthur, Wright King, Ron Kennedy, Bill White, Jr. (Soldiers).

1956

A Ticket for Thaddeus (television). Prod.: Willis Goldbeck, Hal Roach Studios Production (prod. supervis.: Sidney Van Keuren), for Screen Directors' Guild, presented by Eastman Kodak Co. — script: A. I. Bezzerides, from a story by Rose C. Feld — photo: Paul Ivano — asst.-dir.: Arthur Loeker — edit.: Marsh Hendry — art dir.: William Ferrari (art dir.), Rudy Butler (set dec.) — spec. eff.: Jack R. Glass — sound: Jack Goodrich, Joel Moss — makeup: Jack R. Pierce, Carmen Dirigo (hair stylist) — story editor: James J. Geller — cost.: Eric Seelig — casting: Ruth Burch — asst.-dir.: Lew Borzage — length: 25 minutes — premiere: 9 May 1956 NBC-Television (Screen Directors' Playhouse No. 25).

Cast: Edmund O'Brien (Thaddeus [Tadeusz] Kubaczik), Narda Onyx (Kathi Kubaczik), Alan Hale (Ralph Bowen), Clem Bevans (Jessup), Raymond Bailey (Judge), Hayden Rorke (Collier), Russ Conway (Policeman), Frances Robinson (Mrs. Preston).

The Day I Met Caruso (television). Prod.: Willis Goldbeck, Hal Roach Studios Production (prod.

supervis.: Sidney Van Keuren), for Screen Directors' Guild, presented by Eastman Kodak Co.— script: Zoë Akins, from story by Elizabeth Bacon Rodewald — photo: Ed Fitzgerald ASC — mus.: Leon Klatzkin — asst.-dir.: Lew Borzage, Thomas F. Kelly — art dir.: James Vance (art dir.), Rudy Butler (set dec.) — spec. eff.: Jack R. Glass — sound: Jack Goodrich, Joel Moss — makeup: Jack R. Pierce, Carmen Dirigo (hair stylist) — story editor: James J. Geller — cost.: Eric Seelig — casting: Ruth Burch — edit.: Roy Livingston — length: 25 minutes — premiere: 5 Sep 1956 NBC-Television (Screen Director's Playhouse No. 34).

Cast: Lotfi Mansouri (Enrico Caruso), Sandy Descher (Elizabeth), Bill Walker (Black Porter), Emily Lawrence (Cousin Hannah), Walter Coy (Elizabeth's Father), Barbara Eiler (Elizabeth's Mother), Tito Vuolo (Caruso's Valet).

1957

Jeanne Eagels. Prod. & dir.: George Sidney, Columbia — Cast: Kim Novak (Jeanne Eagels), Jeff Chandler, Agnes Moorehead, Virginia Grey ... Frank Borzage (Himself), Lew Borzage (Himself).

1958

China Doll working titles: *Time Is a Memory; The China Doll; The China Story.* Prod.: Frank Borzage (Frank Borzage Productions, Inc.), assoc. prod.: Robert E. Morrison, Romina Production-Batjac Enterprises Inc./d. United Artists — script: Kitty Buhler, [Joel Murcott], from her story "Time Is a Memory," based on a novel by James Benson Nablo and Thomas F. Kelly (1953) — photo: William H. Clothier ASC; photogr. effects: David Koehler — art dir.: Howard Richmond, Jack Mills (set), props: Richard Siegel — asst.-dir.: Lew Borzage, Lou Silverman — makeup: Layne Britton; hair stylist: Lillian Ugrin — mus.: Henry Vars (song: "Suppose," mus. & lyr.: Dunham and Henry Vars) — sound: Earl Crain Sr., Paul M. Holly — edit.: Jack Murray — script supervis.: Catalina Lawrence — techn. advis.: Ltn. Col. Dale E. Bell — prod. manager: Gordon B. Forbes — cost.: Wes Jefferies, Angela Alexander — length: 99 minutes — release: 1 Aug 1958 Los Angeles Preview (Pinewood Theatre, Westwood), 4 Dec 1958 New York (Loew's State); (©27 Jul 1958).

Cast: Victor Mature (Cpt. Cliff Brandon), Li Li Hua (Shu-Jen [Precious Jewel]), Ward Bond (Father Cairns), Bob Mathias (Ltn. Phil Gates), Johnny Desmond (Sgt. Steve Hill), Elaine Curtis (Alice Nichols), Stuart Whitman (Ltn. Dan O'Neill), Ann McCrea (Mona Perkins), Danny Chang (Ellington), Ken Perry (Sgt. Ernie Fleming), Tige Andrews (Cpt. Carlo Menotti), Steve Mitchell (Cpt. Dave Reisner), Don Barry (Sgt. Hal Foster), Ann Paige (Sally), Denver Pyle (Col. Wiley), Tita Aragon (Shiao-Mee Brandon).

1958–1959

The Big Fisherman. Prod.: Rowland V. Lee Productions Inc., A Centurion Films Inc. Presentation (prod. supervisor: Eric G. Stacey)/d. Buena Vista Distribution Co. (Walt Disney) — script: Howard Estabrook, Rowland V. Lee, from the novel by Lloyd Cassel Douglas (Houghton Mifflin Co., Boston 1948) — photo: Lee Garmes ASC (Eastmancolor, Ultra Panavision 70mm); operat.: Eddie Garvin — mus.: Albert Hay Malotte, mus. dir.: Joseph Gershenson, orchestration: David Tamkin — art dir.: John DeCuir (prod. design), Julia Heron (set) — edit.: Paul Weatherwax; assoc. edit.: William Andrews (son), Arnold Schwarzwald (mus.) — cost.: Renie, cost. supervis.: Wesley Jeffries — manager: Edward Dodds — historical advisor: George M. Lamsa — sound: Leslie I. Carey, Frank H. Wilkinson — makeup: Bud and Frank Westmore; hair stylist: Larry Germaine — casting: James Ryan — asst.-dir.: Richard Moder — script supervis.: Anita Speer — length: 180 minutes; (UK: 14,940 ft.; 166 minutes; other versions: 150 minutes and 144 minutes) — release: 23 Jun 1959 Hollywood Preview (Fox Wilshire Theatre); 4 Aug 1959 New York (Rivoli Theatre).

Cast: Howard Keel (Simon Peter), Susan Kohner (Princess Fara), John Saxon (Prince Voldi), Martha Hyer (Herodias), Herbert Lom (Herod Antipas), Ray Stricklyn (Prince Deran), Alexander Scourby (David Ben-Zadok), Beulah Bondi (Hannah), Jay Barney (John the Baptist), Charlotte Fletcher (Queen Rennah), Mark Dana (King Zendi), Rhodes Reason (Andrew), Henry Brandon (Menicus), Brian Hutton (John), Thomas Troupe (James), Marianne Stewart (Ione), Jonathan Harris (Lysias), Leonard Mudie (Ilderan), James Griffith (Beggar), Peter Adams (Herod Phillippus I), Jo Gilbert (Deborah), Michael Mark (Innkeeper), Joe Di Reda (Arab Assassin), Stuart Randall (Aretas

IV, Nabatean King of Petra), Marian Seldes (Princess Arnon, his Daughter), Herbert Rudley (Emperor Tiberius), Phillip Pine (Lucius), Francis J. McDonald (Scribe Spokesman), Perry Ivins (Pharisee Spokesman), Ralph Moody (Aged Pharisee), Tony Jochim (Sadducee Spokesman), Dan Turner (Roman Captain), Bill Borzage, Danny Borzage (Pharisees).

1960–1961

L'Atlantide/Antinea, L'Amante della cittá sepolta France/Italy-USA (1967): *Journey Beneath The Desert; The Lost Kingdom; Queen of Atlantis* — UK (1964): *End of Atlantis; The Lost Kingdom* working title: *Atlantis, City Beneath the Desert.* Prod.: [initially: "A Frank Borzage Production"] Gérard Ducaux-Rupp, Edgar G. Ulmer, Tina & Franz Meyer, C.C.M. Film Roma — Fides, Paris/d. Rank-Film International (F), Titanus (It.), Embassy Pictures (USA) — dir.: [started in Cinecittà by Frank Borzage], Edgar George Ulmer, Giuseppe Masini, [Edmond T. Gréville] — script: Edgar G. Ulmer, Edmond T. Gréville, Ugo Liberatore, Georges André Tabet, Remigio Del Grosso, Amedeo Nazzari, from the novel *L'Atlantide* by Pierre Benoit (Paris 1919) — photo: Bruno Betti, Enzo Serafin (Super-Technirama 70, Technicolor) — mus.: Carlo Rustichelli, mus. dir.: Franco Ferrara — art dir.: Edgar G. Ulmer, Piero Filippone — edit.: Renato Cinquini — cost.: Vittorio Rossi — sound: Enzo Silvestri — spec. eff.: Giovanni Ventimiglia — exec. prod.: Nat Wachsberger, Marquis Luigi Nannerini — length: 105 minutes — release: 5 May 1961 Rome, 2 Aug 1961 Paris (Gaumont-Palace).

Cast: Haya Harareet (Antinea, Queen of Atlantis), Rad Fulton (Robert [=Jean Morhange]), Jean-Louis Trintignan (Pierre [=André de Saint-Avit]), Georges Rivière (John), Amedeo Nazzari (Sheikh Tamal [=Cegheïr ben Cheikh]), Giulia Rubini (Zinah [=Tanit-Zerga]), Gian-Maria Volonté (Tarath), Gabriele Tinti (Max), Ignazio Dolce (Guard).

Notes

Preface

1. *Présence du cinéma* (Paris), March-April 1964, p. 29.

2. Remarks made on Belgian television and reported by Eric de Kuyper, in: *Cinémémoire*, Paris, 1991, p. 82.

3. Cf. Chapter 4, reception of *Humoresque*.

4. *Cinémagazine* (Paris), November 1, 1929, p. 191.

5. *Film Weekly* (London), June 26, 1937, p. 26.

6. Stéphane Bourgoin, *Terence Fisher*, édilig, Paris 1984, p. 25.

7. *Cinéma 59* (Paris), no. 41, November-December 1959, p. 97.

8. *Dictionnaire des cinéastes*, ed. Seuil, Paris 1965, p. 30.

9. *Film Culture* (New York) no. 25, Summer 1962, p. 33.

10. *Histoire du cinéma, 1930–1940*, vol. 4, ed. Delarge, Paris 1980, p. 315.

11. *50 ans de cinéma américain*, ed. Nathan, Paris 1991, p. 305.

12. *Amour-érotisme & cinéma*, Terrain vague-Losfeld, Paris 1966, p. 214.

13. Cf. bibliography at the end of this volume.

14. Linda J. Barth (Griffith Administrative Services, City of Los Angeles, Dept. of Recreation and Parks) helped me find this material, which was handed over to the short-lived Hollywood Museum Collection following the death of the filmmaker and was inaccessible for several years before being loaned to the Academy of Motion Picture Arts and Sciences, Margaret Herrick Library (Special Collections).

Introduction

1. Conversation with the author, Studio City, Los Angeles, July 22, 1990.

2. *Each Man in His Time. The Life Story of a Director*, Farrar, Straus & Giroux, New York 1974, p. 238.

3. *Light Up Your Torches and Pull Up Your Tights*, Arlington House, New Rochelle, 1973, p. 21.

4. Letter to the author, Beverly Hills, August 7, 1989.

5. Conversations of the author with Arthur Jacobson (L.A., October 6, 1990) and Dorothy Wellman (L.A. July 20, 1990).

6. Marlene Dietrich, *Marlene*, Avon Books, New York 1989, p. 113.

7. *Film Dope* (London), no. 4, March 1974, p. 28.

8. *Reader* (New York), Feb. 18, 1983.

9. B. Péret, *Anthologie de l'Amour sublime*, Albin Michel, Paris 1956, 1988, p. 9.

10. *Film Culture* (New York), no. 28, Spring 1963, p. 11.

11. *Le surréalisme au cinéma*, ed. Terrain Vague, Paris 1965, p. 130.

12. "Program Notes," Museum of Modern Art Film Library, New York, Nov. 29, 1956.

13. J.-P. Coursodon, *American Directors*, vol. 1, New York 1983, p. 10.

14. *Écran* (Paris), no. 50, September 15, 1976, p. 69.

15. George C. Pratt, "In Search of the Natural: An Interview with Frank Borzage [1958]," in *Image* (Rochester) 20, nos. 3–4, September-December 1977, p. 43.

16. This phenomenon is particularly noticeable among general film historians such as Paul Rotha, Lewis Jacobs or the team of René Jeanne and Charles Ford who remain impervious to his work. Georges Sadoul and Jerzy Toeplitz neglect it because it doesn't enter into their ideological framework. Borzage is unknown to Friedrich von Zglinicki, Rudolf Oertel, Heinrich Fraenkel, Rune Waldekranz and Werner Arpe, Enno Patalas and Ulrich Gregor.

17. *Histoire du cinéma 1923–1930*, t. 3, ed. Universitaires, Paris 1973, p. 439.

18. J. Segond, "De Cendrillon à Ophélie," in *Positif* (Paris) no. 184/84. Motifs of false appearances, the slatternly girl as a potential princess, "protected" by her fairy godmother), disguises and lures appear more representative of the myth (and of Borzage's films).

19. *Monogram* (London) No. 4, 1972, p. 20–23. A expanded version of this essay appeared in *The Hollywood Professionals vol. 3: Howard Hawks, Frank Borzage, Edgar G. Ulmer*, Tantivy Press, London-Barnes, New York 1974

20. Ed. Albin Michel (Bibliothèque de l'Hermétisme), Paris 1981, p. 135–140.

21. *Positif*, op. cit., p. 13–19.

22. J. Lourcelles, *Dictionnaire du cinéma. Les films*, ed. Laffont (coll. *Bouquins*), Paris 1992, p. 683.

23. Information kindly provided by Head Secretary Robert A. Klinger, Grand Lodge Free and Accepted Masons of California, San Francisco (through the gracious intermediary of the Grande Loge Suisse Alpina, Lausanne).

24. In this regard, Borzage was a rare case in Hollywood: a director whose spiritual leanings spilled over into his work; in this respect only the case of Rex Ingram is comparable; he converted to Islam when filming in North Africa.

25. Marcel Oms, *De quelques thèmes maçonniques dans l'oeuvre de D. W. Griffith*, ed. L'Harmattan, Paris 1984, p. 221–232.

26. See René Guénon, *Fundamental Symbols: The Universal Language of Sacred Science*, Quinta Essentia, Cambridge, 1995; *Études sur la Franc-Maçonnerie et le Compagnonnage*, vol. 1–2, Editions Traditionnelles, Paris 1964.

27. "Directors, like cooks, can't agree on recipes for films. 'Make 'em simply' says Frank Borzage. 'Make 'em hot' says Mervyn LeRoy," in : *Los Angeles Times*, December 3, 1933 and "Santa Barbara Press," December 4, 1933.

28. D. Thomson, *America in the Dark: Hollywood and the Gift of Unreality*, Morrow & Co., New York 1977, p. 216.

29. J. Mitry, *Histoire du cinéma 1930–1940*, t. 4, ed. J.-P. Delarge, Paris 1980, p. 316.

30. See for instance: Edgar Istel, "Mozart's *Magic Flute* and Freemasonery," in *Musical Quarterly* (New York), vol. 13, no. 4, October 1927, p. 519ff.— Daniel Heartz, "La clemenza di Sarastro: Masonic Benevolence in Mozart's last operas" in *The Musical Times*, March 1983, p. 152–157. Bro. W. J. Bunney, "Mozart, the Musician and the Mason" in *The Lodge of Research* No. 2429, Leicester 1919. Paul Nettl, "Masonry and the Magic Flute" in *Opera News* vol. 20, no. 170, Feb. 27, 1956, p. 8ff.

31. See Titus Burckhardt, *Alchemy: Science of the Cosmos, Science of the Soul*, Penguin Books, Baltimore, 1972, p. 149.

32. F. Lamster, *Souls Made Great Through Love and Adversity: The Film Work of Frank Borzage*, Scarecrow Press, Metuchen, N.J., p. 55.

33. "Some Words from Frank Borzage," p. 116–119 in Peter Milne's fundamental work, *Motion Picture Directing: The Facts and Theories of the Newest Art*, Falk Publishing Co., New York 1922 (chapter XII).

34. *Los Angeles Times*, December 3, 1933 (cf. supra).

35. *Cinéma 71* (Paris), no. 161, December 1971, p. 52.

36. *Motion Picture Classic* (New York), vol. XI, no. 1, September 1920, p. 18.

37. *Dictionnaire du cinéma*, op. cit., p. 989.

38. "'Naturalness first requisite of good acting'" says Borzage," Columbia Studios Press Files [September 1933], Microfilm coll. Margaret Herrick Library, A.M.P.A.S., Los Angeles.

39. "Borzage shatters many Film Rules," *New York World Telegram*, April 3, 1937, p. 7 — When we realize that these remarks were made following completion of *History Is Made at Night*, a film whose script was improvised from day to day, and whose shooting was highly unusual (cf. chapter 12), we may ask ourselves if Borzage wasn't being ironic!

40. "Some Words from Frank Borzage," op. cit., p. 112.

41. *San Francisco Call Bulletin*, May 9, 1936.

42. "Directing a Talking Picture," in *How Talkies Are Made* (ed. by Joe Bonica) Hollywood 1930; reappeared in: Richard Koszarski, *Hollywood Directors 1914–1940*, New York — London 1976, p. 235–237.

43. *The Missoulian*, February 11, 1936.

44. "Frank Borzage contra el diálogo en los films," in *Cinegramas* (Madrid) no. 96, July 12, 1936, p. 31 (US source unknown).

45. "Dossiers du cinéma: cinéastes," recueil, Casterman, Tournai 1971, p. 33

46. *The Hollywood Professionals*, op. cit., p. 122–128

47. *Positif* (Paris) no. 142, September 1972, p. 72.

48. *MGM Studio News* (Hollywood), vol. 5, no. 1, January 7, 1938.

49. J. Mitry, *Histoire du cinéma*, t. 4, op. cit., p. 315

50. *Monogram* (London) no. 4, 1972, p. 24.

51. Cecilia Auger, "That Sentimental Gentleman from Hollywood, Frank Borzage, Tells How," *New York Variety*, March 7, 1933.

52. "Columbia Studios Press Files," op. cit.

53. *The Lion's Roar Magazine* (MGM), vol. 2, no. 1, September–October 1942.

54. Dan Thomas, "Borzage called easiest of all Hollywood Directors," in *The Dispatch* (Columbus), January 26, 1937.

55. *The Lion's Roar*, op. cit.

56. Madge Bellamy, *A Darling of the Twenties: Madge Bellamy*, Vestal Press, New York 1989, p. 80.

57. Gary Cooper, "Director Frank Borzage as I Know Him," in *Paramount International News Letter*, New York, March 1, 1936.

58. *Los Angeles Evening Herald*, July 18, 1931.

59. "Columbia Studios Press Files," op. cit.

60. Conversation with the author, November 28, 1990 (Marbella).

61. "Hollywood's Most Popular Man," *Los Angeles Examiner*, December 2, 1934.

62. *N. Y. World Telegram*, op. cit.

63. *Silver Screen* (Hollywood), June 1934.

64. Conversation with the author, October 6, 1990 (New York).

65. *The Film Spectator* (Hollywood), Oct. 15, 1927, p. 7.

66. "'Acting is not acting,' says Frank Borzage," in *Today's News from Universal* (London), May 24, 1934.

67. Conversation with the author, Nyack (New York), August 2, 1990.

Chapter 1

1. *Histoire du cinéma mondial*, Flammarion, Paris 1949, p. 225.

2. *Los Angeles: City of Dreams*, Appleton, New York 1935, p. 186.

3. Henry (1885 Wyoming–October 6,1971 Hollywood) was for over 20 years an electrician and sound technician at 20th Century Fox; he had four children: Frank, Madeline, Mary and William H.

4. Mary died giving birth to twins. Bill [William Felix] (March 4, 1892, Salt Lake City–June 7, 1973, Los Angeles) was an accordionist, who occasionally acted, directed by Henry King (*Way Down East*), Lewis Milestone (*The North Star*), Roger Corman (*House of Usher*) as well as his brother. His son Raymond (1916–1990) was a teen actor in a few movies, circa 1932–36.

5. Information provided by José Luis S. de Pablos, Madrid 1990.

6. Luigi Borzaga died March 16, 1934, in Los Angeles following a car accident. His wife Maria died of cancer June 30, 1947, in Los Angeles.

7. Document kindly provided by Barry E. Kirk, Genealogical Library, The Church of Jesus Christ of Latter-Day Saints, Salt Lake City.

8. Daniel [Dan, Danny] (Dec, 24, 1896–June 17, 1975, Los Angeles) actor and set musician; survived by a son, Donald. Aside from the Ford films, Daniel Borzage can be seen in various westerns with Buck Jones (*The War Horse*), *The Lady and the Cowboy* (H. C. Potter), *The Westerner* (W. Wyler), *True to Life* (G. Marshall), etc. Lew [Lou, Louis, Lewis] (Jan. 30, 1898–December 6, 1974, Santa Ana, Ca.), assistant director and production manager of Frank from 1926 on; in 1933 he married Pearl Cooper, an actress, and is survived by a son, Kenneth, and a daughter, Nicki.

9. Cf. "Picture Shows: Peter Bogdanovich on the Movies," Allen & Unwin, London 1975, p. 172

10. Conversation with the author, Marbella, November 28, 1990.

11. "Cinémonde" (Paris), no. 73, March 13, 1930, p. 165.

12. Sue Williams and Dolly Galla-Rini interviewed by the author in Los Angeles July 14, 1990; Frank Borzage spoke with Harrison Haskins in *Motion Picture Classic* (New York), no. 1 September 1920, p. 18 with *Photoplay Magazine*, September 1920, p. 42, and with Jim Tully in *Vanity Fair*, no. 6, February 1927, p. 50; Borzage interviewed by George Pratt in Hollywood on April 11, 1958 (coll. George Eastman House, Rochester).

13. John Ford spread a rumor to the effect that Borzage was "completely illiterate" (cf. *Positif* no. 82, March 1967). This of course was dead wrong; it would be difficult to imagine memorizing Shakespearean drama or staying afloat in a studio as sophisticated as MGM without knowing how to read or write. On the other hand, it is true that he was, in general, not a bookish sort and had screenplays real aloud to him, which could have started the legend (cf. Part I, "Working on the set," and the beginning of chapter 4).

14. "The New York Dramatic Mirror," August 16, 1911, p. 12. Borzage gave his last performance at the theater two days later in Los Angeles, in "Mr. Aladdin," a comedy written and directed by Thomas Ince (première: October 10, 1914, Majestic Theater). Cf. Davide Turconi, "I film muti di Frank Borzage nella stampa del Tempo," in *Griffithiana* (Gemona) no. 45, December 1992.

15. *Dictionnaire des cinéastes*, Seuil, Paris 1965, p. 117–8.

16. *Hollywood années zéro*, Seghers, Paris, 1972, p. 39.

17. *Photoplay Magazine* (Hollywood), December 1914, p. 16.

18. *Motion Picture Supplement*, October 1915, p. 61.

19. *Picture Play*, January 1917.

20. *Reel Life: The Mutual Film Magazine*, 1914, p. 20 (The Museum of Modern Art, New York; Film: Special Collections).

21. Allan Dwan must have remembered this when shooting *Silver Lode* 40 years later.

22. "Histoire générale du cinéma," vol. 3 (1909–1920), Paris, Denoël, 1975, p. 108.

Chapter 2

1. Ricketts would progressively orient American production from westerns to social drama. Sets were constructed by Edward M. Langley, while C. H. Heimerl supervised the filming done by nine other cameramen. Cf. Timothy James Lyons, *The Silent Partner. The History of the American Film Manufacturing Company 1910–1921*, New York: Arno Press, 1974.

2. Conversations with George Pratt, op. cit.

3. *Image* (Rochester) nos. 3–4, September–December 1977, p. 34.

4. Cf. T.J. Lyons, *The Silent Partner*, op. cit., p. 146.

5. *Photoplay Art* (Los Angeles) no. 2, August 1916, p. 10.

6. *The Moving Picture World*, August 19, 1916.

7. *Vanity Fair*, no. 6, February 1927, p. 50.

8. *The Pittsburgh Reader*, August 6, 1916.

9. *Motography*, September 23, 1916.

10. *Le Film* (Paris) no. 112, June 5, 1918. Restored in 1993 by Medardo Amor at the Filmoteca de la Generalitat Valenciana (3 reels / 500 m. tinted, with Spanish titles). The American Film Institue Catalog" claims that the film was re-edited in 1922 as *Silent Shelby*. Evidently there was a mix-up: this three-reeler directed by Thomas Chatterton (prod: Mustang, distr.: Mutual), opened on April 13, 1916. It had the same screenwriter (K.B. Clarke) and some of the same actors (A. Little, J. Richardson).

11. *The Moving Picture World*, November 25, 1916.

12. *New York Dramatic Mirror*, November 18, 1916.

13. *New York Dramatic News*, July 8, 1916.

14. Lorena Borzage-Rogers made her stage debut in approximately 1908 going on tour singing: "pose & sing"—in California and in Hawaii with Lillian Dolliver, the future mother of Jackie Coogan (*The Kid*). Her first films date from 1914 in Pasadena (*Sherlock Boob, Detective* with Fred Fralick); her film credits, up until 1917, at

which point she abandoned her career, include over 20 titles, mainly short features for Vogue and Universal, including *When Papa Died, His Blowout, Delinquent Bridegrooms, The Iron Mitt, Just for a Kid, A Deep Sea Liar*, all with Ben Turpin (1916). Just before her marriage in June 1916, she had a personal success with the scandalous film, *Where Are My Children?* by feminist Lois Weber, banned in various states (in it she plays a seduced girl who dies while having an abortion). Last film: the lead in the worldly melodrama *The Cricket* (Elsie Jane Wilson, 1917).

Chapter 3

1. *Intolerance* and Ince's *Civilization* both lost a fortune: *Intolerance* cost $424,876 to film over a lengthy period, from October 1914 to July 1916, and *Civilization* cost $97,697, while in 1915–16 the average cost of a full feature was between $16,000 and $30,000. (Cf. *Films in Review*, December 1958, p. 599).

2. The future studios of Metro-Goldwyn-Mayer.

3. Jack Curtis was plagued with bad luck. In 1923, Erich Stroheim gave him the part of McTeague Senior in *Greed*; he played an alcoholic father who dies in a whorehouse suffering from the d.t.'s. Unfortunately for Curtis, the whole episode involving him was cut in editing.

4. *Motion Picture Classic*, vol. 22, no. 6, February 1926.

5. Gloria Swanson, *Swanson on Swanson*, Random House, New York 1980, p. 91.

6. George Eastman House Collection, Rochester, op. cit.

7. Cf., Kalton C. Lahue, *Dreams for Sale: The Rise and Fall of the Triangle Film Corporation*, Barnes, New York 1971, p.181ss.

8. *Motion Picture News*, March 30, 1918. When, in 1919, Frank J. Smith brought the film back to six reels under the title *Ashes of Desire*, the setting of the film was displaced to Malaysia, at the request of the Japanese Embassy.

9. *Variety*, March 22, 1918.

10. A second project of Borzage for Macauley Photoplays, *Just Around the Corner* (March 1919), was never realized.

11. The comic Fred Stone (1873–1959), from Colorado, was one of the pillars of Broadway musical comedy and played the Scarecrow in the world premiere of *The Wizard of Oz* in 1903. His first two films, the farces *The Goat* (story and screenplay by Frances Marion) and *Under the Top*, were produced in the spring of 1919 by Donald Crisp at Paramount. Brother-in-law of writer Rex Beach, Stone was also close friends with Will Rogers (so much so that Rogers named his youngest son Fred Stone Rogers).

Chapter 4

1. Frances Marion (1888–1973) had innumerable successes in Hollywood; including *The Scarlet Letter* and *The Wind* (Sjöström), *Stella Dallas* (King), *Camille* and *Dinner at Eight* (Cukor), *The Champ* (Vidor), etc. DeWitt Bodeen published a substantial file documenting her work as a screenwriter, writer, painter, actress, producer and director in *More from Hollywood*, Barnes-Tantivy, S. Brunwick-London 1976, pp. 91–126.

2. The novella had first been published by Harper in New York in 1918.

3. Frances Marion, *Off with Their Heads! A Serio-*

Comic Tale of Hollywood, MacMillan, New York 1972, p. 71–72.

4. F. Borzage to George Pratt, op. cit. (cf. note 9)

5. *The Moving Picture World,* May 22, 1920.

6. Jim Tully, "Frances Marion" in *Vanity Fair,* January 1927 p. 63. We should mention that the scene described exists only partially in the copy saved and restored at UCLA in 1986.

7. *Motion Picture Classic,* February 1921, p. 59. From 1926 to 1930, Vera Gordon and George Sidney Sr. comprised the Jewish household in the comic-popular series *The Cohens and Kellys.* She also appeared in *Potash and Perlmutter* (1923) and *Abie's Irish Rose* (1946).

8. Robert J. Kelly, who played Leon as a child, worked in the movies since 1912 and already had 53 credits to his name (the *Bobby* series); he died of cardiac insufficiency in 1922, at the age of 13.

9. A three act play staged in February 1923 at the Vanderbilt Theater in Brooklyn with J. Hartley (Sarah Kantor) and Lutha J. Adler (Leon).

10. The second version totally obliterates the Jewish aspect and only remains faithful to the Fannie Hurst novel in its seven first minutes (the purchase of the violin), a beginning botched by Delmer Daves: the remainder of this flamboyant melodrama is based on an unused screenplay by Clifford Odets destined for Irving Rapper's *Rhapsody in Blue* (1945), a "biography" of Gershwin.

11. F. Marion to Kevin Brownlow (1970), quoted in: K. Brownlow, *Behind the Mask of Innocence,* New York: Knopf, 1990, p. 390.

12. *Variety,* June 4, 1920.

13. K. Brownlow, op. cit., p. 391.

14. *Humoresque* was released in the USSR as *In Name of What?* and *Crucified Genius.* Unfinished and previously unpublished article by Eisenstein found in the Archives for Art and Literature of the Federation of Russia (RGALI, f. 1923, op.2, ed. 754). Text and information transmitted to the author by Professor François Albera, Université de Lausanne.

15. Cf. Patricia Erens, *The Jew in American Cinema,* Indiana University Press, Bloomington 1984, p. 77ss.

16. In 1913 *Wallingford's Wallet* by Edgar Lewis, in 1915 the serial *The New Adventures of J. Rufus Wallingford* by Sam Wood.

17. *Variety,* February 17, 1922.

18. *Photoplay Magazine,* April 1922, p. 60.

19. *New York Times,* February 13, 1922.

20. Film buffs may still have a brief image of the haughty Seena Owen, in Stroheim's *Queen Kelly* (1928): she chases Gloria Swanson from her palace with a whip.

21. The last five minutes of the only remaining print (American Film Institute–Library of Congress) are missing. A sound remake of *Back Pay* was filmed in 1930 by William A. Seiter, with Corinne Griffith, Grant Withers and Montagu Love.

22. A 7 minute mini-fragment (one sequence) still exists in the Netherlands Filmmuseum in Amsterdam.

23. *Photoplay Magazine,* July 1922, p. 53.

24. "*Cinémagazine*" (Paris) November 9, 1923.

25. Especially two Canadian films by David M. Hartford, *Back to God's Country* (1919) and *Nomads of the North* (1921), then *Paid in Advance* by Allen J. Holubar. In June 1922, Curwood instituted proceedings against the producers of the film *I Am the Law* (Edwin Carewe) which plagiarized his novel *The Valley of Silent Men.*

26. *Variety,* January 9, 1922.

27. Warner Oland had already portrayed a "Japanese chiseller" in *Patria,* the anti–Japanese serial produced by W. R. Hearst in 1916.

28. William M. Drew, *Speaking of Silents: First Ladies of the Screen,* Vestal Press, New York 1989, p. 168.

29. The last part of the film conforms to Fanny Hurst's original story: a beautiful, married salesgirl cleverly outsmarts and takes full financial advantage of a rake who wines and dines her with the clear expectation of sexual favors in return. Only at the end of the story does it become clear that she has led him on for a higher purpose: to save the life of her tubercular husband and provide for her infant child.

Chapter 5

1. The only Borzage films after 1923 that do not include these words in the credits are *History Is Made at Night* (1937) and *The Big Fisherman* (1959), produced respectively by Walter Wanger and Rowland V. Lee. At Metro-Goldwyn-Mayer, only strong-willed directors such as Victor Fleming, and sometimes King Vidor and Clarence Brown enjoyed this privilege. It was even rarer to maintain it when changing studios.

2. The co-owner of the studio, Michael C. Levee (1889–1972), became Borzage's agent in the '30s and played a decisive role when Borzage temporarily won his independence (cf. chapter 10).

3. Robert Florey, "Filmland," ed. *Cinémagazine,* Paris 1923, p. 171.

4. *Picture Play,* September 1925, p. 98. When the film was released in New York, the screening was preceded by a musical number in which Gladys Rice and Richard Bartlett sang "Memory Lane," the theme of the film.

5. The role of Mary was played in London by Fay Compton. In New York, *Secrets* was staged at the Fulton Theater (December 25, 1922) by Sam H. Harris, with Margaret Lawrence (Mary) and Tom Nesbitt (John) in the leads.

6. Negatives of *Secrets* are in New York (Museum of Modern Art) and Brussels. The film archives in Prague possesses another copy containing several supplementary shots. The integral version, at the Library of Congress (Washington) has not yet been restored.

7. *Variety,* March 26, 1924.

8. Staged at New York's Empire Theater (December 4, 1923), directed by A. H. Woods, with Mary Nash (Polly) and Austin Fairman, then at Curran Theater in San Francisco (January 1925) with Pauline Frederick. The film was remade: *The Secret of Madame Blanche* (MGM 1933) by Charles Brabin, with Irene Dunne, Lionel Atwill and Phillips Holmes.

9. *Cinémagazine* (Paris) no. 29, July 17, 1925, p. 114.

10. The copy in Washington, from the Rohauer collection, is unfortunately incomplete: the second reel is missing (Polly's marriage with Saint-Aubyns, the father's machinations to sabotage their union); the beginning of the third reel has seriously deteriorated.

11. The play opened at the Plymouth Theater New York on August 31, 1921. It was produced by Arthur Hopkins, starring Marjorie Rambeau and Frank Conroy. The first Metro synopsis is dated January 14, 1924; the final script November 8. Paramount filmed a remake in 1931 entitled *Women Love Once,* directed by Edward Goodman and starring Paul Lukas, Eleanor Boardman and Juliette Compton. Borzage's film is unrelated to the Mark Robson's film (1969) of the same name.

12. *Picture-Play Magazine,* April 1925, p. 43.

13. "Looking on with an Extra Girl," in *Picture-Play Magazine,* March 1925, p. 94.

14. Winner of the Pulitzer Prize for *The Old Maid,* which was made into a film with Bette Davis in 1939.

15. *Variety*, February 25, 1925.

16. It premiered September 12, 1921 at the Selwyn Theater and was a success. The cast included Leslie Carter (Lady Catherine), John Drew (Porteous), Estelle Winwood (Elizabeth) and John Halliday (Edward). MGM filmed a discreet mediocre sound remake in 1930 directed by David Burton called *Strictly Unconventional*. It starred Catherine Dale Owen and Lewis Stone and reincorporated the original ending of the play.)

17. Metro-Goldwyn-Mayer Scripts (Special Collections), University of Southern California, Los Angeles.

18. *Joan Crawford*, Pyramid Press, New York 1974; cf. Also *Joan Crawford, the Ultimate Star* by Alexander Walker, Weidenfeld & Nicolson, London 1983, p. 21–22. (Harvey and Walker were fortunate enough to gain access to the MGM files before Ted Turner cut off access to them in Atlanta.)

19. *Variety*, August 12, 1925, p. 28.

20. *Variety*, April 22, 1925, p. 26.

21. "Fun in a Chinese Laundry," Macmillan, New York 1965, p. 210. The inclusion of Frank Capra is an error, as he never worked for MGM. Aside from his famous fistfight with Mayer, his mortal enemy, Stroheim was particularly angry with Rapf (and not Thalberg, who stood up for him). Wellman was hired as Goulding's assistant; his work at Culver city was limited to retakes for Sternberg's *The Exquisite Sinner*, which earned him a promotion to the rank of director. Among the rare artists who adapted to, or temporarily adjusted themselves to Thalberg's methods were Victor Sjöström, Tod Browning and King Vidor (who was on the point of filming, in April–May 1925, his memorable *The Big Parade*).

Chapter 6

1. Cf 20th Century Fox Legal Files, U.C.L.A., Los Angeles

2. When Madge Bellamy was on the verge of going broke, at the end of the silent era, Buck Jones gave her the female lead in his western serial *Gordon of Ghost City* (1933)—in remembrance of *Lazybones*.

3. *A Darling of the Twenties: Madge Bellamy*, op. cit., p. 66–67.

4. Produced by Sam H. Harris, starring George Abbott (Steve) and Beth Merrill (Agnes), *Lazybones* opened at the Vanderbilt Theater in New York on September 22, 1924. The play ended with the revelation of the identity of the baby found eighteen years earlier and Steve's marriage to his protégée Kit.

5. *Cinémagazine* (Paris) December 11, 1925, p. 511.

6. *Cinéma 87* (Paris), October 22, 1987.

7. The play was produced by John Golden (Little Theater, October 20, 1920) and starred Roberta Arnold and Frank Craven. William K. Howard remade *The First Year* for Fox in 1932, with Janet Gaynor and Charles Farrell, Borzage's couple par excellence.

8. Edfried Bingham's script was rewritten by Kenneth B. Clarke, and the actor Jay Hunt was replaced by J. Farrell MacDonald. Remake: *Chicken Wagon Family* (20th Century Fox 1939) by Herbert I. Leeds, with Jane Withers and Leo Carrillo.

9. This was also the working title of a film which was to have starred Alma Rubens, Lou Tellegen (Marcus) and Leslie Fenton (Paul). The play opened in New York September 21, 1925, at the Times Square Theater, produced by A. H. Woods, with Margaret Lawrence, Cecil Humphreys and Sybil Carlisle.

10. "It will be a great honor to work with me, Murnau is reputed to have said to head cameraman Paul Ivano when Ivano offered his services for *Sunrise*. Aggravated by the excessive deference and military tone surrounding the filmmaker's personality, Ivano reportedly retorted: "Maybe it's a great honor for somebody, but I'm working with Emmett Flynn, John Ford and Frank Borzage. Let somebody else have the honor, I don't want it." (cf. "The American Film Institute and American Society of Cinematographers talking with Paul Ivano, A.S.C.," Center for Advanced Studies, Beverly Hills, April 20, 1974, transcript p. 31).

11. As Luciano Berriatúa has shown, Lotte Eisner's comments regarding Murnau's incredible contract with Fox (four films over four years, with an initial salary of $125,000, etc.) are based on erroneous information reported by *Variety*; when Murnau filmed *Sunrise*, his future in the United States was not at all assured, and it was not until March 1927 that he signed a five-year contract with Fox. Cf. *Los proverbios chinos de F. W. Murnau*, vol. 2, Filmoteca española, Madrid 1992, p. 435–37.

Chapter 7

1. Aside from *7th Heaven* (John Golden actually came up with the title and some of the writing), Austin Strong's works are now forgotten, and cinema has only very occasionally made use of them: *A Good Little Devil* (Edwin S. Porter, 1914), *Three Wise Fools* (King Vidor, 1923; Edward Buzzell, 1946) and *Along Came Love* (Bert Lytell, 1937, co-scriptwriter).

2. *MGM Studio News*, no. 2, February 2, 1940.

3. This visit, reported by the press, incited French historians to believe that Borzage co-directed *The Return of Peter Grimm*; nothing could be farther from the truth. Yet strangely enough, the filmmaker had approached Janet Gaynor, Charles Farrell and Madge Bellamy for *The Auctioneer* (May 1926), a project that would follow *Marriage License?*

4. After years of doing extra work, having started in 1923, Charles Farrell got his first big part in the spring of 1926 in James Cruze's *Old Ironsides* (Paramount), where Richard Arlen also appeared. When Farrell got the role of Chico, Arlen was cast in another prestigious picture, Wellman's *Wings*.

5. A music critic, scriptwriter and producer, Benjamin (Barney) Glazer had just finished the script for MGM's *Flesh and the Devil* (starring Greta Garbo) when Fox commissioned him to write *Napoleon and Josephine* (a project for their 1926–27 season that never got off the ground). It was then that Borzage hired him. Later, Glazer would be production manager for Stroheim's *Queen Kelly*.

6. Robert Florey, *Hollywood d'hier et d'aujourd'hui*, Paris 1948, p. 140. Chotin would make several films in France between 1938 and 1946.

7. "A Fox Film Pressbook: *7th Heaven*," New York Public Library, coll. Performing Arts Research Center (Lincoln Center).

8. Ernest G. Palmer (1885–1978) also worked with Murnau (*Four Devils, City Girl*) and won an Oscar in 1941 for his Technicolor photography of Mamoulian's *Blood and Sand*. Harold G. Oliver (1888–1973) studied art history in Rome, designed the Italian sets of *Ben Hur* (1924), worked on Douglas Fairbanks' *Don Q.* and *The Gaucho* and W. Beaudine's *Sparrows*, before linking up with Borzage until 1931 (*Liliom*).

9. "The AFI and ASC talking with Paul Ivano" (1974), Center for Advanced Studies, Beverly Hills, April 20, 1974, transcript p. 31.

10. By kind permission of Kevin Brownlow, ©Thames Television ("Hollywood Series" 1976).

11. Script at UCLA, 20th Century-Fox Film Corp. Collection 010 (Produced Scripts, Box FX-PRS-1027). Photos from Borzage's private albums are at the A.M.P.A.S. (Special Collection, Margaret Herrick Library).

12. Like the original play and Henry King's remake, Glazer's script places great emphasis on the religious elements in the plot and on the munificent presence of the Catholic Church. After the first sequence in the sewers, Chico, Rat and Papa Boule sit discussing religious faith on the pavement outside Sacré-Coeur. While Chico is boasting of his atheism, Boule and Rat glance fearfully at a stained glass window dedicated to St. Anthony which has just lit up. They believe they have witnessed a miracle and make the sign of the cross; in fact, it is Father Chevillon lighting a candle in the chapel! Colonel Brissac, who is looking for Nana and Diane, gives the priest documents which he can use to provide worthy parishioners with jobs in the City Works Dept. When Father Chevillon gets into Boule's temperamental taxi, on his way to look for the two girls, the car sets off by itself. Without a driver, it risks running into a truck — but Chico manages to stop it. The priest is unharmed. Another miracle! Borzage eliminated all this business (the scene with the taxi was shot, then cut).

13. Interview with Ernest Palmer, Sound Archives of the American Society of Cinematographers (A.S.C.), Hollywood.

14. Here Glazer's script slips into a patronizing kind of proselytizing. Boule angrily says: "The trouble with you Chico, is that you don't know the beauty and consolation of religion." The priest then introduces himself to Chico, stating: "God has given me the power to offer you another chance." Then, when the sewer worker observes the medals cost ten francs, he replies: "God has given you back your money. Do you believe in Him now?"

15. Janet Gaynor to Kevin Brownlow, op. cit.

16. Glazer's script differs at this point: When sweeping the street, Chico sees the order for the general mobilization of the armed forces (this scene was shot then cut). In the food shops, prices double ("War is Hunger!"), a woman happily welcomes soldiers ("War is Lust!"), a one-armed veteran of the 1870 Franco-Prussian War bids farewell to his uniformed son ("War is Death!"). Chico discovers that the Registry Office for civil weddings is closed. Aunt Valentine has changed her mind: she sends Brissac to bring Diane to the country so that she can complete her education. Boule transports Chico's bags in his taxi — they encounter Brissac and the aunt who try to prevent the couple's marriage. Brissac offers the sewer worker 10,000 francs to give up Diane (who is now heir to her uncle's money). Diane refuses to return to her family.

17. According to R. Lee Hough, Ford's props man (interview with Kevin Brownlow). Certain sequences were cut — such as the departure of reserve troops from Montmartre, encouraged by Diane waving the tricolored flag! A few days before the film opened, Borzage received a comical invitation from the French Minister of Education to "cooperate in an official French film on the Great War" ("Borzage honored" in *The Moving Picture World*, June 25, 1927, p. 563).

18. The script includes a scene that was shot and then cut: Brissac enters the attic and attempts to seduce Diane, but the arrival of Madame Gobin and her baby saves her. Diane takes the baby in her arms and begins to daydream. (There is no Brissac in King's remake.)

19. In Glazer's script, Diane shouts at the priest: "Your God is nothing!" Left alone, she decides to join her husband in death — and in preparation puts on her wedding dress. Meanwhile, Chico has come to in a military hospital but is suffering from amnesia (this sequence was shot then cut). At the stroke of eleven, like a sleepwalker he removes his bandages, then escapes and blends into the crowd. He enters the attic just as Diane is about to get on the gangway ready to jump to her death.

20. *Histoire du cinéma*, vol. 3, Editions Universitaires, Paris 1973, p. 439.

21. *Comedia* (Paris), February 27, 1928.

22. *The Film Spectator* (Hollywood), May 28, 1927, vol. 3, no. 7, p. 5.

23. *Cinéa-Ciné* (Paris), No 89, January 12, 1927.

24. Hungarian Ernö Rapée (1891–1945), former band leader at the Berlin Ufa Palast, had worked with Murnau, composing the score of *Faust*; he also wrote the scores of *Four Devils*, *Street Angel* and *The River*.

25. Other awards in the U.S.: National Board of Review Award 1927; *New York Times* Ten Best List 1927; *Film Daily's* Ten Best Pictures Annual Poll 1927; No.1 at *The Film Spectator's* Ten Best Pictures of the Year 1927.

26. Along with King's remake, various Chinese versions should be mentioned. The first, directed by Sun Yu, was made in Shanghai in 1930 and included several elements from the plot of Fred Niblo's 1927 *Camille*. It starred Ruan Lingy (Diane) and Jin Yan (Chico), and was called *Yecao Xianhua* (*Wild Grass and Flower of the Field*). The second, *Qi Zhong Tian* (*7th Heaven*) was directed by Zhang Shichuan and starred Zhou Xan (Diane) and Gong Jianong (Chico). At least two other versions were made in Hong Kong. Televised versions: *7th Heaven*, directed by Robert St. Aubrey, with Hurd Hatfield and Geraldine Brooks (The Broadway Television Theater Nr. 61, WOR-TV, October 26, 1953). Radio adaptations: Cecil B. De-Mille's Lux Radio Theater, with Jean Arthur and Don Ameche (CBS, October 17, 1938); and with Van Johnson and Jennifer Jones (CBS, October 16, 1944). Lux Radio Theater, with Janet Gaynor and Charles Farrell (CBS, March 1951 — to mark the twenty-fifth anniversary of the film's release). Charles Farrell also played Chico on the stage, alongside Uta Hagen (Diane) and José Ferrer (Boule) at the Westchester Playhouse, Mount Kisco, N.Y. (August 14, 1939. Director: Harry Ellerbe). There was also a musical version written by Victor Young (music), Victor Wolfson and Stella Unger, which opened on Broadway on May 26, 1955 with Gloria De Haven (Diane) and Ricardo Montalban (Chico) — director John C. Wilson.

27. William K. Everson, "American Silent Films," O.U.P., New York 1978, p. 207.

28. Cf. Paul Willemen in the Programme Notes of the National Film Theater, London, May 1975.

29. "Souvenirs d'un témoin," in *Études cinématographiques* (Paris) No. 38/39, Spring 1965, pp. 12–13.

30. "Le surréalisme au cinéma," *Terrain Vague*, Paris 1963 (new edition), p. 129–130.

31. "Amour-érotisme & cinéma," *Terrain Vague*, Paris 1966, p. 214.

32. *Les cahiers de la Cinémathèque* (Perpignan), no. special 30–31 ("Le cinéma des surréalistes"), summer–autumn 1980, p. 98 and 111.

33. *Les cahiers de la Cinémathèque* (Perpignan), no. 12, winter 1974, p. 28–31.

34. "Difference and Displacement in *7th Heaven*," in *Screen* (London), vol. 12, No. 2, Summer 177, p. 89ff.

35. This information (provided in 1991 by Luciano Berriatua, Madrid) originates from actor José Crespo, who was under contract to Fox at the time.

36. Cf. René Guénon, "Le symbolisme de l'échelle," in *Études Traditionnelles* (Paris), May 1939, p. 175–179. See also Michel Vâlsan, "Les derniers hauts grades de l'Ecossisme," in *ibid.*, June 1953, p. 161ff.

37. The play premiered at the Broadhurst Theater New York December 25, 1922, produced by William Harris, Jr., and starring Fay Bainter and Leslie Howard; it was published in 1926. Hoffe was a screenwriter at MGM from 1932 to 1939.

38. Borzage's technical consultant, Calabrian Alfredo Sabato, had collaborated with DeMille and would direct the first Italian talkie, *Sei Tu L'amore* (Italotone Film Prod.) in Hollywood in 1930, using actors from *Street Angel* such as H. Armetta and A. Rabagliati. Sabato would play the villain in *The River* and a pirate in *The Spanish Main* (1945), both Borzage films.

39. Interview with Harry Oliver, "Oral History Series Transcript" (1968), University of California, Los Angeles (UCLA), Special Collections.

40. [*Street Angel*] was left out of Beverly Heisner's *Hollywood Art: Art Direction in the Days of the Great Studios* (Jefferson, NC: McFarland 1990), a book devoted entirely to American set designers. The only plausible explanation for this omission is that *Street Angel* was long considered lost! (cf. "Lost Film" by Gary Carey, Museum of Modern Art, New York 1970, p. 26ff).

41. "I would much rather have made a film like this one," Murnau reportedly exclaimed, coming out of a screening of *7th Heaven* (reported by *Films Selectos*, Madrid, April 1932).

42. J. Gaynor to Kevin Brownlow, ©Thames Television ("Hollywood Series").

43. *Monthly Film Bulletin* (London) vol. 47, no. 558, July 1980, p. 143–144.

44. *New York Times,* April 10, 1928.

45. John Belton, *The Hollywood Professionals*, op. cit., p. 86.

46. Incidentally, in Shanghai the Chinese director Yuan Muzhi filmed a distant "communist" remake (1937) of the film entitled *Malu Tianshi* (*Angels of the Boulevard*) with Zhao Dan (him) and Zhou Xuan (her).

47. *Variety*, November 14, 1928—*L'angelo Della Strada* was removed from theaters at the orders of the fascist press, who said they were indignant at the negative images of Naples and of an Italy which was now "ordered, hard-working, friendly, passionate, united, walking with forceful steps to the sun of its resurrection" (Mario Carli in *Impero*; cf. *Kines*, no. 46, November 18, 1928). The film was rereleased on October 16, 1929, in an unrecognizable version entitled *Piccola Santa*, with about 30 minutes shaved off. It flopped at the box office.

Chapter 8

1. Cf. *The Film Daily Yearbook*, New York 1929, p. 17, *Film Daily Directors' Annual and Production Guide*, New York 1929, p. 9 and C. Fernández Cuenca, *Historia del cine*, A. Aguado, Madrid, 1950; vol. V, p. 114ff.

2. "*The River—A Fox Campaign Book*," p. 6 (collection of the author).

3. In addition to the remakes in Mandarin mentioned above, we should add various versions (mostly of *7th Heaven*) filmed in Cantonese in Hong Kong starting in 1935. In 1933, progressive Chinese critics referred to Borzage and his "social conscience" to distinguish itself from the local pro–American press that defended "light" entertainment (Information provided by Marco Müller).

4. J.G. Auriol, "Les péchés de Mary Duncan" in *La Revue du cinéma* (Paris) no. 13, August 1, 1930, p. 16–25. The actress made only 15 films. Her career, somewhat similar to that of Louise Brooks, was harmed after unsuccessful Borzage and Murnau films; Fox ended her contract in 1930, and her "vamp" character appeared in innocuous films at Warner, MGM, and finally RKO. In 1933 she played a neurotic actress alongside Katharine Hepburn in *Morning Glory* (L. Sherman), her last screen role. Mary Duncan, widow of the polo player Stephen "Laddie" Sandford, died May 9, 1993, in Palm Beach.

5. Besides the three Borzage films, Tupper sold Paramount the subject for *The First Kiss* (Rowland V. Lee, 1928), to Fox *Christina* (William K. Howard, 1929, with Janet Gaynor) and *Salute* (John Ford, 1929). After an altercation with Sheehan, he became screenwriter at Monogram (*The Phantom Broadcast*, 1933), Warner (*Red Hot Tires*, 1935) and Universal (*Girl Overboard*, 1937), then, disgusted by Hollywood, returned to his forest.

6. Following a misunderstanding, Fox even destroyed the only 35mm nitrate excerpt after having made a 16mm duplicate intended for Everson! The copies in Washington, Luxembourg and Lausanne all come from this duplicate.

7. *Cahiers du Cinéma* (Paris) no. 319, January 1981, p. 40.

8. The novel was published at Grosset & Dunlap, New York 1928 at the time of the film's release. The script and analysis of the sequences are kept at U.C.L.A., 20th Century Fox Corp. Collection 010 (Produced Scripts, Box FX-PRS-61); the stills are part of the "Special Collections" of A.M.P.A.S. (Margaret Herrick Library).

9. In Tupper's book, Rosalie had run away from a convent where she had been sent by her father, a forestry expert, to live with her lover.

10. *L'ami du peuple* (Paris), October 4, 1929.

11. Contrary to what film buffs have written or recopied for decades, *he* is the one who is naked!

12. Both Tupper's novel and the script then include an episode never used by Borzage. The day after Allen John recovers, Rosalee decides to leave her beloved, not having the heart to hurt him any more, nor the strength to forget Marsdon. She leaves for the city (in the novel, the convent) after writing a note to Allen John in which she speaks of a possible return of spring, when things will be clearer. In the film, the lovers spend the rest of the winter together.

13. L. Delaprée, in *Pour Vous* (Paris) no. 47, October 10, 1929, p. 8.

14. *Cinémagazine* (Paris) no. 47, October 10, 1929, p. 8.

15. Jean Mitry, *Histoire du cinéma*, vol. 3, Ed. universitaires, Paris 1973, p. 442.

16. This moment does not exist in Tupper's novel. Marsdon (alias Jorgensen) comes back to the camp as a free man and marries Ellen, a lucky rival of Rosalee who has managed to obtain his pardon. In order to "drown" the very memory of this individual, Rosalee throws herself into the rapids, with the consent of Allen John, who then fishes her out.

17. *The Film Spectator*, vol. 7, no.5, February 9, 1929, p. 10.

18. Erickson and Van Buren were also responsible for the sound sequences in Murnau's *Four Devils* (May 1929) and *Our Daily Bread/City Girl* (June 1929).

19. No. 1171, March 3, 1929, p. 44.

20. Jean Fayard in *Candide*, October 24, 1929 and in *Cinéa* no. 144, November 15, 1929, p. 6.

21. Pierre Villoteau, no. 5, November 15, 1929, p. 70.

22. *L'Ami du Peuple*, October 11, 1929, p. 70.

23. "En marge du cinéma français," ed. *L'Age d'Homme*, Lausanne 1987, p. 73–74.

24. Cf. *Variety*, September 21, 1927, p. 64.

25. *In Old Arizona*, directed by Raoul Walsh and Irving Cummings (fall 1928), was Fox's first sound picture containing filmed exteriors.

26. "Action française" (Paris), June 6, 1930.

27. Conversation with George Pratt, op. cit.

28. Program Note (laudatory and brilliant) of the film, Cinemateca Portuguesa, Lisbon, February 22, 1991.

29. July 7, 1929 and September 22, 1929.

30. *The Film Spectator*, October 5, 1929, p. 191.

31. *Cinémagazine* (Paris) no. 44, November 1, 1929, p. 191.

32. A rediscovery due to Paul Willemen's intuition (London) and to Catherine Gautier's persistence (Madrid).

Chapter 9

1. *Histoire du cinéma* (Denoël and Steele, Paris, 1935), p. 308; updated 1943, 1948 and 1953.

2. *Les grands cinéastes que je propose*, ed. Cerf, Paris 1967, p. 59.

3. Homer Croy, *Our Will Rogers*, Duell, Sloan & Pierce, New York 1953.

4. Pike Peters, his family and friends reappeared in David Butler's *Down to Earth* (1932), also written by Homer Croy; Pike has a replica of a French chateau built in Oklahoma. Rogers and Irene Rich played similar roles in *So This Is London* (John G. Blystone, 1930).

5. Bryan B. and Frances N. Sterling, *Will Rogers in Hollywood*, Crown, New York 1984, p. 104–5.

6. Conversations with George Pratt, op. cit.— *By the Way, Bill*, the Borzage-Rogers project scheduled for October, never materialized.

7. Sheehan married Czech soprano Maria Jeritza in 1935.

8. In comparison, in 1930–31, superstar John Barrymore earned $ 150,000 a film (Warner), baritone Lawrence Tibbett $75,000 for *The Rogue Song* (MGM) and George Arliss $50,000 for *Disraeli* (Warner). McCormack was 45 and his opera career was over when he played in *Song o' My Heart*. Averse to the movies, he would only make one more brief appearance in the British film *Wings of the Morning* by Harold Schuster, in 1937, before retiring the following year. *Photoplay Magazine* (Sept. 1929) polled readers to determine the songs McCormack would sing on screen.

9. Cf. Maureen O'Sullivan-Farrow's interview with John Gallagher, in *Irish America*, February 1989.

10. MGM experimented with the exact same procedure, but renamed "Realife," in *Billy the Kid* (Oct. 1930), King Vidor's western. Cf. Robert E. Carr, R. M. Hayes, *Wide Screen Movies*, Jefferson, NC: McFarland, 1988, p. 6ff.

11. The print (preserved by the A.F.I., 20th Century Fox and The John McCormack Association of Greater Kansas City, Inc.) contains only invasive musical accompaniment (with no relation to the original) and some sound effects. It was actually a version intended for export to non–Anglophone countries where the intertitles would serve as a references for texts in other languages.

12. Born in Ireland to Hungarian parents, Glazer introduced several of Molnár's works to the U.S.;— he also wrote the scripts for *A Trip to Paradise* and *Carousel* (both based on *Liliom*). The American premiere of the play was

at the Garrick Theater in New York on April 20, 1921., starring Joseph Schildkraut and Eva Le Gallienne (Theater Guild). In Europe, the best stage productions of *Liliom* were by Georges Pitoëff (1923) in Paris, Max Pallenberg (1922) and, most of all, Hans Albers (1929, 1946) in Berlin.

13. Richard Fall, prolific author of operettas, operas and symphonies, wrote only two other movie scores: *East Lynne* (1931) by Frank Lloyd and *Sehnsucht 202* (1932) by Max Neufeld, in Vienna.

14. Crowned American box office queen for 1934, Janet Gaynor would definitively retire from the movies five years later. Charles Farrell left Fox in 1933 (a few months after Borzage) to become independent and opened a private club in Palm Springs.

15. Rose Hobart (1906–2000) remained in movies until she got "blacklisted" by McCarthy in 1949. Her most memorable appearance was as the fiancée of the good doctor Frederic March in Mamoulians's *Dr. Jekyll and Mr. Hyde* (1932).

16. Letter from Jason S. Joy to Robert Yost (Fox Film), April 7, 1930, in MPAA Production Code Administration Files (*Liliom* file), A.M.P.A.S., Los Angeles.

17. S. N. Behrman, *People in a Diary*, Boston 1972, p. 145.

18. This title would be used the same year for an adventure film by Irving Cummings.

19. Letter to the author, Woodland Hills (Ca.), December 12, 1991. See also: Rose Hobart, *A Steady Digression to a Fixed Point* (Scarecrow Press, 1994), p. 67–71.

20. "Fox: The Last Word," vol. 1, no. 12, September 13, 1930. In 1935, Fox released Lang's *Liliom* in New York in French with subtitles in a version where 34 minutes were cut (out of the original 120).

21. *New York Times*, October 4, 1930.

22. James Shelley Hamilton, in *Cinema*, vol. 1, no. 8, December 1930, p. 38.

23. Eighty-five performances at the Hudson Theater (October 10, 1930) directed by Marion Gering and Robert V. Newman (producer); Paul Kelly played Eddie, William Pawley recreated his role (Dot's brother)on screen. In Hollywood, Viña Delmar notably wrote the plot of *Sadie McKee* (Clarence Brown, 1934) and the scripts for *The Awful Truth* and *Make Way for Tomorrow* (Leo McCarey, 1937).

24. Cf. William C. deMille, *Hollywood Saga*, Dutton & Co., New York 1939, p. 183–84.

25. Notably, the censors wanted it clearly established that Dot had not slept with Eddie before marrying him; Borzage ignored this and left the viewer free to imagine what he liked! Cf. letter to Mr. Wilson of May 18, 1931, in : MPAA Production Code Administration Files (*Bad Girl* file), A.M.P.A.S., Los Angeles.

26. *New York Times*, August 15, 1931.

27. *Marido y Mujer* (dir: David Howard, Rudolf Sieber [according to other sources: Bert E. Sebell]) starred Conchita Montenegro and George Lewis. In the remake, *Manhattan Heartbeat* (by David Burton), Robert Sterling and Virginia Gilmore played the new marrieds. A second remake was planned in 1948, but never materialized. *Bad Boy* (1935) was directed by John Blystone.

28. Cf. Richard Koszarski, *The Man You Loved to Hate: Erich von Stroheim and Hollywood*, Oxford University Press, New York, 1983, p. 239ff. *Walking Down Broadway*, an initial project of Sidney Lanfield, was first intended for Eilers and Dunn.

29. Staged at the Golden Theater on Broadway (August 26, 1931) by John Golden, with Ross Alexander (Peter) and Barbara Robbins (Sidney).

30. *Variety,* March 8, 1932.

31. *Spencer Tracy … A Biography,* Signet Book, New American Library, New York 1971, p. 83.

32. Cortella was the last name of the first husband of Dolly Borzage, Frank's sister.

33. Ford intended to cast Maureen O'Sullivan, Frank Albertson, Donald Dillaway and William Collier, Sr. The subject (from a John Frederick Ballard play) was filmed twice more: in 1922 by Arthur Berthelet, and in 1942 by Louis King.

34. *Variety,* May 10, 1932.

35. Margaret Herrick Library, Special Collections, A.M.P.A.S. In comparison, John Ford earned $133,980 in 1929, $145,100 in 1930 and $42,000 in 1931.

36. The film would be finally directed by G. W. Pabst at Warners in 1933–34 (cf. chapter 12).

37. Borzage remained nominally under contract to Fox until September 1933, which explained preparations for *Green Dice/There's Always Tomorrow* (summer 1933) with Will Rogers and ZaSu Pitts. Due to the delay in filming of *Man's Castle,* the film would be given to James Cruze; it was released under the title *Mr. Skitch.*

Chapter 10

1. *New York Daily News,* December 6, 1932, p. 40.

2. Particularly *Hemingway and the Movies* by Frank M. Laurence, Da Capo, New York 1982, chapter 3; a more satisfactory evaluation can be found in *The Classic American Novel & the Movies: Exploring the Link between Literature and Film,* ed. Gerald Peary, Roger Shatzkin, Ungar, New York, 1977 (study by William Horrigan, p. 297–304).

3. *New York Times,* December 9, 1932.

4. *Hollywood Reporter,* December 7, 1932.

5. It premiered in Philadelphia (Schubert Theater, September 15, 1930), then in New York (National Theater, September 22, 1930) with Elissa Landi and Glenn Anders.

6. Letter from F.L. Herron to H.A. Bandy (First National Pictures), September 2, 1930. Cf. MPAA Production Code Administration (PCA) Files, file on "A Farewell to Arms," A.M.P.A.S., Los Angeles.

7. Lamar Trotti, August 19, 1932 (PCA Files). At the time, the Hays Office was much more preoccupied by the audacious *She Done Him Wrong* and other Mae West sex comedies at Paramount.

8. In return, Paramount obtained from Warner the rights for *A Connecticut Yankee in King Arthur's Court* for Bing Crosby.

9. For instance, *Hemingway and the Movies* by Frank M. Laurence, University Press of Mississippi, 1981, p. 154–155; *The Encyclopedia of Novels into Film* by John C. Tibbetts and James M. Welsh, Facts on File, New York 1997, p. 120–122. For the cuts, see "A Farewell to Arms and Other Amputations" by Leonard J. Leff, in: *Film Comment* Jan./Feb. 1995, p. 70–73.

10. Here the script contains a scene with strong pacifist tendencies: an Italian soldier hidden in the bushes begs Frederic to help him desert. The American lets himself be persuaded, knocks the soldier out and brings him in as if "wounded" to his ambulance; the scene was probably never filmed (sequence A-17, Final Script, July 7, 1932), Paramount Script Collection, A.M.P.A.S., Los Angeles.

11. Hemingway only mentions Frederic's background briefly, toward the end of the novel ("I wanted to become an architect"), while the screenplay openly emphasizes it.

12. *Los Angeles Examiner,* December 2, 1934.

13. *My Life in Three Acts* (with Katherine Hatch), Harcourt Brace Jovanovich, New York, 1990, p. 70. Although besieged by Hollywood producers, Helen Hayes (who had married scriptwriter Charles MacArthur in 1928) was not principally a movie actress: she made only about twenty films between 1917 and 1978; among them *The Sin of Madelon Claudet* (E. Selwyn 1931), for which she won an Oscar, *Arrowsmith* (John Ford, 1931), *Night Flight* (C. Brown, 1933) and *Airport* (G. Seaton, 1970), for which she won a second Oscar. She worked with Borzage again briefly in *Stage Door Canteen.*

14. This fade-out replaces a shot deemed "too explicit" and cut *in extremis,* two weeks before the film was released in theaters: Frederic takes Catherine by the hand after kissing her and they disappear into the night.

15. "L'initiation maçonnique," in *L'Initiation,* no. 4, janvier 1891.

16. Cf. the file on this ritual in "Speculative Mason" (London), July 1937.

17. In Masonic tradition, the eye symbolizes manifestation of the sun, source of life and light; on an informal level Logos as principal creator; finally, on a purely metaphysical level, the Architect of the Universe. The stone at the top of the dome, the "keystone of the arch," brings us back to Frederic's drunken statement about the arch as the most ancient form, which, seen in relation to the curves of the woman's foot (the "arch" of the foot), leads to his meeting Catherine.

18. This passage implies clearly that Catherine and Frederic are not married in the eyes of the Roman Catholic Church. The priest's blessing was the result of an individual act unrelated to the sacraments of marriage (which in fact the 1938 remake tried to hide). Frank M. Laurence (*Hemingway and the Movies,* op. cit., p. 58, 154–156) ignores this key point, which invalidates most of his argument against the film.

19. "American Directors," vol. 1, New York 1983, p. 21–22.

20. *Positif,* no. 183–184, July–August 1976, p. 22.

21. Paramount Script Collection, op. cit.

22. Conversation with the author (Marbella, November 28, 1990). Newly arrived from Paris, Negulesco had just worked as a camera angle assistant at Paramount on the comedy *This Is the Night* (F. Tuttle), thanks to the intervention of Mischa Auer. In his memoirs, the filmmaker humorously recalls his frustrating experience working on *A Farewell to Arms,* cf. *Things I Did and Things I Think I Did,* Linden Press/Simon & Schuster, New York 1984 (p. 96–100).

23. According to assistant director Arthur Jacobson, who emphasized that Borzage maintained total control over his film until the final editing (conversation with the author, Los Angeles, October 6, 1990).

24. Charles Higham, Joel Greenberg, *The Celluloid Muse,* London 1969.

25. *Films and Filming* (London), July 1982.

26. Robert Arnold, Nicholas Peter Humy, Ana M. Lopez, "Rereading Adaptation: A Farewell to Arm," in *Iris* (Paris), no. 1, 1983, p. 111.

27. On December 7, 1932 a committee of producers including Joseph Schenck, Carl Laemmle Jr., Sol Wurtzel and representatives of the MMPDA such as Jason S. Joy and Joseph I. Breen decided that "due to the film's importance and its excellent direction," the sequence in question did not "contradict the Code." Nevertheless, Hays upheld its objection and on December 14, four days after the film's release, Adolph Zukor, president of Paramount, yielded to the dictate of the censor.

28. Which invalidates Jean Negulesco's comments (*Positif*, October 1986, p. 47); he claims to have directed retakes of this scene after Borzage's departure.

29. "Paramount International News Letter" (New York), March 1, 1936.

30. *Los Angeles Times*, August 1, 1933.

31. As mentioned in chapter 5, the conclusion of *Daddy's Gone a-Hunting* (1925) contains gestures and a final composition that are very similar.

32. *Positif*, no. 183–184, August 1976, p. 14.

33. *Hollywood Professionals*," op. cit., p. 89.

34. The grandiloquent Selznick remake, directed by Charles Vidor (1957), fell into this trap,

35. it was much more faithful to the plot of the novel; Rock Hudson, Jennifer Jones and Vittorio de Sica uninspiringly struggle amidst authentic scenery of the Piave, in Cinemascope and Technicolor. Other remakes: *Force of Arms* (1951) by Michael Curtiz, with William Holden and Nancy Olsen (a very free adaptation); an American TV film by Allen Resiner, adapted by Gore Vidal with Guy Madison and Diana Lynn (*Climax!* CBS, May 26, 1955); a British TV film in two parts by Rex Tucker, with Vanessa Redgrave and George Hamilton (BBC, March 1, 1966). Plans for a film remake by Ted Kotcheff with Nick Nolte never materialized (1977). On radio: Cecil B. DeMille's Radio Lux Theater, preceded by an interview with Borzage, with Clark Gable, Josephine Hutchinson and Adolphe Menjou (CBS April 5, 1937); Orson Welles' production with Katharine Hepburn ("The Campbell Playhouse," CBS, December 1938), a version with Frederic March and Florence Eldridge ("Star Theater," NBC), another with Helen Hayes and Fletcher Markle ("Ford Theater," CBS, June 1949).

36. After being abandoned by her officer, Mae Clarke paces slowly up and down Waterloo Bridge when she is blown up by a German bomb. As viewers reacted very negatively to this tragic ending, many U.S. theaters rectified the situation by cutting the last minute! The preview of *A Farewell* held in Long Beach (November 11) portended a similar reaction.

37. *Variety*, December 13, 1932.

38. *Cyrano* (Paris), November 10, 1933.

39. *L'Echo* (Paris), November 9, 1933.

40. *Mon-Ciné* (Paris) No. 615, November 30, 1933, p. 2.

41. *L'Action française* (Paris), November 4, 1933.

42. *D'Artagnan* (Paris), December 9, 1933.

43. *Debout* (Paris), November 11, 1933.

44. *Vanity Fair* (New York), January, 1933, p. 62.

45. *Le Figaro* (Paris), October 29, 1933.

46. *Ami du film* (Paris), November 10, 1933.

47. Ed. Bordas, Paris 1989, vol. 2, p. 597 (First published 1967).

48. According to her biographer Scott Eyman (*Mary Pickford, America's Sweetheart*, Donald I. Fine, New York 1990, p. 202), the six exposed reels of *Forever Yours* were not burned, but given to the Library of Congress in Washington in 1946.

49. Cooper was a close friend of Mary Pickford and was counting on working again with Borzage immediately, but his studio had already promised him to MGM for Hawks' *Today We Live*.

50. *Cinéma et nouvelle naissance*, Albin Michel, Paris 1981, p. 137.

51. Cf. Jim Heimann, *Out with the Stars: Hollywood's Nightlife in the Golden Era*, Abbeville Press, New York 1985, p. 157.

52. She appeared for instance with Virginia Valli (Mrs. Charles Farrell) in the play *Caprice*, directed by Hope Loring (Beverly Hills Little Theater, May 7, 1934).

53. *Alameda Times*, July 21, 1936.

54. Conversation between Marcel Pereira with Madeline Borzage Matthey, June 8, 2000.

Chapter 11

1. *One Sunday Afternoon* was filmed by Stephen Roberts, with Cooper and Fay Wray, and the melodrama *Another Language* by Edward H. Griffith, with Hayes and Robert Montgomery.

2. In March 1933, Cohn acquired for Borzage the rights to *The Party's Over* (based on a play by Daniel Kusell), with Dorothy Tree in mind as the star; the filmmaker lost interest and the film went to Walter Lang.

3. Interviewed by James Bawden, in *Films in Review* (New York), November 1987, p. 518.

4. The strikes in July 1933, orchestrated by IATSE (International Alliance of Theatrical Stage Employees) responded to salary constraints imposed by the studios after the national bank moratorium, in March.

5. "'Naturalness first requisite of good acting,' says Borzage," in Columbia Studios Press Files (September 1933), Microfilm coll. Margaret Herrick Library, A.M.P.A.S., Los Angeles.

6. *L'Intransigeant* (Paris), March 28, 1934.

7. H. Agel, M. Henry, *Frank Borzage*, op. cit., p. 270.

8. Peter Roffman, Jim Purdy, *The Hollywood Social Problem Film*, Indiana University Press, Bloomington 1981, p. 54. The motif of the miserable shack transformed by love often recurred in movies, notably in H. King's *One More Spring* (1935) and Chaplin's *Modern Times* (1936).

9. Borzage opposes him to Bragg, forced into unemployment after a series of criminal activities and who resentfully blames the system. Michael Henry Wilson mentions, referring to a sequence that disappeared during editing or at the time of release: "Bragg transformed himself into an orator to vilify the 'dirty capitalists' of Wall Street. His appeal for class struggle was met by indifference in the ghetto. After replying to him: 'Perhaps the rich are more evil than us!' Bill ended up discrediting the orator by asking him why he had been laid off by his employer" (*Positif* no. 183/184, July–August 1976, p. 18).

10. *Dictionnaire du cinéma* (Larousse), Paris 1986, p. 73.

11. *Punch* (London), March 21, 1934.

12. Cf. *San Francisco Call-Bulletin*, May 5 and 6, 1938.

13. *Variety,* January 2, 1934.

14. *Comedia*, March 28, 1934.

15. *Le Journal*, April 6, 1934.

16. *Paris Soir*, March 29, 1934.

17. G. Sadoul, *Dictionnair des Films*, éd. Seuil (Microcosme), Paris 1965, p. 42.

18. J. Mitry, *Histoire du cinéma*, tome 4, éd. J.-P. Delarge, Paris 1980, p. 320.

19. *Baqian Li Lu Yun He Yue*, directed by Shi Dongshan, with Tao Jin (the man) and Bai Yang (the woman).—*Man's Castle* was adapted twice for Lux Radio Theater adaptations, broadcast by Cecil B. DeMille, on March 27, 1939 with Spencer Tracy and Loretta Young, and on December 1, 1941, with Tracy and Ingrid Bergman.

20. Interview by Marcel Pereira, March 10, 2000.

21. Aside from the Borzage film, two Hungarian versions, in 1917 and 1924, *A Palutcai Fiuk* (both directed by Bela Balogh with Ernö Verebes), a 16mm Italian version in 1935, *I Ragazzi Della Via Paal* (directed by Mario Monicelli and Alberto Mondadori), and the American-Magyar coproduction *The Boys of Paul Street* in 1969 (directed

by Zoltan Fabri, with Anthony Kemp and Miklos Jancso, Jr.).

22. Jimmy Butler, later one of the famous "Dead End Kids," was killed on the French front on February 18, 1945, at the age of 23.

23. Undated memo in MPAA Production Code Administration Files (file "No Greater Glory"), A.M.P.A.S., Los Angeles.

24. J. Mitry, *Histoire du cinéma*, tome 4, op. cit., p. 323.

25. H. Agel, M. Henry, *Frank Borzage*, op. cit., p. 278.

26. *Action française* (Paris), December 7, 1934.

27. *Le Journal* (Paris), January 13, 1935.

28. *Femmes de France* (Paris), January 13, 1935.

29. *Die Staatszeitung Kalifornien* (Los Angeles), June 9, 1934.

30. "The National Fascist Party's cup for the most artistically accomplished film." Also shown at this same Biennale, outside official competition, was Monicelli and Mondadori's 16mm remake (cf. above).

31. Orazio Bernardinelli, in *Il Messaggero* (Roma), August 16, 1935.

32. Filippo Sacchi, in *Corrière della Sera* (Milano), August 17, 1935.

33. Conversations with George Pratt, op. cit.

34. *Los Angeles Times*, May 13, 1934.

35. *Chicago Tribune*, May 30, 1934.

36. In comparison, John M. Stahl received $60,000 for *Imitation of Life* (June 1934) and James Whale $15,000 for *Bride of Frankenstein* (January 1935). Cf. Universal Collections, Doheny Library, University of Southern California, Los Angeles.

37. In his own words, cf. interview with Peter Bogdanovich, in *Kings of the Bs*, Dutton & Co., New York 1975, p. 388.

38. *Kleiner Mann, was nun?* was also the subject of a three-part miniseries on East German television in 1966 (dir.: Hans Joachim Kasprzik, with Arno Wyzniewski and Jutta Hoffmann). *Altes Herz geht auf die Reise* (Carl Junghans, 1938), inspired by Fallada, was forbidden by the Nazis. After the war, East and West German television adapted the novelist's works five times (e.g., *Der Eiserne Gustaf* by W. Staudte in 1986) and Roland Gräf depicted the novelist's last years in *Fallada — Letztes Kapitel* (with Jörg Gudzuhn, West Germany 1988).

39. *Film-Kurier* (Berlin) July 7, 1934.

40. Christian Viviani, "Margaret Sullavan: un visage dans la foule," in *Positif* no. 183/4, p. 29–35.

41. "Margaret Sullavan makes good," by Frank Borzage, in *Film Weekly* (London), September 14, 1934, p. 8–9.

42. Margaret Sullavan didn't get along at all with her partner whom she found irritating and passive; Montgomery (with whom Borzage was, on the other hand, rather paternalist and protective) treated her as a "wildcat"; according to her biographer, Quirk, the actress was a man-eater, avenging herself for being rejected by the young lead! Cf. Lawrence J. Quirk, *Margaret Sullavan: Child of Fate*, St. Martin's Press, New York 1986, p. 33–35.

43. The Goebbler couple did not exist in Fallada's work and in the film they replace the proletarian in-laws of the Pinnebergs: Lämmchen's father is a militant socialist and her brother a communist.

44. In Fallada's work, Lautenbach is a militant Nazi: the film merely shows him later with his arm in a sling and a black eye after he was beaten up in a demonstration against the Communists.

45. The scene was cut in Massachusetts and Ohio.

46. David Thomson, *America in the Dark*, Morrow & Co., New York 1977, p. 215.

47. In Fallada's work, Heilbutt had Puttbreese's role: when Hans loses his work and can no longer pay the rent on the attic (where the baby had just been born), he lets him stay in a house with a little garden 25 miles east of Berlin; the family survives there. Lämmchen does a bit of sewing. Hans, still unemployed, refuses to steal wood like the others: he wants to remain honest. Only the sight of his home helps him fight despair. And tomorrow? (The character of Lämmchen was based on Anna Issel, Fallada's first wife who helped the writer surmount his difficulties as a "little man.")

48. *Oakland Tribune*, May 27, 1934.

49. *The Times* (London) October 1, 1934.

50. *Film Art* (London) no. 5, winter 1935, p. 36.

51. *New York Times*, June 10, 1934.

52. Henri Agel, *Les grands cinéastes que je propose*, éd. du Cerf, Paris 1967, p. 60.

Chapter 12

1. Cf. Warner Brothers Legal Files, Wisconsin Center for Film and Theater Research, State Historical Society, Madison.

2. Memo dated December 5, 1933, Warner Brothers Archive, Special Collections, University of Southern California, Los Angeles.— On this subject see Jan-Christopher Horak's fascinating study "G.W. Pabst in Hollywood or Every Modern Hero Deserves a Mother" in *Film History* vol. 1, no. 1, New York 1987.

3. "What's Wrong with the Movies," in *Picturegoer Weekly*, London, September 30, 1933, p. 15) and *Motion Picture Magazine* (New York), September 1933.

4. The very first films Warner intended for Borzage — according to a memo dated August 27, 1933 — were *British Agent* with Leslie Howard (taken over by Michael Curtiz), *Dark Hazard* with Edward G. Robinson (dir.: Alfred E. Green) and *Wonder Bar* with Al Jolson (dir.: Lloyd Bacon).

5. While they are walking, Borzage amuses himself at the expense of Kay "Fwancis" and her famous habit of mispronouncing her "r's," which forced scriptwriters to write or rewrite taking her impediment into consideration: like Professor Higgins, Terry gives Amy a lesson in diction.

6. *Los Angeles Examiner*, December 2, 1934.

7. *Variety*, March 13, 1935.

8. The film's publicity still contains the synopsis of the first version (which probably was filmed); after Amy leaves, Terry inaugurates his seaplane, grazing the roofs of buildings and endangering the lives of his passengers. The plane is confiscated, Gibraltar pays the fine. Amy reacts very negatively and Terry decides to kill himself at the wheel.

9. It was actually a Cosmopolitan production distributed by Warner, since Dick Powell, the film's star, had become Marion Davies' attentive escort and favorite partner. *Annapolis Royal* (Paramount), directed by Alexander Hall, was filmed practically simultaneously. Warners reused the script of *Shipmates Forever* for *Dead End Kids on Dress Parade* by William Clemens.

10. Taken from an unpublished play by Hans Székely and Robert A. Stemmle, *Die schönen Tage in Aranjuez* was produced in the summer of 1933 at Berlin-Tempelhof, in Spain (Cordoba, Ronda, Cadiz, San Sebastian) and in France (Biarritz) by Johannes Meyer. Serge de Poligny supervised the French version, *Adieu les beaux*

jours, in which Jean Gabin and Henri Bosc took over the parts played by Liebeneiner and Gustaf Gründgens (Cooper and Halliday in *Desire*).

11. In return, Paramount gave Warner 4500 feet of negative and loaned actors Jack Oakie, William Frawley and Roscoe Karns.

12. Penny Stallings, *Flesh and Fantasy*, Harper & Row, New York, 1978, p. 87.

13. *New York News*, December 10, 1935.

14. The exceptionally high cost (*The Devil Is a Woman* had "only" cost $800,000) was the main reason Lubitsch was stripped of his managerial position, in January 1936.

15. Marlene Dietrich, *Marlene*, Avon Books, New York, 1989, p. 113.

16. Differences with the original German are marked: feigning divine love with Pierre (Tom), Olga (Madeleine) smuggles across the French-Spanish border, on a sailboat; she leads Pierre to believe she is fleeing her husband. But collaboration between police of both countries is very efficient and the gang of thieves is tracked down, step by step. Neither Berlin (already under Hitler) nor Madrid could tolerate this ridiculing of judicial authority; the gang leader, Alexandre (Carlos), is even captured, but is granted a short reprieve thanks to some accomplices. At the end of the story, Olga realizes she cannot erase her past and sends Pierre away, pretending that the officer who has just arrested her is her husband. When Pierre returns sadly to his car, he recognizes Olga's picture on a wanted notice. A melancholy ending for a pleasant, although uneven film, lacking the erotic audaciousness of the remake.

17. Lubitsch prepared *A Royal Scandal* (1945) which he handed over to Preminger after a heart flutter, and his death interrupted shooting of *That Lady in Ermine* (1948), whose direction Preminger took over.

18. John Belton, *The Hollywood Professionals*, op. cit., p. 76.

19. Was this perhaps an inside joke? When they were filming *Desire*, Paramount's relations with Spain were at the breaking point. Offended by the excesses of *The Devil Is a Woman* (alias *Capriccio Espagnol*), the Spanish government demanded the destruction of all prints of the negative of the film; if not, Paramount's Spanish offices would be closed down (November 1935).

20. The delightful song "Awake in a Dream" is one of two tunes composed by Friedrich Hollaender and Leo Robin (lyrics) for *Desire*. The other, "Whispers in the Dark," would be used in Raoul Walsh's *Artists and Models* (1937).

21. *Time Magazine* (New York), March 9, 1936. Besides its "illicit" sexual liaison, *Desire* contravened the Code by making a crime look appealing (the theft) and a criminal sympathetic.

22. In a first version of the script, Duval agreed to take back the necklace and withdraw his complaint because he wanted to sell the pearls to the wife of the Minister of Justice at substantial profit: the censor demanded this passage be cut.

23. Marlene Dietrich, *Marlene*, op. cit., p. 74 (a very unfair remark in regard to Lang, Hitchcock, Wilder, Feyer, Walsh, etc.).— Lux Radio Theatre with Cecil B. DeMille (CBS, March 15, 1937) adapted *Desire* with Marlene Dietrich and Herbert Marshall.

24. *Daily Sketch*, December 24, 1936.

25. *The Spectator* (London) April, 3, 1936, p. 616.

26. "Dietrich Picture Bows Ahead of New York," in *Variety*, May 13, 1936.

27. Alan Crosland's *Glorious Betsy*, one of the first sound films (Vitaphone), with Dolores Costello, Conrad Nagel and John Miljan. The real Jérôme Bonaparte divorced Betsy in 1807 to marry the Princess Catherine of Wurtemberg.

28. Memos of July 21, July 28 and August 7, 1936, Warner Brothers Archive, Special Collections, U.S.C., Los Angeles.

29. In agreement with Hardwicke, Borzage wanted the deadly dull, physically disabled Harcourt, to have an ugly, deformed exterior (as opposed to the "emotionally disabled" Paige), but management at Warners opposed this and demanded the reverend have the features of a saint.

30. Cecil B. DeMille directed the adaptation of the film for Radio Lux Theatre (CBS, January 31, 1938) with Errol Flynn and Olivia de Havilland. In December 1951, Henry Blanke/Warner Bros. announced a Technicolor remake of *Green Light* based on a new script by Harold Medford. It never materialized.

31. Interview with George Pratt, op. cit.

32. *Cahiers du Cinéma* (Paris) no. 150–151, Dec. 1963–Jan. 1964, p. 100.

33. Robert Parish, *Growing Up in Hollywood*, Little, Brown & Co., Boston-Toronto, 1976, p. 93–94 – cf. also: Joshua Logan, *Josh — My Up and Down, In and Out Life*, Delacorte, New York 1976, p. 104–107.

34. According to Gregory Monk, Colin Clive drank suicidally to overcome his own disgust at his homosexuality (his liaison with James Whale); he was unable to work during almost all of 1936. Cf. *Films in Review*, May 1980, p. 265–266.

35. *Film Culture* (New York) no. 28, Spring 1963, p. 12. The justification of the title is found in a sequence cut during editing: roaming around the streets of Paris, Paul enters a bookseller's (Maurice Cass) and meets an old writer friend of his (Oscar Apfel) perusing a rare book. He congratulates him on his recent biography, to which the man of letters asks him: "Paul, when are you going to let me write a biography of you?" Paul replies: "I'm flattered." The writer sallies back: "You're too modest. If I could put into your biography what you have seen and experienced, I'd give a true picture of our times. And I'll tell you a secret — I even have the title, 'History Is Made at Night.'"

36. *New York Times*, March 29, 1937.

37. J.-L. Bourget, *Le mélodrame hollywoodien*, p. 175.

38. *The Singing Marine* (screenplay by Delmer Daves) was filmed in 1937 by Ray Enright, with two Busby Berkeley musical numbers.

Chapter 13

1. Memo, May 16, 1933 in *Memo from: David O. Selznick* (ed. Rudy Behlmer), Avon Books, New York 1973, p. 94. Rather unusual remarks coming from a producer who constantly bullied directors working for him!

2. "Tay Garnett Speaking" by Rick Fernandez in *The Velvet Light Trap* (Madison, WI) no. 18, Spring 1978, p. 16.

3. Interview of James Stewart in *Picture Shows, Peter Bogdanovich on the Movies*, Allen & Unwin, London 1975, p. 132.

4. Jack Dempsey had already appeared in movies, e.g. for Woody S. Van Dyke (the serial *Daredevil Jack* in 1920, *The Prizefighter and the Lady* in 1933) and John McDermott (*Manhattan Madness*, 1926). In *Big City*, his opponents pass out at the very sight of him.

5. *Positif* (Paris) no. 141, September 1972, p. 72.

6. Conversation with the author (Vico-Morcote, Tessin, November 28, 1989).

7. *A Portrait of Joan: The Autobiography of Joan*

Crawford (with Jane Kesner Ardmore), Doubleday, New York 1962, p. 118.

8. Roy Newquist, *Conversations with Joan Crawford*, Citadel Press, Secaucus, N.J. 1980, p. 81.

9. Spencer Tracy and Joan Crawford recreated their roles in *Mannequin* on radio for MGM'S "Maxwell House" broadcast in November 1937.

10. *MGM Studio News*, vol. 5, no. 1, January 7, 1938.

11. This part that MGM had intended for the innocuous Mickey Rooney ended up going to Leo Gorcey, the insolent lout from *Dead End*.

12. A haunting melody by Edward Ward (lyrics by Robert Wright and Chet Forrest) that was nominated for an Oscar in 1938.

13. C. Viviani on "Joan Crawford" in *Dictionnaire du cinéma*, Librairie Larousse, Paris 1986, p. 152.

14. E.M. Remarque became friends with Boyer on the set of *Mayerling* (1936), during a stay in Paris. The two men shared their hatred for Hitler's Germany. Cf. Larry Swindell, *The Reluctant Lover: Charles Boyer*, Doubleday, New York 1983, p. 150–151.

15. The novel first appeared in the U.S. serialized in *Good Housekeeping* (January–May 1937).—Remarque arrived in New York in 1939, but only established himself in the U.S. as of 1941; that same year, Hollywood adapted *So Ends Our Night* with Margaret Sullavan (John Cromwell). Other films based on Remarque's works: *The Other Love* (André De Toth, 1947), *Arch Of Triumph* (Lewis Milestone, 1948), *Der Letzte Akt* (G. W. Pabst, 1956), *A Time to Love and a Time to Die* (Douglas Sirk, 1958), *Die Nacht Von Lissabon* (Zbynek Brynych, tv-ZDF 1971) and *Bobby Deerfield* (Sydney Pollack, 1977).

16. Cf. James Curtis, *James Whale*, Scarecrow Press, Metuchen N.J.—London 1982, p. 150–151.

17. *Hollywood Reporter*, July 10, 1936.

18. Letter dated January 20, 1938, *Fitzgerald Papers* (Carbon Copy Letters, p. 564), Princeton University Library.

19. J. L. Mankiewicz interviewed by Jacques Bontemps and Richard Overstreet, in: *Cahiers du Cinéma* (Paris) no. 178, mai 1966, p. 39.

20. Kenneth L. Geist, *Pictures Will Talk: The Life and Films of Joseph L. Mankiewicz*, Scribner's Sons, New York 1978, p. 89–90.

21. This is notably the case in Aaron Latham's work, *Crazy Sundays: F. Scott Fitzgerald in Hollywood*, Secker & Warburg, London 1971; the author devotes an almost 30-page chapter to the genesis of *Three Comrades*, only mentioning Borzage's name once! (chapter 7, p. 120–149). Cf. also "F. Scott Fitzgerald's Screenplay for *Three Comrades* by Erich Maria Remarque," edited by Matthew J. Bruccoli (Screenplay Library), Southern Illinois University Press, Carbondale-Edwardsville 1978, p. 290. The 94 files of the script changes and transcriptions of conferences between Fitzgerald, Mankiewicz and Paramore (June 4, 1936–May 26, 1938) are conserved in U.S.C.'s "Special Collections" in Los Angeles.

22. Originally from Posen and steeped in Germanic culture, Mankiewicz lived in Berlin in 1919 and 1928.

23. *Présence du cinéma* (Paris), no. 18, November 1963, p. 10.—Fitzgerald worked more or less incognito on 11 films between 1931 and 1940; he had worked at MGM since July 1937, but his contributions to *Marie Antoinette*, *The Women* and *Madame Curie* were all rejected. His only official collaboration (with his name in the credits) was on the Remarque film; it got him a raise and his contract extended for a year.

24. Memos of E. E. Paramore and David Hertz to Mankiewicz; October 23, 1937 and November 27, 1937; revised script January 8, 1938 (U.S.C., Los Angeles).

25. Markus Spieker, *Hollywood unterm Hakenkreuz. Der amerikanishce Spielfilm im Dritten Reich*, Wissenschaftlicher Verlag Trier/Cinémathèque Municipale de Luxembourg, 1999, p. 67, 99.

26. Attending this conference were Louis B. Mayer, Eddie Mannix, Sam Katz, Benjamin Thau and J. L. Mankiewicz; cf. letter from Breen to Mayer, January 27, 1938. On May 16, 1938, Breen even promised Gyssling to cut the shots of the drums during the street fight, and shorten the scenes of confrontation.

27. *New Masses* (New York), February 15, 1938.

28. *The Citizen* (Columbus), May 31, 1938.

29. *L'Action française* (Paris), January 27, 1939.

30. Shooting of *Three Comrades* was delayed six days due to this whim. Cf. Lawrence J. Quirk, *Margaret Sullavan*, op. cit., p. 89.

31. Conversation with the author, July 16, 1990, Beverly Hills.

32. Joëlle Fontaine, in: *Positif* (Paris) no. 269–270, July–August 1983, p. 114.

33. This tune glorifying friendship gives way to a slightly melancholy love theme named "How Can I Leave Thee?" (that we hear on Alfons' record and that Erich plays on the piano). In fact it is an old romantic German melody: "Ach, wie ist's möglich dann, dass ich dich lassen kann" by F. W. Kücken (1827)—that Max Ophüls, the same year (1938), used as the leitmotif in *Werther*. An evocation of a disappeared Germany?

34. An introduction in uniform nonexistent in Remarque's novel or Fitzgerald's script; the latter suggested a political commentary in the form of a metaphor (the German imperial eagle disintegrating under fire from French howitzers) and images of famine and inflation.

35. Breuer is thus clearly denounced as a proto–Nazi. A fleeting figure in Remarque's book, Fitzgerald even makes him a "Gauleiter"—a district chief in Hitler's Germany, who organizes subversion in the region, threatening to shut down the trio's garage if Erich continues to see Pat and seeking to expel the three comrades from the country.

36. An operation which had saved Mankiewicz when he was eight years old (cf. *Pictures Will Talk*, p. 18, n. 8).

37. Latham, *Crazy Sundays*, op. cit., p. 145.

38. Jean-Pierre Coursodon, *American Directors*, vol. 1, op. cit., p. 19.

39. Jean-Loup Bourget, in *Dictionnaire du cinéma américain*, Larousse, Paris 1988, p. 57.

40. Michael Henry Wilson, *Positif* no. 183–184, op. cit., p. 14.

41. Letter to the author, Bedford, N.Y., October 15, 1992.

42. *Ecran* (Paris) no. 50, September 15, 1976, p. 70.

43. Jon Halliday, *Sirk on Sirk*, Secker & Warburg, London 1971, p. 40.

44. Letter to Matthew Josephson, March 11, 1938 (*Lettres de F. Scott Fitzgerald*, Gallimard, Paris 1965).

45. Cf. A. Latham, *Crazy Sundays*, op. cit., chapter 8: "Infidelity: A Picture Worth a Book of Words," p. 150–173.

Chapter 14

1. *MGM Studio News* (Hollywood) vol. 7, no. 2, February 24, 1940, p. 7.

2. Written in 1933, the play was first staged in Canada, then in New York (February 26, 1933, 121 performances), and finally in London (September 4, 1934,

213 performances); Raymond Massey directed and played David, with Gladys Cooper (Judy) and Adrianne Allen (Mariella, in the movie: *Olivia*) alongside him. As for John Keith Winter, he also worked in the movies as a scriptwriter, e.g. *The Strange Affair of Uncle Harry* (Siodmak, 1945) and *The Red Shoes* (Powell and Pressburger, 1948). Gulf's Screen Guild Show produced a radio adaptation of *The Shining Hour* with Melvyn Douglas, Shirley Ross, George Burns and Gracie Allen (February 26, 1939). Televised dramas included: *The Ford Theater Hour* (CBS June 2, 1950, dir.: Marc Daniels) with Lois Wheeler and Margaret Lindsay; *Betty Crocker Star Matinee* (ABC, December 15, 1951) with Neva Patterson and Zachary Scott; *Kraft Theater* (ABC August 19, 1954, dir.: Fred Carney) with Valerie Bettis and Richard Waring.

3. *A Portrait of Joan*, op. cit., p. 122.

4. Quirk, *Margaret Sullavan*, op. cit., p. 96.

5. *A Portrait of Joan*, op. cit., p. 122–123. The uncomplicated pregnancy of Margaret Sullavan (married to agent Leland Hayward) would encourage Joan Crawford to adopt a daughter, Christina, future author of *Mommie Dearest*.

6. Program Note, Cinemateca Portuguesa, Lisbon, May 4, 1990.

7. *Positif*, no. 183–184, op. cit., p. 34.

8. Fred Camper in: *Harvard Film Studies* (Cambridge, Ma.), April 25, 1971, p. 7 (program note).

9. The title is derived from a passage by Walt Whitman, Lloyd C. Douglas's literary idol: "Have you not learned great lessons from those who braced themselves against, and disputed the passage with you."

10. According to William K. Everson, who met the filmmaker in Rochester in 1957 (George Eastman House), Borzage wanted a more "intimate" conclusion. Robert Preston was initially considered for the role of Doctor Beaven. Lux Radio Theater (CBS, March 25, 1940) produced a radio version of *Disputed Passage* with Alan Ladd.

11. The same year Bayard Veiller completed the script of *Barricade* (Gregory Ratoff) which was set in northern China, and would be Frank Capra's collaborator for the propaganda series "Why We Fight," in particular for *The Battle of China* (1944). Chinese activist and aviator Lee Ya-Ching was the technical consultant for *Disputed Passage* and lent her twin-engine airplane for the final scenes.

12. *The Spectator* (London), December 14, 1939.

13. Fred Camper, "*Disputed Passage* by Frank Borzage," *The M.I.T. Film Society* (Cambridge, Ma.), July 6, 1970, 4 p.; reprinted in *Cinema* (London); no. 9, 1971, p. 10–13 (*Essays in Visual Style No. 3*) and in: *Movies and Methods. An Anthology* (published by Bill Nichols), University of California Press, Berkeley–Los Angeles–London 1976, p. 339–343. Camper develops the same theories in his analysis of *The Shining Hour*, op. cit. (cf. above).

14. *The Hollywood Professionals*, op. cit. p. 119–120.

15. Newquist, *Conversations with Joan Crawford*, op. cit. p. 85. The actress forgot she was engaged in open warfare behind the scenes to appear in the credits ahead of Clark Gable!

16. *A Portrait of Joan*, op. cit., p. 125.

17. Richard Bernard Sale published over 400 short stories; in 1944, he went over to movies (scriptwriter at Paramount) and became a director three years later. In Great Britain in the summer of 1956, he filmed *Abandon Ship!/Seven Waves Away* (with Tyrone Power and Mai Zetterling), a film that contains some analogies with *Strange Cargo*: it concerns a handful of shipwrecked prisoners in a rowboat in the middle of the ocean.

18. *Pictures Will Talk*, op. cit., p. 99.

19. *50 ans de cinéma américain*, op. cit., p. 304.

20. Curiously, British critic Paul Willemen sees in *Strange Cargo* "a religious allegory extolling the un–Borzage-like virtues of prudence and moderation," as indicated by the first title, *Not Too Narrow ... Not Too Deep* (in fact, an allusion to the prison graves). "Borzage is not averse to using religion as a symbol for repression and frustration. The ending has Verne, the representative of desire, returning to his prison indefinitely postponing the possibility of erotic satisfaction." (National Film Theater, "Programme Notes," London, May 1975.)

21. *The Hollywood Professionals*, op. cit., p. 102.

22. Letter from Albert Deane (Paramount) to Breen, March 7, 1940, MPAA Production Code Administration, A.M.P.A.S., Los Angeles ("Strange Cargo" file). Cf. also Paul W. Facey, *The Legion of Decency. A Sociological Analysis of the Emergence and Development of a Social Pressure Group*, Arno Press, New York 1974, p. 104–106; *New York Times*, April 26, 1940; *New York Herald Tribune*, April 26, 1940, October 7, 1940 and *The New Republic*, April 22, 1940. *Strange Cargo* was also banned in Australia (May 1940), then authorized two months later after 24 cuts.

23. Cf. René Guénon, "La Stricte Observance et les Supérieurs Inconnus," in *Études sur la Franc-Maçonnerie et le Compagnonnage*, tome II, Éditions traditionnelles, Paris 1964, p. 189ff.

Chapter 15

1. *Daily Variety*, November 30, 1938.

2. Cf. Kevin Brownlow, "Sidney A. Franklin: The Modest Pioneer," in *Focus on Film* (London), no. 19, summer 1972, p. 30–41. George Stevens had proposed *The Mortal Storm* to RKO, who turned it down (February 1938).

3. See chapter 5.3. on *The Mortal Storm* in Jan-Christopher Horak's indispensable documentation, *Anti-Nazi-Filme der deutschprachigen Emigration von Hollywood 1939–1945*, Maks Publikationen, Münster 1984, p. 218ff (interview with Paul Hans Rameau).— On George Froeschel, cf. Hans-Bernhard Moeller's study in *Deutsche Exilliteratur seit 1933, 1. Kalifornien*, A. Francke-Verlag, Berne-Munich 1976, p. 720–730.— One lone German emigrant played in the film, Rudolf Amendt-Anders (pseudonym Robert O' Davis), who also appeared in *Confessions of a Nazi Spy*.

4. Sidney A. Franklin, *We Laughed and We Cried* (unpublished autobiography, n.d.), Kevin Brownlow Coll., London, duplicated manuscript p. 289.

5. *Professor Mamlock* by Adolf Minkin and Herbert Rappaport (Lenfilm 1938); Friedrich Wolf's play premiered at the Zurich Schauspielhaus on November 8, 1934.

6. A disciple of Stanislavski at the Moscow Art Theater as of 1911, Maria Ouspenskaya stayed in New York, under Richard Boleslawski's protection, after a U.S. tour with the company in 1924. She founded the Maria Ouspenskaya School of Dramatic Arts in 1929. She began in Hollywood as of 1936 (as the German countess in William Wyler's *Dodsworth*).

7. Cf. Neal Gabler, *An Empire of Their Own: How the Jews Invented Hollywood*, Crown, New York 1988, p. 272ff. Warner had already gotten around it by showing the word "Jew" scrawled beside Dreyfus's name, but not saying it, in Dieterle's *The Life of Emile Zola* (1937). Only in January 1941, in *So Ends Our Night* (Cromwell) did Hollywood lift the ban: in it emigrant Margaret Sullavan is called a "dirty filthy Jew."

8. Letter of February 7, 1940 to Sidney A. Franklin, MGM Collection, U.S.C.L.A.

9. Quirk, *Margaret Sullavan*, op. cit., p. 107–108. After *Mortal Storm*, Margaret Sullavan, uninterested in the film roles offered to her, would only make five more pictures (including Robert Stevenson's *Back Street*, 1941, with Charles Boyer); she continued working in theater until right before her death in 1960; having become deaf, the actress ended her days.

10. Gene Reynolds would become a multimillionaire producing the televised series M*A*S*H (1972); William T. Orr, future producer for television and for Warner (R. Quine's *Sex and the Single Girl*), played Erich, the brother. Robert Stack (Otto) was on his third film, but would also become a TV celebrity (Eliot Ness in *The Untouchables*, 1959–63).

11. "MGM Pressbook: *The Mortal Storm*," New York Public Library.

12. Robert Stack (with Mark Evans), *Straight Shooting*, Macmillan, New York 1980, p. 77.

13. *Richmond News Reader*, March 18, 1940.

14. *Youngstown Vindicator*, June 2, 1940.

15. Saville produced *The Citadel* (King Vidor, 1938) and *Goodbye Mr. Chips* (Sam Wood, 1939) for MGM in London.

16. Sidney A. Franklin, op. cit., p. 286–87.

17. Conversations of the author with Dorothy Galla-Rini and Susan Williams (Burbank, July 14, 1990), conversation of Marcel Pereira with Juanita Moss (March 10, 2000).

18. Conversation of the author with Nikki and Sean Borzage (Lew's daughter and grandson, March 2001).

19. Rena controlled a large part of their common property (estimated at $444,000), as Frank put almost everything in her name, notably the yacht *Athena* ($25,000), jewelry ($60,000) and the villa ($100,000). Rena and her business executive had been managing the couple's finances for twenty years.

20. John Kobal Archives, London 1969 (republished in the "National Film Theater Programme Notes," December 1972). See also *Evergreen, Victor Saville: In His Own Words* by Roy Moseley, Southern Illinois University Press, 2000.

21. *Los Angeles Examiner*, September 15, 1941. The bombing of Pearl Harbor put an end to the debate. Regarding Nicholas M. Shenck's remarks (president of Loew's/MGM) on *The Mortal Storm*, questioned by Senator Clark, cf. "Propaganda in Motion Pictures. Hearings before a Subcommittee of the Committee on Interstate Commerce, United States Senate. 77th Congress, September 9 to 26, 1941," U.S. Government Printing Office, Washington 1942, p. 324–333.

22. Interview with the author, Hollywood, July 16, 1990.

23. Letter to the author, Bedford, N.Y., October 15, 1992.

24. Letter to the author, Los Angeles, August 5, 1990.

25. Letter to the author, Los Angeles, October 1, 1990.

26. Letter to the author, Beverly Hills, September 12, 1990.

27. Cf. MGM Collection (Victor Saville Papers), U.S.C. Los Angeles. A report from Noerdinger to Saville dated March 5, 1940, dealt with, for example, correcting details concerning table manners, university titles in Germany, Latin sentences of the students, eliminating pastries and ice cream from Bavarian inns in December, etc.

28. Topologically, the place could be Mittenwald or Garmisch-Partenkirchen, but the closest university was in Munich!

29. Coincidentally, Frank Morgan (born Frank Wupperman) was himself Jewish, of German origin.

30. *Souls Made Great by Love and Adversity*, op. cit., p. 96.

31. "In 1937, MGM made inquiries in Berlin regarding use of the SA hymn in *Three Comrades* and those holding the rights asked for $250. In 1939, the company refused to reopen negotiations with Wessel's heirs and the *New York Times* on April 10, 1940 spread a rumor that, for the sequence in the inn, MGM composed a new Nazi hymn entitled the "Adolf Hitler Song." In fact, it actually *was* the "Horst Wessel-Lied," with English lyrics: "Die Fahne hoch, die Reihen dicht geschlossen, SA marschiert mit ruhig festem Schritt" became "Close Up the Ranks," etc. Edward Kane took credit for the music (!); Earl Brent wrote the lyrics.

32. Bonita Granville played the vicious little girl in *These Three* (Wyler) who started the "shameful" rumors about her teacher (nominated for an Oscar in 1936, together with Maria Ouspenskaya for *Dodsworth*, also by Wyler).

33. Richard Rosson and his two cameramen, in charge of the Austrian stock shots for *Florian* (Edwin L. Marin), had been incarcerated for two months for having knowingly filmed exteriors in a German military zone.

34. *Positif*, no. 183–84, p. 31.

35. *Positif*, op. cit., p. 17.

36. "NFT Programme Notes," op. cit. An off-screen voice quotes from Minnie Louise Haskin's "Gate of the Year" heard on Christmas Eve 1939 in King George VI of England's speech broadcast on the radio: "I said to a man who stood at the Gate: 'Give me a light that I may tread safely into the unknown,' and he replied: 'Go out into the darkness, and put your hand into the hand of God. That shall be to you better than a light, and safer than a known way.'"

37. Phyllis Bottome, "Speaking as one who should know. A Novelist talks about the screen version of her book," in: *New York Times*, June 16, 1940.—The author's only regret was the removal of a passage where Roth explains to his son Rudi what makes "a good Jew."

38. "Was stimmt nicht an den Anti-Nazi Filmen?" in *Decision* (New York), August 1941, republished in *Europäische Ideen* (Cologne — London) no. 63, 1986, p. 17.

39. *Aufbau* (New York) no. 26, June 28, 1940, p. 9.

40. "Hollywood Directs the Movies," in *American Scholar*, vol. 10, no. 4, October 1941, p. 497.

41. *The Richmond New Leader*, June 11, 1940.

42. *The New Yorker*, June 22, 1940.

43. *Variety*, June 12, 1940.

44. *New York Times*, June 21, 1940, p. 25 and June 23, 1940.

45. William Boehnel in *The New York World Telegram*, June 21, 1940.

46. Botschaft Washington to AA, July 11, 1940, Bundesarchiv Berlin, R 901, Nr. 60449, p. 3.

47. Cf. *New York Times*, March 9, 1941. In 1939, only Paramount, Fox and MGM still sporadically appeared on German screens, with insipid or low-end products (comedies, musicals, westerns and mystery series). In 1940, MGM was only represented by the Far West operetta *Let Freedom Ring* (Conway), while Paramount showed a half dozen films, including DeMille's *Union Pacific* and *The Plainsman* (a filmmaker very much appreciated by the Nazis since *This Day and Age*, a fetish film of the Hitler youth). The closing of the offices of Loew's/MGM in Berlin also coincided with the founding in Hollywood of the Motion Picture Committee Cooperating for National Defense.

48. *New Statesman* (London), October 19, 1940.

49. *The Spectator* (London), October 4, 1940.

50. *Télérama* (Paris) June 2, 1976. David Seltzer, director of the spy film *Shining Through* (1991), pays homage to *The Mortal Storm* by inserting the final sequence of Martin and Freya's escape.

Chapter 16

1. *GM Pressbook:* Flight Command, New York Public Library (Performing Arts Research Center).

2. Mantz worked on 300 films, beginning with *Hell's Angels* (H. Hughes, 1927–30), then *Air Mail* (Ford), *Test Pilot* (Fleming), *Only Angels Have Wings* (Hawks) and *Flying Leathernecks* (Ray); he died in 1965 in an air stunt for *The Flight of the Phoenix* (Aldrich).

3. Cf. Bruce W. Orriss, *When Hollywood Ruled the Skies: The Aviation Film Classics of World War II*, Aero Associates, Hawthorne, Ca., 1984, p. 13–18.

4. *The Los Angeles Times*, December 17, 1940. Robert Taylor, Walter Pidgeon and Ruth Hussey reenacted their *Flight Command* roles on Radio Lux Theater (CBS, March 24, 1941), directed by Cecil B. DeMille.

5. *Flight Command* was also to be on the list of warmongering propaganda movies incriminated by Senator Gerald Nye ("America First Committee," September 1941; cf. chapter 15).

6. This is the conclusion of the film as it was distributed (an ending with retakes filmed by D. Miller, on April 9, 1941). In the original script, rejected by Breen, Billy removes the cartridges from his weapon before confronting Jim. At the same time, 70 miles away from Flagstaff, Howard Hughes and Howard Hawks were filming their own version of "Billy the Kid," *The Outlaw*, which also met with endless problems from the censor.

7. Monument Valley had just been shown on screen in John Ford's *Stagecoach* (filming: November 1938) and shot a second time — also in black and white — for George B. Seitz's "B" series *Kit Carson* (1940).

8. Performed on stage by Jane Cowl (Kathleen), Henry Stephenson (Sir John) and Orme Caldara (Kenneth), the three-act play with a prologue by Jane Cowl and Jane Murfin (written under the pseudonym of Allan Langdon Martin) opened December 30, 1919, at the Broadhurst Theater in New York. Cecil B. DeMille directed two radio versions of it for Radio Lux Theatre: one with Robert Taylor and Barbara Stanwyck (CBS, April 29, 1940), the other with Borzage's actors: Jeanette MacDonald, Gene Raymond and Brian Aherne (CBS, January 5, 1942). Vincent Youmans and Brian Hooker made it into an operetta in 1932, "Through the Years."

9. "Frank Borzage s'avoue un fervent adepte du procédé Technicolor," in *Ciné-Suisse*, no. 224, May 24, 1945.

10. On stage, the gentle spirits of Moonyean and Sarah Wayne (Kenneth's mother) cooperate in the Beyond to make Sir John yield!

11. James Bawden, "Joe Pasternak," in *Films in Review*, February 1985, p. 67.

12. In 1949, Sol Lesser rereleased *Stage Door Canteen*, cutting 45 minutes (the original ran 134 minutes) giving it an updated commentary. Singer and dancer Lon McCallister, who played the lead (GI "California"), obtained a dramatic role in *The Red House*, produced by Lesser and directed by D. Daves in 1947.

13. Joseph Kraus, "Felix Jackson," in *Deutsche Exilliteratur seit 1933. 1. Kalifornien*, op. cit., p. 734.

14. Hoffenstein worked mainly with Rouben Mamoulian (*Dr. Jeckyll and Mr. Hyde, Love Me Tonight, Song of Songs*); with E. Reinhardt, he would write the script for Preminger's *Laura*. *His Butler's Sister* would be adapted

for radio by Cecil B. DeMille (Radio Lux Theater, CBS, February 7, 1944) with Deanna Durbin, Pat O'Brien and Robert Paige.

15. The script's major incoherence resides in the character of the brother: his rather spineless behavior is motivated by selfish preoccupations, but also by a subconscious hatred for the wealthy class in general, and for his boss in particular. In Martin's eyes, Gerard (whom he fools and manipulates) does not "deserve" his sister's beauty and talent. However, the valet's ignominy is wiped out by the happy ending.

16. *Lettres françaises* (Paris), November 22, 1946.

17. Lewis wrote the famous *Camille* (Cukor) with Greta Garbo in 1937, and *Dark Victory* (Goulding) with Bette Davis; Lenore Coffee had been working in movies since 1919 and her work included tearjerkers destined for Bette Davis, *The Great Lie* (1941) and *Old Acquaintance* (1943). For Borzage, she worked on the screenplay of *The Age of Desire* (1923). She spent her entire childhood in a convent and converted to Catholicism at age twenty. In Maury's rather banal play, the convent houses Jewish children who have escaped deportation; Sister Madeline (alias Clothilde) dreams of being the "mother" of the son of the American, and she feels responsible for all the wounded children. She is shot to death by the Germans. We should mention that there is no link between this film and works of the same name *Till We Meet Again* (or *Forgotten Faces*, 1936) directed by Robert Florey, or Edmund Goulding's *'Til We Meet Again* (1940).

18. Barbara Britton had, for instance, obtained a tiny role alongside Ray Milland in *Reap the Wild Wind* (DeMille, 1942). She did not have a noteworthy career in the movies—*Captain Kidd* (Lee, 1945), *I Shot Jesse James* (Fuller, 1949), many westerns, but she appeared on television and on stage in New York.

19. Lucille Watson also played the Mother Superior in *The Garden of Allah* (Boleslawski) in 1936.

20. *The Star-Spangled Screen: The American World War II Film*, University Press of Kentucky, Lexington 1985, p. 177.

21. MPAA Production Code Administration, A.M.P.A.S., Los Angeles (file "Till We Meet Again"), letters and memos of March 5, March 19, September 8 and October 21, 1943.

22. September 9, 1944.

23. Originally a Joe Pasternak production for Judy Garland, with a script by Joseph L. Mankiewicz. Henry Koster was to be the director. The project would be taken over by Arthur Freed and Vincente Minnelli in February 1947.

24. Cf. Paul Henreid (with Julius Fast), *Ladies' Man: An Autobiography*, St. Martin's Press, New York 1984, p. 167–170.

25. Anne Bonney or Anne Providence plundered the Caribbean with her pirate-companion Jack Rackham and was captured in 1720. Jean Peters played her in Jacques Tourneur's *Anne of the Indies* (1951).

26. "Binnie Barnes: An Interview" by James Bawden, in *Films in Review*, May 1990, p. 289. Among the pirates, we find the sinister-looking Alfredo Sabato, the "villain" in *Street Angel* and *The River*.

27. Cf. *Woman's Home Companion*, September 1945 and MPAA Production Code Administration Files ("The Spanish Main" file), A.M.P.A.S., Los Angeles.

28. *Citizen News*, October 5, 1944, p. 10.

29. "Sunday Dispatch" (Moore Raymond) in *This Year of Films*, London 1946, p. 30.

30. On the strength of his success as a swashbuckler, Paul Henreid would again play pirate Jean Lafitte in *The*

Last of the Buccaneers (Lew Landers, 1950), then the hero of *Pirates of Tripoli* (Felix Feist, 1955). As for Maureen O'Hara, she would clash swords again a third time under the jolly Roger in *Against All Flags* (George Sherman, 1952) with Errol Flynn.

Chapter 17

1. *Citizen News*, September 9, 1945. Republic also produced such curiosities as Gustav Machaty's *Jealousy* (1945) and Ben Hecht's *Spectre of the Rose*.

2. Felix Bressart first refused the part because it seemed too meager (Hassman appears only in the first quarter of the film). According to Catherine McLeod, Borzage then asked Chase to write a long scene between Bressart and Dorn, a scene that he acted before the camera ... without film!

3. In comparison, the budget for a Republic serial would reach a maximum of $50,000 in the fifties; the "Deluxe" productions (often directed by Joseph Kane) were entitled to 21 days and up to $500,000. Among the "Premiere" productions, a film like Ford's *Rio Grande* was granted 32 days and $1,215,000, and Lang's *Secret Beyond the Door* 33 days and $615,000.

4. Charles Laughton would use it for *The Night of the Hunter* (1955), William Wyler set up his Quaker village there for *Friendly Persuasion* (1956).

5. *Technicolor News and Views*, December 1945, p. 2. In 1990, U.C.L.A. restored a Technicolor copy from the original 3-strip negative.

6. The old piano covered in gilt (used earlier by Gloria Swanson at Paramount in the twenties) was also Chopin's instrument in the recent *A Song to Remember*.

7. Myra Hassman was probably a patronym of British pianist Myra Hess.

8. Conversation with the author, Los Angeles, July 28, 1990.

9. Frederick Lamster, op. cit., p. 169.

10. The script is more explicit, with Goronoff saying: "In all music, there is a woman. Without her, there couldn't be any music."

11. John Belton, "Borzage's 'I've Always Loved You': The Spiritualization of Decor and Editing," in *Focus* no. 9, Spring–Summer 1973, p. 42–44; reprinted in *Cinema Stylists* (Filmmakers No. 2), Scarecrow Press, Metuchen 1987, p. 189–194.

12. Borden Chase's definitive script (dated August 3, 1945) contains an infinitely more sugary and conventional ending : Myra sees Goronoff again in his New York apartment and plays with him alone, discovering that her family matters most to her. During this time, Porgy ("Little Myra"), her mother's daughter, plays under Severin's direction (she is in love with him) and obtains deserved triumph. George thinks his wife has abandoned him, but she joins him backstage at the end of the recital to congratulate their child... As usual, Borzage turned the conclusion upside down during the course of filming in order to stress the irrationality of passion. In Chase's novel, Severin asks Porgy's hand in marriage following her successful debut at Carnegie Hall. Myra agrees, now realizing that career and marriage are compatible. What she and Goronoff lacked, she says, was the courage inspired by true love.

13. Richard Maurice Hurst, *Republic Studios: Between Poverty Row and the Majors*, Scarecrow Press, Metuchen, N.J. & London, 1979. On the other hand, the film's entire production history is reconstructed with many details and illustrations in *Republic Confidential. Volume 1— The Studio* by Jack Marthis, Barrington, Illinois, 1999, p. 378–417. Republic would take a final risk with the big-budget musical fiasco *Magic Fire* (*The Story of Richard Wagner*) by William Dieterle, in 1954 — another film forgotten by Hurst.

14. *Los Angeles Times*, October 18, 1946, p. 7.

15. In 1947, Edgar G. Ulmer and Paramount reused the same formula (human drama and classical concerts) for *Carnegie Hall*, in which Arthur Rubinstein, Jascha Heifetz, Leopold Stokowski, Bruno Walter and others appeared.

16. *Cahiers du cinema*, no. 135, septembre 1962, p. 38.

17. H. Agel, *Romance Américaine*, éd. du Cerf, Paris 1963, p. 31–32; *Les grands cinéastes que je propose*, ibid. 1967, p. 61–62.

18. *Guide des Films* (Jean Tulard), vol. 1, Laffont, Paris 1990, p. 1140.

19. Program note, *Cinemateca Portuguesa* (Frank Borzage series, June 25–29, 1990), p. 1.

20. *50 ans de cinéma américain*, op. cit., p. 784.

21. Jack H. Skirball and screenwriter Bruce Manning presided over the independent company Hallmark, founded in 1944. Skirball, for a long time at Education Pictures, had produced two Hitchcock films (*Saboteur, Shadow of a Doubt*), and, for example, Frank Lloyd's *The Howards of Virginia* (1939), a historical-patriotic chronicle of the eighteenth and nineteenth centuries quite close in spirit to *Magnificent Doll*. The conspiracy of Aaron Burr depicted in the last third Borzage's film has been illustrated onscreen in *The Man Without a Country* in 1909 (by Bannister Merwyn), in 1917 (by Ernest C. Warde), in 1925 (by Rowland V. Lee), in 1938 (by Crane Wilbur, short) and on television in 1973 (by Delbert Mann).

22. Ginger Rogers, *Ginger: My Story*, Harper-Collins, New York 1991, p. 277.

23. *Daily Variety*, April 7, 1947.

24. In 1953, Republic released a new cut of the film (94 minutes) entitled *King of the Race Track*.

25. *The New Statesman and Nation* (London), September 24, 1949.

26. In the official papers (and in the credits), the film carries the discouraging notice: "Republic presents a Charles K. Feldman-Group-Marshall Grant production, produced by Charles Haas, directed by Frank Borzage, a Frank Borzage production, a Republic picture"! Charles Haas, who alone wrote the final script, was co-president of Marshall Grant Productions. Haas and Grant, army buddies, left Universal in August 1946, when the studio merged with International Pictures, and tried their luck as independents with *Moonrise*.

27. MPAA Production Code Administration, A.M.P.A.S., Los Angeles ("Moonrise" file), script dated May 3, 1947.

28. Vladimir Pozner claims that he wrote half of it. Cf. "Hollywood, en guerre!" with Vladimir Pozner (interview), in *Cinéma 62* (Paris), March 1962, no. 64, p. 27.

29. Dane Clark (alias Bernard Zanville) appeared in *The Glass Key* (S. Heisler, 1942) based on a work by Dashiell Hammett, and had just appeared opposite Ida Lupino in Negulesco's *Deep Valley* (1947), as another angry man (escaped con) in an unusual romance.

30. Daniel J. Bloomberg's sound recording for *Moonrise* was nominated for an Oscar in 1948.

31. Conversation with the author, Los Angeles, July 7, 1991.

32. *New Chronicle* (London), March 18, 1950.

33. Cf. *The Hollywood Reporter*, June 27, 1945, p. 14 and July 2, 1945; *Citizen News*, June 26, 1945; *Daily Telegraph*, August 11, 1945.

34. R.M. Arlaud, in *Combat* (Paris), August 9, 1950.

35. *Focus,* no. 9, Spring–Summer 1973, p. 30.

Chapter 18

1. Kyrou, *Amour-érotisme & cinéma,* op. cit., p. 217.

2. *Focus* no. 9, spring–summer 1973, p. 26.

3. Along with George Stevens, John Ford, Claude Binyon, Merian C. Cooper, Walter Lang, George Sidney and Mark Robson. Mankiewicz had refused to include the ideological swearing of allegiance that DeMille sought to impose on the entire profession.

4. *New York Times,* September 8, 1957.

5. Among other uncompleted projects of Borzage Productions were *Shadow of Pancho Villa* (1952), *The Boss* (for Samuel Goldwyn Pictures, 1956), *Treasure of Pancho Villa* (in Mexico, for Universal-International, 1957) and *Ghost of the "China"* (for Columbia, 1958). Lew Borzage also worked for other companies, notably in October–November 1955 for Mike Todd's *Around the World in 80 Days,* for which he directed certain exteriors in Lawton, Colorado (the attack of the train by the Indians).

6. *Los Angeles Times,* April 9, 1954.

7. Lotfi Mansouri is the future general director of San Francisco Opera (1988). As for the amazing Sandra Descher, she appeared in 14 films between 1952 and 1958, including *The Cobweb* (Minnelli), *The Prodigal* (Thorpe) and *A Gift for Heidi* (G. Templeton).

8. *Positif* (Paris) no. 341–342, juillet–août 1989, p. 75.

9. *New York Times,* Sept. 8, 1957.

10. William A. Wellman, another member of Borzage's "club," had just collaborated with Batjac-John Wayne on *Blood Alley* (1955) and *Goodbye My Lady* (1956).

11. This is why *China Doll* celebrated its world premiere in Hong Kong. Originally, Li Li Hua came to Hollywood to appear in *The Buccaneer* (DeMille/Quinn), but her role was cut. Li Li Hua was the big star of *Yang Kwei Fei/The Magnificent Concubine* (1962), Run Run Shaw's mega-production.

12. Actress Li Li Hua categorically refused to engage in an action as "vulgar" as kissing Victor Mature. Out of respect for Chinese morals, Borzage had the love scenes rewritten taking these wishes into account.

13. This lack of prejudice is also found on the level of morals: Father Cairns simply frowns when he learns of Brandon's "mistake," but as Brandon assures him it won't happen again, he doesn't see a problem; he quotes Ovid to characterize Shu-Jen's disinterested attitude: "To give is a thing that requires genius."

14. In Pat Kelly and James Benson Nablo's short story and original script, Brandon dies fighting Japanese infantrymen; he leaves behind a little boy.

15. The dialogue alludes to this. Seeing Shiao-Mee, one of Brandon's old army buddies quotes the sentence uttered by the captain at the beginning of the film: "When your dog tags get back to the States, it's my job to see that you're with them." His neighbor replies: "I guess maybe he is with her."

16. "As long as he is not dead, do not say that a man is happy, say, at the very most, that he is lucky. You can only call happy one who has known all possible happiness and has kept it until his death. In everything, Croesus, one must consider the end" (Book I). Cf. Belton, op. cit., p. 122.

17. *New York Times,* September 8, 1957.

18. *The Hollywood Reporter,* August 4, 1958.

19. *The Los Angeles Examiner,* September 11, 1958.

20. *New York Times,* December 4, 1958.

21. In fact, Herod's first wife was the daughter of Aretas IV, the Nabatean of Petra (played in the film by Stuart Randall).

22. The novel dwells at length on events and actions in the life of Jesus, inserting fictional episodes of questionable taste, recalling rationalistic trivialities favored by Ernest Renan. While Lloyd C. Douglas has Christ in person intervene at every opportunity, he is strangely lacking in depth, let alone charisma! Starting out with a timeless, ahistorical Christlike presence (the film evokes neither the crucifixion nor the resurrection of Christ), Borzage achieves the inverse. Other differences in the novel, the execution of John the Baptist (ordered by Salomé) doesn't even give rise to a breeze, Voldi stabs Herod in an ambush before returning to Arabia, and Prince Deran perishes, assassinated by his own subjects.

23. *Arts* (Paris), no. 122, December 14, 1960.

24. *Cahiers du cinéma* (Paris), no. 122, août 1961, p. 24.

25. Charles Higham, *Hollywood Cameramen: Sources of Light,* Indiana University Press, Bloomington-London, 1970, p. 54.

26. *Ben Hur* swept up the three Oscars. Other honors: Blue Ribbon Award of the National Screen Council (November 1959 Box-office), Parents' Family Medal Award 1959, Five Star Award Merit 1959" (Southern California Motion Picture Council), Motion Picture Award of the California Federation of Women's Clubs 1959.

27. In 1921 by Jacques Feyder (*L'Atlantide*), G. W. Pabst in 1932 (*Die Herrin Von Atlantis, D/F*), Arthur Ripley, John Brahm and Gregg Tallas in 1947–49 (*Siren of Atlantis*), Joseph Pevney in 1952–53 (*Desert Legion,* a variant), Jean Kerchbron in 1971–72 (French television drama) and Bob Swaim in 1991 (F/I)—cf. our study "Ayesha et Antinéa. Le mythe de la reine immortelle au cinéma," in *L'Écran fantastique* (Paris) nos. 57–58, June–July 1985.

28. Conversations with the author, March 7, 1992.

29. *The Hollywood Reporter,* December 9, 1960.

30. *Midi-Minuit-Fantastique* (Paris) no. 13, November 1965, p. 7.

31. *Cahiers du cinéma* (Paris) no. 122, August 1961, p. 14–15.

32. *L.A. Herald-Examiner,* June 22, 1962. There was also a separate Masonic ceremony and his blue-colored gravestone bears the traditional Masonic symbols, square and compass. Borzage's golden star is engraved on the "walk of fame" at 6306 Hollywood Boulevard.

Bibliography

Affron, Charles. *Cinema and Sentiment*. Chicago-London: University of Chicago Press, 1982, p. 16–23.

Agel, Henri. "Frank Borzage." *New York Film Bulletin* no.12–14, 1961.

_____. *Romance américaine*. Paris: Editions du Cerf, 1963.

_____. "Frank Borzage." *Les grands cinéastes que je propose*. Paris: Editions du Cerf, 1967, p. 59–62.

_____ and Michael Henry, *Frank Borzage*. Paris: Anthologie du cinéma, vol.7, 1973, p. 241–304.

_____. *Cinéma et nouvelle naissance*. Paris: Albin Michel, Bibliothèque de l'Hermétisme, 1981, chapter IV, p. 135–140.

Ager, Cecelia. "That Sentimental Gentleman from Hollywood, Frank Borzage, Tells How." *New York Variety*, March 7, 1933.

Alpers, Benjamin L. "Anti-Fascism in Soft Focus? Frank Borzage's German Trilogy" http://epsilon3.georgetown.edu/~coventrm/asa2001/panel3/abstracts.html.

Arnold, Robert, Nicholas Peter Humy and Ana M. Lopez, "Rereading Adaptation: A Farewell to Arms." *Iris* (Paris), no. 1, 1983.

Aullo, Juan. "Frank Borzage o el triunfo de la naturalidad." *Camara* (Madrid), no. 63, August 15, 1945, p. 40–41.

Auriol, Jean-Georges. "Un metteur en scène indépendant: Frank Borzage." *L'Ami du Peuple* (Paris), October 11, 1929.

_____. "Les péchés de Mary Duncan." *La Revue du Cinéma* (Paris), no. 13, August 1, 1930, p. 16–25.

Babcock, Muriel. "Hollywood's Most Popular Man. He's Curly-Headed, Sweet-Tempered Frank Borzage." *Los Angeles Examiner*, December 2, 1934.

Baker, Bob. "Frank Borzage." *Film Dope* (London), no. 4, March 1974, p. 26–28.

Bardèche, Maurice and Robert Brasillach. *Histoire du cinéma. 1. Le cinéma muet*. Givors (France): André Martel, 1953.

Bawden, James. "Joe Pasternak." *Films in Review*, February 1985, vol. 36, no. 2, p. 66–81.

_____. "Binnie Barnes: An Interview." *Films in Review*, May 1990, vol. 41, no. 5, p. 280–289.

Bease, A. "Frank Borzage." *Film Journal* (Melbourne), April 1963.

Behlmer, Rudy, ed. *Memo from: David O. Selznick*. New York: Avon Books, 1973.

Behrman, S. N. *People in a Diary*. Boston: Little, Brown, 1972.

Bellamy, Madge. *A Darling of the Twenties: Madge Bellamy*. New York: Vestal Press, 1989.

Belton, John. "Souls Made Great by Love and Adversity: Frank Borzage." *Monogram* (London), no. 4, 1972, p. 20–23.

_____. *Howard Hawks, Frank Borzage, Edgar G. Ulmer. The Hollywood Professionals*, vol. 3. London–New York: Tantivy Press–A.S. Barnes, 1974, p. 74–147.

_____. "Souls Made Great by Love and Adversity" (p. 176–188), "Borzage's 'I've Always Loved You': The Spiritualization of Decor and Editing" (p. 189–194), *Cinema Stylists. Filmmakers no. 2*. Metuchen: Scarecrow Press, 1987.

Bénard da Costa, João. "Ciclo Frank Borzage." Cinemateca Portuguesa, Lisboa (Portugal), May–June 1990; February 1991 (11 Program-texts).

Berriatua, Luciano. *Los proverbios chinos de F. W. Murnau*. Madrid : Filmoteca Española, 1992.

Bescos, José Maria. "Autour de l'hommage Frank Borzage." *Pariscope* (Paris), no. 1300, April 21, 1993, p. 75–76.

Beylie, Claude. "Sur cinq films de Frank Borzage." *Ecran* (Paris) no. 50, September 15, 1976, p. 69–70.

_____. "Frank [Borzage], Douglas [Sirk], Orson [Welles] et les autres." *Cahiers du Cinéma* (Paris), no. 319, January 1981, p. 40.

Bodeen, DeWitt. "Frank Borzage." *Directors/Filmmakers. The International Dictionary of Films and Filmmakers: vol. II*. Chicago–London: Macmillan, St. James Press, 1984, p. 57–59.

Bogdanovich, Peter. *Picture Shows. Peter Bogdanovich on the Movies*. London: Allen & Unwin, 1975.

Borzage, Frank. "Directing a Talking Picture." *How Talkies Are Made*, ed. Joe Bonica, Hollywood 1930 [republished Richard Koszarski. *Hollywood Directors 1914–1940*. London–Oxford–New York: Oxford University Press, 1976, p. 234–237].

_____. "Margaret Sullavan 'Makes Good.'" *Film Weekly* (London), September 14, 1934 (vol. 13, no. 309), p. 8–9.

Bourget, Jean-Loup. "Frank Borzage." *Le mélodrame hollywoodien*. Paris: Stock, 1985, p. 232–240.

_____. "Frank Borzage." *Dictionnaire du cinéma*. Paris: Larousse, 1986, p. 73. [Also *Dictionnaire du cinéma américain*. Paris: Larousse, 1988, p. 56–57.]

Bourgoin, Stéphane. *Terence Fisher*. Paris: édilig, 1984.

Boussinot, Roger. *Encyclopédie du cinéma*. Paris: Bordas, 1967.

Bouyxou, Jean-Pierre. "Frank Borzage: le cinéma serait-il enfin reconnu comme le septième art?" *Paris Match* (Paris), no. 2299, June 17, 1993, p. 18.

Brion, Patrick. "Trois Camarades." *Dossiers du cinéma: films*. Tournai (Belgium): vol. 2, Editions Casterman (vol. 2), 1972, p. 209–212.

_____. "Frank Borzage." *Dossiers du cinéma: cinéastes*, vol. 1. Tournai (Belgium) : Editions Casterman, 1971, p. 33–36.

_____. [André Moreau]. "Borzage le méconnu, cinéaste des gens ordinaires." *Télérama* (Paris), June 2, 1976, p. 20–21.

Brownlow, Kevin. "Sidney A. Franklin. The Modest Pioneer." *Focus on Film* (London), no. 10, Summer 1972, p. 30–41.

____. *Behind the Mask of Innocence*. New York: Knopf, 1990.

Bruccoli, Matthew J. *F Scott Fitzgerald's Screenplay for "Three Comrades" by Erich Maria Remarque*. Carbondale & Edwardsville, London–Amsterdam: Southern Illinois University Press, Feffer & Simon, 1978.

Brunius, Jacques B. *En marge du cinéma français*. Lausanne (Switzerland): L'Age d'Homme, 1987.

Buache, Freddy. "Hommage à Frank Borzage." *La Cinémathèque Suisse* (Lausanne), no. 115, April 26–May 30, 1993, p. 2–26.

Camper, Fred. "Disputed Passage." *Movies and Methods. An Anthology*. Ed. Bill Nichols. Berkeley, Los Angeles, London: University of California Press, 1976, p. 339–343.

____. "The Shining Hour." *Harvard Film Studies* (Cambridge, Mass.), April 25, 1971, p.1–8.

Carreras Kuntz, Maria Elena de las. "Transformed by Love. The Films of Frank Borzage." *Crisis* (Washington, D.C.), vol. 16, no. 7, July–August 1998, p. 16–21.

Carey, Gary. Lost Films. New York: Museum of Modern Art, 1970.

Carr, Harry. *Los Angeles, City of Dreams*. New York: Appleton, 1935.

Carr, Robert E. and R.M. *Wide Screen Movies*. Jefferson, N.C.–London: McFarland, 1988.

Cohen, Harold W. "In Praise of One of the Cinema's Finest Directors: Borzage Incurably Romantic." *Pittsburgh Post-Gazette*, June 30, 1934.

Coons, Robbin. "Love Scene: A Day's Work with Borzage." *Detroit News*, April 11, 1938.

Cooper, Gary. "Director Frank Borzage as I know him." *Paramount International News Letter* (New York), March 1, 1936.

Coursodon, Jean-Pierre. "Frank Borzage." *American Directors. Vol. 1*. New York: McGraw-Hill Paperbacks, 1983, p. 10–22.

Crawford, Joan (with Jane Kesner Ardmore). *A Portrait of Joan. The Autobiography of Joan Crawford*. New York: Doubleday, 1962.

Croy, Homer. *Our Will Rogers*. New York: Duell, Sloan & Pierce, 1953.

Cuenca, Carlos Fernandez. *Historia del cine*. Madrid : A. Aguado, 1950.

Curtis, James. *James Whale*. Metuchen N.J.–London: Scarecrow Press, 1982.

Danel, Isabelle. "Les beaux mariages : Frank Borzage à la Cinémathèque française." *Télérama* (Paris), no. 2255, March 31, 1993, p. 29–30.

D'Arc, James V. "Silent Film Fest Exhibits Work of Native Salt Laker." *Deseret News* (Salt Lake City), November 5–6, 1992.

DeMille, William C. *Hollywood Saga*. New York: Dutton & Co., 1939.

DeWitt, Bodeen. *More from Hollywood*. S. Brunswick: Barnes, London: Tantivy, 1976.

Dick, Bernard F. *The Star Spangled Screen. The American World War II Film*. Lexington: University Press of Kentucky, 1985.

Dietrich, Marlene. *Marlene*. New York: Avon Books, 1989.

Drew, William M. *Speaking of Silents. First Ladies of the Screen*. New York: Vestal Press, 1989.

Dumont, Etienne. "Cycle Frank Borzage au cinéma de minuit de FR3: La rédouverte d'un mythe." *Tribune de Genève* (Geneva), May 6, 1976.

Dumont, Hervé. "Ayesha et Antinéa. Le mythe de la reine immortelle au cinéma." *L'Ecran fantastique* (Paris), no. 57, June 1985, p. 54–69; no. 58, July 1985, p. 54–69.

____. "Frank Borzage" (Program of the *Filmoteca Española*, Madrid), May 1990.

____. *Frank Borzage — Sarastro à Hollywood*. Paris–Milano (Italy): Cinémathèque française — Edizioni Gabriele Mazzotta, 1993.

____. "Echte Leidenschaft für Menschen: Frank Borzage. Schlüssel zu einer kinematographischen Alchemie." *Film Bulletin* (Winterthur), no. 186, May 1993, p. 48–67.

____. "Hommage an Frank Borzage: Vom Mythos zur Wiederentdeckung." *Filmpodium* (Zurich), May 1993, 2–10.

____. *Frank Borzage. Sarastro en Hollywood*. San Sebastian — Madrid : ed. Festival internacional de cine de Donostia-San Sebastian/Filmoteca Española, 2001 (575 p.).

____. "Borzage-Touch oder Poesie und der Samtglanz der Bilder." *Neue Zürcher Zeitung* (Zurich), November 5, 2004.

Edmonds, I. G. and Reiko Mimura, "Frank Borzage." *The Oscar Directors*. San Diego: A.S. Barnes, 1980.

Erens, Patricia. *The Jew in American Cinema*. Bloomington: Indiana University Press, 1984.

Evans, Delight. "'Not That Kid!'" Frank Borzage Often Receives that Appellation but he Hopes to Live it down." *Photoplay Magazine*, September 1920, p. 42–43, 113.

Everson, William K. *American Silent Films*. New York: Oxford University Press, 1978.

____. *Love in the Film*. Secaucus, NJ: Citadel Press, 1979.

Eyman, Scott. *Mary Pickford, America's Sweetheart*. New York: Donald I. Fine, 1990.

Facey, Paul W. *The Legion of Decency. A Sociological Analysis of the Emergence and Development of a Social Pressure Group*. New York: Arno Press, 1974.

Falk, Max. "La vie mouvementée de Frank Borzage." *Cinémonde* (Paris), no. 73, March 13, 1930, p. 165.

Fernandez, Rick. "Tay Garnett Speaking." *The Velvet Light Trap* (Madison, WI), no. 18, Spring 1978.

Ferney, Frédéric. "Frank Borzage, l'oublié." *Le Figaro* (Paris), April 1, 1993.

Finler, Joel W. "Frank Borzage." *The Movie Directors Story*. London: Octopus Books, 1985, p. 14–15.

Florey, Robert. *Filmland*. Paris: Editions Cinémagazine, 1923.

____. *Hollywood d'hier et d'aujourd'hui*. Paris: Prisma, 1948.

____. *Hollywood années zéro*. Paris: Seghers, 1972.

Forestier, François. "Frank Borzage : mélo, rétro, bravo!" *L'Express* (Paris), April 1, 1993, p. 128–129.

Gabler, Neal. *An Empire of Their Own. How the Jews Invented Hollywood*. New York: Crown, 1988.

Galland, Bertil. "Borzage, géant oublié de Hollywood, est ressuscité par un chercheur de Pully." *Le Nouveau Quotidien* (Lausanne), no. 491, April 29, 1993, p. 3.

Gamble, Olivier. Analysis for 25 films of Frank Borzage, *Guide des films*. Ed. Jean Tulard, 2 vol. Paris: Laffont, 1990.

Garnett, Tay. A. *Light Up Your Torches and Pull Up Your Tights*. New Rochelle: Arlington House, 1973.

Geist, Kenneth I. *Pictures Will Talk. The Life and Films of Joseph L. Mankiewicz*. New York: Scribner's Sons, 1978.

George, Alan. "Frank Borzage: The Man Who Will Make "Cavalcade."" *Picturegoer Weekly* (London), May 21, 1932, p. 11.

Guarner, José Luis. "Cine romántico: Borzage o el triunfo del amor sobre la adversidad." *El cine. Enciclopedia del 7° arte*. San Sebastian : Buru Lan S.A., vol. 4, 1973, p. 130–132 [in French: "Le cinéma romantique:

Frank Borzage: le triomphe de l'amour lyrique." *Encyclopédie alpha du cinéma*. Lausanne (Switzerland): Grammont, vol. 1, 1976, p. 21–23].

Guez, Gilbert. "Frank Borzage, un maître méconnu." *Le Figaro* (Paris), February 7, 1987.

Halliday, Jon. *Sirk on Sirk*. London: Secker & Warburg, 1971.

Hardy, Phil. "Borzage and the Power of Love." *Stars of the Silver Screen*. London: Bloomsbury Book, 1984, p. 256–7.

Hartnoll, Gillian. "Frank Borzage." *World Film Directors, vol. I: 1890–1945*. Ed. John Wakeman. New York: W. Wilson Co., 1987, p. 41–47.

Harvey, Stephen. *Joan Crawford*. New York: Pyramid Press, 1974.

Haskins, Harrison. "The Photoplay of the Proletariat. The Realism of Frank Borzage, director of "Humoresque." is explained." *Motion Picture Classic* (New York), vol. XI, no. 1, September 1920, p. 18, 88.

Hayes, Helen (with Katherine Hatch). *My Life in Three Acts*. New York: Harcourt Brace Jovanovich, 1990.

Heimann, Jim. *Out With The Stars. Hollywood's Nightlife in the Golden Era*. New York: Abbeville Press, 1985.

Henreid, Paul (with Julius Fast). *Ladies' Man. An Autobiography*. New York: St. Martin's Press, 1984.

Higham, Charles. *Hollywood Cameramen: Sources of Light*. Bloomington–London: Indiana University Press, 1970.

_____, and Joel Greenberg. *The Celluloid Muse. Hollywood Directors Speak*. London: Angus & Robertson, 1969.

Horak, Jan-Christopher. *Anti-Nazi-Filme der deutschsprachigen Emigration von Hollywood 1939–1945*. Münster (Germany): MAkS Publikationen, 1984.

_____. "G. W. Pabst in Hollywood." *Film History* (New York), vol. I, no. 1, 1987.

Hosman, Harry. "Frank Borzage, meester van het fijnzinnige melodrama." *De Volkskrant* (Amsterdam), October 5, 1991, p. 13.

Howard, William K. "Ten Famous Directors: Sentimental Borzage." *Film Weekly* (London), June 26, 1937, p. 26.

Hurst, Richard Maurice. *Republic Studios. Between Poverty Row and the Majors*. Metuchen N.J.–London: Scarecrow Press, 1979.

Jameux, Charles B. "Frank Borzage, franc-maçon de Rite Ecossais Ancien et Accepté." *Points de vue initiatiques* (Grande Loge de France, Paris) no. 92/1994, p. 37–46.

Jones, Kent. "The Sanctum Sanctorum of Love: Frank Borzage." *Film Comment* (New York), vol. 33, no. 5, September–October 1997, p. 32–43.

Kirkham, Pat. "Loving Men: Frank Borzage, Charles Farrell and Reconstruction of Masculinity in 1920s Hollywood Cinema." *Me Jane: Masculinity, Movies and Women*. Ed. Pat Kirkham, Janet Thumin. New York: St. Martin's Press, 1995, p. 94–112.

Knorr, Wolfram. "Ein Gralshüter der noblen Love-Story. Reine Liebe in schrecklicher Welt: der US-Regisseur Frank Borzage wird wiederentdeckt." *Die Weltwoche* (Zurich), no. 19, May 13, 1993.

Kobal, John. *Romance & the Cinema*. London: Studio Vista, 1973 (chapter "Some Directors: Frank Borzage." p. 128–131).

Koszarski, Richard. *The Man You Loved to Hate. Erich von Stroheim and Hollywood*. Oxford, New York, Toronto, Melbourne: Oxford University Press, 1983.

Kothenschulte, Daniel. "Frank Borzage. Hollywoods siebter Himmel." *Filmpodium* (Zurich), November 16–December 31, 2004.

Kyrou, Ado. "Heures aveuglantes du film d'amour: Frank Borzage." *Amour-érotisme & cinéma*. Paris: Eric Losfeld/Le Terrain Vague, 1957, p. 361–362. Also Paris: Le Terrain Vague, 1966, p. 214–217.

_____. *Le surréalisme au cinéma*. Paris: Le Terrain Vague, 1965.

Lahue, Kalton C. *Dreams for Sale. The Rise and Fall of the Triangle Film Corporation*. New York: Barnes, 1971.

Lamster, Frederick. *Souls Made Great Through Love and Adversity: The Film Work of Frank Borzage*. Metuchen, NJ & London: Scarecrow Press, 1981.

Landrot, Marine. "Le septième art au septième ciel." *Télérama* (Paris), no. 2289, November 24, 1993, p. 152–153.

Latham, Aaron. *Crazy Sundays. F. Scott Fitzgerald in Hollywood*. London: Secker & Warburg, 1971.

Laurence, Frank M. "Screen Romance: A Farewell to Arms." *Hemingway and the Movies*. New York: Da Capo Press, 1981, p. 41–81.

Lecoultre, Cécile and Bernard Chappuis, "Génie éclipsé, Frank Borzage rayonne à nouveau." *24 Heures* (Lausanne), April 23, 1993, p. 72/*Tribune de Genève* (Geneva), April 24, 1993, p. 35.

Lee, Sonia. "Four Directors Tell What's Wrong with the Movies (Mervyn LeRoy, Frank Borzage, Cecil B. DeMille, Ernst Lubitsch)." *Motion Picture Magazine* (New York), September 1933. Also *Picturegoer Weekly* (London), September 30, 1933, p. 15.

Leff, Leonard J. "A Farewell to Arms and Other Amputations." *Film Comment* (New York), Jan./Feb. 1995, p. 70–73.

Le Puyat, Simon. "Frank Borzage et la télé." *Télériné* (Paris), no. 208, May 1976, p. 19–21.

Lightning, Robert K. "We Have Secrets. Borzage, Romance and the Bourgeois State." *CineAction* (Toronto), no. 46/1998, p. 64–72.

Logan, Joshua. *Josh — My Up and Downs, In and Out Life*. New York: Delacorte, 1976.

Lourcelles, Jacques. *Dictionnaire du cinéma. Les films*. Paris: Laffont, coll. Bouquins, 1992 (six films analyzed).

Lyons, Timothy James. *The Silent Partner. The History of the American Film Manufacturing Company 1910–1921*. New York: Arno Press, 1974.

Mank, Gregory. "Colin Clive 1900–1937." *Films in Review*, May 1980, vol. 31, no.5, p. 257–268.

Marcorelles, Louis. "Toulouse redécouvre Frank Borzage." *Le Monde* (Paris), December 26, 1975, p. 12.

Marías, Miguel. "Lágrimas de Frank Borzage" (Program of the *Filmoteca Española*, Madrid), April 1990 Retrospectiva "Fronteras del melodrama: Frank Borzage."

Marion, Frances. *Off With Their Heads ! A Serio-Comic Tale of Hollywood*. New York: MacMillan, 1972.

Mathis, Jack. "The Making of I've Always Loved You." *Republic Confidential. Vol. 1— The Studio*. Barrington, Ill.: Jack Mathis Advertising, 1999, p. 378–417.

McCarthy, Todd and Charles Flynn, ed. *Kings of the Bs. Working within the Hollywood System. An Anthology of Film History and Criticism*. New York: Dutton & Co., 1975.

McElhaney, Joe. "Frank Borzage: Architect of Ineffable Desires." "Great Directors—A Critical Database" (10 p.), http://www.sensesofcinema.com.

Mees, Francis. "Carte blanche: 13 films de Frank Borzage." *Cinémathèque Municipale, Ville de Luxembourg* (Program), September–October 1984.

Mezzena Lona, A. "Mai concludere in tristezza." *Il Piccolo* (Milano), October 16, 1992.

Milne, Peter. "Some Words from Frank Borzage." *Motion Picture Directing: The Facts and Theories of the Newest Art*. New York: Falk Publishing Co., 1922.

Mitry, Jean. *Histoire du cinéma, tome 3 (1923–1930)*. Paris:

Editions Universitaires, 1973 (chapter "Frank Borzage." p. 436–443).

_____. *Histoire du cinéma, tome 4 (1930–1940)*. Paris: J.-P. Delarge, 1980.

_____. "Rencontre avec … Jean Mitry, à propos de Frank Borzage (dossier)." *Les cahiers de la cinémathèque* (Cinémathèque de Toulouse), Toulouse 1975.

Moullet, Luc. "Borzage." *Cahiers du Cinéma* (Paris), no. 135, September 1962, p. 38.

Negulesco, Jean. *Things I Did and Things I Think I Did*. New York: Linden Press–Simon & Schuster, 1984.

Newquist, Roy. *Conversations with Joan Crawford*. Secaucus N.J.: Citadel Press, 1980.

Oliver, W. E. "Bare Foot Boy Has Golf Yearning." *Los Angeles Evening Herald*, July 18, 1931.

Oms, Marcel. "De quelques thèmes maçonniques dans l'œuvre de D. W. Griffith." *Colloque international D. W. Griffith*. Paris: L'Harmattan, 1984, p. 221–232.

Orriss, Bruce W. *When Hollywood Ruled the Skies. The Aviation Film Classics of World War II*. Hawthorne, Ca.: Aero Associates, 1984.

Parrish, Robert. *Growing Up in Hollywood*. Boston–Toronto: Little, Brown & Co., 1976.

Paulau, Jorge. "Frank Borzage." *Films Selectos* (Madrid), April 23, 1932, p.5.

Peary, Gerald, and Roger Shatzkin, ed. *The Classic American Novel & the Movies. Exploring the Link between Literature and Film*. New York: Ungar, 1977.

Perez, Michel. "Frank Borzage enfin sur grand écran." *Le Matin* (Paris), February 4, 1987.

Pozner, Vladimir. "Hollywood en guerre !." *Cinéma 62* (Paris), no. 64, March 1962.

Pratt, George C. "Frank Borzage." *Image* (Rochester), December 1956, vol.5, no. 10, p. 232–233.

_____. "Frank Borzage to George C. Pratt." George Eastman House, Rochester N.Y., Oral History (tape interview made in Hollywood, April 11, 1958).

_____. "In Search of the Natural: An Interview with Frank Borzage" *Image* (Rochester) 20, nos. 3–4 (September–December 1977), p. 34–43 [excerpts from the tape interview mentioned above].

Quinlan, David. "Frank Borzage." *The Illustrated Guide to Film Directors*. London: Batsford, Ltd., 1983, p. 34–35.

Quirk, Lawrence J. *Margaret Sullavan, Child of Fate*. New York: St. Martin's Press, 1986 (Borzage: pp. 31–35, 86–91, 95–100, 105–108).

Richie, Donald. "Hollywood Veteran: Frank Borzage." *Far East Film News* (Tokyo), June 1959, p. 23.

Riou, Alain. "Cent ans d'amour." *Le Nouvel Observateur* (Paris), no. 383, April 1, 1993, p. 10.

Roek, Anton. "Retrospectief Frank Borzage: Arme sloebers die alle tegenslagen doorstaan." *De Filmkrant* (Amsterdam), October 1991, p. 14.

Roffman, Peter and Jim Purdy. "The Borzage Trilogy." *The Hollywood Social Problem Film*. Bloomington: Indiana University Press, 1981, p. 209–212.

Rosen, Philip. "Difference and Displacement in *7th Heaven*." *Screen* (London), vol. 12, no. 2, Summer 1977, p. 89–104.

Sadoul, Georges. *Histoire du cinéma mondial*. Paris: Flammarion, 1949.

_____. *Dictionnaire des cinéastes*. Paris: Seuil, 1965.

_____. *Dictionnaire des films*. Paris: Seuil (coll. Microcosme), 1965.

_____. *Histoire générale du cinéma*, vol. 3 (1909–1920). Paris: Denoël, 1975.

Sarris, Andrew. "First Takes: Frank Borzage." *Film Culture* (New York), no. 25, Summer 1962, p. 33–34.

_____. "Second Line: Frank Borzage." *Film Culture* (New York), no. 28, Spring 1963, p. 11 ("American Directors Issue").

_____. "Borzage 'Eyewash' or Art?" *The Village Voice* (New York), August 16, 1973, p. 6162, 67.

_____. "Frank Borzage." *Cinema: A Critical Dictionary. The Major Film-Makers*. Ed. Richard Roud. London: Secker & Warburg, 1980, p. 136–141.

Savio, Francesco. "Frank Borzage." *Enciclopedia dello spettacolo*. Rome (Italy): Le Maschere, 1954, p. 863–864.

Scheuer, Philip K. "Borzage Gazes at World through Tear-Filled Eyes." *Los Angeles Times*, January 8, 1933.

Schlappner, Martin. "Die romantische Kraft des Alltags. Zur Retrospektive von Frank Borzage im Zürcher Filmpodium." *Neue Zürcher Zeitung* (Zurich), May 7, 1993.

Schneider, Hans W. "Vier Schweizer machen einen Film in Hollywood." *Schweizer Film-Zeitung* (Berne, Switz.), no. 102, January 24, 1942, p.5.

Shapiro, Burton J. "Frank Borzage." *The American Film Heritage (Impressions from the American Film Institute Archives)*. Ed. Kathleen Karr. Washington: Acropolis Books, 1972, p. 172–175.

Sheehan, Henry. "Love in Bloom — Borzage." *The Boston Phoenix*, January 22, 1985, p. 2, 10–11.

Siclier, Jacques. "Les amants de lumière. Une rétrospective Frank Borzage donne l'occasion de réparer un injuste oubli." *Le Monde* (Paris), March 31, 1993, p. 21.

Smith, Robert. "The Films of Frank Borzage." *Bright Lights* (Ohio), part I: vol.1 no.2 (Spring 1975), p. 4–13, part II: vol.1 no.3 (Summer 1975), p. 15–21.

Spalek, J. M. and J. Strelka, ed. *Deutsche Exilliteratur seit 1933, 1. Kalifornien*. Bern (Switzerland)–Munich (Germany): A. Francke-Verlag, 1976.

Stack, Robert (with Mark Evans). *Straight Shooting*. New York: Macmillan, 1980.

Stallings, Penny. *Flesh and Fantasy*. New York: Harper & Row, 1978.

Sterling, Bryan B.; Will, Frances N. *Will Rogers in Hollywood*. New York: Crown, 1984.

Sternberg, Josef von. *Fun in a Chinese Laundry*. New York: Macmillan, 1965.

Swanson, Gloria. *Swanson on Swanson*. New York: Random House, 1980.

Swindell, Larry. *Spencer Tracy. A Biography*. New York: Signet Boot, New American Library, 1971.

_____. *The Reluctant Lover: Charles Boyer*. New York: Doubleday, 1983.

Tavernier, Bertrand and Jean-Pierre Coursodon, "Frank Borzage." *50 ans de cinéma américain*. Paris: Nathan, 1991, p. 301–306.

Tazelaar, Marguerite. "Two Directors Discuss Hollywood: Frank Borzage and Robert Florey." *New York Herald Tribune*, March 5, 1933.

Thomas, Dan. "Borzage called Easiest of All Hollywood Directors." *Dispatch* (Columbus), January 26, 1937.

Thomson, David. *America in the Dark. Hollywood and the Gift of Unreality*. New York: Morrow & Co., 1977.

Tulard, Jean, ed. *Guide des Films*. Paris: Laffont, 1990.

Tully, Jim. "Frances Marion." *Vanity Fair* (New York), January 1927, p. 63.

_____. "Frank BorzageThe Eleventh of a Series of Interviews with Prominent Motion Picture Personages." *Vanity Fair* (New York) vol. 27, no. 6, February 1927, p.50, 96.

Turconi, Davide. "Frank Borzage." *Filmlexicon degli autori e delle opere*. Roma (Italy): Bianco e Nero, 1958, p. 796–798.

_____. "Borzage, una storia d'amore-il più ignorato fra i

'classici.'" *Segnocinema* (Vicenza), no. 27, March 1987, p. 30–31.

Turnbull, Andrew, ed. *The Letters of F. Scott Fitzgerald*. New York: Scribner, 1963.

Veillon, Olivier-René. "Frank Borzage." *Le cinéma américain. Les années trente*. Paris: Seuil, 1986, p. 11–22.

Viviani, Christian. "Margaret Sullavan: un visage dans la foule." *Positif* (Paris), no. 183/184, p. 29–35.

Waintrop, Edouard. "Borzage, l'amour maçon." *Libération* (Paris), April 1, 1993, p. 39.

Walker, Alexander. *Joan Crawford, the Ultimate Star*. London: Weidenfeld & Nicolson, 1983.

Walsh, Raoul. *Each Man in His Time. The Life Story of a Director*. New York: Farrar, Straus & Giroux, 1974.

Watts, Richard, Jr. "Notes in Praise of Several Virtues of *7th Heaven*." *New York Herald Tribune*, June 5, 1927.

Whitaker, Alma. "Dietrich More Than a Trilby, Says Borzage." *Los Angeles Times*, March 8, 1936.

Willemen, Paul. "Frank Borzage." *National Film Theatre* (British Film Institute) Booklet, May–August 1975, p. 2–8.

Wolverton, Joseph. "Frank Borzage American Romantic" (Melnitz Theater Program, *University of California, Los Angeles [U.C.L.A.]*), April 10–June 6, 1987.

Yost, Robert M. "Where Do Movie Stories Come From? An Interview with Director Frank Borzage." *Los Angeles Times*, December 3, 1927.

Collective Issues

"Frank Borzage" (Special Issue, 54 pages). *Focus* (Chicago), no.9, Spring–Summer 1973, with texts by: John Belton, Michael Mahern, David Kehr, Terry Curtis Fox, Burton J. Shapiro and Fred Camper.

"Frank Borzage" (Special Issue). *Positif* (Paris), no. 183/184, July–August 1976: Michael Henry, "Le Fra Angelico du mélodrame" (p. 13–19); Jacques Segond, "De Cendrillon à Ophélie" (p. 20–27); Jean-Loup Bourget, "Au ciel j'irai la voir un jour" (p. 6–12); Christian Viviani, "Margaret Sullavan: un visage dans la foule" (p. 28–35).

Frank Borzage-meester van het melodrama. Amsterdam: Nederlands Filmmuseum-themareeks, no. 1, October 1991 (35 p.), with texts by Hervé Dumont: "Frank Borzage: De herontdekking van een mythe" (p. 6–16); Eric de Kuyper, "Frank Borzage: Regisseur en auteur." "Voor een archeologie van gevoelens" (p. 17–33).

"Frank Borzage" (special Pordenone issue) *Griffithiana* (La Cineteca del Friuli, Gemona, Italy), no. 45, December 1992, 144 p., Italian/English texts by: Davide Turconi, "The Silent Films of Frank Borzage" (p. 4–87); Hervé Dumont, "Jacob's Ladder, or Love and Adversity" (p. 88–114); Richard Koszarski, "Ernest Palmer on Frank Borzage and F.W. Murnau" (p. 115–130); Harrison Haskins, "The Photoplay of the Proletariat" (p. 127–130); Peter Milne," Some Words from Frank Borzage" (p. 131–135).

"Dossier Frank Borzage" *Positif* (Paris), no. 386, April 1993, p. 79–103, texts by: Yann Tobin, "Les voyages fantastiques de Frank Borzage" (p. 81–82); Michael Henry Wilson, "Frank Borzage ou les ailes du désir" (p. 83–91); Jean-Loup Bourget, "L'onde et la flamme" (p. 92–94), "Romantique ou maçonnique?" (p. 97); Hubert Niogret, "Une rencontre exceptionnelle: Frank Borzage et Norma Talmadge" (p. 95–99) and Jean-Pierre Berthomé.

Unsigned articles (in chronological order)

"Motography Gallery of Picture Players: Frank Borzage." *Motography*, October 17, 1914, p. 535.

"Popular Photoplayers: Frank Borzage." *Photoplay Magazine*, December 1914, p. 14.

"Brief Biographies of Popular Players: Frank Borzage." *Motion Picture Supplement*, October 1915, p. 61.

"Frank Borzage Wins High Place as Director." *Photoplay Art* (Los Angeles), no. 2, August 1916, p. 10.

"Borzage's Rise to Directorship Result of Experience and Work." *The Moving Picture World*, April 3, 1920, p. 116.

"Frank Borzage, Director of *Humoresque*: Appeal in Hurst Novel." *The Moving Picture World*, May 20, 1920, p. 1070.

"Borzage Talks to Associated Motion Picture Advertisers." *The Moving Picture World*, June 12, 1920, p. 1496.

"Frank Borzage." *Action française* (Paris), June 6, 1930.

"How Films Should Be Made. Directors, Like Cooks, Can't Agree on Recipes for Films. 'Make Them Simply' Says Frank Borzage. 'Make Them Hot' Says Mervyn LeRoy." *Los Angeles Times*, December 3, 1933.

"Acting Is Not Acting, Says Frank Borzage. Interview with Director of *Little Man, What Now?*" *Today's News from Universal* (London), May 24, 1934.

"Frank Borzage es un modelo de directores." *La Opinion* (Los Angeles), July 8, 1934.

"Frank Borzage contra el diálogo en los films." *Cinegramas* (Madrid), no. 96, July 12, 1936.

"Borzage Shatters Many Film Rules." *New York World Telegram*, April 3, 1937, p. 7A.

"Frank Borzage Speaks." *Metro-Goldwyn-Mayer Studio News*, vol.7, no. 2, February 2, 1940, p.7.

"Frank Borzage: Easy Does It." *The Lion's Roar Magazine* (M-G-M), no. 2, 1941, p. 28.

"Frank Borzage s'avoue un fervent adepte du procédé Technicolor." *Ciné-Suisse* (Berne, Switz.), no. 224, May 24, 1945.

"Frank Borzage." *Current Biography* (New York), vol. 7, no. 11, December 1946, p. 9–11.

"Must Revive Showmanship To Sell Pictures, Says Borzage." *Hollywood Reporter*, June 17,1947, p. 6.

"Frank Borzage: Unique Career" (obituary). *Variety*, June 27, 1962.

"Mr. Frank Borzage, Film Director of Romantic Drama" (obituary). *The Times* (London), June 20, 1961.

"UCLA'S Frank Borzage Film Retrospective. Love Affair: Frank Borzage and His Influence (Nov. 1–29, 2003) (9 p.), on line: http://www.reelclassics.com.

Index

A Nous la Liberté 208
Abel, Walter 162, 242
Adair, Josephine 87
Adrian 190, 254
After Tomorrow 19, 81, 171–173
Against All Flags 5
The Age of Desire 87
Agel, Henri 5, 12, 125, 155, 193, 206, 214, 226, 331
Aherne, Brian 304
Akins, Zoë 95
All Quiet on the Western Front 210, 218
Ameche, Don 333
Anderson, Gene 323
Ankers, Evelyn 310
Antoine, André 208, 214
Aoki, Tsuru 39, 40, 65
The Arab 95
Aragon, Louis 124
Arlen, Richard 112
Armetta, Henry 130
Arnaud, Michel J. 139
Arnold, Jack 288
Around the World in 80 Days 408ch18n5
Arthur, Jean 244, 246, 248
Astor, Gertrude 88
L'Atalante 206
Atkins, Zoë 345
L'Atlantide 356
Atwill, Lionel 262
Auer, Mischa 184
August, Joseph H. 199
Auriol, Jean George 4, 135, 144, 203

Back Pay 19, 102
Bad Girl 19, 81, 106, 167–171, 194, 207
Bainter, Fay 269
Baker, Bob 10
Ball, Lucille 332
Bankhead, Tallulah 308
Banks, Lionel 335
Banton, Travis 238
The Barbarian and the Geisha 5
Bard, Ben 115
Bardèche, Maurice 155
Barker, Reginald 39, 101
Barnes, Binnie 321
Barrymore, Ethel 335, 340
Basevi, James 97
Battista, Miriam 78

Baumann, Charles 37, 39
Baxter, Warner 166
The Beast of Berlin 285, 301
Beaton, Welford 29, 122, 142, 154
Beaudine, William 58
Beaumont, Harry 106
Behrman, S. N. 159, 174
Bell, Monta 97
Bellamy, Madge 25, 101, 104, 105, 107, 111, 395ch6n2
Belton, John 5, 12, 22, 132, 188, 237, 277, 282, 292, 330, 350
Bénard da Costa, Joao 152, 271, 331
Ben-Hur 94, 97
Bennett, Joan 166
Benoit, Pierre 356
Bergman, Ingrid 312
Besier, Rudolf 88, 192
Besserer, Eugenie 99
Beylie, Claude 11, 17, 136, 267
Bezzerides, A.I. 344
Big City 251–253
The Big Fisherman 22, 24, 351–355
The Big Trail 157
Billy Jim 66, 78
Billy the Kid 303–304
Bing, Hermann 110
The Bitter Tea of General Yen 197
Blanke, Henry (Heinrich) 242
Blonde Venus 81
Boardman, Eleanor 97, 176
Boisset, Yves 3
Bond, Ward 347, 348
Booth, John Hunter 146
Borden, Olive 127
Borzage, Bill (William Felix) 12, 32, 146, 336, 351, 352, 392ch1n4
Borzage, Daniel (Dan, Danny) 32, 34, 70, 102, 146, 351, 352, 392ch1n8
Borzage, Dolly 32, 113, 131, 289
Borzage, Frank, Jr. 196, 392ch1n3
Borzage, Henry 31, 32, 196, 351, 392ch1n3
Borzage, Juanita *see* Moss, Juanita
Borzage, Lew 32, 34, 70, 95, 102, 107, 113, 174, 197, 209, 218, 241, 251, 290, 323, 343, 346, 351, 352, 356, 392ch1n8, 408ch18n5
Borzage (Borzaga), Luigi 31, 32, 113, 196, 218, 392ch1n6
Borzage, Madeline 32, 113, 196, 392ch1n3

Borzage (Borzaga-Ruegg), Maria 31, 32, 113, 196, 392ch1n6
Borzage, Mary 196, 392ch1n3, n4
Borzage, Raymond 147, 173, 392ch1n4
Borzage, Rena (Lorena) 57, 78, 102, 194, 195, 289, 343, 393ch1n14, 405ch1n19
Borzage, Susan (Sue) 32, 131, 289
Borzage, William H. 392ch1n3
Bottome, Phyllis 284, 285, 287, 298
Bourget, Jean-Loup 23, 208, 247
Boussinot, Roger 189
Boyer, Charles 165, 244–246, 257
Brasillach, Robert 155
Breakston, George André 209, 211
Bredell, Woody 311
Breen, Joseph I. 177, 228, 238, 260, 282, 318
Brenon, Herbert 134
Brent, George 230, 233
Bressart, Felix 324, 326
Breton, André 3, 124
Brion, Patrick 4, 22, 301
Briskin, Sam 208
Britton, Barbara 312, 313, 318
Brockwell, Gladys 115
Broken Lullaby 176
Brown, Clarence 134, 195, 285, 309, 357
Brown, Gilmore 35
Brownlow, Kevin 7, 75, 114, 290
Brunius, Jacques B. 144
Buache, Freddy 6
Bull, Orville O. (Bunny) 95
Burke, Edwin 171
Butler, David 39, 113, 154, 357
Butler, Jimmy 209, 211
Byington, Spring 306

Cabaret 294
Das Cabinett des Dr. Caligari 152
Calhoun, Rory 344
Camper, Fred 12, 273, 276
Canutt, Yakima 333
Capra, Frank 13, 18, 86, 197, 215
Captain Kid 320
Carillo, Leo 246
Carné, Marcel 3, 154
Carr, Harry 31
Carroll, Nancy 176
Carter, William 324
Cavalcade 174

Chandler, Jeff 34
Chaplin, Charles 75, 77, 86, 134, 285
Chase, Borden 324, 407ch17n12
Chatterton, Ruth 176
Chautard, Emile 113
Children of Dust 19, 343
China Doll 2, 13, 17, 312, 346–351, 408ch18n11
Chotin, André 112
Christmas Holiday 309
The Circle 97–99
City Girl 135
Clair, René 208
Clark, Dane 335, 337, 338
Clarke, Kenneth B. 95
Clive, Colin 244, 245
Clothier, William H. 9, 346
The Code of Honour 53
Cody, Lew 78, 80
Coffee, Lenore 312, 406ch16n17
Cohan, George Michael 76
Cohen, Emanuel 176
Cohn, Harry 197, 208, 209, 214, 215
Colbert, Claudette 176
Collier, William, Jr. 87
Collier, William, Sr. 172, 274
Confessions of a Nazi Spy 285
Connelly, Bobby 72
Connolly, Bobby 229
Conway, Jack 58, 99
Cooper, Gary 25, 29, 176, 178–180, 184, 185, 190, 197, 235, 239
Cooper, Merian C. 13
Cornell, Katharine 308
Costello, Dolores 111
Coursodon, Jean-Pierre 4, 11, 182, 282
The Courtin' of Calliope Crew 53
Coward, Noel 174
Cowl, Jane 304
Craven, Frank 106
Crawford, Joan 97, 98, 111, 251, 254, 256–258, 268, 269, 270, 272, 278–280
Crisp, Donald 13
Croisset, Francis de 189
Cromwell, John 176
Crosby, Bing 195
Crowther, Bosley 300
Croy, Homer 156
Cruze, James 134
The Cup of Life 41
The Curse of Iku 65
Curtis, Alan 254, 257
Curtis, Jack 58, 60, 393ch3n3
Curtiz, Michael 159, 227, 351
Curwood, James Oliver 78

Daddy's Gone a-Hunting 95–97, 102, 343
Dandridge, Dorothy 356
Daniels, William 343, 357
Darling, William 171
Darro, Frankie 209
Daves, Delmer 74, 229, 234, 308, 357
Davidson, Dore 70, 78

Davies, Marion 68, 75, 230, 233, 240, 241
Daw, Marjorie 81
The Day I Met Caruso 27, 343, 345–346
Day Is Done 344
Days of Youth 124
De Cuir, John 352
Delmar, Viña 167, 170
DeMille, Cecil B. 13, 42, 134, 197, 249, 342, 405ch15n47
DeMille, William C. 44
The Demon of Fear 53
Dempsey, Jack 252
Descher, Sandy 345
Desire 17,28, 29, 208, 235–240
Desmond, William 64
De Vinna, Clyde 252
Dick, Bernard F. 318
Dieterle, William 199, 227, 230
Dietrich, Marlene 9, 235, 238–240
Disney, Walt 111, 195, 284, 351
Disputed Passage 74, 274–278, 348
Dix, Richard 195
The Dixie Merchant 107
Doctor's Wives 166–167
Donlevy, Brian 303
Dorn, Philip 324, 326, 327, 334
d'Orsay, Fifi 156, 157
Doucet, Catherine 221
Douchet, Jean 354
Douglas, Lloyd C. 229, 241, 242, 244, 274, 276, 277, 351, 353, 408ch18n22
Douglas, Melvyn 270, 278
Dove, Billy 76
Dozier, William M. 284
Dreier, Hans 177
Driscoll, Bobby 344
The Duke of Chimney Butte 66
Duncan, Mary 127, 135, 138, 141, 144, 397ch8n4
Dunn, James 167, 169, 171
Durbin, Deanna 307, 309, 310
Dvorak, Ann 342
Dwan, Allan 38, 58, 68, 101, 323

Earhart, Amelia 26
Early to Wed 107, 170
Eason, "Breezy" Reeves 320
Edginton, May 88, 192
Edison, Thomas A. 37
Edwards, Walter 39, 41
Eilers, Sally 167, 169, 171, 358
Eisenstein, Sergei M. 3, 75
Eisler, Hanns 319
Epstein, Julius 232
Erickson, A.F. 144
Everson, William K. 124, 136

Fairbanks, Douglas, Jr. 13, 192
Falk, Max 34
Fall, Leo 159
Fall, Richard 159, 160, 162
Fallada, Hans 216, 218, 225, 401ch11n44
Fanck, Arnold 80
A Farewell to Arms 3, 13, 16, 17, 18,

19, 20, 23, 24, 26, 29, 96, 112, 175–189, 207, 228
Farrell, Charles 15, 112, 114, 118, 121, 125, 127, 130, 133, 138, 141,146, 149, 150, 154, 159, 161, 164, 166, 171, 172, 195, 298, 343
Farrell, Glenda 201
Farrow, John 335
Faust 147
Fawcett, George 98, 99
Fegté, Ernst 325
Feld, Fritz 324
Feldman, Charles K. 335
Fenton, Leslie 102
Fields, W.C. 13
The First Year 101, 106, 170
Fisher, Terence 3
Fitzgerald, Scott F. 81, 258–261, 267, 268, 403ch13n21
Fitzroy, Emily 92, 102, 108, 157
Fleming, Victor 134, 155, 195, 250, 251
A Flickering Light 52
Flight Command 302–303
Flirtation Walk 229
Florey, Robert 38, 88, 112, 228, 284
Flying Colors 64
Flynn, Emmet J. 111
Flynn, Errol 230, 242, 244
Folsey, George 22, 254
Ford, John 4, 19, 34, 75, 86, 100, 101, 102, 110, 113, 119, 128, 173, 322, 323, 357
The Forgotten Prayer 53
The Four Devils 127, 135, 145
Four Sons 75, 112, 128, 135
Fox, William 37, 100–102, 110, 111, 142, 145, 159
Francis, Kay 228, 230–233, 234
Frankenstein 218
Franklin, Chester M. 88
Franklin, Sydney A. 286, 288–290, 304, 305
Freund, Karl 261
Froeschel, George 286
Fuller, Samuel 3

Gable, Clark 13, 278, 279
Gamble, Olivier 331
Garfield, John 335
Garland, Judy 306
Garmes, Lee 355
Garnett, Tay 9, 195, 251, 343, 344, 357
Garrett, Oliver H.P. 176
Gaudio, Tony 90, 93, 325
Gautier, Catherine 6
Gaynor, Janet 15, 29, 102, 111, 112, 114, 118, 121, 122, 124, 127, 128, 130, 133, 146, 149, 150, 154, 159, 166, 289, 357
Gerber, Neva 43
Get-Rich-Quick-Wallingford 76
The Ghost River 65
Gibbons, Cedric 97
Gilbert, John 235
Glass, Gaston 69, 241
Glazer, Benjamin 112, 114, 122, 159, 176, 183, 189, 395ch7n5, n12

Gliese, Rochus 110
Godard, Jean-Luc 124
Goldbeck, Willis 357
Golden, John 101, 111, 171
Gombell, Minna 172
The Good Provider 78
Goosson, Stephen 198
Gordon, Alex 136
Gordon, Vera 69, 71, 72, 78
Goulding, Alf 97
Goulding, Edmund 99, 135
Gran, Albert 113
Grant, Marshall 335
Granville, Bonita 295, 405ch15n32
Grayson, Kathryn 306, 307
The Great Dictator 285, 301
The Great Waltz 274
Greed 95
The Green Light 23, 241–244
Greene, Graham 240, 276
Gréville, Edmond T. 357
Grey, Virginia 358
Griffith, D.W. 13, 58, 78, 86, 218
Griffith, Richard 11
Guénon, René 13, 15, 126
Guinan, Texas 61, 62, 63
The Gun Woman 61–64, 79, 317
Gyssling, Georg 258, 260

Haas, Charles 335, 407ch17n26
Hackathorne, George 92, 93
Haines, Donald 211
Hale, Alan 221, 223
Hale, Alan, Jr. 345
Hale, Creighton 97, 106
Hall, Mordaunt 132, 165, 175, 225
Hallelujah, I'm a Bum 206
Harareet, Haya 356
Hardwicke, Sir Cedric 243
Hardy, Oliver 13
Hardy, Sam 76
Hart, William S. 41
Havilland, Olivia de 242
Havoc 119
Hawks, Howard 86, 101, 195
Hayakawa, Sessue 39, 40, 81, 194
Hayes, Helen 26, 29, 30, 176, 177, 180, 189, 197, 289, 308, 399ch10n13
Hays, Will H. 160, 208, 217, 219, 228
Hazard, Lawrence S. 198, 254, 259, 278
He Who Gets Slapped 95
Hearst, William Randolph 67–69, 75, 81, 230, 240
Hearts Divided 76, 240–241
Heflin, Van 307
Helm, Brigitte 235
Hemingway, Ernest 175–177, 183, 184, 186, 188
Henreid, Paul 319–321
Hepburn, Katharine 308
Herczeg, Ferenc 307
Hertz, David 259
His Butler's Sister 23, 75, 309–311
History Is Made at Night 17, 23, 102, 118, 237, 244–249
Hitler, Adolf 208, 240, 259, 260, 261, 285, 288
Hobart, Rose 159–161, 163, 166

Hoffe, Monckton 127
Hoffenstein, Samuel 309
An Honest Man 64
How the West Was Won 5
Howard, John 274, 275
Howard, Leslie 28, 185, 190, 192, 240, 242
Howard, William K. 3, 155
Howe, James Wong 171
Hua, Li Li 346, 347, 348, 349, 408ch18n11
Hull, Josephine 172
Humoresque 19, 24, 68–75, 78, 122, 268, 343
Hunt, Marsha 307
Hunter, Ian 278, 280
Hurst, Fanny 68, 69, 74, 76–78, 81, 85
Hurst, R.M. 331
Hussey, Ruth 303
Huston, John 5, 342
Hutchinson, Samuel S. 43, 44
Hyer, Martha 352
Hyman, Bernard 286

I Take This Woman 25, 273
Idiot's Delight 285
Immediate Lee 57
Ince, Thomas Harper 37–39, 41, 43, 58, 76, 78, 86
Ingram, Rex (actor) 335, 337, 338
Ingram, Rex (director) 95, 391n24
Innocent's Progress 61
The Iron Horse 101, 102
Isn't Life Wonderful? 218
Iturbi, José 324
Ivano, Paul 114, 127, 344, 395ch6n10
I've Always Loved You 2, 27, 158, 311, 324–331, 333

Jack 52
Jackson, Felix 308, 309
Jacobs, Arthur H. 86
Jacobs, Lewis 3
Jacobson, Arthur 29
The Jazz Singer 75, 122
Jeanne Eagels 346
Johnson, Lorimer 54
Johnson Young, Rida 240
Joly, Jacques 354
Jones, Buck 100–103, 105, 106
Journey Beneath the Desert 356
Joyce, Alice 95, 157

Kane, Joseph 324
Kanin, Garson 335
Karger, Maxwell 159
Keaton, Buster 88
Keel, Howard 351, 352
Keeler, Ruby 229, 234
Kehr, David 341
Kelly, Pat 347
Kenyon, Doris 174
Kerry, Norman 65, 76
Kessel, Adam 37, 39
King, Bradley 109
King, Henry 58, 114, 115, 124, 134, 155, 159, 195, 358

King, Joseph (Joe) 59, 78
Kleiner Mann, was nun? 216
Kobal, John 290
Koerner, Charles 319
Kohner, Paul 286
Kohner, Susan 351, 354
Korda, Alexander 155
Koster, Henry 306
Krasna, Norman 251
Kreisler, Fritz 75
Krims, Milton 242
Kyrou, Ado 4, 11, 16, 124, 144, 342

La Cava, Gregory 68, 229, 284
Ladd, Alan 335
The Lady 5, 91–94, 109
Lady Windermere's Fan 98
Laemmle, Carl, Jr. 37, 215, 216, 218
Lamarr, Hedy 273
Lambert, Gavin 334
Lamour, Dorothy 274
Lamster, Frederick 5, 16, 294, 330, 350
Land o' Lizards 54–56
Lang, Charles B. 30, 184, 235
Lang, Fritz 159, 160, 163, 164, 165, 244, 251, 323
Langlois, Henri 4
La Reno, Richard "Dick" 48, 51, 52
La Rue, Jack 182
The Last Laugh 110
Laughton, Charles 153
Laurence, Frank M. 399ch10n18
Lazybones 19, 94, 101–106, 207, 343
Lee, Frankie 87
Lee, Rowland V. 101, 198, 320, 325, 332, 351, 352
Leisen, Mitchell 343
Leonard, Robert Z. 42, 68, 304
LeRoy, Mervyn 227, 357
Lesser, Sol 308, 358
Levee, Michael (Mike) C. 197, 394ch5n2
Levien, Sonya 145, 159, 174, 346
Lewis, David 311
Lewis, Sinclair 285
Life's Harmony 53
Liliom 17, 23, 26,159–166, 207, 209, 340
Lindbergh, Charles 290
Lindsay, Margaret 244
Linow, Ivan 135
Little, Anna 48, 51, 53, 54, 56
Little Man, What Now? 17, 23, 29, 81, 82, 158, 215–226
Litvak, Anatole 285
Living on Velvet 1, 23, 230–233, 312
Livingstone, Margaret 107
Lloyd, Frank 174
Lloyd, Harold 38
Logan, Jacqueline 106
Logan, Joshua 245
Lom, Herbert 351, 355
Loos, Anita 278
Loren, Sophia 209
Lorentz, Pare 189
Lorre, Peter 278

Louise, Anita 242
Lourcelles, Jacques 12, 15, 20
Love, Bessie 111
Loves of Carmen 112, 119
Lubin, Arthur 358
Lubitsch, Ernst 98, 134, 176, 194, 195, 235–237, 309, 314
Lucky Star 3, 5, 11, 16, 19, 23, 24, 27, 74, 83, 86, 134, 145–154, 207, 292
Lyons, Chester A. 76, 77, 95, 98, 147, 160

MacArthur, Charles 273
MacDonald, J. Farrell 107
MacDonald, Jeanette 304, 305, 306, 357
MacDonald, Wallace 92
Mack, William 34
MacKenna, Kenneth 190, 284
MacMurray, Fred 195, 342, 343
The Magic Flute (Mozart) 14–16, 126, 142
Magnificent Doll 332–333
Magnificent Obsession 229
Make Way for Tomorrow 193
Mamoulian, Rouben 176, 194, 235, 343, 357
The Man Who Came Back 166
Mankiewicz, Herman J. 319
Mankiewicz, Joseph L. 251, 253, 258–261, 267, 269, 278, 280, 282, 283, 291, 342, 403ch13n22
Mann, Klaus 299
Mann, Margaret 135
Mannequin 1, 23, 251, 254–257
Mannix, Eddie 251, 259, 289, 358
Manpower 147
Man's Castle 3, 13, 16, 17, 18, 19, 20, 23, 24, 27, 50, 76, 106, 118, 136, 158, 162, 170, 173, 198–209, 221, 228, 247, 347
Mansouri, Lotfi 345, 408ch18n7
Mantz, Paul Albert 303, 406ch16n2
March, Fredric 176
Marido y Mujer 171
Marion, Frances 67–69, 75, 76, 81, 88, 91, 101, 106, 111, 112, 189, 190, 393ch4n1
Marmont, Percy 95
Marriage License? 108–110
Marshall, Virginia 102
Marx, Zeppo 229
Mascolo, Dyonis 125
The Masked Bride 99
Matchin' Jim 53
Mature, Victor 346, 347, 348, 349, 350
Maugham, Somerset W. 97, 99
Mayer, Edwin Justus 235
Mayer, Louis B. 13, 94, 122, 250, 251, 258, 260, 273, 282, 284, 302
McCarey, Leo 18, 155, 193
McCarthy, Joseph 333
McCormack, John 157
McCormick, John 86
McCrea, Joel 112
McDonald, Francis J. 38, 62, 63, 351

McGregor, Malcolm 97
McLaglen, Andrew 358
McLeod, Catherine 324–326, 329, 330, 333, 334
McRae, Henry 101
Meller, Raquel 133
Mellor, William C. 276
Menjou, Adolphe 178
Menken, Helen 111, 122
Menzies, William Cameron 93
Meredith, Burgess 332
The Merry Widow 99
Milestone, Lewis 197, 198, 218, 229, 323
Milland, Ray 312
Miller, David 304
Milne, Tom 132, 184
Minnelli, Vincente 18
Mitry, Jean 4, 11, 23, 122, 142, 209, 212
Mix, Tom 13, 101
Mizoguchi, Kenji 18, 106
A Modern Hero 174, 227
Molnár, Férenc 159, 165, 209
Montgomery, Douglass 218, 219, 225
Moonrise 26, 334–341, 342
Moore, Colleen 81, 82, 84, 86
Moore, Matt 76, 106, 107
Moreno, Antonio 357
Morgan, Frank 286, 288, 306
A Mormon Maid 42
Morrison, Carl, Chick & Peter 44
Morrison, James 82
Morrison, Robert E. 346
The Mortal Storm 2, 17, 19, 23, 80, 284–301
Mosher, John 300
Moss, Juanita 6, 343, 344, 356, 357, 358
Mother Knows Best 145
Moullet, Luc 331
Mowbray, Alan 223
Mozart, Wolfgang Amadeus 14–16
Mulhall, Jack 66
Muni, Paul 159, 227
Murfin, Jane 270, 304
Murnau, Friedrich Wilhelm 18, 22, 110, 112–115, 127, 134, 135, 145, 147, 160, 315, 395ch6n11
Murphy, Audie 13
Mussolini, Benito 34, 133, 145, 183, 188, 214
Mussolini, Vittorio 260
My Man Godfrey 206

Nablo, James Benson 346
Nash, Ogden 270
Nedell, Bernard 112
Negulesco, Jean 19, 27, 34, 74, 183, 184, 188
Neilan, Marshall 97, 99, 189
Nell Dale's Men Folks 53
A New England Idyll 39
Newman, Alfred 190
Newquist, Roy 254
Niblo, Fred 134
The Night of the Hunter 153
Niven, David 332

Nixon, Marian 172
No Greater Glory 19, 23, 27, 28, 198, 209–215, 343
Noerdlinger, Henry S. 287
Novak, Jane 102
Novak, Kim 346
Novalis 11
The Nth Commandment 19, 81–85, 106, 170
Nugent, Frank S. 245
Nugget Jim's Pardner 48–50
Nye, Gerald P. 290

O'Brien, Edmund 344
O'Brien, Eugene 88
O'Brien, George 112
Odets, Clifford 251
O'Hara, Mary 87
O'Hara, Maureen 312, 319–322
Oland, Warner 81
Oliver, Harry 113, 115, 117, 122, 127, 133, 135, 136, 146, 157, 160, 166
Oms, Marcel 13, 125
One Increasing Purpose 107
Ophuls, Max 22, 93
Orsay, Fifi d' 156, 167
Our Daily Bread 135, 145
Ouspenskaya, Maria 286, 324, 404ch15n6
Owen, Seena 76
Ozu, Yasujiro 18, 124

Pabst, G. W. 120, 227, 228
Païni, Dominique 6
Palmer, Ernest 109, 113–115, 127, 133, 395ch7n8
Pandora's Box 128
The Panther 40
Paramore, Edward E. 259
Parrish, Robert 244
Parsons, Louella 289
Party Girl 4
Pasternak, Joseph 306, 307, 309
Pay Back 76–77
Penod, Pascal 346
People on Sunday 84
Pereira, Marcel 6
Perry, Kathryn 106, 107
Philbin, Mary 87
Phillips, Eddie 81
Pichel, Irving 312
Pickford, Mary 28, 111, 174, 189, 190, 192, 193, 231, 343
Pidgeon, Walter 108, 273, 302
The Pilgrim 50–52
Pinthus, Kurt 299
The Pitch o' Chance 44–48, 153
Pitts, ZaSu 102, 106
Polly of the Circus 249
Powell, Dick 195, 229, 234, 240, 241
Pozner, Vladimir 335
Prado, José Maria 6
Pratt, George 65, 185, 343, 351
Previn, André 325
The Pride of Palomar 19, 81
Professor Mamlock 286
Prudence on Broadway 65

The Quicksands of Deceit 53
The Quiet Man 322
Quirk, Lawrence J. 288

Rabagliati, Alberto 127
Rabourdin, Dominique 106
Rainer, Louise 251, 252, 253
Rains, Claude 240
Raintree County 5
Ralston, Vera 323
Rambeau, Marjorie 198
Rameau, Paul Hans 286
Rapée, Ernö 122, 144
Rapf, Harry 95, 97
Rapper, Irving 74
Rasch, Albertina 25
Ratoff, Gregory 124
Ray, Nicholas 4
Raymond, Gene 304
Reicher, Hedwig 147
Reid, Margaret 95
Reid, Wallace 38
Reinhardt, Elizabeth 309
Reinhardt, Max 230
Reisch, Walter 307
Remarque, Erich Maria 258–261,
    267, 285, 403ch13n15
The Return of Peter Grimm 111
Reynolds, Gene 288, 291,
    405ch15n10
Ribentropp, Joachim von 240
Rich, Irene 156, 288
Richardson, Jack 44, 51, 52
Ricketts, Thomas 43
Riefenstahl, Leni 284
Ripley, Arthur Dewitt 244, 245
The River 3, 4, 16, 19, 23, 24, 79,
    86, 151, 113, 134–144, 151, 238,
    347
Roach, Hal 38, 260, 344
The Road Back 258
Robinson, David 77
Robinson, Edward G. 228
Rogers, Ginger 332, 333
Rogers, Lorena B. *see* Borzage,
    Rena
Rogers, Tom 13
Rogers, Will 146, 155–157, 165, 167,
    173, 195, 196
Roland, Gilbert 357
The Romance of the Sawdust Ring
    40
A Romance of the Sea 39
Roos, Bo 343, 344
Roosevelt, Franklin 193, 285
Rosen, Philip 125
Rosher, Charles 42
Rosson, Helene 44, 47, 52
Rosson, Richard 288, 296, 303
Rotha, Paul 3
Rough but Hopeful 343
Rub, Christian 222, 225
Rubens, Alma 65, 69, 78, 80,
    108–110
Rubinstein, Arthur 324, 325, 331
Rubottom, Wade B. 296
Ruegg, Maria *see* Borzage,
    Maria
Ruggles, Charles 357

Russel, Gail 335
Russell, John L. 339
Ruttenberg, Joseph 22, 251, 252

Sabato, Alfredo 135, 397ch7n38
Sadoul, Georges 4, 31, 38, 41, 124,
    208, 311
Sakall, S.Z. *see* Szakall, Szöke
Sale, Richard 278, 404ch14n17
Salt, Waldo 259
Santell, Alfred 323
Sarastro 14–16, 282
Sarris, Andrew 4, 11, 245
Saville, Victor 288–291, 304,
    405ch15n20
Saxon, John 352
Schenck, Joseph M. 87, 88, 94
Schenck, Nicholas M. 94, 250
Schertzinger, Victor 107, 111
Schneiderman, George 102, 111
Die Schönen Tage in Aranjuez 235,
    401ch12n10
Scott, Juanita "Nita" *see* Moss,
    Juanita
Searl, Jackie 211
Secrets (1924) 75, 88–91
Secrets (1933) 26, 91, 189–193, 194,
    197, 321
Segond, Jacques 12, 182
Seitz, George B. 252
Selznick, David O. 249, 250
Sennes, Frank 357
Sennet, Mack 58
Sersen, Fred. W. 119, 135
Seven Sweethearts 306–307
Seventh Heaven see *7th Heaven*
7th Heaven 4, 11, 12, 14, 15, 16, 17,
    18, 19, 20, 22, 23, 24, 29, 93, 99,
    101, 102, 105, 107, 108, 110,
    111–126, 133, 182, 183, 194, 198,
    207, 222, 297, 328, 347, 348
Shantytown 189
Shaw, George Bernard 145
Shearer, Norma 305
Sheehan, Winfield R. 101, 108,
    110–114, 122, 126, 133, 135, 145,
    155, 157, 159, 160, 171, 174
Sherman, Lowell 229
Sherriff, R. C. 216, 258, 259, 302
Sherwood, Robert E. 84, 285
The Shining Hour 24, 264, 269–273
Shipmates Forever 234–235
Shirley, Ann 165
The Shoes That Danced 61
The Shop Around the Corner 237
Show Boat 216
Sidney, George 9, 209, 261, 291,
    343, 346, 357, 358
Sidney, Sylvia 167
The Silken Spider 53
Simon, Simone 124
Siodmak, Robert 84
Sirk, Douglas 5, 18, 268
Sjöström, Victor 95
Skelton, Red 302, 331, 342
Slezak, Walter 312, 320, 321
Smilin' Through 158, 190, 286,
    304–306
Smith, C. Aubrey 190

Society for Sale 64
Sokoloff, Vladimir 312
Song o' My Heart 27, 157–158, 328
The Song of Love 88
Song of Songs 235
A Song to Remember 324
The Spanish Main 319–322
The Sparkuhlodor 314
Stack, Robert 288, 291
Stage Door Canteen 308
Stahl, John M. 18, 29, 97, 99, 215,
    217
Stallings, Laurence 176
Stange, Hugh S. 171
Stanley, Forrest 81
Starke, Pauline 59, 60, 61, 66, 119
Sternberg, Josef von 3, 97, 99, 134,
    194, 235, 273, 357
Stevens, George 357, 404ch15n2
Stewart, James 124, 251, 286, 291,
    294, 299
Stillwell, Edna 331, 343
Stone, Fred 66, 67, 156, 393ch3n11
Stone, Irving 332
Stranded 233
Strange Cargo 17, 23, 278–283
The Straussodore 335
Street Angel 16, 23, 93, 94, 105, 113,
    122, 127–133, 142, 151, 194, 317,
    336
Stroheim, Erich von 87, 95, 99,
    134, 160, 171
Stromberg, Hunt 268
Strong, Austin 111, 114, 122, 124,
    125, 395ch7n1
Sturges, Preston 223
Sullavan, Margaret 29, 157, 216,
    217, 219, 223, 258, 259, 261, 262,
    267–270, 286, 288, 294,
    401ch11n42, 405ch15n9
Sullivan's Travels 223
Sunny Side Up 154
Sunrise 110, 112–114, 119, 122, 127,
    145
Swanson, Gloria 64
Sweet, Blanche 111
Swerling, Jo 198, 209, 216
Swindle, Larry 171
Szakall, Szöke 306

Tacchella, Jean Charles 4, 209
Talmadge, Constance 88
Talmadge, Norma 87–92, 94
Tamiroff, Akim 274, 275, 309
Taurog, Norman 304
Tavernier, Bertrand 4
Taylor, Estelle 162
Taylor, Robert 258, 262, 302–304
Tearle, Gordfey 122
Tess of the D'Urbervilles 99
Thalberg, Irving G. 94–97, 99, 176,
    250
That Gal of Burke's 53
That's My Man 107, 333–334
They Had to See Paris 156
Thomas, Olive 65, 67
Thomson, David 14
Three Comrades 3, 17, 19, 22, 23,
    24, 27, 258–268, 273, 298

A Ticket for Thaddeus 344
Till We Meet Again 2, 13, 23, 284, 300, 311–319, 346
Toland, Gregg 246
Tone, Franchot 258, 259, 261, 262, 267, 269, 309, 310
Tools of Providence 41
Toton 65, 343
Tourneur, Maurice 99, 127
Tracy, Lee 162
Tracy, Spencer 155, 167, 173, 195, 198, 202, 203, 205, 206, 208, 251–254, 256, 273, 357
Travelling avant 209
The Treasure of the Sierra Madre 342
Trento, Guido 127
Trintignant, Jean-Louis 356
A Trip to Paradise 160
Truffaut, François 170
Tupper, Tristram 86, 135, 144, 145, 397ch8n5
Turconi, Davide 5, 36
The Typhoon 40

Ulmer, Edgar G. 216, 356, 357
Unlucky Luke 53
Until They Get Me 58–61, 78, 119, 153
Urban, Joseph 70

The Valley of Silent Men 78–80, 135, 194
Van Buren, A. H. 144
Van Dyke, W. S. 100, 273
The Vanishing Virginian 306
Varconi, Victor 166, 276, 281
Veiller, Bayard 274
Velez, Lupe 195
Vidor, Charles 324

Vidor, King 18, 97, 134, 197, 229, 241, 250
Viertel, Berthold 216
Vigo, Jean 206, 208, 214
Vinneuil, François 188, 214, 261
Viviani, Christian 256, 271, 297

Wages for Wives 106
Wagner, Richard 184, 186
Wald, Jerry 232
Walker, Robert 343
Walking Down Broadway 171
Wallace, Richard 176
Wallis, Hal B. 227, 228, 233, 242, 244
Walsh, Raoul 9, 19, 100, 101, 110, 112, 134, 147, 157, 166
Wanger, Walter 195, 197, 244
Warner, H. B. 165
Warner, Jack 13, 227, 230, 240, 242, 249, 285
Warrenton, Gilbert 69, 70
Waterloo Bridge 188, 218
Watson, Lucille 312, 313
Wayne, John 323, 333, 342, 343, 346, 347
Wee Lady Betty 58
Weinberg, Herman G. 236
Weissmuller, Johnny 195, 308, 342, 343
Welles, Orson 22, 323
Wellman, William A. 9, 97, 99, 195, 206, 335, 343, 357
Werker, Alfred 171
West, Claudine 286, 299
West, Raymond B. 39, 41
Westfront 1918 120
Westmore, George 88
Whale, James 208, 216, 258
What Price Glory? 101, 110, 119, 122

Whitebait, Colin 301
Who Is to Blame? 64
Whom the Gods Would Destroy 66
Wilde, Cornel 324
Wilder, Billy 5
Wilky, L. Guy 44, 45
Willemen, Paul 12, 404ch13n20
William, Warren 230, 233
Williams, Guinn 146, 251
Wilson, Michael Henry 5, 12, 125, 187, 214, 265, 298
The Wind 134
Wingate, James 208
Winter, John Keith 269, 271
The Wizard of Oz 274
Wolf, Friedrich 286
Wolff, Pierre 208
A Woman in Paris 77
The Wrath of the Gods 39
Wright, Basil 301
Wurtzel, Sol M. 101, 113, 114, 126, 145, 160, 171
Wyler, William 13

Yates, Herbert J. 323, 324, 325, 334
You Only Live Once 244
Young, Loretta 198, 202, 204, 205, 206, 249
Young, Robert 261, 262, 269, 286, 288
Young America 173–174, 343
Young as You Feel 167
Youngerman, Joe 343, 357

Zanuck, Darryl F. 13, 124
Zavattini, Cesare 18
Zéro de conduite 214
Zoo in Budapest 198, 207
Zukor, Adolph 37, 75, 235